OpenGL™
Programming for the
X Window System

Mark J. Kilgard

Addison-Wesley Developers Press

Reading, Massachusetts • Menlo Park, California • New York
Don Mills, Ontario • Harlow, England • Amsterdam
Bonn • Sydney • Singapore • Tokyo • Madrid • San Juan
Paris • Seoul • Milan • Mexico City • Taipei

Library of Congress Cataloging-in-Publication Data

Kilgard, Mark J.
    OpenGL programming for the X Window System / Mark J. Kilgard.
        p.   cm.
    Includes bibliographical references and index.
    ISBN 0-201-48359-9
    1. Computer graphics.   2. X Window System (Computer system)
    3. OpenGL.   I. Title.
    T385.K347   1996
    006.6'—dc20   96-23162
                                                               CIP

Sponsoring Editor: Mary Treseler
Project Manager: John Fuller
Production Assistant: Melissa Lima
Cover design: Jean Seal
Text design: Kim Arney
Set in 10-point Sabon by Pure Imaging Publishing

1 2 3 4 5 6 7 8 9 -MA- 0099989796
First printing, July 1996

Addison-Wesley books are available for bulk purchases by corporations, institutions, and other organizations. For more information please contact the Corporate, Government, and Special Sales Department at (800) 238-9682.

Find A-W Developers Press on the World-Wide Web at:
http://www.aw.com/devpress/

For Sharon and Dana

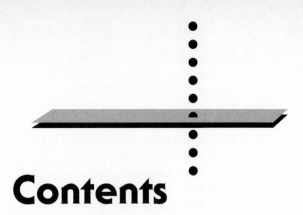

Contents

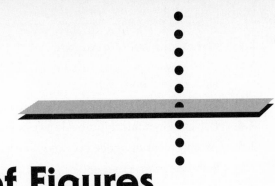

List of Figures

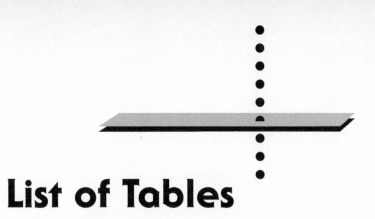

List of Tables

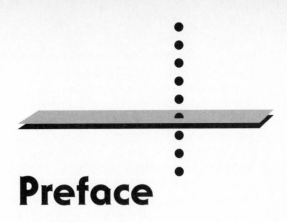

Preface

The past decade and a half has shown that standard software interfaces are the catalysts for launching mature and successful computer technologies. PostScript has enabled laser printing to change the way people print documents. Graphical user interfaces such as the Macintosh toolbox, Microsoft Windows, and OSF/Motif have reinvented the way we interact with our computers. Networking software such as TCP/IP has opened up the worldwide Internet to anyone who wants access.

None of these software interfaces "invented" the technologies they popularized. Laser printing, graphical user interfaces, and computer networks were developed years ahead of the software standards that would eventually popularize each technology. In each case, it was a widely adopted software standard that ignited the widespread use of the technology.

Three-dimensional graphics has come of age with the widespread adoption of OpenGL as a common programming interface for interactive 3D graphics. OpenGL currently supports the X Window System, Microsoft Windows 95 and NT, OS/2, and the Power Macintosh. This means 3D graphics applications can be developed for inexpensive PCs and for the most sophisticated high-performance workstations using the same software model and programming interface.

This book is about OpenGL, specifically about how to write OpenGL programs for the X Window System. OpenGL is "window system independent," meaning that it defines a model for using 3D graphics and the programming interface to use OpenGL, but it does not define the way windows are created and other "window system" operations. These window system specific operations are left to the window system. For the X Window System, OpenGL is supported using the GLX extension. OpenGL can be used in conjunction with standard X libraries and tool-kits such as Xlib and OSF/Motif.

What you will learn by reading this book is not just how to use OpenGL, but how to integrate your OpenGL applications tightly with the X Window System. Previous knowledge of OpenGL is not required, but the coverage of OpenGL's functionality is hardly complete. This book is not an introduction to the X Window System. It assumes that the reader programs in C and has experience with the Xlib and/or Motif programming interfaces. A background in computer graphics is not assumed, but is helpful. A basic knowledge of geometry and trigonometry is useful for some sections.

A typical reader of this book is expected to fall into one or more of the following categories:

- An Xlib or Motif programmer who wants to use OpenGL to implement 3D graphics applications.

- A programmer proficient in IRIS GL, the predecessor to OpenGL, who would like to migrate to OpenGL for more portability and access to the fastest current and future hardware.

- A non-X programmer (using Windows NT or another window system) who wants to understand X and OpenGL in order to port graphics applications from X to Windows or to other non-X window systems.

- A student of computer graphics who wants to develop practical 3D programming skills.

- A technical decision maker who wants to assess the value of using OpenGL with X for 3D graphics applications.

Unlike previous books in Addison-Wesley's OpenGL series, which present OpenGL outside the context of a particular window system, this book delves into the ways real OpenGL applications for the X Window System should be designed and constructed. Each chapter contains source code (written in ANSI C and, in one instance, C++) demonstrating the techniques described. The overriding goal is to allow the reader to construct real and useful 3D applications using OpenGL and X.

The material is presented in seven chapters. These chapters are tutorial in nature and each builds on the material in previous chapters. Chapter 1 is an introduction to OpenGL and to using OpenGL with X. Chapter 2 explains the GLX model for integrating OpenGL and X using Xlib. Chapter 3 explains how to use OpenGL with Motif and other widget sets. Chapter 4 describes an Xlib-based toolkit, known as the OpenGL Utility Toolkit (or GLUT), for constructing quick-and-dirty OpenGL programs to explore 3D programming. Chapter 5 explores OpenGL's features with examples using GLUT. Chapter 6 presents advanced topics for OpenGL application writers: revisions of OpenGL, how to use alternative input devices, how to use overlays, how to ensure OpenGL portability and interoperability, approaches to OpenGL hardware acceleration, and performance tuning. Chapter 7 combines the techniques explained in earlier chapters to develop a practical OpenGL application using Motif. The appendices explain how to obtain the book's source code examples and the GLUT library source code via the Internet and provide a full description of the OpenGL Utility Toolkit programming interface.

Acknowledgments

I began my software engineering career writing window system software. I was not particularly interested in computer graphics. OpenGL and Silicon Graphics changed that for me. My introduction to both OpenGL and Silicon Graphics was through Kurt Akeley and Phil Karlton. I am greatly indebted to them for my opportunity to work on X, and later on OpenGL, at Silicon Graphics. Kurt's contributions to computer graphics are widely acknowledged. While Kurt has been the guiding force for well over a decade of Silicon Graphics's high-end computer graphics hardware architectures, his work on OpenGL, as a software standard, is sure to be more important than any single hardware design. Kurt is a personal inspiration to me. Phil managed and directed the early development of OpenGL's implementation. His vision for combining Silicon Graphics's 3D graphics experience with the X Window System gave me a wonderful opportunity to parlay my window system expertise into a rewarding career at Silicon Graphics. Thanks, Phil.

Anyone associated with Silicon Graphics realizes quickly that the dedication, talent, and vision of its engineers and technical managers are the company's greatest strengths. I know this personally from working with Allen Akin, David Blythe, Sharon Clay, Peter Daifuku, Celeste Fowler, Ziv Gigus, Deanna Hohn, Robert Keller, Allen Leinwand, Dan McLachlan, Brian McClendon, Tom McReynolds, Tom Paquin, Mark Segal, Dave Spalding, Tom Weinstein, Paula Womack, Mark Young, and David Yu. These individuals and all the others at Silicon Graphics created the systems, the software, and, most important, the environment that made this book possible.

Craig Groeschel, Randi Rost, and many of the aforementioned Silicon Graphics engineers and managers provided invaluable feedback by reviewing this work. Mark Segal deserves special thanks for his thorough proofreading and suggestions. Brian Paul and a host of OpenGL Utility Toolkit users on the Internet assisted in the debugging much of the source code developed for this book.

Much of the material in this book was developed in conjunction with my "OpenGL and X" column, published in *The X Journal*. I thank the staff at SIGS Publications for their publishing efforts, particularly Seth Bookey, Charles Bowman, Kristina Jukodahr, and Steve Mikes.

Deirdre Tiffany's feedback, patience, and support meant the world to me. Words cannot say enough.

There are others who have influenced this book indirectly, but fundamentally, through their influence on my life. I count among these Nancy Denmark, John Deuel, Michael Hicks, Thomas Kulick, Bernie Luksich, Peter Ostrin, my brothers Mike and Matt, and certainly my parents Chris and Brenda. Thanks, and play safe!

—*MJK*

Introduction

This chapter, which introduces OpenGL and describes its relationship to the X Window System, is organized into the following six sections:

1. "What is OpenGL?" explains what OpenGL is, how it came about, and what functionality it provides.

2. "OpenGL's Rendering Functionality" describes the set of operations provided by OpenGL for rendering 2D and 3D color images.

3. "GLX: The Glue Between OpenGL and X" describes OpenGL's GLX extension to the X Window System and how GLX integrates OpenGL with X.

4. "The GLU Library" describes the OpenGL Utility library, which provides a standard API to higher-level functionality layered on top of OpenGL's core rendering functionality.

5. "An Example Xlib-based OpenGL Program" presents a simple OpenGL example using the Xlib programming interface.

6. "Comparing OpenGL to PEX" compares and contrasts OpenGL with the other standard for 3D in the X Window System, known as PEX.

1.1 WHAT IS OPENGL?

The OpenGL graphics system is a high-performance, window system independent software interface to graphics hardware. OpenGL was designed by Silicon Graphics,

Inc. (SGI), based on a decade of experience in computer graphics hardware and software design. The *GL* in *OpenGL* stands for *Graphics Library*. To a graphics programmer, OpenGL is exactly that—a library of approximately 350 distinct graphics routines. These routines allow a programmer to generate high-quality color images efficiently. While OpenGL is well suited for interactive rendering of 3D graphics, it can also be used for 2D graphics and imaging.

OpenGL is a *standard* originally developed by Silicon Graphics. Silicon Graphics has turned over control of the OpenGL standard to the OpenGL Architectural Review Board (ARB), which consists of leaders in the computer industry. Its founding members included DEC, IBM, Intel, Microsoft, and Silicon Graphics. The board has since expanded to include (at the time of this writing) two more prominent computer graphics companies: Intergraph and Evans & Sutherland. The collective vision underlying OpenGL is that through a common, fast software interface for programming graphics, 3D graphics can rapidly become a mainstream computer technology. Much to the benefit of those using interactive 3D computer graphics, OpenGL has realized this goal. Implementations of OpenGL are widely available, and applications based on OpenGL are commonplace. In particular, OpenGL implementations are now available from every major X Window System vendor.

OpenGL provides a layer of abstraction between graphics hardware and an application program. Together, OpenGL's routines form an application programming interface (API). The routines allow graphics primitives (points, lines, polygons, bitmaps, and images) to be rendered to a frame buffer. Using the available primitives and the operations that control their rendering, high-quality color images of 3D objects can be generated.

The most commonly used programming languages for OpenGL are C and C++. The OpenGL API is the same for both languages. Nearly all the programs in this book are written in ANSI C; in Section 5.7, which discusses Open Inventor, a C++ program also appears. OpenGL bindings exist for other languages such as Ada and FORTRAN. These bindings merely provide a way to call OpenGL routines from these languages; the functionality of OpenGL is the same in any language.

1.1.1   OpenGL's Design

The designers of OpenGL specify the graphics system as a *state machine* [36]* that controls a well-defined set of drawing operations. The routines that OpenGL supplies provide a means to manipulate OpenGL's state machine to generate the desired graphics output. Figure 1.1 shows a simplified view of OpenGL's abstract state machine.

Don't be intimidated by the term "state machine"; it is not that complicated. Think of OpenGL as a virtual device with lots of knobs and levers that controls the way it operates. You feed geometric descriptions of what you want rendered (in the form of vertices and images) into OpenGL. Based on the ways the levers and knobs are set, OpenGL generates a pixelized 2D rendering of your data. For example, one

---

* References to the Bibliography appear in square brackets throughout this book.

Figure 1.1 High-level, abstract OpenGL machine.

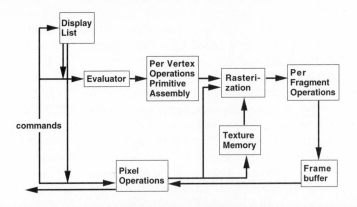

lever controls whether lighting calculations are done on your data, and a knob controls the way your data is blended with other data already rendered. The OpenGL state machine is not a black box. You can read back the value of almost every piece of OpenGL state you can set. OpenGL's state machine has lots of advantages for implementation and conceptual reasons. Specifying OpenGL as a state machine results in a consistent, precise specification and eliminates ambiguity about what a given operation does and does not do.

The model used for interpretation of OpenGL commands is *client-server*. This is an abstract model; it does not demand that OpenGL be implemented as distinct client and server processes. A client-server approach means that the boundary between a program and the OpenGL implementation is well defined, to specify clearly how data is passed between the application using OpenGL and the OpenGL implementation. This allows OpenGL to operate over a *wire protocol*, the way the X protocol operates, but OpenGL does not require that OpenGL rendering take place in a separate process. Using a wire protocol means that all OpenGL operations can be encoded in a stream of bytes that can be sent across a network. Not requiring a wire protocol means that OpenGL can bypass the use of the protocol when direct access to the graphics hardware is available.

In the case of the X Window System, OpenGL is implemented as an extension to X, meaning that there is an X extension protocol for OpenGL (the GLX protocol). So just as basic X programs can run on a remote computer while the results are displayed to a local workstation, X programs using OpenGL can do the same.

The OpenGL specification is *window system independent,* meaning that it provides rendering functionality but does not specify how to manipulate windows or receive events from the window system. This allows the OpenGL interface to be implemented for different window systems. For example, OpenGL has been implemented for the X Window System, Windows 95 and NT, OS/2, and the Power Macintosh. While OpenGL itself is window system independent, for each window system, a window system dependent interface must be used to coordinate OpenGL's functionality with that of the window system. Each distinct window system has its own interface, but the basic functionality performed by this window system dependent interface is very similar to what other window systems provide. The window system dependent interface for the X Window System is called GLX. Note that GLX is both the name of OpenGL's window system dependent programming interface for X and the name of OpenGL's X extension protocol.

One thing to keep in mind about OpenGL, particularly for the X Window System, is that OpenGL is generally an extension to the base window system. While OpenGL is becoming a standard feature of most current workstations, some workstations (typically older workstations and many X terminals) will not support the GLX extension that provides OpenGL support.[1] Section 1.3 provides further discussion of OpenGL's X support and how to determine whether the GLX extension, and therefore OpenGL, is supported by your workstation.

Graphics systems are often classified as one of two types: *procedural* or *descriptive*. With a procedural interface, the program specifies exactly what to draw by issuing a specific sequence of commands. With a descriptive interface, the programmer sets up a model of the scene to be rendered and leaves the method of drawing the scene up to the graphics system. OpenGL is a procedural interface. In a descriptive system, the programmer gives up control of exactly how the scene is to be rendered. Being procedural allows the programmer a high degree of control over the way rendering is performed. Descriptive graphics systems are typically implemented as a layer above a procedural interface. Two popular descriptive graphics systems that render using OpenGL are Open Inventor [40] and IRIS Performer [35], both developed by Silicon Graphics. Open Inventor is highly object-oriented and easy to use. IRIS Performer is designed to optimize the rendering performance of visual simulation applications, such as flight simulators.

An overriding goal of OpenGL is to allow the construction of *portable* and *interoperable* graphics programs. For this reason, OpenGL's rendering functionality must be implemented in its entirety. This means all the complex rendering functionality mandated by the OpenGL specification can be used with any OpenGL implementation. Previous graphics standards often allowed subsetting, meaning that not all rendering functionality was mandated; often the results were programs that could not be expected to work on distinct implementations. To ensure compliant implementations, every OpenGL vendor must validate its implementation using a comprehensive set of conformance tests.

In practice, well-written OpenGL programs for the X Window System are quite portable among X workstations from different vendors. All the programs presented

---

1. For such machines, the freely available Mesa library written by Brian Paul at the University of Wisconsin, provides an implementation of the OpenGL programming interface that does not require the GLX extension. While Mesa is portable and free, it does not benefit from accelerated graphics hardware and cannot emulate some details of GLX's operation. To find out how to obtain Mesa, see Appendix A.

in this book have been tested to ensure that they are good examples of writing portable OpenGL programs for X.

While OpenGL is portable, it is also fast, because OpenGL leverages Silicon Graphics's design experience, acquired from a decade of building high-performance graphics workstations. Specialized hardware for 3D rendering greatly improves graphics performance. OpenGL is designed with such hardware in mind. As computer technology advances, you can expect higher OpenGL performance from newer hardware for the same money or less. Many of the ways in which hardware can accelerate OpenGL performance are discussed in Section 6.5.

OpenGL is *extensible,* meaning that additional functionality can be added to OpenGL incrementally as new features are warranted. While any OpenGL implementor can add a new extension, OpenGL's ARB coordinates a set of common extensions. Many of the available extensions to OpenGL are described later, in Section 5.6. By their nature, extensions will not exist in all OpenGL implementations. Please note that extensions to OpenGL are distinct from extensions to the X Window System. While GLX is an X extension to support OpenGL, OpenGL extensions do not require new X extensions.

1.1.2 History of OpenGL

OpenGL is the successor to a graphics library known as IRIS GL, developed by Silicon Graphics as a device-independent graphics interface for use across a full line of graphics workstations. IRIS GL [27] is used by more than 1,500 3D graphics applications. IRIS GL has evolved over the last decade and has been implemented on numerous graphics devices of varying sophistication.

OpenGL is not backward compatible with IRIS GL. OpenGL has removed dated IRIS GL functionality and made functionality more general in places. The most visible difference to programmers is that the routines and symbols that make up the OpenGL API all start with either `gl` or `GL`, to avoid name space conflicts. IRIS GL provides routines for managing windows and obtaining user input. To gain window system independence and focus OpenGL on rendering functionality, IRIS GL's windowing functionality was not made part of OpenGL. All window system dependent portions of IRIS GL have been eliminated from OpenGL. What has been preserved is the spirit of the API. OpenGL retains IRIS GL's ability to render 3D objects quickly and efficiently. IRIS GL is network-extensible, but only by means of a proprietary protocol called Distributed GL (DGL). In contrast, OpenGL's GLX protocol is both network-extensible and an open standard.

Before OpenGL, every vendor of 3D graphics workstations invented its own functionally similar, but incompatible, programming interfaces for accessing that vendor's 3D hardware (IRIS GL was just one such proprietary interface). The result was that 3D graphics programs for various makes of computer workstations were quite incompatible.

OpenGL was proposed as a standard to bring 3D graphics programming into the mainstream of application programming by providing a standard, common, high-performance interface to interactive 3D graphics hardware. This was the reason that the OpenGL ARB was formed. Silicon Graphics turned over the OpenGL standard to the ARB, which now directs and approves OpenGL's further development. Currently, over 30 companies have licensed OpenGL and many commercial implementations are available. Numerous universities have also licensed OpenGL for educational and research purposes. Table 1.1 presents a short time line of important events in the history of OpenGL.

OpenGL continues to evolve as a standard, and the ARB continues to standardize extensions for OpenGL, enhance the core OpenGL standards, provide bindings

Table 1.1 Important milestones in the development of the OpenGL standard

Year	Event
1982	Initial development of the IRIS GL.
1987	IRIS GL adds `glVertex3f`-style vertex commands.
1989	Kurt Akeley attempts detailed IRIS GL specification.
	Distributed GL (DGL) protocol released (precursor of GLX protocol).
	IRIS GL "mixed model" interface released (precursor of GLX API).
	Silicon Graphics commits itself to an OpenGL effort.
1990	Kurt Akeley and Mark Segal begin work on OpenGL specification.
1991	First OpenGL Architectural Review Board (ARB) meetings held.
1992	First OpenGL sample implementation released to licensees.
	OpenGL Reference Manual published.
	First commercial OpenGL released by DEC and Silicon Graphics.
1993	*OpenGL Programming Guide* published.
	Open Inventor toolkit (based on OpenGL) released.
	OpenGL specification and manual pages distributed via the Internet.
1994	Microsoft releases Windows NT 3.5, including OpenGL.
	Work on standard OpenGL extensions begins.
	OpenGL Utility Toolkit distribution announced.
1995	GLX 1.1 approved.
	Brian Paul releases Mesa, a free implementation of the OpenGL API.
	Intergraph and Evans & Sutherland join the ARB.
	GLU 1.2 approved.
	Sun and Hewlett-Packard announce plans to adopt OpenGL.
	OpenGL add-on to Microsoft Windows 95 made available.
1996	OpenGL 1.1 and GLX 1.2 publicly released.

for additional computer languages (such as those for Ada and FORTRAN), and promote the OpenGL standard.

The original OpenGL specification was version 1.0. Since that time, the ARB has approved the upwardly compatible version 1.1. Most of the additions to 1.1 were extensions to 1.0 that were deemed useful enough to be made part of the OpenGL standard itself. This practice of integrating proven extensions into the core OpenGL standard allows new features to be released and tested before their inclusion in the core OpenGL standard. By regularly integrating successful extensions into the core OpenGL, the ARB can ensure that the OpenGL standard will stay current and coherent.

The GLX specification has also been revised. GLX 1.1 and GLX 1.2 further enhance OpenGL's integration with the X Window System. Section 6.1 explains the various revisions of OpenGL and GLX. The revisions of the OpenGL standards mostly add advanced features. Unless otherwise noted, the material in this book applies to the OpenGL 1.0 and GLX 1.0 standards and compatible revisions.

1.2 OpenGL's Rendering Functionality

OpenGL is not a high-level 3D graphics interface. When you build a graphics program using OpenGL, you start with a few simple geometric and image primitives. The sophistication comes from combining the primitives and using them in various modes. This section describes OpenGL's rendering functionality. For now, assume that OpenGL is initialized and things are set up so that OpenGL commands render to an onscreen window. The details of initializing OpenGL for rendering are discussed later.

1.2.1 Geometric Primitives

A geometric primitive renders a simple shape, such as a point, a line, or a triangle. Using these primitives, complex 3D scenes can be rendered. Often scenes are constructed using thousands of individual triangles. Figure 1.2 shows the available geometric primitives in OpenGL. Notice the ordering of the vertices, in particular for primitives such as the GL_TRIANGLE_STRIP and the GL_TRIANGLE_FAN.

A primitive is described using a set of vertices. Figure 1.3 shows one way a polygon might be specified. To begin a geometric primitive, the glBegin routine passes in the primitive type as an argument. Then a list of vertex coordinates are specified. Each glVertex3f call sends a vertex represented as three floating-point values (hence the 3f suffix).

Along with the coordinates of each vertex, per-vertex information such as color, normals, edge drawing, and texturing can be specified between a glBegin and a glEnd. Notice how glColor3f is used to change the current color. Each vertex is

Figure 1.2 OpenGL geometric primitives.

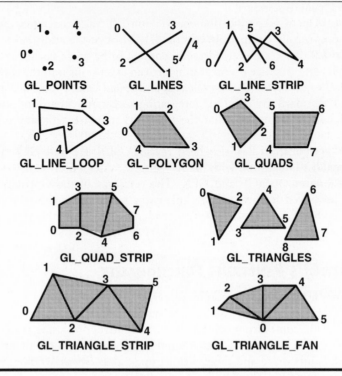

Figure 1.3 Example of generating a 3D polygon with smooth shading between vertices.

```
glShadeModel(GL_SMOOTH);
glBegin(GL_POLYGON); /* pentagon */
  glColor3f(0.0, 1.0, 0.0); /* green */
  glVertex3f(0.0, 1.0, 0.0);
  glVertex3f(0.7, 1.0, 0.0);
  glColor3f(0.0, 0.0, 1.0); /* blue */
  glVertex3f(1.4, 0.6, 0.0);
  glVertex3f(1.4, 0.4, 0.0);
  glVertex3f(0.0, 0.0, 0.0);
glEnd();
```

drawn according to the current color. An OpenGL primitive is completed by calling glEnd.

Looking at the way OpenGL routines are used, you can see OpenGL's naming convention. All OpenGL routines begin with gl, and the remainder of each routine name is in mixed case (for example, glCopyPixels). The OpenGL constants all begin with GL_, and use only capital letters, and words are separated by underscores (for example, GL_TRIANGLE_FAN). OpenGL defines its own set of basic data types, all of which begin with GL but are otherwise lowercase (for example, GLfloat and GLsizei). While these OpenGL basic data types are not guaranteed to be based on the built-in C language types, they typically are for most OpenGL implementations. All 14 data types used by OpenGL can be found in Table 1.2

OpenGL tends to be function call intensive. Instead of using a single routine with many complex parameters, OpenGL's API favors multiple function calls with simple

Table 1.2 The OpenGL data types. Because ANSI C allows the sizes of basic data types to be implementation-dependent, OpenGL uses these types to ensure that its data types are properly sized. For Unix workstations, the OpenGL data types' mapping to C data types is straightforward—for example, GLfloat to float and GLushort to unsigned short. Types such as GLclampf are different from GLfloat in the assumptions OpenGL makes about values considered valid, but not in the underlying type used to represent the types. Typically, ANSI C prototypes and default type conversions make explicit casting between OpenGL and C data types unnecessary.

OpenGL Type	Minimum Number of Bits	Description
GLboolean	1	Boolean
GLbyte	8	Signed integer
GLubyte	8	Unsigned integer
GLshort	16	Signed integer
GLushort	16	Unsigned integer
GLint	32	Signed integer
GLuint	32	Unsigned integer
GLsizei	32	Nonnegative integer
GLenum	32	Enumerated integer value
GLbitfield	32	Bit field
GLfloat	32	Floating-point value
GLclampf	32	Floating-point value clamped between 0 and 1
GLdouble	64	Floating-point value
GLclampd	64	Floating-point value clamped between 0 and 1

parameters. OpenGL primitives are constructed by calling multiple OpenGL routines. Calling multiple routines gives the program more flexibility and more control over the primitives generated.

In many cases, OpenGL is flexible about the format that can be used to pass data to OpenGL. For many basic operations, there are multiple versions of the same basic routine and each version accepts data in a different format. For example, glVertex3i accepts integers, while glVertex3f and glVertex3d take single- and double-precision floating-point, respectively. For routines in a family such as glVertex, which generates vertices, or glColor, which sets the current color, the suffix of routines in a given family determines the data format and the number of parameters passed to the routine. So glVertex2f takes a two-dimensional vertex, while glVertex3f takes a three-dimensional vertex. The f suffix indicates that a GLfloat is expected. Table 1.3 shows the correspondences between suffix letters and OpenGL parameter types.

The v suffix indicates that the parameters for a routine are passed via a pointer to a vector. For example, you could call

```
static GLfloat vertex[3] = { 1.0, 5.5, -32.0 };
glVertex3fv(vertex);
```

Having several functionally equivalent routines that accept different data types allows the programmer flexibility in deciding how to store the data. A programmer whose data is in integer format does not want to convert it to floating-point to pass it to the graphics system. Another programmer does not want to convert floating-point data into integers. Conversions between data types can be expensive. High-performance graphics hardware can be designed to accept multiple data formats and offload the task of format conversion from the host processor.

You can start to see why it makes sense to consider OpenGL as a state machine. Commands such as glColor3f change the state of the current color. Subsequent

Table 1.3 Correspondences between OpenGL routine name suffix letters and OpenGL parameter types

Suffix Letters	Corresponding OpenGL Type
b	GLbyte
ub	GLubyte
s	GLshort
us	GLushort
i	GLint
ui	GLuint
f	GLfloat
d	GLdouble

vertices use the updated current color. `glBegin` puts OpenGL into a state in which it can start drawing the specified primitive. The multiple `glVertex` routines load the vertices one at a time for a given primitive. Nearly all of OpenGL's state that can be set by the programmer can also be queried by the programmer. For example, the `glGetFloatv(GL_CURRENT_COLOR, &float_array)` call will retrieve the setting of the current color.

1.2.2   Pixel Path Operations

In addition to OpenGL's geometric primitives, the other way to get pixels rendered (and the way to read them back) is to use OpenGL's pixel operations. Images (2D arrays of pixel data) are displayed using `glDrawPixels` and are retrieved from the frame buffer using `glReadPixels`. (The frame buffer is the place where rendered pixels are stored.) OpenGL also provides a means to copy pixel data from one region of the frame buffer to another with `glCopyPixels`. In addition to rectangular images, OpenGL provides a bitmap primitive, generated by `glBitmap`. Bitmaps are like images, but instead of an array of pixel values, a bitmap is an array of bits that serves as a drawing mask. Typically, bitmaps are used for rendering characters. The location at which an image or bitmap is rendered is determined by the *current raster position* which is set by the `glRasterPos` family of routines.

While transferring an image to and from the screen can be quite simple, OpenGL has a sophisticated *pixel path* that allows pixel data to be zoomed, biased, scaled, looked up, and further processed on the way to and from the frame buffer. This makes OpenGL useful not just for 3D graphics, but for image processing tasks as well. There are OpenGL extensions that give OpenGL still more image-processing capabilities, allowing it to perform operations such as histograms and convolutions. OpenGL's pixel path is discussed in more detail in Section 5.4.

OpenGL's geometric primitives and pixel operations find a special synergy in OpenGL's texture mapping facilities. Texture mapping is a feature that allows an image to be projected onto a geometric primitive such as a 3D triangle. You can think of texture mapping as the logical equivalent of stretching virtual wallpaper over polygons you render. Texture mapping is discussed in more detail in Section 5.2. The important point here is that when texture images are downloaded into OpenGL, they are passed through the same pixel path used by images, so all the facilities that bias, scale, and perform lookup table operations can be applied to textures.

1.2.3   Two Color Models

OpenGL has two different color models: *RGBA* and *color index*. RGBA is generally the preferred model.

The `glColor3f` call has already been demonstrated, but not explained. This call assumes OpenGL's RGBA color mode. The routine takes three floating-point parameters between 0.0 and 1.0, which specify the degree of red, green, and blue for the current color. For X users, RGBA corresponds roughly to the `TrueColor` visual type, while color index corresponds to `PseudoColor`. The color model for a given window is fixed, just as X windows are created with a fixed visual.

You may be able to guess that the *RGB* in *RGBA* stands for *red, green, and blue*. The *A* may be unfamiliar. It stands for *alpha*. The alpha value is used when two colors are to be combined for blending operations. Alpha represents the opacity of the color. 1.0 is totally opaque; 0.0 is totally transparent. For example, using alpha, you could render a scene that includes translucent green glass. Some frame buffers actually store alpha values so they can be used in blending or compositing. In such a case, each pixel in the frame buffer would have an associated alpha value. The alpha value is not visible on the display. It is just used to determine how a pixel to be drawn is blended with the current pixel value in the frame buffer. The `glAlphaFunc` and `glBlendFunc` routines control precisely the way alpha blending operates. The `glColor4f` command is a variation on `glColor3f` that takes a fourth parameter specifying alpha (`glColor3f` implicitly sets alpha to 1.0).

RGBA supports a trilinear palette for a broad range of colors, which makes it very useful for rendering realistic scenes. OpenGL supports lighting, fog, and smooth shading most effectively in RGBA mode. Since inexpensive hardware may have limited color resolution, an application can use *dithering* for better color resolution (at the expense of spatial resolution). Figure 1.4 demonstrates how dithering can improve the quality of shaded images on machines with limited color resolution.

The color index model assumes a readable and writable linear colormap. Usually window systems specify how colors are allocated and arranged, so OpenGL does

Figure 1.4 Shaded images with dithering enabled and disabled at different color resolutions.

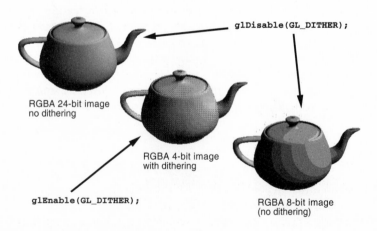

not have any specific routines to allocate colors. For example, in X, an Xlib color allocation routine such as XAllocColor would be used. The glIndex family of routines is used to set the current color index. The advantage of color index is that the color of a given pixel value can be dynamically changed. There is a level of indirection (the colormap) between the pixel values in the frame buffer and the colors on the screen. Typically, color index windows will not support more than 8 or 12 bits of index resolution per pixel, simply because the size of the required colormaps. Because color index lacks a fixed relationship for the colors available for display, facilities such as lighting, fog, and shading are more complicated than in RGBA mode. In color index mode, these facilities, require proper setup of the colormap for them to operate correctly; other facilities such as texture mapping and alpha blending, are not available at all.

Color index mode is typically used on graphics hardware that does not have enough color resolution to adequately represent an RGB color space. For example, a machine with 8 bits of pixel resolution has to split up those 8 bits among red, green, and blue components to form an RGB color space. This is typically done by giving 3 bits to red, 3 bits to green, and 2 bits to blue. This means there are 8 gradations of red and green and 4 gradations of blue. The resulting color space makes 8-bit RGBA scenes exhibit quantization errors, so subtle color variations are lost.

A benefit of color index is that those same 8 bits of resolution permit a palette of 256 distinct colors that can be determined based on the scene being displayed. A scene showing a rosy sunset could fill the palette with many red, yellow, and orange shades and few green shades and accurately capture the colors of the scene. However, RGBA has a fixed colormap arrangement that does not have enough red, yellow, and orange shades to represent the scene adequately with only 8 bits of resolution.

With plenty of bits of resolution per pixel (24 bits or more), color representation is no longer an issue, and the complications and limitations of color index make RGBA far superior. Also, the writability of color index colormaps becomes a serious drawback when multiple applications simultaneously attempt to display windows that set up differently loaded logical colormaps. Windows whose requested colors are not loaded will display unexpected colors.

As technology continues to drive down video memory prices, graphics hardware with higher resolution frame buffers will become common. For this reason and because color index is harder to use and more limiting, nearly all the examples in this book will use the RGBA color model.

1.2.4 OpenGL Modes and Other State

Many modes in OpenGL, such as dithering, are enabled and disabled using the glEnable and glDisable commands, respectively. For example, dithering is enabled by calling glEnable(GL_DITHER). Afterwards, drawing is done with dithering enabled. You can think of `glEnable` and `glDisable` as ways to affect the operation of the OpenGL state machine. The enable/disable state of OpenGL modes can be retrieved using `glIsEnabled`.

Many modes have additional parameters that control the way the mode operates. For example, lighting calculations are based on many different lighting parameters. Parameters associated with the lighting model are controlled using `glLightModelf`; the characteristics of individual light sources are controlled using `glLightf`. OpenGL's lighting model is described in Section 5.1, but here is an example in which lighting is enabled with various lighting parameters being set:

```
GLfloat position[] = {0.0, 0.0, 1.5, 1.0};

glLightModelf(GL_LIGHT_MODEL_LOCAL_VIEWER, GL_TRUE);
glLightModelf(GL_LIGHT_MODEL_TWO_SIDE, GL_FALSE);
glLightfv(GL_LIGHT0, GL_POSITION, position);
glEnable(GL_LIGHTING);
```

The first argument of `glLightModelf` indicates which OpenGL lighting parameter to update; the final argument supplies the new parameter value. Complex facilities such as lighting, fog, and texture mapping have many different parameters to control their operation and are activated by calling `glEnable`. There are also much simpler facilities for things such as controlling the width (in pixels) of rendered lines. The `glLineWidth` routine sets the line width. Because line width is something inherent in lines, there is no need for a `glEnable` option for line width; there is simply a reasonable default (1.0).

While there are many OpenGL routines for setting parameters for various OpenGL capabilities, a single family of routines retrieves most OpenGL state: `glGetBooleanv`, `glGetDoublev`, `glGetFloatv`, and `glGetIntegerv`. For example:

```
GLint state;
glGetIntergerv(GL_LIGHT_MODEL_TWO_SIDE, &state);
```

After calling `glGetIntergerv`, `state` is updated with the current two-sided lighting state.

OpenGL state that requires more than one enumerant to name it (for example, light zero's position, which takes `GL_LIGHT0` and `GL_POSITION` to specify the state) requires a special retrieval routine (such as `glGetLightv`).

OpenGL is designed to have sensible default state. When you first instantiate a context for OpenGL rendering (an instance of an OpenGL state machine that programs use for rendering), all OpenGL state is initialized to predefined default values. Typically, most modes are disabled by default.

State changes immediately affect subsequent rendering. For the most part, the commands to change OpenGL state can be executed in whatever order makes sense to the program. There are exceptions, however. State changes are not allowed when a geometric primitive is being specified (meaning within a `glBegin`-and-`glEnd` pair).

Often, programs change various OpenGL state and later need to revert to the state prior to the changes. Sometimes (often in the case of software libraries layered on OpenGL), the program does not know OpenGL's current state. While the program can retrieve the current values of any state it intends to change, retrieving state can be slow relative to the rate at which commands can be sent to fast graphics hardware. The `glPushAttrib` and `glPopAttribute` calls manage an attribute stack that allows groupings of OpenGL state (such as all the lighting-related state) to be saved (pushed onto the stack) and later restored (popped from the stack). The argument of `glPushAttrib` is a bit mask indicating what state to push. `glPopAttrib` needs no argument, since it just restores the state before the last `glPushAttrib`. For example:

```
glPushAttrib(GL_LIGHTING_BIT);
  modifyOpenGLlightingState();
  doSomeRenderingWithChangedState();
glPopAttrib();
```

After execution of this code fragment, OpenGL's lighting state is what it was before `glPushAttrib` was called. This is a good deal more convenient than attempting to retrieve and restore each piece of lighting state individually.

1.2.5 Ancillary Buffers

Typically, the results of OpenGL rendering are directed to a window displayed on a user's computer. It is also possible to render OpenGL into an in-memory data structure (such as an X pixmap) or into dedicated memory within a graphics hardware device that cannot be displayed.

OpenGL treats the image it renders as an array (or grid) of pixels. The term *frame buffer* refers to the memory within a graphics hardware device that maintains the image displayed on a user's computer screen. OpenGL also uses the term to refer to the array of pixel state maintained by a drawing surface regardless of its hardware representation. For example, memory for an X pixmap is considered a frame buffer by OpenGL.

For most 2D rendering interfaces (such as Xlib), the frame buffer simply contains pixel values that represent a displayable image. OpenGL permits considerably more state to be maintained within the frame buffer. OpenGL considers the frame buffer to be a set of buffers. Each pixel within the frame buffer has an associated value in each buffer. The most important type of buffer is the color (or image) buffer, which contains the color information that represents a displayable image. OpenGL can actually support more than one image buffer within a single frame buffer. As will be explained, multiple image buffers make possible double-buffered animation and stereoscopic display.

OpenGL also supports nonimage buffers, which are often referred to as *ancillary*, or helper, buffers. Several types of ancillary buffers are supported by OpenGL. The next subsections will explain how OpenGL's various ancillary and image buffers are used.

The set of image and ancillary buffers supported by a given frame buffer type is referred to as a *frame buffer configuration*. A window system may support multiple frame buffer configurations, each supporting a different set of buffers. Typically, multiple windows of different configurations can be displayed at one time. Every X window or pixmap has a single frame buffer configuration, though.

1.2.5.1 The Depth Buffer

In the rendering of a 3D scene, there is a general need to ensure that objects that should be obscured by closer objects in the scene are not displayed. This is the problem of *hidden line and hidden surface removal* (HLHSR).

A general method for solving this problem is the use of a *depth buffer* (also commonly referred to as a *Z buffer*). Though the screen has only two dimensions (width and height), 3D graphics attempts to simulate a third dimension. The depth buffer maintains a depth value for every pixel. When 3D primitives are rendered by OpenGL, they are rasterized into a collection of *fragments*. Each fragment corresponds to a single pixel to be updated and includes color and depth information. The X and Y locations corresponding to a fragment determine which pixel in the frame buffer the fragment is intended to update. A fragment's depth (or Z value) is used to determine how "near" the fragment is to the viewer. When OpenGL's depth testing mode is properly enabled, the fragment is drawn only if its Z value is "nearer" than the current Z value for the corresponding pixel in the depth buffer. When the fragment is drawn into the frame buffer, its Z value replaces the previous value in the depth buffer. Normally, when the scene starts to be rendered, the entire depth buffer is cleared to the "farthest" value. As a 3D scene is rendered, the depth buffer automatically sorts the fragments being drawn so only the nearest fragment at each pixel location remains. Objects visually behind other objects are automatically eliminated from the scene. The resolution of the depth buffer improves the accuracy of depth testing; most depth buffers have from 24 to 32 bits of precision per pixel.

You can see the benefit of using depth buffering in Figure 1.5. It shows two versions of a scene that displays intersecting 3D gears. In one window, OpenGL's depth testing is enabled with `glEnable(GL_DEPTH_TEST)`, while in the other window depth testing is disabled with `glDisable(GL_DEPTH_TEST)`. The window using depth testing looks as it should, but the one with depth testing disabled shows portions of a gear that should be behind the second gear. There are also places where the "back" of a gear is displayed where the "front" should be showing (this is the reason the lighting looks incorrect).

Figure 1.5 A 3D scene rendered with and without depth testing enabled.

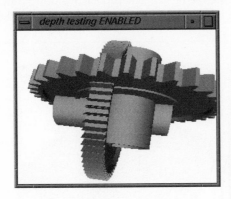

1.2.5.2 The Stencil Buffer

Another buffer supported by OpenGL is the stencil buffer. Like the depth buffer, the stencil buffer can be used to prevent certain pixels from being drawn. The stencil buffer acts in much the same way as a cardboard stencil used with a can of spray paint. You can "draw" values into the stencil buffer using the normal OpenGL rendering primitives. Then a stencil test can be defined and stenciling enabled. Figure 1.6 demonstrates the use of the stencil buffer.

One application of the stencil buffer is in a flight simulator. Imagine that the view outside the plane is to fit into an irregularly shaped windshield. The rendering of the view "outside" the plane should not interfere with the rendering of the instruments "inside" the cockpit. If the windshield area is drawn in the stencil buffer, then a stencil test can be set up to make sure the windshield view is drawn only where the windshield stencil has been drawn.

Though stenciling is the stencil buffer's most common use, this feature's full functionality is useful for far more. Other applications include constructive solid geometry. Stencil buffers typically range from 1 to 8 bits of precision per pixel.

1.2.5.3 The Accumulation Buffer

Yet another buffer supported by OpenGL is the accumulation buffer [16], which can be used for antialiasing, motion blur, simulating photographic depth of field, and rendering soft shadows from multiple light sources. Images are not rendered into the accumulation buffer. Rather, they are first rendered into an image buffer and then are added to the contents of the accumulation buffer after rendering. This process can be repeated to accumulate multiple scenes. Then the accumulated result

Figure 1.6 The bottom window shows a scene using stenciling to limit the rendering of a scene to a pattern loaded into the stencil buffer. The top left window shows the stencil pattern (rendered to the image buffer). The top right window shows the scene rendered without stenciling.

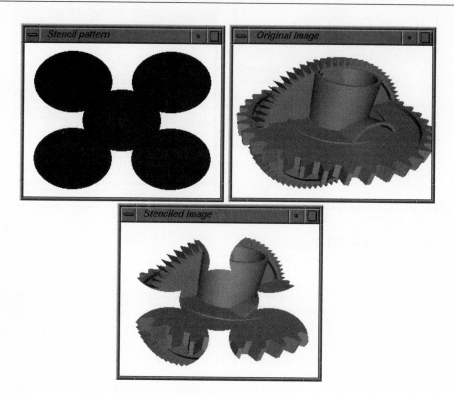

image can be transferred back into the image buffer for display. The effect is much the same as the one a photographer gets from exposing a piece of film several times.

Accumulation buffers generally have more bits of resolution than image buffers, typically twice the resolution. This extended range helps to ensure that image precision is not lost when many images are accumulated.

Here is how an accumulation buffer could be used to achieve an effect similar to the motion blur seen in photographs of quickly moving objects: Draw a scene several times, with each frame corresponding to a slightly advanced point in time. By accumulating all the frames (with reduced intensity for earlier frames), you can achieve the appearance of motion blur, since motionless objects are sharp but moving objects are blurred by their accumulation in slightly differing locations.

1.2.5.4 Double Buffering

Double buffering means having two image buffers, one visible *front* buffer and another, nonvisible, *back* buffer. Unlike simple 2D rendering, generating 3D images may take substantial time. Also, use of the depth, stencil, and accumulation buffers all means that the image being drawn at any moment may be quite different from the final image. It would be quite distracting for the viewer to see each scene while it was "under construction" and would destroy the illusion of a smoothly animated scene. Double buffering allows one image to be rendered while another is being displayed.

OpenGL supports this use of front and back image buffers. The `glDrawBuffer` routine can be used to specify which buffer is the target of rendering operations. To render to the back buffer, a program calls `glDrawBuffer(GL_BACK)`. A window system specific routine makes the back buffer visible. For X, that routine is `glXSwap-Buffers`.

Double buffering is often achieved by rendering into a nonvisible image buffer in main memory and then quickly copying the buffer's contents to screen memory. A better alternative is to build hardware that actually supports two sets of image buffers. Then the cost of a buffer swap can be extremely low, since no data has to be copied. Instead, the video controller just changes to scanning image pixels out of the other buffer. This technique is shown in Figure 1.13 and is further discussed in Section 6.5.5.

1.2.5.5 Stereo

Stereo is similar to double buffering in that more than one image buffer is supported. In addition to front and back buffers, left and right buffers are provided. (Typically stereo and double buffering are combined, requiring four image buffers; this is sometimes called *quad-buffering.*) Special stereo video hardware can alternate between scanning out the left and right buffers for every screen refresh. Viewing goggles that synchronize with the vertical refresh of the screen alternately open and close LCD shutters so that the left eye sees the left frame and the right eye sees the right frame. If a program carefully draws the scene twice with slightly different perspectives in the left and right buffers, the viewer experiences an optical illusion of 3D.

While double buffering is common on graphics workstations, stereo requires special hardware and tends to be rather expensive, so most OpenGL implementations do not support stereo.

1.2.6 Modeling and Viewing

One of the most difficult initial hurdles in learning 3D graphics programming is how to properly set up a scene and the parameters to define a reasonable view of that scene. It is very easy to get a blank window because the viewing parameters for the scene are not properly initialized.

Figure 1.7 Stages of vertex transformation.

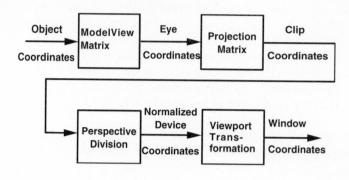

3D computer graphics uses matrix transformations to orient, view, clip, and map the model to the screen. OpenGL's various stages in mapping vertices in object coordinates into pixels in window coordinates are shown in Figure 1.7 .

An OpenGL programmer is responsible for loading the *modelview* and *projection* matrices. The modelview matrix determines how the vertices of OpenGL primitives are transformed to eye coordinates. The projection matrix transforms vertices in eye coordinates to clip coordinates.

A number of OpenGL routines deal with manipulating these matrices. The glMatrixMode routine is called with an argument of GL_MODELVIEW or GL_PROJECTION to specify the matrix to be modified. Then glLoadIdentity may be called to set the currently modifiable matrix to the identity matrix. Routines such as glRotatef, glTranslatef, and glScalef may be called to manipulate the currently modifiable matrix. glLoadMatrixf loads a specific matrix; glMultMatrixf multiplies the current matrix by some specified matrix and stores the result as the current matrix. This book will not explain the theory behind modelview and projection matrices and will not provide much tutorial material on their use. Any introductory 3D graphics text will cover the topic in detail.

OpenGL provides matrix stacks that, like the attribute stack, allow you to save and restore the modelview and projection matrices. Use glPushMatrix and glPopMatrix to save and restore matrices.

OpenGL and its utility library, called GLU (described in Section 1.4), include several routines for initializing the modelview and perspective matrices: glFrustum, glOrtho, gluOrtho2D, gluPerspective, and so on. To help initialize the modelview matrix, the gluLookAt routine defines a base viewing transformation. Figure 1.8 shows how changing the projection matrix and the base modelview matrix affects the way a scene is rendered.

The final step in establishing a view of your scene is the *viewport* transformation. It determines how the scene will be mapped onto the computer screen. The

Figure 1.8 The upper left view shows an initial view of a set of objects. The other views show how changing OpenGL's projection and modelview matrices changes the view of the objects.

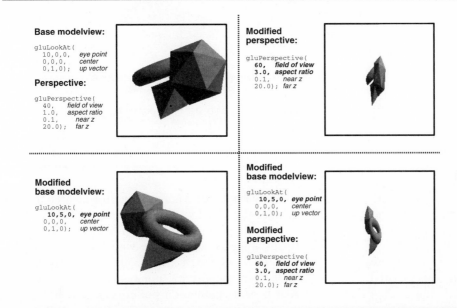

glViewport routine specifies the rectangle in the window into which the final image is to be mapped. By default, the entire window is used. glViewport is commonly invoked when an OpenGL window is resized.

1.2.7 Further Capabilities

Simply specifying 3D primitives and determining how to map them to the screen is not enough to achieve realistic images. Some features that improve image quality, such as lighting, have already been hinted at. OpenGL supports a number of lighting models that simulate the effects of lighting on primitives. Light sources can be defined and material properties can be specified to achieve realistic lighting effects. Lighting is discussed further in Section 5.1.

OpenGL supports polygons that are flat-shaded or smooth-shaded, as shown in Figure 1.9. Flat-shaded means the entire polygon is a single, uniform color. Smooth-shaded (or *Gouraud shaded*) means the polygon color varies continuously across the surface based on colors assigned to the vertices.

In addition to providing these shading models, OpenGL allows primitives to be rendered that have a 1D or 2D texture mapped onto the polygon. For example, the

Figure 1.9 Comparing flat and smooth polygon shading.

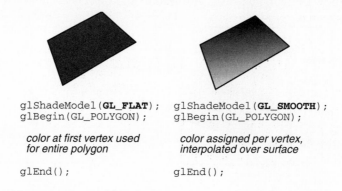

```
glShadeModel(GL_FLAT);        glShadeModel(GL_SMOOTH);
glBegin(GL_POLYGON);          glBegin(GL_POLYGON);
```

color at first vertex used   *color assigned per vertex,*
for entire polygon   *interpolated over surface*

```
glEnd();                      glEnd();
```

surface of a desk could be textured with a wood-grain image for greater realism. Texture mapping can greatly enhance the visual impact of a scene without increasing its geometric complexity. Texture mapping is discussed further in Section 5.2.

Because 3D rendering eventually appears on a screen with limited resolution, OpenGL provides various techniques to eliminate the "jaggies" that result from aliasing. OpenGL provides *antialiasing* support for points, lines, and polygons. Techniques using the alpha, stencil, or accumulation buffers can also be used to minimize aliasing problems.

Computer images often appear unrealistically sharp and well-defined. OpenGL supports *fog* to provide an effect that simulates atmospheric effects. Haze, mist, smoke, and pollution can all be simulated. When fog is enabled, objects farther away begin to fade into the specified fog color. Fog can be used in the rendering of wireframe objects to show which lines are more distant in the scene. This technique is called *depth cueing*. Antialiasing, fog, and blending are related topics and will be discussed in Section 5.3.

Many graphics applications, such as computer-aided design tools, need to draw curves and surfaces. Polygons are flat, so it takes many small polygons to approximate a curved surface. Also, it takes many small lines to approximate a curve. OpenGL provides an *evaluator* facility for the efficient rendering of curves and surfaces. Curves and surfaces are discussed further in Section 5.5.

Users of 3D want to do more than just see 3D images; they want to interact with them. For example, an application may let a user click on an object in a 3D scene to indicate that this is the object to be manipulated. This is often called *picking*. To support picking, OpenGL supports a *selection* mechanism that returns the objects that are rendered at a given location on the screen. OpenGL also has a *feedback* mechanism that returns the results of transformation calculations.

Often a sequence of OpenGL commands is rendered repeatedly. OpenGL supports *display lists*, which allow commands to be compiled for later execution. Dis-

Figure 1.10 Example of hierarchical display list usage. The single `glCallList(3)` call will generate 17 OpenGL commands.

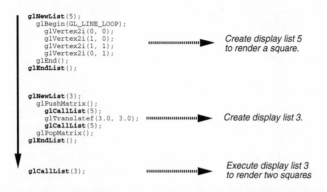

```
glNewList(5);
   glBegin(GL_LINE_LOOP);
      glVertex2i(0, 0);                              Create display list 5
      glVertex2i(1, 0);                              to render a square.
      glVertex2i(1, 1);
      glVertex2i(0, 1);
   glEnd();
glEndList();


glNewList(3);
   glPushMatrix();
      glCallList(5);                                 Create display list 3.
      glTranslatef(3.0, 3.0);
      glCallList(5);
   glPopMatrix();
glEndList();


glCallList(3);                                       Execute display list 3
                                                     to render two squares
```

play lists can even call other display lists, allowing hierarchies of display lists as shown in Figure 1.10. For networked 3D applications, display lists can greatly minimize the network protocol bandwidth needed and increase performance. The routines `glNewList` and `glEndList` are used to create a display list. A created display list can be executed using the `glCallList` routine.

One thing to keep in mind about OpenGL is that the features described above are not isolated functionalities. Each feature can be combined with others for advanced effects. For example, lighting, fog, display lists, texture mapping, and double buffering can all be used simultaneously.

OpenGL has still more capabilities, but their full introduction is beyond the scope of this chapter. Explanations and sample code in later chapters, particularly Chapter 5, provide more explanation of many of OpenGL's features and demonstrate their use.

1.3   GLX: The Glue Between OpenGL and X

As explained earlier, OpenGL is *window system independent*. This means that the basic OpenGL routines do not describe how an OpenGL context is created or how to create a window for use with OpenGL rendering. Instead, OpenGL leaves the details of window creation and other window management tasks to the native window system. This means OpenGL can be implemented for the X Window System, Windows NT, or any future window system.

Since the OpenGL specification does not describe the way OpenGL integrates with the window system, a supplemental specification must describe the way OpenGL integrates with a particular window system. GLX is an extension to the core X protocol for communicating OpenGL commands to the X server. It also supports window system specific operations such as creating rendering contexts for OpenGL rendering and binding those contexts to windows.

You can tell whether a particular X server supports OpenGL by running the xdpyinfo (X display info) command and looking for GLX in the list of supported extensions. For example, on Unix systems, you can use the command

```
xdpyinfo | grep GLX
```

If GLX is printed, OpenGL is supported.

GLX defines an API that provides the routines (all prefixed by glx) for interfacing OpenGL with X. GLX also defines a byte-stream protocol for supporting OpenGL as an X server extension. The GLX protocol allows 3D applications running on workstations from different vendors to interoperate in the same way as the X protocol provides network-extensible 2D graphics interoperability. Be aware that the term *GLX* is sometimes used to describe the GLX protocol and sometimes the API. Because the API hides the details of the GLX protocol from the programmer, most of the time *GLX* is used to refer to the API.

1.3.1   A Quick Survey of GLX

GLX permits OpenGL rendering into both X windows and pixmaps. An X server can support different visuals to describe the different types of windows supported by the server. When a window is created, a visual is specified that determines the visual type and frame buffer capabilities of the newly created window. For the core X protocol, a visual determines how pixel values are mapped to colors on the screen. X treats a drawable as basically a 2D array of pixels, but OpenGL has a much more sophisticated view of a drawable's frame buffer capabilities. GLX overloads the core X notion of a visual by associating additional information about OpenGL's frame buffer capabilities. In addition to an image buffer, OpenGL can support the types of ancillary buffers discussed in Section 1.2.5. For example, an OpenGL-capable window might also have a stencil buffer and a depth buffer. Multiple different frame buffer configurations can be supported by a single X server by exporting multiple visuals. The specific OpenGL-capable visuals an X server provides depend on the OpenGL implementation and the available graphics hardware resources.

All OpenGL implementations for the X Window System *must* support at least one RGBA visual. A color index visual is also required if the X server supports PseudoColor or StaticColor visuals. These required visuals must support a stencil buffer of at least 1 bit and a depth buffer of at least 12 bits. The required RGBA visual must have an accumulation buffer. The alpha component of the image buffer is not required for the RGBA visual (but alpha is still used in all rendering calculations). Many implementations will supply many more than two visuals.

The GLX API supplies two routines, glxGetConfig and glxChooseVisual, to help programmers select an appropriate visual. Once the appropriate visual is selected, XCreateWindow creates the window with the selected visual.

GLX supports offscreen rendering to pixmaps. First create a standard X pixmap of the desired depth, using `XCreatePixmap`. Then call `glXCreateGLXPixmap` with the desired OpenGL visual. A new drawable of type `GLXPixmap` is returned; it can be used for drawing OpenGL into the pixmap.

To render using OpenGL, an OpenGL *rendering context* must be created. The `glXCreateContext` routine creates such a context. The object returned by `glXCreateContext` is of type `GLXContext`. Each rendering context is a bundle of all the state that affects OpenGL rendering. Think of a rendering context as an instance of an OpenGL state machine.

Before any OpenGL rendering can occur, a rendering context must be *bound* to the desired OpenGL-capable frame buffer resource using `glXMakeCurrent`. The term *GLX drawable* describes any "frame buffer" resource into which OpenGL rendering can be directed. Two types of GLX drawables are mandated by GLX: X windows and GLX pixmaps (the `GLXPixmap` object returned by `glXCreatePixmap`).[2] All GLX drawables are of type `GLXDrawable`. All OpenGL rendering commands implicitly use the currently bound rendering context and drawable.

Just as a program can create multiple windows, a program can create multiple OpenGL rendering contexts. A single *thread* of control within an OpenGL process can be bound only to one rendering context and drawable at a time. (A thread is an independently scheduled unit of processor execution; standard Unix processes have a single thread.) Once the thread is bound, OpenGL rendering can begin. `glXMakeCurrent` can be called again to bind to a different window and/or rendering context. This is rather different from the standard Xlib rendering model, in which every X rendering routine (such as `XPutImage`, for example) is given both the X drawable and the X graphics context as explicit arguments, instead of being implicitly determined by the current bound drawable and rendering context as in OpenGL. Unlike `XPutImage`, an OpenGL rendering routine such as `glDrawPixels` takes neither the GLX drawable nor the rendering context as an argument. The difference between the two approaches is shown in Figure 1.11. OpenGL's approach is faster, since fewer arguments are passed with each rendering routine called. Also, changing rendering contexts is expensive, particularly when hardware is used to maintain OpenGL's state. `glXMakeCurrent` discourages unnecessary graphics context switches by making them explicit to the programmer.

The analogy shown in Figure 1.12 compares a GLX rendering context and a GLX drawable to a crayon and a sheet of paper. Just as the crayon's color and the pressure with which the crayon is used determine how the sheet of paper is drawn on, the state of an OpenGL rendering context determines how pixels in the frame buffer of a GLX drawable will be updated.

The GLX stream of commands is considered distinct from the stream of X requests. Sometimes you may want to mix OpenGL and X rendering into the same window. If so, synchronization can be achieved using the `glXWaitGL` and `glXWaitX` routines. For

---

2.   It is possible for other types of GLX drawables to be supported through extensions to GLX. For example, another type of GLX drawable may support hardware-accelerated rendering into off screen frame buffer memory.

Figure 1.11 Implicit OpenGL drawable and rendering context specification versus the explicit specification of drawable and graphics context used by Xlib.

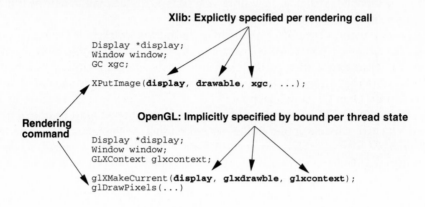

most X applications, this synchronization is not an issue, because applications typically segregate X and OpenGL rendering into distinct windows. OpenGL rendering is typically done to windows created specifically for 3D rendering, while other X windows for the user interface are rendered with X rendering requests.

To swap the buffers of a double buffered window, `glXSwapBuffers` can be called. Figure 1.13 shows how `glXSwapBuffers` is used for animation.

Figure 1.12 A visual analogy comparing X and GLX rendering objects.

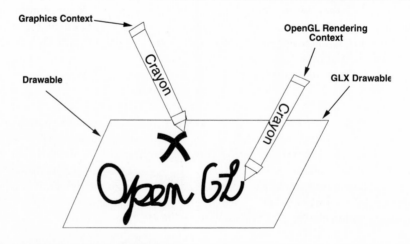

Figure 1.13 Animation through hardware double buffering.

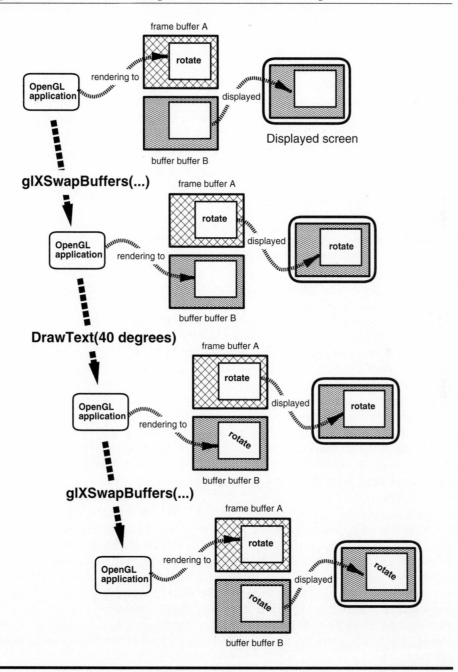

X fonts can be converted into per-glyph OpenGL display lists using the `glXUseXFont` routine. This means that the same fonts available for X rendering are available for OpenGL rendering.

GLX does not demand that OpenGL commands be executed by the X server. The GLX specification explicitly allows OpenGL to render directly to the hardware if this feature is supported by the implementation. This is referred to as *direct rendering*, as opposed to *indirect rendering*, in which rendering requests are passed to the X server for execution. Direct rendering is possible when the program is running on the same machine as the graphics hardware. When available, direct rendering allows extremely high-performance rendering, because OpenGL commands do not need to be sent through the X server to get to the graphics hardware.

1.3.2 The GLX Protocol

The GLX protocol is an X extension protocol embedded in the X11 protocol stream, like other X extension protocols such as the Shape extension or the X Input extension. In the same way that the Xlib API hides the X11 protocol encoding from X programmers, OpenGL programmers do not need to be aware of the protocol encoding because the OpenGL and GLX APIs are transparently translated into GLX protocol as necessary.

OpenGL rendering requests are combined in `GLXRender` requests to reduce overhead. The batching of GLX protocol, just like the batching of normal X11 protocol, allows the context switch overhead between the client and the server to be amortized over multiple calls and it allows larger chunks of protocol to be transported for greater efficiency.

The overhead of transporting GLX protocol from OpenGL programs to the X server may be high enough that it can impinge on OpenGL rendering performance. The use of display lists to download sequences of OpenGL commands within the X server can help balance the overhead of issuing OpenGL requests. Programmers should minimize the number of state retrieving calls such as `glGetIntegerv`, since these demand a roundtrip between the OpenGL client and the X server.

Using direct rendering, when it is available, can eliminate the use of GLX protocol for OpenGL rendering when programs are running on the local workstation. Direct rendering can be a tremendous performance boon if it is available. While all OpenGL implementations for X are required to support indirect rendering so that OpenGL can work across a network, support for direct rendering is not required. Your program may request that direct rendering be used if available, but whether OpenGL rendering is done directly or indirectly will not affect the way your program runs or how it is written, only the speed at which it renders OpenGL. OpenGL's architecture for direct and indirect rendering is shown in Figure 1.14.

Figure 1.14 The GLX architecture supports both direct rendering (for high-performance rendering by local programs) and indirect rendering (for remote programs or when direct rendering is not supported). Indirect programs use the X server as a proxy for OpenGL rendering.

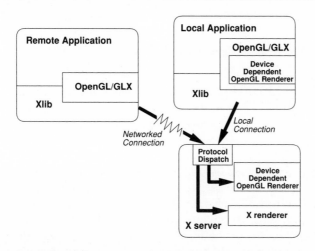

1.4 THE GLU LIBRARY

The core OpenGL library is a software interface to graphics hardware, so the implementation is naturally dependent on the available graphics hardware. In other words, the core OpenGL library is *device-dependent*. However, a number of tasks are common to many OpenGL programs that are *device-independent*. The OpenGL Utility library (GLU) collects a set of routines that implement useful operations common to many OpenGL programs. The GLU routines (all prefixed with glu) fall into the following areas:

- Manipulating images for use in texturing (see Section 5.2).
- Transforming coordinates.
- Polygon tessellation (see Section 2.1.2).
- Rendering spheres, cylinders, and disks.
- Non-Uniform Rational B-Spline (NURBS) curves and surfaces (see Section 5.5).
- Describing errors (see Section 2.8).

While GLU is not part of the core OpenGL library, it is a standard interface available to all OpenGL programs. The GLU library is window system independent, so the GLU library is available on other window systems as well as on X. There is nothing in the GLU library that you could not implement yourself, but by using the GLU library, you save time by not rewriting common (though sometimes involved) graphics operations.

1.5 AN EXAMPLE XLIB-BASED OPENGL PROGRAM

This section presents the source code for a simple OpenGL program using Xlib and GLX. This example demonstrates what is involved in programming OpenGL with Xlib and GLX. Most X programmers do not program at the Xlib level, but instead use widgets, such as the Motif widget set. Chapter 3 discusses using OpenGL with the Motif widget set. However, whether you program using the Motif or the Xlib interface, the GLX routines you will use are the same.

The program, named `glxsimple`, creates a window and draws a 3D cube (missing two faces) and allows the user to rotate the cube around the X, Y, and Z axes, using the mouse buttons. Figure 1.15 shows what the program displays.

Besides demonstrating how to establish an X window for OpenGL rendering, the example demonstrates the use of double buffering, display lists, and establishing the proper viewing parameters. The point of `glxsimple` is to provide a quick tour of what OpenGL programs for X must do. The program does the bare minimum required to render OpenGL into a window.

Figure 1.15 Screen snapshot of `glxsimple`.

1.5.1 Initialization

The following is a walk through the steps that set up a window for OpenGL rendering. The same numbers are used later to discuss the way `glxsimple.c` performs each step.

1. As in all X programs, `XOpenDisplay` should be called to open a connection to the X server.

2. Using `glXQueryExtension`, make sure the OpenGL GLX extension is supported by the X server.

3. Before creating the window, the program needs to select an appropriate visual. The GLX routine `glXChooseVisual` makes it easy to find the right visual. In the example, an RGBA (and `TrueColor`) visual with a depth buffer is desired: if possible, it should support double buffering.

4. Create an OpenGL rendering context by calling `glXCreateContext`.

5. Create a window with the selected visual. Most X programs always use the default visual, but OpenGL programmers will need to be comfortable with using visuals other than the default. The selected visual is passed to `XCreateWindow`.

6. Using `glXMakeCurrent`, bind the rendering context to the window. Subsequent OpenGL rendering commands will use the current window and rendering context.

7. To display the window, `XMapWindow` should be called.

8. Set the desired OpenGL state. Depth buffering is enabled, the clear color is set to black, and the 3D viewing volume is specified.

9. Begin dispatching X events.

Button presses change the angle of rotation for the object to be viewed and cause a redraw. Expose events also cause a redraw (without changing the rotation). Window resizes call `glViewport` to ensure that the OpenGL viewport corresponds to the maximum dimensions of the window.

1.5.2 Example: `glxsimple.c`

Here is the `glxsimple.c` program. First include the necessary header files for Xlib and GLX. The `<stdio.h>` and `<stdlib.h>` headers include basic C library declarations. The `<X11/Xlib.h>` header includes declarations for the Xlib library. The `<GL/glx.h>` header includes declarations for the GLX interface; the `<GL/gl.h>` header includes declarations for OpenGL's core interface. Note that there are distinct header files for GLX and for the core of OpenGL.

```
#include <stdio.h>
#include <stdlib.h>
```

```
#include <X11/Xlib.h>
#include <GL/glx.h>
#include <GL/gl.h>
```

Declare needed global variables and variables used by main. The snglBuf and dblBuf arrays specify a list of frame buffer capabilities to be passed to glXChoose-Visual to determine what visual to use.

```
static int snglBuf[] = {GLX_RGBA, GLX_RED_SIZE, 1, GLX_GREEN_SIZE,
                1, GLX_BLUE_SIZE, 1, GLX_DEPTH_SIZE, 12,
                None};
static int dblBuf[] = {GLX_RGBA, GLX_RED_SIZE, 1, GLX_GREEN_SIZE,
                1, GLX_BLUE_SIZE, 1, GLX_DEPTH_SIZE, 12,
                GLX_DOUBLEBUFFER, None};


Display *dpy;
Window win;
Bool doubleBuffer = True;
/* Initial 3D box orientation. */
GLfloat xAngle = 42.0, yAngle = 82.0, zAngle = 112.0;


void
main(int argc, char **argv)
{
  XVisualInfo *vi;
  Colormap cmap;
  XSetWindowAttributes swa;
  GLXContext cx;
  XEvent event;
  Bool needRedraw = False, recalcModelView = True;
  int dummy;
```

Step 1. Open a connection to the X server. If an unexpected condition occurs, fatalError will print an explanation and exit.

```
  dpy = XOpenDisplay(NULL);
  if (dpy == NULL)
    fatalError("could not open display");
```
• • • • • • • • • • • •

Step 2. Make sure OpenGL's GLX extension is supported. The `glXQuery-Extension` also returns the GLX extension's error base and event base. For almost all OpenGL programs, this information is irrelevant; hence the use of `dummy`.

```
if (!glXQueryExtension(dpy, &dummy, &dummy))
  fatalError("X server has no OpenGL GLX extension");
```
• • • • • • • • • • • •

Step 3. Find an appropriate OpenGL-capable visual. Look for double buffering first; if it is not found, settle for a single buffered visual.

```
vi = glXChooseVisual(dpy, DefaultScreen(dpy), dblBuf);
if (vi == NULL) {
  vi = glXChooseVisual(dpy, DefaultScreen(dpy), snglBuf);
  if (vi == NULL)
    fatalError("no RGB visual with depth buffer");
  doubleBuffer = False;
}
if (vi->class != TrueColor)
  fatalError("TrueColor visual required for this program");
```
• • • • • • • • • • • •

Step 4. Create an OpenGL rendering context.

```
cx = glXCreateContext(dpy, vi,
  /* No sharing of display lists */ None,
  /* Direct rendering if possible */ True);
if (cx == NULL)
  fatalError("could not create rendering context");
```
• • • • • • • • • • • •

Step 5. Create an X window with the selected visual. Since the visual selected is likely not to be the default, create an X colormap for use.

```
cmap = XCreateColormap(dpy, RootWindow(dpy, vi->screen),
  vi->visual, AllocNone);
swa.colormap = cmap;
swa.border_pixel = 0;
swa.event_mask = ExposureMask | ButtonPressMask |
  StructureNotifyMask;
```

```
win = XCreateWindow(dpy, RootWindow(dpy, vi-screen), 0, 0, 300,
                    300, 0, vi->depth, InputOutput, vi->visual,
                    CWBorderPixel | CWColormap | CWEventMask,
                    &swa);
XSetStandardProperties(dpy, win, "glxsimple", "glxsimple", None,
                       argv, argc, NULL);
```

• • • • • • • • • • • • •

Step 6. Bind the rendering context to the window.

```
glXMakeCurrent(dpy, win, cx);
```

• • • • • • • • • • • • •

Step 7. Request that the X window be displayed on the screen.

```
XMapWindow(dpy, win);
```

• • • • • • • • • • • • •

Step 8. Configure the OpenGL context for rendering.

```
/* Enable depth buffering */
glEnable(GL_DEPTH_TEST);
/* Set up projection transform. */
glMatrixMode(GL_PROJECTION);
glLoadIdentity();
glFrustum(-1.0, 1.0, -1.0, 1.0, 1.0, 10.0);
```

• • • • • • • • • • • • •

Step 9. Dispatch X events. The program handles only three event types. A mouse `ButtonPress` event will rotate the cube. Each button updates a different axis of rotation and sets the `recalcModelView` flag. A `ConfigureNotify` event informs the program when the window is resized. In response, the program updates the OpenGL viewport to render to the full size of the window. If an `Expose` event is received, indicating that the window needs to be redrawn, this is noted with the `needRedraw` flag. To minimize the work to be done, we read as many events as are ready to be received before acting on the events.

```
while (1) {
  do {
    XNextEvent(dpy, &event);
    switch (event.type) {
```

```
    case ButtonPress:
      recalcModelView = True;
      switch (event.xbutton.button) {
      case 1:
        xAngle += 10.0;
        break;
      case 2:
        yAngle += 10.0;
        break;
      case 3:
        zAngle += 10.0;
        break;
      }
      break;
    case ConfigureNotify:
      glViewport(0, 0, event.xconfigure.width,
        event.xconfigure.height);
      /* Fall through... */
    case Expose:
      needRedraw = True;
      break;
    }
  } while (XPending(dpy)); /* Loop to compress events. */
```
• • • • • • • • • • • • •

Once the outstanding events have been read, we update the OpenGL modelview
matrix if the `recalcModelView` flag is set. This ensures that any rotations from button presses will be applied. Any time the modelview matrix changes, the scene
should also be redrawn so `needRedraw` is set.

After updating the modelview matrix, determine whether a redraw is needed by
checking the `needRedraw` flag. If it is, call the `redraw` routine to update the window's scene.

```
  if (recalcModelView) {
    glMatrixMode(GL_MODELVIEW);
    /* Reset modelview matrix to the identity matrix. */
    glLoadIdentity();
    /* Move the camera back three units. */
    glTranslatef(0.0, 0.0, -3.0);
    /* Rotate by X, Y, and Z angles. */
    glRotatef(xAngle, 0.1, 0.0, 0.0);
    glRotatef(yAngle, 0.0, 0.1, 0.0);
    glRotatef(zAngle, 0.0, 0.0, 1.0);
    recalcModelView = False;
```

```
      needRedraw = True;
    }
    if (needRedraw) {
      redraw();
      needRedraw = False;
    }
  }
}
```

1.5.3 Scene Update

The redraw routine does all the OpenGL rendering. The code is slightly complicated by constructing a display list to draw the cube. The first time redraw is called, glNewList and glEndList are used to construct a display list for the object to be rendered. Subsequent redraws call the display list instead of rendering the object each time.

Creating a display list potentially allows improved performance, since the commands can be compiled for faster execution. Display lists save having to send all the commands to render the scene whenever the window is redrawn.

```
void
redraw(void)
{
  static Bool displayListInited = False;

  if (displayListInited) {
    /* If display list already exists, just execute it. */
    glCallList(1);
  } else {
    /* Otherwise, compile and execute to create the display
       list. */
    glNewList(1, GL_COMPILE_AND_EXECUTE);
```

The commands for rendering the object consist of four 3D rectangles of different colors. Notice that the rectangles are generated by first calling glBegin(GL_QUADS) and are ended with glEnd. Each rectangle is specified by four glVertex3f calls, which specify the four vertices of that rectangle. The glColor3f invocations tell in what color each rectangle should be rendered.

```
    glClear(GL_COLOR_BUFFER_BIT | GL_DEPTH_BUFFER_BIT);
    glBegin(GL_QUADS);
      /* Front face */
      glColor3f(0.0, 0.7, 0.1); /* Green */
```

```
      glVertex3f(-1.0, 1.0, 1.0);
      glVertex3f(1.0, 1.0, 1.0);
      glVertex3f(1.0, -1.0, 1.0);
      glVertex3f(-1.0, -1.0, 1.0);
      /* Back face */
      glColor3f(0.9, 1.0, 0.0); /* Yellow */
      glVertex3f(-1.0, 1.0, -1.0);
      glVertex3f(1.0, 1.0, -1.0);
      glVertex3f(1.0, -1.0, -1.0);
      glVertex3f(-1.0, -1.0, -1.0);
      /* Top side face */
      glColor3f(0.2, 0.2, 1.0); /* Blue */
      glVertex3f(-1.0, 1.0, 1.0);
      glVertex3f(1.0, 1.0, 1.0);
      glVertex3f(1.0, 1.0, -1.0);
      glVertex3f(-1.0, 1.0, -1.0);
      /* Bottom side face */
      glColor3f(0.7, 0.0, 0.1); /* Red */
      glVertex3f(-1.0, -1.0, 1.0);
      glVertex3f(1.0, -1.0, 1.0);
      glVertex3f(1.0, -1.0, -1.0);
      glVertex3f(-1.0, -1.0, -1.0);
    glEnd();
  glEndList();
  displayListInited = True;
}
```

If the window is double buffered, glXSwapBuffers is called on the window. By default, rendering to double buffered windows takes place in the nonvisible back buffer. Swapping buffers will quickly swap the front and back buffers, avoiding any visual artifacts (the contents of the back buffer should be considered undefined after a swap). In effect, the rendering of each frame can be done "behind the scenes."

glFlush is called to ensure that the OpenGL rendering commands are actually sent to the graphics hardware. A flush is implicitly done by glXSwapBuffers, so the glFlush is needed explicitly only in the single-buffered case.

```
  if (doubleBuffer)
    /* Buffer swap does implicit glFlush. */
    glXSwapBuffers(dpy, win);
  else
    /* Explicit flush for single buffered case. */
    glFlush();
}
```

1.5.4 Compiling the Example

When you compile OpenGL programs, you will need to link your program with both OpenGL libraries and X libraries. To compile `glxsimple` on a Unix workstation, your compile command would look something like this:

```
cc -o glxsimple glxsimple.c -lGL -lXext -lX11
```

The `-lGL` option tells the compiler to link with the OpenGL library. The OpenGL library includes both the core OpenGL routines (those prefixed with `gl`) and the GLX routines (those prefixed with `glx`). The `-lXext` option tells the compiler to link with the X extension library. Remember that GLX is an extension to X. The implementation of GLX uses routines in the X extension library to initialize use of the GLX extension. Finally, the `-lX11` option tells the compiler to link with the Xlib routines for communicating with the X server.

The routines that make up the OpenGL Utility (GLU) library, discussed in Section 1.4, are not part of the core OpenGL library, because they are utility routines that are not part of the core OpenGL or GLX interfaces. Instead, the routines are found in a distinct library. If your program uses routines with the `glu` prefix, you will need to supply an additional `-lGLU` option to the compiler, telling it to link with the GLU library.

The OpenGL library is typically implemented as a *shared* library, meaning that the code and data associated with the library are not made part of the executable file that you compile. Instead, the library implementation is dynamically linked into your program when your program starts execution. The major benefit of shared libraries (and the reason for their name) is that several programs on the same machine can share a single copy of the library code instead of each program's having its own copy.

Another benefit of shared libraries that is typically used by OpenGL implementations is that the library implementation itself may be different on different workstations because different workstations may have different graphics hardware. This is very important when direct rendering is supported by an OpenGL implementation, because the way direct rendering is done depends on the graphics hardware available on a given workstation.

When you compile your OpenGL program with your workstation vendor's shared OpenGL library that supports direct rendering, this makes it possible for that same program (without any recompilation) to be copied to another machine supported by your workstation vendor, but with different graphics hardware, and still run your OpenGL program. Because the device-dependent OpenGL rendering code is within the shared library, rather than in your program's executable file, your program can run on current and future graphics hardware without recompilation. It also means your vendor can fix bugs and improve the speed of its OpenGL implementation and your program can immediately benefit from new versions of the OpenGL shared library.

The `glxsimple` example is very basic. Section 2.1 has a more involved example that demonstrates how to better take advantage of OpenGL with the X Window System.

1.6 COMPARING OPENGL TO PEX

OpenGL is not the only means for extending the X Window System to support 3D. PEX [45] is an extension developed by the X Consortium to add 3D capabilities to X. Readers familiar with PEX may be interested in a brief comparison of OpenGL and PEX; other readers can proceed to the next chapter.

The most commonly available version of PEX is 5.1. An updated release, PEX 5.2, is intended to address many of PEX 5.1's problems that are discussed here, but multiple complete PEX 5.2 implementations are not currently available. An in-depth analysis of PEX 5.1 and OpenGL 1.0 is presented by Akin [3]. The following discussion focuses on some of the most prominent distinctions between OpenGL and PEX.

1.6.1 Subsets and Baselines

One thing that makes PEX difficult to compare to OpenGL is that PEX allows much of its functionality to be optionally implemented. PEX classifies its functionality into one or more of three subsets: the immediate mode subset, the structure subset, and the PHIGS workstation subset. (PHIGS is a 3D graphics standard; the abbreviation stands for Programmer's Hierarchical Interactive Graphics System.) The PEX specification *explicitly* allows implementations to support one, two, or all three subsets. The result is that an application cannot depend on any given PEX server to supply the subset functionality the application might require.

OpenGL requires that all its rendering functionality be supported. Even advanced features such as depth buffering, fog, lighting, antialiasing, and texturing must be supported in *all* implementations.

Still, not all OpenGL implementations are totally identical. Rendering functionality is not a complete picture of OpenGL's capability. Rendering performance will depend on the implementation, and OpenGL frame buffer capabilities will vary among implementations. Different depths of ancillary buffers will be supported; stereo and double-buffering hardware may or may not actually be present; a frame buffer may or may not support the alpha component. Despite the possibility of variation, OpenGL's GLX standard does *mandate* an RGBA visual with frame buffer capabilities that are sufficient for most common 3D applications. When color index is supported by the hardware, a color index visual with suitable frame buffer capabilities must also be supported. Stencil and depth buffers must be supported for these required visuals, and an accumulation buffer must be supported for the RGBA visual. These required visuals guarantee that all OpenGL implementations have a standard baseline of both rendering and frame buffer functionality that applications can rely on to be present.

1.6.2 Programming Interfaces

There is an essential difference between PEX and OpenGL, which lies in the ways the two graphics systems are specified. OpenGL is fundamentally specified as an application programming interface. As with the X Window System, the fundamental specification for PEX is a wire protocol.

In PEX, the choice of programming interface is left to the programmer. In X11R5, a PHIGS-style API has been supplied, but this API for PEX has not gained much acceptance. Currently, the PEX community is standardizing on the PEXlib API, which more readily exposes the wire protocol and can be implemented independent of the PEX protocol (like OpenGL direct rendering). The disadvantage of PEXlib is that implementation dependencies are also exposed, leaving the programmer to work around the absence of functionality that is missing because of subsetting in PEX implementations.

With OpenGL there is a single API, which promises to be standard even across differing window systems (such as X and Windows NT), and the full functionality of this API is available in all OpenGL implementations. The GLX specification does provide a wire protocol for network-transparent operation, but the wire protocol is not the fundamental specification of OpenGL.

1.6.3 Rendering Functionality

PEX and OpenGL both support basic 3D rendering functionality. Both allow 3D and 2D lines and polygons to be rendered using standard modeling and viewing methods. PEX (depending on the implementation) and OpenGL also support picking, lighting, depth cueing, and hidden-line and -surface removal.

OpenGL supports a number of sophisticated rendering features that PEX 5.1 lacks. Alpha blending, texture and environment mapping, antialiasing, accumulation buffer methods, and stencil buffering are all missing from PEX (though some PEX implementations supply these as nonstandard extensions).

PEX does support features not available in OpenGL. PEX has extensive text support for stroke fonts that are fully transformable in 3D. B-Spline surfaces and curves are supported directly by PEX, whereas OpenGL supports NURBS functionality via routines that are part of the GLU library. PEX can support cell arrays, but the functionality is seldom implemented. Markers and quadrilateral meshes are supported by PEX as rendering primitives; neither is supported as a primitive by OpenGL. PEX supports self-intersecting contours and polygon lists with shared geometry; OpenGL does not.

1.6.4 Display Lists

PEX and OpenGL both provide means to store commands for later execution. In PEX (for implementations that support the structure or PHIGS workstation subsets), editable *structures* can be created and edited. A structure contains graphics primitives, such as a polygon. Structures may also contain calls to execute other structures, allowing them to be arranged in a hierarchical fashion. An entire 3D model can be constructed out of a hierarchy of structures, so that a redraw requires only retraversing the structure hierarchy.

OpenGL does not support structures in the same way as PEX does. Instead, *display lists* can be constructed that contain sequences of OpenGL commands. Like structures, a display list can contain a command to execute another display list, effectively allowing display lists to be combined into arbitrary networks. Unlike structures, OpenGL display lists are *not* editable. Once one is created, it is sealed and cannot be changed (except by destroying and recreating it). This write-only nature allows optimizations to be performed on display lists that are unavailable to structures. The commands in a display list can be optimized for faster execution.

Even though display lists cannot be edited, this should not be considered a disadvantage. The same effect as that of editing can be achieved by rewriting display lists called by other display lists.

Display lists and structures both minimize the amount of transfer overhead when PEX or OpenGL is run over a network, since the commands in a structure or display list can be executed repeatedly by only calling the "structure or" display list by name. The commands themselves need to be transferred across the wire only once.

1.6.5 Portability

While PEX was designed to be vendor-independent and portable, the subsetting allowed by the PEX standard allows implementations of greatly varying functionality to claim to be "standard" PEX implementations. The fact that PEX explicitly allows multiple subsets perhaps indicates the PEX standard may be too large to implement fully and completely in a timely fashion. Anyone who has been disappointed by the functionality of the X Consortium's sample implementation will understand this problem.

OpenGL does not allow any subsetting of rendering functionality and therefore can expect much greater application portability. The need for interoperability testing for OpenGL is greatly reduced because OpenGL demands more consistent implementations.

Neither OpenGL nor PEX is *pixel exact*. This means neither specification is completely explicit about what pixels must be modified by each rendering operation (the core X protocol is largely pixel exact). Pixel exactness is not a desirable feature for 3D since much 3D graphics is done with floating-point where limited numerical precision make exactness nearly impossible. However, the OpenGL specification is much more rigorous than PEX about what is considered conformant behavior. Not only does this make conformance test design easier, but OpenGL programmers can have high confidence that their scene will be rendered accurately on all compliant OpenGL implementations.

The OpenGL release kit includes a suite of conformance tests to verify rendering accuracy. No standard test suites exist to validate PEX implementations.

1.6.6 Window System Dependency

PEX is very tightly coupled to the X Window System. Not only was it designed in the context of X but its semantics depend on X notions of drawables, events, and execution requirements.

But X is not the only significant window system on the market. For this reason, OpenGL was designed to be window system independent. This means its API can also be used with Windows NT and future window systems. Application developers wishing to develop 3D applications for both X and Windows machines will appreciate having a consistent model for 3D across the two window systems.

2

Integrating X and OpenGL

This chapter, which explains OpenGL's integration with the X Window System at the Xlib level, is organized into the following eight sections:

1. "A More Involved Xlib Example" shows how to use the Xlib, GLX, GLU, and OpenGL interfaces to construct a simple but complete OpenGL example to view a 3D dinosaur model.

2. "OpenGL and X Visuals" further explains how X visuals advertise frame buffer configurations and gives advice for selecting the right visual.

3. "More about Colormaps" presents more details about using X colormaps for OpenGL windows.

4. "Using GLX Contexts" explains how to create and manage GLX contexts.

5. "Rendering X Fonts with OpenGL" explains how to create display lists containing characters from X fonts.

6. "Rendering OpenGL into Pixmaps" explains how to use GLX pixmaps for offscreen rendering.

7. "Mixing X and OpenGL Rendering" explains how to synchronize OpenGL and X rendering into the same window or pixmap.

8. "Debugging Tips" presents techniques to help you debug OpenGL programs.

2.1 A MORE INVOLVED XLIB EXAMPLE

This section walks through a more involved Xlib example program, called `glx-dino`, which renders a 3D dinosaur model using OpenGL. Like `glxsimple`, discussed in the preceding chapter, the program uses the Xlib interface for communicating with the X server. However, `glxsimple` does little beyond getting a window onto the screen, rendering the scene, and rudimentary interaction. More sophisticated OpenGL programs need to do more to abide by X Window System conventions.

The `glxdino` program accepts the common X command line options: **–display**, **–geometry**, and **–iconic**. The user rotates the model using mouse motion instead of just button presses. Well-behaved X programs are also expected to communicate with the window manager about the way the window should be treated by the window manager. The conventions for doing this are specified in a document called the Inter-Client Communication Convention Manual (ICCCM for short). ICCCM is an X Consortium standard. `glxdino` uses the conventions specified in the ICCCM to inform the window manager of the application's name, requested size and position on the screen, and iconification state. These properties are also used to request a constant aspect ratio for the window. ICCCM conventions are also used to minimize use of colormap resources.

For the most part, you do not have to understand the ICCCM conventions, because Xlib routines exist for making your requests as to the way your application's windows should be treated.

The program also makes more extensive use of OpenGL. Once again, hidden surfaces are removed using depth buffering, but the dinosaur model used has substantially more polygons than are used by `glxsimple`. A technique known as *backface culling* improves rendering performance by not rendering back-facing polygons. Hierarchical modeling is used to construct the dinosaur and render it via OpenGL display lists. The OpenGL Utility (GLU) library polygon tessellation routines divide complex polygons into simpler polygons that are renderable by OpenGL. Sophisticated lighting lends realism to the dinosaur. And, if available, double buffering smoothes animation. Figure 2.1 shows a screen snapshot of `glxdino`.

2.1.1 Initialization

The program's initialization proceeds through steps that parallel those used by `glx-simple`, though there are some additional steps and some steps are more involved.

1. Process the standard X command line options.

2. Open the connection to the X server.

3. Determine whether OpenGL's GLX extension is supported.

Figure 2.1 Screen snapshot of `glxdino`.

4. Find the appropriate X visual and colormap.
5. Create an OpenGL rendering context.
6. Create an X window for OpenGL rendering.
7. Bind the rendering context to the window.
8. Make the display list hierarchy for the dinosaur model.
9. Configure OpenGL rendering state.
10. Map the window.
11. Begin dispatching X events.

Keep these steps in mind during the following discussion of `glxdino.c`'s initialization code. The step numbers are referenced as the corresponding steps are discussed.

The program begins by including header files for the interfaces to be used by the program:

```
/* C library header files. */
#include <stdio.h>
#include <stdlib.h>
```

```
#include <string.h>
#include <math.h>

/* OpenGL header files. */
#include <GL/gl.h>
#include <GL/glx.h>
#include <GL/glu.h>

/* X header files. */
#include <X11/Xlib.h>
#include <X11/Xatom.h>
#include <X11/Xmu/StdCmap.h>
#include <X11/keysym.h>
```

Also, the program uses several global variables to keep track of program state:

```
Display *dpy;
Window win;
GLfloat angle = -150; /* in degrees */
Bool doubleBuffer = True, iconic = False, keepAspect = False;
  int W = 300, H = 300;
XSizeHints sizeHints = {0};
GLdouble bodyWidth = 2.0;
int configuration[] = {GLX_DOUBLEBUFFER, GLX_RGBA, GLX_DEPTH_SIZE, 12,
  GLX_RED_SIZE, 1, GLX_BLUE_SIZE, 1, GLX_GREEN_SIZE, 1, None};
```

Step 1. After declaring the variables used by main, the first task is to process any command line arguments. Users of the X Window System should be familiar with -display, which specifies the X server to use, -geometry, which specifies the initial size and location of the program's main window, and -iconic, which requests that the window be initially iconified.

While there is no requirement for an X program to accept standard X options, most do as a matter of consistency and convenience. Most X toolkits automatically parse the standard set of X options.

An additional -keepaspect option is not a standard X command line option. When specified, it requests that the window manager ensure that the ratio between the initial width and height of the window be maintained. Often, a 3D program may benefit from a constant aspect ratio for its rendering window.[1] The -single

---

1. Programmers familiar with IRIS GL (OpenGL's predecessor) may recall a routine, named keepaspect, that would maintain the aspect ratio of a window. OpenGL has no similar routine, since OpenGL only supports rendering, so functionality such as maintaining the window aspect ratio must be implemented via X interfaces.

option requests a single-buffered window even if a double-buffered window is available. Without the option, `glxdino` tries to use a double-buffered window, but will use a single-buffered window if a double-buffered visual is not available. The `-keepaspect` and `-single` options are not standard X or OpenGL options; they are simply used to demonstrate how additional options for OpenGL programs might be implemented.

```
void
main(int argc, char **argv)
{
  XVisualInfo *vi;
  Colormap cmap;
  XSetWindowAttributes swa;
  XWMHints *wmHints;
  Atom wmDeleteWindow;
  GLXContext cx;
  XEvent event;
  KeySym ks;
  Bool needRedraw = False, recalcModelView = True;
  char *display = NULL, *geometry = NULL;
  int flags, x, y, width, height, lastX, i;

  for (i = 1; i < argc; i++) {
    if (!strcmp(argv[i], "-geometry")) {
      if (++i >= argc)
        fatalError("follow -geometry option with geometry parameter");
      geometry = argv[i];
    } else if (!strcmp(argv[i], "-display")) {
      if (++i >= argc)
        fatalError("follow -display option with display parameter");
      display = argv[i];
    } else if (!strcmp(argv[i], "-iconic"))
      iconic = True;
    else if (!strcmp(argv[i], "-keepaspect"))
      keepAspect = True;
    else if (!strcmp(argv[i], "-single"))
      doubleBuffer = False;
    else
      fatalError("bad option");
  }
```

• • • • • • • • • • • •

The `fatalError` routine is used to abort `glxdino` if there is an error such as a bad command line option. The routine prints out the message and then exits the program.

Steps 2 and 3. Next, a connection to the X server is established, using `XOpen-Diplay`. Since `glxdino` requires OpenGL's GLX extension, the program checks that the extension exists, using `glXQueryExtension`. The routine indicates whether the GLX extension is supported. As is the convention for X routines that query extensions, the routine can also return the *base error code* and *base event code* for the GLX extension. The current version of GLX supports no extension events, but does define eight protocol errors. Most OpenGL programs will need neither of these numbers. You can pass in `NULL`, as `glxdino` does, to indicate that you do not need the event or error base.

```
dpy = XOpenDisplay(display);
if (dpy == NULL)
  fatalError("could not open display");


if (!glXQueryExtension(dpy, NULL, NULL))
  fatalError("X server has no OpenGL GLX extension");
```
• • • • • • • • • • • •

While `glxdino` uses only base OpenGL and GLX functionality, OpenGL is designed for future extensibility. The `glXQueryVersion` routine returns the major and minor versions of the OpenGL implementation. GLX 1.0 returns a major version of 1 and a minor version of 0; GLX 1.1 returns 1 and 1; GLX 1.2 returns 1 and 2, and so on.

`glxdino` does not use `glXQueryVersion`, but it is useful for any program that requires functionality available only in later versions of OpenGL. Note that the version returned depends on both the OpenGL client program *and* the X server. The number returned is the less recent of the two versions if the versions are different. So a client expecting GLX 1.2 might connect to a server supporting only GLX 1.0, in which case `glXQueryVersion` would return 1.0. The client would need to be careful not to use any GLX 1.1 (or later) functionality. The later revisions of the OpenGL, GLX, and GLU standards are discussed in Section 6.1.

2.1.1.1 Choosing a Visual and Colormap

Step 4. The GLX extension overloads X visuals to denote supported frame buffer configurations. Before you create an OpenGL window, you should select a visual that supports the frame buffer features you intend to use. GLX guarantees that an RGBA mode visual with a depth buffer, a stencil buffer, and an accumulation buffer must be supported. Also, if color index is supported, a color index mode visual with a depth buffer and stencil buffer must be available. More and less capable visuals are likely to be supported as well, depending on the implementation.

To make it easy to select a visual, glXChooseVisual takes a list of the capabilities you are requesting and returns an XVisualInfo* for a visual meeting your requirements. NULL is returned if such a visual is not available. To ensure that your application will run with any OpenGL GLX server, your program should be written to support the baseline required GLX visuals. Also, you should ask for only the minimum set of frame buffer capabilities you require. For example, if your program never uses a stencil buffer, you will probably waste resources if you request one anyway.

Since glxdino rotates the dinosaur in response to user input, the program will run better if double buffering is available. Double buffering helps create the illusion of smooth animation. Since double buffering support is not required for OpenGL implementations, glxdino resorts to single buffering if no double buffer visuals are available. The program's configuration integer array tells what capabilities glX-ChooseVisual should look for. Notice that if a double buffer visual is not found, another attempt is made, which does not request double buffering by starting after the GLX_DOUBLBUFFER token. And when the -single option is specified, the code looks only for a single buffered visual.

glxdino does require a depth buffer (of at least 12 bits of accuracy, the minimum required by GLX) and uses the RGBA color model. The RGBA baseline visual must support at least a 12-bit depth buffer, so glxdino should always find a usable visual. Here is how glxdino finds an appropriate visual and colormap:

```
/* Find an OpenGL-capable RGB visual with depth buffer. */
if (!doubleBuffer)
  goto SingleBufferOverride;
vi = glXChooseVisual(dpy, DefaultScreen(dpy), configuration);
if (vi == NULL) {
SingleBufferOverride:
  vi = glXChooseVisual(dpy, DefaultScreen(dpy), &configuration[1]);
  if (vi == NULL)
    fatalError("no appropriate RGB visual with depth buffer");
  doubleBuffer = False;
}
cmap = getShareableColormap(vi);
```

• • • • • • • • • • • •

X has a default visual for each screen; most non-OpenGL X programs default to using this visual. You should *not* assume that the visual you need is the default visual. Using a nondefault visual means that any window created using the visual will require a colormap matching the visual. Since the window we are interested in uses OpenGL's RGBA color model, we want a colormap configured for using RGB. The ICCCM establishes a means for sharing RGB colormaps between clients. XmuLookupStandard-Colormap is used to set up a colormap for the specified visual. The routine reads the ICCCM RGB_DEFAULT_MAP property on the X server's root window. If the property does not exist or does not have an entry for the specified visual, a new RGB colormap is created for the visual and the property is updated (creating it if necessary). Once the colormap has been created, XGetRGBColormaps finds the newly created colormap. The work for finding a colormap is done by the getShareableColormap routine:

```
Colormap
getShareableColormap(XVisualInfo * vi)
{
  Status status;
  XStandardColormap *standardCmaps;
  Colormap cmap;
  int i, numCmaps;

  /* Be lazy; using DirectColor too involved for this example. */
  if (vi->class != TrueColor)
    fatalError("No support for non-TrueColor visual.");
  /* if no standard colormap but TrueColor, just make an
    unshared one */
  status = XmuLookupStandardColormap(dpy, vi->screen, vi->visualid,
    vi->depth, XA_RGB_DEFAULT_MAP,
  /* replace */ False, /* retain */ True);
  if (status == 1) {
    status = XGetRGBColormaps(dpy, RootWindow(dpy, vi->screen),
      &standardCmaps, &numCmaps, XA_RGB_DEFAULT_MAP);
    if (status == 1)
      for (i = 0; i < numCmaps; i++)
        if (standardCmaps [i].visualid == visualid) {
          cmap = standardCmaps[i].colormap;
          XFree(standardCmaps);
          return cmap;
        }
  }
  cmap = XCreateColormap(dpy, RootWindow(dpy, vi->screen),
    vi->visual, AllocNone);
  return cmap;
}
```

If a standard colormap cannot be allocated, glxdino will create an unshared colormap. For some servers, it is possible (though unlikely) that a DirectColor visual will be returned (the GLX specification requires that a `TrueColor` visual be returned in precedence to a `DirectColor` visual if available). To shorten the example code by handling only the most likely case, the code bails if a `DirectColor` visual is encountered. A more portable (and longer) program would be capable of initializing an RGB `DirectColor` colormap.

2.1.1.2 Creating a Rendering Context

Step 5. Once a suitable visual and colormap are found, the program can create an OpenGL rendering context using `glXCreateContext`.

```
/* Create an OpenGL rendering context. */
cx = glXCreateContext(dpy, vi,
  /* No sharing of display lists */ NULL,
  /* Direct rendering if possible */ True);
if (cx == NULL)
  fatalError("could not create rendering context");
```

• • • • • • • • • • • •

The last parameter allows the program to request a direct rendering context if the program is connected to a local X server, as discussed in Section 1.3.2. An OpenGL implementation is not required to support direct rendering, but if it does, faster rendering is possible, since OpenGL will render directly to the graphics hardware. Direct rendered OpenGL requests do not have to be sent to the X server. Even when on the local machine, you may not want direct rendering in some cases. For example, if you want to render to X pixmaps, you should render through the X server.

GLX rendering contexts support sharing of display lists with one another. To this end, the third parameter for `glXCreateContext` is another, already created GLX rendering context, or `NULL` can be specified to create an initial rendering context. If an existing rendering context is specified, the display list indices and definitions are shared by the two rendering contexts. The sharing is transitive, so a share group can be formed among a whole set of rendering contexts.

To share, all the rendering contexts must exist in the *same* address space. This means direct renderers cannot share display lists with renderers rendering through the X server. Likewise, direct renderers in separate programs cannot share display lists. Sharing display lists between renderers can help to minimize the memory requirements of applications that need the same display lists.

2.1.1.3 Setting Up a Window

Step 6. Because OpenGL uses visuals to distinguish various frame buffer capabilities, programmers using OpenGL need to be aware of the steps required to create a window with a nondefault visual. As mentioned earlier, a colormap created for the visual is necessary. But the most irksome thing to remember about creating a window with a nondefault visual is that the border pixel value *must* be specified if the window's visual is not the same as its parent's visual. The border pixel (or border pixmap) determines the border's color (or pattern); nearly all X windows specify a border width of zero, so borders are rarely actually displayed. Still, if a border pixel is not specified, a BadMatch is generated.

Before the window is actually created, the argument of the -geometry option should be parsed, using XParseGeometry, to obtain the user's requested size and location. The size will be needed when the window is created by XCreateWindow. Both the size and the location are needed to set up the ICCCM size hints for the window manager. If a fixed aspect ratio is requested by the user specifying -keepaspect, the right size hints for preserving the aspect ratio are also established.

```
flags = XParseGeometry(geometry, &x, &y,
  (unsigned int *) &width, (unsigned int *) &height);
if (WidthValue & flags) {
  sizeHints.flags |= USSize;
  sizeHints.width = width;
  W = width;
}
if (HeightValue & flags) {
  sizeHints.flags |= USSize;
  sizeHints.height = height;
  H = height;
}
if (XValue & flags) {
  if (XNegative & flags)
    x = DisplayWidth(dpy, DefaultScreen(dpy)) + x - sizeHints.width;
  sizeHints.flags |= USPosition;
  sizeHints.x = x;
}
if (YValue & flags) {
  if (YNegative & flags)
    y = DisplayHeight(dpy, DefaultScreen(dpy)) + y -
      sizeHints.height;
  sizeHints.flags |= USPosition;
  sizeHints.y = y;
}
if (keepAspect) {
  sizeHints.flags |= PAspect;
  sizeHints.min_aspect.x = sizeHints.max_aspect.x = W;
  sizeHints.min_aspect.y = sizeHints.max_aspect.y = H;
```

```
  }
  swa.colormap = cmap;
  swa.border_pixel = 0;
  swa.event_mask = ExposureMask | StructureNotifyMask |
    ButtonPressMask | Button1MotionMask | KeyPressMask;
  win = XCreateWindow(dpy, RootWindow(dpy, vi->screen),
    sizeHints.x, sizeHints.y, W, H,
    0, vi->depth, InputOutput, vi->visual,
    CWBorderPixel | CWColormap | CWEventMask, &swa);
```

• • • • • • • • • • • •

After the hints are determined and the window is created, an X *property* is established on the window. An X property is a named piece of data associated with the window that can be queried by other X clients, most commonly the window manager. XSetStandardProperties establishes a standard set of ICCCM-specified properties. XSetWMHints also sets up properties used by the window manager for determining the window's state. This is how the -iconic option takes effect.

```
  XSetStandardProperties(dpy, win, "OpenGLosaurus", "glxdino",
    None, argv, argc, &sizeHints);
  wmHints = XAllocWMHints();
  wmHints->initial_state = iconic ? IconicState : NormalState;
  wmHints->flags = StateHint;
  XSetWMHints(dpy, win, wmHints);
  wmDeleteWindow = XInternAtom(dpy, "WM_DELETE_WINDOW", False);
  XSetWMProtocols(dpy, win, &wmDeleteWindow, 1);
```

The final addition to the window is the WM_PROTOCOLS property, which indicates window manager protocols that the client understands. The most commonly used protocol defined by ICCCM is WM_DELETE_WINDOW. If this atom is listed in the WM_PROTOCOLS property of a top-level window, then when the user requests that the program be quit from the window manager, the window manager will politely send a WM_DELETE_WINDOW message to the client instructing the client to delete the window. If the window is the application's main window, the client is expected to terminate. If this property is not set, the window manager will ask the X server to terminate the client's connection unilaterally, without notice to the client. By default, a terminated connection is reported by Xlib with an ugly message like this:

```
X connection to :0.0 broken
(explicit kill or server shutdown).
```

Asking to participate in the WM_DELETE_WINDOW protocol allows the client to safely handle requests to quit from the window manager.

The property has another advantage for OpenGL programs. Many OpenGL programs doing animation will use XPending to check for pending X events and otherwise draw their animation. But if all a client's animation is direct OpenGL rendering and the client does not otherwise perform any X requests, the client never sends requests to the X server. Because of a problem in XPending's implementation on many Unix operating systems,[2] such an OpenGL program may not notice that its X connection has been terminated for some time. Using the WM_DELETE_WINDOW protocol eliminates this problem, because the window manager notifies the client by using a message (tripping XPending) and the client is expected to drop the connection. Using the WM_DELETE_WINDOW protocol is good practice even if you do not use XPending and the Xlib message does not bother you.

All these steps (besides creating a window with a nondefault visual) are standard for creating a top-level X window. A *top-level* window is a window created as a child of the root window (the window manager may choose to reparent the window when it is mapped to add a border). Note that the properties discussed are placed on the top-level window, not necessarily the same window into which OpenGL renders. While glxdino creates a single window, a more complicated program might nest windows used for OpenGL rendering inside the top-level window. The ICCCM window manager properties belong on top-level windows only. Most of the work setting window manager X properties will be done for you if you use a toolkit layered on top of Xlib such as Motif or the GLUT library discussed in Chapter 4.

Step 7. At this point, a window and an OpenGL rendering context exist. In OpenGL (unlike Xlib), you do not pass the rendering destination into every rendering call. Instead, a given OpenGL rendering context is *bound* to a window using glXMakeCurrent:

```
glXMakeCurrent(dpy, win, cx);
```
• • • • • • • • • • • •

Once it is bound, all OpenGL rendering calls operate using the current OpenGL rendering context and the current bound window. A thread can be bound to only one window and one rendering context at a time. A context can be bound to only a single thread at a time. If you call glXMakeCurrent again, it unbinds from the old context and window and then binds to the newly specified context and window. You can unbind a thread from a window and a context by passing NULL for the context and None for the drawable.

---

2. Operating systems using FIONREAD ioctl calls on file descriptors using Berkeley nonblocking I/O cannot differentiate between no data to read and a broken connection; both conditions cause the FIONREAD ioctl to return zero. MIT's standard implementation of XPending uses Berkeley nonblocking I/O and FIONREAD ioctls. Occasionally, Xlib does make an explicit check on the socket to see if it is closed, but only after a few hundred calls to XPending.

2.1.2 The Dinosaur Model

Step 8. The task of figuring out how to describe the 3D object you wish to render is called *modeling*. Much as a plastic airplane model is constructed from little pieces, a computer-generated 3D scene must also be built from little pieces. In the case of 3D rendering, the pieces are generally polygons.

The dinosaur model to be displayed is built from a hierarchy of display lists. Rendering the dinosaur is accomplished by executing a single display list. The make-Dinosaur routine creates the display lists, then contextInit initializes OpenGL state such as enabling lighting so the dinosaur model can be rendered properly:

```
makeDinosaur();
contextInit();
```

• • • • • • • • • • • •

The strategy for modeling the dinosaur is to construct solid pieces for the body, arms, legs, and eyes. Figure 2.2 shows the 2D sides of the solids used to construct the dinosaur. Making these pieces solid is done by *extruding* the sides (stretching the

Figure 2.2 2D complex polygons used to model the dinosaur's arm, leg, eye, and body sides.

2D sides into the third dimension). When the solid pieces are correctly situated relative to each other, they form the complete dinosaur.

The work of building the dinosaur model is done by the `makeDinosaur` routine. A helper routine, `extrudeSolidFromPolygon`, is used to construct each solid extruded object. The dinosaur model itself requires raw data to represent the model. The following arrays encode the vertices for the polygons to be extruded that are shown in Figure 2.2:

```
GLfloat body[][2] = { {0, 3}, {1, 1}, {5, 1}, {8, 4}, {10, 4}, {11, 5},
   {11, 11.5}, {13, 12}, {13, 13}, {10, 13.5}, {13, 14}, {13, 15},
   {11, 16}, {8, 16}, {7, 15}, {7, 13}, {8, 12}, {7, 11}, {6, 6},
   {4, 3}, {3, 2}, {1, 2}};
GLfloat arm[][2] = { {8, 10}, {9, 9}, {10, 9}, {13, 8}, {14, 9},
   {16, 9}, {15, 9.5}, {16, 10}, {15, 10}, {15.5, 11}, {14.5, 10},
   {14, 11}, {14, 10}, {13, 9}, {11, 11}, {9, 11}};
GLfloat leg[][2] = { {8, 6}, {8, 4}, {9, 3}, {9, 2}, {8, 1}, {8,
   0.5}, {9, 0}, {12, 0}, {10, 1}, {10, 2}, {12, 4}, {11, 6}, {10,
   7}, {9, 7}};
GLfloat eye[][2] = { {8.75, 15}, {9, 14.7}, {9.6, 14.7}, {10.1,
   15}, {9.6, 15.25}, {9, 15.25}};
```

The display list numbers used to capture the dinosaur model are described by a set of symbolic values. Values declared with enum begin with zero (an invalid OpenGL display list name) unless otherwise reassigned; this is why the first enum value is RESERVED.

```
typedef enum {
  RESERVED, BODY_SIDE, BODY_EDGE, BODY_WHOLE, ARM_SIDE, ARM_EDGE,
  ARM_WHOLE, LEG_SIDE, LEG_EDGE, LEG_WHOLE, EYE_SIDE, EYE_EDGE,
  EYE_WHOLE, DINOSAUR
} displayLists;
```

Using the vertex data, the display list names, and the `extrudeSolidFromPolygon` routine for generating extruded polygons, `makeDinosaur` is implemented like this:

```
GLfloat skinColor[] = {0.1, 1.0, 0.1, 1.0}; /* Green */
GLfloat eyeColor[] = {1.0, 0.2, 0.2, 1.0}; /* Red */

void
makeDinosaur(void)
{
  GLfloat bodyWidth = 3.0;
```

```
extrudeSolidFromPolygon(body, sizeof(body), bodyWidth,
  BODY_SIDE, BODY_EDGE, BODY_WHOLE);
extrudeSolidFromPolygon(arm, sizeof(arm), bodyWidth / 4,
  ARM_SIDE, ARM_EDGE, ARM_WHOLE);
extrudeSolidFromPolygon(leg, sizeof(leg), bodyWidth / 2,
  LEG_SIDE, LEG_EDGE, LEG_WHOLE);
extrudeSolidFromPolygon(eye, sizeof(eye), bodyWidth + 0.2,
  EYE_SIDE, EYE_EDGE, EYE_WHOLE);
glNewList(DINOSAUR, GL_COMPILE);
  glMaterialfv(GL_FRONT, GL_DIFFUSE, skinColor);
  glCallList(BODY_WHOLE);
  glPushMatrix();
    glTranslatef(0.0, 0.0, bodyWidth);
    glCallList(ARM_WHOLE);
    glCallList(LEG_WHOLE);
    glTranslatef(0.0, 0.0, -bodyWidth - bodyWidth / 4);
    glCallList(ARM_WHOLE);
    glTranslatef(0.0, 0.0, -bodyWidth / 4);
    glCallList(LEG_WHOLE);
    glTranslatef(0.0, 0.0, bodyWidth / 2 - 0.1);
    glMaterialfv(GL_FRONT, GL_DIFFUSE, eyeColor);
    glCallList(EYE_WHOLE);
  glPopMatrix();
glEndList();
}
```

First the body, arm, leg, and eye display lists are built by extruding the complex polygons defining the sides of each object. Then the dinosaur object is built from these display lists.

2.1.2.1 The GLU Tessellator

The polygons in Figure 2.2 are irregular and complex. For performance reasons, OpenGL directly supports drawing only convex polygons. The complex polygons that make up the sides of the dinosaur need to be broken into smaller convex polygons. Figure 2.3 shows how the complex polygons shown in Figure 2.2 dinosaur can be broken down into simple triangles suitable for rendering with OpenGL.

Since rendering complex polygons is a common need, OpenGL supplies a set of utility routines in OpenGL's GLU library that make it easy to *tessellate* complex polygons. In computer graphics, tessellation is the process of breaking a complex geometric surface into simple convex polygons.

Figure 2.3 Resulting GLU tessellation of the dinosaur polygons.

The GLU library routines for tessellation are as follows:

gluNewTess	Create a new tessellation object.
gluTessCallback	Define a callback for a tessellation object.
gluBeginPolygon	Begin a polygon description to tessellate.
gluTessVertex	Specify a vertex for the polygon to tessellate.
gluNextContour	Mark the beginning of another contour for the polygon to tessellate.
gluEndPolygon	Finish a polygon being tessellated.
gluDeleteTess	Destroy a tessellation object.

These routines are used by `glxdino.c` to tessellate the sides of the dinosaur based on the arrays of 2D vertices that specify the dinosaur's body, arm, leg, and eye polygons.

To use the tessellation package, you first create a tessellation object with `gluNewTess`. An opaque handle of type `GLUtriangulatorObj*` is returned that is passed into the other polygon tessellation routines. You do not need a tessellation object for every polygon you tessellate. You might need more than one tessellation object if you were trying to tessellate more than one polygon at a time. In the sample program, a single tessellation object is used for all the polygons that need tessellation.

Once you have a tessellation object, you should set up callback routines using `gluTessCallback`. The way the GLU tessellation package works is that you feed in vertices. Then the tessellation is performed and your registered callbacks are called to indicate the beginning, the end, and all the vertices for the convex polygons that tessellate the points you feed to the tessellator.

Here is the `extrudeSolidFromPolygon` routine. Observe how it uses the GLU tessellation routines:

```
void
extrudeSolidFromPolygon(GLfloat data[][2], unsigned int dataSize,
  GLdouble thickness, GLuint side, GLuint edge, GLuint whole)
{
  static GLUtriangulatorObj *tobj = NULL;
  GLdouble vertex[3], dx, dy, len;
  int i;
  int count = dataSize / (2 * sizeof(GLfloat));

  if (tobj == NULL) {
    tobj = gluNewTess(); /* Create and initialize a GLU polygon
                            tessellation object. */
    gluTessCallback(tobj, GLU_BEGIN, glBegin);
    gluTessCallback(tobj, GLU_VERTEX, glVertex2fv); /* Tricky. */
    gluTessCallback(tobj, GLU_END, glEnd);
  }
  glNewList(side, GL_COMPILE);
    glShadeModel(GL_SMOOTH); /* Smooth minimizes seeing
                                tessellation. */
    gluBeginPolygon(tobj);
    for (i = 0; i < count; i++) {
      vertex[0] = data[i][0];
      vertex[1] = data[i][1];
      vertex[2] = 0;
      gluTessVertex(tobj, vertex, &data[i]);
    }
    gluEndPolygon(tobj);
  glEndList();
  glNewList(edge, GL_COMPILE);
    glShadeModel(GL_FLAT); /* Flat shade keeps angular hands from
                              being "smoothed".*/
    glBegin (GL_QUAD_STRIP);
    for (i = 0; i <= count; i++) {
      /* mod function handles closing the edge. */
      glVertex3f(data[i % count][0], data[i % count][1], 0.0);
```

```
      glVertex3f(data[i % count][0], data[i % count][1], thickness);
      /* Calculate a unit normal by dividing by Euclidean distance.
         We could be lazy and use glEnable(GL_NORMALIZE)
         so we could pass in arbitrary normals for a very slight
         performance hit. */
      dx = data[(i + 1) % count][1] - data[i % count][1];
      dy = data[i % count][0] - data[(i + 1) % count][0];
      len = sqrt(dx * dx + dy * dy);
      glNormal3f(dx / len, dy / len, 0.0);
    }
    glEnd();
  glEndList();
  glNewList(whole, GL_COMPILE);
    glFrontFace(GL_CW);
    glCallList(edge);
    glNormal3f(0.0, 0.0, -1.0); /* Constant normal for side. */
    glCallList(side);
    glPushMatrix();
      glTranslatef(0.0, 0.0, thickness);
      glFrontFace(GL_CCW);
      glNormal3f(0.0, 0.0, 1.0); /* Reverse normal for other side. */
      glCallList(side);
    glPopMatrix();
  glEndList();
}
```

To understand exactly why the callbacks are specified as they are, consult the *OpenGL Reference Manual* [30]. The point to notice is the way a single tessellation object is set up once and callbacks are registered for it. Then gluBeginPolygon is used to start tessellating a new complex polygon. The vertices of the polygon are specified using gluTessVertex. The polygon is finished by calling gluEndPolygon.

Notice that the code for tessellating the polygon lies between a glNewList and a glEndList; these routines begin and end the creation of a display list. The callbacks will generate glVertex2fv calls specifying the vertices of convex polygons needed to represent the complex polygon being tessellated. Once it is completed, a display list is available that can render the desired complex polygon. Figure 2.3 shows the resulting GLU tessellation for the dinosaur body, eyes, legs, and arms.

Consider the performance benefits of OpenGL's polygon tessellator as compared with a graphics system that supplies a polygon primitive that supports nonconvex polygons. A polygon primitive that supported nonconvex polygons would likely need to tessellate each complex polygon on the fly. Calculating a tessellation is not without cost. If you are drawing the same complex polygon more than once, it is better to do the tessellation only once. This is exactly what is achieved by creating a display list for the tessellated polygon. But if you are rendering continuously changing complex polygons, the GLU tessellator is fast enough for generating vertices on the fly for immediate-mode rendering.

Having a tessellation object not directly tied to rendering is also more flexible. Your program might need to tessellate a polygon but not actually need to render it. The GLU system of callbacks just generates vertices. You can call OpenGL glVertex calls to render the vertices or supply your own special callbacks to save the vertices for your own purposes. The tessellation algorithm is accessible for your own use.

The GLU tessellator also supports multiple contours, allowing disjoint polygons or polygons with holes to be tessellated. The gluNextContour routine begins a new contour.

The tessellation object is just one example of functionality in OpenGL's GLU library that supports 3D rendering without complicating the basic rendering routines in the core OpenGL API. Other GLU routines support rendering of curves and surfaces using Non-Uniform Rational B-Splines (NURBS) and tessellating boundaries of solids such as cylinders, cones, and spheres. All the GLU routines are a standard part of OpenGL.

2.1.2.2 Hierarchical Display Lists

After generating the complex polygon display list for the sides of a solid object, the extrudeSolidFromPolygon routine creates another display list for the perimeter edge of the extruded solid. The perimeter edge is generated using a QUAD_STRIP primitive. Along with the vertices, normals are calculated for each quad along the edge. Later, these normals will be used for lighting the dinosaur. The normals are computed to be unit vectors. Having normals specified as unit vectors is important for correct lighting. An alternative would be to use glEnable(GL_NORMALIZE), which ensures that all normals are properly normalized before use in lighting calculations. Specifying unit vectors to begin with and not using glEnable(GL_NORMALIZE) saves time during rendering. Be careful when using scaling transformations (often set up using glScalef), since scaling transformations will scale normals too. If you are using scaling transformations, glEnable(GL_NORMALIZE) is almost always required for correct lighting.

Once the edge and side display lists are created, the solid is formed by calling the edge display list, then filling in the solid by calling the side display list twice (once translated over by the width of the edge). The makeDinosaur routine will use extrudeSolidFromPolygon to create solids for each body part needed for the dinosaur.

Then makeDinosaur combines these display lists into a single display list for the entire dinosaur. Translations are used to position the display lists to form the complete dinosaur. The body display list is called; then arms and legs for the right side are added; then arms and legs for the left side are added; then the eye is added (it is one solid, which pokes out from each side of the dinosaur's head a little bit).

2.1.2.3 Context Initialization

Step 9. Once the dinosaur model has been created using a hierarchy of display lists, the OpenGL context to render the model should be initialized. The `contextInit` routine takes care of enabling back-face culling, enabling depth testing, establishing and enabling lighting state, and initializing the modelview and projection matrices. The explanation of the way this state is used follows the implementation of `contextInit`:

```
GLfloat lightZeroPosition[] = {10.0, 4.0, 10.0, 1.0};
GLfloat lightZeroColor[] = {0.8, 1.0, 0.8, 1.0}; /* green-tinted */
GLfloat lightOnePosition[] = {-1.0, -2.0, 1.0, 0.0};
GLfloat lightOneColor[] = {0.6, 0.3, 0.2, 1.0}; /* red-tinted */

void
contextInit(void)
{
  glEnable(GL_CULL_FACE); /* Up to 50% better performance than no
                             back-face culling. */
  glEnable(GL_DEPTH_TEST); /* Enable depth buffering. */
  glLightModeli(GL_LIGHT_MODEL_LOCAL_VIEWER, 1);
  glLightfv(GL_LIGHT0, GL_POSITION, lightZeroPosition);
  glLightfv(GL_LIGHT0, GL_DIFFUSE, lightZeroColor);
  glLightf(GL_LIGHT0, GL_CONSTANT_ATTENUATION, 0.1);
  glLightf(GL_LIGHT0, GL_LINEAR_ATTENUATION, 0.05);
  glLightfv(GL_LIGHT1, GL_POSITION, lightOnePosition);
  glLightfv(GL_LIGHT1, GL_DIFFUSE, lightOneColor);

  /* Enable both lights. */
  glEnable(GL_LIGHT0);
  glEnable(GL_LIGHT1);
  glEnable(GL_LIGHTING);

  /* Set up projection transform. */
  glMatrixMode(GL_PROJECTION);
  gluPerspective(
    40.0,      /* Field of view in degree */
    1.0,       /* Aspect ratio */
    1.0,       /* Z near */
    40.0);     /* Z far */

  /* Now change to modelview. */
  glMatrixMode(GL_MODELVIEW);
  gluLookAt(
```

```
    0.0, 0.0, 30.0,   /* Eye is at (0,0,30) */
    0.0, 0.0, 0.0,    /* Center is at (0,0,0) */
    0.0, 1.0, 0.);    /* Up is in positive Y direction */

  glPushMatrix();     /* Dummy push so we can pop on model
                         recalc. */
}
```

• • • • • • • • • • • •

The lighting initialization is explained in Section 2.1.3 in conjunction with Figure 2.5. The view selection is explained in Section 2.1.4 in conjunction with Figure 2.6.

2.1.2.4 Back-Face Culling

A common optimization in 3D graphics is a technique known as *back-face culling*. The idea is to treat polygons as essentially one-sided entities. A front-facing polygon needs to be rendered, but a back-facing polygon can be eliminated.

Consider the dinosaur model. When the model is rendered, the back side of the dinosaur will not be visible. If the direction in which each polygon "faced" were known, OpenGL could simply eliminate approximately half the polygons (the back-facing ones) without ever rendering them.

Notice the calls to `glFrontFace` when each solid display list is created in `extrudeSolidFromPolygon`. The argument to the call is either `GL_CW` or `GL_CCW`, meaning clockwise or counterclockwise. If the vertices of a polygon, when they are projected onto the screen, are listed in counterclockwise order and `glFrontFace` is set to `GL_CCW`, the generated polygon is front-facing; if the vertices, when they are projected onto the screen, are listed in clockwise order, the polygon is back-facing.

Figure 2.4 The clockwise and counterclockwise orientations of polygon vertices and the eye-pointing viewing the scene can be used to determine whether a polygon is front- or back-facing. Based on this determination, back-facing polygons can be culled.

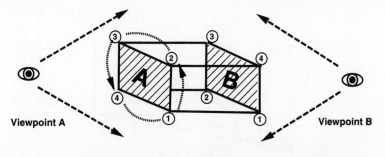

Face A
Counterclockwise (*front-facing*) to Viewpoint A
Clockwise (*back-facing*) to Viewpoint B

Face B
Clockwise (*back-facing*) to Viewpoint A
Counterclockwise (*front-facing*) to Viewpoint B

Figure 2.5 Arrangement of lights, eyes, and dinosaur in modeling space.

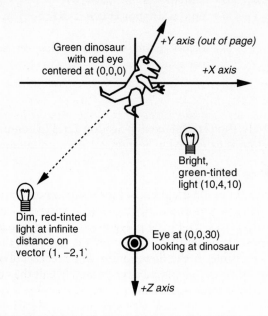

Figure 2.6 Static view for `glxdino`.

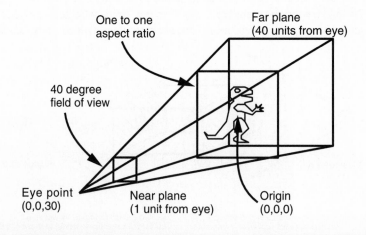

By calling `glFrontFace` with `GL_CW`, you reverse the sense of which polygons face front and which face back. Figure 2.4 shows how the clockwise and counterclockwise orientations (and hence whether a face is back- or front-facing) depend on the location of the eye-point.

When the OpenGL state is set up by `contextInit`, as shown previously, `glEnable(GL_CULL_FACE)` is used to enable back-face culling. Any back-facing polygons will be eliminated or culled before they are rasterized. Like most modes that are enabled and disabled using `glEnable` and `glDisable`, it is disabled by default.[3] Actually, OpenGL is not limited to back-face culling. The `glCullFace` routine can be used to specify that either the back or the front should be culled when face culling is enabled.

The static data specifying the vertices of the complex polygons is listed in counterclockwise order. To make the quads in the quad strip face outward, `glFrontFace(GL_CW)` is specified. The same mode ensures that the far side faces outward. But `glFrontFace(GL_CCW)` is needed to make sure the front of the other side faces outward (logically, it needs to be reversed from the opposite side because the vertices were laid out counterclockwise for both sides, since they are from the same display list).

When you are developing your 3D program, it is often helpful to disable back-face culling. That way, both sides of every polygon will be rendered. Then, once you have your scene correctly rendering, you can go back and optimize your program to use back-face culling.

Do not be left with the misconception that enabling or disabling back-face culling (or any other OpenGL feature) must be done for the duration of the scene or program. You can enable and disable back-face culling at will. It is possible to draw part of your scene with back-face culling enabled, then disable it, and then later re-enable culling, but this time for front faces.

2.1.3 Lighting

The realism of a computer-generated 3D scene is greatly enhanced by adding lighting. In the `glxsimple` example, `glColor3f` was used to add color to the faces of the 3D cube. This adds color to rendered objects but does not use lighting. When the cube moves, the colors do not vary as those of a real cube would as it is affected by real-world lighting. The dinosaur model rendered by `glxdino` uses OpenGL's lighting model to make the scene a bit more realistic.

OpenGL supports a basic 3D lighting model to achieve higher realism. When you look at a real object, its color is affected by lights, by the material properties of the object, and by the angle at which the light shines on the object. OpenGL's lighting model approximates the real world.

---

3.   Dithering is the only core OpenGL capability enabled by default.

Complicated effects such as the reflection of light and shadows are not supported by OpenGL's lighting model, though OpenGL-based algorithms are available to simulate such effects. Such advanced OpenGL rendering techniques are beyond the scope of this book.

2.1.3.1   Types of Lighting

The effects of light are complex. In OpenGL, lighting is greatly simplified by dividing the effect of lighting into four different categories: *emitted*, *ambient*, *diffuse*, and *specular*. All four categories can be computed independently and then added together.

Emitted light is the simplest. It is light that originates from an object and is unaffected by any light sources. Self-luminous objects can be modeled using emitted light.

Ambient light is light that has been scattered so much by the environment that its direction is impossible to determine. Even a directed light, such as a flashlight, may have some ambient light associated with it.

Diffuse light comes from some direction. The brightness of the light bouncing off an object depends on the light's angle of incidence with the surface it is striking. Once it hits a surface, the light is scattered equally in all directions, so it appears equally bright independent of the location of the eye.

Specular light comes from some direction and tends to bounce off the surface in a certain direction. Shiny metal or plastic objects have a high specular component. Chalk and carpet have almost none. Specularity corresponds to the everyday notion of how shiny an object is.

A single OpenGL light source has some combination of ambient, diffuse, and specular components. OpenGL supports multiple lights simultaneously. The programmer can control the makeup of a light as well as its position, direction, and attenuation. Attenuation is the way a light's intensity decreases as the distance from the light increases. A more thorough exploration of OpenGL's lighting model is given in Section 5.1.

2.1.3.2   Lighting in the Example

The example uses two lights. Both use only the diffuse component. A bright, slightly green-tinted *positional* light is to the right front of the dinosaur. A dim, red-tinted *directional* light is coming from the left front of the dinosaur. Figure 2.5 shows how the dinosaur, the lights, and the eye-point are arranged. A positional light is located at some finite position in modeling space. A directional light is considered to be located infinitely far away. Using a directional light allows OpenGL to consider the emitted light rays to be parallel by the time the light reaches the object. This simplifies the lighting calculations that must be done by OpenGL.

The `lightZeroPosition` and the `lightOnePosition` static variables indicate the positions of the two lights. You will notice that each has not three but four coordinates. This is because the light location is specified in *homogeneous* coordinates.

The fourth value divides the X, Y, and Z coordinates to obtain the true coordinate. Notice that `lightOnePosition` (the infinite light) has the fourth value set to zero. This is how an infinite light is specified.[4]

The dinosaur can rotate around the Y axis based on the user's mouse input. The idea behind the example's lighting arrangement is that when the dinosaur is oriented so that its side faces to the right, it should appear green because of the bright light. When its side faces leftward, the dinosaur should appear poorly lighted, but the red infinite light should catch the dinosaur's red eye.

Here, again, is the code from `contextInit` that sets up the lighting state:

```
glLightModeli(GL_LIGHT_MODEL_LOCAL_VIEWER, 1);
glLightfv(GL_LIGHT0, GL_POSITION, lightZeroPosition);
glLightfv(GL_LIGHT0, GL_DIFFUSE, lightZeroColor);
glLightf(GL_LIGHT0, GL_CONSTANT_ATTENUATION, 0.1);
glLightf(GL_LIGHT0, GL_LINEAR_ATTENUATION, 0.05);
glLightfv(GL_LIGHT1, GL_POSITION, lightOnePosition);
glLightfv(GL_LIGHT1, GL_DIFFUSE, lightOneColor);

/* Enable both lights. */
glEnable(GL_LIGHT0);
glEnable(GL_LIGHT1);
glEnable(GL_LIGHTING);
```

The `glEnable(GL_LIGHTING)` turns on lighting support. The lights' positions and diffuse components are set via calls to `glLightfv` using the `GL_POSITION` and `GL_DIFFUSE` parameters. Each light is enabled using `glEnable`.

The attenuation of the green light is adjusted. This determines how the light intensity fades with distance and demonstrates how individual lighting parameters can be set. It would not make sense to adjust the attenuation of the red light, since it is an infinite light that shines with uniform intensity.

Neither ambient nor specular lighting is demonstrated in this example, so that the effect of the diffuse lighting will be clear. Specular lighting might be used to give the dinosaur's eye a glint.

Recall that when the edge of each solid was generated, normals were calculated for each vertex along the quad strip. Also, a single normal was given for each complex-polygon side of the solid. These normals are used in the diffuse-lighting calculations to determine how much light should be reflected. If you rotate the dinosaur,

---

4. Actually, all coordinates are logically manipulated by OpenGL as three-dimensional homogeneous coordinates. The *OpenGL Programming Guide*'s Appendix G [28] briefly explains homogeneous coordinates. A more involved discussion of homogeneous coordinates and why they are useful for 3D computer graphics can be found in Foley and van Dam [13].

you will notice that the color intensity changes as the angle of incidence for the light varies.

Also notice the calls to `glShadeModel`. OpenGL's shade model determines whether flat or smooth shading should be used on polygons. The dinosaur model uses different shading depending on whether a side or an edge is being rendered. There is a good reason for this. The `GL_SMOOTH` mode is used on the sides. If flat shading were used instead of smooth, each convex polygon composing the tessellated complex polygon side would be a single color. The viewer could notice exactly how the sides had been tessellated. Smooth shading prevents this, since the colors are interpolated across each polygon.

But for the edge of each solid, `GL_FLAT` is used. Because the edge is generated as a quad strip, quads along the strip share vertices. If we used a smooth shading model, each edge between two quads would have a single normal. Some of the edges are very sharp (for instance, the claws in the hand and the tip of the tail). Interpolating across such varying normals would lead to an undesirable visual effect. The fingers would appear rounded if they were seen straight on. Instead, with flat shading, each quad gets its own normal and there is no interpolation, so the sharp angles are clearly visible.

2.1.4 View Selection

In 3D graphics, *viewing* is the process of establishing the perspective and orientation with which the scene should be rendered. Like a photographer properly setting up his camera, an OpenGL programmer should establish a view. Figure 2.6 shows how the view is set up for `glxdino`.

In OpenGL, establishing a view means loading the projection and modelview matrices with the right contents. To modify the projection matrix, call `glMatrix-Mode(GL_PROJECTION)`. Calculating the right matrix by hand can be tricky. The GLU library has two useful routines that make the process easy.

GLU's `gluPerspective` routine allows you to specify a field-of-view angle, an aspect ratio, and near and far clipping planes. It multiplies the current projection matrix with one created according to the routine's parameters. Since initially the projection matrix is an identity matrix, `glxdino`'s `gluPerspective` call effectively loads the projection matrix.

Another GLU routine, `gluLookAt`, can be used to orient the eye-point for the modelview matrix. Notice how `glMatrixMode(GL_MODELVIEW)` is used to switch to the modelview matrix. Using `gluLookAt` requires you to specify the eye-point's location, a location to look at, and a vector to determine which way is up. Like `gluPerspective`, `gluLookAt` multiplies the matrix it constructs from its parameters with the current matrix. The initial modelview matrix is the identity matrix, so `glxdino`'s call to `gluLookAt` effectively loads the modelview matrix.

Check Section 2.1.2 again to see how `contextInit` uses `gluLookAt` and `glu-Perspective`. After the `gluLookAt` call, `glPushMatrix` is called. Both the modelview and projection matrices exist on stacks that can be pushed and popped. Calling `glPushMatrix` pushes a copy of the current matrix onto the stack. When a rotation occurs, this matrix is popped off and another `glPushMatrix` is done. This newly pushed matrix is composed with a rotation matrix to reflect the current absolute orientation. Every rotation pops off the top matrix and replaces it with a newly rotated matrix.

Notice that the light positions are not set until after the modelview matrix has been properly initialized. Because the location of the viewpoint affects the calculations for lighting, separate the projection transformation in the projection matrix and the modeling and viewing transformations in the modelview matrix.

2.1.5 Event Dispatching

Steps 10 and 11. At this point, the window has been created, the OpenGL renderer has been bound to it, the display lists have been constructed, and OpenGL's state has been configured. All that remains is to request that the window be mapped using `XMapWindow` and begin handling any X events sent to the program. Mapping the window is straightforward:

```
XMapWindow(dpy, win);
```

When the window was created, it was requested that five types of window events be sent to the program: `Expose` events, reporting regions of the window to be drawn; `ButtonPress` events, indicating mouse button status; `KeyPress` events, indicating that a keyboard key has been pressed; `MotionNotify` events, indicating mouse movement; and `ConfigureNotify` events, indicating that the window's size or position has changed.

X event dispatching is usually done in an infinite loop. Most X programs do not stop dispatching events until the program terminates. `XNextEvent` can be used to block waiting for an X event. When an event arrives, its type is examined to determine what event has been received.

```
for (;;) {
  do {
    XNextEvent(dpy, &event);
    switch (event.type) {
    case ConfigureNotify:
      glViewport(0, 0,
        event.xconfigure.width, event.xconfigure.height);
      /* fall through... */
    case Expose:
      needRedraw = True;
      break;
```

```
        case MotionNotify:
          recalcModelView = True;
          angle -= (lastX - event.xmotion.x);
        case ButtonPress:
          lastX = event.xbutton.x;
          break;
        case KeyPress:
          ks = XLookupKeysym((XKeyEvent *)event, 0);
          if (ks == XK_Escape)
            exit(0);
          break;
        case ClientMessage:
          if (event.xclient.data.l[0] == wmDeleteWindow)
            exit(0);
          break;
        }
    } while (XPending(dpy)); /* Loop to compress events. */
    if (recalcModelView) {
      glPopMatrix(); /* Pop old rotated matrix (or dummy matrix if *
                        first time). */
      glPushMatrix();
      glRotatef(angle, 0.0, 1.0, 0.0);
      glTranslatef(-8, -8, -bodyWidth / 2);
      recalcModelView = False;
      needRedraw = True;
    }
    if (needRedraw) {
      redraw();
      needRedraw = False;
      }
    }
}
```

• • • • • • • • • • •

Now consider how the different types of events are handled.

2.1.5.1 Expose Handling

For an Expose event, the example program just sets a flag indicating that the window needs to be redrawn. The reason is that Expose events indicate a single subrectangle in the window that must be redrawn. The X server will send a number of Expose events if a complex region of the window has been exposed.

For a normal X program using 2D rendering, you may be able to minimize the rendering needed to redraw the window by carefully examining the rectangles for each `Expose` event. For 3D programs, this is usually too difficult to be worthwhile, since it is hard to determine what would need to be done to redraw some subregion of the window. In practice, the window is usually redrawn in its entirety. For the dinosaur example, redrawing involves calling the dinosaur display list with the right view. It is not helpful to know that only a subregion of the window actually needs to be redrawn. For this reason, an OpenGL program should not begin redrawing until it has received all the `Expose` events most recently sent to the window. This practice, known as *expose compression*, helps you avoid redrawing more than you should.

Notice that all that is done to handle an expose immediately is to set the `need-Redraw` flag. Then `XPending` is used to determine whether more events are pending. Not until the stream of events pauses is the `redraw` routine really called (and the `needRedraw` flag reset).

```
void
redraw(void)
{
  glClear(GL_COLOR_BUFFER_BIT | GL_DEPTH_BUFFER_BIT);
  glCallList(DINOSAUR);
  if (doubleBuffer)
    glXSwapBuffers(dpy, win);
  else
    glFlush();
}
```

The `redraw` routine does three things: it clears the image and depth buffers, executes the dinosaur display list, and either calls `glXSwapBuffers` on the window if double buffered or calls `glFlush` (`glXSwapBuffers` performs an implicit `glFlush`). The current modelview matrix determines at what angle the dinosaur is drawn.

2.1.5.2 Window Resizing

The server sends a `ConfigureNotify` event to indicate a window resize. Handling the event for an OpenGL window generally requires changing the associated OpenGL rendering context's viewport. The sample program calls `glViewport`, specifying the window's new width and height. A resize also necessitates a screen redraw, so the code "falls through" to the expose code, which sets the `needRedraw` flag.

When you resize the window, its aspect ratio may change (unless you have negotiated a fixed aspect ratio with the window manager, as the `-keepaspect` option does). If you want the aspect ratio of your final image to remain constant, you may need to respecify the projection matrix with an aspect ratio to compensate for the window's changed aspect ratio. `glxdino.c` does not do this, but it is easy to add by updating the `ConfigureNotify` case to say

```
glViewport(0, 0,
  event.xconfigure.width, event.xconfigure.height);
glMatrixMode(GL_PROJECTION);
glLoadIdentity();
gluPerspective( /* field of view in degree */ 40.0,
  /* aspect ratio */ (float) event.xconfigure.width /
      event.xconfigure.height,
  /* Z near */ 1.0, /* Z far */ 40.0);
glMatrixMode(GL_MODELVIEW);
```

Notice that the aspect ratio has been changed to reflect the window's aspect ratio.

2.1.5.3   Handling Input

The example program allows the user to rotate the dinosaur while moving the mouse by holding down the first mouse button. We record the current angle of rotation whenever a mouse button state changes. As the mouse moves while the first mouse button is held down, the angle is recalculated. A `recalcModelView` flag is set, indicating that the scene should be redrawn with the new angle.

When there is a lull in events, the modelview matrix is recalculated and then the `needRedraw` flag is set, forcing a redraw. The `recalcModelView` flag is cleared. As discussed earlier, recalculating the modelview is done by popping off the current top matrix, using `glPopMatrix`, and pushing on a new matrix. This new matrix is composed with a rotation matrix using `glRotatef` to reflect the new absolute angle of rotation. An alternative approach would be to multiply the current matrix by a rotation matrix reflecting the change in angle of rotation, but such a relative approach to rotation can lead to inaccurate rotations owing to accumulated floating-point round-off errors.

2.1.5.4   Quitting

Because the `WM_DELETE_WINDOW` atom was specified on the top-level window's list of window manager protocols, the event loop should also be ready to handle an event sent by the window manager's asking the program to quit. If `glxdino` receives a `ClientMessage` event whose first data item is the `WM_DELETE_WINDOW` atom, the program calls `exit`.

When a `KeyPress` event is received and it is the **Esc** key, `glxdino` will also exit.

2.1.5.5   Compiling `glxdino`

The command line to compile `glxdino.c` would look something like this:

```
cc -o glxdino glxdino.c -lGLU -lGL -lXmu -lXext -lX11 -lm
```

More options are required than with the command line to compile `glxsimple`. The `-lGLU` option requests linking with the OpenGL Utility library. The `-lXmu` option requests linking with the X Miscellaneous Utilities library. The `-lm` option requests linking with the Unix math library.

2.2 OpenGL and X Visuals

X visuals are very important to OpenGL and GLX. GLX overloads the X visual concept with additional OpenGL-related frame buffer capabilities. Before GLX and OpenGL overloaded X visuals, the core X visual really described the *visual* characteristics a window could have. Each X visual described a method by which pixel values in the frame buffer were converted to colors on the screen. For the purpose of review, Table 2.1 compares the basic X visual classes.

In addition to the core X function of visuals, GLX uses X visuals to define a *frame buffer configuration* consisting of a set of *frame buffer attributes* named by GLX attributes. The basic GLX attributes are described in Table 2.2. For example, the GLX attributes for a visual can specify that the visual is OpenGL-capable, uses the RGBA color model, has a 20-bit depth buffer, and has a 4-bit stencil buffer. A window created with this example visual will have those same GLX attributes.

X visuals provide a way for an OpenGL-capable X server to "advertise" the frame buffer configurations that are supported by the X server. All possible frame buffer configurations are listed. The choice of the configuration to be used is made by selecting the appropriate visual. The `glXGetConfig` and `glXChooseVisual` routines allow you to query what GLX attributes various visuals provide.

Before GLX, many X servers supported only a single visual; sophisticated X servers before GLX may have supported 4 or 5 different visuals. Because GLX associates a good deal more information with each visual, OpenGL-capable X servers are likely to support many more visuals. Most OpenGL-capable X servers will support from 4 to 12 visuals, though extremely configurable graphics hardware exists that advertises 80 or more visuals.

Table 2.1 Classification of Core X Visual Classes.

Type of Colormap	Modifiable	Fixed
Monochrome/gray	GrayScale	StaticGray
Indexed color	PseudoColor	StaticColor
Decomposed RGB color	DirectColor	TrueColor

Table 2.2 GLX Visual Attributes for Use with `glXChooseVisual` and `glXGetConfig`.

Attribute	Type	Notes
GLX_USE_GL	Boolean	True if OpenGL rendering is supported.
GLX_BUFFER_SIZE	Integer	Depth of the color buffer.
GLX_LEVEL	Integer	Frame buffer level, > 0 is overlay.
GLX_RGBA	Boolean	True if RGBA color model supported.
GLX_DOUBLEBUFFER	Boolean	True if front/back color buffer pairs.
GLX_STEREO	Boolean	True if left/right color buffer pairs.
GLX_RED_SIZE	Integer	Number of bits of red in RGBA color model.
GLX_GREEN_SIZE	Integer	Number of bits of green in RGBA color model.
GLX_BLUE_SIZE	Integer	Number of bits of blue in RGBA color model.
GLX_ALPHA_SIZE	Integer	Number of bits of alpha in RGBA color model.
GLX_DEPTH_SIZE	Integer	Number of bits in the depth buffer.
GLX_STENCIL_SIZE	Integer	Number of bits in the stencil buffer.
GLX_AUX_BUFFERS	Integer	Number of auxiliary color buffers.
GLX_ACCUM_RED_SIZE	Integer	Accumulation buffer red component.
GLX_ACCUM_GREEN_SIZE	Integer	Accumulation buffer green component.
GLX_ACCUM_BLUE_SIZE	Integer	Accumulation buffer blue component.
GLX_ACCUM_ALPHA_SIZE	Integer	Accumulation buffer alpha component.

A disadvantage of OpenGL's overloading of X visuals is that many more visuals must be supported (though in practice there is no practical problem with supporting a large number of visuals). The advantage is that X servers are fully explicit about the frame buffer configurations their graphics hardware provides. The idea of overloading visuals was not invented by GLX. Other X extensions and conventions that predated GLX also associated additional information with X visuals.[5]

The additional information associated with X visuals by GLX does not change the operation of a visual if OpenGL is not used with windows created using the visual. That is, a non-OpenGL X program could use an OpenGL-capable visual and expect the visual to work like any other X visual. The overloading may mean that there are multiple visuals that are indistinguishable based on their core X visual information, but the visuals could be distinguished based on their GLX attributes. For example, an X server might advertise three 24-bit TrueColor visuals, but they might have different GLX attributes. An X program unaware of GLX could use any of these three visuals without noticing a difference, because the differences among the visuals are made apparent only when OpenGL is being used.

---

5. PEX's **PEXMatchRenderTargets** request, the MVEX video extension's **QueryVideo** request, and the **SERVER_OVERLAY_VISUALS** convention for advertising overlays are a few examples.

As specified, X permits a visual to be supported at multiple depths, though few X servers take advantage of this allowance. Because GLX associates capabilities that are heavily dependent on window depth, GLX permits GLX-capable visuals to support only a single depth.

It is important to note that not all X visuals on an OpenGL-capable X server must support OpenGL rendering. This is the purpose of the `GLX_USE_GL` boolean attribute. It is possible for some visuals not to support OpenGL rendering. Even so, every OpenGL-capable X server is required to have certain guaranteed GLX configurations.

2.2.1   The Visuals Whose Existence Is Guaranteed by GLX

The GLX extension is very specific about what OpenGL-capable visuals must be supported by an X server that supports GLX. GLX-capable X servers must export at least one visual that supports RGBA rendering. If the X server exports a `Pseudo-Color` or `StaticColor` visual on frame buffer level 0 (the main image planes), a visual that supports color index rendering is also required. One of the visuals that supports RGBA rendering must have at least one color buffer, a stencil buffer at least 1 bit deep, a depth buffer at least 12 bits deep, and an accumulation buffer. Alpha bitplanes (sometimes called *destination alpha*) are optional in this visual. However, its color buffer size must be as large as the deepest `TrueColor`, `Direct-Color`, `PseudoColor`, or `StaticColor` visual supported on frame buffer level 0, and it must itself be made available on frame buffer level 0. If a color index visual is required, one such visual must have at least one color buffer, a stencil buffer at least 1 bit deep, and a depth buffer at least 12 bits deep.

2.2.2   Example: `glxvisuals.c`

This section presents a simple program, called `glxvisuals`, that outputs an X server's OpenGL-capable visuals and their capabilities. Using a program such as `glxvisuals`, you can determine a great deal about the capabilities of a particular OpenGL implementation and the hardware it uses. The X Window System's standard `xdpyinfo` ("X display info") command serves a similar purpose, but its output is limited to non-OpenGL visual information.

Figure 2.7 shows an example of the output returned by `glxvisuals`. The information returned is kept terse so the results are compact. Table 2.3 explains the column abbreviations.

```
#include <stdlib.h>
#include <stdio.h>
#include <X11/Xlib.h>
#include <GL/glx.h>
```

Figure 2.7 Output of glxvisuals showing the OpenGL-capable visuals supported on a 24-bit Silicon Graphics Indy.

```
display: :0.0
  using GLX version: 1.1

      visual bf lv rg d st  r  g  b  a ax dp st accum buffs
   id dep cl sz l  ci b ro sz sz sz sz bf th cl r  g  b  a
   -------------------------------------------------------------
   0x20 2  pc   2  2  c  .  .  .  .  .  .  .  .  .  .  .  .  .
   0x21 4  pc   4  .  c  y  .  .  .  .  .  24 8  .  .  .  .
   0x22 4  tc   4  .  r  y  .  1  2  1  .  .  24 8  16 16 16 16
   0x23 8  pc   8  .  c  .  .  .  .  .  .  24 8  .  .  .  .
   0x25 8  tc   8  .  r  .  .  3  3  2  .  .  24 8  16 16 16 16
   0x26 8  pc   8  1  c  .  .  .  .  .  .  .  .  .  .  .  .
   0x27 12 pc  12  .  c  .  .  .  .  .  .  24 8  .  .  .  .
   0x28 12 pc  12  .  c  y  .  .  .  .  .  24 8  .  .  .  .
   0x29 12 tc  12  .  r  y  .  4  4  4  .  .  24 8  16 16 16 16
   0x2a 24 tc  24  .  r  .  .  8  8  8  .  .  24 8  16 16 16 16
   OpenGL vendor string: SGI
   OpenGL renderer string: NEWPORT 24
   OpenGL version string: 1.0 Irix 5.3
   direct rendering: supported
```

```c
static char *ClassOf(int c);
static char *Format(int n, int w);

void
main(int argc, char *argv[])
{
  Display *dpy;
  XVisualInfo match, *visualList, *vi, *visualToTry;
  int errorBase, eventBase, major, minor, found;
  int glxCapable, bufferSize, level, renderType, doubleBuffer,
  stereo, auxBuffers, redSize, greenSize, blueSize, alphaSize,
  depthSize, stencilSize, acRedSize, acGreenSize, acBlueSize,
  acAlphaSize;

  dpy = XOpenDisplay(NULL);
  if (!dpy) {
    fprintf(stderr, "Could not connect to %s.\n",
      XDisplayName(NULL));
```

Table 2.3 `glxvisuals` Column Abbreviations and Their Meanings

Column Name	Meaning or Corresponding GLX Attribute
`visual id`	X visual ID
`visual dep`	X visual depth
`visual cl`	X visual class:
	pc= *PseudoColor*, tc= *TrueColor*, gs= *GrayScale*,
	sg= *StaticGray*, sc= *StaticColor*, dc= *DirectColor*
`bf sz`	`GLX_BUFFER_SIZE`
`lvl`	`GLX_LEVEL`
`rg/ci`	`GLX_RGBA`
`db`	`GLX_DOUBLEBUFFER`
`stro`	`GLX_STEREO`
`r sz`	`GLX_RED_SIZE`
`g sz`	`GLX_GREEN_SIZE`
`b sz`	`GLX_BLUE_SIZE`
`a sz`	`GLX_ALPHA_SIZE`
`ax bf`	`GLX_AUX_BUFFERS`
`dpth`	`GLX_DEPTH_SIZE`
`stcl`	`GLX_STENCIL_SIZE`
`accum buffs r`	`GLX_ACCUM_RED_SIZE`
`accum buffs g`	`GLX_ACCUM_GREEN_SIZE`
`accum buffs b`	`GLX_ACCUM_BLUE_SIZE`
`accum buffs a`	`GLX_ACCUM_ALPHA_SIZE`

```
    exit(1);
  }
  if (glXQueryExtension(dpy, &errorBase, &eventBase) == False) {
    fprintf(stderr, "OpenGL not supported by X server.\n");
    exit(1);
  }
```

The first thing `glxvisuals` does is connect to the X server and determine whether OpenGL's GLX extension is supported. Unlike most OpenGL or X programs, `glxvisuals` never maps or renders to an X window. It uses its connection to the X server only to query information.

```
glXQueryVersion(dpy, &major, &minor);
printf("display: %s\n", XDisplayName(NULL));
printf("using GLX version: %d.%d\n\n", major, minor);


match.screen = DefaultScreen(dpy);
visualList = XGetVisualInfo(dpy, VisualScreenMask, &match, &found);
```

glXQueryVersion reports the version of GLX *being used*. Note that the version of GLX used is negotiated between the client and the X server in order to agree on a compatible GLX version. If the client and the server both have the same major version, they are compatible and the minor version that is returned is the minimum of the two minor version numbers. Thus, if a GLX 1.1 client connects to a GLX 1.0 server, glXQueryVersion will indicate that version 1.0 is in use.

After the outputting of the display name and the version of GLX being used, all the visuals for the default screen are queried. For each visual that supports OpenGL rendering, the associated GLX capabilities are output. Note that glxvisuals returns information about visuals only on the default screen. If you wanted visual information on another screen, you would need to change your DISPLAY to default to a different screen (for example, :0.1). If desired, the program could be enhanced to retrieve the OpenGL visual information for all supported screens.

If an X server supports OpenGL and multiple screens, do not assume that each screen supports the same OpenGL capabilities or X visuals. It is possible for what is known as a *heterogenous* X server to support multiple screens where each screen has different hardware capabilities.

Here is how glxvisuals reports the GLX attributes of each visual on the default screen:

```
printf("  visual bf lv rg d st  r  g  b  a ax dp st accum buffs\n");
printf(" id dep cl sz l  ci b ro sz sz sz sz bf th cl r g b a\n");
printf("-----------------------------------------------------\n");

visualToTry = NULL;
for(vi = visualList; found > 0; found--, vi++) {
  glXGetConfig(dpy, vi, GLX_USE_GL, &glxCapable);
  if (glxCapable) {
    printf("0x%x %2d %s", vi->visualid, vi->depth,
        ClassOf(vi->class));
    glXGetConfig(dpy, vi, GLX_BUFFER_SIZE, &bufferSize);
    glXGetConfig(dpy, vi, GLX_LEVEL, &level);
    glXGetConfig(dpy, vi, GLX_RGBA, &renderType);
    glXGetConfig(dpy, vi, GLX_DOUBLEBUFFER, &doubleBuffer);
    glXGetConfig(dpy, vi, GLX_STEREO, &stereo);
    glXGetConfig(dpy, vi, GLX_AUX_BUFFERS, &auxBuffers);
    glXGetConfig(dpy, vi, GLX_RED_SIZE, &redSize);
    glXGetConfig(dpy, vi, GLX_GREEN_SIZE, &greenSize);
    glXGetConfig(dpy, vi, GLX_BLUE_SIZE, &blueSize);
    glXGetConfig(dpy, vi, GLX_ALPHA_SIZE, &alphaSize);
    glXGetConfig(dpy, vi, GLX_DEPTH_SIZE, &depthSize);
    glXGetConfig(dpy, vi, GLX_STENCIL_SIZE, &stencilSize);
    glXGetConfig(dpy, vi, GLX_ACCUM_RED_SIZE, &acRedSize);
    glXGetConfig(dpy, vi, GLX_ACCUM_GREEN_SIZE, &acGreenSize);
```

```
    glXGetConfig(dpy, vi, GLX_ACCUM_BLUE_SIZE, &acBlueSize);
    glXGetConfig(dpy, vi, GLX_ACCUM_ALPHA_SIZE, &acAlphaSize);
    printf(" %2s %2s %1s %1s %1s ",
      Format(bufferSize, 2), Format(level, 2),
      renderType ? "r" : "c",
    doubleBuffer ? "y" : ".",
    stereo ? "y" : ".");
    printf("%2s %2s %2s %2s ",
      Format(redSize, 2), Format(greenSize, 2),
    Format(blueSize, 2), Format(alphaSize, 2));
    printf("%2s %2s %2s %2s %2s %2s %2s",
      Format(auxBuffers, 2), Format(depthSize, 2),
      Format(stencilSize, 2),
      Format(acRedSize, 2), Format(acGreenSize, 2),
      Format(acBlueSize, 2), Format(acAlphaSize, 2));
    printf("\n");
    visualToTry = vi;
  }
}
```

First the X-specific visual information is output: the visual ID, depth, and visual class. Then multiple calls to `glXGetConfig` retrieve the value of each core GLX attribute for each visual. The routine `ClassOf` is used to output an abbreviation of the visual class. The routine `Format` ensures that numbers are printed with the appropriate width and that a zero is output as a period to make the output easier to read. These routines are listed later.

Once the visual capabilities have been output, information about the OpenGL implementation is output. The `glGetString` routine can be used to query the OpenGL implementation vendor, a renderer name specifying the hardware the implementation utilizes, and the version of the OpenGL implementation.

However, to use `glGetString` (or any other core OpenGL routine), the calling process must be made current to an OpenGL context and drawable. Otherwise, there is no context from which the information can be retrieved. During the output of OpenGL visual capabilities, an OpenGL-capable visual is saved (it does not matter which one). Based on this visual, an OpenGL context and window are created. There is no need to render to the window, so the window is never mapped to appear on the screen. `glXMakeCurrent` is used to bind to the context and the window, and `glGetString` is used to retrieve the OpenGL implementation information.

```
  if (visualToTry) {
    GLXContext context;
    Window window;
    Colormap colormap;
    XSetWindowAttributes swa;
```

```
    context = glXCreateContext(dpy, visualToTry, 0, GL_TRUE);
    colormap = XCreateColormap(dpy,
      RootWindow(dpy, visualToTry->screen),
      visualToTry->visual, AllocNone);
    swa.colormap = colormap;
    swa.border_pixel = 0;
    window = XCreateWindow(dpy, RootWindow(dpy, visualToTry-screen),
      0, 0, 100, 100, 0, visualToTry->depth, InputOutput,
      visualToTry->visual, CWBorderPixel | CWColormap, &swa);
    glXMakeCurrent(dpy, window, context);
    printf("\n");
    printf("OpenGL vendor string: %s\n", glGetString(GL_VENDOR));
    printf("OpenGL renderer string: %s\n", glGetString(GL_RENDERER));
    printf("OpenGL version string: %s\n", glGetString(GL_VERSION));
    if (glXIsDirect(dpy, context))
      printf("direct rendering: supported\n");
  } else
    printf("No GLX-capable visuals!\n");
  XFree(visualList);
}
```

glXIsDirect can be used to determine whether a created context supports indirect or direct rendering. When the OpenGL context is created, a direct context is requested. Therefore, glXIsDirect can be used to report whether the OpenGL implementation can support direct rendering. If glxvisuals was run from a remote machine, direct rendering would not be available. It is also possible that some OpenGL implementations may limit the number of simultaneous direct rendering contexts. So the fact that a given context does not support direct rendering does not let you conclude that the OpenGL implementation has no support for direct rendering. For this reason, an indication about direct rendering support is output *only* if the created context does support direct rendering.

Finally, here are ClassOf and Format. The Format routine is interesting because it uses a recirculating buffer pool for the formatted strings it returns for use by printf.

```
static char *
ClassOf(int c)
{
  switch (c) {
  case StaticGray:    return "sg";
  case GrayScale:     return "gs";
  case StaticColor:   return "sc";
  case PseudoColor:   return "pc";
  case TrueColor:     return "tc";
```

```
    case DirectColor:    return "dc";
    default: return "??";
  }
}

static char *
Format(int n, int w)
{
  static char buffer[256];
  static int bufptr;
  char *buf;

  if (bufptr >= sizeof(buffer) - w)
    bufptr = 0;
  buf = buffer + bufptr;
  if (n == 0)
    sprintf(buf, "%*s", w, ".");
  else
    sprintf(buf, "%*d", w, n);
  bufptr += w + 1;
  return buf;
}
```

The command line to compile glxvisuals would look something like this:

```
cc -o glxvisuals glxvisuals.c -lGL -lXext -lX11
```

2.2.3 glXChooseVisual and glXGetConfig

Two GLX routines supply information about OpenGL-capable visuals. glXGet-Config will retrieve an associated GLX attribute for a specified visual. glXChoose-Visual is a utility routine providing an easy means to find a visual matching a set of specified GLX attribute criteria. For most OpenGL programs, glXChooseVisual is adequate for selecting the right OpenGL-capable visual. The routines have the following prototypes:

```
int glXGetConfig(Display *dpy,
  XVisualInfo *vis, int attrib, int *value);
XVisualInfo *glXChooseVisual(Display *dpy,
  int screen, int *attriblist);
```

glXGetConfig returns zero if it succeeds (with correct parameters, it can be expected always to succeed) and updates the contents of *value* with the GLX attribute named *attrib* for the specified visual *vis*. glXChooseVisual will return an XVisualInfo* for the visual on the specified *screen* matching the GLX attribute criteria listed by *attriblist*. The *attriblist* is a list of boolean and integer GLX attribute value/pairs terminated by the value None.

If an attribute is not specified, a default is used. The selection criteria used for each attribute vary. Table 2.4 lists the default and selection criteria for all the core GLX attributes. For integer attributes, when the value 0 is specified (and 0 is the integer default value if the attribute is not explicitly specified), glXChooseVisual attempts to match a visual with the smallest amount of the attribute. For example, if the GLX_DEPTH_SIZE is not specified, glXChooseVisual will prefer a visual with no depth buffer.

This can have unexpected (but documented) consequences when a program fails to specify nonzero amounts for GLX_RED_SIZE, GLX_GREEN_SIZE, and GLX_BLUE_SIZE. If the amounts are not specified, glXChooseVisual will favor the visual with the smallest red, green, and blue components. This is rarely desired.

Also, note that the boolean attributes match exactly. This means it is possible for you to search for a single buffered visual and find none, even though there might be a double buffered visual, meeting all the other requirements, that you could use by rendering only into the front buffer. It is generally a good idea to use multiple calls to glXChooseVisual in case a given X server does not support your application's most appropriate frame buffer configuration. For example, if you would like a sin-

Table 2.4 Defaults and Selection Criteria Used by glXChooseVisual

Attribute	Default	Selection Criteria
GLX_USE_GL	True	Exact
GLX_BUFFER_SIZE	0	Minimum, smallest
GLX_LEVEL	0	Exact
GLX_RGBA	False	Exact
GLX_DOUBLEBUFFER	False	Exact
GLX_STEREO	False	Exact
GLX_RED_SIZE	0	Minimum, largest
GLX_GREEN_SIZE	0	Minimum, largest
GLX_BLUE_SIZE	0	Minimum, largest
GLX_ALPHA_SIZE	0	Minimum, largest
GLX_DEPTH_SIZE	0	Minimum, largest
GLX_STENCIL_SIZE	0	Minimum, smallest
GLX_AUX_BUFFERS	0	Minimum, smallest
GLX_ACCUM_RED_SIZE	0	Minimum, largest
GLX_ACCUM_GREEN_SIZE	0	Minimum, largest
GLX_ACCUM_BLUE_SIZE	0	Minimum, largest
GLX_ACCUM_ALPHA_SIZE	0	Minimum, largest

gle buffered visual, request one using `glXChooseVisual`, but if the call fails, try again, requesting a double buffered visual. By calling `glDrawBuffer(GL_FRONT)`, you can use a double buffered visual as you would a single buffered visual. There are some OpenGL implementations that provide only double buffered visuals.

It should be stressed that the `glXChooseVisual` algorithm merely makes calls to `glXGetConfig` to determine the GLX attributes of the visuals it considers. You could write `glXChooseVisual` yourself, but you do not have to. Because `glX-ChooseVisual` returns only a single matching visual, it does have to provide a heuristic for choosing a visual when multiple visuals match the specified attribute list.

The heuristic used can vary among different `glXChooseVisual` implementations. Do not rely on different implementations to behave identically when more than one visual matches the specified attribute list.

2.3 MORE ABOUT COLORMAPS

Using X colormaps is more complicated for OpenGL programs, for a number of reasons. OpenGL programs typically use multiple visuals, and different OpenGL visuals require different colormaps. Because OpenGL applications use nondefault visuals, OpenGL windows cannot rely on using the default colormap. This means OpenGL programs must find other means to share multiple colormaps. Because colormaps are a limited hardware resource, sharing is very important to prevent *colormap flashing*. Colormap flashing occurs when the number of logical colormaps displayed on the screen exceeds the number of physical colormaps available. The undesirable result is that some windows are displayed without their correct colormaps installed.

2.3.1 Colormap Sharing

The ICCCM conventions for RGB colormaps help X clients share RGB colormaps. Section 2.1.1 presented a method for sharing colormaps using the ICCCM conventions. Using these conventions is strongly recommended for OpenGL programs using the RGBA color model.

Unfortunately, there is no standard way of sharing color index colormaps between OpenGL applications. However, if you are unable to share color index colormaps between clients, you can reduce some potential for colormap flashing by sharing color index colormaps within your application.

2.3.2 Managing Multiple Colormaps

Often OpenGL programs require more than one colormap. A typical OpenGL program may do OpenGL rendering in a subwindow, but most of the program's user interface is implemented using normal X 2D rendering. If the OpenGL window is 24 bits deep, it would be expensive to require that all the user interface windows also be 24 bits deep. Among other things, pixmaps for the user interface windows would need to be 32 bits per pixel instead of the typical 8 bits per pixel, since pixmap pixels must be padded out to either 1, 2, or 4 bytes for efficient access. So the program may use the server's (probably default) 8-bit `PseudoColor` visual for its user interface, but use a 24 bit `TrueColor` visual for its OpenGL subwindow. Multiple visuals demand multiple colormaps. Many other situations may arise when an OpenGL program needs multiple colormaps within a single top-level window hierarchy.

Normally, window managers assume that the colormap needed by a top-level window and all its subwindows is the colormap used by the top-level window. A window manager automatically notices the colormap of the top-level window and tries to ensure that the colormap is installed when the window gains user input focus.

With multiple colormaps used inside a single top-level window, the window manager needs to be informed of the other colormaps being used. The Xlib routine `XSetWMColormapWindows` can be used to place a standard property on your top-level window to indicate all the colormaps used by the top-level window and its descendants.

Be careful about using multiple colormaps. It is possible that a server will not have enough colormap resources to support the set of visuals and its associated colormaps that you desire. Unfortunately, there is no standard way to determine what sets of visuals and colormaps can be simultaneously installed when multiple visuals are supported. Xlib provides two calls, `XMaxCmapsOfScreen` and `XMinCmapsOfScreen`, but these do not express hardware conflicts between visuals.

Here are some guidelines:

- If `XMaxCmapsOfScreen` returns 1, you are guaranteed a single hardware colormap. Colormap flashing is quite likely. You should write your entire application to use a single colormap.

- If an 8-bit `PseudoColor` visual and a 24-bit `TrueColor` visual are supported on a single screen, it is extremely likely that a different colormap for each of the two visuals can be installed simultaneously.

- If `XMaxCmapsOfScreen` returns a number greater than 1, it is possible that the hardware supports multiple colormaps for the same visual. A rule of thumb is that the higher the number is, the more likely it is that multiple hardware colormaps exist for the same visual. If the number is greater than the total number of visuals on the screen, it must be true for at least one visual (but you cannot find out which one via Xlib requests).

It is hoped that multiple hardware colormaps will become more prevalent and, perhaps, that a standard mechanism to detect colormap and visual conflicts will become available. If you need to know the exact colormap resources for a particular graphics subsystem, ask the vendor.

2.3.3   Initializing Writable Colormaps

Loading of colormap entries is a window system dependent operation, so OpenGL leaves it to the native window system to supply the mechanism for loading colormap cells. OpenGL programs using color index mode with `PseudoColor` visuals or RGBA mode with `DirectColor` visuals must use X's colormap allocation routines to install colormap entries. `XAllocColor` and `XAllocNamedColor` allocate read-only color cells within an X colormap. Private writable colormap cells are allocated with `XStoreColor`, `XStoreColors`, and `XStoreNamedColor`. Ranges of writable colormap cells are allocated with `XAllocColorPlanes`. For `PseudoColor` color index visuals, most OpenGL programs allocate their own private colormaps, even though this tends to create colormap flashing. Because color index lighting, fog, and antialiasing require carefully laid out colormap ramps, it is difficult to share color index colormaps between different clients. This is one more reason to avoid color index windows if possible.

2.4   Using GLX Contexts

OpenGL commands are executed within the context of an OpenGL rendering context. GLX encapsulates this OpenGL rendering state within GLX contexts. Before any OpenGL commands can be executed, a rendering context must be created and "made current" to an OpenGL drawable. A process can create multiple OpenGL contexts, but only a single GLX context can be made current to a given thread of execution with the process. The contexts are created by `glXCreateContext`, prototyped as follows:

```
GLXContext glXCreateContext(Display *dpy,
  XVisualInfo *vis, GLXContext shareList, Bool direct);
```

The `GLXContext` handle returned by `glXCreateContext` names the newly created GLX context. If a GLX context cannot be created, `NULL` is returned. The visual named by *vis* must be an OpenGL-capable visual, and it determines the visual of the created GLX context. The `GLX_USE_GL` attribute value for an OpenGL-capable visual is `True`. A GLX context can be made current only to a GLX drawable that has the same visual as the context.[6]

---

6. It is possible a future version of GLX will relax this similarity constraint. One approach to doing this is SGI's `GLX_SGIX_fbconfig` GLX extension.

The *direct* parameter to `glXCreateContext` requests that a direct rendering context be created. A direct rendering context requires that the process be running local to the graphics display, since direct rendering implies direct access to the graphics hardware. The alternative to direct rendering is indirect rendering. Not all GLX implementations will support direct rendering. When available, direct rendering provides a rendering performance advantage, because commands are sent directly to the graphics hardware rather than being relayed to the X server for execution. You can determine whether a GLX context, once created, supports direct rendering using `glXIsDirect`. For example:

```
GLXContext context;

context = glXCreateContext(dpy, vis, NULL,
  /* request direct rendering */ True);
if (glXIsDirect(dpy, context)) {
  printf("context uses direct rendering\n");
} else {
  printf("context uses indirect rendering\n");
  printf("direct rendering NOT supported by context\n");
}
```

2.4.1 Sharing Display Lists

Whether a GLX context uses direct or indirect rendering controls the *address space* in which the GLX context resides. Indirect rendering contexts reside within the X server's address space. Direct rendering contexts reside within the address space of the process creating the context. The address space in which a context resides determines the set of contexts with which the context can share OpenGL display lists.[7] The *shareList* parameter to `glXCreateContext` names an existing GLX context that must reside in the same address space as the context being created. Also, the shareList context and the context being created must reside on the same screen. The named and newly created context will share the set of display lists they can use. These shared display lists are known as a *display list arena*. Any number of contexts can share display lists. Figure 2.8 shows an example of two contexts sharing display lists. Keep in mind that sharing display lists does not imply the sharing of OpenGL rendering state.

The chief reason to share display lists is to reduce the amount of memory devoted to display lists when multiple GLX contexts are in use. The memory used

---

7. OpenGL 1.1 introduces texture objects. GLX contexts that share display lists also share texture objects. See Section 6.1.1.

Figure 2.8 Sharing of OpenGL display lists between two GLX contexts.

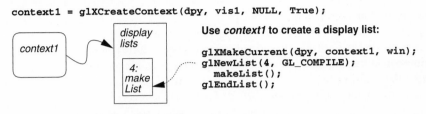

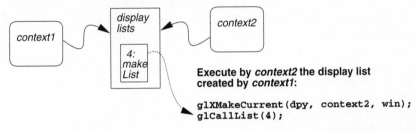

to maintain a shared display list arena is not destroyed until all the contexts sharing the arena have been destroyed.

Most OpenGL commands are not atomic with respect to the execution of other OpenGL commands by other contexts. glEndList and glDeleteLists are exceptions. The list named in a glNewList call is not created or superseded until glEndList is called. If one rendering context is sharing a display list arena with another, it will continue to use the existing definition while the second context is in the process of redefining it.

2.4.2 Binding to GLX Contexts

For a thread to make current to a GLX context and an OpenGL-capable drawable, glXMakeCurrent is called. The routine is prototyped as

```
Bool glXMakeCurrent(Display *dpy, GLXDrawable drawable,
  GLXContext context);
```

The call returns True if it is successful, False otherwise. If False is returned, the previously current rendering context and drawable (if any) remain unchanged. Once bound to a context, subsequent OpenGL commands use the *context* to modify the *drawable*. Only one thread can be made current to a given context at any given point in time. You can release the current context without assigning a new one; call

```
glXMakeCurrent(dpy, None, NULL);
```

It is possible for multiple threads of contexts using different GLX contexts to be simultaneously rendering to a window. While it is possible, do not assume that two threads of execution, even on a multiprocessor workstation, will be able to render concurrently faster than a single thread. Particularly when OpenGL is accelerated by graphics hardware, there are often hidden costs associated with context-switching the graphics hardware.

Changing the current context and drawable and glXMakeCurrent is a moderately expensive operation. For good performance, do not call glXMakeCurrent more than necessary. For example, the following code to redraw two windows simultaneously is extremely inefficient:

```
for (i=0; i<200; i++) {
  glXMakeCurrent(dpy, win1, ctx1);
  renderItemNumber(i);
  glXMakeCurrent(dpy, win2, ctx2);
  renderItemNumber(i);
}
```

Instead, the code could be rewritten to run much faster as

```
glXMakeCurrent(dpy, win1, ctx1);
for (i=0; i<200; i++)
  renderItemNumber(i);

glXMakeCurrent(dpy, win2, ctx2);
for (i=0; i<200; i++)
  renderItemNumber(i);
```

One practice that is acceptable is to call glXMakeCurrent on the same context and drawable already made current. The first check made by glXMakeCurrent is to see whether the context and drawable to make current to are already current and, if so, simply to return. This can occur frequently in callback-driven programs using multiple windows; different callbacks render to different windows without knowing what context and drawable might be current. It is often faster and less error-prone to call glXMakeCurrent for a context and drawable that are probably already made current than to try to cache the current context and drawable within your application code to avoid calling glXMakeCurrent.

You can find out what the GLX context and drawable are currently made current by calling the following routines:

```
GLXContext glXGetCurrentContext(void);
GLXDrawable glXGetCurrentDrawable(void);
```

A GLX context can be destroyed by calling `glXDestroyContext`, prototyped as follows:

```
void glXDestroyContext(Display *dpy, GLXContext context);
```

If the context being destroyed is currently made current to by another thread, the context is destroyed when that thread unbinds from its context; otherwise, the context is destroyed immediately. In either case, the name used to access the context is deleted immediately, so no further binds or actions on the context are possible.

2.4.3   Copying Context State

GLX provides the capability to copy OpenGL state with the `glXCopyContext` routine, prototyped as

```
void glXCopyContext(Display *dpy, GLXContext source,
  GLXContext destination, unsigned long mask);
```

When invoked, OpenGL state variables are copied from the *source* GLX context to the *destination* context. The *mask* parameter is a bitwise *or*-ing of the same symbolic names used for `glPushAttrib` to describe various categories of OpenGL state. For example, specifying `GL_LIGHTING_BIT` for *mask* would just copy the lighting related state. The single symbolic constant `GL_ALL_ATTRIB_BITS` can be specified to copy the maximum possible portion of rendering state.

The source and destination contexts must reside in the same address space and use the same screen. The destination context cannot be made current while the copy occurs. An implicit `glFlush` is performed on the *source* context before being copied.

While `glXCopyContext` can be useful, it is also very expensive. Avoid calling `glXCopyContext` frequently if you call it at all. For many GLX implementations, it will be faster to initialize the OpenGL state in two contexts so that it is the same rather than to initialize the state for one context and copy it to the other.

2.5   RENDERING X FONTS WITH OPENGL

Programs rendering 3D scenes with OpenGL often still need to render 2D text for example, to annotate a 3D scene. OpenGL provides no specialized support for rendering text. However, GLX provides the `glXUseXFont` routine, which lets you create a range of display lists with each individual display list containing a `glBit-map` command to render the bitmap representing a single character in a specified X bitmap font. The `glXUseXFont` routine is prototyped like this:

```
void glXUseXFont(Font font,
  int start, int count, int listBase);
```

The *font* argument is an X Font ID, obtained using `XLoadFont` or `XLoadQuery-Font`. The *start* argument names a font character within the font. Calling `glXUseXf-Font` creates a range of *count* display lists, one for each of the characters of the named font over the range of characters beginning with the *start* character in the font.

One of the chief advantages of `glXUseXFont` is ensuring that text rendered with an X font is rendered identically using both X and OpenGL. This means the text in an application's user interface can exactly match text in a 3D rendering window.

Here is an example of creating a range of display lists for all the displayable ASCII characters:

```
XFontStruct *font;
Font fid;

font = XLoadQueryFont(dpy,
  "-adobe-courier-bold-o-normal--14-140-75-75-m-90-iso8859-1");
fid = font->fid;
glXMakeCurrent(dpy, win, context);
glXUseXFont(dpy, fid, 32, 96, 2000 + 32);
```

The result of this call is to create a range of display lists from 2032 to 2127 (32 through 127), which is the range of displayable 7-bit ASCII characters. The value 2000 is used as the "base" for the font. Adding 2000 to the ASCII value of a character gives the display list to render that character. For example, the ASCII value for a capital B is 66, so to render a capital B call:

```
callList(2066);
```

OpenGL provides a way to call a sequence of display lists using `glCallLists`. While `glCallLists` is a general-purpose routine that works for any type of display list, it makes rendering lines of text very easy. Another routine, `glListBase`, lets you specify an integer offset to the values passed to `glCallLists`. Using this offset makes it possible for ASCII characters to be mapped easily into display-list names. Continuing the example shown previously, here is code rendering a string of text with `glCallLists` and `glListBase`:

```
char *message = "hello world";
glListBase(2000);
glCallLists(strlen(message), GL_UNSIGNED_BYTE, message);
```

Each character (to OpenGL, each character is an unsigned byte) in the array message is called as a display list offset by 2000.

The place where the text is positioned on the screen is determined by the *current
raster position*, set by glRasterPos2f or by other routines in the glRasterPos
family. The details of establishing a raster position are described in Section 5.4.1.
The glBitmap command in each display list has parameters that will advance the
raster position by the width of the character. This ensures that the raster position is
moved forward by the width of each character after that character is rendered.

You can use the font information contained in Xlib's XFontStruct structure to
calculate how high or wide (in pixels) characters or strings of characters will be
when rendered, just as you do for X. For example, to find the pixel width of the
message text shown previously, call

```
int pixel_width;

pixel_width = XTextWidth(font, message, strlen(message));
```

glXUseXFont-created display lists position characters just as X does. The character
is rendered relative to a baseline determined by the raster position. The character's
ascent, descent, left bearing, and right bearing are properly accounted for.

For Asian character sets in which characters are either 16-bit or 32-bit values,
you can use GL_2_BYTES or GL_4_BYTES as the second argument to glCallLists.
Note that for large character sets or character sets with large bitmaps, you should
instantiate only ranges of characters you plan to use with glXUseXFont, to save
memory. Arabic or other character sets that render right to left can be handled by
glXUseXFont, because the raster position will be adjusted leftward instead of right-
ward.

2.6 RENDERING OPENGL INTO PIXMAPS

OpenGL is typically used for rendering directly into displayed windows on a computer's video screen, but GLX also supports OpenGL rendering into X pixmaps. An
X pixmap is an X drawable residing in offscreen memory as an array of pixel values.
Core X rendering operations can be used to render into both windows and pixmaps.
Rendering OpenGL into pixmaps has advantages over rendering directly to windows. Pixmaps are not obscured or damaged, unlike windows, which can overlap
and obscure each other. This means if you render into pixmaps, you need not be con-
cerned with handling Expose events. Expose events are not generated for pixmaps,

because the pixmap image is always retained. Another benefit of pixmaps is that, unlike the situation with windows, the renderable area of a pixmap is not bounded by the screen size.

X pixmaps cannot be used directly for OpenGL rendering. Consider that the `XCreateWindow` call takes a `Visual*` as one of its parameters. When a window is created, its visual determines what OpenGL frame buffer capabilities (such as ancillary buffers) the window provides. Xlib's `XCreatePixmap` routine for creating a pixmap, however, does not take a `Visual*` as a parameter. For the core X Window System, this is quite reasonable, because pixmaps are never displayed and, therefore, need no *visual* attributes. However, OpenGL overloads visuals by associating OpenGL frame buffer capabilities with X visuals, so a pixmap will need some associated visual for OpenGL rendering to the pixmap to be possible.

GLX provides the `glXCreateGLXPixmap` routine to associate a frame buffer configuration with a pixmap. The routine is prototyped as

```
GLXPixmap glXCreateGLXPixmap(
  Display *dpy,
  XVisualInfo *visual,
  Pixmap pixmap);
```

`glXCreateGLXPixmap` is passed a *pixmap* XID (returned by `XCreatePixmap`) and a `XVisualInfo*` *visual* (typically found using `glXChooseVisual`); the routine returns a GLX pixmap XID that has the frame buffer configuration (including associated ancillary buffers) determined by the `XVisualInfo*` parameter. The X pixmap passed to `glXCreateGLXPixmap` is used as the front left buffer of the resulting offscreen area (any back buffers for double-buffering or right stereo buffers cannot be rendered to with X). Other than the left front buffer, no OpenGL ancillary buffer has an associated XID for X rendering. The visual must be OpenGL-capable and the depth of the pixmap must match the depth of the visual. This process is shown in Figure 2.9.

You can think of creating a GLX pixmap as "wrapping" a standard X pixmap with an OpenGL-described frame buffer configuration. X rendering can be done to the pixmap XID, and OpenGL rendering can be done to the GLX pixmap XID.

OpenGL rendering contexts can be bound to a GLX pixmap created by `glX-CreateGLXPixmap`. As in the case of windows, the GLX pixmap and the rendering context must share the same screen and visual. Direct rendering to GLX pixmaps is not necessarily supported. For this reason, OpenGL contexts created for use with GLX pixmaps should be created as indirect contexts. The only way to determine whether direct rendering to a GLX pixmap is possible is to create the direct context and GLX pixmap and attempt a `glXMakeCurrent`; if this succeeds, direct rendering to GLX pixmaps is supported.

Since pixmaps are not displayed, it is almost certainly the case that applications will read back or copy to the screen the images rendered into GLX pixmaps. The

Figure 2.9 How OpenGL-capable `GLXPixmaps` are created from X `Pixmaps`.

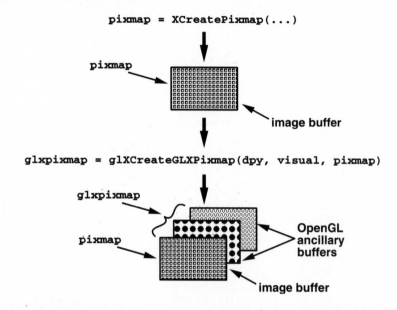

core X `XGetImage` and `XCopyArea` routines and OpenGL's `glReadPixels` routine can be used to read back and copy, respectively, the contents of a pixmap.

Keep in mind that OpenGL window rendering performance may be appreciably faster than GLX pixmap rendering performance. Whether GLX pixmaps benefit from OpenGL graphics hardware acceleration is implementation dependent; in most implementations, they do not. GLX pixmaps typically reside in host memory; in such cases, GLX pixmap rendering gets no benefit from graphics hardware acceleration, and OpenGL pixmap rendering is implemented with relatively slow "soft" OpenGL code running on the host processor. On some very fast OpenGL implementations, the difference between OpenGL rendering performance to a window and GLX pixmap rendering performance may be a factor of 50 or more.

Because the contents of a pixmap are retained, a pixmap requires an amount of memory proportional to its area and pixel depth. Because GLX pixmaps require additional memory for any supported OpenGL ancillary buffers, GLX pixmaps typically consume considerably more memory than standard X pixmaps. Generally, the memory for GLX pixmaps is allocated within the address space of the X server. Keep in mind the memory demands that GLX pixmaps make on the operating system and window system. For example, an 800-by-800-pixel 24-bit double-buffered pixmap using a 32-bit depth buffer and an accumulation buffer with 16-bit components would require about 12 megabytes of memory!

To destroy a GLX pixmap (and deallocate its associated memory), call `glX-DestroyGLXPixmap`, prototyped as follows:

```
void glXDestroyGLXPixmap(
  Display *dpy,
  GLXPixmap pix);
```

Be aware of the visual used to create a GLX pixmap. While double buffered visuals are extremely useful for supporting on-screen animation, double buffered visuals are not generally advised for GLX pixmaps. There are two reasons:

1. Allocating both a front and a back buffer for a pixmap is generally a waste of memory. GLX pixmaps do not need a front displayed buffer distinct from the back rendering buffer, because GLX pixmaps have no displayed buffer.

2. Hardware double buffering on some machines limits the color resolution to half the single buffered color resolution (see Section 6.5.5). This is reflected in the available GLX pixmap color resolution, since the same visuals for on-screen windows are used for GLX pixmaps. For GLX pixmap uses, the more color resolution, the better.

Everything that OpenGL can render into a window can be rendered into a GLX pixmap.[8] Even so, OpenGL does not require that an image rendered to the screen be pixel-per-pixel identical to the GLX pixmap-rendered image. The specifics of on-screen rendering and GLX pixmap rendering can vary within the bounds of the OpenGL specification.

2.6.1 Generating Encapsulated PostScript

OpenGL is mostly used for interactive output of graphics to a video screen; however, applications often need to generate 3D scenes and images for direct output to color or black-and-white printers or to be embedded in documents. Rendering OpenGL into GLX pixmaps is a straightforward way to capture OpenGL-rendered images. Such images can then be converted to Encapsulated PostScript (EPS) so that the image can be inserted into other documents or printed to a PostScript printer.

The `pixmap2eps` example that follows renders the dinosaur scene from `glxdino` into a GLX pixmap. The image in the GLX pixmap is then read from the pixmap, using `glReadPixels`, and written to a file as EPS. EPS is just an example image for-

---

8. In isolated instances, some OpenGL extensions may not be supported for use with GLX pixmaps, but *all* of OpenGL's core functionality must be supported when rendering to pixmaps. An example of an extension not supported for pixmaps is Silicon Graphic's multisampling extension (see page 254).

mat. The image read from the GLX pixmap could also be written to any of the other popular image formats, such as TIFF, GIF, or the Silicon Graphics RGB image format.

The routine `generateEPS` writes out an EPS file of the specified width and height. The `inColor` parameter determines whether the EPS should be color or black-and-white. Here is the `pixmap2eps.c` example using `generateEPS`:

```
int generateEPS(char *filename, int inColor, unsigned int width,
    unsigned int height);

void
main(int argc, char **argv)
{
  static int configuration[] = { GLX_DOUBLEBUFFER, GLX_RGBA,
      GLX_DEPTH_SIZE, 16, GLX_RED_SIZE, 1, GLX_GREEN_SIZE, 1,
      GLX_BLUE_SIZE, 1, None};
  Display *dpy;
  XVisualInfo *vi;
  GLXContext cx;
  Pixmap pmap;
  GLXPixmap glxpmap;
  int imageWidth = 400, imageHeight = 400;

  dpy = XOpenDisplay(NULL);
  if (dpy == NULL)
    fatalError("could not open display");

  if (!glXQueryExtension(dpy, NULL, NULL))
    fatalError("X server has no OpenGL GLX extension");
```

So far, an X server connection is made and verified to be OpenGL-capable.

```
  /* Find an OpenGL-capable RGB visual with depth buffer */
  vi = glXChooseVisual(dpy, DefaultScreen(dpy), &configuration[1]);
  if (vi == NULL) {
    vi = glXChooseVisual(dpy, DefaultScreen(dpy), &configuration[0]);
    if (vi == NULL) {
      fatalError("No appropriate RGB visual with depth buffer.");
  }
}
```

Unlike `glxdino`, which attempts to use a double buffered visual in preference to a single buffered visual, `pixmap2eps` prefers a single buffered visual, because single buffered GLX pixmaps use less memory and are likely to have more color resolution.

```
/* Create an OpenGL rendering context */
cx = glXCreateContext(dpy, vi,
    NULL,    /* no sharing of display lists */
    False);  /* direct rendering if possible */
if (cx == NULL)
    fatalError("Could not create rendering context");
```

Unlike glxdino, pixmap2eps does not attempt to allocate a direct OpenGL rendering context since OpenGL rendering contexts are not always required to support direct rendering to GLX pixmaps.

```
pmap = XCreatePixmap(dpy, RootWindow(dpy, vi->screen),
  imageWidth, imageHeight, vi->depth);
glxpmap = glXCreateGLXPixmap(dpy, vi, pmap);
glXMakeCurrent(dpy, glxpmap, cx);
```

Create a 400-by-400-pixel pixmap, then create a GLX pixmap from it with the visual selected earlier. Make current to the GLX pixmap.

```
contextInit();
makeDinosaur();
glViewport(0, 0, imageWidth, imageHeight);
redraw();
```

Now that we are bound to the GLX pixmap, initialize the rendering context and the display lists for the dinosaur model by calling the same routines used in glxdino. Set the viewport and draw the scene by calling redraw. Unlike glxdino, which watches for a ConfigureNotify to set the viewport and an Expose event to draw the scene, pixmap2eps renders without waiting for any events, since the pixmap is retained.

```
  generateEPS("dino.rgb.eps", /* color */ 1, imageWidth,
      imageHeight);
  generateEPS("dino.bw.eps", /* black&white */ 0, imageWidth,
      imageHeight);
}
```

Now that the GLX pixmap contains the image of the dinosaur, call generateEPS to generate EPS. The second parameter of generateEPS determines if the generated

EPS is color or grayscale. If the output is destined for a black-and-white printer, the black-and-white EPS is one-third the size of the color version.

The routine `grabPixels` reads the raw pixel color data from the current bound OpenGL context and drawable. With it, `generateEPS` is implemented as follows:

```
GLvoid *grabPixels(int inColor, unsigned int width, unsigned int
    height);

int
generateEPS(char *filename, int inColor, unsigned int width,
unsigned int height)
{
  FILE *fp;
  GLvoid *pixels;
  char *curpix;
  int components, pos, i;

  pixels = grabPixels(inColor, width, height);
```

Grab all the color pixels from the GLX pixmap by calling `grabPixels`.

```
if (pixels == NULL)
   return 1;
 if (inColor)
   components = 3; /* Red, green, blue. */
 else
   components = 1; /* Luminance. */
```

A color EPS file has three components, for red, green, and blue. A black-and-white file uses a single luminance (grayscale) component.

```
fp = fopen(filename, "w");
if (fp == NULL) {
   return 2;
}
fprintf(fp, "%%!PS-Adobe-2.0 EPSF-1.2\n");
fprintf(fp, "%%%%Creator: OpenGL pixmap render output\n");
fprintf(fp, "%%%%BoundingBox: 0 0 %d %d\n", width, height);
fprintf(fp, "%%%%EndComments\n");
fprintf(fp, "gsave\n");
fprintf(fp, "/bwproc {\n");
fprintf(fp, "    rgbproc\n");
```

```
fprintf(fp, "    dup length 3 idiv string 0 3 0 \n");
fprintf(fp, "    5 -1 roll {\n");
fprintf(fp, "    add 2 1 roll 1 sub dup 0 eq\n");
fprintf(fp, "    { pop 3 idiv 3 -1 roll dup 4 -1 roll dup\n");
fprintf(fp, "      3 1 roll 5 -1 roll } put 1 add 3 0 \n");
fprintf(fp, "    { 2 1 roll } ifelse\n");
fprintf(fp, "    }forall\n");
fprintf(fp, "    pop pop pop\n");
fprintf(fp, "} def\n");
fprintf(fp, "systemdict /colorimage known not {\n");
fprintf(fp, "   /colorimage {\n");
fprintf(fp, "        pop\n");
fprintf(fp, "        pop\n");
fprintf(fp, "        /rgbproc exch def\n");
fprintf(fp, "        { bwproc } image\n");
fprintf(fp, "    } def\n");
fprintf(fp, "} if\n");
fprintf(fp, "/picstr %d string def\n", width * components);
fprintf(fp, "%d %d scale\n", width, height);
fprintf(fp, "%d %d %d\n", width, height, 8);
fprintf(fp, "[%d 0 0 %d 0 0]\n", width, height);
fprintf(fp, "{currentfile picstr readhexstring pop}\n");
fprintf(fp, "false %d\n", components);
fprintf(fp, "colorimage\n");
```

Open the named file and output an EPS header. This header informs a PostScript engine that an image follows, and tells a program supporting the embedding of EPS what the image's bounding box is.

```
curpix = (char *) pixels;
pos = 0;
for (i = width * height * components; i > 0; i--) {
  fprintf(fp, "%02hx", *curpix++);
  if (++pos >= 32) {
    fprintf(fp, "\n");
    pos = 0;
  }
}
if (pos)
  fprintf(fp, "\n");
```

Once the header has been written, output each byte of the raw image as a hexadecimal value.

```
    fprintf(fp, "grestore\n");
    free(pixels);
    fclose(fp);
    return 0;
}
```

Finally, output the EPS footer, free the pixels returned by grabPixels, and close the file.

Here is how grabPixels is written:

```
GLvoid *
grabPixels(int inColor, unsigned int width, unsigned int height)
{
  GLvoid *buffer;
  GLint swapbytes, lsbfirst, rowlength;
  GLint skiprows, skippixels, alignment;
  GLenum format;
  unsigned int size;

  if (inColor) {
    format = GL_RGB;
    size = width * height * 3;
  } else {
    format = GL_LUMINANCE;
    size = width * height * 1;
  }

  buffer = (GLvoid *) malloc(size);
  if (buffer == NULL)
    return NULL;
```

Based on whether the image to grab is color or not, determine the OpenGL format to be used for glReadPixels and the size of the buffer. The GL_RGB format returns color pixels. The GL_LUMINANCE format returns luminance (grayscale) pixels.

```
  glGetIntegerv(GL_UNPACK_SWAP_BYTES, &swapbytes);
  glGetIntegerv(GL_UNPACK_LSB_FIRST, &lsbfirst);
  glGetIntegerv(GL_UNPACK_ROW_LENGTH, &rowlength);
  glGetIntegerv(GL_UNPACK_SKIP_ROWS, &skiprows);
  glGetIntegerv(GL_UNPACK_SKIP_PIXELS, &skippixels);
  glGetIntegerv(GL_UNPACK_ALIGNMENT, &alignment);
  glPixelStorei(GL_UNPACK_SWAP_BYTES, GL_FALSE);
  glPixelStorei(GL_UNPACK_LSB_FIRST, GL_FALSE);
```

```
glPixelStorei(GL_UNPACK_ROW_LENGTH, 0);
glPixelStorei(GL_UNPACK_SKIP_ROWS, 0);
glPixelStorei(GL_UNPACK_SKIP_PIXELS, 0);
glPixelStorei(GL_UNPACK_ALIGNMENT, 1);

glReadPixels(0, 0, width, height, format,
  GL_UNSIGNED_BYTE, (GLvoid *) buffer);
```

Save all the current pixel storage unpack modes so they can be restored after the glReadPixels. Load the pixel storage unpack modes for reading the pixmap's contents in a tight block of data. The only nondefault pixel storage mode is the GL_UNPACK_ALIGNMENT mode. Finally, read the pixmap's contents into the allocated buffer.

```
glPixelStorei(GL_UNPACK_SWAP_BYTES, swapbytes);
glPixelStorei(GL_UNPACK_LSB_FIRST, lsbfirst);
glPixelStorei(GL_UNPACK_ROW_LENGTH, rowlength);
glPixelStorei(GL_UNPACK_SKIP_ROWS, skiprows);
glPixelStorei(GL_UNPACK_SKIP_PIXELS, skippixels);
glPixelStorei(GL_UNPACK_ALIGNMENT, alignment);
return buffer;
}
```

Restore the original pixel storage unpack modes and return the buffer. Reading and manipulating images are discussed further in Section 5.4.

The result of running pixmap2eps is the creation of two files: dino.rgb.eps and dino.bw.eps, containing the color and grayscale images, respectively. No windows appear when the program is run, since all the rendering is done to the GLX pixmap. The beginning of dino.rgb.eps appears in Figure 2.10.

2.7 MIXING X AND OPENGL RENDERING

OpenGL allows its rendering to be mixed with core X rendering into the same window.[9] You should be careful in doing so, because X and OpenGL rendering requests are logically issued in two distinct streams. If you want to ensure proper rendering, you *must* synchronize the streams. Calling glXWaitGL will ensure that all OpenGL

---

9. In IRIS GL, the predecessor of OpenGL, rendering into an X window using core X rendering after IRIS GL has been bound to the window is undefined. This precludes mixing core X rendering with GL rendering in the same window, but OpenGL specifies that X and OpenGL rendering can be mixed with predictable results *if* the right synchronization is performed.

Figure 2.10 First 34 lines of `dino.rgb.eps` generated by `pixmap2eps`.

```
Adobe-2.0 EPSF-1.2
%%Creator: OpenGL pixmap render output
%%BoundingBox: 0 0 400 400
%%EndComments
gsave
/bwproc {
  rgbproc
  dup length 3 idiv string 0 3 0
  5 -1 roll {
  add 2 1 roll 1 sub dup 0 eq
  { pop 3 idiv 3 -1 roll dup 4 -1 roll dup
    3 1 roll 5 -1 roll put 1 add 3 0 }
  { 2 1 roll } ifelse
  } forall
  pop pop pop
} def
systemdict /colorimage known not {
  /colorimage {
    pop
    pop
    /rgbproc exch def
    { bwproc } image
  } def
} if
/picstr 1200 string def
400 400 scale
400 400 8
[400 0 0 400 0 0]
{currentfile picstr readhexstring pop}
false 3
colorimage
000000000000000000000000000000000000000000000000000000000000000
000000000000000000000000000000000000000000000000000000000000000
000000000000000000000000000000000000000000000000000000000000000
```

rendering has finished before subsequent X rendering takes place. Calling `glXWaitX` will make sure all core X rendering has finished before subsequent OpenGL rendering takes place. Both routines take no arguments. During indirect rendering, these requests do not require a protocol round-trip to the X server.

Here is an example in which synchronization would be necessary to ensure the expected rendering:

```
glXMakeCurrent(dpy, win, glxcontext);
glClear(GL_COLOR_BUFFER_BIT);
XDrawLine(dpy, win, gc, 0, 0, 10, 10);
```

The problem is that the OpenGL color buffer clear could be done *after* the XDraw-Line request is rendered, because OpenGL and X are not synchronized. The problem can be solved by adding a glXWaitGL call like this:

```
glXMakeCurrent(dpy, win, glxcontext);
glClear(GL_COLOR_BUFFER_BIT);
glXWaitGL();
XDrawLine(dpy, win, gc, 0, 0, 10, 10);
```

The glXWaitGL ensures that the glClear completes before the XDrawLine executes.

The core OpenGL API also includes the glFinish and glFlush commands, which are useful for rendering synchronization. glFinish ensures that all rendering has appeared on the screen when the routine returns (similar to XSync). glFlush ensures only that the queued commands will eventually be executed (similar to XFlush).

Understand that mixing OpenGL and X in the same drawable is not normally necessary. Many OpenGL programs will use a toolkit such as Motif for their 2D user interface component and use a distinct X window for OpenGL rendering. This requires no synchronization, since OpenGL and core X rendering go to distinct X windows. Only when OpenGL and core X rendering are directed at the same window is synchronization of rendering necessary.

Also, OpenGL can be used for extremely fast 2D as well as 3D. When you feel a need to mix core X and OpenGL rendering into the same window, consider rendering what you would do in core X using OpenGL. Not only do you avoid the synchronization overhead, but you can potentially achieve faster 2D using direct rendered OpenGL as opposed to core X rendering. While mixing OpenGL and X into the same drawable is possible if correctly synchronized, it is usually not necessary and not recommended.

2.8 DEBUGGING TIPS

Bugs can creep into OpenGL programs just as they do into any other program. Many times, programming bugs in OpenGL or X are reported as errors by OpenGL or X. Looking for such errors in your programs and understanding them is the first step toward eliminating the bugs that originated the errors.

2.8.1 Finding OpenGL Errors

The OpenGL state machine records errors when erroneous commands are issued. One way to cause an error is to pass an invalid enumerate to an OpenGL routine. For example:

```
glBegin(GL_LINE);
  glVertex2i(45, 12);
  glVertex2i(4, 13);
glEnd();
```

While this may appear at first glance to be reasonable, the GL_LINE enumerant is invalid when it is passed to glBegin. The programmer probably intended to call glBegin(GL_LINES).

Another source of errors is overflowing or underflowing the matrix or attribute stack. Errors can also occur when an out-of-range value is passed to a command argument (for example, trying to create a display list zero) or when a requested operation is illegal in the current state (for example, trying to change lighting parameters in the middle of a glBegin/glEnd pair). An error can also occur when OpenGL runs out of memory. In all cases except for running out of memory, OpenGL will ignore the erroneous command. If an out-of-memory error occurs, the results of subsequent OpenGL operations may be undefined.

A correct OpenGL program should not generate any OpenGL errors, but during debugging it is helpful to check explicitly for errors. A good time to check for errors is at the end of each frame. Errors in OpenGL are not reported unless you explicitly check for them, unlike X protocol errors, which are always reported to the client.

OpenGL errors are recorded by setting "sticky" flags. Once an error flag is set, it will not be cleared until glGetError is used to query the error. An OpenGL implementation may have several error flags internally that can be set (since OpenGL errors may occur in different stages of the OpenGL rendering pipeline). When you look for errors, you should call glGetError repeatedly until it returns GL_NO_ERROR, indicating that all the error flags have been cleared.

The OpenGL error model is suited for high-performance rendering, since error reporting does not slow down the error-free case. Because OpenGL errors should not be generated by bug-free code, you will probably want to remove error querying from your final program, since querying errors will slow down your rendering speed.

When an OpenGL error is generated, the command that generated it is not recorded, so you may need to add more error queries to your code to isolate the source of the error.

The gluErrorString routine in the OpenGL Utility library (GLU) converts an OpenGL error number into a human-readable string and helps you output a reasonable error message.

Here is a routine you can call within your OpenGL program to isolate locations where OpenGL errors are being generated:

```
void
sniff_for_opengl_errors(void)
{
  int error;

  while ((error = glGetError()) != GL_NO_ERROR)
    fprintf(stderr, "GL error: %s\n", gluErrorString(error));
}
```

The possible OpenGL error codes are shown in Table 2.5. In all cases except GL_OUT_OF_MEMORY, the behavior of OpenGL is defined to ignore the offending command when an error occurs. Be aware that if a GL_OUT_OF_MEMORY error occurs, the state of the OpenGL context is undefined.

2.8.2   X11 Protocol Errors

Unlike OpenGL errors, which must be actively queried with glGetError to be detected, X11 protocol errors are actively sent by the X server to the X program responsible for the error. X errors arrive as asynchronous error protocol packets. If an X protocol error is received by Xlib, Xlib's default behavior is to report the error and exit.

Here is an example of what Xlib might output:

```
X Error of failed request: BadMatch (invalid parameter attributes)
  Major opcode of failed request: 1 (X_CreateWindow)
  Serial number of failed request: 19
  Current serial number in output stream: 20
```

Typically, X protocol errors are caused by passing bad parameters to Xlib or GLX routines. For OpenGL programs, BadMatch is a common X protocol error. The error

Table 2.5 OpenGL Error Codes

Error Code	Description
GL_INVALID_ENUM	GLenum argument out of range.
GL_INVALID_VALUE	Numeric argument out of range.
GL_INVALID_OPERATION	Operation illegal in current state.
GL_STACK_OVERFLOW	Command would cause a stack overflow.
GL_STACK_UNDERFLOW	Command would cause a stack underflow.
GL_OUT_OF_MEMORY	Not enough memory left to execute command.

indicates that parameters were not of the expected matching types. `BadMatch` is easy to generate if you do not make sure that windows, visuals, colormaps, pixmaps, and GLX contexts properly match each other. For example, if you try to create a window of a depth not supported by the specified visual, a `BadMatch` error will result. One difficulty of debugging `BadMatch` errors is that the error is not specific about exactly what fails to match. Incorrect use of the `XCreateWindow` and `XCreateColormap` Xlib calls is the most common source of X protocol errors for OpenGL programmers.

Table 2.6 Reasons for X protocol errors resulting from `XCreateWindow` and `XCreateColormap` Xlib calls. The errors that tend to be encountered frequently by OpenGL programmers are marked with a • symbol.

Xlib Call	Error	Cause
XCreateWindow	BadMatch	• Visual must support requested depth.
		Parent window is `InputOnly`.
		For `InputOnly` windows, depth must be zero.
		Visual must be supported on the screen.
		For `InputOnly` windows, border width must be zero.
		Background pixmap must have same depth and root as window.
		For `ParentRelative` background pixmap, window requires parent's depth.
		• Border pixmap must have same depth and root as window.
		Border pixel required if no border pixmap and window's visual is different from parent.
		For `CopyFromParent` border pixmap, window requires parent's depth.
		Colormap must match window's visual and root.
		For `CopyFromParent` colormap window requires parent's visual.
	BadValue	Window width and height must be positive.
		Attribute value out of range.
	BadAlloc	X server out memory.
	BadCursor	Invalid cursor specified.
	BadWindow	Invalid root window specified.
	BadPixmap	Invalid background or border pixmap specified.
XCreateColormap	BadMatch	`AllocNone` required for `StaticGray`, `StaticColor`, and `TrueColor`.
	BadWindow	Invalid window specified.
	BadAlloc	• Attempted `AllocAll` creating overlay colormap with reserved transparent pixel, use `AllocNone` instead.
		X server out memory.

To help you debug these situations, Table 2.6 provides a checklist of all the possible reasons for X protocol errors when are called these routines.

A good way to debug these problems is to call `XSynchronize(dpy, True)` in your program. This will ensure that all X protocol requests are performed synchronously (X protocol errors arrive asynchronously by default). While this slows down performance, it will also ensure that the error is delivered immediately after the Xlib call generating the error. In a debugger, put a breakpoint at `exit`, since the default X protocol error handler calls `exit` to terminate the program when an error occurs. Run your program and when an X protocol error occurs, you should drop into the debugger and examine the place in your code where the error is being generated.

Be sure not to enable X request synchronization for your final program.

2.8.3 Specialized OpenGL Debugging Tools

Beyond the error reporting facilities built into OpenGL, many OpenGL vendors will supply further debugging and profiling tools specifically for OpenGL programs. One such tool is the Silicon Graphics `ogldebug` tool. With `ogldebug`, you can single-step through the execution of OpenGL routines, break when a given OpenGL routine is called, examine OpenGL state (including the contents of display lists), and collect traces of OpenGL commands executed, all through a graphical user interface and without modifying or specially compiling your application. A snapshot of `ogldebug` in use is shown in Figure 2.11 .

Figure 2.11 Screen snapshot of IRIX 5.3's `ogldebug` OpenGL debugger halted while debugging the rendering of a program called `material`. The History Panel shows the history of all OpenGL commands executed; the Count Panel tracks the number of times each OpenGL routine has been called.

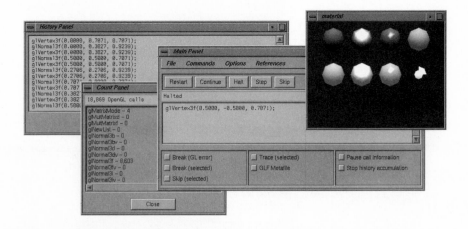

Another type of OpenGL development tool is a profiling system that understands the performance characteristics of certain graphics hardware configurations to let you get the optimum performance from your OpenGL application for a particular piece of hardware. Consult your vendor's OpenGL development documentation to determine whether `ogldebug` or other OpenGL development tools are available.

Using OpenGL with Widgets

This chapter, which explains OpenGL application programming using X Toolkit widgets, particularly the OSF/Motif widget set, is organized into the following sections:

1. "About the X Toolkit and Motif" provides a brief introduction to widget-based X application programming.
2. "Using OpenGL Drawing Area Widgets" describes the issues involved with integrating OpenGL rendering with widgets, including a short example.
3. "Specifics of the OpenGL Drawing Area Widgets" describes the functionality provided by the standard OpenGL drawing area widgets and some common widget pitfalls.
4. "A More Involved Widget Example" walks through a more significant widget-based OpenGL program.

3.1 ABOUT THE X TOOLKIT AND MOTIF

Most X applications are written using not the low-level Xlib interface described in the previous chapters, but the X Toolkit, often called simply Xt or the Xt Intrinsics. This chapter discusses using OpenGL with the X Toolkit and associated widget sets, in particular OSF/Motif. A full introduction to the X Toolkit and the Motif widget set is beyond the scope of this book. Beyond a brief introduction, the reader is assumed to be knowledgeable about X Toolkit and Motif programming.

The X Toolkit provides an object-oriented framework for the graphical user interface of an X application. A programmer can build a program from scroll bars, buttons, and menus instead of the involved and often cumbersome level of X windows, visuals, and events. The X Toolkit provides the structure and mechanisms for user interface objects known as *widgets*. The X Toolkit also provides its own event dispatch loop so that programmers use what is called an "inverted" or callback-driven, programming style, common in graphical user interface programming. This means programmers register functions to be called by the toolkit when high-level events occur.

The X Toolkit also takes care of details such as cut-and-paste and most window manager conventions, and provides extensive customizability through the X resource mechanism.

Widgets for scroll bars, buttons, menus, and other user interface objects are not supplied by the X Toolkit itself. Its designers carefully avoided the specification of a specific "look and feel." Instead, the X Toolkit leaves the construction of a useful set of widgets up to other libraries layered on top of the X Toolkit. Though it is not the only available widget set, OSF/Motif is the industry standard widget set used by most X application writers. Figure 3.1 shows how Motif and the X Toolkit libraries are layered.

Using OpenGL with the X Toolkit and Motif is a good choice for most 3D application writers. The application's graphical user interface can use Motif widgets for a standard look and feel, while OpenGL can be used for rendering 3D scenes.

Today's 3D graphics applications typically have all the trappings of graphical user interfaces: pulldown menus, dialog boxes, scroll bars, panels with buttons and sliders. Creating and managing common user interface objects is what Motif does well. Generally, 3D rendering is confined to one or more 3D rendering areas. This

Figure 3.1 Basic software library layering for Motif-based programs (not including OpenGL).

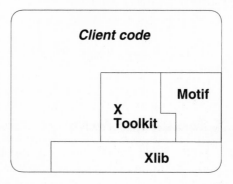

type of application is typically constructed using standard Motif widgets for all the user interface objects and using special OpenGL drawing area widgets for the 3D rendering areas.

Using OpenGL with Motif has numerous advantages over using Xlib only, as described in Chapters 1 and 2. First and most important, Motif provides a well-documented, standard widget set that gives your application a consistent look and feel. Second, Motif and the X Toolkit take care of routine but complicated issues such as cut-and-paste and window manager conventions. Third, the X Toolkit's work procedure and timeout mechanisms make it easy to animate a 3D window without blocking out user interaction with your application.

3.2 USING OPENGL DRAWING AREA WIDGETS

The easiest way to create an OpenGL rendering area is by instantiating a special OpenGL widget within your Motif application. After that, you can create an OpenGL rendering context, bind it to the OpenGL widget's window, and be ready to render OpenGL.

Motif's drawing area widget would seem a natural widget for OpenGL rendering. Unfortunately, the X Toolkit's design, on which Motif relies, allows programmers to specify a widget's visual only if the widget's class is derived from the shell widget class. Shell widgets are often called *top-level* widgets because they are designed to communicate with the window manager and act as containers for other widgets. A nonshell widget inherits the depth and visual of its parent widget. The Motif drawing area widget class (like most widget classes) is not derived from the shell widget class. It is impossible, without resorting to programming widget internals, to set the visual of a nonshell Motif widget differently from that of its ancestor shell widget.

The problem is that OpenGL uses X visuals to determine the OpenGL frame buffer capabilities of an X window. In many cases, an application's 3D viewing area is likely to demand a deeper, more capable visual than the X server's default visual, which Motif normally uses.

If this seems confusing, do not worry. It is confusing, and it is the reason that there are special OpenGL drawing area widgets. You have two options:

1. You can use the standard Motif drawing area widget for your OpenGL rendering area and make sure that the top-level shell widget is created with the correct visual for OpenGL's use. This is both limiting and involved.

2. You can use an OpenGL drawing area widget that is specially programmed to overcome the X Toolkit's inability to set the visual and depth of a nonshell widget.

Either approach can work, but the OpenGL widget is much simpler and more flexible.

Figure 3.2 Screen snapshot of `glw` OpenGL drawing area widget example.

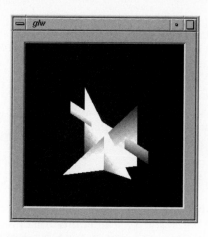

There are actually two different OpenGL widgets, but they are almost identical. One is specific to the Motif widget set; the other is not part of any particular widget set. Section 3.3.1 discusses the two widgets in more detail.

The OpenGL widgets are not part of the GLX standard because GLX interfaces OpenGL and X at a level below that of the X Toolkit. However, vendor-supplied OpenGL development environments for X generally include the OpenGL-specific widget library and header files. Also, the OpenGL-specific widget source code is available via the Internet. (See Appendix A.)

3.2.1   A Short OpenGL-specific Widget Example

The `glw` example program listed below renders three smooth-shaded 3D polygons within an OpenGL drawing area widget. The 3D drawing area resides within a Motif frame widget. Figure 3.2 shows the appearance of `glw`. The polygons can be rotated in 3D. A user keystroke starts and stops the polygon's rotation. The program stops rotating the polygons when iconified.

The `glw.c` source code for the example begins with a list of ANSI C library, Xlib, Motif, and OpenGL header files:

```
#include <stdlib.h>
#include <stdio.h>
#include <Xm/Form.h>    /* Motif Form widget. */
#include <Xm/Frame.h>   /* Motif Frame widget. */
#include <X11/keysym.h>
#include <X11/Xutil.h>
```

```
#include <X11/Xatom.h>  /* For XA_RGB_DEFAULT_MAP. */
#include <X11/Xmu/StdCmap.h>  /* For XmuLookupStandardColormap. */
#include <GL/gl.h>
#include <GL/glu.h>
#include <GL/glx.h>
```

The OpenGL-specific Motif drawing area widget's header file is then included:

```
#include <X11/GLw/GLwMDrawA.h>  /* Motif OpenGL drawing area. */
```

3.2.1.1 *Widget Initialization*

Next, a set of global variables are defined. These variables include two sets of GLX attributes that are used when the OpenGL rendering area is being created. Also, a list of X Toolkit fallback resources supplies reasonable defaults for the program's widgets.

```
static int snglBuf[] = {GLX_RGBA, GLX_DEPTH_SIZE, 12,
  GLX_RED_SIZE, 1, None};
static int dblBuf[] = {GLX_RGBA, GLX_DEPTH_SIZE, 12,
  GLX_DOUBLEBUFFER, GLX_RED_SIZE, 1, None};
static String fallbackResources[] = {
  "*glxarea*width: 300", "*glxarea*height: 300",
  "*frame*x: 20", "*frame*y: 20",
  "*frame*topOffset: 20", "*frame*bottomOffset: 20",
  "*frame*rightOffset: 20", "*frame*leftOffset: 20",
  "*frame*shadowType: SHADOW_IN", NULL
};
Display *dpy;
XtAppContext app;
XtWorkProcId workId = 0;
Widget toplevel, form, frame, glxarea;
XVisualInfo *visinfo;
GLXContext glxcontext;
Colormap cmap;
Bool doubleBuffer = True, spinning = False;
```

The main routine initializes the program's widget hierarchy through the following steps:

1. Call XtAppInitialize[1] to initialize the X Toolkit and return a top-level widget for the program. Among other things, this starts a connection to the X server.

---

1. In X11R6, XtAppInitialize and XtVaAppInitialize have been superseded by XtOpenApplication and XtVaOpenApplication, respectively.

2. Register the `mapStateChanged` callback to be triggered when the top-level window changes iconification state.

3. Find an appropriate GLX-capable visual based on the `dblBuf` GLX attribute list (falling back on the `snglBuf` list if a double-buffered visual is not available).

4. Embed a Motif frame widget in a Motif form widget. The OpenGL-specific Motif drawing area widget is placed within the frame.

5. Obtain a colormap for the OpenGL-specific widget using the algorithm presented in Section 2.1.1. The OpenGL-specific widget creates a colormap automatically if one is not specified explicitly, but the widget lacks an intelligent colormap allocation algorithm such as the one implemented by `getShareableColormap`.

6. Create the OpenGL-specific Motif drawing area widget using the colormap and visual information determined earlier.

7. Register four callbacks to handle graphics initialization, widget exposes, widget resizes, and user input.

8. Finally, realize the complete widget hierarchy and begin event processing.

Comments in the code mark each step. Once event processing begins, the registered callbacks (discussed after the `main` routine) are called as appropriate to handle window system events from the X server.

```
int
main(int argc, char **argv)
{
  /* Step 1. */
  toplevel = XtAppInitialize(&app, "Glw", NULL, 0, &argc, argv,
    fallbackResources, NULL, 0);

  /* Step 2. */
  XtAddEventHandler(toplevel, StructureNotifyMask,
    False, mapStateChanged, NULL);

  /* Step 3. */
  dpy = XtDisplay(toplevel);
  visinfo = glXChooseVisual(dpy, DefaultScreen(dpy), dblBuf);
  if (visinfo == NULL) {
    visinfo = glXChooseVisual(dpy, DefaultScreen(dpy), snglBuf);
    if (visinfo == NULL)
      XtAppError(app, "no good visual");
    doubleBuffer = False;
  }
```

```
/* Step 4. */
form = XmCreateForm(toplevel, "form", NULL, 0);
XtManageChild(form);
frame = XmCreateFrame(form, "frame", NULL, 0);
XtVaSetValues(frame,
  XmNbottomAttachment, XmATTACH_FORM,
  XmNtopAttachment, XmATTACH_FORM,
  XmNleftAttachment, XmATTACH_FORM,
  XmNrightAttachment, XmATTACH_FORM,
  NULL);
XtManageChild(frame);

/* Step 5. */
cmap = getShareableColormap(visinfo);
```

The `getShareableColormap` algorithm is not shown here. See page 50.

```
/* Step 6. */
glxarea = XtVaCreateManagedWidget("glxarea",
  glwMDrawingAreaWidgetClass, frame,
  GLwNvisualInfo, visinfo,
  XtNcolormap, cmap,
  NULL);

/* Step 7. */
XtAddCallback(glxarea, GLwNginitCallback, graphicsInit, NULL);
XtAddCallback(glxarea, GLwNexposeCallback, expose, NULL);
XtAddCallback(glxarea, GLwNresizeCallback, resize, NULL);
XtAddCallback(glxarea, GLwNinputCallback, input, NULL);

/* Step 8. */
XtRealizeWidget(toplevel);
XtAppMainLoop(app);
return 0; /* ANSI C requires main to return int. */
}
```

Figure 3.3 shows the instance hierarchy of the four nested widgets created during main.

3.2.1.2 Callbacks

The `graphicsInit` callback is called after the OpenGL drawing area widget is realized, so that an OpenGL context can be created and its state initialized. The OpenGL drawing area widget does not automatically create an associated GLX

Figure 3.3 The nested widget hierarchy within `glw`. After each widget's name is the widget's class in parentheses. The `glw` and `form` widgets have the same dimensions as the `frame` widget.

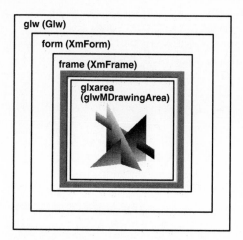

context. This is the responsibility of the application. So `graphicsInit` determines the widget's visual, using `XtVaGetValues`, then creates a GLX context. After making current to the context, the context's state is initialized for rendering.

```
void
graphicsInit(Widget w, XtPointer clientData, XtPointer call)
{
  XVisualInfo *visinfo;

  /* Create OpenGL rendering context. */
  XtVaGetValues(w, GLwNvisualInfo, &visinfo, NULL);
  glxcontext = glXCreateContext(XtDisplay(w), visinfo,
    0,         /* No sharing. */
    True);     /* Direct rendering if possible. */
  /* Set up OpenGL state. */
  glXMakeCurrent(XtDisplay(w), XtWindow(w), glxcontext);
  glEnable(GL_DEPTH_TEST);
  glClearDepth(1.0);
  glClearColor(0.0, 0.0, 0.0, 0.0); /* clear to black */
  glMatrixMode(GL_PROJECTION);
  gluPerspective(40.0, 1.0, 10.0, 200.0);
  glMatrixMode(GL_MODELVIEW);
```

```
  glTranslatef(0.0, 0.0, -50.0);
  glRotatef(-58.0, 0.0, 1.0, 0.0);
}
```

The `resize` callback is called when the OpenGL drawing area widget is resized. The new size of the window can be extracted from the `GLwDrawingAreaCallback-Struct` (defined later in Figure 3.6) that is passed to the callback as the `call` parameter. Notice that it must first be cast to the correct type. Then the OpenGL viewport is adjusted.

```
void
resize(Widget w,
  XtPointer clientData, XtPointer call)
{
  GLwDrawingAreaCallbackStruct *callData;

  callData = (GLwDrawingAreaCallbackStruct *) call;
  glXMakeCurrent(XtDisplay(w), XtWindow(w), glxcontext);
  glXWaitX();
  glViewport(0, 0, callData->width, callData->height);
}
```

While `glw` has only a single window, `glXMakeCurrent` is called to demonstrate that callbacks are responsible for ensuring that the intended OpenGL context and drawable are made current before calling OpenGL routines. This is vital if there are multiple OpenGL rendering areas or contexts in use, to avoid unintentionally rendering with the wrong context or to the wrong drawable.

Notice that `glXWaitX` is called before `glViewport`. This is one of the few situations in which the OpenGL and X request streams need to be synchronized (see Section 2.7). The resizing of the widget window is a potential problem. The resizing is done with an X request that may execute *after* the `glViewport` call updates the viewport. Potentially, the viewport could get updated based on the window's previous size. Calling `glXWaitX` prevents this unintended execution order.

The `expose` callback is called when the OpenGL drawing area widget is exposed and needs to be redrawn. Handling the expose consists of calling the `draw` routine to redraw the window.

```
void
expose(Widget w,
  XtPointer clientData, XtPointer call)
{
  draw();
}
```

The `draw` routine redraws the OpenGL drawing area's contents. The routine clears the color and depth buffers, then renders the three polygons. If the window is double-buffered, `glXSwapBuffers` shows the newly rendered scene. If the window is single-buffered, `glFlush` is called to make sure all issued OpenGL commands get processed. If indirect rendering is called, `glFinish` makes sure complete scenes are not sent faster than they are rendered.

```
void
draw(void)
{
  glXMakeCurrent(dpy, XtWindow(glxarea), glxcontext);
  glClear(GL_COLOR_BUFFER_BIT | GL_DEPTH_BUFFER_BIT);
  glBegin(GL_POLYGON);
    glColor3f(0.0, 0.0, 0.0);
    glVertex3f(-10.0, -10.0, 0.0);
    glColor3f(0.7, 0.7, 0.7);
    glVertex3f(10.0, -10.0, 0.0);
    glColor3f(1.0, 1.0, 1.0);
    glVertex3f(-10.0, 10.0, 0.0);
  glEnd();
  glBegin(GL_POLYGON);
    glColor3f(1.0, 1.0, 0.0);
    glVertex3f(0.0, -10.0, -10.0);
    glColor3f(0.0, 1.0, 0.7);
    glVertex3f(0.0, -10.0, 10.0);
    glColor3f(0.0, 0.0, 1.0);
    glVertex3f(0.0, 5.0, -10.0);
  glEnd();
  glBegin(GL_POLYGON);
    glColor3f(1.0, 1.0, 0.0);
    glVertex3f(-10.0, 6.0, 4.0);
    glColor3f(1.0, 0.0, 1.0);
    glVertex3f(-10.0, 3.0, 4.0);
    glColor3f(0.0, 0.0, 1.0);
    glVertex3f(4.0, -9.0, -10.0);
    glColor3f(1.0, 0.0, 1.0);
    glVertex3f(4.0, -6.0, -10.0);
  glEnd();

  if (doubleBuffer)
    glXSwapBuffers(dpy, XtWindow(glxarea));
  else
    glFlush();
```

```
  /* Avoid indirect rendering latency from queuing. */
  if (!glXIsDirect(dpy, glxcontext))
    glFinish();
}
```

An expose from the window system is not the only reason the `draw` routine might be called. It can also be called when the scene is rotating. The continuous rotation of the polygons occurs when an X Toolkit work proc is registered in response to a user keystroke. An X Toolkit work proc is a callback that is continuously called while it remains registered and whenever there are no other pending callbacks. Work procs are good for continuous animation.

The `input` callback adds and removes the work proc to rotate `glw`'s polygons. The spacebar is used to start and stop the rotation. The actual work proc routine is called `spin`.

```
void
input(Widget w, XtPointer clientData, XtPointer callData)
{
  XmDrawingAreaCallbackStruct *cd = (XmDrawingAreaCallbackStruct *)
    callData;
  char buffer[1];
  KeySym keysym;

  switch (cd->event->type) {
  case KeyPress:
    if (XLookupString((XKeyEvent *) cd->event, buffer, 1, &keysym,
      NULL) > 0) {
      switch (keysym) {
      case XK_space: /* The spacebar. */
        if (spinning) {
          XtRemoveWorkProc(workId);
          spinning = False;
        } else {
          workId = XtAppAddWorkProc(app, spin, NULL);
          spinning = True;
        }
        break;
      }
    }
    break;
  }
}
```

The `spin` work proc callback adjusts the modelview matrix with a rotation, then redraws the scene by calling `draw`. By returning `False`, the work proc remains registered so that the animation will continue.

```
Boolean
spin(XtPointer clientData)
{
  glXMakeCurrent(dpy, XtWindow(glxarea), glxcontext);
  glRotatef(2.5, 1.0, 0.0, 0.0);
  draw();
  return False; /* Leave work proc active. */
}
```

The last callback is `mapStateChanged`. This callback is called when the top-level widget's window is unmapped and mapped. This corresponds to when `glw` is iconified and restored. This callback will remove the `spin` work proc if registered when the top-level window is unmapped, to keep the animation from occurring when the window is iconified. Animating an iconified window just wastes processing time, since the window is not visible. When the window is restored, and if the scene should be spinning, the `spin` work proc is added again.

```
void
mapStateChanged(Widget w, XtPointer clientData,
  XEvent * event, Boolean * cont)
{
  switch (event-type) {
  case MapNotify:
    if (spinning && workId != 0)
    workId = XtAppAddWorkProc(app, spin, NULL);
    break;
  case UnmapNotify:
    if (spinning)
    XtRemoveWorkProc(workId);
    break;
  }
}
```

3.2.1.3 Compiling `glw`

The command line to compile `glw.c` would look something like this:

```
cc -o glw glw.c -lGLw -lGLU -lGL -lXm -lXt -lXmu -lXext -lX11
```

Figure 3.4 Software libraries used by OpenGL widget-based programs.

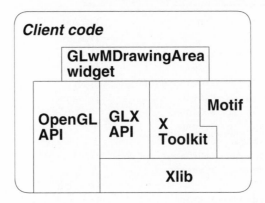

The -1GLw option links with the OpenGL widget library. The OpenGL widgets are not a standard part of Motif, so they reside in a distinct library from the Motif widget set.

3.3 SPECIFICS OF THE OPENGL DRAWING AREA WIDGETS

When a Motif program uses OpenGL with the OpenGL widgets, the layering of software libraries is more involved than what was shown in Figure 3.1. Figure 3.4 shows the layering for an application using the OpenGL widgets.

3.3.1 The Motif and Non-Motif OpenGL Widget Differences

It has already been mentioned that the OpenGL widget library has both a Motif and a generic or *widget-set-independent* OpenGL widget. The Motif widget class is called glwMDrawingAreaWidgetClass, the generic widget class is called glwDrawingAreaWidgetClass. The subtle difference between the names is the addition of a capital M in the Motif name. The implementation difference is that the Motif widget has the additional resources associated with Motif's XmPrimitive widget class. The XmPrimitive resources are shown in Table 3.1. There is no OpenGL functionality difference between the two widgets. For programs not using the XmPrimitive resources, the widgets are interchangeable.

To use the generic widget, you would include its header like this:

```
#include <X11/GLw/GLwDrawA.h>
```

Table 3.1 The XmPrimitive resources listed here are available only to the Motif version of the OpenGL-specific drawing area widget.

Name	Type	Default
XmNbottomShadowColor	Pixel	Dynamic
XmNbottomShadowPixmap	Pixmap	Dynamic
XmNforeground	Pixel	Dynamic
XmNhelpCallback	XtCallbackList	NULL
XmNhighlightColor	Pixel	Dynamic
XmNhighlightOnEnter	Boolean	False
XmNhighlightPixmap	Pixmap	Dynamic
XmNhighlightThickness	Dimension	2
XmNnavigationType	XmNavigationType	XmNONE
XmNshadowThickness	Dimension	2
XmNtopShadowColor	Pixel	Dynamic
XmNtopShadowPixmap	Pixmap	Dynamic
XmNtraversalOn	Boolean	True
XmNunitType	unsigned char	Dynamic
XmNuserData	Pointer	NULL

The difference between this header file name and the Motif header file name is, again, a capital M. When instantiating your OpenGL drawing area widget, use the widget class name without the capital M. These two changes could be made to glw.c and they would not change the operation of glw in any way, since glw does not make use of any XmPrimitive resources.

While Motif programs can use either widget, Motif programmers are encouraged to use the Motif version of the widget. Programs using non-Motif widget sets such as X Consortium's Athena widget set must use the generic version of the OpenGL widget.

3.3.2 OpenGL Widgets and the Widget Class Hierarchy

Every widget instance has a particular widget class. These widget classes are object-oriented, meaning that widget classes are derived or subclassed from simpler base widget classes. The various widget classes form a widget hierarchy that indicates how various widget classes are derived from simpler widget classes. All widgets are derived from the X Toolkit's core widget class.

To appreciate how the two OpenGL widget classes fit into the X Toolkit and Motif widget class hierarchy, see Figure 3.5. Notice that the generic widget (GLw-DrawingArea) is derived directly from the core widget class, but the Motif-specific OpenGL widget (GLwMDrawingArea) is derived from XmPrimitive.

Notice that Motif's XmDrawingArea widget has no direct relation to the OpenGL widgets. Also, neither the Motif drawing area widget nor either of the OpenGL widgets is derived from the X Toolkit's shell widget class. Except for the special case of the OpenGL widgets, only shell and shell-derived widget classes have a resource for selecting their widget windows' visuals. Because the `XmDrawingArea` widget class is not derived from the shell widget class and is not specially written like the OpenGL widgets, its visual cannot be independently specified. This is why the Motif drawing area widget is difficult to use with OpenGL.

3.3.3 OpenGL Widget Resources

Both OpenGL widgets provide a common set of OpenGL drawing area widget resources. These resources are shown in Table 3.2. Both OpenGL widgets also provide the core widget resources shown in Table 3.3 The core resources are common to all widgets. As described above, the Motif-specific OpenGL widget also supports the XmPrimitive resources in Table 3.1.

   The following are descriptions of resources specific to the OpenGL widgets. The various OpenGL widget callbacks are all passed a pointer to a call data structure of type `GLwDrawingAreaCallbackStruct`. This structure is shown in Figure 3.6.

   `GLwNallocateBackground` If this resource is `True`, the background pixel and pixmap resources are allocated based on the widget's visual and colormap. If it is `False`, the widget's background information will be calculated using the parent's visual and colormap during widget initialization.

Figure 3.5 Partial widget class hierarchy showing the standard OpenGL widgets. Widgets beginning with an `Xm` prefix are Motif widgets; the `GLw` prefix is for the OpenGL widgets; other widgets are part of the X Toolkit intrinsics.

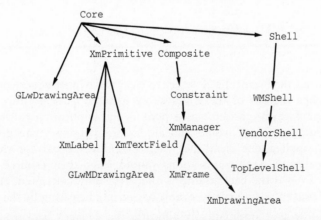

Table 3.2 The resources specific to the GLwMDrawingArea and GLwDrawingArea widgets. The lower set of resources provides an alternate means of visual selection in addition to GLwNvisualInfo resource. If the lower resources fail to select an acceptable visual, the widget immediately exits your application with an error message. For this reason, use of the lower resource set is not recommended.

Name	Type	Default
GLwNallocateBackground	Boolean	False
GLwNinstallBackground	Boolean	True
GLwNallocateOtherColors	Boolean	False
GLwNinstallColormap	Boolean	True
GLwNginitCallback	XtCallbackList	NULL
GLwNexposeCallback	XtCallbackList	NULL
GLwNinputCallback	XtCallbackList	NULL
GLwNresizeCallback	XtCallbackList	NULL
GLwNvisualInfo	VisualInfo*	NULL
GLwNattribList	int*	NULL
GLwNbufferSize	int	0
GLwNlevel	int	0
GLwNrgba	Bool	False
GLwNdoublebuffer	Bool	False
GLwNstereo	Bool	False
GLwNauxBuffers	int	0
GLwNredSize	int	0
GLwNgreenSize	int	0
GLwNblueSize	int	0
GLwNalphaSize	int	0
GLwNdepthSize	int	0
GLwNstencilSize	int	0
GLwNaccumRedSize	int	0
GLwNaccumGreenSize	int	0
GLwNaccumBlueSize	int	0
GLwNaccumAlphaSize	int	0

Applications that want the X server to clear the widget window's front color buffer when regions of the window are exposed must set this resource to True. Enabling the resource also permits the application to determine the pixel value that Motif would allocate for the window's background. Most OpenGL applications clear the widget window as part of the window's expose callback. Such applications should leave this resource False (the default). Even if the background is allocated, the GLwNinstallBackground resource must also be True to enable background clearing by the X server.

When the widget automatically allocates the widget's background color, it uses the window's associated colormap. You may find that this automatic

Table 3.3 The core widget resources shared by all widgets

Name	Type	Default
XmNaccelerators	XtAccelerators	NULL
XtNancestorSensitive	Boolean	Dynamic
XtNbackground	Pixel	Dynamic
XtNbackgroundPixmap	Pixmap	XtUnspecifiedPixmap
XtNborderColor	Pixel	XtDefaultForeground
XtNborderPixmap	Pixmap	XtUnspecifiedPixmap
XtNcolormap	Colormap	Dynamic
XtNdepth	int	Dynamic
XtNdestroyCallback	XtCallbackList	NULL
XtNheight	Dimension	Dynamic
XtNinitialResourcesPersistent	Boolean	True
XtNmappedWhenManaged	Boolean	True
XtNscreen	Screen*	Dynamic
XtNsensitive	Boolean	True
XtNtranslations	XtTranslations	NULL
XtNwidth	Dimension	Dynamic
XtNx	Position	0
XtNy	Position	0

allocation is undesirable if you are using color index windows and need to control the allocation of color cells within the colormap.

GLwNinstallBackground   If this resource and the GLwNallocate-Background resource are True, the widget requests that the X server immediately clear any exposed region of the widget's window. When either is False, the widget's window has no background specified, leaving exposed window regions undefined until the window is redrawn by the client.

GLwNallocateOtherColors   This resource is similar to GLwNallocate-Background, but enabling it allocates the additional colors for the foreground, highlight color, and highlight pixmap. Though the OpenGL widget

Figure 3.6 GLwDrawingAreaCallbackStruct structure.

```
typedef struct {
    int reason;
    XEvent *event;
    Dimension width;
    Dimension height;
}  GLwDrawingAreaCallbackStruct;
```

does not use these other colors, the application may query them to match colors between the drawing area and the rest of the Motif user interface. Because the additional colors are resources belonging to Motif's `XmPrimitive` widget, this resource is used only by the Motif version of the OpenGL widgets.

`GLwNinstallColormap`   If this resource is `True`, the widget takes responsibility for using `XSetWMColormapWindows`, as described in Section 2.3.2, so that the window manager will install the widget window's colormap when the window's shell has focus. If the resource is disabled, it is up to the application to ensure that the window manager is informed of the widget's colormap installation needs.

For applications with multiple OpenGL widgets sharing a single colormap, it is more efficient for exactly one of the sharing widgets to enable this resource.

`GLwNginitCallback`   This resource specifies a list of callbacks that are called when the widget is first realized. OpenGL rendering context creation and initialization are often done within this callback. The callback reason is `GLwCR_INIT`.

`GLwNexposeCallback`   This resource specifies a list of callbacks that are called when the widget receives an `Expose` event for redrawing the widget's window. By default, multiple `Expose` events are automatically compressed into a single callback. The expose callback reason is `GLwCR_EXPOSE`; the callback structure also includes an `Expose` event.

`GLwNinputCallback`   This resource specifies a list of callbacks for keyboard and mouse input events. The widget's default translation table reports key press and release events, button press and release events, and mouse motion via this callback. The translation table specifies

```
<Key>osfHelp:   PrimitiveHelp() \n\
<KeyDown>:      glwInput() \n\
<KeyUp>:        glwInput() \n\
<BtnDown>:      glwInput() \n\
<BtnUp>:        glwInput() \n\
<BtnMotion>:    glwInput()
```

The `PrimitiveHelp` action is provided only by the Motif version of the OpenGL widgets. The `glwInput` action invokes this resource's set of input callbacks. The callback structure includes the associated X input event, and the callback reason is `GLwCR_INPUT`.

This input callback resource is provided as a programming convenience for receiving a basic set of X input events through a single callback. If necessary, a more sophisticated program can specify its own translation table and actions, overriding the functionality of the `GLwNinputCallback` resource.

`GLwNresizeCallback` This resource specifies a list of callbacks that are called when the OpenGL drawing area is resized. The callback structure includes the new width and height, and the callback reason is `GLwCR_RESIZE`. The associated X `ConfigureNotify` event is not in the callback structure.

`GLwNvisualInfo` This resource specifies an `XVisualInfo*` pointer indicating the visual the widget should use. This visual determines the GLX attributes for the drawing area. Typically, this pointer is obtained by calling `glXChoose-Visual`.

The remainder of the resources provide an alternate means of visual selection for the OpenGL widget based on GLX attributes instead of requesting a visual explicitly with `GLwNvisualInfo`. Using the remaining resources is *not* recommended. The problem with them is that if they fail to match a visual successfully, the widget immediately exits your application. The X Toolkit is not designed for widget creation to fail, and the widget provides no backup when no visual matching the specified GLX attributes can be found. Unfortunately, the widget's only effective option is to print an error message and exit.

Instead of using GLX attribute selection resources, always determine the widget's intended visual before creating the widget and specify the visual with the `GLw-NvisualInfo` resource.

3.3.4   OpenGL Widget Advice

The caveat about visual selection in the preceding section is one important piece of advice for using the OpenGL widgets. Here is some more advice for using the OpenGL widgets effectively:

- You cannot make current to the drawing area widget's window until the widget has been realized. It is not until after it is realized that the widget has an associated X window.

  The graphics initialization (`ginit`) callback is called when the widget is realized. This makes it a very appropriate place to initialize a rendering context for the widget.

- To determine the widget's window and display, use the `XtWindow` and `Xt-Display` macros. For example, you can make current to an OpenGL widget's window like this:

```
glXMakeCurrent(XtDisplay(glxwidget), XtWindow(glxwidget),
    context);
```

  Note that `XtWindow` does not return a valid window ID until the widget is realized.

- It is up to the application to create a rendering context for rendering into the widget's window. You can get the widget's `GLwNvisualInfo` resource value and then use the returned `XVisualInfo*` to create an OpenGL rendering context with `glXCreateContext`.

- The graphics initialization (`ginit`) callback should be registered before the widget is realized. If it is registered after the widget is realized, the callbacks will never be called.

- If the OpenGL widget's `GLwNinputCallback` callback does not meet your needs for user input, feel free to add your own actions and translations to the OpenGL widgets. The default actions and translations are only conveniences.

- In your callbacks, be sure to call `glXMakeCurrent` at the beginning of every OpenGL widget callback if your application uses multiple OpenGL contexts. The order in which callbacks for different windows are called is not predictable. Making current to the already current rendering context and drawable is cheap, so always be safe, not sorry.

- If your shell widget's keyboard focus policy is `XmEXPLICIT` (Motif's default), as opposed to `XmPOINTER`, you may find that your Motif OpenGL widget fails to receive keyboard input. The problem is simply that another widget has the keyboard focus.

  The idea behind the explicit keyboard focus policy is that the keyboard focus is moved among widgets as appropriate under the application's control. For example, pressing the **Tab** key advances the focus to the next widget in a tab group.

  One solution is to change the keyboard focus policy to `XmPOINTER`, where the keyboard focus is always directed to the widget where the pointer is currently located. However, the advantage of the explicit keyboard focus policy is that the user can interact with the application without continually moving the mouse.

  The better solution that is consistent with the explicit focus policy is to call `XmProcessTraversal` when you want keyboard input to be directed to your OpenGL widget. For example:

```
XmProcessTraversal(glxwidget, XmTRAVERSE_CURRENT);
```

  This ensures that the keyboard focus is on your OpenGL widget. You might call the above routine whenever the user clicks a mouse button inside the widget. Clicking on the OpenGL widget would then always ensure keyboard focus. The Motif-specific OpenGL widget can also use its `XmNtraversalOn` (disabled by default) and `XmNnavigationType` to participate in keyboard traversal.

  Consult a Motif reference for more details about Motif's keyboard focus policy.

- If you do not specify a colormap when your OpenGL widget is realized, the widget creates a colormap of the appropriate visual type for you. Other OpenGL widgets within your application that share the same visual will automatically share the same colormap. Unfortunately, the widget does not automatically share colormaps between applications using the ICCCM conventions.

  This is why the `glw.c` example uses its `getShareableColormap` routine to obtain a shared colormap. Using a routine such as `getShareableColormap` is recommended for OpenGL widgets, to minimize colormap usage.

- X Toolkit work procs are good for animation. The X Toolkit's `XtAppAddWorkProc` is used for continuous animation by `glw`. If you want to pace the rate of animation within your program, you can use `XtAppAddTimeout` to schedule redraws at set intervals.

- Because 3D programs often take more time to redraw than the period between input events, it is recommended that you not redraw OpenGL windows every time an input event is received. Instead, update application data structures that control the way the scene is rendered and schedule a work proc, if one is not already scheduled, to render the scene based on the current scene state.

  Here's an example of routines to do this:

```
static int redisplayPending = 0;
static XtWorkProcId redisplayID;

Boolean
handleRedisplay(XtPointer closure)
{
  renderScene(); /* Render scene based on current state. */
  redisplayPending = 0;
  return True; /* Remove this work proc. */
}

void
postRedisplay(void)
{
  if (!redisplayPending) {
    redisplayID = XtAppAddWorkProc(app, handleRedisplay, 0);
    redisplayPending = 1;
  }
}
```

Assuming that `renderScene` will render the scene based on the current state of the application's data structures describing the scene, callbacks should merely update the scene's data structure and call `postRedisplay` to ensure that the scene is updated. The actual redraw is done by the `handleRedisplay` work proc.

The advantage of this approach is that if a scene update callback is called right after another, they result in a single redraw. This also means your expose callback can be written as a single call to `postRedisplay`. This way, a scene update and the handling of an `Expose` event can result in a single redraw. Avoiding redundant and stale redraws is crucial to the interactivity of your application.

A more complicated version of this technique is demonstrated in Chapter 7's example application. Also, the GLUT library, discussed in Chapter 4, supplies a `glutPostRedisplay` routine for this same purpose.

- The OpenGL widget library also provides two utility routines:

```
void GLwDrawingAreaMakeCurrent(Widget w, GLXContext ctx)
void GLwDrawingAreaSwapBuffers(Widget w)
```

The routines exactly correspond to the following calls, respectively:

```
glXMakeCurrent(XtDisplay(w), XtWindow(w), ctx)
glXSwapBuffers(XtDisplay(w), XtWindow(w))
```

Using the OpenGL widget utility routines has no actual advantage over calling the GLX routines.

Once you understand how to use the OpenGL widgets within Motif programs, you can build extremely sophisticated user interfaces around your 3D viewing areas.

3.4 A MORE INVOLVED WIDGET EXAMPLE

This section presents a more involved OpenGL example, using the X Toolkit and Motif. The `paperplane` example displays paper airplanes that fly in 3D figure-eight patterns. The program lets the user stop and start the animating, add and remove planes, and quit using Motif pulldown menus.

The code can be compiled three different ways: using the Motif OpenGL widget, using the generic OpenGL widget, and using the standard Motif drawing area widget. To use the Motif OpenGL widget, the program is compiled like this:

```
cc -o paperplane paperplane.c -lGLw -lGL -lXm -lXt -lXext -lX11 -lm
```

By defining the `noMotifGLwidget` C preprocessor symbol, you can compile a version that uses the generic OpenGL widget. You'll note that the source code differ-

Figure 3.7 Screen snapshot of `paperplane`.

ences are minimal, since the features of the XmPrimitive widget class are not used. To compile using the non-Motif OpenGL widget, add the `-DnoMotifGLwidget` option to the previous compile command.

You can also compile `paperplane.c` to use Motif's drawing area widget. To do so, compile the program like this:

```
cc -o paperplane paperplane.c -DnoGLwidget -lGL -lXm -lXt -lXext \
    -lX11 -lm
```

Note that `-DnoGLwidget` is specified, but that the `-lGLw` option for compiling with the OpenGL widget library is not specified. You can see in the following listing that additional code is required to coax the X Toolkit and Motif to create the entire widget hierarchy in the visual desired for OpenGL rendering.

Here is `paperplane.c`:

```
#include <stdlib.h>
#include <stdio.h>
#include <unistd.h>
#include <math.h>
#include <Xm/MainW.h>
#include <Xm/RowColumn.h>
```

```
#include <Xm/PushB.h>
#include <Xm/ToggleB.h>
#include <Xm/CascadeB.h>
#include <Xm/Frame.h>

#ifdef noGLwidget
#include <Xm/DrawingA.h>  /* Motif drawing area widget. */
#else
#ifdef noMotifGLwidget
#include <X11/GLw/GLwMDrawA.h>  /* Pure Xt OpenGL drawing area
    widget. */
#else
#include <X11/GLw/GLwMDrawA.h>  /* Motif OpenGL drawing area
    widget. */
#endif
#endif

#include <X11/keysym.h>
#include <GL/gl.h>
#include <GL/glu.h>
#include <GL/glx.h>

#define PI 3.14159265358979323846
#define PI_2 1.57079632679489661923

static int dblBuf[] = {
  GLX_DOUBLEBUFFER, GLX_RGBA, GLX_DEPTH_SIZE, 16,
  GLX_RED_SIZE, 1, GLX_GREEN_SIZE, 1, GLX_BLUE_SIZE, 1,
  None
};
static int *snglBuf = &dblBuf[1];
static String fallbackResources[] = {
  "*sgiMode: true", /* Enable SGI Indigo Magic lookfeel */
  "*useSchemes: all", /* and SGI schemes. */
  "*title: OpenGL paper plane demo",
  "*glxarea*width: 300", "*glxarea*height: 300", NULL
};

Display *dpy;
Bool doubleBuffer = True, moving = False, made_current = False;
XtAppContext app;
XtWorkProcId workId = 0;
Widget toplevel, mainw, menubar, menupane, btn, cascade, frame,
  glxarea;
```

```
GLXContext cx;
XVisualInfo *vi;
#ifdef noGLwidget
Colormap cmap;
#endif
Arg menuPaneArgs[1], args[1];

#define MAX_PLANES 15

struct {
  float speed; /* Zero speed means not flying. */
  GLfloat red, green, blue;
  float theta;
  float x, y, z, angle;
} planes[MAX_PLANES];

void
draw(Widget w)
{
  GLfloat red, green, blue;
  int i;

  glClear(GL_DEPTH_BUFFER_BIT);

  /* Paint black to blue smooth-shaded polygon for background. */
  glDisable(GL_DEPTH_TEST);
  glShadeModel(GL_SMOOTH);
  glBegin(GL_POLYGON);
  glColor3f(0.0, 0.0, 0.0);
  glVertex3f(-20, 20, -19);
  glVertex3f(20, 20, -19);
  glColor3f(0.0, 0.0, 1.0);
  glVertex3f(20, -20, -19);
  glVertex3f(-20, -20, -19);
  glEnd();

  /* Render planes. */
  glEnable(GL_DEPTH_TEST);
  glShadeModel(GL_FLAT);
  for (i = 0; i <MAX_PLANES; i++)
    if (planes[i].speed != 0.0) {
      glPushMatrix();
      glTranslatef(planes[i].x, planes[i].y, planes[i].z);
      glRotatef(290.0, 1.0, 0.0, 0.0);
```

```
      glRotatef(planes[i].angle, 0.0, 0.0, 1.0);
      glScalef(1.0 / 3.0, 1.0 / 4.0, 1.0 / 4.0);
      glTranslatef(0.0, -4.0, -1.5);
      glBegin(GL_TRIANGLE_STRIP);
      /* Left wing. */
      glVertex3f(-7.0, 0.0, 2.0);
      glVertex3f(-1.0, 0.0, 3.0);
      glColor3f(red = planes[i].red, green = planes[i].green,
        blue = planes[i].blue);
      glVertex3f(-1.0, 7.0, 3.0);
      /* Left side. */
      glColor3f(0.6 * red, 0.6 * green, 0.6 * blue);
      glVertex3f(0.0, 0.0, 0.0);
      glVertex3f(0.0, 8.0, 0.0);
      /* Right side. */
      glVertex3f(1.0, 0.0, 3.0);
      glVertex3f(1.0, 7.0, 3.0);
      /* Final tip of right wing. */
      glColor3f(red, green, blue);
      glVertex3f(7.0, 0.0, 2.0);
      glEnd();
      glPopMatrix();
    }
  if (doubleBuffer)
    glXSwapBuffers(dpy, XtWindow(w));
  if (!glXIsDirect(dpy, cx))
    glFinish();  /* Avoid indirect rendering latency
                    from queuing. */
#ifdef DEBUG
  {              /* For help debugging, report any
                    OpenGL errors that occur per frame. */
    GLenum error;
    while ((error = glGetError()) != GL_NO_ERROR)
     fprintf(stderr, "GL error: %s\n", gluErrorString(error));
  }
#endif
}
```

If you compile with -DDEBUG, any OpenGL errors will be reported at the end of each frame. This is good practice when you are debugging your OpenGL widget applications.

```
void
tick_per_plane(int i)
{
  float theta = planes[i].theta += planes[i].speed;
  planes[i].z = -9 + 4 * cos(theta);
  planes[i].x = 4 * sin(2 * theta);
  planes[i].y = sin(theta / 3.4) * 3;
  planes[i].angle = ((atan(2.0) + PI_2) * sin(theta) - PI_2) * 180 /
    PI;
  if (planes[i].speed < 0.0)
    planes[i].angle += 180;
}


void
add_plane(void)
{
  int i;

  for (i = 0; i < MAX_PLANES; i++)
    if (planes[i].speed == 0) {

#define SET_COLOR(r,g,b) \
      planes[i].red=r; planes[i].green=g; planes[i].blue=b; break

    switch (rand() % 6) {
    case 0:
      SET_COLOR(1.0, 0.0, 0.0); /* red */
    case 1:
      SET_COLOR(1.0, 1.0, 1.0); /* white */
    case 2:
      SET_COLOR(0.0, 1.0, 0.0); /* green */
    case 3:
      SET_COLOR(1.0, 0.0, 1.0); /* magenta */
    case 4:
      SET_COLOR(1.0, 1.0, 0.0); /* yellow */
    case 5:
      SET_COLOR(0.0, 1.0, 1.0); /* cyan */
     }
    planes[i].speed = (rand() % 20) * 0.001 + 0.02;
    if (rand() & 0x1)
      planes[i].speed *= -1;
    planes[i].theta = ((float) (rand() % 257)) * 0.1111;
```

```
      tick_per_plane(i);
      if (!moving)
        draw(glxarea);
      return;
    }
  XBell(dpy, 100); /* Cannot add any more planes. */
}

void
remove_plane(void)
{
  int i;

  for (i = MAX_PLANES - 1; i >= 0; i--)
    if (planes[i].speed != 0) {
      planes[i].speed = 0;
      if (!moving)
        draw(glxarea);
      return;
    }
  XBell(dpy, 100); /* No more planes to remove. */
}

void
resize(Widget w, XtPointer data, XtPointer callData)
{
  if (made_current) {
#ifdef noGLwidget
    Dimension width, height;

    /* Unfortunately, drawing area resize callback does not give
       height and width via its parameters. */
    glXWaitX();
    XtVaGetValues(w, XmNwidth, &width, XmNheight, &height, NULL);
    glViewport(0, 0, (GLint) width, (GLint) height);
#else
    GLwDrawingAreaCallbackStruct *resize =
      (GLwDrawingAreaCallbackStruct *) callData;

    glXWaitX();
    glViewport(0, 0, (GLint) resize->width, (GLint) resize->height);
#endif
  }
}
```

```
void
tick(void)
{
  int i;

  for (i = 0; i < MAX_PLANES; i++)
    if (planes[i].speed != 0.0)
      tick_per_plane(i);
}

Boolean
animate(XtPointer data)
{
  tick();
  draw(glxarea);
  return False; /* Leave Xt work proc active. */
}

void
toggle(void)
{
  moving = !moving; /* Toggle. */
  if (moving)
    workId = XtAppAddWorkProc(app, animate, NULL);
  else
    XtRemoveWorkProc(workId);
}

void
quit(Widget w, XtPointer data, XtPointer callData)
{
  exit(0);
}

void
input(Widget w, XtPointer data, XtPointer callData)
{
  XmDrawingAreaCallbackStruct *cd = (XmDrawingAreaCallbackStruct *)
    callData;
  char buf[1];
  KeySym keysym;

  if (cd->event->type == KeyPress)
    if (XLookupString((XKeyEvent *) cd->event, buf, 1, &keysym, NULL)
      == 1)
```

```
      switch (keysym) {
      case XK_space:
        if (!moving) { /* Advance one frame if not in motion. */
          tick();
          draw(w);
        }
        break;
      case XK_Escape:
        exit(0);
      }
    }

void
map_state_changed(Widget w, XtPointer data, XEvent * event, Boolean
  * cont)
{
  switch (event->type) {
  case MapNotify:
    if (moving && workId != 0)
      workId = XtAppAddWorkProc(app, animate, NULL);
    break;
  case UnmapNotify:
    if (moving)
      XtRemoveWorkProc(workId);
    break;
  }
}
```

The widget instance hierarchy created by `paperplane` is shown in Figure 3.8. Notice that the `glxarea` widget can be one of three different widget classes, depending on how `paperplane.c` is compiled.

```
int
main(int argc, char *argv[])
{
  toplevel = XtAppInitialize(&app, "Paperplane", NULL, 0, &argc, argv,
    fallbackResources, NULL, 0);
  dpy = XtDisplay(toplevel);

  /* Find an OpenGL-capable RGB visual with depth buffer. */
  vi = glXChooseVisual(dpy, DefaultScreen(dpy), dblBuf);
  if (vi == NULL) {
    vi = glXChooseVisual(dpy, DefaultScreen(dpy), snglBuf);
    if (vi == NULL)
```

Figure 3.8 Diagram of the widget instance hierarchy for paperplane. The glxarea widget is the only widget rendered using OpenGL.

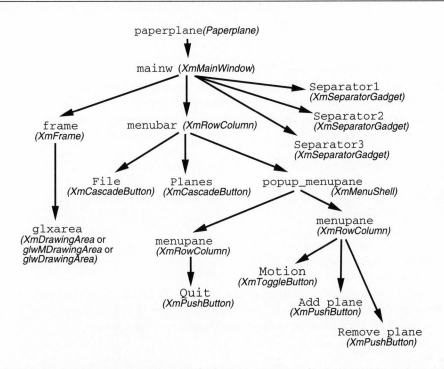

```
  XtAppError(app, "no RGB visual with depth buffer");
  doubleBuffer = False;
}

/* Create an OpenGL rendering context. */
cx = glXCreateContext(dpy, vi,
  /* No display list sharing. */ None,
  /* Favor direct rendering. */ True);
if (cx == NULL)
  XtAppError(app, "could not create rendering context");
/* Create an X colormap since probably not using default
  visual. */
#ifdef noGLwidget
cmap = XCreateColormap(dpy, RootWindow(dpy, vi->screen),
  vi->visual, AllocNone);
```

```
    /* Must establish the visual, depth, and colormap of the toplevel
      widget before the widget is realized. */
    XtVaSetValues(toplevel, XtNvisual, vi->visual, XtNdepth, vi->depth,
      XtNcolormap, cmap, NULL);
#endif
```

For simplicity, paperplane.c does not try to find a sharable colormap. Instead, the OpenGL widget will automatically create an appropriate colormap if none is specified. However, compiling to use the standard Motif drawing area, the right colormap, depth, and visual must all be specified for the top-level widget. Then Motif's drawing area widget can inherit its visual from the top-level widget.

```
    XtAddEventHandler(toplevel, StructureNotifyMask, False,
      map_state_changed, NULL);
    mainw = XmCreateMainWindow(toplevel, "mainw", NULL, 0);
    XtManageChild(mainw);
    /* Create menu bar. */
    menubar = XmCreateMenuBar(mainw, "menubar", NULL, 0);
    XtManageChild(menubar);
#ifdef noGLwidget
    /* Hack around Xt's unfortunate default visual inheritance. */
    XtSetArg(menuPaneArgs[0], XmNvisual, vi->visual);
    menupane = XmCreatePulldownMenu(menubar, "menupane",
      menuPaneArgs, 1);
#else
    menupane = XmCreatePulldownMenu(menubar, "menupane",
      NULL, 0);
#endif
    btn = XmCreatePushButton(menupane, "Quit", NULL, 0);
    XtAddCallback(btn, XmNactivateCallback, quit, NULL);
    XtManageChild(btn);
    XtSetArg(args[0], XmNsubMenuId, menupane);
    cascade = XmCreateCascadeButton(menubar, "File", args, 1);
    XtManageChild(cascade);
#ifdef noGLwidget
    menupane = XmCreatePulldownMenu(menubar, "menupane",
      menuPaneArgs, 1);
#else
    menupane = XmCreatePulldownMenu(menubar, "menupane",
      NULL, 0);
#endif
    btn = XmCreateToggleButton(menupane, "Motion", NULL, 0);
    XtAddCallback(btn, XmNvalueChangedCallback,
      (XtCallbackProc) toggle, NULL);
```

```
    XtManageChild(btn);
    btn = XmCreatePushButton(menupane, "Add plane", NULL, 0);
    XtAddCallback(btn, XmNactivateCallback,
      (XtCallbackProc) add_plane, NULL);
    XtManageChild(btn);
    btn = XmCreatePushButton(menupane, "Remove plane", NULL, 0);
    XtAddCallback(btn, XmNactivateCallback,
      (XtCallbackProc) remove_plane, NULL);
    XtManageChild(btn);
    XtSetArg(args[0], XmNsubMenuId, menupane);
    cascade = XmCreateCascadeButton(menubar, "Planes", args, 1);
    XtManageChild(cascade);
    /* create framed drawing area for OpenGL rendering */
    frame = XmCreateFrame(mainw, "frame", NULL, 0);
    XtManageChild(frame);
#ifdef noGLwidget
    glxarea = XtVaCreateManagedWidget("glxarea",
      xmDrawingAreaWidgetClass, frame, NULL);
#else
#ifdef noMotifGLwidget
    /* notice glwDrawingAreaWidgetClass lacks an 'M'. */
    glxarea = XtVaCreateManagedWidget("glxarea",
      glwDrawingAreaWidgetClass, frame,
      GLwNvisualInfo, vi, NULL);
#else
    glxarea = XtVaCreateManagedWidget("glxarea",
      glwMDrawingAreaWidgetClass, frame,
      GLwNvisualInfo, vi, NULL);
#endif
#endif
    XtAddCallback(glxarea, XmNexposeCallback, (XtCallbackProc) draw,
      NULL);
    XtAddCallback(glxarea, XmNresizeCallback, resize, NULL);
    XtAddCallback(glxarea, XmNinputCallback, input, NULL);
    /* Set up application's window layout. */
    XmMainWindowSetAreas(mainw, menubar, NULL, NULL, NULL, frame);
    XtRealizeWidget(toplevel);
```

Notice that the graphics initialization (ginit) callback is not used. You do not have to use it. If you wait until after XtRealizeWidget realizes the drawing area widget, you can bind to the window and initialize the OpenGL context then.

```
    glXMakeCurrent(dpy, XtWindow(glxarea), cx);
    made_current = True;
```

```
/* Set up OpenGL state. */
glClearDepth(1.0);
glClearColor(0.0, 0.0, 0.0, 0.0);
glMatrixMode(GL_PROJECTION);
glFrustum(-1.0, 1.0, -1.0, 1.0, 1.0, 20);
glMatrixMode(GL_MODELVIEW);

/* Add three initial random planes. */
srand(getpid());
add_plane();
add_plane();
add_plane();

XtAppMainLoop(app);
return 0; /* ANSI C requires main to return int. */
}
```

An even more involved Motif-based OpenGL example is the subject of Chapter 7. Other Motif code is presented in Section 6.2.8, on the X Input extension, and in Section 6.3.8, on using overlays for Motif menus.

4

A Simple Toolkit
for OpenGL

Most of the complexity of integrating OpenGL and X can be hidden using a simple windowing toolkit. This chapter introduces one such toolkit for writing OpenGL programs, which makes such programs significantly more compact and easier to write. This chapter is organized into the following sections:

1. "Introducing GLUT" describes the OpenGL Utility Toolkit with a brief example and provides an overview of GLUT's functionality.
2. "More GLUT Functionality" delves further into the features GLUT provides.
3. "Advice and Hints on Use" gives tips and techniques for constructing GLUT programs.
4. "A Substantial GLUT Example" demonstrates practical GLUT programming, including animation, overlays, and pop-up menus.

4.1   INTRODUCING GLUT

The previous chapters have discussed using OpenGL with the native X Window System APIs. This chapter discusses a toolkit for using OpenGL with X that raises the OpenGL programmer above the details of using the Xlib and GLX APIs. This toolkit is called the OpenGL Utility Toolkit, or GLUT. It has two purposes:

- GLUT provides a way to write OpenGL programs without the complexity entailed by the details of the native window system APIs. While the toolkit described may not be satisfactory for full-featured OpenGL applications, it can let you explore OpenGL without worrying about the involved window system integration issues presented in the previous chapters. This chapter discusses using GLUT's API for easily constructing OpenGL programs.

- GLUT's implementation demonstrates proper handling of a wide variety of OpenGL and X integration issues. GLUT's implementation makes concrete many of the topics discussed earlier. Because the GLUT library source code is freely available, it is a valuable resource for learning how OpenGL and X interface.

A tangent purpose for GLUT is its existence as a *window system independent* API for writing OpenGL programs. *Window system independent* means the GLUT interface can be implemented on any number of window systems supporting OpenGL. So a GLUT program could be recompiled to run using X, Windows NT, OS/2, or some other window system supporting OpenGL. For this reason, GLUT is careful to limit the functionality it supports to functionality that can be portably supported across other window systems.

The remainder of this chapter discusses the GLUT API and its theory of operations. The GLUT programming interface is fully described in Appendix B. Examples are presented in this chapter and in later chapters to demonstrate the use of GLUT. Source code for the GLUT implementation for X is readily available on the Internet. See Appendix A for details on obtaining GLUT.

4.1.1 A Short Example

Here is a short, simple GLUT example, called `glutsphere.c`:

```
#include <GL/glut.h>

GLfloat light_diffuse[] = {1.0, 0.0, 0.0, 1.0};
GLfloat light_position[] = {1.0, 1.0, 1.0, 0.0};
GLUquadricObj *qobj;

void
display(void)
{
  glClear(GL_COLOR_BUFFER_BIT | GL_DEPTH_BUFFER_BIT);
  glCallList(1); /* Render sphere display list. */
  glutSwapBuffers();
}

void
gfxinit(void)
{
```

```
  qobj = gluNewQuadric();
  gluQuadricDrawStyle(qobj, GLU_FILL);
  glNewList(1, GL_COMPILE); /* Create sphere display list. */
  gluSphere(qobj, /* Radius */ 1.0,
    /* Slices */ 20, /* Stacks */ 20);
  glEndList();
  glLightfv(GL_LIGHT0, GL_DIFFUSE, light_diffuse);
  glLightfv(GL_LIGHT0, GL_POSITION, light_position);
  glEnable(GL_LIGHTING);
  glEnable(GL_LIGHT0);
  glEnable(GL_DEPTH_TEST);
  glMatrixMode(GL_PROJECTION);
  gluPerspective( /* Field of view in degree */ 40.0,
    /* Aspect ratio */ 1.0,
    /* Z near */ 1.0, /* Z far */ 10.0);
  glMatrixMode(GL_MODELVIEW);
  gluLookAt(0.0, 0.0, 3, /* Eye is at (0,0,3). */
    0.0, 0.0, 0.0, /* Center is at (0,0,0). */
    0.0, 1.0, 0.); /* Up is in positive Y direction. */
  glTranslatef(0.0, 0.0, -1.0);
}

void
main(int argc, char **argv)
{
  glutInit(&argc, argv);
  glutInitDisplayMode(GLUT_DOUBLE | GLUT_RGB | GLUT_DEPTH);
  glutCreateWindow("sphere");
  glutDisplayFunc(display);
  gfxinit();
  glutMainLoop();
}
```

The `glutsphere` program draws a lighted sphere, as shown in Figure 4.1. The program renders the sphere when the window needs redrawing. Though simple, the example demonstrates the basics of opening a window with GLUT and rendering an image into it. Starting with `main`, here are the GLUT routines used and what they do:

```
glutInit(&argc, argv);
```

This routine initializes GLUT. `glutInit` processes any command line arguments GLUT understands (for X, this would be options such as `-display` and `-geometry`). Any command line arguments recognized by GLUT are stripped out, leaving the

Figure 4.1 Screen snapshot of `glutsphere` program.

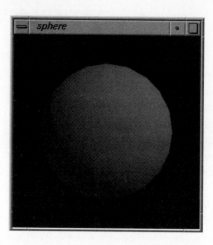

remaining options for your program to process. A connection to the X server is established, and GLUT makes sure the X server supports OpenGL. Typically, GLUT programs call `glutInit` before any other GLUT routine.

```
glutInitDisplayMode(GLUT_DOUBLE | GLUT_RGB | GLUT_DEPTH);
```

When a window is created, its type is determined by GLUT's current *display mode*. The display mode is a set of indicators that determines the frame buffer capabilities of the window. The above call to `glutInitDisplayMode` means that a window should be created subsequently with the following capabilities:

- Double buffering
- An RGBA color model
- A depth buffer (or Z buffer) for hidden surface elimination

Other indicators, such as `GLUT_STENCIL`, can be bitwise *or*-ed into the display mode value to request additional capabilities such as a stencil buffer.

```
glutCreateWindow("sphere");
```

Create a window for OpenGL rendering, called "sphere." Details such as choosing the correct visual and colormap and communicating information such as the window name to the window manager are all handled by GLUT. Along with the window, an associated OpenGL rendering context is created. This means that each window has its own private set of OpenGL state.

While this example does not use it, `glutCreateWindow` actually returns an integer identifier for the window. For an application with multiple windows, this feature lets you control multiple windows. Because of GLUT's design, you will rarely need a window's identifier. This is because GLUT keeps a *current window* as part of its state. Most window operations implicitly affect the current window. When a window is created, the current window is implicitly set to the new window. This is why the OpenGL routines in `gfxinit` implicitly affect the OpenGL context for the newly created window.

If you do need to change the current window, you can call `glutSetWindow`- (winnum), where `winnum` is a window identifier. You can also call `glutGetWindow()` to return the current window identifier.

The way GLUT informs a program when operations need to be performed on particular windows is by triggering a *callback*. A callback is a routine that the GLUT program registers to be called when a certain condition is true. For example, GLUT lets programs specify a callback to be triggered when a GLUT program needs to display a given window. Other GLUT callbacks will also be introduced.

The redisplay callback is registered as follows:

```
glutDisplayFunc(display);
```

`glutDisplayFunc` registers the `display` function as the routine to be called when the current window needs to be redisplayed. Whenever a callback is made for a specific window (any window callback, not just a display callback), the current window is implicitly set to the window prompting the callback. So when the `display` callback registered with `glutDisplayFunc` is called, you know that GLUT has implicitly changed the current window to the window that needs to be redisplayed. This means `display` can call OpenGL rendering routines and the routines will affect the correct window.

The `gfxinit` routine takes care of initializing OpenGL rendering state. It uses a set of GLU routines, including `gluSphere`, to make a display list for rendering a sphere. Lighting parameters are established and depth buffering is enabled. Finally, the projection and modelview matrices are set up for rendering the sphere. After `gfxinit` has executed, the `display` callback can render the scene by clearing the color and depth buffers with `glClear`, calling the sphere display lists, and swapping the buffers to display the red sphere. But before this can be done, GLUT must show the window and begin dispatching callbacks.

GLUT begins managing windows and dispatching callbacks when the program enters GLUT's main loop:

```
glutMainLoop();
```

For those familiar with Motif and the X Toolkit, this routine serves the same purpose as the X Toolkit's `XtAppMainLoop` routine. It begins event processing and shows any windows that have been created. It never exits. Callback functions registered with GLUT are called as necessary. For example, the `display` routine in the example will be called whenever `Expose` events are received by the program from the X server.

All the GLUT routines called by `glutsphere.c`'s `main` routine have now been shown. The other GLUT routine called by the program is in the `display` callback to swap buffers:

```
glutSwapBuffers();
```

When the window was being created, the display mode was set to request a double-buffered window. After `display` renders the sphere using OpenGL routines, `glutSwapBuffers` is called to swap the current window's buffers to make the image rendered into the back buffer visible. Double buffering lets the sphere be displayed without displaying the rendering in progress.

Supporting more than one window is easy. To create a second window showing the same red sphere, add the following calls just before `glutMainLoop`:

```
glutCreateWindow("a second window");
glutDisplayFunc(display);
gfxinit();
```

Because of the implicit update of the current window, `display` will also be registered for the second window and `gfxinit` will initialize the second window's OpenGL context. Also, remember that when a callback such as `display` is called, the current window is implicitly set to the window that needs the callback, so the rendering done by `display` will be directed into the correct window. The output of the resulting program is shown in Figure 4.2.

4.1.1.1 Compiling `glutsphere`

The command line to compile `glutsphere.c` would look something like this:

```
cc -o glutsphere glutsphere.c -lglut -lGLU -lGL -lXmu -lXext -lX11
```

The `-lglut` option links with the GLUT library.

4.1.2 User Input and Other Callbacks

An interactive 3D program needs a way to get input from the user. GLUT provides callback routines to be registered for each window for keyboard and mouse input.

```
glutKeyboardFunc(keyboard);
```

Figure 4.2 The two windows generated by the modified version of `glutsphere`.

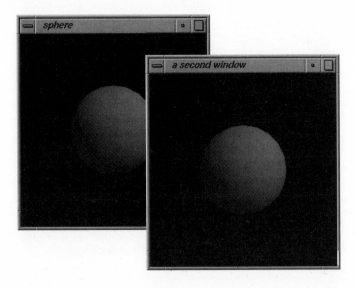

This routine registers a callback for keyboard input for the current window. The function `keyboard` might be written like this:

```
void
keyboard(unsigned char key, int x, int y)
{
  printf("key '%c' pressed at (%d,%d)\n",
    key, x, y);
}
```

If the `keyboard` callback is registered for a window, the `keyboard` routine will be called when a key is pressed in the window. The ASCII character generated by the key press is passed in along with the location of the cursor within the window (relative to an origin at the upper left-hand corner of the window). Another routine, called `glutSpecialFunc`, registers another callback, which is triggered when non-ASCII keys, such as arrow and function keys, are pressed.

```
glutSpecialFunc(special);
```

Here is an example callback for handling special keys:

```
void
special(int key, int x, int y)
{
  if(key == GLUT_KEY_INSERT)
    printf("The insert key pressed at (%d,%d)\n",
      x, y);
}
```

Callbacks for mouse events can also be registered:

```
glutMouseFunc(mouse);
glutMotionFunc(motion);
glutPassiveMotionFunc(passive);
```

These routines register callbacks for mouse button changes and mouse motion for the current window. The following are example callbacks:

```
void
mouse(int btn, int state, int x, int y)
{
  printf("button %d is %s at (%d,%d)\n",
    btn, state == GLUT_DOWN ? "down" : "up",
    x, y);
}

void
motion(int x, int y)
{
  printf("button motion at (%d,%d)\n",
    x, y);
}

void
passive(int x, int y)
{
  printf("non-button mouse motion at (%d,%d)\n",
    x, y);
}
```

The motion callback is generated by mouse motion when one or more mouse buttons are pressed; the passive motion callback is generated when all mouse buttons are released.

GLUT supports many other types of callbacks. The `glutDisplayFunc` routine, already introduced, lets you know when to redraw the window. The callback registered by `glutReshapeFunc` is called when a window is resized. A default handler exists for handling window resizes that calls `glViewport(0,0,w,h)`, where w and h are the new width and height of the window. This makes the entire window available for OpenGL rendering. Usually this is appropriate, but you can call `glutReshapeFunc` to specify your own reshape callback if necessary.

Also, callbacks can be registered for timeouts and when the program is "idling." A program doing continuous animation redraws each new scene as fast as the system will permit. This can be done by specifying an idle function using

```
glutIdleFunc(idle);
```

The function `idle` will be called whenever there is nothing else to do. If each time `idle` is called the program renders a new scene, the window is continuously animated. Event processing happens between calls to your idle function, so be careful not to spend too much time in your idle function or you risk compromising your program's interactivity. Only one idle function can be registered at a time. If you call `glutIdleFunc` with `NULL`, the idle function is disabled. Idle callbacks are very much like X Toolkit work procedures.

Here is an example idle callback for animating a scene:

```
void
idle(void)
{
  advanceSceneStateOneFrame();
  glutPostRedisplay();
}
```

Notice that the `idle` routine does not actually render using OpenGL. `idle` calls the `advanceSceneStateOneFrame` routine to update the program's state variables determining how the scene should be rendered. The `glutPostRedisplay` tells GLUT that the window's display callback should be triggered; that is, a redisplay is necessary. This ensures that the window is rerendered. The display callback will redisplay the scene based on the state variables updated by `advanceSceneStateOneFrame`.

The practice of "posting a redisplay" on a window makes it easier to control when your program needs to redisplay its windows. You should write your display callback to be *idempotent*, meaning that it can be called repeatedly and will rerender the same scene, assuming that the program state determining the scene has not changed. This ensures that if your program is sent an `Expose` event informing the program that it should redraw the scene, the scene will be redrawn the same as before the window was damaged.

Multiple calls to `glutPostRedisplay` and any pending `Expose` events will be combined, if possible, to minimize the number of redisplays necessary. This causes GLUT programs to redraw their windows more efficiently than if the window were redrawn every time any state changed or any `Expose` event was delivered. This same technique is described for Motif programs on page 129.

GLUT programs can register a callback to be notified of changes in window visibility:

```
glutVisibilityFunc(visibility)
```

Because a program doing continuous animation is wasting its time if the window it is rendering into is completely obscured or unmapped, GLUT's `glutVisibility-Func` routine registers a callback for the current window that is called when the window's visibility status changes. Here is an example visibility callback:

```
void
visibility(int status)
{
  if(status == GLUT_VISIBLE)
    glutIdleFunc(animate);
  else /* stop animating */
    glutIdleFunc(NULL);
}
```

Another type of callback is the timer callback that is registered by calling `glut-TimerFunc` as follows:

```
glutTimerFunc(1000, timer, value);
```

The first parameter indicates the number of milliseconds to wait before calling the `timer` callback function. The second parameter is the callback routine. Depending on the calling of other callbacks and the program's scheduling by the operating system, it may take longer than the specified time for the callback to be triggered. The third parameter is an integer that will be passed to the timer callback. You can register multiple timer functions. Timer callbacks are very much like X Toolkit timeout callbacks.

The timer callback could be implemented like this:

```
void
timer(int value)
{
  printf("One second passed since glutTimerFunc called.\n");
  printf("Value is %d\n", value);
}
```

4.1.3 Menus

A common need for 3D programs is to turn various modes on or off based on user input. Pop-up menus provide a simple mechanism for this type of input.

GLUT provides an easy-to-use API for cascading pop-up menus. Menus can be created, changed, and "attached" to a mouse button within a window. If a pop-up menu is "attached" to a button in a window, pressing the button will trigger the menu. If a menu entry is selected, the callback function for the menu is called. The callback is passed the associated value for the selected menu entry. Here's an example:

```
glutCreateMenu(choice_selected);
glutAddMenuEntry("Enable lighting", 1);
glutAddMenuEntry("Disable lighting", 2);
glutAttachMenu(GLUT_RIGHT_BUTTON);
```

The result is a menu with two options to enable or disable lighting. The menu is associated with the current window and will be triggered when the right mouse button is pressed within the window. Selecting a menu item will call the `choice_selected` callback, which might look like this:

```
void
choice_selected(int value)
{
  if(value == 1) glEnable(GL_LIGHTING);
  if(value == 2) glDisable(GL_LIGHTING);
  glutPostRedisplay();
}
```

Notice that instead of naively redrawing the window with lighting appropriately enabled or disabled, `glutPostRedisplay` is called. The advantage of "posting a redisplay" instead of performing the redraw explicitly is that removing the pop-up menu is likely to damage the current window.[1] A "posted redisplay" can be combined with any pending Expose events caused by unmapping the pop-up menu.

Like windows, GLUT maintains a *current menu* and the `glutCreateMenu` routines returns an integer identifier for the menu being created. The `glutSetMenu` and `glutGetMenu` routines set and query the current menu. Also, menu callbacks implicitly set the current menu to the menu generating the callback. The routines `glutAddMenuEntry` and `glutAttachMenu` operate on the current menu.

---

1. Actually, GLUT will try to put the pop-up menu in the overlay planes (if overlays are supported) to avoid the window damage normally generated by pop-up menus. GLUT also has support for OpenGL rendering into overlays. (See Section 4.2.10.)

Figure 4.3 An example of GLUT cascaded pop-up menus.

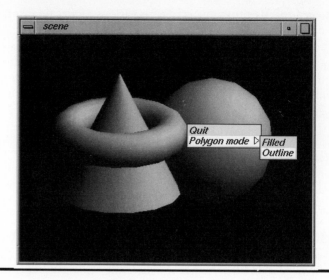

The menu identifier of a submenu is required for creating cascaded menus where one menu item can trigger the display of a submenu. Here is an example of creating a cascaded menu:

```
submenu = glutCreateMenu(polygon_mode);
glutAddMenuEntry("Filled", 1);
glutAddMenuEntry("Outline", 2);
glutCreateMenu(main_menu);
glutAddMenuEntry("Quit", 666);
glutAddSubMenu("Polygon mode", submenu);
glutAttachMenu(GLUT_RIGHT_BUTTON);
```

Figure 4.3 shows what this menu would look like. Menus can be cascaded arbitrarily deeply (but menu recursion is not permitted).

When menus are activated, the GLUT main loop continues to process events, handle timeouts, and call the idle function. Sometimes a program might want to suspend activity such as the idle callback when a menu is in use. The `glutMenuStatusFunc` can register a callback for this purpose; the callback routine might look like this:

```
void
menu_status(int status, int x, int y)
{
```

```
   if(status == GLUT_MENU_IN_USE)
     glutIdleFunc(NULL);
   else
     glutIdleFunc(animate);
}
```

4.2 MORE GLUT FUNCTIONALITY

So far, GLUT has been used to create and configure windows for OpenGL rendering and to deliver callbacks for input, pop-up menus, redisplays, and animation. For a lot of example programs and demos, this is all that is required. However, there is more to GLUT. A full description of the GLUT API is given in Appendix B.

4.2.1 Subwindows

A *top-level* window is a window created by `glutCreateWindow` that can be moved independently of other windows. Not only are multiple top-level windows supported, but GLUT can also manage multiple subwindows within top-level windows. A *subwindow* resides within a top-level window. Subwindows are created with GLUT's `glutCreateSubwindow` call. A subwindow can become the current window, just like a top-level window, using `glutSetWindow`.

Subwindows are logically distinct from their parent windows. A subwindow can have a different display mode from its top-level parent window and have its own independent set of menu and input callbacks. Subwindows can even be nested within other subwindows. The drawable region of a subwindow is limited by its parent window, and when a parent window moves, the subwindow moves too.

Subwindows have the following benefits:

- Subwindows can have differing display modes, so a subwindow can be RGBA double-buffered while its parent is color index, single-buffered. Double-buffered subwindows can be swapped independent of other windows on the screen.

- Input events are distributed to subwindows, so you can use subwindows to partition or limit the ways events are distributed.

- As described in the next section, subwindows can be positioned, reshaped, pushed down, and popped up relative to sibling subwindows, shown, and hidden. These operations work in essentially the same way as they work on top-level windows.

Subwindows provide a flexible way to partition top-level windows to suit your application's needs.

4.2.2 Window Management

In addition to the window operations already introduced for creating windows, registering callbacks, swapping buffers, and associating menus with windows, GLUT provides routines to manage windows relative to other windows.

You can control the initial size and position of a top-level window with `glut-InitWindowSize` and `glutInitWindowPosition`. These routines update the *initial window size* and the *initial window position*, respectively. When a top-level window is created with `glutCreateWindow`, its size and position are determined by GLUT's initial window size and initial window position. The following code requests a top-level window be created as a 500-by-400-pixel window at screen location (100,100):

```
glutInitWindowSize(500, 400);
glutInitWindowPosition(100, 100);
glutCreateWindow("Positioned and sized window");
```

Note that when a user specifies the `-geometry` option to a GLUT program, its effect is to set the initial window size and initial window position to the user's requested size and/or position.

`glutDestroyWindow` will destroy the specified window, destroying its associated colormap and OpenGL state. If the destroyed window is the current window, the current window becomes invalid. The routine is called as follows:

```
int window;
window = glutCreateWindow("hello");
glutDestroyWindow(window);
```

`glutPositionWindow` and `glutReshapeWindow` change the location and size of the current window. Examples:

```
glutPositionWindow(50, 50);
glutReshapeWindow(400, 300);
```

The positions and dimensions are specified in pixels.

`glutPopWindow` and `glutPushWindow` change the *stacking order* of the current window relative to its window siblings. The stacking order determines how windows overlap one another; lower windows in the stacking order are overlapped by higher windows. A pop places the window at the top of the stack; a push places the window at the bottom of the stack. Figure 4.4 shows how pushing and popping windows affect the way they are overlapped. `glutShowWindow` and `glutHide-Window` change the display status of the current window. For example:

Figure 4.4 The stacking order of sibling windows can be changed with `glutPop-Window` and `glutPushWindow`.

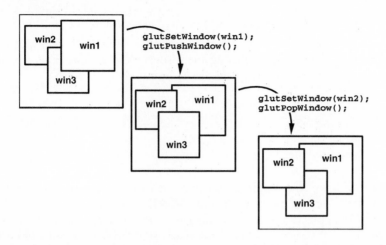

```
glutPopWindow();
glutPushWindow();
glutShowWindow();
glutHideWindow();
```

Visibility and display callbacks may be called as a side effect of performing these operations.

There are window management operations that are limited to top-level windows. These are iconifying the window and setting the window or icon title. `glutIconify-Window` will iconify the current window if it is a top-level window. The `glut-SetWindowTitle` and `glutSetIconTitle` routines change the window and icon titles of the current window if it is a top-level window. Here is an example of the use of these routines:

```
glutSetWindow(someWindow);
glutIconifyWindow();
glutSetIconTitle("Setting icon title to this");
glutSetWindowTitle("Setting window title to this");
```

When most of these window management operations are performed on top-level windows, they should be considered "requests" (not automatic operations), because

the management of top-level windows within the X Window System is the responsibility of the window manager. This means that for an operation such as `glut-`
`ReshapeWindow`, programs should wait for a reshape callback to be generated to
indicate that the request was actually processed and acknowledged by the window
manager.

Window management operations are also compressed by GLUT. This means that
if you call several GLUT window management routines in a short time, it is likely
that GLUT will process only the most recent operation. For example:

```
glutPushWindow();
glutPositionWindow(45, 45);
glutPopWindow();
glutPositionWindow(10, 10);
```

This sequence will pop the window and move it to location (10,10), optimizing
away the first push and the move to location (45,45).

Sometimes 3D applications want to take over the entire screen. Often this is
called "becoming full-screen." Games and visual simulation programs often have
this need. This implies disabling the window manager's border decorations so that
every pixel on the screen belongs to the application. You can use `glutPosition-`
`Window` and `glutReshapeWindow` to make a GLUT window as large as the screen,
but this will not disable the window manager decorations. To accomplish this, call
`glutFullScreen` when the application's top-level window is current. For example:

```
glutSetWindow(mainWindow);
glutFullScreen();
```

Note that the exact behavior of `glutFullScreen` depends on the window manager
you are using.[2] Also be aware that `glutFullScreen` does not prevent other windows from obscuring your application. Even though the window is full-screen,
other windows can appear on top of it. A subsequent call to `glutPositionWindow`
or `glutReshapeWindow` will re-enable window manager decorations. `glut-`
`FullScreen` should be called only on top-level windows.

4.2.3 Controlling the Cursor Shape

The shape of the mouse cursor is often used as an indication of application status or
to indicate the active mouse operation. GLUT provides a means of changing the

---

2. To implement full-screen support, the GLUT implementation for X uses the Motif mwm window manager's `_MOTIF_WM_HINTS` property to disable all window decoration. The window is also resized
to cover the entire screen.

cursor shape within GLUT windows. For example, the following will change the cursor shape in the current window to that of a spray can (like one a paint program might use):

```
glutSetCursor(GLUT_CURSOR_SPRAY);
```

The available cursor shapes are described in Table 4.1.

By default, windows are created with a cursor of type GLUT_CURSOR_INHERIT. Note that a subwindow can have a distinct cursor from its parent (though GLUT_CURSOR_INHERIT lets a window share its parent's cursor). When you want to hide the cursor while in a window, use GLUT_CURSOR_NONE. Some display hardware supports a full-screen crosshair cursor, meaning that the vertical and horizontal lines intersecting at the cursor stretch all the way to the sides of the screen. GLUT_CURSOR_FULL_CROSSHAIR will enable such a cursor if supported; otherwise,

Table 4.1 Available GLUT cursor shapes for use with glutSetCursor and their descriptions.

Parameter	Description
GLUT_CURSOR_RIGHT_ARROW	Arrow pointing up and to the right.
GLUT_CURSOR_LEFT_ARROW	Arrow pointing up and to the left.
GLUT_CURSOR_INFO	Pointing hand.
GLUT_CURSOR_DESTROY	Skull and crossbones.
GLUT_CURSOR_HELP	Question mark.
GLUT_CURSOR_CYCLE	Arrows rotating in a circle.
GLUT_CURSOR_SPRAY	Spray can.
GLUT_CURSOR_WAIT	Wristwatch.
GLUT_CURSOR_TEXT	Insertion point cursor for text.
GLUT_CURSOR_CROSSHAIR	Simple crosshair.
GLUT_CURSOR_UP_DOWN	Bidirectional pointing up and down.
GLUT_CURSOR_LEFT_RIGHT	Bidirectional pointing left and right.
GLUT_CURSOR_TOP_SIDE	Arrow pointing to top side.
GLUT_CURSOR_BOTTOM_SIDE	Arrow pointing to bottom side.
GLUT_CURSOR_LEFT_SIDE	Arrow pointing to left side.
GLUT_CURSOR_RIGHT_SIDE	Arrow pointing to right side.
GLUT_CURSOR_TOP_LEFT_CORNER	Arrow pointing to top left corner.
GLUT_CURSOR_TOP_RIGHT_CORNER	Arrow pointing to top right corner.
GLUT_CURSOR_BOTTOM_RIGHT_CORNER	Arrow pointing to bottom left corner.
GLUT_CURSOR_BOTTOM_LEFT_CORNER	Arrow pointing to bottom right corner.
GLUT_CURSOR_NONE	Invisible cursor.
GLUT_CURSOR_FULL_CROSSHAIR	Full-screen crosshair cursor (if available).
GLUT_CURSOR_INHERIT	Use parent's cursor.

it is the same as GLUT_CURSOR_CROSSHAIR. The blank and full-screen crosshair cursors are often used in conjunction with glutFullScreen.

4.2.4 Color Index Mode

While most GLUT programs are expected to use the RGBA color model, support is also provided for using the color index model. Color index windows are created with glutCreateWindow or glutCreateSubwindow just like RGBA windows. The difference is in the way the *display mode* is set. The value GLUT_INDEX is bitwise *or*-ed into the display mode bitmask set by glutInitDisplayMode to request a color index window.

Each color index GLUT window has an implicit colormap associated with it. Three routines are provided for manipulating the colormaps of color index GLUT windows. glutSetColor will assign an RGB triple to a specified colormap index. For example:

```
/* Set index 5 to red. */
glutSetColor(5, 1.0, 0.0, 0.0);
```

Color components of various indices can be retrieved using glutGetColor. To retrieve the RGB triple previously assigned to index 5, call

```
GLfloat red, green, blue;
red = glutGetColor(5, GLUT_RED);
green = glutGetColor(5, GLUT_GREEN);
blue = glutGetColor(5, GLUT_BLUE);
```

Physical color index colormaps are a limited resource. Not every window can have its colormap installed simultaneously if there are enough windows using different colormaps. Because each GLUT window uses its own logical colormap, a GLUT program may find it difficult even to share colormaps between its own color index windows. To help in this situation, GLUT provides the glutCopyColormap routine. It copies the logical colormap from a specified window to the current window. The GLUT implementation can then share a single X colormap between the two windows if possible (until one window modifies its colormap).

To promote sharing of GLUT color index colormaps among multiple windows, programs should create a color index window, allocate cells in that window's colormap, and, when creating any new color index window, immediately call glutCopy-Colormap after creating the new window.

This approach makes it possible for GLUT color index windows to share colormaps, but still permits a GLUT program to maintain distinct color index colormaps per-window if required.

4.2.5 Other Input Device Callbacks

Previously, only a few limited input callbacks were demonstrated. `glutKeyboard-Func`, `glutMouseFunc`, and `glutMotionFunc` register callbacks for ASCII character input, mouse button changes, and mouse motion when buttons are held down. GLUT can indicate when special keys, such as function keys and arrow keys, are used by registering a callback with `glutSpecialFunc`.

An example special keyboard callback looks like this:

```
special_key(int key, int x, int y)
{
  if(key == GLUT_PAGE_UP) {
    doPageUp();
  }
}
```

Other special key values are of the form `GLUT_KEY_F3` for the **F3** key and `GLUT_KEY_LEFT` for the left arrow key.

GLUT also provides callbacks to be registered for nonstandard input devices that are often associated with 3D applications. GLUT generates input callbacks from events generated by tablet, dial-and-button box, and Spaceball devices.

`glutSpaceballMotionFunc`, `glutSpaceballRotateFunc`, and `glutSpaceball-ButtonFunc` register callbacks for a 3D input device known as a Spaceball. This device provides 6 degrees of freedom to support 3D rotation and 3D translation as well as a set of buttons.

`glutButtonBoxFunc` and `glutDialsFunc` register callbacks for a common computer-aided design (CAD) input device known as a dial-and-button box. The device consists of a set of dials (or knobs) and a set of buttons. The dials turn independently.

`glutTabletMotionFunc` and `glutTabletButtonFunc` register callbacks for a 2D tablet input device. A tablet reports the absolute location of the tablet's puck (or locator) on the tablet surface. The puck also has a set of buttons.

More thorough descriptions of these devices are given in Section 6.2. The specific characteristics of Spaceballs, dial-and-button boxes, and tablets can vary among various models. For example, the number of buttons on a tablet puck may vary. The `glutDeviceGet` routine returns model-dependent device information and tells you whether the current system has a given device available. To determine whether a tablet is available and get the number of buttons on the tablet puck, call

```
has_tablet = glutDeviceGet(GLUT_HAS_TABLET);
if(has_tablet) {
  tablet_btns = glutDeviceGet(GLUT_NUM_TABLET_BUTTONS);
}
```

You can register callbacks for devices that do not exist, though the callback will obviously never be called. These callbacks are like other input callbacks in that they register a callback for the current window. Input from a nonstandard device is typically distributed (like keyboard input) to the window currently containing the mouse cursor.

4.2.6   State Retrieval

The `glutDeviceGet` routine demonstrated in the preceding section is one way to retrieve state from GLUT. GLUT maintains global, per-window, and per-menu state that can be retrieved by GLUT applications. (See Appendix C.) Unlike the OpenGL API, where almost all application-visible state can be queried, GLUT has a more limited set of retrievable state.

Whereas `glutDeviceGet` returns input device related state, `glutGet` returns more basic GLUT state. Table 4.2 describes the state returned by `glutGet`; Table 4.3 describes the state returned by `glutDeviceGet`. Per-window and per-menu state returned by `glutDeviceGet` corresponds to the current window and menu, respectively.

`glutExtensionSupported` is a helper routine to determine whether a given OpenGL extension is supported. An application can itself parse the string returned by `glGetString(GL_EXTENSIONS)`, but `glutExtensionSupported` provides a convenient interface to this common operation. Here is an example:

```
if (glutExtensionSupported("GL_EXT_texture3D")) {
  printf("3D textures are supported.\n");
}
```

Because GLUT is designed as a window system independent interface, GLX extensions (introduced with GLX 1.1) are not returned by `glutExtensionSupported`. Typically, such extensions would be supported by extending the GLUT API. For example, the `GLUT_MULTISAMPLE` display mode mask provides access to the `GLX_SGIS_multisample` extension supporting hardware antialiasing.

4.2.7   More Menu Management

GLUT's pop-up menus provide a convenient way to manipulate the state of your application. Section 4.1.3 introduced the basics of creating a menu, adding entries and submenus to it, and attaching it to a window's mouse button.

In addition to the basics, you can manipulate existing menus. You can change an arbitrary menu item within a menu to a menu entry using the `glutChangeToMenuEntry` routine. A symmetric `glutChangeToSubmenu` routine changes an arbitrary menu item to a submenu trigger. You can also remove menu items from a menu by calling `glutRemoveMenuItem`. The menu item affected by these routines is specified as an index into the menu items of the current menu. The topmost menu item is 1. Remember that if you remove a menu item from a menu, it will change the indices of all menu items below the removed item.

Table 4.2 Available `glutGet` parameters and their descriptions

Parameter	Description
GLUT_WINDOW_X	X offset from parent window or screen origin (if top-level).
GLUT_WINDOW_Y	Y offset from parent window or screen origin (if top-level).
GLUT_WINDOW_WIDTH	Width of window in pixels
GLUT_WINDOW_HEIGHT	Height of window in pixels
GLUT_WINDOW_BUFFER_SIZE	Total number of bits in each color buffer.
GLUT_WINDOW_STENCIL_SIZE	Number of bits in stencil buffer.
GLUT_WINDOW_DEPTH_SIZE	Number of bits in depth buffer.
GLUT_WINDOW_RED_SIZE	Bits of red in color buffer (RGBA).
GLUT_WINDOW_GREEN_SIZE	Bits of green in color buffer (RGBA).
GLUT_WINDOW_BLUE_SIZE	Bits of blue in color buffer (RGBA).
GLUT_WINDOW_ALPHA_SIZE	Bits of alpha in color buffer (RGBA).
GLUT_WINDOW_ACCUM_RED_SIZE	Bits of red in accumulation buffer.
GLUT_WINDOW_ACCUM_GREEN_SIZE	Bits of green in accumulation buffer.
GLUT_WINDOW_ACCUM_BLUE_SIZE	Bits of blue in accumulation buffer.
GLUT_WINDOW_ACCUM_ALPHA_SIZE	Bits of alpha in accumulation buffer.
GLUT_WINDOW_DOUBLEBUFFER	If window is double buffered.
GLUT_WINDOW_RGBA	If window uses RGBA color model.
GLUT_WINDOW_PARENT	Window number of parent (zero if top-level).
GLUT_WINDOW_NUM_CHILDREN	Number of direct descendant subwindows.
GLUT_WINDOW_COLORMAP_SIZE	Size of color index colormap (zero if RGBA).
GLUT_WINDOW_NUM_SAMPLES	Number of samples for multisampling.
GLUT_WINDOW_STEREO	If window is stereo.
GLUT_WINDOW_CURSOR	Window cursor name.
GLUT_SCREEN_WIDTH	Width of screen in pixels.
GLUT_SCREEN_HEIGHT	Height of screen in pixels.
GLUT_SCREEN_WIDTH_MM	Width of screen in millimeters.
GLUT_SCREEN_HEIGHT_MM	Height of screen in millimeters.
GLUT_MENU_NUM_ITEMS	Number of items in current menu.
GLUT_DISPLAY_MODE_POSSIBLE	If window can be created with current display mode.
GLUT_INIT_WINDOW_X	X value of initial window position.
GLUT_INIT_WINDOW_Y	Y value of initial window position.
GLUT_INIT_WINDOW_WIDTH	Width value of initial window size.
GLUT_INIT_WINDOW_HEIGHT	Height value of initial window size.
GLUT_INIT_DISPLAY_MODE	Initial display mode bitmask.
GLUT_ELAPSED_TIME	Number of milliseconds since GLUT initialized.

Here's one way you might manipulate a menu with these routines:

```
new_menu = glutCreateMenu(menu_callback);
glutAddMenuEntry("Top entry", 45);
glutAddSubmenu("A submenu trigger", some_submenu_id);
```

Table 4.3 Available GLUT `glutDeviceGet` parameters and their descriptions.

Parameter	Description
GLUT_HAS_KEYBOARD	If the workstation has a keyboard.
GLUT_HAS_MOUSE	If the workstation has a mouse.
GLUT_HAS_SPACEBALL	If the workstation has a Spaceball.
GLUT_HAS_DIAL_AND_BUTTON_BOX	If the workstation has a dial-and-button box.
GLUT_HAS_TABLET	If the workstation has a tablet.
GLUT_NUM_MOUSE_BUTTONS	Number of mouse buttons.
GLUT_NUM_SPACEBALL_BUTTONS	Number of Spaceball buttons.
GLUT_NUM_BUTTON_BOX_BUTTONS	Number of dial-and-button box buttons.
GLUT_NUM_DIALS	Number of dials.
GLUT_NUM_TABLET_BUTTONS	Number of tablet buttons.

```
glutChangeToMenuEntry(2, "Was a submenu trigger",
  another_submenu_id);
glutChangeToSubmenu(1, "Was a menu entry", 36);
glutRemoveMenuItem(1);
/* Menu now has just "Was a menu entry" submenu trigger. */
```

A menu is destroyed with a `glutDestroyMenu` routine. To destroy a menu, the menu to be destroyed is specified by its menu ID. For example:

```
glutDestroyMenu(new_menu);
```

An important thing to remember when manipulating GLUT menus is that you should not modify menus while they are in use (that is, popped up). This restriction avoids complications that might arise from doing so. The `glutMenuStatusFunc` routine (previously used to demonstrate how to stop animation when menus are in use) can also be used to track menu use and avoid modifying menus while they are in use. This restriction does not usually complicate programs.

4.2.8 Font Rendering

OpenGL's sophisticated 3D graphics capabilities do not obviate the need for displaying text. Since OpenGL has no explicit routines for rendering text, GLUT provides a small set of routines to render text either as bitmaps or as vectors using OpenGL's underlying rendering routines (`glBitmap` for bitmap characters and `GL_LINE_STRIP` primitives for stroke characters). Examples of font rendering using the GLUT routines are shown in Figure 4.5.

A bitmap character is a single-color image containing a representation of the character. The image of a character is often referred to as a *glyph*. Bitmap glyphs can be rendered quickly, but are not well suited for rendering rotated, scaled, or projected text.

Figure 4.5 Screen snapshot of GLUT program using both bitmap and stroke fonts. The stroke font could be improved by enabling line smoothing for antialiasing (see Section 5.3).

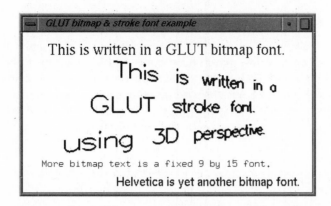

A stroke font uses a set of line segments to represent each glyph. Because a stroke glyph has a geometric representation, text rendered with a stroke font can be rotated, scaled, and projected in 3D. Stroke text can be combined into a 3D scene. Because they must be rendered as the constituent lines forming each character, stroke glyphs are considerably slower to render than bitmap glyphs.

GLUT supplies routines that generate both bitmap and stroke glyphs. It is up to the GLUT program to combine the rendering of individual characters into words or lines of text.

Here is an example of rendering a string with GLUT bitmap characters using the `glutBitmapCharacter` routine:

```
glRasterPos2f(x, y);
for (i = 0; string[i] != '\0'; i++) {
  glutBitmapCharacter(GLUT_BITMAP_9_BY_15, string[i]);
}
```

`GLUT_BITMAP_9_BY_15` names the font to be used. Other choices would be `GLUT_BITMAP_TIMES_ROMAN_10` and `GLUT_BITMAP_HELVETICA_12`. Each call to `glutBitmapCharacter` generates a `glBitmap` call that draws a bitmap representing the specified ASCII character. Notice that `glRasterPos2f` is called before the text is rendered. Each `glBitmap` call renders a character at the current raster position and then advances the current raster position by the width of the character. Each subsequent call to `glutBitmapCharacter` renders with the newly adjusted current raster position to output the full text of the string.

OpenGL state that affects the rendering of `glBitmap` will affect the operation of `glutBitmapCharacter`. For example, `glColor3f` will change the color of the bitmaps rendered by `glutBitmapCharacter`.

4.2.9 Geometric Shape Rendering

GLUT includes a number of routines for generating easily recognizable geometric shapes. These routines allow short and succinct GLUT programs to be written that render scenes with identifiable objects. Each of the nine geometric shapes has two associated GLUT routines: one for wireframe rendering, the other for solid rendering. Examples of the available shapes are shown in Figures 4.6 and 4.7 .

Here are the GLUT calls to generate the wireframe shapes shown in Figure 4.6:

```
glutWireSphere(1.0, 20, 20);
glutWireCone(1.0, 1.3, 20, 20);
glutWireCube(1.0);
glutWireTorus(0.5, 1.0, 15, 15);
```

Figure 4.6 Example renderings using each of the nine GLUT wireframe geometric shape rendering routines.

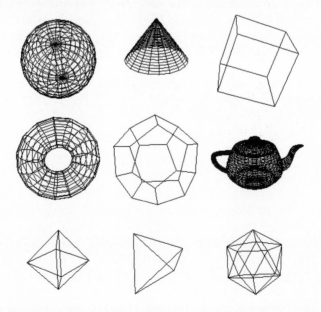

Figure 4.7 Example renderings using each of the nine GLUT solid geometric shape rendering routines.

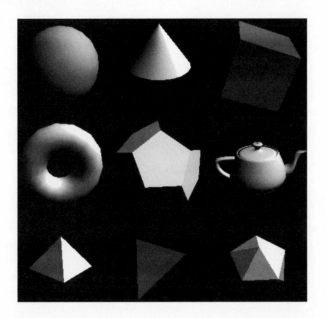

```
glutWireDodecahedron();
glutWireTeapot(1.0);
glutWireOctahedron();
glutWireTetrahedron();
glutWireIcosahedron();
```

Here are the GLUT calls to generate the solid shapes shown in Figure 4.7:

```
glutSolidSphere(1.0, 20, 20);
glutSolidCone(1.0, 1.3, 20, 20);
glutSolidCube(1.0);
glutSolidTorus(0.5, 1.0, 15, 15);
glutSolidDodecahedron();
glutSolidTeapot(1.0);
glutSolidOctahedron();
glutSolidTetrahedron();
glutSolidIcosahedron();
```

The sphere routines require a radius and number of slices and stacks as parameters. The cone routines require a base radius, height, the number of slices, and the number of stacks. The torus routines require an inner radius, an outer radius, and number of sides and rings. The cube and teapot routines take a scaling factor.

The routines do *not* generate display lists for the objects they create. If you render these objects frequently, consider capturing their OpenGL command sequences in a display list to speed their rendering. The routines generate normals appropriate for lighting, but do not generate texture coordinates (except in the case of the teapot rendering routines). For example:

```
glNewList(40, GL_COMPILE);
glutSolidIcosahedron();
glEndList();
```

4.2.10 Overlay Support

Some graphics hardware supports more than one frame buffer layer. An extra frame buffer layer "above" the main frame buffer layer is commonly referred to as an *overlay*. The overlay is displayed preferentially to the main frame buffer layer (often called the *normal plane*). A special overlay pixel value is called the *transparent* pixel value. When an overlay pixel has the transparent value, the color on the screen for that pixel is the color determined by the normal plane pixel value.

Normally, the overlay is cleared to the transparent pixel value so that what the user sees on the screen is the contents of the normal plane. You can think of the overlay being "stacked on top of" the normal plane. Because overlay rendering goes to a different frame buffer level, you can render into the overlay without disturbing the image in the normal plane. This makes overlays ideal for tasks such as text annotation, pop-up menus and dialog boxes, and "rubber-banding," in which an overlaid rectangle can be stretched across a region of the screen.[3]

Overlays rely on graphics hardware support, so not all workstations support overlays. Typically, you will find overlays on more expensive graphics hardware.

GLUT automatically makes use of overlays if they exist for pop-up menus. This means that if the user "pops up" a menu within a window, the menu is rendered in the overlays. When the menu "pops down" when the user is finished with it, this means that the contents of the normal plane window were never disturbed and no display callback will need to be generated. This makes GLUT programs more interactive when

---

3. Typically, the way rubber-banding is accomplished without overlays is to render using the *XOR* logic function. When a pixel is so rendered, its value is updated with the *exclusive or* of the pixel value currently in the frame buffer and the value to be rendered. If the pixel is updated again using *XOR* with the same previously rendered value (that is, rendering again what was just rendered), the pixel resumes its previous value. This means you can generate rubber-banding effects without explicitly reading and restoring the frame buffer continually. The problem with this approach is that the *xor*-ed pixel appearance is unpredictable in practice.

you are displaying on hardware that supports overlays, because pop-up menus can be used without forcing expensive redraws of windows they momentarily obscure.

GLUT also has explicit overlay support for purposes such as annotation and rubber-banding. If overlays are supported, you can call `glutEstablishOverlay` to enable an overlay for the current window. Like a subwindow, an overlay has its own independent OpenGL context and display mode. Unlike a subwindow, an overlay is not a distinct window with its own unique callbacks and window name. Also, the overlay completely overlaps the window it belongs to. You should find out whether the window can support an overlay before you try to establish one. For example:

```
glutInitDisplayMode(GLUT_SINGLE | GLUT_INDEX);
if(glutLayerGet(GLUT_OVERLAY_POSSIBLE))
  glutEstablishOverlay();
else
  reportError("No overlay supported.");
```

Notice that `glutInitDisplayMode` is used to request a single-buffered, color index overlay. Typically, you will find that most overlay-capable hardware supports single buffered, color index overlays. Only the highest-end graphics hardware is likely to provide double buffered and RGB overlays. `glutLayerGet` is a special state retrieval routine that returns layer-related state. Other layer state that can be retrieved with `glutLayerGet` is shown in Table 4.4.

Every GLUT window has a current layer, either the normal plane or the overlay (the current layer is always the normal plane if no overlay is established). You can switch a window's current layer by calling `glutUseLayer`. The layer that is current determines where OpenGL rendering is directed. For example:

```
glutUseLayer(GLUT_OVERLAY);
renderOverlay(); /* Update what is in the overlay. */
glutUseLayer(GLUT_NORMAL);
renderNormalPlane(); /* Update what is in the normal plane. */
```

When you establish an overlay, the current layer is implicitly changed to the overlay.

Table 4.4 GLUT `glutLayerGet` parameters

Parameter	Description
GLUT_OVERLAY_POSSIBLE	Whether an overlay could be established.
GLUT_LAYER_IN_USE	Either GLUT_NORMAL or GLUT_OVERLAY, depending on which is in use.
GLUT_HAS_OVERLAY	If the *current window* has an overlay established.
GLUT_TRANSPARENT_INDEX	The transparent pixel value for the overlay.
GLUT_NORMAL_DAMAGED	If the normal plane needs redrawing because of damage.
GLUT_OVERLAY_DAMAGED	If the overlay needs redrawing because of damage.

Transparent rendering is very important for using the overlays. You can query the transparent color index by calling `glutLayerGet(GLUT_TRANSPARENT_INDEX)`. The index that is transparent may vary among vendors, so make sure you query the value. Also, be sure to avoid accidentally using the transparent index value when you mean to render opaque pixels. Here is an example of the correct use of overlay color indices:

```
int transparent, opaque;

glutEstablishOverlay();
transparent = glutLayerGet(GLUT_TRANSPARENT_INDEX);
glClearIndex(transparent);
opaque = (transparent + 1) % glutGet(GLUT_WINDOW_COLORMAP_SIZE);
glutSetColor(opaque, 1.0, 0.0, 0.0); /* Red. */
glIndexi(opaque);
```

With this initialization, `glClear` can be used to clear the overlay, and rendering the `opaque` index will appear in red. Note how `opaque` is guaranteed to be a valid index, but a different index from `transparent`.

`glutOverlayDisplayFunc` registers a special overlay display callback that will be called when the overlay needs to be redrawn. A redisplay can be posted for the overlay by calling `glutOverlayDisplayFunc`. If the overlay callback is not registered but an overlay is established for a window, the window's display callback will do "double duty" as both the normal plane and the overlay callback. When either the normal plane or the overlay for the window is damaged or a redisplay is posted, the window's display callback will be called if no overlay display callback is registered. If the overlay is being animated with overlay, it may not be necessary to have two distinct callbacks.

You can remove an overlay that has been established by calling

```
glutRemoveOverlay();
```

Destroying an overlay implicitly sets the current layer back to the normal plane. When you do not want to display the overlay (for example, when rubber-banding is not active), you can hide and show an overlay without having to remove and re-establish it. For example:

```
glutShowOverlay();
glutHideOverlay();
```

Overlays are discussed further in Section 6.3, which explains how to program overlays with Xlib, and in Section 6.5.5, which explains overlays in the context of graphics hardware acceleration features.

4.3 ADVICE AND HINTS ON USE

Here are a number of points to keep in mind when writing GLUT programs. Some of these are strong recommendations; others are simply hints and tips.

4.3.1 Callback Advice

- Do not change state that will affect the way a window will be drawn in a window's display callback. Your display callback should be idempotent. This will ensure that you can correctly redraw your scene if it is damaged.

- If you need to redisplay a window, instead of rendering in whatever callback you happen to be in, call `glutPostRedisplay`. As a general rule, code that renders directly to the screen should be called only from display callbacks; other types of callbacks should not be rendering to the screen.

- If you use an idle callback to control your animation, use a visibility callback to determine when the window is fully obscured or iconified and do not waste processing time rendering during these times.

- If you register a single function as a callback routine for multiple windows, you can call `glutGetWindow` within the callback to determine what window is generating the callback. Likewise, `glutGetMenu` can be called to determine what menu is generating a menu callback.

- Do not select for more input callbacks than you actually need. For example, if you do not need motion or passive motion callbacks, disable them by passing NULL to their callback register functions. Disabling input callbacks allows the GLUT implementation to limit the window system input events that must be processed.

- Use the passive motion callback with care. If you register a passive motion callback for a window, your program receives motion events whenever the mouse moves across the window. You can remove a passive motion callback when it is not needed by calling `glutPassiveMotionFunc(NULL)`.

- Remember that it is illegal to create or destroy menus or to change, add, or remove menu items while a menu (and any cascaded submenus) is in use (that is, "popped up"). Use the menu status callback to determine when to avoid menu manipulation.

- By default, timer and idle callbacks may be called while a pop-up menu is active. On slow machines, slow rendering in an idle callback will compromise menu performance. Also, depending on how menus are used, it may be desirable for motion to stop immediately when a menu is triggered. In this case, use the menu entry/exit callback set with `glutMenuStateFunc` to track the use of pop-up menus.

- The backspace, **Del**, and **Esc** keys generate ASCII characters, so detect key presses for these keys using the `glutKeyboardFunc` callback, not the `glutSpecialFunc` callback.

4.3.2 Window Management Advice

- Neither GLUT nor the window system automatically reshapes subwindows. If subwindows should be reshaped to reflect a reshaping of the top-level window, the GLUT program is responsible for doing this.

- Not every OpenGL implementation supports the same range of frame buffer capabilities, though minimum requirements for frame buffer capabilities do exist. If `glutCreateWindow` or `glutCreateSubWindow` is called with an *initial display mode* not supported by the OpenGL implementation, a fatal error will be generated with an explanatory message. To avoid this, `glutGet(GLUT_DISPLAY_MODE_POSSIBLE)` should be called to determine whether the initial display mode is supported by the OpenGL implementation.

- Keep in mind that when a window is damaged, you should assume that *all* of the ancillary buffers are damaged and redraw them all.

- Keep in mind that after a `glutSwapBuffers`, you should assume that the state of the back buffer becomes undefined.

4.3.3 Current Window/Menu Management Advice

- Do not call any GLUT routine that affects the *current window* or *current menu* if no current window or current menu is defined. This can be the case at initialization time (before any windows or menus have been created) and if you destroy the current window or current menu. GLUT implementations should not be expected to generate a warning or otherwise ignore this case, because checking for this error would slow down the operation of properly written GLUT programs.

- For most callbacks, the *current window* and/or *current menu* is set appropriately at the time of the callback. Timer and idle callbacks are exceptions. If your application uses multiple windows or menus, make sure that you explicitly set the window or menu appropriately, using `glutSetWindow` or `glutSetMenu`, in idle and timer callbacks.

- It is more efficient to use `glutHideOverlay` and `glutShowOverlay` to control the display state of a window's overlay instead of removing and re-establishing an overlay every time an overlay is needed.

4.3.4 Miscellaneous Advice

- Avoid using the color index color model if possible (using overlays requires color index, though). The RGBA color model is more functional and is less likely to cause colormap swapping effects.

- If you are not using `glutSwapBuffers` for double-buffered animation, remember to use `glFlush` to ensure that rendering requests are dispatched to the frame buffer. While many OpenGL implementations will automatically flush pending commands, this is specifically not mandated.

- Few workstations have support for multiple simultaneously installed overlay colormaps. For this reason, if an overlay is cleared or otherwise not being used, it is best to hide it using `glutHideOverlay`, to keep other windows with active overlays from being displayed with the wrong colormap. If your application uses multiple overlays, use `glutCopyColormap` to promote colormap sharing.

- GLUT has no special routine for exiting the program. GLUT programs should use ANSI C's `exit` routine. If a program needs to perform special operations before quitting the program, use the ANSI C `onexit` routine to register exit callbacks. GLUT will exit the program unilaterally when fatal errors occur or when the window system requests the program to terminate. For this reason, avoid calling any GLUT routines within an exit callback.

- If you are encountering GLUT warnings or fatal errors in your programs, try setting a debugger breakpoint in the internal `__glutWarning` or `__glutFatalError` routines to determine where the error occurred within your program.

- Definitely, definitely use the `-gldebug` option to look for OpenGL errors when OpenGL rendering does not appear to be operating properly. OpenGL errors are reported only if you explicitly look for them! See Section 2.8 for additional debugging tips.

4.4 A Substantial GLUT Example

Now that you have seen the GLUT programming interface and considered advice about using GLUT effectively, this section demonstrates the practice of GLUT programming.

This section presents a GLUT example program called `zoomdino`. The intent of the program is to show good GLUT programming practice so you can write clean, efficient GLUT programs. The program renders the dinosaur model presented in Chapter 2. Like the `glxdino` example, `zoomdino` lets the user spin the dinosaur, but, in addition, the user can impart momentum to the dinosaur so that it keeps spinning. Spinning is good, but when `zoomdino`'s view window is not visible or iconified, the rendering is automatically suspended to avoid wasting rendering

Figure 4.8 Zooming in on rubber-banded subregions in `zoomdino`.

First subregion
zoom defined by the rubber band

Second subregion
zoom defined by the rubber band

effort when no one can see it. Well-behaved animation programs should avoid rendering to nonvisible windows. Also, you can control your view of the dinosaur by "zooming in" on subregions of the scene. A rubber-banded rectangle rendered in the overlay planes (if available) helps you set the view rectangle defining your next view. Figure 4.8 shows how `zoomdino` lets the user zoom in on subregions using rubber-banding. Finally, GLUT's pop-up menu facility is used to control the lights shining on the dinosaur.

The `makeDinosaur` routine used by `zoomdino.c` is identical to the code presented in Section 2.1.2, so it is not repeated here.

```
void
main(int argc, char **argv)
{
  glutInit(&argc, argv);
  glutInitDisplayMode(GLUT_RGB | GLUT_DOUBLE | GLUT_DEPTH);
  glutCreateWindow("zoomdino");
  glutDisplayFunc(redraw);
  glutReshapeFunc(reshape);
  glutMouseFunc(mouse);
  glutMotionFunc(motion);
  glutVisibilityFunc(vis);
```

`zoomdino` uses a single double-buffered window using the RGBA color model and a depth buffer. GLUT callbacks are registered. The `redraw` callback takes care of rendering the dinosaur model in the normal plane. The `reshape` callback takes care of reconfiguring the viewport and perspective matrices of both the normal plane and the overlay (if an overlay is supported). The `mouse` and `motion` routines implement both the spinning of the model (using the left mouse button) and the rubber-banding to zoom the viewing area (using the middle mouse button). The `vis` callback is used to ensure that the idle callback registered when the dinosaur continues to spin is deregistered when the window becomes nonvisible and is reregistered when the window becomes visible again. The code for these routines follows the explanation of `main`.

```
glutCreateMenu(controlLights);
glutAddMenuEntry("Toggle right light", 1);
glutAddMenuEntry("Toggle left light", 2);
glutAttachMenu(GLUT_RIGHT_BUTTON);
```

A two-entry menu attached to the right button lets the user toggle on and off the two lights that shine on our model. The `controlLights` callback, shown later, enables and disables the lights.

```
makeDinosaur();
resetProjection();
gluLookAt(0.0, 0.0, 30.0, /* eye is at (0,0,30) */
  0.0, 0.0, 0.0, /* center is at (0,0,0) */
  0.0, 1.0, 0.); /* up is in positive Y direction */
glEnable(GL_CULL_FACE);
glEnable(GL_DEPTH_TEST);

glLightModeli(GL_LIGHT_MODEL_LOCAL_VIEWER, 1);
glLightfv(GL_LIGHT0, GL_POSITION, lightZeroPosition);
glLightfv(GL_LIGHT0, GL_DIFFUSE, lightZeroColor);
glLightf(GL_LIGHT0, GL_CONSTANT_ATTENUATION, 0.1);
glLightf(GL_LIGHT0, GL_LINEAR_ATTENUATION, 0.05);
glLightfv(GL_LIGHT1, GL_POSITION, lightOnePosition);
glLightfv(GL_LIGHT1, GL_DIFFUSE, lightOneColor);
glEnable(GL_LIGHT0);
glEnable(GL_LIGHT1);
glEnable(GL_LIGHTING);
```

The code above initializes OpenGL state for rendering the dinosaur model. This state is basically like the state setup in `glxdino.c`'s `contextInit` routine. The only difference is that `resetProjection` is used to establish the projection matrix instead of calling `gluPerspective`. Here is what `resetProjection` does:

```
float viewX, viewY, viewX2, viewY2, viewWidth, viewHeight;

void
resetProjection(void)
{
```

```
glMatrixMode(GL_PROJECTION);
glLoadIdentity();
viewX = -1.0;
viewWidth = 2.0;
viewY = -1.0;
viewHeight = 2.0;
glFrustum(viewX, viewX + viewWidth, viewY, viewY + viewHeight,
    1.0, 40);
glMatrixMode(GL_MODELVIEW);
}
```

The various `view-` variables keep track of the near clipping plane rectangle. This initial perspective projection shows the dinosaur model from a distance. These variables will be adjusted to zoom a new viewing subregion after the user finishes rubber-banding a new region in the `mouse` callback.

4.4.1 Establishing an Overlay for Rubber-Banding

Continuing with `main`, the code attempts to establish an overlay for rendering the rubber-banding effect used to zoom a new subregion. Overlays are typically single-buffered and color index, so the initial display mode is modified to make it appropriate for establishing an overlay. Then `glutLayerGet(GLUT_OVERLAY_POSSIBLE)` can determine whether an overlay can be established. If `glutEstablishOverlay` is called and an overlay is not possible for the current window, GLUT will immediately exit (`glutEstablishOverlay`, like `glutCreateWindow`, has no way to report failure). The lesson is to look before you leap.

If an overlay is not possible, a message is printed informing the user that overlay rubber-banding will not be enabled. The `overlaySupport` variable is checked later in the program to decide whether the overlay rubber-banding code should be avoided because an overlay is not established.

```
glutInitDisplayMode(GLUT_SINGLE | GLUT_INDEX);
overlaySupport = glutLayerGet(GLUT_OVERLAY_POSSIBLE);
if (overlaySupport == 0) {
  printf("Sorry, no whizzy zoomdino overlay usage!\n");
} else {
  glutEstablishOverlay();
  glutHideOverlay();
```

If an overlay can be established, `glutEstablishOverlay` is called to do so. The overlay is hidden immediately, because until the user attempts to use rubber-banding, we do not need to display the overlay. It is good practice not to show an overlay unless you are using it for rendering. This is because overlays complicate the calculations done by the X server to manage window real estate, and colormap resources for overlays are often limited (typically, overlays support color index, not RGBA).

```
      transparent = glutLayerGet(GLUT_TRANSPARENT_INDEX);
      glClearIndex(transparent);
      red = (transparent + 1) % glutGet(GLUT_WINDOW_COLORMAP_SIZE);
      glutSetColor(red, 1.0, 0.0, 0.0); /* Red. */
      glutOverlayDisplayFunc(redrawOverlay);
      glutSetWindowTitle("zoomdino with rubber-banding");
    }
    glutMainLoop();
}
```

Because the overlay uses color index, the colormap cells must be loaded with the correct colors. The overlay reserves a cell for the transparent pixel so that the code retrieves that transparent index. When you are initializing the overlay colormap, be careful not to attempt to allocate the transparent index. A safe index can be determined by adding 1 to the transparent index modulo the number of colormap cells. Once the index is determined, `glutSetColor` loads red into the index's colormap cell.

Establishing an overlay also means that the program takes responsibility for rendering the overlay when an overlay redisplay is required. If the overlay and normal plane are being animated in lockstep, the window's default display callback could do "double duty" updating both the overlay and normal plane layers. In the case of `zoomdino`, the overlay and normal plane are independently updated. For example, when the user is using rubber-banding to define a subregion, the dinosaur model may or may not be spinning. In this case, it is best to register a distinct overlay display callback using `glutOverlayDisplayFunc`.

To let the user know that rubber-banding is supported, the window's title is updated to say "zoomdino with rubber-banding."

4.4.2 Normal Plane and Overlay Rendering

The window is created, the callbacks have been registered, a pop-up menu is created and attached to the window, and an overlay has been established if possible. When `glutMainLoop` is entered, the window will be shown and the user can begin interacting with `zoomdino`. Now the implementation of the callbacks is important.

```
void
redraw(void)
{
  glClear(GL_COLOR_BUFFER_BIT | GL_DEPTH_BUFFER_BIT);
  glPushMatrix();
  glRotatef(angle, 0.0, 1.0, 0.0);
```

```
  glTranslatef(-8, -8, -bodyWidth / 2);
  glCallList(DINOSAUR);
  glPopMatrix();
  glutSwapBuffers();
}
```

The normal plane `redraw` routine clears the back color and depth buffers, rotates the modelview based on the current angle for the displaying dinosaur model, and executes the display list created by `makeDinosaur`. Finally, the rotation is undone and the buffer is swapped. Observe that `redraw` is idempotent as long as `angle` is not changing and no OpenGL state is changed. This ensures that if the window is damaged, it will be redrawn exactly as it should appear. It is also true that `redraw` is the only callback that actually *renders* to the normal plane. Other callbacks update OpenGL state or change `angle`, but they do no actual rendering. Instead, when rendering is required, `glutPostRedisplay` is called to trigger the display callback.

```
void
reshape(int w, int h)
{
  if (overlaySupport) {
    glutUseLayer(GLUT_OVERLAY);
    glViewport(0, 0, w, h);
    glMatrixMode(GL_PROJECTION);
    glLoadIdentity();
    gluOrtho2D(0, w, 0, h);
    glScalef(1, -1, 1);
    glTranslatef(0, -h, 0);
    glMatrixMode(GL_MODELVIEW);
    glutUseLayer(GLUT_NORMAL);
  }
  glViewport(0, 0, w, h);
  W = w;
  H = h;
}
```

The `reshape` callback updates the normal plane and overlay viewports as well as the overlay projection matrix. Note that the overlay is updated only if `overlay-Support` indicates that the overlay is supported. The overlay projection matrix is set so that OpenGL can be rendered using window-relative coordinates with the origin positioned in the upper left-hand corner of the window. This means that window coordinates reported by input events can be directly used for overlay OpenGL rendering. `gluOrtho2D` will create a viewing plane of the correct size, but the origin will be in the lower left-hand corner. `glScalef` flips the Y axis, and `glTranslatef` moves the origin to the window's upper left-hand corner.

For both the overlay and normal plane, `glViewport` sets the viewport rectangle to cover the entire window.

```
void
redrawOverlay(void)
{
  static int prevStretchX, prevStretchY;

  if (glutLayerGet(GLUT_OVERLAY_DAMAGED)) {
    /* Damage means we need a full clear. */
    glClear(GL_COLOR_BUFFER_BIT);
  } else {
    /* Undraw last rubber-band. */
    glIndexi(transparent);
    glBegin(GL_LINE_LOOP);
    glVertex2i(anchorX, anchorY);
    glVertex2i(anchorX, prevStretchY);
    glVertex2i(prevStretchX, prevStretchY);
    glVertex2i(prevStretchX, anchorY);
    glEnd();
  }
  glIndexi(red);
  glBegin(GL_LINE_LOOP);
  glVertex2i(anchorX, anchorY);
  glVertex2i(anchorX, stretchY);
  glVertex2i(stretchX, stretchY);
  glVertex2i(stretchX, anchorY);
  glEnd();
  prevStretchX = stretchX;
  prevStretchY = stretchY;
}
```

The overlay displays only the rubber-band used to sweep out a new view subregion; the reset of the overlay should remain cleared to the transparent index. To keep the rubber-band rendering highly interactive and eliminate rubber-band flickering, `redrawOverlay` tries to clear the overlay only when the overlay contents have been damaged. If the entire overlay is cleared every time the overlay has been redrawn, the user may notice a flicker (remember, the overlay is not double-buffered) when the window is large, because a clear leaves the rubber-band undrawn for a reasonably long time. The interaction and visual appearance are greatly improved when zoomdino draws the old rubber-band using the transparent pixel (clearing only the pixels known not to be transparent), then draws the rubber-band in its new location.

The only problem with this approach is that if the window is damaged, the overlay's frame buffer state becomes undefined. In this case, a full clear of the overlay is needed, but this is infrequent and does not typically happen when the user is actively using rubber-banding. The glutLayerGet(GLUT_OVERLAY_DAMAGED) informs the callback as to whether the callback was generated to repair damage reported by the window system. If the only reason redrawOverlay is being called is that an overlay redisplay posted using glutPostOverlayRedisplay, the frame buffer will not report being damaged and a clear will not be necessary.

The prevStretchX and prevStretchY variables keep track of the location where the last rubber-band was rendered so it can be cleared the next time redraw-Overlay is used (assuming no damage).

4.4.3   Spinning and Rubber-Banding

The mouse callback handles both the spinning of the dinosaur using the left mouse button and the zooming of a subregion view using the middle mouse button.

```
void
mouse(int button, int state, int x, int y)
{
  if (button == GLUT_LEFT_BUTTON) {
    if (state == GLUT_DOWN) {
      glutSetCursor(GLUT_CURSOR_LEFT_RIGHT);
      spinning = 1;
      spinBegin = x;
      angleDelta = 0;
    } else if (state == GLUT_UP) {
      glutSetCursor(GLUT_CURSOR_INHERIT);
      spinning = 0;
      if (angleDelta == 0)
        glutIdleFunc(NULL);
    }
  }
}
```

The dinosaur can begin spinning when the left mouse button is pressed in the window. When this occurs, spinning is set to indicate that mouse motion will spin the dinosaur. The current mouse X position is recorded as spinBegin. The angleDelta records the rotational velocity of the dinosaur. When spinning is initiated (that is, the left button is first pressed down), the rotational velocity is zero. This lets the user halt the spinning by clicking the left mouse button without moving the mouse.

When the left button is released, spinning is unset. As will be seen when the motion callback is described, when mouse motion occurs while spinning is enabled, the rotational velocity is updated based on the direction and distance of the mouse motion. Also, an `idle` callback is registered that continuously updates angle based on the current rotational velocity. `idle` is implemented as follows:

```
idle(void)
{
  angle += angleDelta;
  glutPostRedisplay();
}
```

Every time the `angle` is updated, a redisplay is posted for the normal plane to render the newly rotated dinosaur.

When the left mouse button is released, if the angular velocity is zero, the `idle` callback is deregistered. Otherwise, it is left registered to keep the dinosaur spinning. Maintaining the angular velocity of the dinosaur when the button is released is similar to imparting angular momentum to the object.

To help indicate to the user that the dinosaur can be rotated while the left mouse button is held down, `glutSetCursor` is called to make the cursor appear as a left-and-right arrow. The default cursor image is restored when the left mouse button is released.

When the middle button is pressed, rubber-banding begins as the user sweeps out a new subregion for zooming the view of the dinosaur. The `mouse` callback continues:

```
if (button == GLUT_MIDDLE_BUTTON) {
    if (state == GLUT_DOWN) {
      rubberBanding = 1;
      anchorX = x;
      anchorY = y;
      stretchX = x;
      stretchY = y;
      if (overlaySupport)
        glutShowOverlay();
```

`rubberBanding` is set to indicate that rubber-banding is active so that mouse motion in the `motion` callback will redisplay the rubber-band. The `anchorX` and `anchorY` variables maintain the location where the rubber-band is initiated. `stretchX` and `stretchY` indicate the region over which the rubber-band is stretched.

If overlays are supported, the overlay is shown. Since the overlay is hidden when rubber-banding is not being done, showing the overlay will generate an overlay display callback to first render the rubber-band. In the `motion` callback, the rubber-banded region is redrawn as the mouse position changes.

When the middle button is released, the new projection matrix must be calculated to show the newly zoomed view.

```
    } else if (state == GLUT_UP) {
      if (overlaySupport)
        glutHideOverlay();
      rubberBanding = 0;
      glutUseLayer(GLUT_NORMAL);

#define max(a,b) ((a) > (b) ? (a) : (b))
#define min(a,b) ((a) < (b) ? (a) : (b))

      windowX = min(anchorX, stretchX);
      windowY = min(H - anchorY, H - stretchY);
      windowX2 = max(anchorX, stretchX);
      windowY2 = max(H - anchorY, H - stretchY);
      windowW = windowX2 - windowX;
      windowH = windowY2 - windowY;
      if (windowW == 0 || windowH == 0) {
        resetProjection();
      } else {
        viewX2 = windowX2 / W * viewWidth + viewX;
        viewX = windowX / W * viewWidth + viewX;
        viewY2 = windowY2 / H * viewHeight + viewY;
        viewY = windowY / H * viewHeight + viewY;
        viewWidth = viewX2 - viewX;
        viewHeight = viewY2 - viewY;
        glMatrixMode(GL_PROJECTION);
        glLoadIdentity();
        glFrustum(viewX, viewX + viewWidth, viewY, viewY + viewHeight,
            1.0, 40);
        glMatrixMode(GL_MODELVIEW);
      }
      glutPostRedisplay();
    }
  }
}
```

When the middle mouse button is released, the overlay (if supported) is hidden again and rubberBanding is unset. The normal plane projection matrix should now be zoomed based on the subregion swept during rubber-banding. The layer in use is not set when an input callback is entered (only display callbacks change the layer in use), so glutUseLayer(GLUT_NORMAL) ensures that the normal plane projection matrix, and not the overlay projection matrix, is updated. When you are using overlays, remember to set the layer in use when in doubt. If the region is empty (that is, it has zero width or height), `resetProjection` is used to fall back to the original view. This lets the user click and release the middle mouse button without sweeping a region to get back to starting view, *and* intelligently handles the degenerate case of an empty view region.

Once the subregion originally in window coordinates is converted to the normal plane's modeling coordinate space, the new perspective projection can be loaded. Calling `glutPostRedisplay` ensures that the normal plane is redisplayed with the newly zoomed view.

The mouse callback `motion` must handle both spinning and rubber-banding motion.

```
void
motion(int x, int y)
{
  if (rubberBanding) {
    stretchX = x;
    stretchY = y;
    if (overlaySupport)
     glutPostOverlayRedisplay();
  }
```

If `rubberBanding`, the new `stretchX` and `stretchY` are recorded and an overlay redisplay is requested by calling `glutPostOverlayRedisplay` if an overlay is supported.

```
  if (spinning) {
    angleDelta = (x - spinBegin) / 2;
    if (angleDelta)
      glutIdleFunc(idle);
    else
      glutIdleFunc(NULL);
    spinBegin = x;
  }
}
```

If `spinning`, a new rotational velocity is calculated based on the change in the mouse's X position from the last sampled position. If the rotational velocity is nonzero, the `idle` callback will be registered to begin spinning the dinosaur. If the velocity is zero, the idle callback should be deregistered. Finally, a new `spinBegin` is recorded based on the current X position.

Notice that for neither spinning nor rubber-banding does rendering actually happen in the `motion` callback. Instead, the `redraw` and `redrawOverlay` do all rendering based on state updated by other callbacks. This means that generating redisplays will regenerate the overlay and normal plane contents whether the reason for the redisplay is an explicit redisplay posted by the program or a redisplay generated by the window system to repair window damage.

4.4.4 Suspending Animation and Pop-up Menus

The ability to leave the dinosaur model spinning means that `zoomdino` continues rendering after user interaction stops. If the resulting animation is visible to the user, the animation is worthwhile. However, if `zoomdino`'s window is hidden, obscured by other windows, or iconified, the visual effect of animating the window is lost. A well-behaved animated program should disable rendering when its window is not visible or is iconified.

```
void
vis(int visible)
{
  if (visible != GLUT_VISIBLE) {
    if (angleDelta)
      glutIdleFunc(NULL);
  } else {
    if (angleDelta)
      glutIdleFunc(idle);
  }
}
```

The `vis` callback is triggered when the visibility of the window changes. If the window becomes nonvisible (that is, iconified, hidden, or completely obscured), the idle callback should be deregistered. When the window becomes visible again, the animation should begin again if the rotational velocity is nonzero. In this case, the `idle` callback should be reregistered.

This callback lets the user spin the dinosaur, then iconify the `zoomdino` window, and know that the program will not uselessly waste workstation resources rendering to no effect.

The final routine is the `controlLights` menu callback. As with `glxdino`, two light sources illuminate the dinosaur model. Using a pop-up menu, these light sources can be toggled on and off.

```
int lightZeroSwitch = 1, lightOneSwitch = 1;

void
controlLights(int value)
{
  glutUseLayer(GLUT_NORMAL);
  switch (value) {
  case 1:
    lightZeroSwitch = !lightZeroSwitch;
    if (lightZeroSwitch)
      glEnable(GL_LIGHT0);
    else
      glDisable(GL_LIGHT0);
    break;
  case 2:
    lightOneSwitch = !lightOneSwitch;
    if (lightOneSwitch)
      glEnable(GL_LIGHT1);
    else
      glDisable(GL_LIGHT1);
    break;
  }
  glutPostRedisplay();
}
```

The lightZeroSwitch and lightOneSwitch keep track of the current states of the light sources. The lights are initially on. Selecting a menu item will toggle the appropriate light. Notice that glutUseLayer(GLUT_NORMAL) is used to ensure that the layer to use is the normal plane. Remember that it is all right to call glutUse-Layer(GLUT_NORMAL) even when no overlay exists, since the normal layer of a window always exists. However, glutUseLayer(GLUT_OVERLAY) should be used only when an overlay is established.

5

Exploring OpenGL with GLUT

To give the reader a better feel for using GLUT and OpenGL, this chapter explores various OpenGL capabilities using GLUT-based examples. Each section includes an example program to demonstrate the ideas presented. The chapter is organized into the following sections:

1. "Exploring Lighting with GLUT" explains OpenGL's lighting model.
2. "Exploring OpenGL Texture Mapping with GLUT" explains OpenGL's texture mapping support.
3. "Exploring Blending Operations with GLUT" explains OpenGL's functionality for blending, antialiasing, and fog.
4. "Exploring Images and Bitmaps with GLUT" explains pixel operations and OpenGL's pixel path.
5. "Exploring Curves and Surfaces with GLUT" describes OpenGL's evaluator and NURBS routines for rendering curves and surfaces.
6. "Exploring the OpenGL Extensions with GLUT" discusses use of OpenGL extensions, focusing on the polygon offset extension (made standard in OpenGL 1.1).
7. "Exploring Open Inventor with GLUT" shows how to combine GLUT with the object-oriented Open Inventor 3D toolkit layered on top of OpenGL.

5.1 EXPLORING LIGHTING WITH GLUT

This section uses GLUT to demonstrate OpenGL's support for lighting as a technique to improve the realism of OpenGL-generated graphics. When 3D graphics are generated on a computer, realism is almost always an underlying goal. If the 3D image is to be effective, it needs to convey a sense of realism to the viewer. Lighting is a means to improve the realism of a 3D scene.

5.1.1 The OpenGL Lighting Model

Anyone who has studied optics knows that the physical behavior of light is quite complicated. OpenGL cannot and does not try to capture the phenomenon of light completely. Computer-generated graphics is often a trade-off between realism and interactivity. OpenGL is designed primarily for interactive graphics and therefore does not go to extremes to simulate the effects of lighting. The point is not to simulate light precisely, but to achieve realistic effects without too much computational burden.

The *lighting model* used by OpenGL approximates real-world lighting effects by breaking colors into red, green, and blue components. Of course, this is not an accurate representation of light's physical nature.

OpenGL light sources are described by the proportions of red, green, and blue light they emit. The materials of surfaces described by OpenGL geometric primitives can be described by the percentages of red, green, and blue light they reflect in various directions. OpenGL uses a set of lighting equations to approximate the effect of lighting. The equations are relatively easy to compute and provide a fairly reasonable lighting effect.

OpenGL allows multiple light sources to be established. They can be separately enabled and disabled. The effects of the different (enabled) light sources interact with each other. For example, if you have two lights, a red light and a blue light, shining on a white object, the object should appear magenta.

OpenGL supports four distinct types of lighting:

Emissive lighting. This is the simplest type of lighting. The object itself emits light of a certain color. In the real world, this might correspond to something like pixels on your computer monitor, which emit light of a given color independent of the lighting in the room. Using emissive light is simple: assign an emissive color to a surface.

Ambient lighting. Ambient lighting corresponds to light so scattered that it can be considered equally uniform and coming from every direction. An example of ambient lighting is the effect of backlighting in a room. Backlighting keeps the light from shining directly on most objects in the room, but objects are still visible by the indirect or ambient light.

Diffuse lighting. Unlike ambient lighting, diffuse lighting comes from a given direction. The amount of the light that is reflected is proportional to the light's incidence to the surface. Light shining directly on the surface will be reflected more brightly than light striking the surface at an angle. But once the light encounters the surface, it is reflected evenly in all directions.

Specular lighting. Specular lighting is like diffuse lighting, but the light tends to be reflected from the surface in a preferred, reflected direction. Think of a silver ball held up outside with the sun shining. When you look at the ball such that the sun reflects directly on it, you can see a bright shiny spot. This is called a *specular highlight*. Specularity corresponds well to the everyday notion of "shininess." For example, chalk has almost no specular component, while a shiny metal or plastic has a high specular component.

A single light source may actually be composed of several different types of lighting. For example, a flashlight will have both diffuse and specular components (corresponding to the flashlight's directed light), but there is also a small amount of ambient light (corresponding to the environmental light added by the flashlight).

Lights in OpenGL have an effect on the scene only when they interact with surfaces in the scene. If you enable a red light, but do not render any geometric primitives, do not expect anything to happen. A light source is not itself rendered; it affects only the way the scene is rendered.

OpenGL provides a reasonable lighting model in that if used effectively, OpenGL lighting can enhance the illusion of 3D. For example, a moving positional light source in an animated scene will change the coloration of the objects in the scene in a reasonably realistic manner.

There are limitations to OpenGL's lighting model. For example, shadows and reflective surfaces cannot be generated automatically. This does not mean you cannot generate shadows or reflective surfaces in OpenGL, just that you have to do much of the work yourself. But to OpenGL's advantage, the machinery for such effects is a standard part of OpenGL (features such as blending and environment mapping of textures). It is just that OpenGL does not build support for shadows or reflection into its lighting model.

5.1.2   Using OpenGL's Lighting Model

OpenGL's lighting is disabled by default. To enable lighting, call

```
glEnable(GL_LIGHTING);
```

Without lighting enabled, color is assigned by the *current color* established by the `glColor3f` family of calls. With lighting disabled, the color you assign to geometric primitives is the color you get (though options such as smooth shading or fog can affect the color). The more involved case is when lighting is enabled.

5.1.2.1 Defining Light Sources

OpenGL supports (at least) eight simultaneously active light sources. Light sources can be enabled and disabled individually. For example, to enable light source number 0, a program would call

```
glEnable(GL_LIGHT0);
```

Because each light you enable complicates the lighting equations, performance is likely to be better with fewer lights enabled.

Each light source has an ambient, a diffuse, and a specular intensity. You can think of each intensity as the color that the light source emits for each type of light. The intensity is specified as color with red, green, blue, and alpha components between 0 and 1. (Alpha is used in blending operations and will be discussed in detail in Section 5.3; for now, ignore it.) For example, a light with a bright white diffuse and specular intensity and a dimmer ambient intensity would be specified like this:

```
GLfloat amb[] =  /* dim white */
                 { 0.3, 0.3, 0.3, 1.0 };
GLfloat dif[] =  /* bright white */
                 { 1.0, 1.0, 1.0, 1.0 };
GLfloat spec[] = /* bright white */
                 { 1.0, 1.0, 1.0, 1.0 };

glLightfv(GL_LIGHT1, GL_AMBIENT, amb);
glLightfv(GL_LIGHT1, GL_DIFFUSE, dif);
glLightfv(GL_LIGHT1, GL_SPECULAR, spec);
```

White light is generated by supplying equal amounts of red, green, and blue. The closer each component is to 1.0, the more intense the light source. Unless alpha is being explicitly used, alpha is usually specified as 1.0.

Light sources also have a position. Sometimes the position can be "at infinity." In such a case, the light source is called *infinite*, or *directional*. The sun can be considered a directional, or infinite, light source because of its great distance from the earthly objects it illuminates.

In a number of cases, you will find that "simplifications" exist in the OpenGL lighting model to make the mathematics of calculating lighting effects easier. For example, the effect of a directional light (positioned "at infinity") is easier to calculate than that of a directional light at some absolute position. For a distant light, you can get better performance by setting up the light as an infinite, directional light with little effect on the rendered scene.

You can specify a light source's position like this:

```
GLfloat pos_= { 2.0, 3.0, 5.0, 1.0 };

glLightfv(GL_LIGHT1, GL_POSITION, pos);
```

Notice that a vector of four values (x,y,z,w) is specified. The x, y, and z parameters are divided by w to determine the actual (x,y,z) location of the light source. If w is zero, this indicates that the light is an infinite light (notice the division by zero!). A light with a zero w would have a direction, but not a position. Readers with a mathematical background may recognize these as homogeneous coordinates.

5.1.2.2   Defining the Surface Material

Lights are useless without surfaces to shine on. Two types of information about the surface are used in OpenGL lighting calculations:

> **Material properties.** These are colors specified as red, green, blue, and alpha components between 0 and 1 for each type of light: ambient, diffuse, specular, and emissive. Each color type is combined with the light source's color type intensity to determine what color of light to reflect off the surface. A *specular exponent* is also part of the material properties and is roughly a measure of the surface's shininess.

> **Surface normals.** The normal to a surface at a point is a 3D vector at that point, determining the orientation of the surface. The diffuse and specular lighting calculations use the angle of incidence between the light and the surface normal to determine the amount of light reflected. For specular lighting, the amount of reflection also depends on the viewer's "eye" position.

The material properties are set using the `glMaterialfv` family of calls. For example:

```
GLfloat amb[] = { 0.33, 0.22, 0.03, 1.0 };
GLfloat dif[] = { 0.78, 0.57, 0.11, 1.0 };
GLfloat spec[] = { 0.99, 0.91, 0.81, 1.0 };

glMaterialfv(GL_FRONT, GL_AMBIENT, amb);
glMaterialfv(GL_FRONT, GL_DIFFUSE, dif);
glMaterialfv(GL_FRONT, GL_SPECULAR, spec);
glMaterialf(GL_FRONT, GL_SHININESS, 27.8);
```

The values in this example are chosen to give the appearance of brass. Notice that the blue color components are lower than the red and green components to give a yellowish tint, and the specular color is rather bright.

Per-vertex normals for geometric primitives are specified using the `glNormal3f` family of calls. For the lighting calculations to work as expected, the normals should be unit vectors. Even when you specify unit vectors in your calls to `glNormal3f`, modeling operations such as scaling can denormalize your normal vectors. To avoid this problem (at a slight performance penalty), the following call will assure that your normal vectors are always properly normalized before lighting calculations are performed:

```
glEnable(GL_NORMALIZE);
```

When `GL_NORMALIZE` is disabled (the default), it is up to you to make sure that lighting calculations are done with unit normals.

5.1.2.3 Other Lighting Concepts

OpenGL's lighting model has a number of other interesting features that are beyond the scope of this book to describe in detail, but they are worth mentioning for completeness.

> **Spotlights.** OpenGL allows positional lights to be restricted so that the shape of the light generated is a cone. The *spotlight direction* and *cutoff angle* can be specified.

> **Two-sided lighting.** OpenGL can support distinct lighting for the fronts and backs of polygons. This explains the `GL_FRONT` parameter in the example calls to `glMaterialfv`.

> **Attenuation.** In the real world, the intensity of a light source drops off with distance. OpenGL allows a similar attenuation effect to be specified for positional light sources.

> **Global ambient light.** A global ambient light source can be established.

> **Color index mode lighting.** OpenGL supports lighting in color index mode. In general, OpenGL lighting is considerably more straightforward in RGBA mode.

The lighting parameters for a scene do not have to be static. For example, you may want to move a positional light source for each frame of an animated scene (perhaps the light is on a swinging pendulum). Or you could render part of a scene with lights 1 and 2 enabled, then later disable light 2 for the remainder of the frame. While normally you will want to keep your light sources fixed for the duration of the frame you are rendering, this is by no means required.

Abstractly, you can think of OpenGL lighting as a large set of equations for determining the color of rendered geometric primitives. It is beyond the scope of this book to examine the mathematical equations for the OpenGL lighting model in detail, but mathematically inclined readers are invited to read the discussion of

OpenGL lighting in the *OpenGL Programming Guide* [28] or the OpenGL specification itself [36].

This section's GLUT example, called `lightlab`, allows you to change the material and lighting characteristics of a scene containing a teapot, a torus, and an icosahedron. The objects in the scene can be rendered to appear to be made of brass, red plastic, emerald, or slate. Two directional lights, coming from the left and right, can shine red, white, green, or not at all. Figures 5.1, 5.2, 5.3, and 5.4 show various lighting configurations using `lightlab`. GLUT menus are used to control the various lighting parameters. The program's source code is a good start for exploring OpenGL lighting features.

5.1.3 Example: `lightlab.c`

```
#include <stdlib.h>
#include <stdarg.h>
#include <stdio.h>
#include <GL/glut.h>
```

Figure 5.1 `lightlab`'s initial appearance. Both lights enabled so that the teapot has two specular highlights. The left side of the teapot catches the left side's red light; the right side catches the right side's green light.

Figure 5.2 The right light is off; the left light shines red. Notice that the emerald torus is hardly visible because there is no green light in the scene. Also, because there is only one light shining, the teapot has a single specular highlight.

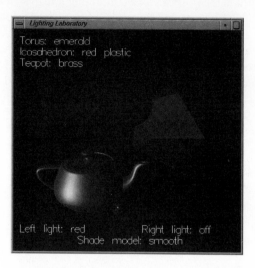

Figure 5.3 Both lights are shining white and the picture is bright. Flat shading is being used instead of smooth shading. This makes it apparent that the torus is not tessellated very finely. Lighting with smooth shading gives it a rounder appearance.

Figure 5.4 Slate is not very shiny, so the teapot's specular highlights are spread widely across its surface. The specular highlight for the icosahedron is caught by the entire front triangle. The left side of the icosahedron appears redder because of the left red light.

```
enum {
  BRASS, RED_PLASTIC, EMERALD, SLATE
} MaterialType;
enum {
  TORUS_MATERIAL = 1, TEAPOT_MATERIAL = 2, ICO_MATERIAL = 3
} MaterialDisplayList;
enum {
  LIGHT_OFF, LIGHT_RED, LIGHT_WHITE, LIGHT_GREEN
} LightValues;

GLfloat redLight[] = {1.0, 0.0, 0.0, 1.0},
    greenLight[] = {0.0, 1.0, 0.0, 1.0,}
    whiteLight[] = {1.0, 1.0, 1.0, 1.0};
GLfloat leftLightPosition[] = {-1.0, 0.0, 1.0, 0.0},
    rightLightPosition[] = {1.0, 0.0, 1.0, 0.0};
GLfloat brassAmbient[] = {0.33, 0.22, 0.03, 1.0},
    brassDiffuse[] = {0.78, 0.57, 0.11, 1.0},
    brassSpecular[] = {0.99, 0.91, 0.81, 1.0},
    brassShineiness = 27.8;
```

```
GLfloat redPlasticAmbient[] = {0.0, 0.0, 0.0},
  redPlasticDiffuse[] = {0.5, 0.0, 0.0},
  redPlasticSpecular[] = {0.7, 0.6, 0.6},
  redPlasticShininess = 32.0;
GLfloat emeraldAmbient[] = {0.0215, 0.1745, 0.0215},
  emeraldDiffuse[] = {0.07568, 0.61424, 0.07568},
  emeraldSpecular[] = {0.633, 0.727811, 0.633},
  emeraldShininess = 76.8;
GLfloat slateAmbient[] = {0.02, 0.02, 0.02,}
  slateDiffuse[] = {0.02, 0.01, 0.01},
  slateSpecular[] = {0.4, 0.4, 0.4},
  slateShininess = .78125;
int shadeModel = GL_SMOOTH;
char *leftLight, *rightLight;
char *icoMaterial, *teapotMaterial, *torusMaterial;

/* printf-style interface for rendering text using a GLUT
   stroke font. */
void
output(GLfloat x, GLfloat y, char *format,...)
{
  va_list args;
  char buffer[200], *p;

  /* Use stdarg.h macros for variable argument list processing. */
  va_start(args, format);
  vsprintf(buffer, format, args);
  va_end(args);
  glPushMatrix();
  glTranslatef(x, y, 0);
  for (p = buffer; *p; p++)
    glutStrokeCharacter(GLUT_STROKE_ROMAN, *p);
  glPopMatrix();
}

void
display(void)
{
  glClear(GL_COLOR_BUFFER_BIT | GL_DEPTH_BUFFER_BIT);
  glMatrixMode(GL_MODELVIEW);
  glPushMatrix();
    glScalef(1.3, 1.3, 1.3);
    glRotatef(20.0, 1.0, 0.0, 0.0);
    glPushMatrix();
```

```
        glTranslatef(-0.65, 0.7, 0.0);
        glRotatef(90.0, 1.0, 0.0, 0.0);
        glCallList(TORUS_MATERIAL);
        glutSolidTorus(0.275, 0.85, 10, 15);
      glPopMatrix();
      glPushMatrix();
        glTranslatef(-0.75, -0.8, 0.0);
        glCallList(TEAPOT_MATERIAL);
        glutSolidTeapot(0.7);
      glPopMatrix();
      glPushMatrix();
        glTranslatef(1.0, 0.0, -1.0);
        glCallList(ICO_MATERIAL);
        glutSolidIcosahedron();
      glPopMatrix();
    glPopMatrix();
    glPushAttrib(GL_ENABLE_BIT);
      glDisable(GL_DEPTH_TEST);
      glDisable(GL_LIGHTING);
      glMatrixMode(GL_PROJECTION);
      glPushMatrix();
        glLoadIdentity();
        gluOrtho2D(0, 3000, 0, 3000);
        glMatrixMode(GL_MODELVIEW);
        glPushMatrix();
          glLoadIdentity();
          output(80, 2800, "Torus: %s", torusMaterial);
          output(80, 2650, "Icosahedron: %s", icoMaterial);
          output(80, 2500, "Teapot: %s", teapotMaterial);
          output(80, 250, "Left light: %s", leftLight);
          output(1700, 250, "Right light: %s", rightLight);
          output(850, 100, "Shade model: %s",
            shadeModel == GL_SMOOTH ? "smooth" : "flat");
        glPopMatrix();
        glMatrixMode(GL_PROJECTION);
      glPopMatrix();
    glPopAttrib();
    glutSwapBuffers();
}

void
lightSelect(GLenum which, int value, char **label)
{
  glEnable(which);
```

```
  switch (value) {
  case LIGHT_OFF:
    *label = "off";
    glDisable(which);
    break;
  case LIGHT_RED:
    *label = "red";
    glLightfv(which, GL_DIFFUSE, redLight);
    break;
  case LIGHT_WHITE:
    *label = "white";
    glLightfv(which, GL_DIFFUSE, whiteLight);
    break;
  case LIGHT_GREEN:
    *label = "green";
    glLightfv(which, GL_DIFFUSE, greenLight);
    break;
  }
  glutPostRedisplay();
}

void
leftLightSelect(int value)
{
  lightSelect(GL_LIGHT0, value, &leftLight);
}

void
rightLightSelect(int value)
{
  lightSelect(GL_LIGHT1, value, &rightLight);
}
void
material(int dlist, GLfloat * ambient, GLfloat * diffuse,
  GLfloat * specular, GLfloat shininess)
{
  glNewList(dlist, GL_COMPILE);
    glMaterialfv(GL_FRONT, GL_AMBIENT, ambient);
    glMaterialfv(GL_FRONT, GL_DIFFUSE, diffuse);
    glMaterialfv(GL_FRONT, GL_SPECULAR, specular);
    glMaterialf(GL_FRONT, GL_SHININESS, shininess);
  glEndList();
}
```

```
char *
materialSelect(int object, int value)
{
  glutPostRedisplay();
  switch (value) {
  case BRASS:
    material(object, brassAmbient,
      brassDiffuse, brassSpecular, brassShineiness);
    return "brass";
  case RED_PLASTIC:
    material(object, redPlasticAmbient, redPlasticDiffuse,
      redPlasticSpecular, redPlasticShininess);
    return "red plastic";
  case EMERALD:
    material(object, emeraldAmbient, emeraldDiffuse,
      emeraldSpecular, emeraldShininess);
    return "emerald";
  case SLATE:
    material(object, slateAmbient, slateDiffuse,
      slateSpecular, slateShininess);
    return "slate";
  }
  return NULL; /* avoid bogus warning! */
}

void
torusSelect(int value)
{
  torusMaterial = materialSelect(TORUS_MATERIAL, value);
}

void
teapotSelect(int value)
{
  teapotMaterial = materialSelect(TEAPOT_MATERIAL, value);
}

void
icoSelect(int value)
{
  icoMaterial = materialSelect(ICO_MATERIAL, value);
}
```

```c
void
mainMenuSelect(int value)
{
  if (value == 666)
    exit(0);
  glShadeModel(shadeModel = value);
  glutPostRedisplay();
}

int
main(int argc, char **argv)
{
  int leftLightMenu, rightLightMenu, torusMenu, teapotMenu, icoMenu;

  glutInitWindowSize(400, 400);
  glutInit(&argc, argv);
  glutInitDisplayMode(GLUT_DOUBLE | GLUT_RGB | GLUT_DEPTH);
  glutCreateWindow("Lighting Laboratory");
  glutDisplayFunc(display);

#define LIGHT_MENU_ENTRIES() \
    glutAddMenuEntry("Disable", LIGHT_OFF); \
    glutAddMenuEntry("Red", LIGHT_RED); \
    glutAddMenuEntry("White", LIGHT_WHITE); \
    glutAddMenuEntry("Green", LIGHT_GREEN);
#define MATERIAL_MENU_ENTRIES() \
    glutAddMenuEntry("Brass", BRASS); \
    glutAddMenuEntry("Red plastic", RED_PLASTIC);\
    glutAddMenuEntry("Emerald", EMERALD); \
    glutAddMenuEntry("Slate", SLATE);

  leftLightMenu = glutCreateMenu(leftLightSelect);
  LIGHT_MENU_ENTRIES();
  rightLightMenu = glutCreateMenu(rightLightSelect);
  LIGHT_MENU_ENTRIES();
  torusMenu = glutCreateMenu(torusSelect);
  MATERIAL_MENU_ENTRIES();
  teapotMenu = glutCreateMenu(teapotSelect);
  MATERIAL_MENU_ENTRIES();
  icoMenu = glutCreateMenu(icoSelect);
  MATERIAL_MENU_ENTRIES();

  glutCreateMenu(mainMenuSelect);
  glutAddMenuEntry("Smooth shading", GL_SMOOTH);
```

```
glutAddMenuEntry("Flat shading", GL_FLAT);
glutAddSubMenu("Left light", leftLightMenu);
glutAddSubMenu("Right light", rightLightMenu);
glutAddSubMenu("Torus", torusMenu);
glutAddSubMenu("Teapot", teapotMenu);
glutAddSubMenu("Icosahedron", icoMenu);
glutAddMenuEntry("Quit", 666);
glutAttachMenu(GLUT_RIGHT_BUTTON);
glLightfv(GL_LIGHT0, GL_POSITION, leftLightPosition);
glLightfv(GL_LIGHT0, GL_SPECULAR, whiteLight);
glLightfv(GL_LIGHT1, GL_POSITION, rightLightPosition);
glLightfv(GL_LIGHT1, GL_SPECULAR, whiteLight);
leftLightSelect(LIGHT_RED);
rightLightSelect(LIGHT_GREEN);
torusSelect(RED_PLASTIC);
teapotSelect(BRASS);
icoSelect(EMERALD);
glEnable(GL_LIGHTING);
glEnable(GL_DEPTH_TEST);
glEnable(GL_NORMALIZE);
glLineWidth(1.0);
glMatrixMode(GL_PROJECTION);
gluPerspective( /* degrees field of view */ 50.0,
  /* aspect ratio */ 1.0, /* Z near */ 1.0, /* Z far */ 10.0);
glMatrixMode(GL_MODELVIEW);
gluLookAt(0.0, 0.0, 5.0, /* eye is at (0,0,5) */
  0.0, 0.0, 0.0, /* center is at (0,0,0) */
  0.0, 1.0, 0.); /* up is in positive Y direction */
glTranslatef(0.0, 0.0, -1.0);

glutMainLoop();
return 0; /* ANSI C requires main to return int. */
}
```

5.2 EXPLORING OPENGL TEXTURE MAPPING WITH GLUT

Texture mapping (often called simply texturing) is the process of applying an image to the surface of a geometric primitive. In the real world, most surfaces are not just shaded or a single color. For example, a wooden table has a wood-grain pattern across its surface. If a computer were to render such a table, attempting to render the intricate wood-grain surface using simple triangles and rectangles, it would likely be too slow. Instead, we can use a 2D image of a wood-grain pattern and *texture* the

Figure 5.5 Cow model texture mapped with a red brick texture.

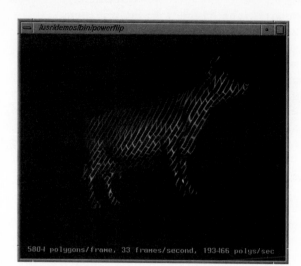

image onto the model of the table. You can think of a texture as a form of "wallpaper" for rendered 3D polygons.

OpenGL is very careful to apply textures in such a way that even if a textured polygon is rotated, translated, scaled, or even projected, the texture is rendered appropriately.

Texturing can make the difference between a realistic scene and one that is flat and obviously computer-generated. If you look at the world around you, most surfaces can be thought of as having some texture. For example, a brick wall, the label on a can of soup, and a reflection in a mirror can all be rendered using textures.

Texture mapping is useful for more purposes than simply adding a surface image to rendered polygons. Texturing can also greatly reduce the geometric complexity of a scene. Imagine a tree in the distance. Rendering such a tree with all its leaves and limbs could take a long time. Instead, you could render a single rectangle and texture the image of a tree onto it. Or a flight simulator could render forest-covered ground by texturing the aerial image of a forest onto a few polygons representing the ground. Figures 5.5, 5.8, and 5.9 show examples of the use of texture mapping.

5.2.1 Using Textures with OpenGL

Textured objects are rendered with the same OpenGL routines used to render geometric primitives. Additional OpenGL calls specify a texture image and how the texture is applied to the geometry you render. The procedure for using texture mapping can be broken up into four steps:

1. Enabling texture mapping.
2. Specifying the texture image.
3. Specifying how the texture is to be applied to the surface.
4. Rendering the primitives, supplying both geometric coordinates *and* texture coordinates.

5.2.1.1 Enabling Texturing

Like other OpenGL capabilities, texturing is enabled and disabled using the `glEnable` and `glDisable` calls. Texturing is initially disabled when an OpenGL rendering context is created. The following call enables texturing:

```
glEnable(GL_TEXTURE_2D);
```

Because not everything in your scene may require texturing (and textured primitives typically render more slowly than nontextured primitives), disable texturing when it is not needed.

5.2.1.2 Specifying a Texture

The simplest texture is defined by a single 2D image (1D and even 3D textures are also possible). The routine `glTexImage2D` specifies a 2D image texture. The parameters for `glTexImage2D` are an array of pixel values for the texture itself, along with the texture's height, width, type, format, internal resolution, border width, and level-of-detail. The width and height of a texture must be some (possibly different) power of 2.

Where do the texture images themselves come from? They can be programmatically generated, but it is more likely that they are generated with a paint program, a scanner, or a digital camera. The texture of a face used in this section's example program (see Figure 5.8) was generated with a Silicon Graphics Indy workstation's standard digital video camera.

The individual cells that make up a texture image are called *texels* (texture elements). OpenGL's texture mapping functionality is supported only for the RGBA color model and not for the color index model.

Because polygons can be arbitrarily scaled, the final size of a textured polygon on the screen may vary. To avoid the visual artifacts of undersampling a texture to fit a small polygon in window coordinates (relative to the texture size), OpenGL supports a technique called *mipmapping* that allows several versions of the texture image at smaller sizes to be used. Figure 5.6 shows how mipmaps are organized as a set of prefiltered textures at diminishing resolutions. Without mipmapping, small textured objects might shimmer and flash as they move. When mipmap filtering is used, OpenGL automatically chooses or interpolates the right level-of-detail from

Figure 5.6 Multiple levels of detail for a texture using mipmaps.

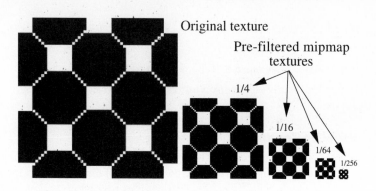

the set of available mipmaps. The GLU utility routine `gluBuild2DMipmaps` can assist you in building correctly filtered mipmaps.

There are a large number of texture image formats and types. A texture image is loaded through OpenGL's pixel path. Configuring the pixel path's operation is discussed in Section 5.4. Further information about constructing textures using `glTexImage2D` and `gluBuild2DMipmaps` is given in the *OpenGL Programming Guide* [28] and in the OpenGL manual pages for these routines.

5.2.1.3 Specifying Texture Modes

Once a texture is specified, OpenGL also needs to be informed as to how you want the texture to be applied to each pixel. OpenGL provides a number of texture filtering methods and texture modes to control the way geometric primitives are textured.

OpenGL's texture mode determines how the texture values are combined with the primitive's color values (those generated by lighting calculations or by explicit vertex color assignment) when you are generating textured fragments. Fragments are generated during the rasterization of an OpenGL primitive. A fragment is the bundle of information necessary to update a specific pixel location in the frame buffer. In particular, it determines how the color of a pixel is updated. The *texture environment* determines how texture values affect the color of a fragment. The texture environment can be one of the following:

GL_DECAL The color of a textured fragment in decal mode is determined directly by the texture's color components. The texture values override the color values for the fragment. Specify decal mode with the following call:

```
glTexEnvi(GL_TEXTURE_ENV,
    GL_TEXTURE_ENV_MODE, GL_DECAL);
```

GL_MODULATE The color of a textured fragment in modulate mode is a combination of the texture color and the color values generated by lighting calculations or explicit vertex color assignment. Using the modulate mode allows texturing to interact with colors determined by OpenGL's lighting model.

```
glTexEnvi(GL_TEXTURE_ENV,
    GL_TEXTURE_ENV_MODE, GL_MODULATE);
```

GL_BLEND Blend mode is useful for a texture that represents luminance (brightness). The color of a textured pixel in blend mode is a combination of the color values generated by lighting calculations or explicit vertex color assignment blended with a *texture environment color*, with the blending factor based on the texture's luminance values.

```
glTexEnvi(GL_TEXTURE_ENV,
    GL_TEXTURE_ENV_MODE, GL_MODULATE);
glTexEnvfv(GL_TEXTURE_ENV,
    GL_TEXTURE_ENV_COLOR, &rgba_vector);
```

Typically, if you use an RGB texture, you should use the modulate mode if you want texture and lighting to interact. Otherwise, use the decal mode. The default texture mode is GL_MODULATE.

OpenGL also allows control over the filtering algorithms used to determine texture values. When the rendered primitive in screen space is smaller than the actual texture, a *minification* filter determines how and which texels determine the texture color for a fragment. For example, the GL_NEAREST filter chooses the texel in texture coordinates nearest the center of the pixel, ignoring mipmaps. GL_LINEAR performs a weighted sum of the four texels nearest in texture coordinates to the center of the pixel, ignoring mipmaps. More sophisticated and computationally expensive filtering methods use mipmaps. For example, GL_NEAREST_MIPMAP_LINEAR (the default minification filter) samples the nearest texel in each of the two nearest mipmap images, then uses a weighted sum of the two samples. The most expensive, but highest-quality, mode is GL_LINEAR_MIPMAP_LINEAR.

Filtering may also be necessary when the rendered primitive is larger in screen space than the texture. The texture *magnification* filter controls this case. Mipmapping works only for minification, so the only magnification filtering options are GL_NEAREST and GL_LINEAR (the default).

Better texture filtering can avoid some of the visual artifacts associated with animated texture-mapped scenes. A poor filter may allow the texture to "swim" or jitter, particularly when a textured object is moving slowly. Better filtering is traded off against texture-rendering performance.

5.2.1.4 Rendering Textured Primitives

Once a texture and the necessary texturing parameters are specified, rendering of textured primitives can begin. In addition to object coordinates generated by the `glVertex3f` family of routines, a textured primitive requires that per-vertex *texture coordinates* be specified. Texture coordinates determine which location within the texture map is assigned to each vertex. The complete texture is mapped onto the surface of the primitive by interpolating the texture coordinates between vertices. Figure 5.7 shows how texture coordinates map texture information to the surface of a polygon.

Texture coordinates are explicitly assigned with the `glTexCoord2f` family of routines. Usually, texture coordinate values range between 0.0 and 1.0. The following is an example of generating texture coordinates for a triangle.

```
glBegin(GL_TRIANGLES);
  glTexCoord2f(0.1, 0.2); glVertex3f(0, 1, 3);
  glTexCoord2f(0.2, 0.7); glVertex3f(2, 9, 2);
  glTexCoord2f(0.8, 0.5); glVertex3f(7, 6, 8);
glEnd():
```

Texels for texture coordinates falling outside the range 0 to 1 can either be clamped to 0 or 1 or *repeated* by using only the fractional components of the texture coordi-

Figure 5.7 Texture coordinates determine how texels in the texture are mapped to the surface of a triangle in object coordinates.

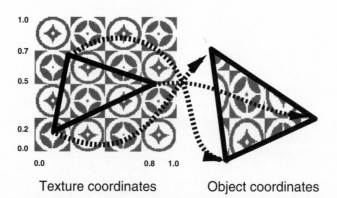

Texture coordinates   Object coordinates

nates. The texture for a brick pattern can probably be repeated; the texture for a billboard should be clamped.

5.2.1.5 More Texturing Features

OpenGL texturing also supports a number of features beyond the scope of this book, but these features are worth mentioning briefly. OpenGL supports the automatic generation of texture coordinates based on the object coordinates of vertices. This saves you the overhead of specifying texture coordinates when the texture coordinates can be generated based on the object coordinates. Like modeling coordinates, texture coordinates can be transformed by a *texture matrix* before use. As mentioned previously, OpenGL supports 1D textures. One-dimensional textures are useful for scientific visualization, where the 1D texture coordinate might be used to represent, for example, temperature over the surface of an object. Proposed extensions to OpenGL also permit 3D textures, which are useful for volumetric rendering of information such as 3D seismic and medical imaging data (see page 254).

If you switch textures repeatedly, it is useful to make a display list for each texture you use frequently. This allows OpenGL to avoid copying the texture and other overhead every time `glTexImage2D` is executed. This is particularly useful when OpenGL direct rendering is not available.

5.2.2 Fun with Textures

The `mjkwarp` example program listed at the end of this section demonstrates using texture mapping to rotate, contort, and shatter a 2D image, all while the image spins. The effects are reminiscent of MTV video effects. The point of including these effects is to demonstrate a few of the possibilities of texture mapping. Figure 5.8 shows `mjkwarp` in its various texturing modes:

Elastic sheet.   The scene is a 12-by-12 grid of squares with a portion of a face textured to each square in the grid. The local *x* and *y* vertex components of each square are fixed while the local *z* component varies sinusoidally over time, with the amplitude higher near the center of the grid.

The result is a spinning image that appears to stretch inward and outward as if the image were affixed to a pulsating elastic sheet of rubber.

If "patches" of a texture are rendered onto smaller polygons composing a smooth surface, textures can appear to deform smoothly over a complex surface.

Spinning cube.   A simpler texturing effect; a face is textured onto four sides of a spinning cube. The texture is correctly rendered in perspective even when a cube side is rotated almost out of view.

The distance from the cube to the viewer also varies sinusoidally with time, so the size of the textured image on the screen varies. Mipmapping avoids undersampling artifacts when the cube's size in the window is small.

Figure 5.8 Various modes of `mjkwarp`. Texturing techniques can be used to rotate, contort, and shatter an image.

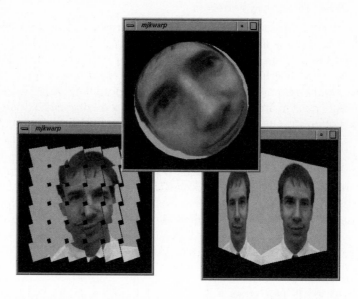

Rotating squares.   The scene is a 6-by-6 grid of squares, each with a portion of a face. Each square is separately rotated around its center. The result is an image that appears to shatter into a confused pattern of squares, only to rotate back again to the recognizable image of a face.

Along with demonstrating texturing effects, `mjkwarp` allows the minification filtering method to be changed via pop-up menus. Because using a higher-quality filtering method is computationally more expensive, better filtering methods are likely to slow the rendering rate of textured geometry.

The speed of texture mapping can vary greatly among OpenGL implementations. Workstations with hardware texturing support achieve much better texturing performance than workstations with no hardware texturing support. Without texturing hardware, texturing calculations (which are expensive because they must be done for each pixel) must be implemented in software. For this reason, `mjkwarp` permits the user to select an appropriate animation rate. The animation advances in real time with frames calculated no faster than the animation rate via pop-up menus. Without this support, `mjkwarp` can vary wildly in its frame rate as the texturing overhead of the scene varies.

Figure 5.9 Formula 1 racing simulation making extensive use of texture mapping, including texture-mapped trees.

mjkwarp is a fairly simple example of using texture mapping. The example uses no lighting effects. For this reason, the GL_DECAL texture mode is used. Also, only a single texture is used. The actual data for the 256-by-256 pixel RGB image used for mjkwarp's texture is declared externally and is contained in an mjkimage.c source file (not listed here, since it is merely a large encoded image).

5.2.3 More on Texture Mapping

Texture mapping is a versatile rendering technique [17]. It is likely that you will hear the term more and more frequently because of the sophistication and realism texturing adds to 3D graphics. For example, texture mapping is becoming quite common in the latest crop of 3D video games. But the utility of texture mapping is hardly limited to video games and visual simulation applications. Texture mapping also has applications in scientific and technical visualization [42] as well as in image processing [26]. Those interested in a more detailed technical explanation of texture mapping, can consult Paul Heckbert's survey of the topic [19].

5.2.4 Example: mjkwarp.c

```
#include <stdio.h>
#include <stdlib.h>
#include <string.h>
#include <math.h> /* for cos(), sin(), and sqrt() */
#include <GL/glut.h>
```

```
/* External texture image array found in mjkimage.c */
extern unsigned char mjk_image[];
extern int mjk_depth, mjk_height, mjk_width; /* 3, 256, 256 */

float tick1 = 0, tick2 = 0, angle, size;
int set_timeout = 0, interval = 100, minify_menu, rate_menu;
#define CUBE 1
#define SQUARES 2
#define DRUM 3
int mode = SQUARES, spinning = 1, scaling = 1, visible = 0;

void
animate(int value)
{
  if (visible) {
    if (spinning || scaling)
      if (value) {
        if (spinning) {
          tick1 += 4 * (interval / 100.0);
          angle = ((int) tick1) % 360;
        }
        if (scaling) {
          tick2 += 2 * (interval / 100.0);
          size = .7 - .5 * sin(tick2 / 20.0);
        }
      }
  }
  glutPostRedisplay();
  set_timeout = 1;
}

void
redraw(void)
{
  int begin, end, elapsed;
  int i, j;
  float amplitude;

  if (set_timeout)
    begin = glutGet(GLUT_ELAPSED_TIME);
  glClear(GL_COLOR_BUFFER_BIT | GL_DEPTH_BUFFER_BIT);
  glPushMatrix();
  if (mode != DRUM)
    glScalef(size, size, size);
```

```
  switch (mode) {

#define SQ_COLS 6
#define SQ_TILE_TEX_W (1.0/SQ_COLS)
#define SQ_ROWS 6
#define SQ_TILE_TEX_H (1.0/SQ_ROWS)
  case SQUARES:
    glTranslatef(-SQ_COLS / 2.0 + .5, -SQ_ROWS / 2.0 + .5, 0);
    for (i = 0; i < SQ_COLS; i++)
      for (j = 0; j < SQ_ROWS; j++) {
        glPushMatrix();
          glTranslatef(i, j, 0);
          glRotatef(angle, 0, 1, 1);
          glBegin(GL_QUADS);
            glTexCoord2f(i * SQ_TILE_TEX_W, j * SQ_TILE_TEX_H);
            glVertex2f(-.5, -.5);
            glTexCoord2f((i + 1) * SQ_TILE_TEX_W, j * SQ_TILE_TEX_H);
            glVertex2f(.5, -.5);
            glTexCoord2f((i + 1) * SQ_TILE_TEX_W, (j + 1) *
                SQ_TILE_TEX_H);
            glVertex2f(.5, .5);
            glTexCoord2f(i * SQ_TILE_TEX_W, (j + 1) * SQ_TILE_TEX_H);
            glVertex2f(-.5, .5);
          glEnd();
        glPopMatrix();
      }
    break;

#define DR_COLS 12
#define DR_TILE_TEX_W (1.0/DR_COLS)
#define DR_ROWS 12
#define DR_TILE_TEX_H (1.0/DR_ROWS)
#define Z(x,y) (((DR_COLS-(x))*(x) + (DR_ROWS-(y))*(y)) \
    * amplitude) - 28.0
  case DRUM:
    glRotatef(angle, 0, 0, 1);
    glTranslatef(-DR_COLS / 2.0 + .5, -DR_ROWS / 2.0 + .5, 0);
    amplitude = 0.4 * sin(tick2 / 6.0);
    for (i = 0; i < DR_COLS; i++)
      for (j = 0; j < DR_ROWS; j++) {
        glPushMatrix();
          glTranslatef(i, j, 0);
          glBegin(GL_QUADS);
            glTexCoord2f(i * DR_TILE_TEX_W, j * DR_TILE_TEX_H);
```

```
            glVertex3f(-.5, -.5, Z(i, j));
            glTexCoord2f((i + 1) * DR_TILE_TEX_W, j * DR_TILE_TEX_H);
            glVertex3f(.5, -.5, Z(i + 1, j));
            glTexCoord2f((i + 1) * DR_TILE_TEX_W, (j + 1)
                * DR_TILE_TEX_H);
            glVertex3f(.5, .5, Z(i + 1, j + 1));
            glTexCoord2f(i * DR_TILE_TEX_W, (j + 1) * DR_TILE_TEX_H);
            glVertex3f(-.5, .5, Z(i, j + 1));
          glEnd();
        glPopMatrix();
      }
    break;
  case CUBE:
    glRotatef(angle, 0, 1, 0);
    glBegin(GL_QUADS);
      /* Front. */
      glTexCoord2f(0.0, 0.0);
      glVertex3f(-1.0, -1.0, 1.0);
      glTexCoord2f(1.0, 0.0);
      glVertex3f(1.0, -1.0, 1.0);
      glTexCoord2f(1.0, 1.0);
      glVertex3f(1.0, 1.0, 1.0);
      glTexCoord2f(0.0, 1.0);
      glVertex3f(-1.0, 1.0, 1.0);
      /* Back. */
      glTexCoord2f(0.0, 1.0);
      glVertex3f(-1.0, 1.0, -1.0);
      glTexCoord2f(1.0, 1.0);
      glVertex3f(1.0, 1.0, -1.0);
      glTexCoord2f(1.0, 0.0);
      glVertex3f(1.0, -1.0, -1.0);
      glTexCoord2f(0.0, 0.0);
      glVertex3f(-1.0, -1.0, -1.0);
      /* Left. */
      glTexCoord2f(0.0, 0.0);
      glVertex3f(-1.0, -1.0, -1.0);
      glTexCoord2f(1.0, 0.0);
      glVertex3f(-1.0, -1.0, 1.0);
      glTexCoord2f(1.0, 1.0);
      glVertex3f(-1.0, 1.0, 1.0);
      glTexCoord2f(0.0, 1.0);
      glVertex3f(-1.0, 1.0, -1.0);
      /* Right. */
```

```
      glTexCoord2f(0.0, 1.0);
      glVertex3f(1.0, 1.0, -1.0);
      glTexCoord2f(1.0, 1.0);
      glVertex3f(1.0, 1.0, 1.0);
      glTexCoord2f(1.0, 0.0);
      glVertex3f(1.0, -1.0, 1.0);
      glTexCoord2f(0.0, 0.0);
      glVertex3f(1.0, -1.0, -1.0);
    glEnd();
  }
  glPopMatrix();
  glutSwapBuffers();
  if (set_timeout) {
    set_timeout = 0;
    end = glutGet(GLUT_ELAPSED_TIME);
    elapsed = end - begin;
    if(elapsed > interval)
      glutTimerFunc(0, animate, 1);
    else
      glutTimerFunc(interval - elapsed, animate, 1);
  }
}


void
visibility(int state)
{
  if (state == GLUT_VISIBLE) {
    visible = 1;
    animate(0);
  } else {
    visible = 0;
  }
}


void
minify_select(int value)
{
  glTexParameterf(GL_TEXTURE_2D, GL_TEXTURE_MIN_FILTER, value);
  gluBuild2DMipmaps(GL_TEXTURE_2D, mjk_depth, mjk_width, mjk_height,
    GL_RGB, GL_UNSIGNED_BYTE, mjk_image);
  glutPostRedisplay();
}
```

```
void
rate_select(int value)
{
  interval = value;
}

void
menu_select(int value)
{
  switch (value) {
  case 1:
    spinning = !spinning;
    if (spinning)
      animate(0);
    break;
  case 2:
    scaling = !scaling;
    if (scaling)
      animate(0);
    break;
  case 3:
    mode++;
    if (mode > DRUM)
      mode = CUBE;
    switch (mode) {
    case CUBE:
      glEnable(GL_CULL_FACE);
      glDisable(GL_DEPTH_TEST);
      break;
    case SQUARES:
      glDisable(GL_CULL_FACE);
      glDisable(GL_DEPTH_TEST);
      break;
    case DRUM:
      glEnable(GL_DEPTH_TEST);
      glDisable(GL_CULL_FACE);
      break;
    }
    glutPostRedisplay();
    break;
  case 666:
    exit(0);
  }
}
```

```
int
main(int argc, char **argv)
{
  glutInit(&argc, argv);
  glutInitDisplayMode(GLUT_RGB | GLUT_DOUBLE | GLUT_DEPTH);
  glutCreateWindow("mjkwarp");
  glutDisplayFunc(redraw);
  glMatrixMode(GL_PROJECTION);
  gluPerspective( /* field of view in degree */ 40.0,
    /* aspect ratio */ 1.0, /* Z near */ 1.0, /* Z far */ 70.0);
  glMatrixMode(GL_MODELVIEW);
  gluLookAt(0.0, 0.0, 5.0, /* eye is at (0,0,30) */
    0.0, 0.0, 0.0, /* center is at (0,0,0) */
    0.0, 1.0, 0.); /* up is in positive Y direction */

  /* Image data packed tightly. */
  glPixelStorei(GL_UNPACK_ALIGNMENT, 1);

  gluBuild2DMipmaps(GL_TEXTURE_2D, mjk_depth, mjk_width, mjk_height,
    GL_RGB, GL_UNSIGNED_BYTE, mjk_image);
  glTexParameterf(GL_TEXTURE_2D, GL_TEXTURE_WRAP_S, GL_CLAMP);
  glTexParameterf(GL_TEXTURE_2D, GL_TEXTURE_WRAP_T, GL_CLAMP);
  glTexParameterf(GL_TEXTURE_2D, GL_TEXTURE_MAG_FILTER, GL_NEAREST);
  glTexParameterf(GL_TEXTURE_2D, GL_TEXTURE_MIN_FILTER, GL_NEAREST);
  glTexEnvi(GL_TEXTURE_ENV, GL_TEXTURE_ENV_MODE, GL_DECAL);
  glEnable(GL_TEXTURE_2D);
  glutVisibilityFunc(visibility);
  minify_menu = glutCreateMenu(minify_select);
  glutAddMenuEntry("Nearest", GL_NEAREST);
  glutAddMenuEntry("Linear", GL_LINEAR);
  glutAddMenuEntry("Nearest mipmap nearest",
      GL_NEAREST_MIPMAP_NEAREST);
  glutAddMenuEntry("Linear mipmap nearest",
      GL_LINEAR_MIPMAP_NEAREST);
  glutAddMenuEntry("Nearest mipmap linear",
      GL_NEAREST_MIPMAP_LINEAR);
  glutAddMenuEntry("Linear mipmap linear",
      GL_LINEAR_MIPMAP_LINEAR);
  rate_menu = glutCreateMenu(rate_select);
  glutAddMenuEntry(" 2/sec", 500);
  glutAddMenuEntry(" 6/sec", 166);
  glutAddMenuEntry("10/sec", 100);
  glutAddMenuEntry("20/sec", 50);
  glutAddMenuEntry("30/sec", 33);
```

```
glutCreateMenu(menu_select);
glutAddMenuEntry("Toggle spinning", 1);
glutAddMenuEntry("Toggle scaling", 2);
glutAddMenuEntry("Switch mode", 3);
glutAddSubMenu("Minimum frame rate", rate_menu);
glutAddSubMenu("Minify modes", minify_menu);
glutAddMenuEntry("Quit", 666);
glutAttachMenu(GLUT_RIGHT_BUTTON);
menu_select(3);
glutMainLoop();
return 0; /* ANSI C requires main to return int. */
}
```

5.3   EXPLORING BLENDING OPERATIONS WITH GLUT

This section uses GLUT in describing OpenGL's blending operations for effects like transparency, antialiasing, and atmospheric effects such as fog. It also explains what *alpha* is in more detail.

Passing references have been made to a color component known as alpha. This section finally addresses the questions: What is alpha? How does one use it?

OpenGL's RGBA (for red, green, blue, and alpha) color model represents colors as four floating-point components clamped to between 0.0 and 1.0. The red, green, and blue components are simple; they measure the intensity of each respective color component. A pixel with R, G, and B each at 1.0 appears white; a pixel with R, G, and B each at 0.0 appears black. Indeed, the red, green, and blue color components readily translate into the RGB color space generated by standard color monitors.

X programmers will likely recognize the R, G, and B as very similar to the core X notion of a TrueColor visual. But in core X, TrueColor visuals have no associated alpha component. So what is the alpha component?

Alpha is not a displayed component like the red, green, and blue components. Instead, alpha is used to control color blending. It is a measure of the opaqueness of the color. An alpha value of 1.0 implies complete opacity; an alpha value of 0.0 implies complete transparency. Normally, most objects are rendered with an alpha of 1.0 because most objects are opaque, but objects such as colored glass or a sheer fabric can be rendered with an alpha component of less than 1.0 to indicate that the material is not completely opaque.

Two examples of situations where alpha could be used are in the rendering of blurred, spinning helicopter rotor blades and the rendering of 3D scientific data where transparency is used to see through otherwise opaque objects.

OpenGL's RGBA color model logically involves alpha throughout the entire OpenGL rendering pipeline. The glColor3f routine is really a specialized version of the more general glColor4f routine, in which the fourth parameter is alpha (`glColor3f` implicitly generates an alpha component of 1.0). Lighting and material parameters involving color all require an alpha component. Textures and images logically contain an alpha component. For image and texture formats without an explicit alpha component, 1.0 is assumed. OpenGL's generalized RGBA lighting equations detail the way alpha and lighting interact. The point is that the alpha component is a first-class component of the OpenGL RGBA color model throughout the OpenGL rendering pipeline.

Note that alpha exists only in the RGBA color model. There is no support for alpha in the OpenGL color index model.

If alpha is a part of every RGBA color, when is alpha used? It is used for blending operations. Alpha blending is a per-pixel operation in which the color value from an incoming OpenGL rendering fragment[1] (the *source*) is combined with the color value of the corresponding currently stored pixel value (the *destination*). When blending is enabled, this combining is based on the source and destination blending factors set using the `glBlendFunc` routine.

Blending is relatively expensive because it can require several multiplications and additions per pixel depending on the blending factors. For this reason, blending is not enabled by default in OpenGL. To use blending, you must enable it:

```
glEnable(GL_BLEND);
```

Every OpenGL implementation supports red, green, and blue components within the frame buffer to support RGB pixels. Some hardware also supports an alpha component within the frame buffer in addition to the RGB components. This is often referred to as *destination alpha*. Supporting destination alpha is not required by OpenGL implementations. While there are a few techniques in which destination alpha is useful, many common blending operations can be supported using only *source alpha*.

OpenGL programs that do not need destination alpha should avoid selecting a visual that has destination alpha. Selecting a visual with destination alpha can hurt performance because alpha values will be written to the frame buffer even when blending is disabled. For GLUT, this means you should not specify the `GLUT_ALPHA` bitmask when setting the *display mode*. For Xlib and Motif, this means you should request a `GLX_ALPHA_SIZE` of 0 (the default) when calling `glXChooseVisual`.

Alpha can also be used to accept or reject fragments based on their alpha values in much the same way as the depth and stencil tests work. OpenGL's `glAlphaFunc` controls the operation of the alpha test and is enabled by calling

```
glEnable(GL_ALPHA_TEST);
```

---

1. For review, a fragment in OpenGL is generated during the rasterization of geometry; each fragment contains the information (color, depth) needed to update the pixel to which the fragment corresponds.

To discard any fragment with an alpha of 0, enable alpha testing and call

```
glAlphaFunc(GL_GREATER, 0.0);
```

5.3.1 Uses for Blending

The discussion so far has explained alpha and blending, but not uses for blending. Blending has been described in general terms. In practice, using blending in an OpenGL application is reasonably straightforward.

The most common blending mode is to use the source alpha value for each component of the source blend factor and to use 1.0 minus the source alpha value for each component of the destination blend factor. This is done by calling

```
glBlendFunc(
  GL_SRC_ALPHA, /* Source blend */
  GL_ONE_MINUS_SRC_ALPHA); /* Destination blend */
```

This blending function combines the source image with the destination based on alpha. For example, if the source alpha value is 0.75, 75% of the source fragment color will be blended with 25% of the destination pixel color to determine the new pixel color.

This section's example program uses this blending function to blend together two rotating icosahedrons. The alpha component used to render each icosahedron varies periodically. The code for `blender.c` can be found at the end of the section. Notice, in Figure 5.10, how the two icosahedrons are blended where they overlap. The effect is a time-varying transparency of the two icosahedrons.

Figure 5.10 Screen snapshot showing `blender` example program. Notice how the red and green icosahedrons are blended.

Another example using alpha blending would be a paint program that supports a painting mode in which the brush color is gradually blended with the canvas color. Using the same blend function as before (GL_SRC_ALPHA for the source blend factor and GL_ONE_MINUS_SRC_ALPHA for the destination blend factor), drawing the brush at 10% alpha would allow brush strokes to gradually blend the brush color with the canvas color. Alpha could even be varied across the brush shape to blend more of the brush color at the brush center (higher alpha) and less at the edges (lower alpha).

OpenGL specifies images and textures as rectangular arrays of pixels. Alpha can also be used to render nonrectangular raster images and textures. By using a pixel format with an alpha component, an alpha of 0 can be used for "invisible" portions of the image or texture. As an example of this technique, textures with alpha permit the rendering of a leafy tree using a single textured rectangle. Though a tree is tree-shaped and not rectangular, a rectangular tree texture image can be constructed with an alpha of 0 where the tree is not present. When the textured rectangle for the tree is rendered with alpha testing enabled to eliminate texels with 0 alpha, only the tree shape is rendered.

Something to be careful about when using blending, particularly in 3D scenes, is that blending operations tend to be order-dependent. This means that the blending is affected by the order in which the primitives in the scene are drawn. Using depth buffering, most 3D scenes can be drawn without much regard to ordering (the depth buffer sorts objects in the scene based on their depth values). However, when you combine blending and depth buffering, you may find that you need to be careful about rendering order within your scene. Techniques do exist to combine depth buffering and blending, but they are beyond the scope of this book. A more involved discussion of blending can be found in Chapter 6, "Blending, Antialiasing, and Fog," in the *OpenGL Programming Guide* [28].

5.3.2 Antialiasing through Blending

The term *aliasing*, in computer graphics, refers to visual artifacts caused by mapping ideal geometry onto a finite array of pixels. The most common example of aliasing is informally called "jaggies." This is when a line or the edge of a polygon appears jagged because the rasterized line or edge is only a set of pixels that approximates an ideal line.

Techniques to reduce the effect of aliasing are known as *antialiasing* techniques. Basic line-drawing techniques make a binary decision about whether a given pixel should be rendered when drawing a line. A more sophisticated line-drawing technique might calculate the line's *coverage* value for each pixel. This coverage value is the fraction of the pixel that the ideal line would cover.

OpenGL can automatically calculate coverage values for points, lines, and polygons. OpenGL can then multiply this coverage value by the alpha value of each fragment generated by the primitive. The resulting alpha value can be used, in conjunction with alpha blending, to antialias the primitive.

Figure 5.11 Magnified view of the `blender` example's text. Notice the jaggies in the lower line.

Figure 5.11 is a magnified view of the example program's text message. The top line is rendered using antialiasing; the lower line is rendered without antialiasing. The text is rotated slightly to make jaggies more evident.

Coverage-based antialiasing is also available in OpenGL's color index mode, but is complicated by the lack of alpha. This discussion of antialiasing is limited to RGBA mode using coverage-based alpha blending.

Antialiasing for lines, points, and polygons is not on by default, but can be enabled using `glEnable` for each type of antialiasing:

```
glEnable(GL_LINE_SMOOTH);
glEnable(GL_POINT_SMOOTH);
glEnable(GL_POLYGON_SMOOTH);
```

To effectively make use of the coverage-multiplied alpha values, you will also need to enable blending like this:

```
glEnable(GL_BLEND)
glBlendFunc(GL_SRC_ALPHA,
            GL_ONE_MINUS_SRC_ALPHA);
```

Be careful when using antialiasing through alpha blending. The warnings about order-dependent rendering when using blending also apply to blending-based antialiasing.

Note that the coverage- and blending-based techniques discussed here are not the only antialiasing techniques. For example, multisampling and accumulation buffer techniques can also be used to reduce aliasing artifacts.

5.3.3 Fog and Atmospheric Effects

Lighting, texturing, and antialiasing can help make computer-generated images appear more realistic. Even so, images can still appear too sharp. In computer-generated images, usually objects in the background are just as sharp as objects in the foreground. We generally expect objects in the distance to have lower contrast than closer objects. In OpenGL, a technique known as *fog* can approximate the atmospheric effects that make distant objects appear less sharp. Fog is a general technique and can be used to simulate atmospheric effects such as smoke, haze, pollution, and mist. Fog is important to visual simulation applications such as flight and battle simulators.

Fog can be thought of as another type of blending, orthogonal to alpha blending. Fog blends a fog color with each rasterized fragment's color. The blending factor is a function of the distance in eye coordinates from the eye-point to the fragment being fogged. In effect, the farther away the fragment, the closer the fragment's color comes to the fog color. So if the fog color is gray, the farther away objects are from the viewer, the more they blend to gray. Figure 5.12 demonstrates the use of fog.

Fog can be useful not just for simulating atmospheric effects, but also as a straightforward hint to the viewer about the distance to an object. Sometimes this technique is called depth cueing; it is often used in wireframe rendering so that lines in the distance are dimmer than closer lines.

Fog is not enabled by default, but can be enabled with `glEnable`. The `glFog` family of routines controls the fog parameters. The following demonstrates enabling fog:

```
GLfloat fogColor[4]={0.5, 0.5, 0.5, 1.0};
glEnable(GL_FOG);
```

Figure 5.12 Screen snapshot showing five teapots growing more distant from left to right. The black background provides high contrast for the white fog color into which the distant teapots fade.

```
glFogi(GL_FOG_MODE, GL_EXP);
glFogfv(GL_FOG_COLOR, fogColor);
glFogf(GL_FOG_DENSITY, 0.35);
```

This sequence enables fog and sets the fog blending factor to decay exponentially with the fogging distance. The fog color is a medium gray. The fog density determines the rate of exponential decay.

The other available fog modes are GL_LINEAR and GL_EXP2. The GL_LINEAR mode is typically used for depth cueing. The GL_EXP2 mode is often used for simulating smoke.

Fog is available in OpenGL's color index mode, but, like coverage-based antialiasing, fog is complicated in color index mode.

5.3.4 Hints

Fog and generating coverage values for antialiasing are relatively expensive and logically per-pixel operations, but optimizations at the expense of quality can be used to speed fog and coverage calculations. OpenGL provides a way to hint to the implementation whether speed or correctness is more important by calling glHint. For example, to obtain the nicest fog result, call

```
glHint(GL_FOG_HINT, GL_NICEST);
```

And to generate coverage values optimized for efficiency, call

```
glHint(GL_POINT_SMOOTH_HINT,
      GL_FASTEST);
glHint(GL_LINE_SMOOTH_HINT,
      GL_FASTEST);
glHint(GL_POLYGON_SMOOTH_HINT,
      GL_FASTEST);
```

Exact interpretation of the hints is implementation-dependent. Implementations can even ignore glHint. In practice, the glHint call provides a way for an application to indicate whether efficiency or correctness is more important. By default, hints are set to GL_DONT_CARE, indicating that the OpenGL application has no preference.

5.3.5 Example: blender.c

```
#include <GL/glut.h>
#include <stdio.h>
#include <math.h>
```

```
GLfloat light0_ambient[] = {0.2, 0.2, 0.2, 1.0};
GLfloat light0_diffuse[] = {0.0, 0.0, 0.0, 1.0};
GLfloat light1_diffuse[] = {1.0, 0.0, 0.0, 1.0};
GLfloat light1_position[] = {1.0, 1.0, 1.0, 0.0};
GLfloat light2_diffuse[] = {0.0, 1.0, 0.0, 1.0};
GLfloat light2_position[] = {-1.0, -1.0, 1.0, 0.0};
float s = 0.0;
GLfloat angle1 = 0.0, angle2 = 0.0;


void
output(GLfloat x, GLfloat y, char *text)
{
  char *p;

  glPushMatrix();
    glTranslatef(x, y, 0);
    for (p = text; *p; p++)
      glutStrokeCharacter(GLUT_STROKE_ROMAN, *p);
  glPopMatrix();
}

void
display(void)
{
  static GLfloat amb[] =
  {0.4, 0.4, 0.4, 0.0};
  static GLfloat dif[] =
  {1.0, 1.0, 1.0, 0.0};

  glClear(GL_COLOR_BUFFER_BIT | GL_DEPTH_BUFFER_BIT);
  glEnable(GL_LIGHT1);
  glDisable(GL_LIGHT2);
  amb[3] = dif[3] = cos(s) / 2.0 + 0.5;
  glMaterialfv(GL_FRONT, GL_AMBIENT, amb);
  glMaterialfv(GL_FRONT, GL_DIFFUSE, dif);

  glPushMatrix();
    glTranslatef(-0.3, -0.3, 0.0);
    glRotatef(angle1, 1.0, 5.0, 0.0);
    glCallList(1); /* Render icosahedron display list. */
  glPopMatrix();

  glClear(GL_DEPTH_BUFFER_BIT);
```

```
    glEnable(GL_LIGHT2);
    glDisable(GL_LIGHT1);
    amb[3] = dif[3] = 0.5 - cos(s * .95) / 2.0;
    glMaterialfv(GL_FRONT, GL_AMBIENT, amb);
    glMaterialfv(GL_FRONT, GL_DIFFUSE, dif);
    glPushMatrix();
      glTranslatef(0.3, 0.3, 0.0);
      glRotatef(angle2, 1.0, 0.0, 5.0);
      glCallList(1); /* Render icosahedron display list. */
    glPopMatrix();

    glPushAttrib(GL_ENABLE_BIT);
      glDisable(GL_DEPTH_TEST);
      glDisable(GL_LIGHTING);
      glMatrixMode(GL_PROJECTION);
      glPushMatrix();
        glLoadIdentity();
        gluOrtho2D(0, 1500, 0, 1500);
        glMatrixMode(GL_MODELVIEW);
        glPushMatrix();
          glLoadIdentity();
          /* Rotate text slightly to help show jaggies. */
          glRotatef(4, 0.0, 0.0, 1.0);
          output(200, 225, "This is antialiased.");
          glDisable(GL_LINE_SMOOTH);
          glDisable(GL_BLEND);
          output(160, 100, "This text is not.");
        glPopMatrix();
        glMatrixMode(GL_PROJECTION);
      glPopMatrix();
    glPopAttrib();
    glMatrixMode(GL_MODELVIEW);
    glutSwapBuffers();
}

void
idle(void)
{
  angle1 = fmodf(angle1 + 0.8, 360.0);
  angle2 = fmodf(angle2 + 1.1, 360.0);
  s += 0.05;
  glutPostRedisplay();
}
```

```
void
visible(int vis)
{
  if (vis == GLUT_VISIBLE)
    glutIdleFunc(idle);
  else
    glutIdleFunc(NULL);
}


int
main(int argc, char ** argv)
{
  glutInit(&argc, argv);
  glutInitDisplayMode(GLUT_DOUBLE | GLUT_RGB | GLUT_DEPTH);
  glutCreateWindow("blender");
  glutDisplayFunc(display);
  glutVisibilityFunc(visible);

  glNewList(1, GL_COMPILE); /* Create ico display list. */
  glutSolidIcosahedron();
  glEndList();

  glEnable(GL_LIGHTING);
  glEnable(GL_LIGHT0);
  glLightfv(GL_LIGHT0, GL_AMBIENT, light0_ambient);
  glLightfv(GL_LIGHT0, GL_DIFFUSE, light0_diffuse);
  glLightfv(GL_LIGHT1, GL_DIFFUSE, light1_diffuse);
  glLightfv(GL_LIGHT1, GL_POSITION, light1_position);
  glLightfv(GL_LIGHT2, GL_DIFFUSE, light2_diffuse);
  glLightfv(GL_LIGHT2, GL_POSITION, light2_position);
  glEnable(GL_DEPTH_TEST);
  glEnable(GL_CULL_FACE);
  glEnable(GL_BLEND);
  glBlendFunc(GL_SRC_ALPHA, GL_ONE_MINUS_SRC_ALPHA);
  glEnable(GL_LINE_SMOOTH);
  glLineWidth(2.0);

  glMatrixMode(GL_PROJECTION);
  gluPerspective(
    40.0,     /* Field of view in degree */
    1.0,      /* Aspect ratio */
    1.0,      /* Z near */
    10.0);    /* Z far */
```

```
glMatrixMode(GL_MODELVIEW);
gluLookAt(
  0.0, 0.0, 5.0,    /* Eye is at (0,0,5) */
  0.0, 0.0, 0.0,    /* Center is at (0,0,0) */
  0.0, 1.0, 0.);    /* Up is in positive Y direction */
glTranslatef(0.0, 0.6, -1.0);

glutMainLoop();
return 0; /* ANSI C requires main to return int. */
}
```

5.4 Exploring Images and Bitmaps with GLUT

So far, OpenGL has been used for rendering 3D scenes described with "geometry"; that is, vertices describing lines, points, and polygons. OpenGL also provides accelerated image and bitmap rendering. This section describes the facilities OpenGL provides for rendering images and bitmaps.

OpenGL's imaging capabilities are fairly rich. OpenGL can draw, read, and copy pixel data. When pixel data is transferred, the data can be altered using color lookup tables and linear transformation of color values. Pixels can be converted between different formats (for example, luminance data can be expanded into RGB data) and all of OpenGL's fragment operations can be performed: blending, masking, and clipping. OpenGL is also very flexible about how pixel data is extracted from and placed into host memory.

5.4.1 The Pixel Path

The flow of pixel data through OpenGL is referred to as OpenGL's *pixel path* or *pixel pipeline*. Either term gives the correct impression that pixel data "flows" from a source to a destination, with the possibility of applying a set of pixel conversions and transformations to the data as it is transferred. For now, consider the source to be an image residing in host memory, using the frame buffer as the destination.

OpenGL's glDrawPixels command transfers an image in host memory to the frame buffer. Here is the prototype for glDrawPixels:

```
void glDrawPixels(GLsizei width, GLsizei height,
  GLenum format, GLenum type, const GLvoid *pixels);
```

When called, glDrawPixels will draw a block of pixels of size width by height to the frame buffer. The pixel data to be transferred is read from pixels as a sequence of bytes, integers, or floating-point values, depending on the type parameter. The way the pixel data is interpreted is determined by the format parameter. For example, the data format could be RGB values, luminance values, color indexes, or depth values. The pixels parameter specifies where the pixel data is located within the program's address space.

Here is an example use of glDrawPixels:

```
glDrawPixels(100, 100, GL_RGB, GL_UNSIGNED_BYTE, data);
```

This call draws a 100-by-100 pixel image located at data to the frame buffer. The pixels in memory are formatted as a sequence of unsigned bytes, one byte for each red, green, and blue color component. This call does not specify how the image data is packed in memory, how the data should be converted and transformed as it flows through the pixel path, or at what location within the frame buffer the image should be placed. Other routines, described below, configure OpenGL state that determines these modes.

This section's example program, called splatlogo, uses glDrawPixels to draw varying OpenGL logo images. The source code for splatlogo.c is given at the end of this section. The user places a logo by clicking the left mouse button. The right mouse button activates a menu letting the user change pixel path parameters. Figure 5.13 shows splatlogo with its pop-up menu active.

5.4.1.1 Unpacking and Converting Pixels

OpenGL gives programs a fair degree of flexibility about the way image data is arranged in host memory. The glPixelStoref and glPixelStorei routines configure

Figure 5.13 splatlogo example with menu displayed.

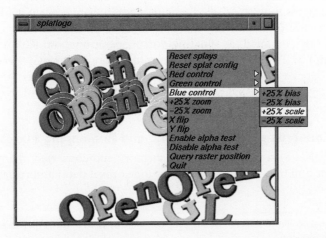

OpenGL's pixel storage modes, which determine how images are "unpacked" from memory. Based on the unpack pixel storage modes, `glDrawPixels` converts "raw" bytes in memory to pixels for transfer to their destinations. Here is an example of configuring OpenGL's unpack pixel storage modes:

```
glPixelStorei(GL_UNPACK_SWAP_BYTES, GL_FALSE);
glPixelStorei(GL_UNPACK_ROW_LENGTH, 0);
glPixelStorei(GL_UNPACK_SKIP_ROWS, 0);
glPixelStorei(GL_UNPACK_SKIP_PIXELS, 0);
glPixelStorei(GL_UNPACK_ALIGNMENT, 1);
```

The `GL_UNPACK_SWAP_BYTES` mode controls the byte order of the image data. Usually, this mode should be false unless you are transferring multibyte data generated on a computer with a different byte order. The `GL_UNPACK_ROW_LENGTH` mode determines the number of pixels within each row of the image. You can also think of this as the pixel *stride* of your image data. Specifying a row length of 0 means the *width parameter of* `glDrawPixels` will be used for the pixel stride. The `GL_UNPACK_SKIP_ROWS` and `GL_UNPACK_SKIP_PIXELS` modes provide a way to offset by the specified number of rows and pixels into the image.[2] The `GL_UNPACK_ALIGNMENT` mode specifies the alignment requirements for the start of each pixel row in memory. Allowed values are 1, 2, 4, and 8. For example, an alignment of 4 (the default) indicates that each row begins at a memory address that is a multiple of 4. Figure 5.14 shows how these modes and the parameters for `glDraw-Pixels` define the way an image will be unpacked from host memory.

Once the pixels are unpacked, OpenGL will convert the data as necessary. Each possible pixel format represents either *component* or *index* values. RGB and depth values are examples of component values; stencil values and color indexes are index values. Formats that describe colors need to be expanded to RGBA form. For example, if the format is luminance, the luminance component value would be expanded as red, green, and blue with alpha set to 1. Later pixel processing operations on components are specified as floating-point operations on RGBA components between 0 and 1. To implement these transformations, OpenGL needs to convert component data to floating-point representations. Keep in mind that the conversions and transformations being specified are generally optimized by real OpenGL implementations to avoid trivial conversions and transformations.

5.4.1.2 Converting, Scaling, Biasing, and Remapping Pixels

Once the pixels are unpacked from host memory and converted, there is an opportunity to scale and bias (shift and offset for index pixel data) and remap the data via

---

2. The same effect could be achieved by adjusting the pointer passed to `glDrawPixels`; these modes exist for convenience.

lookup tables. Scaling color components gives you the opportunity to multiply the red, green, blue, and alpha components of each color pixel by scaling factors. Biasing color components lets you add a bias amount to each component. For example, if you wanted to reduce the blue component in an image being transferred and amplify the red component of the image, you could do the following:

```
glPixelTransferf(GL_BLUE_BIAS, -0.1);
glPixelTransferf(GL_RED_SCALE, 1.3);
```

This will subtract 0.1 from the blue component of each pixel transferred and multiply the red component of each pixel by 1.3. If the bias is 0.0 and the scale is 1.0 for each component (the default), pixel data is effectively passed through unchanged.

The pixel map facility lets color components, color indices, and stencil values be remapped using lookup tables defined by the `glPixelMap*` family of routines. There are 10 different maps, as shown in Table 5.1. Here is an example showing how to use RGBA pixel transfer maps to zero any components less than 0.5:

```
GLfloat map[32];

/* Construct the bottom half of the map. */
for(i = 0; i<16; i++)
  map[i] = 0.0;
```

Figure 5.14 How an image will be unpacked from host memory by `glDrawPixels`.

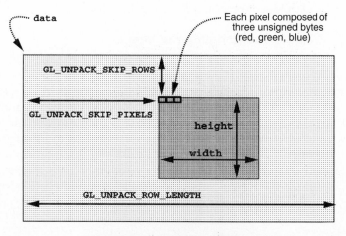

```
glDrawPixels(width, height,
    GL_RGB, GL_UNSIGNED_BYTE, data);
```

Table 5.1 OpenGL's various pixel transfer maps

Map Name	Map Function
GL_PIXEL_MAP_I_TO_I	Maps color indices to color indices
GL_PIXEL_MAP_S_TO_S	Maps stencil indices to stencil indices.
GL_PIXEL_MAP_I_TO_R	Maps color indices to red components.
GL_PIXEL_MAP_I_TO_G	Maps color indices to green components.
GL_PIXEL_MAP_I_TO_B	Maps color indices to blue components.
GL_PIXEL_MAP_I_TO_A	Maps color indices to alpha components.
GL_PIXEL_MAP_R_TO_R	Maps red components to red components.
GL_PIXEL_MAP_G_TO_G	Maps green components to green components.
GL_PIXEL_MAP_B_TO_B	Maps blue components to blue components.
GL_PIXEL_MAP_A_TO_A	Maps alpha components to alpha components.

```
/* Construct the top half of the map. */
for(i = 16; i<32; i++)
  map[i] = 1/32.0 * i;
glPixelTransferi(GL_MAP_COLOR, GL_FALSE);
glPixelMapfv(GL_PIXEL_MAP_R_TO_R, 32, map);
glPixelMapfv(GL_PIXEL_MAP_G_TO_G, 32, map);
glPixelMapfv(GL_PIXEL_MAP_B_TO_B, 32, map);
glPixelMapfv(GL_PIXEL_MAP_A_TO_A, 32, map);
```

Each component will be sampled to one of 32 values. Values of less than 16 will be mapped to 0; values of 16 or greater will be mapped back to the original value (though perhaps with loss of precision due to quantizing the components).

5.4.1.3 Positioning and Zooming the Image

Once all the pixel values have been converted and transformed, the image can be rasterized. The location in the frame buffer where glDrawPixels should draw its pixels is determined by OpenGL's *current raster position*, which is set with the glRasterPos3f family of routines. The coordinates of the raster position are specified in modeling coordinates (like vertices). OpenGL transforms the raster position into window coordinates just as if the location was supplied to glVertex3f. Once transformed, the raster position either defines a valid pixel location within the frame buffer for drawing images *or* an invalid raster position because the raster position coordinate lies outside the current viewing volume. An invalid raster position means no image can be drawn. Here is an example of setting the current raster position:

```
glRasterPos2f(10.0, 10.0);
```

The advantage of this approach is that images can be positioned in the same way that geometry is positioned. Unfortunately, it can also be very frustrating when your image is clipped because the raster position you specified is invalid. You can query if the current raster position's location is valid and query its transformed location by calling

```
GLfloat rpos[4];
GLboolean valid;

glGetFloatv(GL_CURRENT_RASTER_POSITION, rpos);
glGetBooleanv(GL_CURRENT_RASTER_POSITION_VALID, &valid);
printf("Raster position (%g,%g,%g,%g) is %s\n",
  rpos[0], rpos[1], rpos[2], rpos[3],
  valid ? "valid" : "INVALID");
```

Keep in mind that the image rendered by `glDrawPixels` has its origin in the lower left-hand corner of the image, rather than in the upper left-hand corner as in X's `XPutImage` rendering routine.

OpenGL lets you scale the image you are rendering in both the x and y directions with `glPixelZoom`, prototyped as

```
void glPixelZoom(GLfloat xfactor, GLfloat yfactor);
```

The default *xfactor* and *yfactor* values are 1.0 and 1.0, meaning that the image is not rescaled. Larger magnitudes of *xfactor* and *yfactor* will expand the image; smaller magnitudes will shrink the image. Negative zoom factors reflect the resulting image about the current raster position.

5.4.1.4 Fragment Operations

Once the image has been rasterized, each resulting fragment is processed just as if it had been generated by the rasterization of a geometric primitive. This means that alpha blending, dithering, stenciling, masking, and all the other per-fragment operations supported by OpenGL can be performed on images. If enabled, even operations such as fog and depth testing that are not typical imaging operations are still performed when images are rasterized.

Rendering images often does not require these operations. If you have any of these operations enabled when you do not require them, they may slow down your image rendering performance. Be sure to disable options you do not require. For example, if you do not want depth testing performed, make sure you disable it before calling `glDrawPixels`.[3]

One handy per-fragment operation that is useful when drawing images is alpha testing. OpenGL images are pixel rectangles, but using the alpha component of

---

3. When `glDrawPixels` is called, the current raster position's *z* value is used as the uniform depth for the image when depth testing and fog generation are being performed.

Figure 5.15 `splatlogo` demonstrating pixel zooming, scaling, and biasing.

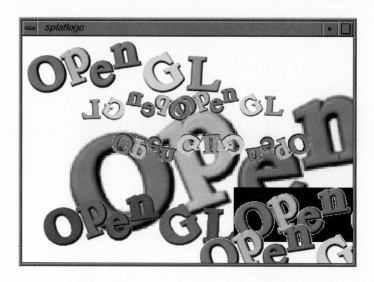

images, you can render irregularly shaped images. Assign an alpha of 0 to any pixel within the image you do not want rendered. Assign an alpha value of 1 to any pixel you want rendered. Then enable alpha testing to render only pixels with an alpha greater than or equal to 0.5, like this:

```
glAlphaFunc(GL_GEQUAL, 0.5);
glEnable(GL_ALPHA_TEST);
```

The pixels in the image that are assigned an alpha value of 0 are discarded during alpha testing.

Figure 5.15 shows `splatlogo`'s use of the pixel-zooming functionality for both zooming and reflection. The pixel-transfer stage is also used to scale and bias the color components for a few of the logos. The logo surrounded by a black rectangle has alpha testing disabled; the pixels with an alpha of 0 are colored black.

5.4.2 Bitmaps

In addition to image pixel rectangles, OpenGL supports rendering *bitmaps* with the `glBitmap` routine. A bitmap is a rectangular array of 0s and 1s that acts as a drawing mask. When a bitmap is rendered, every 1 in the pixel array is rasterized using OpenGL's current color (or current index, in color index mode); every 0 is discarded. The most common use for bitmaps is to render characters of text. The GLUT bitmap font rendering routines described in Section 4.2.8 use `glBitmap`. `glBitmap` is prototyped as

```
void glBitmap(GLsizei width, GLsizei height,
  GLfloat xorig, GLfloat yorig,
  GLfloat xmove, GLfloat ymove,
  const GLubyte *bitmap);
```

Notice that `glBitmap` lacks the type and format parameters passed to `glDrawPixels`; however, there are additional parameters. The *xorig* and *yorig* arguments specify the pixel offset of the image's origin relative to the current raster position. This is useful for text rendering when some character's bitmap descends below the origin (like the letter j). The *xmove* and *ymove* parameters specify the *x* and *y* pixel offsets to be added to the current raster position. This is used to advance the raster position by the width of the character when rendering text.

   `glBitmap`'s ability to move the raster position in window-relative coordinates is handy apart from actually rendering a bitmap. You can use this ability to adjust the current raster position without risking making the raster position invalid because the raster position falls outside the window's viewport. For example, you can adjust a valid current raster position like this:

```
glBitmap(0, 0, 0, 0, 20, -10, 0);
```

This will move the raster position 20 pixels to the right and 10 pixels down. Notice that the width and height of the bitmap are specified as 0, meaning that no bitmap image will be rendered.

   Pixel transfer state does not affect bitmap image data, though the pixel storage modes are used. This means you cannot scale, bias, map, or zoom bitmaps.

5.4.3   Reading and Copying Pixels

So far, all the discussion has been about drawing pixels where an image in host memory is transferred to the screen. OpenGL also allows pixels to be read from the frame buffer, as well as copied from one region of the frame buffer to another.

   The routine to read pixels is `glReadPixels`, prototyped as

```
void glReadPixels(GLint x, GLint y,
  GLsizei width, GLsizei height,
  GLenum format, GLenum type, GLvoid *pixels);
```

The *x* and *y* arguments are window-relative pixel coordinates (where the origin is the lower left-hand corner of the window) specifying the location to read from; the current raster position is not used for specifying where to read pixels. The *width* and *height* arguments specify the width and height, in pixels, of the frame buffer region to be read. The *type* parameter specifies the data type of the pixel data to be read. For example, GL_RGB reads the red, green, and blue color components, while GL_DEPTH_COMPONENT reads depth values from the depth buffer. The *pixels* pointer tells where in host memory to transfer the pixel data.

Just like the pixel unpack storage modes, there is an identical set of pixel *pack* storage modes that control the way pixels are packed by glReadPixels into host memory.

Also, all the pixel transfer modes operate on pixels being read back from the frame buffer. This means you can scale and bias (shift and offset for index data), remap, and convert the pixel data you read in exactly the same manner as you can transform pixel data being drawn.

The routine to copy pixels from one region of the frame buffer to another is glCopyPixels, prototyped as

```
void glCopyPixels(GLint x, GLint y,
  GLsizei width, GLsizei height, GLenum type);
```

A region of pixels of size *width* by *height* is copied from the current raster position to the location specified by the *x* and *y* window-relative pixel coordinates. The *type* parameter specifies the type of data to be copied (one of GL_COLOR, GL_DEPTH, or GL_STENCIL). Results of copies from outside the window region, or from regions of the window that are not exposed, are undefined.

The glDrawBuffer routine determines the color buffer in which pixels are drawn. The glReadBuffer routine determines the color buffer from which pixels are read. Using glCopyPixels, you can read from the buffer specified by glRead-Buffer and copy the data into the buffer specified by glDrawBuffer.

As with reading and drawing pixels, copied pixels pass through the pixel transfer stage. This means you can scale and bias (shift and offset for index data), remap, and convert the pixel data you copy in exactly the same manner as you can transform pixel data being drawn or read. Because copied pixels are never transferred to host memory, the pack and unpack pixel storage modes are irrelevant when copying pixels.

5.4.4 Texturing as the Merging of Geometry and Imagery

Texture maps are images. Therefore, it should not be surprising that when you load a texture with glTexImage2D or glTexImage1D, the OpenGL pixel path's unpack pixel storage modes and the pixel transfer modes are used when the texture image is transferred from host memory to texture memory. All the functionality described in this section also applies to loading texture images. Figure 5.16 shows how drawing pixels, reading pixels, copying pixels, and loading textures all make use of OpenGL's pixel path functionality.

Figure 5.16 OpenGL's pixel path functionality is used to draw pixels, read pixels, copy pixels, and load textures.

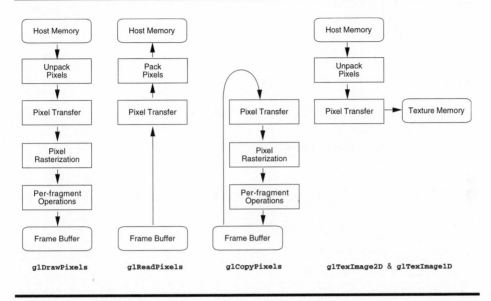

In a very real sense, textures provide a way to "drape" images over geometry. One of the achievements of OpenGL is its ability to merge the rendering of geometry with the rendering of images. For example, you can rotate an image by loading it into texture memory and then rendering a rotated rectangle with the texture applied to it. Images can also be scaled, panned, and even projected by rendering images out of texture memory.

5.4.5 Example: `splatlogo.c`

```
#include <stdlib.h>
#include <stdio.h>
#include <GL/glut.h>

#define MAX_SPLATS 20

/* From logo.c containing the data for an OpenGL logo image. */
extern int logo_width; /* = 317 */
extern int logo_height; /* = 85 */
extern unsigned char logo_image[];
```

```
typedef struct _SplatInfo {
  int x, y;
  GLboolean alphaTest;
  GLfloat xScale, yScale;
  GLfloat scale[3];
  GLfloat bias[3];
} SplatInfo;

int winHeight;
int numSplats = 0;
SplatInfo splatConfig;
SplatInfo splatList[MAX_SPLATS];
SplatInfo splatDefault =
{
  0, 0,
  GL_TRUE,
  1.0, 1.0,
  1.0, 1.0, 1.0,
  0.0, 0.0, 0.0,
};

void
reshape(int w, int h)
{
  glViewport(0, 0, w, h);
  glMatrixMode(GL_PROJECTION);
  glLoadIdentity();
  gluOrtho2D(0, w, 0, h);
  glMatrixMode(GL_MODELVIEW);
  winHeight = h;
}

void
renderSplat(SplatInfo * splat)
{
  glRasterPos2i(splat->x, splat->y);
  if (splat->yScale >= 0)
    glBitmap(0, 0, 0, 0, 0, -logo_height * splat->yScale, 0);
  if (splat->xScale <0)
    glBitmap(0, 0, 0, 0, logo_width * -splat->xScale, 0, 0);
  glPixelZoom(splat-xScale, splat->yScale);
  glPixelTransferf(GL_RED_SCALE, splat->scale[0]);
  glPixelTransferf(GL_GREEN_SCALE, splat->scale[1]);
```

```
  glPixelTransferf(GL_BLUE_SCALE, splat->scale[2]);
  glPixelTransferf(GL_RED_BIAS, splat->bias[0]);
  glPixelTransferf(GL_GREEN_BIAS, splat->bias[1]);
  glPixelTransferf(GL_BLUE_BIAS, splat->bias[2]);
  if (splat->alphaTest)
    glEnable(GL_ALPHA_TEST);
  else
    glDisable(GL_ALPHA_TEST);
  glDrawPixels(logo_width, logo_height, GL_RGBA,
    GL_UNSIGNED_BYTE, logo_image);
}

void
display(void)
{
  int i;

  glClear(GL_COLOR_BUFFER_BIT);
  for (i = 0; i<numSplats; i++) {
    renderSplat(&splatList[i]);
  }
}

void
mouse(int button, int state, int x, int y)
{
  if (button == GLUT_LEFT_BUTTON) {
    if (state == GLUT_DOWN) {
      if (numSplats<MAX_SPLATS) {
        splatConfig.x = x;
        splatConfig.y = winHeight - y;
        renderSplat(&splatConfig);
        splatList[numSplats] = splatConfig;
        numSplats++;
      } else {
        printf("out of splats!\n");
      }
    }
  }
}

void
mainSelect(int value)
```

```
{
  GLfloat rpos[4];
  GLboolean valid;

  switch (value) {
  case 0:
    numSplats = 0;
    glutPostRedisplay();
    break;
  case 1:
    splatConfig = splatDefault;
    break;
  case 2:
    splatConfig.xScale *= 1.25;
    splatConfig.yScale *= 1.25;
    break;
  case 3: splatConfig.xScale *= 0.75;
    splatConfig.yScale *= 0.75;
    break;
  case 4: splatConfig.xScale *= -1.0;
    break;
  case 5:
    splatConfig.yScale *= -1.0;
    break;
  case 6:
    splatConfig.alphaTest = GL_TRUE;
    break;
  case 7:
    splatConfig.alphaTest = GL_FALSE;
    break;
  case 411:
    glGetFloatv(GL_CURRENT_RASTER_POSITION, rpos);
    glGetBooleanv(GL_CURRENT_RASTER_POSITION_VALID, &valid);
    printf("Raster position (%g,%g) is %s\n",
      rpos[0], rpos[1], valid ? "valid" : "INVALID");
    break;
  case 666:
    exit(0);
    break;
  }
}

void
scaleBiasSelect(int value)
{
```

```c
  int color = value >> 4;
  int option = value & 0xf;

  switch (option) {

  case 1:
    splatConfig.bias[color] += 0.25;
    break;
  case 2:
    splatConfig.bias[color] -= 0.25;
    break;
  case 3:
    splatConfig.scale[color] *= 2.0;
    break;
  case 4:
    splatConfig.scale[color] *= 0.75;
    break;
  }
}

int
scaleBiasMenu(int mask)
{
  int menu;

  menu = glutCreateMenu(scaleBiasSelect);
  glutAddMenuEntry("+25% bias", mask | 1);
  glutAddMenuEntry("-25% bias", mask | 2);
  glutAddMenuEntry("+25% scale", mask | 3);
  glutAddMenuEntry("-25% scale", mask | 4);
  return menu;
}

int
main(int argc, char *argv[])
{
  int mainMenu, redMenu, greenMenu, blueMenu;

  glutInitWindowSize(680, 440);
  glutInit(&argc, argv);
  splatConfig = splatDefault;

  glutCreateWindow("splatlogo");

  glutReshapeFunc(reshape);
  glutDisplayFunc(display);
  glutMouseFunc(mouse);
```

```
glPixelStorei(GL_UNPACK_ALIGNMENT, 1);
glAlphaFunc(GL_GEQUAL, 0.5);
glDisable(GL_ALPHA_TEST);
glEnable(GL_DITHER);
glClearColor(1.0, 1.0, 1.0, 0.0);

redMenu = scaleBiasMenu(0 << 4);
greenMenu = scaleBiasMenu(1 << 4);
blueMenu = scaleBiasMenu(2 << 4);

mainMenu = glutCreateMenu(mainSelect);
glutAddMenuEntry("Reset splays", 0);
glutAddMenuEntry("Reset splat config", 1);
glutAddSubMenu("Red control", redMenu);
glutAddSubMenu("Green control", greenMenu);
glutAddSubMenu("Blue control", blueMenu);
glutAddMenuEntry("+25% zoom", 2);
glutAddMenuEntry("-25% zoom", 3);
glutAddMenuEntry("X flip", 4);
glutAddMenuEntry("Y flip", 5);
glutAddMenuEntry("Enable alpha test", 6);
glutAddMenuEntry("Disable alpha test", 7);
glutSetMenu(mainMenu);
glutAddMenuEntry("Query raster position", 411);
glutAddMenuEntry("Quit", 666);
glutAttachMenu(GLUT_RIGHT_BUTTON);
glutMainLoop();
return 0;      /* ANSI C requires main to return int. */
}
```

5.5 EXPLORING CURVES AND SURFACES WITH GLUT

Rendering smooth curves and surfaces efficiently is very important to professionals, such as mechanical engineers and computer special-effects animators, who work with objects that are typically modeled with curves and surfaces. Applications for computer-aided design (CAD) often depend on fast rendering of 3D curves and surfaces.

Examples of curves are splines, circles, and spiral paths. What distinguishes a surface from a curve is that a surface has area, while a curve has length. A surface can be a sphere, or a curved patch, or even a flat surface such as a rectangle (though for this discussion, we generally assume a curved surface, since flat surfaces need no special support to be rendered with OpenGL).

The basic 3D rendering primitive used by OpenGL is the polygon. These polygons are *flat*. Complex objects are typically modeled as tens, hundreds, or even thousands of individual polygons (typically triangles). An elephant, a V-8 engine, or a DNA molecule can be rendered as the amalgamation of enough triangles that the viewer can recognize the modeled object.

5.5.1   Why Curves and Surfaces?

While triangles are sufficient to model any 3D solid object, they are generally not the most convenient, compact, or accurate graphical representation. Representing something like a sphere or a torus (doughnut) with hundreds of triangles works, but mathematical representations of these objects as surfaces are both smaller and easier to manipulate. Also, using triangles to represent a curved surface is always an approximation.

OpenGL does not support curves and surfaces as fundamental rendering primitives. Instead, OpenGL provides facilities to break curves and surfaces up into lines or polygons for efficient rendering. Curves and surfaces are specified by *control points* that shape the curve or surface. Control points may act as "anchors" that the curve or surface must pass through, or they may act as "magnets" that simply attract the curve. From these control points, OpenGL can automatically generate (for any specified precision) a set of lines or polygons that approximates the curve or surface. Figure 5.17 shows how a set of control points defines a 3D spiraling curve.

Figure 5.17 Two views of the control points for a spiral B-spline curve. Note how the control points pull the curve into a descending spiral. The knot multiplicity for the endpoints is 4, ensuring that the endpoints of the spiral match the beginning and end control points.

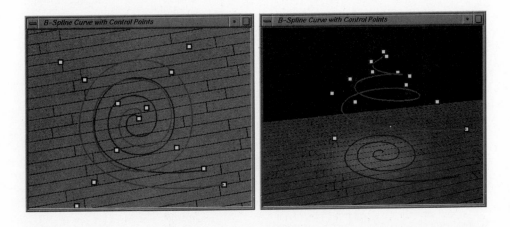

This approach has several advantages:

- An application can treat curves and surfaces as pure mathematical representations, meaning that they are compact and exact (not approximated).
- When converting a surface to polygons for rendering, the application can control the precision with which the surface is rendered. An application can trade off rendering accuracy for rendering speed.
- Hardware acceleration for OpenGL need not be burdened by supporting specialized curve and surface primitives. Curve and surface rendering make use of the speed of accelerated line- and polygon-rendering hardware.
- Even though curve and surface primitives are not supported directly, OpenGL has an *evaluator* facility for generating vertices, normals, colors, and texture coordinates from polynomial mappings that aids rendering curves and surfaces *and* that can be accelerated with hardware. The evaluator facility is not limited to supporting curves and surfaces and has other applications (such as image warping).

OpenGL supports curves and surfaces in two ways: low-level evaluators and utility routines in the GLU library for generating Non-Uniform Rational B-Splines (NURBS).

Do not let yourself be intimidated by the mathematical basis of these techniques; the intuition that underlies the use of evaluators and NURBS for generating curves and surfaces is not exceedingly complicated. You can use curves and surfaces in OpenGL without a rigorous mathematical background. A straightforward, intuitive explanation of curves and surfaces can be found in the "Curves and Surfaces" chapter of *The Inventor Mentor* [44]. The purpose of this section is to provide a conceptual overview of evaluators and NURBS to get you started. The section concludes with a simple GLUT program that calls the GLU library to render a few NURBS surfaces. If you are looking for more detail about OpenGL's programming interface to evaluators and NURBS, see the "Evaluators and NURBS" chapter in the *OpenGL Programming Guide* [28].

5.5.2 Evaluators

OpenGL evaluators provide a means to use polynomial or rational polynomial mappings[4] to generate vertices, normals, texture coordinates, and/or colors. Conceptually, evaluators supply a level of indirection between parameterized values (typically describing a curve or surface) and the generation of per-vertex information.

Bézier curves and surfaces are convenient representations of curves and surfaces. Commonly used in computer graphics, Bézier curves and surfaces are easily generated with evaluators. Pierre Bézier developed the theory of Bézier curves and sur-

---

4. Evaluators are based on *Bernstein* polynomials.

faces for use in designing automobiles at Renault. These curves and surfaces are described with a set of control points that define the endpoints and shape of the curve or surface.

Evaluat or polynomial mappings are set up by calling one of the `glMap` family of routines. Both 1D and 2D evaluators are supported. A 1D evaluator describes a curve; a 2D evaluator describes a surface. `glEnable` and `glDisable` are used to enable and disable the various available evaluators.

Here is an example of generating a Bézier surface with OpenGL evaluators:

```
GLfloat controlPts[4][4][3] = { /* Not listed. */ };

glMap2f(GL_MAP2_VERTEX_3,
  /* min u */ 0.0, /* max u */ 1.0,
  /* u stride */ 3, /* u order */ 4,
  /* min v */ 0.0, /* max v */ 1.0,
  /* v stride */ 3, /* v order */ 4,
  &controlPts[0][0][0]);
glEnable(GL_MAP2_VERTEX_3);
glEnable(GL_AUTO_NORMAL);
```

This code sets up and enables the `GL_MAP2_VERTEX_3` evaluator map so that x, y, and z vertices will be generated when the map is evaluated. Assume that the variables u and v are the values over which the evaluator mapping varies. The `glMap2f` call specifies that u and v vary over the range 0 to 1. Sixteen (4×4) control points are supplied. Each point is an x, y, and z float packed tightly in the `controlPts` array, so the stride for extracting points from the array is 3. The splines for both u and v on the surface are order 4. Enabling `GL_AUTO_NORMAL` will compute surface normal vectors analytically when `GL_MAP2_VERTEX_3` is used to generate vertices (this makes lighting of surfaces easy!). Next, call

```
glMapGrid2f(
  8,          /* u partitions */
  0.0, 1.0,   /* range over u */
  8,          /* v partitions */
  0.0, 1.0    /* range over v */);
```

This establishes a 9×9 grid (8×8 steps) over the full u and v range of the mapping. The evaluator is now set up and ready to use. To render the surface, call

```
glEvalMesh2(GL_FILL, 0, 8, 0, 8);
```

This command generates quad strips that will render the Bézier surface defined by the `controlPts` and automatically generates surface normals across the entire grid.

The same surface could be evaluated and rendered explicitly by an OpenGL program, but using evaluators has two important advantages:

- The single `glEvalMesh2` call above replaces 144 `glVertex3f` and 144 `glNormal3f` calls. This may greatly reduce the bus bandwidth to the graphics hardware (or network bandwidth, if you are using OpenGL on a remote machine) required to render the surface.

- If the OpenGL implementation supports evaluators in the graphics hardware subsystem, evaluators offload significant amounts of computation from the host CPU when rendering curves and surfaces. In the example above, a fourth-order polynomial evaluation is required for each of 81 grid points.

In addition to supplying parameterized values as a mesh with `glEvalMesh2` or `glEvalMesh1`, the `glEvalCoord` family of routines generate evaluated per-vertex information for explicit parameterized values.

5.5.3   The GLU NURBS Routines

You can use evaluators to describe any polynomial or rational polynomial splines or surfaces of any degree, including Bézier curves and surfaces, Hermite splines, uniform B-splines, and NURBS; however, evaluators operate at a low level. Higher-level interfaces for rendering curves and surfaces can use evaluators for efficient implementation, but provide a more sophisticated interface for generating curves and surfaces. The GLU library provides a powerful set of NURBS routines that make use of evaluators for actual rendering.

Nonuniform rational B-splines provide a general and convenient description for curves and surfaces.[5] A NURBS curve or surface can be converted to an evaluator-based description. The GLU NURBS routines provide a standard interface to do just that. This means you can use the GLU NURBS routines to describe curves and surfaces conveniently and still obtain the potential for hardware acceleration of evaluators.

To specify a NURBS curve, you need a set of *control points*, a *knot sequence*, and the *order* of the curve.

Control points are points in object space that affect the shape of the curve in some way. The knot sequence lists nondecreasing values in the parameter domain that divide the parameter domain into segments. Conceptually, each knot serves as a boundary for the influence of corresponding control points. Having a knot value repeated multiple times in the sequence can eliminate the influence of neighboring control points and thereby decrease the continuity of the curve. The number of times a knot is repeated for a given control point is called the *knot multiplicity* of the control point.

---

5. The Bézier curves and surfaces renderable with evaluators are a limited case of NURBS curves and surfaces.

The order is implicitly determined by the number of knots *minus* the number of control points. The order affects how "smooth" the curve will be. Mathematically, the order is one more than the largest exponent in the parametric polynomial equations describing the curve.

Particular knot sequences specify various important classes of curves:

Uniform cubic B-splines. Knots are uniformly spaced and each knot is unique. For example: 0, 1, 2, 3, 4, 5, 6, 7.

Cubic Bézier curves. There are four control points. Knot multiplicity is 4 at the beginning and end. A knot multiplicity of 4 for the beginning and ending control points ensures that the curve must pass through the endpoints. For example: 0, 0, 0, 0, 1, 1, 1, 1.

Uniform cubic B-splines that pass through the endpoints. Multiplicity of 4 at the beginning and ending control points; uniformly spaced single knots between. For example: 0, 0, 0, 0, 1, 2, 3, 4, 5, 5, 5, 5.

A NURBS surface varies with two parameters (u and v), so there are two knot sequences (one for each parameter). The control points are arranged logically as a grid of points over u and v.

The phrase "non-uniform rational B-spline" denotes a set of mathematical properties of the NURBS curve or surface description:

Non-Uniform   Knot spacing need not be uniform.

Rational   The parametric equations describing the spline can have a polynomial denominator (that is, they can be ratios). One nice advantage of rational splines is that, unlike nonrationals, conic sections can be represented exactly.

B-Spline   The influence of the control points is based on the B-spline basis function.

The `molehill.c` sample program at the end of this section demonstrates using the GLU NURBS routines to generate four different NURBS surfaces. The control points are modified differently for each NURBS surface to demonstrate how differing control points manipulate the generated surface. Lighting is enabled because good lighting helps distinguish the curvature across surfaces. The result is shown in Figure 5.18.

The GLU NURBS routines make it straightforward to generate NURBS curves and surfaces. First, allocate a NURBS renderer:

```
nurbsHandle = gluNewNurbsRenderer();
```

All other NURBS routines manipulate the NURBS renderer to perform NURBS operations. Either curves or surfaces can be generated. Since curves are a simplification of

Figure 5.18 Screen snapshot of `molehill`. The four colored NURBS surfaces have control points in different configurations.

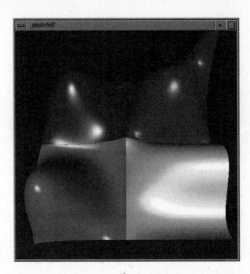

the procedure for rendering surfaces, the discussion that follows deals only with surfaces.

`gluBeginSurface` and `gluEndSurface` delimit a surface definition. Within a surface definition, calling `gluNurbsSurface` generates a NURBS surface. The routine is passed a set of control points, two knot sequences (for the u and v directions), and the order for the NURBS surface to be generated. In addition, an evaluator-type parameter (such as `GL_MAP2_VERTEX3` or `GL_MAP2_TEXTURE_CORD2`) determines what type of per-vertex information will be generated. You always need to generate vertices, but additional calls to `gluNurbsSurface` can be used to generate texture coordinates, normals, or colors.

You can change properties that control the way NURBS are rendered with `gluNurbsProperty`. For example, to change the sampling tolerance used when tessellating a NURBS surface, call

```
gluNurbsProperty(nurbsHandle,
  GLU_SAMPLING_TOLERANCE, 25.0);
```

You can see in Figure 5.19 the effect of large changes in the sampling tolerance when tessellating a NURBS surface.

GLU's NURBS support includes a sophisticated capability for *trimming* NURBS surfaces. During a NURBS surface definition (not in a curve definition), you can

Figure 5.19 The sampling tolerance when tessellating a NURBS surface or curve can be adjusted to trade off accuracy of the approximation against rendering speed. Notice that the left-hand version of `molehill` is a considerably more accurate rendering of the surfaces, but it contains substantially more polygons. While less accurate, the right-hand image can be redrawn much faster than the left-hand image.

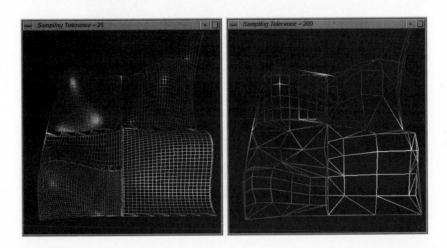

specify one or more trim curves. Conceptually, trimming permits you to "cut away" areas from a NURBS surface. You can cut "holes" in a surface (see Figure 5.20) or create an irregular (nonrectangular) boundary for the surface. The region to be trimmed is specified as a set of closed trimming loops specified by more GLU calls within a surface definition. Use the calls `gluBeginTrim`, `gluPwlCurve` (specifies a piecewise linear curve), `gluNurbsCurve`, and `gluEndTrim`. You can see in Figure 5.21 how trimming affects the resulting tessellation of the surface.

Be aware that converting NURBS descriptions to OpenGL evaluators is reasonably expensive. If your program renders the same NURBS surface repeatedly, it may be to your advantage to capture the OpenGL commands generated by the GLU NURBS routines within a display list. Then you can execute the display list to render the NURBS surface to avoid recomputing the surface on each rendering. The `molehill` example demonstrates this practice.

5.5.4 More Information

Most computer graphics textbooks devote a chapter to the mathematical aspects of representing curves and surfaces. There are also entire books on the subject [4, 9]. A dissertation by Derrick Burns [5] describes efficient surface trimming. To get a "hands-

Figure 5.20 Example of a trimmed NURBS surface. Notice NURBS surfaces may be texture-mapped.

Figure 5.21 Wireframe rendering of the trimmed NURBS surface to show the tessellation into polygons.

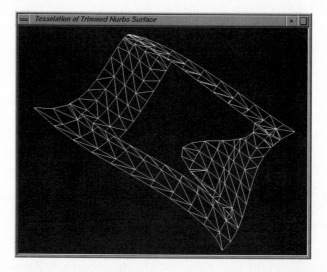

on" feel for how NURBS surfaces operate, try changing the molehill.c sample program (and other OpenGL NURBS examples) to use different control points and knot multiplicities. Also, the Open Inventor toolkit, which is layered on top of OpenGL, contains an object-oriented interface to rendering NURBS curves and surfaces.

5.5.5 Example: `molehill.c`

```c
#include <GL/glut.h>

GLfloat mat_red_diffuse[] = { 0.7, 0.0, 0.1, 1.0 };
GLfloat mat_green_diffuse[] = { 0.0, 0.7, 0.1, 1.0 };
GLfloat mat_blue_diffuse[] = { 0.0, 0.1, 0.7, 1.0 };
GLfloat mat_yellow_diffuse[] = { 0.7, 0.8, 0.1, 1.0 };
GLfloat mat_specular[] = { 1.0, 1.0, 1.0, 1.0 };
GLfloat mat_shininess[] = { 100.0 };
GLfloat knots[8] = { 0.0, 0.0, 0.0, 0.0, 1.0, 1.0, 1.0, 1.0 };
GLfloat pts1[4][4][3], pts2[4][4][3];
GLfloat pts3[4][4][3], pts4[4][4][3];
GLUnurbsObj *nurb;
int u, v;

static void
display(void)
{
  glClear(GL_COLOR_BUFFER_BIT | GL_DEPTH_BUFFER_BIT);
  glCallList(1);
  glFlush();
}

void
main(int argc, char **argv)
{
  glutInit(&argc, argv);
  glutCreateWindow("molehill");
  glMaterialfv(GL_FRONT, GL_SPECULAR, mat_specular);
  glMaterialfv(GL_FRONT, GL_SHININESS, mat_shininess);
  glEnable(GL_LIGHTING);
  glEnable(GL_LIGHT0);
  glEnable(GL_DEPTH_TEST);
  glEnable(GL_AUTO_NORMAL);
  glEnable(GL_NORMALIZE);
  nurb = gluNewNurbsRenderer();
```

```
gluNurbsProperty(nurb, GLU_SAMPLING_TOLERANCE, 25.0);
gluNurbsProperty(nurb, GLU_DISPLAY_MODE, GLU_FILL);

/* Build control points for NURBS molehills. */
for(u=0; u<4; u++) {
  for(v=0; v<4; v++) {
    /* Red. */
    pts1[u][v][0] = 2.0*((GLfloat)u);
    pts1[u][v][1] = 2.0*((GLfloat)v);
    if((u==1 || u == 2) && (v == 1 || v == 2))
      /* Stretch up middle. */
      pts1[u][v][2] = 6.0;
    else
      pts1[u][v][2] = 0.0;

    /* Green. */
    pts2[u][v][0] = 2.0*((GLfloat)u - 3.0);
    pts2[u][v][1] = 2.0*((GLfloat)v - 3.0);
    if((u==1 || u == 2) && (v == 1 || v == 2))
      if(u == 1 && v == 1)
        /* Pull hard on single middle square. */
        pts2[u][v][2] = 15.0;
      else
        /* Push down on other middle squares. */
        pts2[u][v][2] = -2.0;
    else
      pts2[u][v][2] = 0.0;

    /* Blue. */
    pts3[u][v][0] = 2.0*((GLfloat)u - 3.0);
    pts3[u][v][1] = 2.0*((GLfloat)v);
    if((u==1 || u == 2) && (v == 1 || v == 2))
    if(u == 1 && v == 2)
      /* Pull up on single middle square. */
      pts3[u][v][2] = 11.0;
    else
      /* Pull up slightly on other middle squares. */
      pts3[u][v][2] = 2.0;
    else
      pts3[u][v][2] = 0.0;

    /* Yellow. */
    pts4[u][v][0] = 2.0*((GLfloat)u);
```

```
      pts4[u][v][1] = 2.0*((GLfloat)v - 3.0);
      if((u==1 || u == 2 || u == 3) && (v == 1 || v == 2))
        if(v == 1)
          /* Push down front middle and right squares. */
          pts4[u][v][2] = -2.0;
        else
          /* Pull up back middle and right squares. */
          pts4[u][v][2] = 5.0;
      else
        pts4[u][v][2] = 0.0;
    }
  }
  /* Stretch up red's far right corner. */
  pts1[3][3][2] = 6;
  /* Pull down green's near left corner a little. */
  pts2[0][0][2] = -2;
  /* Turn up meeting of four corners. */
  pts1[0][0][2] = 1;
  pts2[3][3][2] = 1;
  pts3[3][0][2] = 1;
  pts4[0][3][2] = 1;

  glMatrixMode(GL_PROJECTION);
  gluPerspective(55.0, 1.0, 2.0, 24.0);
  glMatrixMode(GL_MODELVIEW);
  glTranslatef(0.0, 0.0, -15.0);
  glRotatef(330.0, 1.0, 0.0, 0.0);

  glNewList(1, GL_COMPILE);
    /* Render red hill. */
    glMaterialfv(GL_FRONT, GL_DIFFUSE, mat_red_diffuse);
    gluBeginSurface(nurb);
      gluNurbsSurface(nurb, 8, knots, 8, knots,
        4 * 3, 3, &pts1[0][0][0],
        4, 4, GL_MAP2_VERTEX_3);
    gluEndSurface(nurb);

    /* Render green hill. */
    glMaterialfv(GL_FRONT, GL_DIFFUSE, mat_green_diffuse);
    gluBeginSurface(nurb);
      gluNurbsSurface(nurb, 8, knots, 8, knots,
        4 * 3, 3, &pts2[0][0][0],
        4, 4, GL_MAP2_VERTEX_3);
    gluEndSurface(nurb);
```

```
      /* Render blue hill. */
      glMaterialfv(GL_FRONT, GL_DIFFUSE, mat_blue_diffuse);
      gluBeginSurface(nurb);
        gluNurbsSurface(nurb, 8, knots, 8, knots,
          4 * 3, 3, &pts3[0][0][0],
          4, 4, GL_MAP2_VERTEX_3);
      gluEndSurface(nurb);

      /* Render yellow hill. */
      glMaterialfv(GL_FRONT, GL_DIFFUSE, mat_yellow_diffuse);
      gluBeginSurface(nurb);
      gluNurbsSurface(nurb, 8, knots, 8, knots,
        4 * 3, 3, &pts4[0][0][0],
        4, 4, GL_MAP2_VERTEX_3);
      gluEndSurface(nurb);
    glEndList();

  glutDisplayFunc(display);
  glutMainLoop();
}
```

5.6 EXPLORING THE OPENGL EXTENSIONS WITH GLUT

Compared with other similar graphics standards, OpenGL mandates a rather high baseline of supported rendering functionality. This is good, because it means you will not find OpenGL outdated in a year or two. OpenGL's rendering functionality is state-of-the-art, even for today's most powerful graphics workstations, but computer graphics is a rapidly evolving field. For this reason, OpenGL has been designed so it can be extended with additional rendering capabilities.

5.6.1 OpenGL Extension Naming

An OpenGL extension defines additional OpenGL functionality beyond what the OpenGL core defines. An OpenGL implementation may implement 0 or more OpenGL extensions. Each extension has a unique name. While OpenGL implementors are free to implement their own extensions, OpenGL's governing body, the OpenGL Architectural Review Board (ARB), works to coordinate standard OpenGL extensions and makes sure vendor-specific extensions do not clash.

Names for extensions are designed to make it clear if an extension is proposed by only a single vendor or if multiple vendors have endorsed the extension. The EXT_ prefix is used to indicate that multiple vendors have endorsed the extension. This may or may not mean that multiple implementations of the extension currently exist. Vendor-specific extensions are prefixed by a vendor identifier such as `HP_` or `SGI_`. For vendor-specific extensions, further conventions may exist to distinguish classes of vendor-specific extensions. For example, Silicon Graphics uses a trailing S after its vendor identifier (such as `SGIS_`) to indicate that the extension is likely to be supported only on certain hardware configurations. A trailing X after SGI's vendor identifier (such as `SGIX_`) indicates that the extension is considered experimental and may not be supported in future releases.

The OpenGL extensions supported by an OpenGL implementation are determined by calling

```
extensions = glGetString(GL_EXTENSIONS);
```

The returned string is a space-separated list of OpenGL extension names supported by the implementation. By convention, every extension name listed in the string is prefixed by `GL_`. The application program is responsible for parsing the string to determine whether a particular extension is supported before using it.

An extension adds new routines, constants, and/or types to the OpenGL API. The names of added routines, types, or constants are suffixed with the extension name's prefix. A routine, constant, or type with an `EXT_` prefix would be named, respectively:

```
glRoutineEXT
GL_CONSTANT_EXT
GLtypeEXT
```

The specification for an extension documents the way the extension affects the OpenGL state machine. An OpenGL extension is not limited to adding new routines to establish new functionality. An extension may provide new enumerants to be passed to existing OpenGL routines. An extension may also establish new OpenGL state that can affect the operation of existing OpenGL routines.

5.6.2 Available Extensions

There are currently several dozen specified OpenGL extensions for which implementations exist or are planned. Extensions are proposed for numerous reasons, including adding new capabilities, generalizing existing functionality, improving rendering quality, improving performance, and overcoming design shortcomings. Vendors are now releasing OpenGL implementations that implement extensions. Discussing every proposed OpenGL extension is beyond the scope of this book. Instead, only a few important extensions will be discussed briefly:

> `GL_EXT_abgr` is a simple extension to augment the available host-memory image formats. It provides a reverse-order alternative to the RGBA image

format. ABGR refers to the order in which the red, green, blue, and alpha components are represented in memory. IRIS GL, OpenGL's predecessor, used the ABGR image format, so many existing applications and their file formats rely on an image format reversed from OpenGL's default. This extension allows OpenGL to efficiently support images in the ABGR format.

`GL_EXT_polygon_offset` allows depth values of polygon fragments to be displaced so that lines, points, and polygons that lie in the same plane can be rendered without interaction. The polygon offset extension is useful to avoid artifacts that occur when lines are used to draw outlines around polygons or when multiple coplanar polygons need to be rendered. This extension is covered in more detail later, because this section's example demonstrates the `GL_EXT_polygon_offset` extension.

OpenGL 1.1 includes an updated interface for polygon offset. See Section 6.1.1.2.

`GL_SGIS_multisample` provides a mechanism to antialias all primitives. The technique is to sample all primitives multiple times at different locations within each pixel (rather than just at the pixel center). The color sample values are resolved to a single displayable color each time a pixel is updated, so antialiasing appears automatic at the application level. Multisampling enables extremely high-quality animated scenes. Currently, multisampling is implemented only in high-end graphics hardware such as Silicon Graphic's RealityEngine and InfiniteReality.

`GL_EXT_texture3D` supports three-dimensional texture mapping. In the core OpenGL, texture coordinates are already logically manipulated as (homogeneous) 3D coordinates. This extension defines in-memory formats for 3D images and adds pixel formats to support them. 3D textures are useful for volumetric rendering. For example, a 256-×-256-×-256 cube of medical or seismic data could be sliced arbitrarily if it were represented as a 3D texture (potentially rendered in real time if 3D textures are supported by hardware!).

`GL_EXT_texture_object` supports named texture objects whose contents and parameters may be changed after they are defined. Texture objects are designed to make up for deficiencies in efficiently using display lists to package textures. For machines with special texture memories, the extension also provides simple texture memory management. OpenGL 1.1 includes an updated interface for texture objects. See Section 6.1.1.6.

`GL_EXT_convolution` adds 1D and 2D convolution operations to OpenGL's pixel transfer process. Thus, pixel drawing, reading, and copying, as well as texture image definition, are all candidates for convolution. Convolution is an important image processing operation, useful for sharpening, blurring, and detecting edges in images.

`GL_HP_image_transform` adds support for scaling, rotation, and translation of images to the pixel transfer process. Different resampling methods can be selected. The extension includes a color table to look up posttransformed pixel values.

`GL_SGI_color_matrix` provides a method for reassigning and duplicating color components and performing simple color space conversions by transforming RGBA pixel values with a 4-by-4 color matrix. As with other matrices supported by OpenGL, there is a stack of color matrices. After the 4-by-4 matrix transformation, components can be scaled, biased, and looked up in a color table.

`GL_EXT_histogram` accumulates image statistics for pixels passed through the pixel path. Occurrences of specific pixel component values can be counted, and minimum and maximum pixel component values can be calculated. Pixels can be discarded before rasterization if only the statistics are desired.

`GL_SGIS_sharpen_texture` introduces texture magnification filters that sharpen the resulting image when it is greatly magnified. Instead of simply magnifying the texture's highest level-of-detail (the level-0 mipmap), by extrapolating from the texture's second highest level-of-detail (the level 1 mipmap) to the texture's highest level-of-detail (the level-0 mipmap), an apparently sharper resulting texture can be rendered. Texture sharpening can be specified on a per-component basis. Often the alpha component of a texture is used to define a pattern such as a tree shape. Texture sharpening of the alpha component of such "shaped" textures can be used to avoid blurring shape edges that otherwise result from a simpler sampling of the alpha values at the edges.

`GL_SGIS_detail_texture` is yet another texture magnification filter that blends the texture's highest level-of-detail with a separately defined "detail" image. The texture for a stretch of road, complete with yellow dividing lines, might use detail texture to blend a gravel pattern into the road surface. This way, if the road were viewed up close (that is, if the texture were highly magnified), the gravel detail would be visible.

`GL_EXT_vertex_array` adds the ability to specify multiple geometric primitives with very few subroutine calls. Instead of calling an OpenGL procedure for each individual vertex, normal, or color, arrays of vertices, normals, and colors are prespecified and dispatched via a single subroutine call. The vertex array extension promises to improve performance for *extremely* fast graphics hardware where host overhead may be a potential bottleneck or on CPUs where the cost of a subroutine call is relatively expensive (like the Intel x86 architecture). OpenGL 1.1 includes an updated interface for vertex arrays. See Section 6.1.1.1.

Note that many of the extensions we have discussed here are either new texture mapping capabilities or new pixel path capabilities. This is one indication that OpenGL is expanding to encompass hardware accelerated image processing

Figure 5.22 OpenGL's extended image processing pipeline.

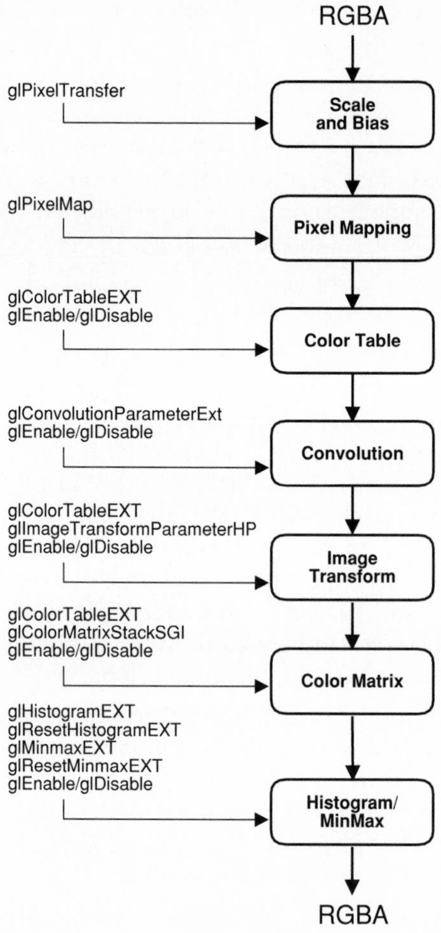

functionality. Figure 5.22 shows how OpenGL image processing extensions provide a very sophisticated imaging pipeline.

5.6.3 Extension Interoperability

OpenGL is logically a client/server system. For a program to use an OpenGL extension, the extension must be supported by both the OpenGL client library and the OpenGL server implementation. A given extension might not be supported for a number of reasons. For example, the OpenGL server implementation might be running a previous release of OpenGL that predated the extension, or the OpenGL server might be from a vendor that does not support the extension. OpenGL programs that use extensions should be careful to properly query the existence of extensions they will be using. This is not different from what X programs should do before using X extensions.

In general, applications should ensure that they operate when a given extension is not available. For example, a program using the `GL_EXT_vertex_array` extension should fall back to the more conventional means of generating vertex, normal, and color data. Programs using extensions such as `GL_SGIS_multisample` or `GL_SGIS_sharpen_texture` can generally operate without the extension, admittedly at reduced image quality.

5.6.4 GLX Extensions

So far, this discussion has focused on OpenGL extensions, but it is also possible to extend the OpenGL window system support API—for example, GLX in the case of the X Window System. The original GLX 1.0 did not provide support for extensions, but GLX 1.1 adds support for GLX extensions. Section 6.1.2 describes GLX 1.1 and various available GLX extensions. GLX extensions involve window system dependent capabilities, while OpenGL extensions are window system independent.

5.6.5 Extensions as OpenGL's Future

Revisions to the OpenGL specification (for example, OpenGL 1.1, described in Section 6.1.1) will "roll up" successful OpenGL extensions into the core of OpenGL's functionality. In this sense, OpenGL extensions are a testing ground for new functionality and a glimpse of what a future revision to OpenGL might contain.

Advances in graphics hardware and rendering support happen quickly. The OpenGL extension mechanism provides a framework that lets OpenGL vendors develop new rendering functionality in a controlled and consistent manner. To find out more about the extensions supported by a given OpenGL implementation, consult the vendor's documentation. Information on supported extensions is often found on the `glIntro` and `glXIntro` manual pages.

5.6.6 The Polygon Offset Extension

This section's example folds and unfolds a paper airplane as the airplane spins in 3D. The `origami` program works by modeling the paper airplane using eight polygons, as shown in Figure 5.23. The program then translates and rotates these polygons to animate the folding and unfolding of the paper plane. The airplane

Figure 5.23 The paper airplane is divided into eight polygons, defined by the fold lines of the folded plane.

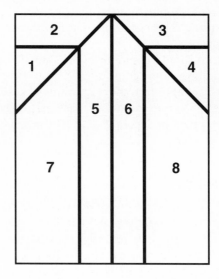

polygons are rendered in a single color, so outlines around each polygon help delineate the folds and edges of the airplane.

The polygon offset extension is used for this section's example program because it was one of the early extensions to OpenGL (meaning that many vendors have had time to implement the extension) and it helps remedy an annoying visual artifact common to depth-buffered programs. The extension was made an official part of the OpenGL standard in version 1.1. Actually, the polygon offset functionality that was made part of OpenGL 1.1 improved on the original extension's design, demonstrating how extensions can provide a valuable testing ground for new functionality migrating into the core OpenGL standard.

In the example, the `GL_EXT_polygon_offset` extension is used (if available) to outline the folds and edges of the paper properly. Without the polygon offset extension, unsightly artifacts are generated when the outline folds and edges are rendered, as shown in Figure 5.24. If the polygons and outlines are rendered naively with the same vertex coordinates, each polygon may obscure its associated outline in some orientations because of the way the depth buffering sorts fragments. One way to avoid these artifacts is to translate the outline slightly closer to the viewer, but this can lead to different artifacts. When translated slightly forward, the outline may sometimes appear to "float" above its polygon at some orientations. The polygon offset extension can be used to avoid both types of outlining artifacts by providing a way to offset depth values for polygons without changing the polygon vertices.

Figure 5.24 The origami example program and three different outline modes. Notice that using the polygon offset extension gives the cleanest result. Rendering the fold and edge outlines using either "nothing" or the "translate hack" method results in noticeable artifacts, visible in the magnified views.

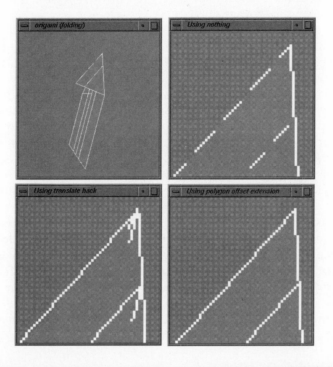

The polygon offset extension is enabled like other OpenGL modes. The following statements enable and disable operation of the polygon offset extension:

```
glEnable(GL_POLYGON_OFFSET_EXT);
glDisable(GL_POLYGON_OFFSET_EXT);
```

When enabled, the polygon offset extension displaces the depth values of fragments generated by rendering polygons by an amount that is proportional to the maximum absolute value of the depth slope of the polygon, measured and applied in window coordinates. This displacement allows lines (or points) and polygons in the same plane to be rendered without interaction, meaning that the lines can be rendered either completely in front of or behind the polygons (depending on the sign of the offset factor). It also allows multiple coplanar polygons to be rendered without interaction, if different offset factors are used for each polygon.

The extension's `glPolygonOffsetEXT` routine takes two parameters, specifying the scaling factor which is used to create a variable depth offset for each polygon, and the bias, which is a constant depth offset. For example:

```
glPolygonOffsetEXT(/*factor*/ 0.5,
                   /*bias*/ 0.001);
```

Initially, the factor and the bias are both zero. Polygon offset is useful for rendering hidden line images, for applying decals to surfaces, and for rendering surfaces with highlighted edges.

Notice that in `origami.c` all code related to using the polygon offset extension is guarded by `#ifdef` C preprocessor directives. This ensures that the code will compile cleanly on an OpenGL library implementation that does not provide the polygon offset extension. By convention, each system's OpenGL header file advertises what extensions the system's OpenGL client library provides based on C preprocessor `#defines`. The `GL_EXT_polygon_offset` macro is defined only if the polygon offset extension is supported by the client library OpenGL implementation.

In addition to the compile-time check, a runtime check should also be made if the OpenGL server supports the polygon offset extension. As a rule, do not call an OpenGL extension routine unless you have verified that the extension is supported. The `glutExtensionSupported` routine (part of the OpenGL Utility Toolkit) makes it easy to query whether a named extension is supported. When the extension is supported, `origami` will use it; when it is not supported, `origami` will still run but will use the "translate hack" instead of the cleaner polygon offset extension.

5.6.7 Example: `origami.c`

```
#include <stdlib.h>
#include <stdio.h>
#include <GL/glut.h>

enum {
  FLAT,              /* Completely flat sheet of paper */
  FLAP1,             /* Left flap being folded in */
  FLAP2,             /* Right flap being folded in */
  CENTER2,           /* Right side folded up at center */
  WING2,             /* Right wing folded down */
  CENTER1,           /* Left side folded up at center */
  WING1,             /* Left wing folded down */
  FOLDED             /* Fully folded paper airplane */
} States;
```

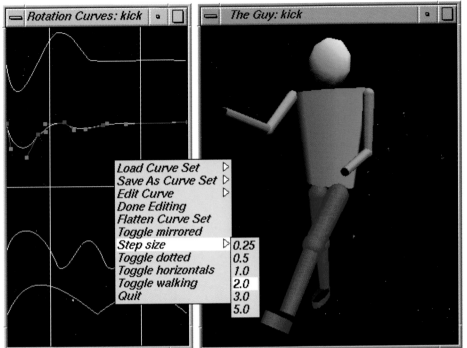

Plate 1: *walker* is a human kinetics program written by Kanishka Agarwal and Philip Winston using the OpenGL Utility Toolkit described in Chapter 4. The curves in the left window describe the rotations in time for the figure's joints. The program shows GLUT can be used to develop reasonably involved applications.

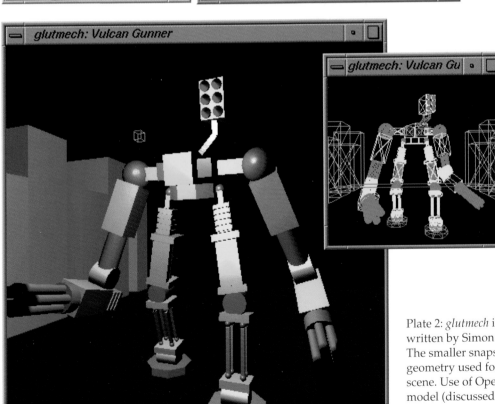

Plate 2: *glutmech* is a GLUT program written by Simon Parkinson-Bates. The smaller snapshot shows the geometry used for the robot and scene. Use of OpenGL's lighting model (discussed in Section 5.1) heightens the robot's realism.

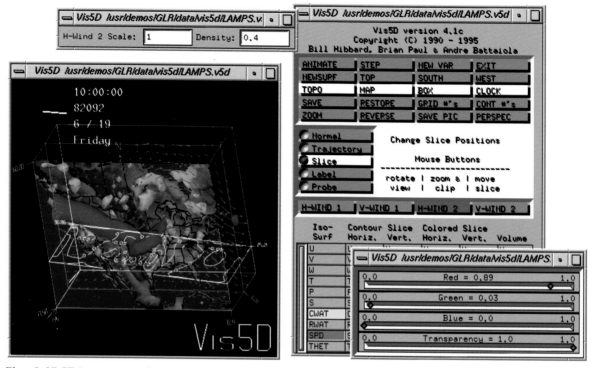

Plate 3: *Vis5D* is a program for visualization of weather simulation results written by Bill Hibbard and Brian Paul at the University of Wisconsin in Madison. The program uses OpenGL for rendering the annotated weather map and Xlib for the user interface. Chapter 2 describes using OpenGL with Xlib.

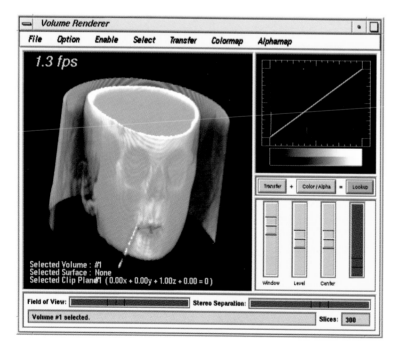

Plate 4: *volren* is an OpenGL-based volume rendering application written by Brian Cabral and Todd Kulick. The program has a sophisticated Motif user interface. Chapter 3 describes using OpenGL with Motif.

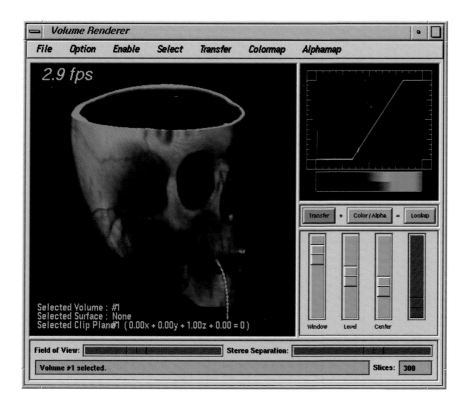

Plate 5: Another view of *volren* shows the same data set shown in Plate 4 but with the transfer function set to show data at the density of bone. Notice the skull. *volren* uses the 3D texture mapping extension mentioned in Section 5.6.2 to interactively render volumetric data.

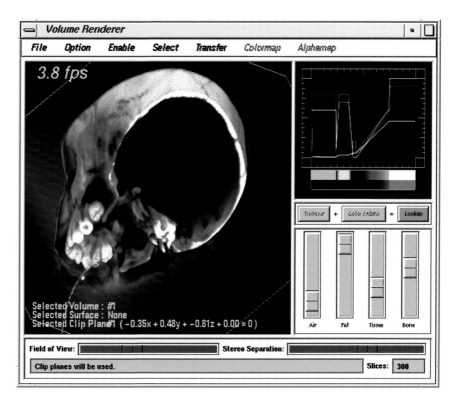

Plate 6: Using clipping planes, *volren* lets a researcher slice into the data set to see internal features. The volume rendering capabilities of *volren* are an extension of OpenGL's texture mapping capability described in Section 5.2.

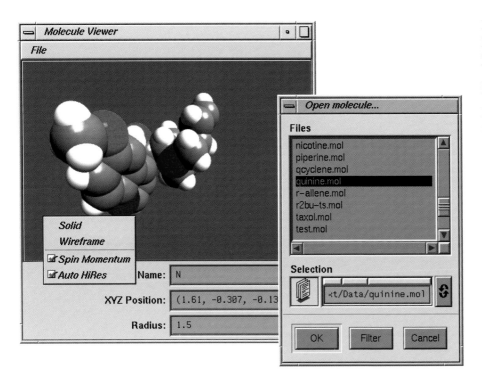

Plate 7: The *molview* program is fully described in Chapter 7. The quinine molecule is rendered with OpenGL, but the user interface is Motif. The popup menu is rendered in the overlay planes (see Section 6.3.8) to improve menu interaction.

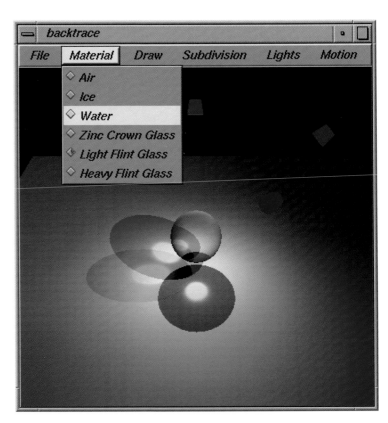

Plate 8: The *backtrace* program by Celeste Fowler demonstrates clever lighting effects generated using OpenGL's lighting model. Lighting effects are discussed in Section 5.1.

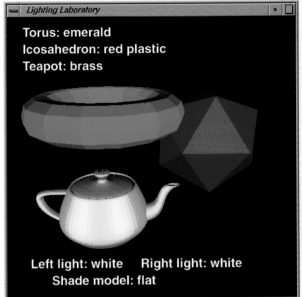

Plate 9: *lightlab*'s initial appearance. Both lights are enabled so the teapot has two specular highlights. The left side of the teapot catches the left side's red light; the right side catches the green from the right side's green light. See the program in Section 5.1.3.

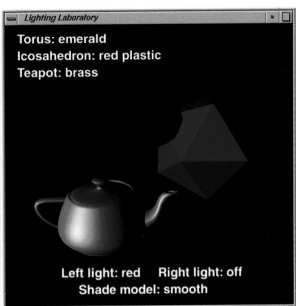

Plate 10: The right light is off; the left side shines red. Notice the emerald torus is hardly visible because there is no green light in the scene. Also, because there is only one light shining, the teapot has a single specular highlight.

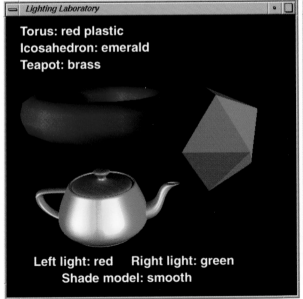

Plate 11: Both lights are shining white and the picture is bright. Flat shading is being used instead of smooth shading. This makes it apparent that the torus is not tessellated that finely. Lighting with smooth shading gives it a rounder appearance.

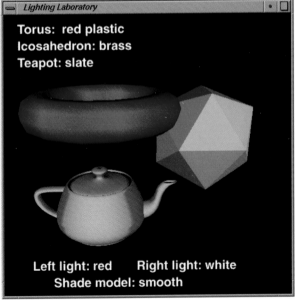

Plate 12: Slate is not very shiny, so the teapot's specular highlights are spread across the teapot's surface. The specular highlight for the icosahedron appears redder because of the left red light.

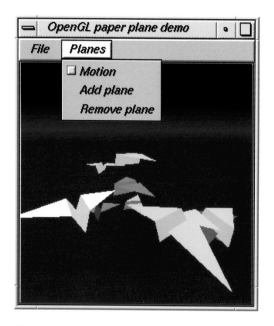

Plate 13: *paperplane* shows 3D paper airplanes flying. The program has a simple Motif user interface. See Section 3.4.

Plate 14: Notice how the red and green icosahedrons blend where they overlap in the *blender* example. See Section 5.3.

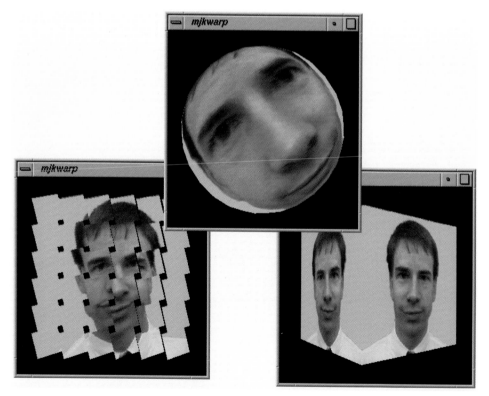

Plate 15: The author's face texture mapped to a rotating cube rendered by the *mjkwarp* example program described in Section 5.2.4.

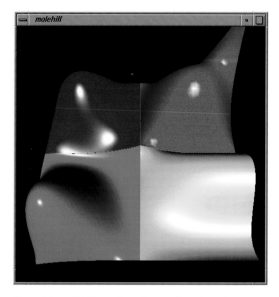

Plate 16: *molehill* renders four colored surfaces described by non-rational uniform B-splines (or simply NURBS). Notice the effects of lighting. See Section 5.5.

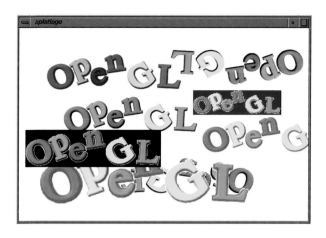

Plate 17: *splatlogo* uses glDrawPixels to render the OpenGL logo. The logos are scaled, biased, and zoomed by OpenGL's *pixel path* to demonstrate simple imaging operations. See Section 5.4.

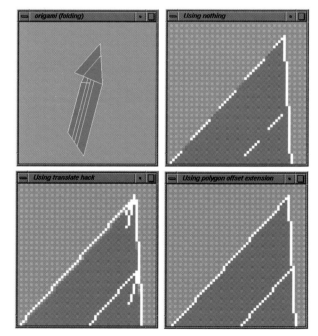

Plate 18: The *origami* program folds and unfolds a paper airplane. The edges on the plane are rendered to reduce depth buffer aliasing artifacts with the polygon offset extension if supported See Section 5.6.

Plate 19: The *glutduck* program shows how to combine the OpenGL Utility Toolkit (GLUT) with the Open Inventor toolkit and OpenGL for object-oriented 3D rendering. See Section 5.7.

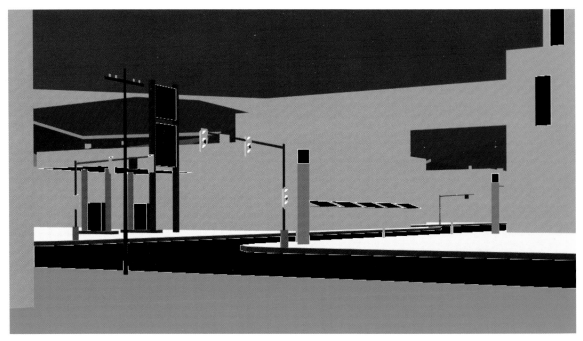

Plate 20: This visual simulation program uses IRIS Performer to render a detailed town with OpenGL. Extensive use of OpenGL texture mapping greatly increases the visual realism.

Plate 21: Here is the same view of the town shown in Plate 20 but with texture mapping disabled. Notice how much realism is added by texture mapping. OpenGL's texture mapping capability is described in Section 5.2.

```c
#if GL_EXT_polygon_offset
int polygon_offset;
#endif
int motion = 1;
int spinning = 1;
int state = FLAT;
int click = 0;
int delay = 0;
int direction;
float flap1_angle = 0;
float flap2_angle = 0;
float center1_angle = 0;
float center2_angle = 0;
float wing1_angle = 0;
float wing2_angle = 0;

typedef GLfloat Point[2];

Point poly1[] =
{
  {-1, 0},
  {-1 / 3.0, 2 / 3.0},
  {-1, 2 / 3.0}
};
Point poly2[] =
{
  {-1, 1},
  {-1, 2 / 3.0},
  {-1 / 3.0, 2 / 3.0},
  {0, 1}
};
Point poly3[] =
{
  {0, 1},
  {1, 1},
  {1, 2 / 3.0},
  {1 / 3.0, 2 / 3.0}
};
Point poly4[] =
{
  {1 / 3.0, 2 / 3.0},
  {1, 2 / 3.0},
  {1, 0}
```

```
};
Point poly5[] =
{
  {-1 / 3.0, 2 / 3.0},
  {0, 1},
  {0, -1.5},
  {-1 / 3.0, -1.5}
};
Point poly6[] =
{
  {0, 1},
  {1 / 3.0, 2 / 3.0},
  {1 / 3.0, -1.5},
  {0, -1.5}
};
Point poly7[] =
{
  {-1, 0},
  {-1 / 3.0, 2 / 3.0},
  {-1 / 3.0, -1.5},
  {-1, -1.5}
};
Point poly8[] =
{
  {1, 0},
  {1 / 3.0, 2 / 3.0},
  {1 / 3.0, -1.5},
  {1, -1.5}
};


void
polydlist(int dlist, int num, Point points[])
{
  int i;

  glNewList(dlist, GL_COMPILE);
  glBegin(GL_POLYGON);
  for (i = 0; i < num; i++)
    glVertex2fv(&points[i][0]);
  glEnd();
  glEndList();
}
```

```
void
idle(void)
{
  if (spinning)
    click++;
  switch (state) {
  case FLAT:
    delay++;
    if (delay >= 80) {
      delay = 0;
      state = FLAP1;
      glutSetWindowTitle("origami (folding)");
      direction = 1;
    }
    break;
  case FLAP1:
    flap1_angle += 2 * direction;
    if (flap1_angle >= 180) {
      state = FLAP2;
    } else if (flap1_angle <= 0) {
      state = FLAT;
    }
    break;
  case FLAP2:
    flap2_angle += 2 * direction;
    if (flap2_angle >= 180) {
      state = CENTER2;
    } else if (flap2_angle <= 0){
      state = FLAP1;
    }
    break;
  case CENTER2:
    center2_angle += 2 * direction;
    if (center2_angle >= 84) {
      state = WING2;
    } else if (center2_angle <= 0) {
      state = FLAP2;
    }
    break;
  case WING2:
    wing2_angle += 2 * direction;
    if (wing2_angle>= 84) {
      state = CENTER1;
```

```
      } else if (wing2_angle <= 0) {
        state = CENTER2;
      }
      break;
    case CENTER1:
      center1_angle += 2 * direction;
      if (center1_angle >= 84) {
        state = WING1;
      } else if (center1_angle <= 0) {
        state = WING2;
      }
      break;
    case WING1:
      wing1_angle += 2 * direction;
      if (wing1_angle >= 84) {
        state = FOLDED;
      } else if (wing1_angle <= 0) {
        state = CENTER1;
      }
      break;
    case FOLDED:
      delay++;
      if (delay >= 80) {
        delay = 0;
        glutSetWindowTitle("origami (unfolding)");
        direction = -1;
        state = WING1;
      }
      break;
  }
  glutPostRedisplay();
  }

void
draw_folded_plane(void)
{
  glPushMatrix();
    glRotatef(click, 0, 0, 1);
    glRotatef(click / 5.0, 0, 1, 0);
    glTranslatef(0, .25, 0);
    glPushMatrix();
      glRotatef(center1_angle, 0, 1, 0);
      glPushMatrix();
        glTranslatef(-.5, .5, 0);
```

```
      glRotatef(flap1_angle, 1, 1, 0);
      glTranslatef(.5, -.5, 0);
      glCallList(2);
    glPopMatrix();
    glCallList(5);

    glPushMatrix();
      glTranslatef(-1 / 3.0, 0, 0);
      glRotatef(-wing1_angle, 0, 1, 0);
      glTranslatef(1 / 3.0, 0, 0);

      glCallList(7);
      glPushMatrix();
        glTranslatef(-.5, .5, 0);
        glRotatef(flap1_angle, 1, 1, 0);
        glTranslatef(.5, -.5, 0);
        glCallList(1);
      glPopMatrix();
    glPopMatrix();
  glPopMatrix();

  glPushMatrix();
    glRotatef(-center2_angle, 0, 1, 0);
    glPushMatrix();
      glTranslatef(.5, .5, 0);
      glRotatef(-flap2_angle, -1, 1, 0);
      glTranslatef(-.5, -.5, 0);
      glCallList(3);
    glPopMatrix();
    glCallList(6);

    glPushMatrix();
      glTranslatef(1 / 3.0, 0, 0);
      glRotatef(wing2_angle, 0, 1, 0);
      glTranslatef(-1 / 3.0, 0, 0);

      glCallList(8);
      glPushMatrix();
        glTranslatef(.5, .5, 0);
        glRotatef(-flap2_angle, -1, 1, 0);
        glTranslatef(-.5, -.5, 0);
        glCallList(4);
      glPopMatrix();
    glPopMatrix();
  glPopMatrix();
```

```
    glPopMatrix();
}
void
display(void)
{
  glClear(GL_COLOR_BUFFER_BIT | GL_DEPTH_BUFFER_BIT);
  glPolygonMode(GL_FRONT_AND_BACK, GL_FILL);
  glColor3ub(67, 205, 128);
#if GL_EXT_polygon_offset
  if (polygon_offset) {
    glPolygonOffsetEXT(0.5, 0.0);
    glEnable(GL_POLYGON_OFFSET_EXT);
  }
#endif
  draw_folded_plane();
  glPolygonMode(GL_FRONT_AND_BACK, GL_LINE);
  glColor3ub(255, 255, 255);
#if GL_EXT_polygon_offset
  if (polygon_offset) {
    glPolygonOffsetEXT(0.0, 0.0);
    glDisable(GL_POLYGON_OFFSET_EXT);
  } else {
    glPushMatrix();
    glTranslatef(0, 0, .05);
  }
#else
  glPushMatrix();
  glTranslatef(0, 0, .05);
#endif
  draw_folded_plane();
#if GL_EXT_polygon_offset
  if (polygon_offset)
    glPopMatrix();
#else
  glPopMatrix();
#endif
  glutSwapBuffers();
}

void
visible(int state)
{
  if (state == GLUT_VISIBLE) {
    if (motion)
```

```
    glutIdleFunc(idle);
  } else {
    glutIdleFunc(NULL);
  }
}

void
menu(int value)
{
  switch (value) {
  case 1:
    direction = -direction;
    if (direction > 0)
      glutSetWindowTitle("origami (folding)");
    else
      glutSetWindowTitle("origami (unfolding)");
    break;
  case 2:
    motion = 1 - motion;
    if (motion)
      glutIdleFunc(idle);
    else
      glutIdleFunc(NULL);
    break;
  case 3:
      spinning = 1 - spinning;
      break;
  case 666:
    exit(0);
  }
}
int
main(int argc, char **argv)
{
  glutInit(&argc, argv);
  glutInitDisplayMode(GLUT_RGB | GLUT_DEPTH | GLUT_DOUBLE);
  glutCreateWindow("origami");
  glutDisplayFunc(display);
  glutVisibilityFunc(visible);
  glClearColor(.488, .617, .75, 1.0);
  glMatrixMode(GL_PROJECTION);
  gluPerspective(40.0, 1.0, 0.1, 10.0);
  glMatrixMode(GL_MODELVIEW);
  gluLookAt(0, 0, 5.5,
```

```
      0, 0, 0,
       0, 1, 0);
   glEnable(GL_DEPTH_TEST);
   glDepthFunc(GL_LEQUAL);
   glLineWidth(2.0);
   polydlist(1, sizeof(poly1) / sizeof(Point), poly1);
   polydlist(2, sizeof(poly2) / sizeof(Point), poly2);
   polydlist(3, sizeof(poly3) / sizeof(Point), poly3);
   polydlist(4, sizeof(poly4) / sizeof(Point), poly4);
   polydlist(5, sizeof(poly5) / sizeof(Point), poly5);
   polydlist(6, sizeof(poly6) / sizeof(Point), poly6);
   polydlist(7, sizeof(poly7) / sizeof(Point), poly7);
   polydlist(8, sizeof(poly8) / sizeof(Point), poly8);
   glutCreateMenu(menu);
   glutAddMenuEntry("Reverse direction", 1);
   glutAddMenuEntry("Toggle motion", 2);
   glutAddMenuEntry("Toggle spinning", 3);
   glutAddMenuEntry("Quit", 666);
   glutAttachMenu(GLUT_RIGHT_BUTTON);
#if GL_EXT_polygon_offset
   polygon_offset = glutExtensionSupported("GL_EXT_polygon_offset");
#endif
   glutMainLoop();
   return 0; /* ANSI C requires main to return int. */
}
```

5.7   EXPLORING OPEN INVENTOR WITH GLUT

Programming graphics with OpenGL is fairly low-level. This section describes the Open Inventor toolkit, which makes it possible to render 3D scenes without all the rendering details required by OpenGL. Actually, Open Inventor is layered on top of OpenGL.

5.7.1   Procedural versus Descriptive

The OpenGL graphics system is a *procedural* standard for interactive 3D graphics. This means that a sequence of OpenGL commands describes a specific procedure for drawing a 3D scene. An alternative to a procedural graphics system is a *descriptive* system. An example of a descriptive graphics system is the object-oriented Open Inventor library (or simply Inventor), developed and licensed by Silicon Graphics. Implementations of Open Inventor are available for both Silicon Graphics and non-

Silicon Graphics workstations. Open Inventor is related to OpenGL because Inventor is layered on top of OpenGL.

With a procedural graphics system such as OpenGL, you draw a scene by executing a series of graphics commands—for example, "Enable depth buffering, set up the projection and modelview matrices, set up lighting parameters, set the viewport, clear the color and depth buffers, generate a triangle strip with these vertices, push the modelview matrix," and so on. On the other hand, with a descriptive system, you specify a scene as a description of what is to be rendered—for example, "There is a light source shining down on the scene, there is a green plastic cylinder at the origin, there is a brass cube three units left of the cylinder," and so on—in brief, a descriptive specification of a 3D scene is about objects, while a procedural specification is about rendering.

Because a descriptive graphics system permits a higher-level description of 3D scenes than a procedural one, programmers often find descriptive graphics systems easier to use.

A descriptive graphics system does not eliminate procedural rendering. When a descriptive specification of a scene is to be rendered, a procedural specification must be generated and executed from the higher-level descriptive specification. Also, an application using procedural graphics systems may still achieve better performance through efficient use of the lower-level procedural interface.

The efficiency of a descriptive graphics system is largely dependent on how well the descriptive system's rendering model is adapted to the lower-level procedural system it is used with. Open Inventor is specifically designed to efficiently makes use of OpenGL's rendering functionality. When necessary, Open Inventor still provides access to the lower-level OpenGL library.

5.7.2 Open Inventor in Brief

Open Inventor is an object-oriented 3D toolkit. Language bindings for both C++ and ANSI C are provided (though the C++ binding is more convenient and extensible). The library itself is written in C++.

Programs use Open Inventor to manipulate *scene graphs* constructed from *node* objects. Each node is an object that holds information, such as a surface material, a shape, a light, or a camera. A scene graph is a tree of nodes describing a 3D scene. An example scene graph is presented graphically in Figure 5.25.

The node objects are extensible, meaning that specialized nodes can be subclassed from existing nodes. Advanced Inventor programmers are encouraged to develop their own nodes if necessary. Rendering the scene described by the scene graph is done by traversing the scene graph and performing the rendering action associated with each node.

Inventor metafiles provide a way to share 3D scene information between applications. An Inventor metafile encodes an Inventor scene graph in an ASCII or binary

Figure 5.25 Graphical representation of a partial Inventor scene graph. When rendering a scene graph, Inventor generally traverses the nodes in a depth-first, left-to-right order (though specialized nodes permit more sophisticated traversal methods). To simplify the diagram, the leftmost and rightmost group nodes are not expanded to show the nodes below them.

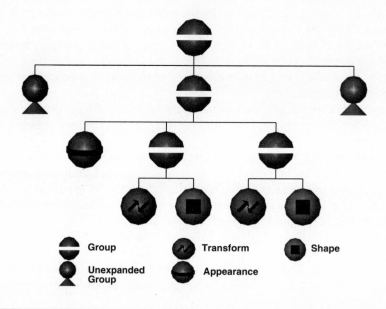

Group

Unexpanded
Group

Transform

Appearance

Shape

file.[6] It is easy for an Inventor program to read or write Inventor metafiles, which are generally suffixed with the .iv extension. A portion of the metafile used in this section's example is shown in Figure 5.26.

The Inventor toolkit is window system independent (like OpenGL itself), but a component library helps make Inventor more useful for a specific window system. The X Window System implementation of Inventor has a component library (lib-InventorXt) that integrates Inventor with Xt/Motif. This is how most X-based Inventor programs are written. Figure 5.27 shows how the Inventor libraries fit into the context of related X libraries. This section's sample program demonstrates that it is also possible to use the base Inventor library (libInventor) without the component library.

---

6. The Inventor file format is the basis for the VRML 1.0 data format used to interact with 3D virtual worlds via the World Wide Web.

Figure 5.26 First 25 lines of the `duck.iv` Open Inventor metafile containing a 3D duck model.

```
#Inventor V2.0 ascii

Separator {
  Separator {
    Material {
      ambientColor   0.25396 0.25396 0
      diffuseColor   1 1 0
      specularColor  0.89987 0.89310 0.89682
      emissiveColor  0 0 0
      shininess      0.68108
      transparency   0
    }
    Separator {
    ShapeHints {
      vertexOrdering  COUNTERCLOCKWISE
      shapeType       SOLID
      faceType        CONVEX
    }
    NormalBinding {
      value PER_VERTEX_INDEXED
    }
    Coordinate3 {
      point [ 0.43192 -0.48431 -0.061775,
              0.42836 -0.47830 -0.078645,
              0.38222 -0.50567 -0.78644
```

5.7.3 Open Inventor with GLUT

The `glutduck.c++` source code at the end of this section combines Open Inventor with GLUT. The program draws a duck in a pond. The duck swims a circle in the pond, either in response to user input or if continuous animation of the scene is enabled. Figure 5.28 shows how the program appears onscreen. Since GLUT does not use the X Toolkit or Motif, the `libInventorXt` library is not used; `glutduck`'s windowing support is supplied by GLUT.

Looking at the source code, you will notice a host of Inventor related header files. All the header files named `<Inventor/nodes/...>` declare C++ classes for Inventor's scene graph nodes. A second type of Inventor C++ classes are *actions*. The header files called `<Inventor/actions/...>` declare C++ classes for Inventor's action objects. Actions are applied to Inventor scene graphs to perform operations on

Figure 5.27 Relationship of Open Inventor libraries and OpenGL and X libraries.

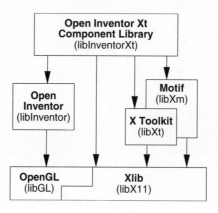

the scene graph. The most common action is to render the scene graph into a window, but other possible actions include calculating a subgraph's bounding box, writing the scene graph to a file, and dispatching input events to the scene graph's nodes. The rendering action is optimized for OpenGL's interface. For example, Inventor automatically uses OpenGL display lists to cache the OpenGL commands generated by repeatedly rendered Inventor nodes. While nodes and actions are the most common

Figure 5.28 Screen snapshot of `glutduck` using Open Inventor.

Inventor objects, many other object types are supported by Inventor; these are beyond the scope of this book. The *Inventor Mentor* [44] is an excellent book for learning more about Open Inventor.

glutduck's use of Inventor is fairly simple. The program's duckScene routine creates a scene graph containing the duck in the pond. While the duck model is read from the duck.iv Inventor file, the pond and the composition of the duck relative to the pond are done programmatically by calling the necessary Inventor routines.

Updating the scene can be performed by editing and/or manipulating the scene graph nodes. The animation in glutduck is done by updating the angle of the duck's rotation node within the scene graph and then redrawing the scene. Inventor also has sophisticated facilities for more automated mechanisms for controlling and updating the scene graph, such as sensors, engines, draggers, and manipulators.

To redraw its window, glutduck does the following:

1. Uses glClear to clear the screen.

2. Instantiates a SoGLRenderAction with its viewport set correctly to the size of the rendering window.

3. Applies the SoGLRenderAction object's action to the root of the duck pond scene graph. The action performed by SoGLRenderAction is to traverse the scene graph invoking each node's OpenGL render action. This process renders the duck pond.

4. The window is double-buffered; to display the newly rendered scene, glutSwapBuffers is called to swap the window's buffers.

The SoGLRenderAction action causes the necessary OpenGL rendering commands to be issued. The action assumes that the OpenGL library is already bound to the correct context and window.

The user can interact with glutduck in several ways. A pop-up menu controls the animation of the scene. Mouse motion when the left mouse button is held down controls the duck's rotation, and pressing the spacebar advances the duck's rotation in steps.

Not demonstrated in the glutduck program is Open Inventor's Xt-based component library. This library makes it easy to use Inventor with Motif. Some of the facilities provided by the library are:

- An SoXtRenderArea object that encapsulates an OpenGL drawing area widget for easy use with Inventor.

- Support for overlay planes.

- User interface components such as a directional light editor, a material editor, and a scene viewer.

- Clipboard support for passing 3D Inventor scene graph information between applications.

Open Inventor is a powerful tool for utilizing OpenGL. Because Inventor has a high-level, object-oriented descriptive model, Inventor simplifies developing programs that manipulate 3D data. In addition, Open Inventor is designed to efficiently generate OpenGL commands, so Inventor leverages the low-level tuning and hardware acceleration of the underlying OpenGL implementation.

5.7.4 Example: `glutduck.c++`

```
// Based on an example from the Inventor Mentor chapter 13, example 5.

#include <stdio.h>
#include <unistd.h>
#include <GL/glut.h>
#include <Inventor/SoDB.h>
#include <Inventor/SoInput.h>
#include <Inventor/SbViewportRegion.h>
#include <Inventor/actions/SoGLRenderAction.h>
#include <Inventor/nodes/SoSeparator.h>
#include <Inventor/nodes/SoCylinder.h>
#include <Inventor/nodes/SoDirectionalLight.h>
#include <Inventor/nodes/SoMaterial.h>
#include <Inventor/nodes/SoPerspectiveCamera.h>
#include <Inventor/nodes/SoRotationXYZ.h>
#include <Inventor/nodes/SoTransform.h>
#include <Inventor/nodes/SoTranslation.h>

int spinning = 0, moving = 0, begin;
SoSeparator *root;
SoRotationXYZ *duckRotXYZ;
float angle = 0.0;
SbViewportRegion myViewport;

void
reshape(int w, int h)
{
  glViewport(0, 0, w, h);
  myViewport.setWindowSize(w,h);
}

void
renderScene(void)
{
```

```
  glClear(GL_COLOR_BUFFER_BIT | GL_DEPTH_BUFFER_BIT);
  SoGLRenderAction myRenderAction(myViewport);
  myRenderAction.apply(root);
}

void
redraw(void)
{
  renderScene();
  glutSwapBuffers();
}

int
duckScene(void)
{
  root = new SoSeparator;
  root->ref();

  // Add a camera and light
  SoPerspectiveCamera *myCamera = new SoPerspectiveCamera;
  myCamera->position.setValue(0., -4., 8.0);
  myCamera->heightAngle = M_PI/2.5;
  myCamera->nearDistance = 1.0;
  myCamera->farDistance = 15.0;
  root->addChild(myCamera);
  root->addChild(new SoDirectionalLight);

  // Rotate scene slightly to get better view
  SoRotationXYZ *globalRotXYZ = new SoRotationXYZ;
  globalRotXYZ->axis = SoRotationXYZ::X;
  globalRotXYZ->angle = M_PI/9;
  root->addChild(globalRotXYZ);

  // Pond group
  SoSeparator *pond = new SoSeparator;
  root->addChild(pond);
  SoMaterial *cylMaterial = new SoMaterial;
  cylMaterial->diffuseColor.setValue(0., 0.3, 0.8);
  pond->addChild(cylMaterial);
  SoTranslation *cylTranslation = new SoTranslation;
  cylTranslation->translation.setValue(0., -6.725, 0.);
  pond->addChild(cylTranslation);
```

```
   SoCylinder *myCylinder = new SoCylinder;
   myCylinder->radius.setValue(4.0);
   myCylinder->height.setValue(0.5);
   pond->addChild(myCylinder);

   // Duck group
   SoSeparator *duck = new SoSeparator;
   root->addChild(duck);

   // Read the duck object from a file and add to the group
   SoInput myInput;
   if (!myInput.openFile("duck.iv")) {
     if (!myInput.openFile(
       "/usr/share/src/Inventor/examples/data/duck.iv"))
       return 1;
   }
   SoSeparator *duckObject = SoDB::readAll(&myInput);
   if (duckObject == NULL) return 1;

   // Set up the duck transformations
   duckRotXYZ = new SoRotationXYZ;
   duck->addChild(duckRotXYZ);
   duckRotXYZ->angle = angle;
   duckRotXYZ->axis = SoRotationXYZ::Y; // rotate about Y axis
   SoTransform *initialTransform = new SoTransform;
   initialTransform->translation.setValue(0., 0., 3.);
   initialTransform->scaleFactor.setValue(6., 6., 6.);
   duck->addChild(initialTransform);
   duck->addChild(duckObject);
   return 0;
}

void
updateModels(void)
{
  duckRotXYZ->angle = angle;
  glutPostRedisplay();
}

void
animate(void)
{
  angle += 0.1;
  updateModels();
}
```

```
void
setAnimation(int enable)
{
  if(enable) {
    spinning = 1;
    glutIdleFunc(animate);
  } else {
    spinning = 0;
    glutIdleFunc(NULL);
    glutPostRedisplay();
  }
}

void
keyboard(unsigned char ch, int x, int y)
{
  if(ch == ' ') {
    setAnimation(0);
    animate();
  }
}

void
menuSelect(int item)
{
    switch(item) {
  case 1:
    setAnimation(0);
    animate();
    break;
  case 2:
    if(!spinning) setAnimation(1);
      else setAnimation(0);
    break;
  }
}

void
vis(int visible)
{
  if (visible == GLUT_VISIBLE) {
    if (spinning) glutIdleFunc(animate);
  } else {
    if (spinning) glutIdleFunc(NULL);
```

```
  }
}

void
mouse(int button, int state, int x, int y)
{
  if (button == GLUT_LEFT_BUTTON && state == GLUT_DOWN) {
    setAnimation(0);
    moving = 1;
    begin = x;
  }
  if (button == GLUT_LEFT_BUTTON && state == GLUT_UP) {
    moving = 0;
    glutPostRedisplay();
  }
}

void
motion(int x, int y)
{
  if (moving) {
    angle = angle + .01 * (x - begin);
    begin = x;
    updateModels();
  }
}

int
main(int argc, char **argv)
{
  glutInit(&argc, argv);
  glutInitDisplayMode(GLUT_RGB | GLUT_DOUBLE | GLUT_DEPTH |
      GLUT_MULTISAMPLE);
  SoDB::init();
  if(duckScene()) {
    fprintf(stderr, "couldn't read IV file\");
    exit(1);
  }
  glutCreateWindow("GLUT Inventor Duck Pond");
  glutReshapeFunc(reshape);
  glutDisplayFunc(redraw);
  glutCreateMenu(menuSelect);
  glutAddMenuEntry("Step", 1);
```

```
glutAddMenuEntry("Toggle animation", 2);
glutAttachMenu(GLUT_RIGHT_BUTTON);
glutKeyboardFunc(keyboard);
glutMouseFunc(mouse);
glutMotionFunc(motion);
glutVisibilityFunc(vis);
glEnable(GL_DEPTH_TEST);
glClearColor(0.132, 0.542, 0.132, 1.0);
glutMainLoop();
return 0; /* ANSI C requires main to return int. */
}
```

The command line to compile `glutduck.c++` would look something like this:

```
CC -o glutduck glutduck.c++ -lglut -lInventor -lGLU -lGL -lXmu \
    -lXext -lX11 -lm
```

The `-lInventor` option links with the Open Inventor library.

Advanced Topics

This chapter, which covers a set of advanced topics for OpenGL and X programmers, is organized into the following sections:

1. **"Revisions to OpenGL, GLX, and GLU"** describes the additions and changes that have been made to OpenGL in version 1.1, the new functionality provided by GLX 1.1 and 1.2, and additions to the OpenGL Utility (GLU) library.

2. **"X Input Extension"** explains this extension for managing specialized input devices such as a tablet or a Spaceball, because OpenGL programs often need access to sophisticated input devices.

3. **"Using Overlays"** explains the convention agreed on by most X workstation vendors to advertise overlay visuals.

4. **"Portability and Interoperability"** provides guidance for ensuring that the OpenGL code you write is portable to other workstations and interoperable so that you can expect your code to work on different OpenGL implementations.

5. **"Hardware for Accelerating OpenGL"** discusses the ways specialized graphics hardware is used to accelerate OpenGL rendering operations.

6. **"Maximizing OpenGL"** Performance provides advice for tuning OpenGL applications for maximum performance, including an approach for developing application-specific benchmarks.

6.1   REVISIONS TO OPENGL, GLX, AND GLU

OpenGL and its related GLX and GLU standards continue to evolve under the auspices of the OpenGL Architectural Review Board (ARB). The updates are based on feedback from users and implementors of OpenGL. The revisions are upward-compatible, so old programs will continue to work with new OpenGL, GLX, and GLU revisions. For example, any program that runs with a 1.0 OpenGL implementation will also run unchanged with a 1.1 OpenGL implementation. Programs using newer OpenGL programs can operate with older OpenGL-capable X servers, but such programs need to avoid using newer features not supported by the older X servers. Programs should query support for newer revisions before using the functionality they contain.

6.1.1   OpenGL 1.1

OpenGL 1.0 was first released on July 1, 1992. During 1995, Kurt Akeley led an effort by the ARB to update the OpenGL specification for release as OpenGL 1.1. Several additions were made to OpenGL, especially to the texture-mapping capabilities, but also to the geometry and fragment operations. Figure 6.1 shows the relationship of OpenGL 1.1 to the base OpenGL functionality. All the OpenGL 1.1 additions were based on experience with extensions to OpenGL 1.0, meaning that the new OpenGL 1.1 functionality was proven before its inclusion in the core of OpenGL.

Figure 6.1 OpenGL 1.1 additions.

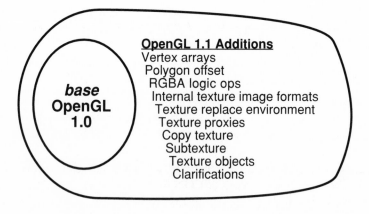

Because GLX allows OpenGL programs to connect to a remote X server that may or may not support OpenGL 1.1, even if the system on which you compile your OpenGL program supports OpenGL 1.1, it is always a good idea to make sure that OpenGL 1.1 is supported before you use any OpenGL 1.1 features. This is done by querying the `GL_VERSION` using `glGetString` once bound to an OpenGL rendering context. The following routine returns true if OpenGL 1.1 or higher is supported:

```
int
supportsOneDotOne(void)
{
  const GLubyte *version;
  int major, minor;

  version = glGetString(GL_VERSION);
  if (sscanf(version, "%d.%d", &major, &minor) == 2)
    return major > 1 || minor >= 1;
  return 0; /* OpenGL version string malformed! */
}
```

If a program uses OpenGL 1.1 functionality when OpenGL 1.1 is not supported, the OpenGL 1.1 calls will likely be detected via OpenGL's error mechanism (probably `GL_INVALID_OPERATION` or `GL_INVALID_ENUM`).

6.1.1.1   Vertex Arrays

OpenGL's vertex specification command groups (`glVertex`, `glNormal`, `glTexCoord`, `glColor`, `glIndex`, and `glEdgeFlag`) accept data in any combination of supported formats. This approach has the advantages of being both flexible and straightforward. An OpenGL program can send vertex data to OpenGL based on what is most convenient to the program. The disadvantage of the approach is that every piece of vertex data sent to OpenGL requires the expense of a separate procedure call.

OpenGL 1.1's *vertex array* addition provides an alternative, more structured way to send vertex data to OpenGL. Arrays of vertex data may be transferred to OpenGL with far fewer OpenGL procedure calls than have previously been necessary. Six arrays are defined, one each for vertex positions, normal coordinates, colors, color indices, texture coordinates, and edge flags. The arrays may be specified and enabled independently, or one of a set of predefined configurations may be selected with a single command.

The primary goal is to decrease the number of procedure calls required to transfer non-display-listed geometry data to OpenGL. A second goal was to improve the efficiency of the transfer, especially to allow direct memory access (DMA) hardware to be used to affect the transfer. OpenGL 1.1's vertex array facility is an updated version of the `GL_EXT_vertex_array` extension.

   The routines to describe the locations and organizations of the six arrays are prototyped as follows:

```
void glVertexPointer(GLint size, GLenum type,
  GLsizei stride, GLvoid *pointer);
void glNormalPointer(GLenum type, GLsizei stride,
  GLvoid *pointer);
void glTexCoordPointer(GLint size, GLenum type,
  GLsizei stride, GLvoid *pointer);
void glColorPointer(GLint size, GLenum type,
  GLsizei stride, GLvoid *pointer);
void glIndexPointer(GLenum type, GLsizei stride,
  GLvoid *pointer);
void glEdgeFlagPointer(GLsizei stride, GLvoid *pointer);
```

The *size* parameter specifies how many values are sent for each vertex when using
vertex position, texture coordinate, and color arrays (the parameters of the other
arrays are of fixed size). For example, to specify vertices as (x,y,z) coordinates, the
size would be 3. The *type* parameter specifies the type of the values sent. For example, to specify single-precision floating-point values, the type would be GL_FLOAT.
The glEdgeFlagPointer routine has no type parameter, because GLboolean is the
only accepted type for the edge flag. The values that make up each array element are
packed sequentially. The *stride* parameter specifies the distance in machine units
(typically bytes) between elements within each array. For example, a stride of 32 for
the vertex array indicates that the beginning of the next vertex position to follow a
given vertex position is 32 bytes after the beginning of the given vertex position. A
stride of 0 indicates that elements are stored sequentially. The *pointer* parameter
specifies the location in memory of the first value of the first element of the array
being specified.

   An individual array is enabled or disabled by calling one of the following:

```
void glEnableClientState(GLenum array);
void glDisableClientState(GLenum array);
```

The possible *array* values are GL_VERTEX_ARRAY, GL_NORMAL_ARRAY, GL_TEXTURE_
COORD_ARRAY, GL_COLOR_ARRAY, GL_INDEX_ARRAY, and GL_EDGE_ FLAG_ARRAY.
Here is an example of how the vertex position and color arrays could be set up and
enabled:

```
static GLint vertex[][2] = {
  { 0, 0 },
  { 0, 1 },
```

```
  { 1, 1 }
};
static GLfloat color[][3] = {
  { 0.5, 0.0, 0.3 },
  { 1.0, 0.0, 0.0 },
  { 0.7, 0.7, 0.7 }
};

glVertexPointer(2, GL_INT, 0, vertex);
glColorPointer(3, GL_FLOAT, 0, color);
glEnableClientState(GL_VERTEX_ARRAY);
glEnableClientState(GL_COLOR_ARRAY);
```

Now the data from the vertex and color arrays are ready to be efficiently transferred. The simplest way to transfer data from vertex arrays is with

```
void glArrayElement(GLint i);
```

This routine transfers the ith element of the currently enabled vertex arrays. For each enabled array, it is as though the array's corresponding vertex generation routine were called for element i. If the vertex position array is enabled, the element's vertex position is issued last, after the data for other enabled arrays is transferred. If the vertex array state were established as described earlier, calling `glArrayElement(2)` would be equivalent to executing the following:

```
glTexCoord3fv(texCoord[2]);
glVertex3fv(vertex[2]);
```

When the vertex position array is enabled, `glArrayElement` calls should be between a `glBegin` and a `glEnd`. For example:

```
glBegin(GL_LINES);
  glArrayElement(0);
  glArrayElement(1);
  glArrayElement(2);
glEnd();
```

Avoid changing the data within vertex arrays between a `glBegin` and a `glEnd`, because changes to the data may affect the parameters sent by `glArrayElement` in nonsequential ways. That is, a call to `glArrayElement` that precedes a change to array data may access the changed data, and a call that follows a change to array data may access the original data. The rule of thumb is to avoid changing vertex array data between a `glBegin` and a `glEnd`. Outside of `glBegin` and `glEnd`, changes to the array contents can be made and subsequent vertex transfers will use the updated values.

When a complete geometric primitive can be entirely generated with sequential data from vertex arrays, you can use the call

```
void glDrawArrays(GLenum mode, GLint first, GLsizei count);
```

With `glDrawArrays`, you can render the same lines generated by the `glArray-Element` example above by calling:

```
glDrawArrays(GL_LINES, 0, 3);
```

This single call to `glDrawArrays` replaces calling `glBegin`, three `glVertex2iv` calls, three `glColor3fv` calls, and `glEnd`. Using larger vertex arrays results in even greater efficiency.

You can also execute vertex array elements contained in a list of array elements with

```
glDrawElements(GLenum mode, GLsizei count, GLenum type,
  GLvoid *indices);
```

This routine lets you execute vertex array elements in arbitrary sequences and repeat duplicated vertex element data by referencing a single copy. The vertex elements in the preceding example can be executed in reverse order, like this:

```
static GLint reversedList[] = { 2, 1, 0 };

glDrawElements(GL_LINES, 3, GL_UNSIGNED_INT, reversedList);
```

The index list *type* can be `GL_UNSIGNED_INT`, `GL_UNSIGNED_SHORT`, or `GL_UNSIGNED_BYTE`.

One caveat about the use of `glDrawElements` and `glDrawArrays` is that OpenGL's current edge flag, texture coordinates, color, color index, and normal coordinates are each indeterminate after the execution of these two routines. This caveat and the earlier caveat about changing vertex array contents between a `glBegin` and a `glEnd` facilitate implementing OpenGL's vertex array facility using direct memory access (DMA) hardware support. Using specialized graphics DMA and OpenGL direct rendering, the vertex array calls may direct specialized graphics hardware to "pull" vertex data directly from the program's address space. This *pull model* for transferring vertex data is in contrast to OpenGL's traditional *push model*, in which the vertex data is first loaded from memory into the CPU running the OpenGL program, then transferred to the graphics hardware. The pull model can achieve higher bandwidth, and sometimes lower latency, by moving data from main memory directly to the graphics hardware. Not all OpenGL implementations will support DMA transfers for vertex arrays. Even so, vertex arrays reduce the procedure call overhead of sending vertex data to OpenGL and may improve performance by allowing the OpenGL implementation to take advantage of data coherence.

To improve the efficiency of initializing vertex arrays, the `glInterleaved-Arrays` routine sets up the six arrays to one of 14 common configurations. The idea is that most programs will use only a small number of the possible vertex array configurations and the arrays used will often be *interleaved*. Interleaving means that all enabled arrays have the same stride and that same-numbered elements of different arrays are stored together and sequentially.

An example supported configuration is `GL_C3F_V3F`. It supplies a color specified by three `GLfloats` and a vertex position specified by three `GLfloats` for each vertex, and the vertex position and color data are interleaved in memory. Here is an example using `glInterleavedArrays`:

```
static GLfloat data[][6] = {
  { 1.0, 0.5, 0.0,    /* color 0 */
    0.0, 5.0, 0.0 },  /* vertex 0 */
  { 0.0, 0.3, 1.0,    /* color 1 */
    5.0, 5.0, 0.0 },  /* vertex 1 */
  { 0.3, 0.5, 0.3,    /* color 2 */
    5.0, 0.0, 1.0 }   /* vertex 2 */
};

glInterleavedArrays(GL_C3F_V3F, 0, data);
```

The single `glInterleavedArrays` has the same effect as setting up the vertex arrays like this:

```
glDisableClientState(GL_EDGE_FLAG_ARRAY);
glDisableClientState(GL_INDEX_ARRAY);
glDisableClientState(GL_TEXTURE_COORD_ARRAY);
glDisableClientState(GL_NORMAL_ARRAY);

glEnableClientState(GL_COLOR_ARRAY);
glColorPointer(3, GL_FLOAT, 0, &data[0][0]);

glEnableClientState(GL_VERTEX_ARRAY);
glVertexPointer(3, GL_FLOAT, 0, &data[0][3]);
```

Figure 6.2 shows how the vertex parameters in the `data` array are interleaved. You are encouraged to use the configurations supported by `glInterleaved-Arrays`, because they are likely to be better optimized than other vertex configurations.

Figure 6.2 Vertex data interleaved for `glInterleavedArrays`'s `GL_C3F_V3F` configuration.

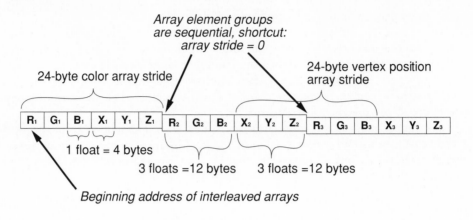

Vertex arrays operate on memory within the address space of the OpenGL program, as the routine called `glEnableClientState` implies. Vertex arrays are considered part of the OpenGL client state. Because of this, vertex array commands cannot be compiled into display lists. Instead, vertex array routines are executed immediately between `glCallList` and `glEndList`, with the resulting vertex and other commands accumulated in the display list.

On very fast OpenGL implementations, vertex arrays may substantially improve the rendering performance of some applications by comparison with using OpenGL's standard vertex generation routines. However, this does not justify rewriting all your OpenGL code to use vertex arrays. Organizing your application's data into vertex arrays may be more cumbersome than using OpenGL's standard vertex generation routines.

Vertex arrays are just one of several options for improving the efficiency of sending vertex data to OpenGL. Depending on your application, the standard vertex generation routines, vertex arrays, display lists, and evaluators are each worth considering on their relative merits. For example, vertex arrays may be of little benefit if you are using indirect rendering, while executing display lists that contain sets of repeatedly executed vertices will greatly improve the performance of indirect rendering applications (because indirect rendered display lists reside *within* the X server's address space). On the other hand, data within display lists cannot be changed the way data within vertex arrays can. Evaluators also have their place. If your vertex data can be described with polynomial mappings (typical of curves and surfaces), evaluators can be considerably more efficient than vertex arrays.

6.1.1.2 Polygon Offset

The polygon offset extension has already been discussed in Section 5.6.6. This extension's functionality was added to OpenGL 1.1; however, the functionality was updated based on experience using the `GL_EXT_polygon_offset` extension. This is an excellent example of OpenGL extensions' being used as a "functionality testing ground" before making new functionality a part of the core OpenGL standard.

Enabling polygon offset allows depth values of fragments generated by the rasterization of a polygon to be shifted toward or away from the origin, as an affine function of the window coordinate depth slope of the polygon. Shifted depth values allow coplanar geometry, especially facet outlines, to be rendered without depth buffer artifacts. They can also be used by sophisticated shadow algorithms.

The additions match those of the previously discussed `GL_EXT_polygon_offset` extension, with two exceptions. First, the offset is enabled separately for `GL_POINT`, `GL_LINE`, and `GL_FILL` rasterization modes, all sharing a single affine function definition. (Shifting the depth values of the outline fragments, instead of the fill fragments, allows the contents of the depth buffer to be maintained correctly.) Second, the offset bias is specified in units of depth buffer resolution, rather than in the [0,1] depth range. Recall from Section 5.6.6 that specifying the offset as a depth range was somewhat arbitrary because an appropriate bias depended on the depth buffer's resolution. The OpenGL 1.1 approach avoids this complication.

The OpenGL 1.1 routine for changing the polygon depth offset is

```
glPolygonOffset(GLfloat factor, GLfloat units);
```

Unlike the extension version, this routine has no `EXT` prefix, since it is not an extension but a standard part of OpenGL 1.1.

Here is how polygon offset is enabled for each polygon mode:

```
glEnable(GL_POLYGON_OFFSET_FILL);
glEnable(GL_POLYGON_OFFSET_LINE);
glEnable(GL_POLYGON_OFFSET_POINT);
```

6.1.1.3 RGBA Logical Operations

Fragments generated by RGBA rendering can be merged into the frame buffer using a logical operation, just as color index fragments can be in OpenGL 1.0. Blending is disabled during such operations because it is rarely desired, because many systems could not support it, and to match the semantics of the `GL_EXT_blend_logic_op` extension, on which this addition is loosely based.

The logical operation is set with `glLogicOp` and enabled for RGBA mode using

```
glEnable(GL_COLOR_LOGIC_OP);
```

For consistency, GL_INDEX_LOGIC_OP is enabled and disabled to control the logical operation applied to color indices (for compatibility with OpenGL 1.0, the old symbolic constant GL_LOGIC_OP may also be used).

6.1.1.4 Internal Texture Image Formats

In OpenGL 1.1, textures have an *internal format*, rather than a simple count of components as in OpenGL 1.0. The internal format is represented as a single enumerated value, indicating both the organization of the image data (GL_LUMINANCE, GL_RGB, GL_RGBA, and so on) and the number of bits of storage for each image component. OpenGL applications can use the internal format specification to suggest the desired storage precision of texture images.

While the prototype of the OpenGL 1.1 routines for texture image specification (glTexImage2D and glTexImage1D) is identical to that of OpenGL 1.0, the interpretation of the third parameter has been expanded to specify the texture's internal image format. glTexImage2D now names its arguments accordingly:

```
void glTexImage2D( GLenum target,
  GLint level,
  GLint internalformat, /* was components in 1.0 */
  GLsizei width,
  GLsizei height,
  GLsizei border,
  GLenum format, GLenum type, GLvoid *data);
```

The *internal format* can be either a *base internal format*, such as GL_RGB or GL_INTENSITY, or a *sized internal format*, such as GL_RGB8 or GL_INTENSITY16. (For compatibility with OpenGL 1.0, *internal format* values 1, 2, 3, and 4 are equivalent to the base internal formats GL_ALPHA, GL_LUMINANCE_ALPHA, GL_RGB, and GL_RGBA, respectively.) A base internal format permits OpenGL to store the resulting texture using an internal component resolution of its own choosing. The internal component resolution is the number of bits allocated to each value in a texture image. By specifying a sized internal format when defining a texture, an application is requesting that OpenGL allocate the texture's internal format to be as close as possible to the internal component resolution specified by the internal format.

A sized internal format requests OpenGL to assign the texture component memory allocation to be as close as possible to the internal component resolution requested.

These additions to OpenGL 1.1 match those of a subset of the GL_EXT_texture extension.

6.1.1.5 Texture Replace Environment

A common use of texture mapping is to replace the color values of generated fragments with texture color data. This could be specified only indirectly in OpenGL

1.0, which required that the OpenGL program specify that "white" geometry be modulated by a texture. OpenGL 1.1 allows such replacements to be specified explicitly, possibly improving performance.

To use the replace texture environment, call

```
glTexEnvf(GL_TEXTURE_ENV,
  GL_TEXTURE_ENV_MODE, GL_REPLACE);
```

This addition matches a subset of the GL_EXT_texture extension.

6.1.1.6 Texture Proxies

In OpenGL 1.0, it is difficult to determine whether a texture will fit into texture memory on a given system. The GL_MAX_TEXTURE_SIZE returned by glGet-Integerv assumes the worst case for texture allocation and is therefore insufficient to query the maximum texture size at the various possible texture formats, component resolutions, and shapes. The texture proxy mechanism addresses this problem.

Texture proxies allow an OpenGL implementation to advertise different maximum texture image sizes as a function of some other texture arguments, especially of the internal image format. An OpenGL program may use the proxy query mechanism to tailor its use of texture resources at runtime. The proxy interface is designed to allow such queries without adding new routines to the OpenGL interface.

The following shows how to use a proxy texture to determine whether a 512-by-512 texture with no border at mipmap level 0 requesting an RGB internal format with 4 bits per component can fit in texture memory.

```
GLint internalFormat;

glTexImage2D(GL_PROXY_TEXTURE_2D, /*level*/ 0, GL_RGB4,
  512, 512, /*border*/ 0,
  GL_RGB, GL_UNSIGNED_BYTE,
  /* no data */ NULL);
glGetTexLevelParameteriv(GL_PROXY_TEXTURE_2D, 0,
  GL_TEXTURE_INTERNAL_FORMAT, &internalFormat);

if (internalFormat != GL_RGB4) {
  /* Should be the format requested if texture fits, not zero. */
  printf("Texture won't fit!");
} else {
  printf("Texture will fit.");
}
```

The GL_PROXY_TEXTURE_2D target requests a proxy texture. The texture image, format, and type (the last three arguments) are ignored when a proxy texture is specified, since no actual texture image is loaded. If a texture as specified by `glTexImage2D` can be allocated, the proxy state values for the specified level-of-detail are updated. Otherwise, if the texture is too large, no error is generated, but the proxy width, height, border width, and internal format are set to 0.

Note that the proxy texture mechanism reports what the texture memory can handle based on the current texture parameters, not the available resources. It is still possible to run out of resources when you try to allocate the real texture.

These additions match those of a subset of the `GL_EXT_texture` extension, except that implementations return allocation information consistent with support for complete mipmap arrays.

6.1.1.7 Copy Texture and Subtexture

In OpenGL 1.0, textures can be defined only with image data stored in host memory. OpenGL 1.1 adds the ability to define textures with image data taken directly from the frame buffer. Two new routines for 2D and 1D textures are provided:

```
void glCopyTexImage2D(GLenum target, GLint level,
  GLenum internalformat,
  GLint x, GLint y,
  GLsizei width, GLsizei height,
  int border);
void glCopyTexImage1D(GLenum target, GLint level,
  GLenum internalformat,
  GLint x, GLint y,
  GLsizei width,
  int border);
```

The *x*, *y*, *width*, and *height* arguments specify the window coordinates and dimensions for a pixel rectangle within the frame buffer to be used as the source for texture image data.

In OpenGL 1.0, to respecify a texture, the entire texture needs to be reloaded. However, OpenGL 1.1 adds the capability to respecify rectangular subregions of existing texture images. One use of subtexture loading is to "roam" through a large texture. Two new routines support subtexture loading for 2D and 1D textures:

```
void glTexSubImage2D(GLenum target, GLint level,
  GLint xoffset, GLint yoffset,
  GLsizei width, GLsizei height,
  GLenum format,
  GLenum type, GLvoid *data);
void glTexSubImage1D(GLenum target, GLint level,
  GLint xoffset,
  GLsizei width,
```

```
GLenum format,
GLenum type, GLvoid *data);
```

The *xoffset* and *yoffset* arguments specify the lower left texel coordinates of the *width*-wide by *height*-high rectangular subregion of the texture array. The texture's internal format is unchanged. The other arguments correspond to the arguments of `glTexImage2D` and `glTexImage1D` respectively.

OpenGL 1.1's `glCopyTexSubImage2D` and `glCopyTexSubImage1D` routines combine copying texture image data from the frame buffer *and* subtexture loading.

These additions match those defined by the `GL_EXT_copy_texture` and `GL_EXT_subtexture` extensions.

6.1.1.8 Texture Objects

OpenGL 1.0 was designed with the assumption that display lists could be used to cache textures on systems that provide dedicated texture memory. In practice, this approach proved infeasible; more explicit support for texture management was needed. OpenGL 1.1 adds *texture objects* to provide better support for managing texture memory. A set of texture arrays and its related texture state can be treated as a single object. Such treatment allows greater implementation efficiency when multiple arrays are used. In conjunction with the subtexture capability, it also allows clients to make gradual changes to existing texture arrays, rather than completely redefining them.

Like display lists, texture objects are named by unsigned integers. However, the name spaces for texture objects and display lists are independent. A texture object is created by *binding* an unused name to TEXTURE_1D or TEXTURE_2D. The binding is done with the routine

```
void glBindTexture(GLenum target, GLuint textureObject);
```

When an unused texture object is first bound, it acquires new default texture state. If bound to the GL_TEXTURE_2D, the texture object becomes a 2D texture until deleted; likewise for a texture object bound to GL_TEXTURE_1D.

Calling `glBindTexture` on an already existing texture object rebinds the texture to the specified target (and breaks the binding of the previously bound texture).

While a texture object is bound, OpenGL operations on the target to which it is bound affect the bound object, and queries of the target to which the texture object is bound return the state of the bound object. If texture mapping of the object's dimensionality is enabled, the state of the bound texture directs the texturing operation.

Texture objects can be deleted with `glDeleteTextures`. Unused texture object names can be generated with `glGenTextures`. `glIsTexture` determines whether a specified unsigned integer names an existing texture object. These routines parallel the display list functionality provided by `glDeleteLists`, `glGenLists`, and `glIsList`.

OpenGL implementations for graphics hardware with dedicated texture memory can choose to provide a working set of *resident* texture objects on which binding operations are carried out with higher performance. When a texture object is already loaded into texture memory, it will be faster to bind to than if the texture had to be downloaded from the computer's main memory. The routine `glAreTextures-Resident` provides a means to query whether a set of textures are resident.

To help guide an OpenGL implementation to determine what texture objects should be resident, `glPrioritizeTextures` lets a program assign *priorities* in the range of [0,1] to texture objects. Zero indicates the lowest priority, with the least likelihood of being resident; 1 indicates the highest priority, with the greatest likelihood of being resident.

Texture objects are shared between contexts that are configured to share display lists.

These additions match those of the `GL_EXT_texture_object` extension, with slight additions to the texture residency semantics.

6.1.1.9 Miscellaneous Changes

OpenGL 1.1 also makes a number of miscellaneous minor changes and clarifications:

- Color indices may now be specified as unsigned bytes.
- Texture coordinates s, t, and r are divided by q during the rasterization of points, pixel rectangles, and bitmaps. This division was documented only for lines and polygons in OpenGL 1.0.
- The line rasterization algorithm has been changed so that vertical lines on pixel borders rasterize correctly.
- Texture alpha values are returned as in OpenGL 1.0 if there is no alpha channel in the texture array. However, this behavior was unspecified in OpenGL 1.0, and was incorrectly documented in the *OpenGL Reference Manual*.
- Fog start and end values may now be negative.
- Evaluated color values direct the evaluation of the lighting equation if `glColorMaterial` is enabled.

6.1.2 GLX 1.1 and GLX 1.2

GLX 1.1 adds a mechanism for providing vendor-specified GLX extensions. GLX 1.2 adds `glXGetCurrentDisplay` to return the current X server display (previously, the current drawable and context could be queried, but not the display). Most of the other changes in the 1.1 and 1.2 revisions to GLX are clarifications of the operation of GLX. Figure 6.3 shows the relationship of GLX 1.1 and GLX 1.2 to the base GLX functionality.

Figure 6.3 GLX 1.1 and 1.2 additions.

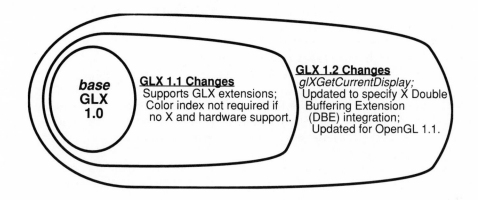

6.1.2.1 Vendor-specific GLX Extensions

GLX 1.0 anticipated the need to query the version of GLX using `glXQuery-Version`. However, no mechanism like OpenGL's `glGetString(GL_EXTENSIONS)` support was provided for vendor-specific extensions to GLX. GLX 1.1 adds such a mechanism.

Like core OpenGL extensions, GLX extensions are advertised by a text string naming the available extensions. The routine that returns this string is

```
const char *glXQueryExtensionsString(Display *dpy, int screen);
```

The string returned is zero-terminated and contains a space-separated list of extension names. The character pointer returned by `glXQueryExtensionsString` does not need to be deallocated and should not be modified. Note that different X screens may support different sets of GLX extensions. This can be the case if the graphics hardware used by the two screens is different and does not provide the same extension capabilities.

To help you determine when a GLX extension is supported, here is a function that returns true if a named GLX extension is supported:

```
int
glxExtensionSupported(Display * dpy, int screen, char *extension)
{
  int major, minor;
  const char *extensions, *start;
  char *where, *terminator;
```

```
if (glXQueryVersion(dpy, &major, &minor)) {
  if (minor >= 1 || major > 1) {
    extensions = glXQueryExtensionsString(dpy, screen);
    start = extensions;
    for (;;) {
      where = strstr(start, extension);
      if (!where)
        return 0;
      terminator = where + strlen(extension);
      if (where == start || *(where - 1) == ' ')
        if (*terminator == ' ' || *terminator == '0')
          return 1;
      start = terminator;
    }
  }
}
return 0;
}
```

Because `glXQueryExtensionsString` is a GLX 1.1 routine, the query above first makes sure GLX 1.1 is supported.

GLX extension names use the same naming conventions used by OpenGL extensions described in Section 5.6.1, except that GLX extension names are typically prefixed with `GLX_` to help distinguish them from core OpenGL extensions. To provide a flavor of the types of GLX extensions possible, a set of GLX extensions endorsed by multiple OpenGL vendors and a few Silicon Graphics-specific extensions are described here:

> `GLX_EXT_visual_info` enhances the standard GLX mechanism for querying information about visuals to better distinguish visuals. `glXChooseVisual` as originally specified does not have attributes to select a specific X visual type (`TrueColor` versus `DirectColor` for RGBA, and `PseudoColor` versus `Static-Color` for color index) or to obtain information about transparent pixels.
>
> Here is an example of using the extension to match only `DirectColor` visuals:
>
> ```
> int attrib_list[] = {
>   GLX_RGBA,
>   GLX_X_VISUAL_TYPE_EXT, GLX_DIRECT_COLOR_EXT,
>   None
> };
>
> visual = glXChooseVisual(dpy, DefaultScreenOfDisplay(dpy),
>   attrib_list);
> ```

Without the new `GLX_X_VISUAL_TYPE_EXT` attribute, `glXChooseVisual` returns `TrueColor` visuals in preference to `DirectColor` visuals. This makes it difficult to retrieve OpenGL-capable `DirectColor` visuals.

`GLX_EXT_visual_rating` gives X servers a way to export GLX-capable visuals with improved features or image quality, but lower performance or greater system burden, without having these visuals selected in preference to faster, lighter-weight visuals.

This extension introduces a new visual attribute, `GLX_VISUAL_CAVEAT_EXT`, that can be used by `glXChooseVisual` and `glXGetConfig`. This attribute distinguishes visuals as either slow (`GLX_SLOW_EXT`) or without caveats (`GLX_NONE_EXT`). If the attribute is not specified, `glXChooseVisual` gives preference to visuals without caveats.

`GLX_SGI_make_current_read` allows programs to make current with a different "read" drawable that is distinct from the drawable used for writing pixels. Normally, the same drawable used for writing pixels is used for reading pixels. When a read drawable is specified, the source pixel data for `glCopyPixels` and `glDrawPixels` comes from the read drawable. A different read and write drawable let pixels be copied from one window or pixmap to another. To select a read drawable, call

```
glXMakeCurrentReadSGI(Display *dpy, GLXDrawable write,
  GLXDrawable read, GLXContext context);
```

The current read drawable can be retrieved with `glXGetCurrentReadDrawableSGI`.

`GLX_SGI_swap_control` allows an application to set a minimum period for buffer swaps (counted in display retrace periods) performed by `glXSwapBuffers`. This lets the application maintain a constant frame rate, even when some frames could be rendered faster than the application's sustained frame rate. Maintaining a constant frame rate is desirable because the animation may otherwise appear jerky or uneven and distract the viewer.

As an example, an application with a sustained frame rate of 30 frames per second with a 60-hertz display retrace rate may benefit by calling `glXSwapIntervalSGI(2)`. Even though the application may occasionally render a frame in less than a single display retrace, the frame rate will be held to 30 frames per second.

`GLX_SGI_video_sync` allows an application to synchronize drawing (or another activity, such as audio) to the vertical retrace of a monitor. `glXWaitVideoSyncSGI` lets a process sleep until a counter corresponding to a number of screen refreshes reaches a desired value. The current counter value can be queried with `glXGetVideoSyncSGI`.

`GLX_SGIS_multisample` adds a new visual attribute used to find visuals that support *multisampling*, a frame buffer feature that automatically reduces rendering artifacts caused by aliasing. Multisampling is generally superior to other antialiasing techniques such as those described in Section 5.3.2, because rendering primitives do not have to be sorted back-to-front (a hard task for arbitrary 3D scenes). Multisampling works by maintaining multiple color, depth, and stencil *samples* per pixel; the displayed pixel is the average of all the samples. Because these multiple samples require substantial amounts of frame buffer memory and more computation to render multisampled primitives, multisampling is likely to be supported only on expensive high-end graphics hardware.

Multisampling is used by creating a window using a multisample-capable visual. The `GLX_SAMPLE_SGIS` visual attribute requests a visual with the given number of multisamples. For example:

```
int attributes[] = { GLX_RGB, GLX_SAMPLES_SGIS, 4,
  GLX_DEPTH_SIZE, 24, None};

visual = glXChooseVisual(dpy, screen, attributes);
```

If `visual` is not `NULL`, a multisampled visual exists. Windows created with it will automatically render with multisampling enabled.

For a more detailed description of these GLX extensions, consult the GLX manual pages for the extension routines.

6.1.2.2 GLX Implementation Information

The list of available GLX extensions is one type of GLX implementation information that can be retrieved. GLX 1.1 has other new routines to retrieve GLX implementation information.

The `glXGetClientString` routine returns a character pointer to strings indicating the version, vendor, and GLX extensions supported by the client GLX implementation. Here is how the routine is used:

```
const char *client_version, *client_vendor, *client_extensions;

client_version = glXGetClientString(dpy, GLX_VERSION);
client_vendor = glXGetClientString(dpy, GLX_VENDOR);
client_extensions = glXGetClientString(dpy, GLX_EXTENSIONS);
```

Note that the list of GLX extensions returned by `glXQueryExtensionsString` shows extensions that are supported by *both* the GLX client and GLX server implementations. This is because an extension is available for use only if the extension is supported by both the client and the server.

Another routine, `glXQueryServerString`, allows GLX server implementation information to be returned:

```
const char *server_version, *server_vendor, *server_extensions;

server_version = glXQueryServerString(dpy, screen, GLX_VERSION);
server_vendor = glXQueryServerString(dpy, screen, GLX_VENDOR);
server_extensions = glXQueryServerString(dpy, screen,
  GLX_EXTENSIONS);
```

Notice that the GLX server information can vary with the X screen.

6.1.2.3 Retrieving the Current Display

GLX 1.2 adds a routine named `glXGetCurrentDisplay` that fixes a glaring omission in previous GLX versions. While the current bound drawable and rendering context could be retrieved, before GLX 1.2, there was no way to return the currently bound X server connection. With GLX 1.2, the current bound display can be returned like this:

```
current_display = glXGetCurrentDisplay();
```

If no X display is currently bound, NULL is returned.

6.1.2.4 Minor GLX Updates

GLX versions 1.1 and 1.2 have made a few minor clarifications and updates to GLX:

- **GLX 1.1:** Not all X servers support `PseudoColor` and `StaticColor` visuals, though most do. For X servers without such visuals, OpenGL's color index color model cannot be provided. GLX no longer mandates a color index-capable visual when the graphics hardware is incapable of supporting color index. But if the X server supports `PseudoColor` or `StaticColor` visuals, color index is still required.

- **GLX 1.2:** GLX 1.0 specified that double-buffering window state could be consistent with X's Multi-Buffering Extension (also known as MBX). This extension was never standardized, and the X Consortium has since abandoned it in favor of the X Double Buffering Extension (DBE). GLX reflects this state of affairs by mandating conformance with DBE.

- **GLX 1.2:** GLX rendering contexts with shared display lists also share OpenGL 1.1 texture objects.

- **GLX 1.2:** GLX protocol definitions have been added for new OpenGL 1.1 rendering commands.

6.1.3 GLU 1.1 and GLU 1.2

The OpenGL Utility (GLU) library has been updated twice. The GLU 1.1 revision added a routine to query the GLU library version and GLU extensions that are supported. GLU 1.1 also improved the Non-Uniform Rational B-Splines (NURBS) support. The GLU 1.2 revision reimplemented the polygon tessellator with a new interface (the old interface, described in Section 2.1.2, remains for backward compatibility). Figure 6.4 shows the relationships of GLU 1.1 and 1.2 to the base GLU functionality.

6.1.3.1 GLU Implementation Information

GLU 1.1 adds a routine to query the GLU library version and any GLU extensions supported (no GLU extensions exist at the time of this writing). The routine is very similar to the OpenGL `glGetString` routine. The routine can be called two ways:

```
const char *glu_version, *glu_extensions;

glu_version = gluGetString(GLU_VERSION);
glu_extensions = gluGetString(GLU_EXTENSIONS);
```

6.1.3.2 Improved NURBS Support

GLU 1.1 adds more options for the NURBS tessellation support described in Section 5.5.3. Instead of a single sampling method based on path length, three different methods can be selected:

> `GLU_PATH_LENGTH` (the default) makes sure the maximum length, in pixels, of the edges of the tessellation polygons are no greater than the sampling tolerance (specified by `GLU_SAMPLING_TOLERANCE`).

Figure 6.4 GLU 1.1 and 1.2 additions.

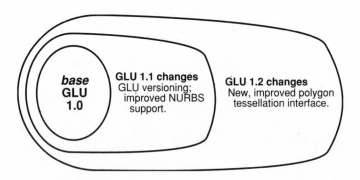

`GLU_PARAMETRIC_ERROR` specifies that the surface is rendered in such a way that the parametric tolerance (specified by `GLU_PARAMETRIC_TOLERANCE`) describes the maximum distance, in pixels, between the tessellation polygons and the surfaces they approximate.

`GLU_DOMAIN_DISTANCE` allows programs to control, in parametric coordinates, the number of sample points per unit length (specified by `GLU_U_STEP` and `GLU_V_STEP`) that are taken in the *u* and *v* dimensions.

The sampling method and related sampling method parameters are controlled with `gluNurbsProperty`. For example:

```
GLUnurbsObj *surface_gen;

surface_gen = gluNewNurbsRenderer();
gluNurbsProperty(surface_gen,
  GLU_SAMPLING_METHOD, GLU_DOMAIN_DISTANCE);
gluNurbsProperty(surface_gen, GLU_U_STEP, 50);
gluNurbsProperty(surface_gen, GLU_V_STEP, 25);
```

The sampling method that is best depends on the surface or curve being tessellated and is beyond the scope of this book.

6.1.3.3 Updated Polygon Tessellator

GLU 1.2 reimplements the polygon tessellation routines to be more robust and more functional, and to give more programmable control. The interface and features of the new tessellator are described briefly here.

The new tessellator uses the same `gluNewTess` and `gluDeleteTess` routines to create and destroy tessellation objects used by the rest of the interface. Input contours are specified in a slightly different fashion with the following new routines:

```
void gluTessBeginPolygon(GLUtesselator *tess, void *polygon_data);
void gluTessBeginContour(GLUtesselator *tess);
void gluTessVertex(GLUtesselator *tess, GLdouble coords[3], void
  *vertex_data);
void gluTessEndContour(GLUtesselator *tess);
void gluTessEndPolygon(GLUtesselator *tess);
```

A polygon tessellation is initiated with `gluTessBeginPolygon` and ended with `gluTessEndPolygon`. Between these calls, there must be one or more contours. Each contour is initiated with `gluTessBeginContour` and ended with `gluTess-EndContour`. Each contour is defined by 0 or more calls to `gluTessVertex` to define a closed contour (the last vertex of each contour is automatically linked to the first). At the end of the polygon definition, a set of callbacks is made (registered by `gluTessCallback`) to generate the resulting tessellation.

The following are new features and advantages of the GLU 1.2 tessellator:

- There are two versions of each callback: one with user-specified polygon data (the opaque handle passed to `gluTessBeginPolygon`) and one without it.

- A new *combine* callback exists for combining or merging features. This might occur, for example, when the tessellator detects an intersection between two input vertices. The callback allows the program to combine other vertex data (such as color) between the points being combined.

- A tolerance for merging features to reduce the size of the output tessellation can be established. The tolerance is specified like this:

```
GLUtesselator *poly_gen;

gluTessProperty(poly_gen, GLU_TESS_TOLERANCE, 0.00001);
```

The default tolerance is 0.

- The contours partition a plane into regions. The tessellator's *winding rule* specifies which of these regions are inside the polygon to be tessellated. The winding rule can be set like this:

```
gluTessProperty(poly_gen, GLU_TESS_WINDING_RULE,
    GLU_TESS_WINDING_NONZERO);
```

The default winding rule is `GLU_TESS_WINDING_ODD`. The two other rules have *constructive solid geometry* (CSG) applications for computing polygon intersections (`GLU_TESS_WINDING_ABS_GEQ_TWO`), unions (`GLU_TESS_WINDING_POSITIVE`), and differences (`GLU_TESS_WINDING_POSITIVE`).

- Also for CSG applications, the tessellator can be used to compute a set of closed contours separating the polygon interior and exterior instead of a tessellation. The "boundary only" mode can be enabled like this:

```
gluTessProperty(poly_gen, GLU_TESS_BOUNDARY_ONLY, GL_TRUE);
```

- The `gluGetTessProperty` can be used to retrieve tessellator properties:

```
GLdouble tolerance;

gluGetTessProperty(poly_gen, GLU_TESS_TOLERANCE, &tolerance);
```

- To ensure that the vertices are planar, all input data is projected to a plane perpendicular to a *polygon normal* before tessellation and all output triangles will be oriented counterclockwise with respect to the normal. The polygon normal can be specified like this:

```
gluTessNormal(poly_gen, 0.0, 0.0, 1.0);
```

If you do not specify a normal, the normal will be calculated automatically (expecting that the vertices are coplanar or approximately so).
- The GLU 1.2 tessellator is generally more robust and faster than in the previous implementation.

For a more thorough explanation of the GLU 1.2 tessellator, see the manual pages for the routines listed above.

6.2 X INPUT EXTENSION

OpenGL applications often use input devices in addition to the standard keyboard and mouse. Such programs access input devices such as tablets, dial boxes, button boxes, and exotic 3D input sources such as the Spaceball (see Figure 6.5). For example, an application constructing 3D models may assign different axes of rotation and translation to each knob on a dial box so the user can manipulate 3D objects more naturally.

Because input is beyond the scope of OpenGL's rendering model, OpenGL leaves it to the window system to determine how such input devices are accessed. For the X Window System, the X Input extension is used. The extension was designed by engineers at Ardent Computer and Hewlett-Packard and is an X Consortium standard.

Figure 6.5 Sophisticated input devices often used by 3D applications.

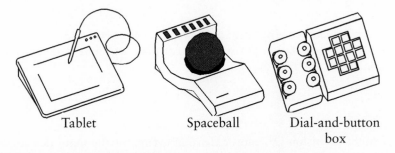

Tablet   Spaceball   Dial-and-button
                                         box

The X Input extension's approach is to define requests and events analogous to, but distinct from, the core requests and events for mouse and keyboard input. This allows extension input devices to be individually distinguishable from each other and from the core input devices. The extension can support a wide variety of input devices. This section introduces the X Input extension's structure and API. Examples are shown using the X Input extension with both Xlib- and Motif-based OpenGL programs.

Programs using the X Input extension should link with the extension's client library, known as `libXi`. Normally, this is done by adding `-lXi` to your program's link line. The X extension library (`libXext`) and Xlib are required to use `libXi`, so the `-lXext` and `-lX11` link options should follow the `-lXi` option. Source code using the extension's API should include the following header file:

```
#include <X11/extensions/XInput.h>
```

6.2.1 Querying the Extension

The first step in using the X Input extension is to query whether the extension is supported by your X server. Like all X extensions, the X Input extension is not necessarily supported on all X servers, so programs should query the existence of the extension before using it. The following routine determines whether the X Input extension is supported and returns the extension's event base:

```
int
isXInputSupported(Display *dpy, int *event_base)
{
  Bool exists;
  int opcode, error_base,
  XExtensionVersion *version;

  exists = XQueryExtension(dpy, "XInputExtension", &opcode,
    event_base, &error_base);
  if(!exists)
    return 0;
  version = XGetExtensionVersion(dpy, "XInputExtension");
  if (version == NULL || ((int) version) == NoSuchExtension)
    return 0;
  XFree(version);
  return 1;
}
```

The X Input extension generates extension events for the input devices it manages. Unlike core events, which are always identified by constant integers for each core event type, an X extension's events are dynamically assigned a range of integer event types for however many events the extension provides. The base of this range is returned when the extension is queried with XQueryExtension. Your program should retain the returned event_base value, since it will be necessary to interpret correctly and dispatch X Input events. Similar to event_base, error_base returns the base of the dynamically assigned range of extension protocol error types, but this value is not often needed by applications. The opcode is the dynamically assigned extension request opcode, and, like the error_base, is rarely required by applications.[1]

The XGetExtensionVersion routine returns the X server's X Input extension version information. As of the writing of this book, the major version was 1 and the minor version was 3 for the extension. Though currently not very useful, the version information could be used to distinguish future revisions of the X Input extension. XGetExtensionVersion is passed the text string XInputExtension as a parameter; this suggests that versions of other extensions could be queried. This is not currently the case, nor is it likely to be.

6.2.2 Types of Extension Devices

The core X protocol supports only a pointer and a keyboard as input devices. The X pointer is usually implemented as a mouse device. The X pointer has two functions: (1) It generates motion events that client programs can detect, and (2) it can be used to indicate the current focus and location for events generated by the X keyboard. When the keyboard is not explicitly focused, the keyboard events track the pointer's location.

The keyboard and pointer are referred to as the *core devices*, and the input events they generate (KeyPress, KeyRelease, ButtonPress, ButtonRelease, and MotionNotify) are known as the *core input events*. All other input devices are referred to as *extension input devices* and the input events they generate are known as *extension input events*. The X Input extension does not change the behavior or functionality of the core input device or core events.

In the policy-free X tradition, the X Input extension provides a programming interface for the use of additional input devices, but the extension does not provide support for particular input devices. Instead, input devices are abstracted as logical devices. Any kind of input device may be used as an extension input device. Extension input devices may have zero or more keys, zero or more buttons, and zero or more valuators (axes of motion). Motion may be reported as relative movements from a previous position or as an absolute position.

All valuators reporting motion information for a given extension input device will report the same kind of motion information (absolute or relative). An example

---

1. This X convention is the reason glXQueryExtension also returns the GLX extension event and error bases.

of a device that returns absolute information is a tablet. A tablet returns absolute positions along two axes (*x* and *y*) identifying the location of the puck. A Spaceball returns relative information based on the rotation (*x*, *y*, and *z*) and translation (*x*, *y*, and *z*) forces on the ball.

By treating an input device abstractly as a collection of keys, buttons, and valuators, the extension can accommodate a wide variety of possible input devices within the X Input extension framework. The disadvantage of this flexibility is that there are no standards for the ways vendors advertise functionally identical input devices.

6.2.2.1 Input Classes

The possible information returned by an extension input device is determined by the *input classes* the device supports. The X Input extension defines these input classes:

> `Key` The device reports key events.
>
> `Button` The device reports button events.
>
> `Valuator` The device reports valuator data in motion events.
>
> `Proximity` The device reports proximity events. An input device, such as a graphics tablet, or touch tablet may send a proximity event to indicate that a stylus has moved into or out of contact with a positional sensing surface.
>
> `Focus` The device can be focused and reports focus events.
>
> `Feedback` The device supports feedback, such as key clicks, bells, or LEDs.

Each extension input device may support multiple input classes. For example, a joystick would support a button class and a valuator class with two axes. The extension allows server implementors to add new input classes without changing the extension protocol. For this reason, client programs that use functions such as `XListInputDevices`, which return information by input class should avoid using data for input classes not understood by the client. This allows new classes to be added without forcing existing clients to be recompiled.

6.2.3 Querying Supported Devices

Once support for the X Input extension has been determined, an application using the extension should determine whether the devices that the program supports are supported by the X server. The `XListInputDevices` routine returns a list of all devices that can be opened by the X server. The routine returns a pointer to an array of `XDeviceInfo` structures, or `NULL` if there are no input devices to list. `XFreeDeviceList` frees the non-`NULL` list returned by `XListInputDevices` once the list is no longer needed. The `XDeviceInfo` structure is shown in Figure 6.6.

The `type` field in the `XDeviceInfo` structure is an `Atom`, which can be converted to the text string naming the device type using `XGetAtomName`. Possible device type names are listed in Figure 6.7. The `name` field provides a character string naming the

Figure 6.6 XDeviceInfo structure.

```
typedef struct _XDeviceInfo *XDeviceInfoPtr;
typedef struct _XDeviceInfo {
  XID              id;
  Atom             type;
  char             *name;
  int              num_classes;
  int              use;
  XAnyClassPtr     inputclassinfo;
} XDeviceInfo;
```

device instance. Using the type and name fields, the desired device can be determined.

The X pointer device and keyboard device, as well as all available input devices, are reported by XListInputDevices. The use field in the structure specifies the current use of the device. If the value of the use field is IsXPointer, the device is the X pointer device. If the value of the field is IsXKeyboard, the device is the X keyboard device. If the value is IsXExtensionDevice, the device is available for use as an extension input device. The X Input extension allows clients to change the physical device that is used as the X pointer or X keyboard with XChangeKeyboardDevice and XChangePointerDevice.

Each XDeviceInfo entry contains a pointer to a list of structures that describe characteristics of each class of input supported by the device. The inputclassinfo field is the pointer to this list. The num_classes field contains the number of entries in this list. The entries in the list vary in length. A length field in each class information structure determines how many bytes to skip forward to find the next class information structure. This design permits input classes to be expanded or added in future revisions to the X Input extension. The XKeyInfo, XButtonInfo,

Figure 6.7 Possible device type names.

BARCODE	ID_MODULE	QUADRATURE
BUTTONBOX	KEYBOARD	SPACEBALL
CURSORKEYS	KNOB_BOX	TABLET
DATAGLOVE	MOUSE	TOUCHPAD
EYETRACKER	NINE_KNOB	TOUCHSCREEN
FOOTMOUSE	ONE_KNOB	TRACKBALL

and `XValuatorInfo` structures describe the characteristics of the key, button, and valuator input classes, respectively. These structures are shown in Figure 6.8.[2]

6.2.3.1 `xdevices.c`

The following program connects to an X server supporting the X Input extension and lists the characteristics of all supported devices:

```
#include <stdlib.h>
#include <stdio.h>
#include <X11/Xlib.h>
#include <X11/extensions/XInput.h>
```

After the required headers, the `list_input_devices` routine calls `XListInput-Devices` to determine what devices are supported by the X server. The remainder of the routine decodes and outputs the device list.

```
XDeviceInfoPtr
list_input_devices(Display * display, int *ndevices)
{
  int i, j, k;
  XDeviceInfoPtr list, slist;
  XAnyClassPtr any;
  XKeyInfoPtr key;
  XButtonInfoPtr b;
  XValuatorInfoPtr v;
  XAxisInfoPtr a;

  list = (XDeviceInfoPtr) XListInputDevices(display, ndevices);
  slist = list;
  printf("The number of available input devices is %d\n", *ndevices);
  for (i = 0; i < *ndevices; i++, list++) {
    printf("\nDevice id is %d\n", list->id);
    printf("Device type is %s\n", XGetAtomName(display, list->type));
    printf("Device name is %s\n", list->name);
    printf("Num_classes is %d\n", list->num_classes);
    if (list->num_classes > 0) {
      any = (XAnyClassPtr) (list->inputclassinfo);
      for (j = 0; j < list->num_classes; j++) {
        printf("\tInput class is %d\n", any->class);
        printf("\tLength is %d\n", any->length);
```

---

2. These structures, as originally defined, have fields called `class`. C++ uses the word class as a keyword, so in C++, the field is remapped to `c_class`.

Figure 6.8 The XKeyInfo, XButtonInfo, and XValuatorInfo structures describing additional device characteristics. XAnyClassInfo is a generic header for all class info structures. Notice that the XValuatorInfo structure has an array of axes information.

```
typedef struct _XKeyInfo *XKeyInfoPtr;
typedef struct _XKeyInfo {
  XID                class;
  int                length;
  unsigned short     min_keycode;
  unsigned short     max_keycode;
  unsigned short     num_keys;
} XKeyInfo;

typedef struct _XButtonInfo *XButtonInfoPtr;
typedef struct _XButtonInfo {
  XID                class;
  int                length;
  short              num_buttons;
} XButtonInfo;

typedef struct _XAxisInfo *XAxisInfoPtr;
typedef struct _XAxisInfo {
  int                resolution;
  int                min_value;
  int                max_value;
} XAxisInfo;

typedef struct _XValuatorInfo *XValuatorInfoPtr;
typedef struct _XValuatorInfo {
  XID                class;
  int                length;
  unsigned char      num_axes;
  unsigned char      mode;
  unsigned long      motion_buffer;
  XAxisInfoPtr       axes;
  } XValuatorInfo;

typedef struct _XAnyClassinfo *XAnyClassPtr;
typedef struct _XAnyClassinfo {
  XID                class;
  int                length;
} XAnyClassInfo;
```

```
switch (any->class) {
case KeyClass:
  key = (XKeyInfoPtr) any;
  printf("\tNum_keys is %d\n", key->num_keys);
  printf("\tMin_keycode is %d\n", key->min_keycode);
  printf("\tMax_keycode is %d\n", key->max_keycode);
  break;
```

A device with a `KeyClass` input class has a specified number of keys; the generated keycodes range between the `min_keycode` and `max_keycode` fields.

```
case ButtonClass:
  b = (XButtonInfoPtr) any;
  printf("\tNum_buttons is %d\n", b->num_buttons);
  break;
```

A device with a `ButtonClass` input class has a given number of buttons. Generally, a key is distinguished from a button by whether the face of the key is marked with a symbol giving it meaning. Keys also tend to auto-repeat, while buttons do not. Buttons support tracking of valuator motion when held down.

```
case ValuatorClass:
  v = (XValuatorInfoPtr) any;
  a = (XAxisInfoPtr) ((char *) v +
    sizeof(XValuatorInfo));
  printf("\tMode is %d\n", v->mode);
  printf("\tNum_axes is %d\n\n", v->num_axes);
  for (k = 0; k < v->num_axes; k++, a++) {
    printf("\t\tMin_value is %d\n", a->min_value);
    printf("\t\tMax_value is %d\n", a->max_value);
    printf("\t\tResolution is %d\n\n", a->resolution);
  }
  break;
```

A device with a `ValuatorClass` input class has a specified number of valuators; each axis has a potentially independent `min_value`, `max_value`, and `resolution`.

```
default:
  printf("unknown class\n");
}
any = (XAnyClassPtr) ((char *) any + any->length);
```

Notice how the `length` field is used to skip to the next class info entry.

```
      }
    }
  }
  return slist;
}

main(int argc, char **argv)
{
  int ndevices;
  Display *display;
  XDeviceInfoPtr slist;
```

`xdevices` opens a connection to the X server, but is unlike most X applications in that no windows are created. This is because `xdevices` simply queries the X server for its supported devices and has no graphical user interface.

```
  display = XOpenDisplay(NULL);
  if (display == NULL) {
    printf("Could not open display.\n");
    exit(1);
  }
  slist = list_input_devices(display, &ndevices);
  if (slist) {
    XFreeDeviceList(slist);
  }
}
```

The routine `XFreeDeviceList` is used to free the non-`NULL` list returned by `XListInputDevices` when the list is no longer needed.

6.2.4 Sample Devices

Because the X Input extension does not mandate the ways specific types of devices should be advertised, each vendor decides how the devices they wish to support are advertised. This subsection gives guidance to programmers desiring to use X Input devices by describing how one vendor, Silicon Graphics, supports various devices. The information for the described devices can be obtained with the `xdevices` program shown in the preceding subsection, except for the information on the specific physical layout of the device, which cannot be determined by extension requests.

6.2.4.1 Silicon Graphics Dial-and-button Box

Silicon Graphics's dial-and-button box, manufactured by Seiko, consists of eight dials and a separate button pad with 32 buttons, each with an LED indicator. The device is advertised through the X Input extension as follows:

```
Device type:          KNOB_BOX
Device name:          dial+buttons
Classes:              2
  ButtonClass
    Number buttons:     32
  ValuatorClass
    Device mode:        Absolute
    Number axes:        8
    Axis 1 through 8
      Minimum value:    -32768
      Maximum value:    32767
      Resolution:       200
```

The physical layout of Silicon Graphics's dial-and-button box is shown in Figure 6.9.

6.2.4.2 Silicon Graphics Spaceball

Silicon Graphics's Spaceball, manufactured by Spatial Systems, Inc., is a pedestal supporting a palm-sized ball with an inset button and two rows of four buttons

Figure 6.9 Physical layout of the valuators and buttons for the dial-and-button-box device supported by Silicon Graphics.

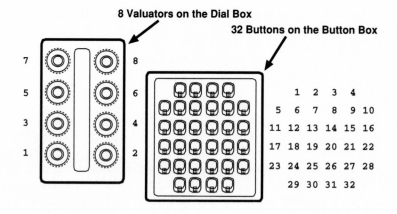

positioned on a shelf forward from the ball. Applying pressure to the ball causes valuator events to be generated in six axes of freedom. Twisting the ball generates rotations; lightly pushing or pulling the ball generates translations. A seventh axis measures the device's period. The buttons also generate input. The device is advertised through the X Input extension as follows:

```
Device type:          SPACEBALL
Device name:          spaceball
Classes:              2
  ButtonClass
    Number buttons:   9
  ValuatorClass
    Device mode:      Absolute
    Number axes:      7
    Axis 1 through 7
      Minimum value:  -18000
      Maximum value:  18000
      Resolution:     200
```

The physical layout of Silicon Graphics's Spaceball device is shown in Figure 6.10.

Figure 6.10 Physical layout of the valuators and buttons for the Spaceball device supported by Silicon Graphics.

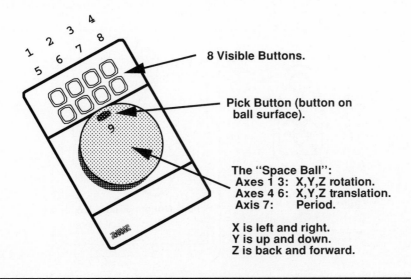

8 Visible Buttons.

Pick Button (button on ball surface).

The "Space Ball":
Axes 1 3: X,Y,Z rotation.
Axes 4 6: X,Y,Z translation.
Axis 7:   Period.

X is left and right.
Y is up and down.
Z is back and forward.

6.2.4.3 Silicon Graphics Tablet

Silicon Graphics's tablet, manufactured by Hitachi, has a large square surface on which a four-button puck with a crosshair slides. The device returns the absolute location of the puck on the tablet surface with high resolution.

```
Device type:          TABLET
Device name:          tablet
Classes:              2
  ButtonClass
    Number buttons:   4
  ValuatorClass
    Device mode:      Absolute
    Number axes:      2
    Axis 1
      Minimum value:  0
      Maximum value:  2206
      Resolution:     200
    Axis 2
      Minimum value:  0
      Maximum value:  2206
      Resolution:     200
```

The physical layout of Silicon Graphics's tablet puck is shown in Figure 6.11.

Figure 6.11 Physical layout of the valuators and buttons for the tablet device supported by Silicon Graphics.

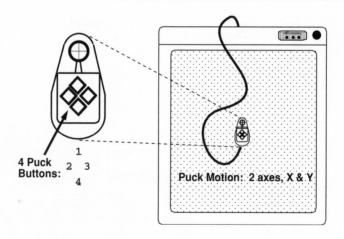

4 Puck Buttons: 1 2 3 4

Puck Motion: 2 axes, X & Y

6.2.5 Opening and Selecting Events from a Device

Once the desired device is determined, a client program must request that the X server open the device. This is done with the `XOpenDevice` routine. Multiple clients can all have the same device open. A `device_id` parameter uniquely identifies the device to be opened. The `device_id` is obtained from the `id` field of an `XDevice-Info` structure, returned by `XListInputDevices`. Successfully opening a device returns an `XDevice*`. The `XDevice` structure contains a pointer to an array of `XInputClassInfo` structures. Each element in that array contains information about events of a particular input class supported by the input device. The `XDevice` and `XInputClassInfo` structures are shown in Figure 6.12.

A client program determines the event type and event class for a given device event by using macros defined in `<X11/extensions/XInput.h>`. The name of the macro corresponds to the desired event (for example, `DeviceButtonPress`). The macro is passed an `XDevice*` returned by `XOpenDevice`.

The macro fills in the value of the event class. The event class is an integer that is used by a client program to indicate to the X server which events the client program wants to receive. The macro also fills in the value of the event type. The event type is an integer that a client uses to determine what kind of event it has received from `XNextEvent`. The client compares the type field of the event structure with known event types to make this determination.

The core event types are constants and are defined in the header file `<X11/X.h>`; however, extension event types are not constants. Extension event types are dynamically allocated by the X server when the extension is initialized. For this reason, extension event types must be obtained by the client from the server at runtime.

Figure 6.12 The `XDevice` structure returned by `XOpenDevice`.

```
typedef struct {
  unsigned char          input_class;
  unsigned char          event_type_base;
} XInputClassInfo;

typedef struct {
  XID                    device_id;
  int                    num_classes;
  XInputClassInfo        *classes;
} XDevice;
```

For example, the event type and class for a tablet device are determined as follows:

```
XDeviceInfoPtr tablet_info;
XDevice *tablet;
int tablet_button_press, tablet_button_release;
XEventClass tablet_press_class, tablet_release_class,
  tablet_press_grab_class;

tablet = XOpenDevice(dpy, tablet_info->id);
DeviceButtonPress(tablet, tablet_button_press,
  tablet_press_class);
DeviceButtonPressGrab(tablet, unused_by_macro,
  tablet_press_grab_class);
DeviceButtonRelease(tablet, tablet_button_release,
  tablet_release_class);
```

Table 6.1 describes the X Input extension's event categories, associated event types, and event structures. The macro name for determining the integer values for the event type and class is the same as the event class name.

Device input events are selected using the `XSelectExtensionEvent` routine. The routine is passed the window from which events are to be selected and a list of `XEventClass` values that define the desired event classes and devices.

Continuing with the tablet example, `XSelectExtensionEvent` would be used to select for tablet motion events on a window like this:

```
XEventClass event_classes[3];

event_classes[0] = tablet_press_class;
event_classes[1] = tablet_press_grab_class;
event_classes[2] = tablet_release_class;
XSelectExtensionEvent(dpy, window, event_classes, 3);
```

The X Input extension's event classes are analogous to the core input events. The one event class with no corresponding equivalent is the `DeviceButtonPressGrab`. The event class does not select any event by itself, but instead controls the way the button release event after a button press is delivered. For core pointer button presses and releases, the pointer is automatically grabbed between the `ButtonPress` and `ButtonRelease` events on behalf of the client for which `ButtonPress` was selected. However, this is not necessarily the case for device button press and release events. Only when `DeviceButtonPressGrab` is selected will an implicit passive grab be enacted between a device button press and release. Because most programs will want to receive both the `DeviceButtonPress` *and* the `DeviceButtonRelease`

Table 6.1 The event categories, types, classes, and structures for the X input extension.

Event Category	Event Type/Class	Event Structure
Device key events	DeviceKeyPress	XDeviceKeyPressedEvent
	DeviceKeyRelease	XDeviceKeyReleasedEvent
Device button events	DeviceButtonPress	XDeviceButtonPressedEvent
	DeviceButtonRelease	XDeviceButtonReleasedEvent
	DeviceOwnerGrabButton	n/a
	DeviceButtonPressGrab	n/a
Device motion events	DeviceMotionNotify	XDeviceMotionEvent
	DevicePointerMotionHint	
	DeviceButton1Motion	
	DeviceButton2Motion	
	DeviceButton3Motion	
	DeviceButton4Motion	
	DeviceButton5Motion	
	DeviceButtonMotion	
Device input focus events	DeviceFocusIn	XDeviceFocusInEvent
	DeviceFocusOut	XDeviceFocusOutEvent
Device proximity events	ProximityIn	XProximityInEvent
	ProximityOut	XProximityOutEvent
Device state notification event	DeviceStateNotify	XDeviceStateNotifyEvent
Device mapping event	DeviceMappingNotify	XDeviceMappingEvent
Device change event	ChangeDeviceNotify	XChangeDeviceNotifyEvent

as a pair of events, selecting for `DeviceButtonPressGrab` is generally recommended whenever `DeviceButtonPress` and `DeviceButtonRelease` are selected.

A word of warning: If any client has selected the `DeviceButtonPressGrab` event class on some window for a specific device, any requests by other clients to select for either `DeviceButtonPress` or `DeviceButtonPressGrab` on the same window and device will cause an X protocol error to be delivered to the newly selecting client. Because typically only one client selects for device button presses and releases on a given window, this is usually not a problem.

`XSelectExtensionEvent` can be called multiple times for a given window and device. Subsequent calls replace the previous selected events. `XGetSelectedExtensionEvents` queries two lists of currently selected event classes for a specified window. One list contains the currently selected events for the calling client; the second list contains the list of all events selected by any clients.

Once a client has selected X Input extension events using `XSelectExtension-Event`, the X server will deliver X Input extension events to the client as appropriate. `XNextEvent` and the other Xlib routines for receiving X events will return X Input events just like other events. You can identify X Input extension events by comparing the event type field in the `XEvent` structure with the (dynamically assigned) event type of selected X Input extension events.

6.2.6   Other X Input Extension Features

The remainder of the X Input extension functionality is fairly analogous to the core X protocol's keyboard and pointer handling. The remaining functionality can be grouped into various categories:

> **Control of event propagation.** See `XChangeDeviceDontPropagateList` and `XGetDeviceDontPropagateList`.
>
> **Sending events.** See `XSendExtensionEvent`.
>
> **Getting motion history.** See `XGetDeviceMotionEvents` and `XFreeDevice-MotionEvents`.
>
> **Grabbing an extension device.** See `XGrabDevice`, `XUngrabDevice`, `XGrab-DeviceKey`, `XUngrabDeviceKey`, `XGrabDeviceButton`, `XUngrabDevice-Button`, and `XAllowDeviceEvents`.
>
> **Device focus.** See `XSetDeviceFocus` and `XGetDeviceFocus`.
>
> **Device feedbacks.** For controlling key clicks, bells, and LED displays. See `XGet-FeedbackControl`, `XFreeFeedbackList`, `XChangeFeedbackControl`, and `XDeviceBell`.
>
> **Device encoding.** See `XGetDeviceKeyMapping`, `XChangeDeviceKeyMapping`, `XGetDeviceModifierMapping`, `XSetDeviceModifierMapping`, `XSet-Device-ButtonMapping`, and `XGetDeviceButtonMapping`.
>
> **Device state.** See `XQueryDeviceState` and `XFreeDeviceState`.
>
> **Device mode.** See `XSetDeviceMode` and `XSetDeviceValuators`.
>
> **Device controls.** For controlling device resolution. See `XChangeDevice-Control`, `XGetDeviceControl`, and `XFreeDeviceControl`.

Further information on the X Input extension is available [31, 32, 10, 11].

6.2.7   An Xlib-based OpenGL Example

The following example demonstrates how to use OpenGL with an Xlib program. The program takes input from the dial-and-button box device described in Section

6.2.4. The program's window displays the state of the dials and buttons as shown in Figure 6.13.

The Xlib and OpenGL code for creating the window and OpenGL context is a simplified version of `glxdino.c`'s code (described in Section 2.1). The program uses the X Input extension to scan the supported input devices for a dial-and-button box. If one is found, `dials` selects for dial-and-button box input events and handles the returned events in its event processing loop.

To compile `dials`, use the following command line:

```
cc -o dials dials.c -lGLU -lGL -lXi -lXext -lXmu -lX11 -lm
```

The source code for `dials.c` follows

```
#include <string.h>
#include <stdio.h>
#include <stdlib.h>
#include <math.h>
```

Figure 6.13 Screen snapshot showing the `dials` example. Each dial shows the current rotation of the dials; the currently depressed buttons are darkened.

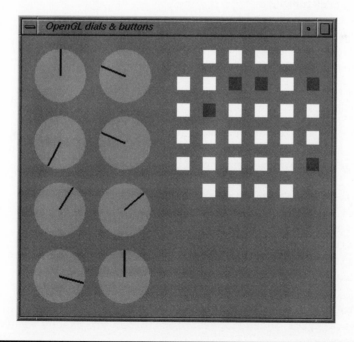

```
#include <GL/gl.h>
#include <GL/glu.h>
#include <GL/glx.h>
#include <X11/Xatom.h>  /* for XA_RGB_DEFAULT_MAP atom */
#include <X11/Xmu/StdCmap.h>  /* for XmuLookupStandardColormap */
#include <X11/extensions/XInput.h>
```

These headers are identical to those required by glxdino.c, with the addition of
the X Input extension header file.

```
#define PI              3.14159265358979323846
#define NUM_DIALS       8
#define NUM_BUTTONS     32
#define RELEASE         0
#define PRESS           1
```

The program assumes that 8 dials and 32 buttons are arranged on the device, as
shown in Figure 6.9.

```
Display *dpy;
Window win;
Atom wmDeleteWindow;
XDevice *dialsDevice;
int deviceMotionNotify = 0, deviceButtonPress = 0,
  deviceButtonPressGrab = 0, deviceButtonRelease = 0;
int dials[NUM_DIALS], buttons[NUM_BUTTONS];
```

dialsDevice is a handle to the dial-and-button box device. deviceMotionNotify,
deviceButtonPress, deviceButtonPressGrab, and deviceButtonRelease are
used to store dynamic event type values for the X Input events the program selects.
The dials and buttons arrays hold the program's most recent snapshot of the
device's state for use when displaying the window.

```
static void fatalError(char *message);
static Colormap getShareableColormap(XVisualInfo * vi);
static void display(void);
static void resize(int width, int height);
static void initDialsAndButtons(void);
static void processEvents(void);
```

The main routine creates dials's rendering window and associated resources. The
routines fatalError and getShareableColormap are exactly identical to the
glxdino.c versions.

```
void
main(int argc, char **argv)
{
  XVisualInfo *vi;
  Colormap cmap;
  XSetWindowAttributes swa;
  GLXContext cx;
  int width = 480, height = 420;
  int configuration[] = {
    GLX_DOUBLEBUFFER, GLX_RGBA,
    GLX_RED_SIZE, 1, GLX_GREEN_SIZE, 1, GLX_BLUE_SIZE, 1,
    None};

  dpy = XOpenDisplay(NULL);
  if (dpy == NULL)
    fatalError("Could not open display.");

  if (!glXQueryExtension(dpy, NULL, NULL))
    fatalError("X server has no OpenGL GLX extension.");

  /* Find an OpenGL-capable RGB visual with depth buffer.*/
  vi = glXChooseVisual(dpy, DefaultScreen(dpy), configuration);
  if (vi == NULL)
    fatalError("No appropriate double buffered RGB visual.");
  cmap = getShareableColormap(vi);

  /* create an OpenGL rendering context */
  cx = glXCreateContext(dpy, vi,
    NULL, /* No sharing of display lists */
    True); /* Direct rendering if possible */
  if (cx == NULL)
    fatalError("Could not create rendering context.");

  swa.colormap = cmap;
  swa.border_pixel = 0;
  swa.event_mask = ExposureMask | StructureNotifyMask;
  win = XCreateWindow(dpy, RootWindow(dpy, vi->screen),
    0, 0, width, height,
    0, vi->depth, InputOutput, vi->visual,
    CWBorderPixel | CWColormap | CWEventMask, &swa);
  XSetStandardProperties(dpy, win, "OpenGL dials & buttons",
    "dials", None, argv, argc, NULL);
  wmDeleteWindow = XInternAtom(dpy, "WM_DELETE_WINDOW", False);
  XSetWMProtocols(dpy, win, &wmDeleteWindow, 1);
```

```
    glXMakeCurrent(dpy, win, cx);
    glClearColor(0.5, 0.5, 0.5, 1.0);
    glLineWidth(3.0);
    resize(width, height);
    initDialsAndButtons();

    XMapWindow(dpy, win);
    processEvents();
}
```

All the work of finding and initializing the dial-and-button box device and selecting for the desired input events is isolated in the `initDialsAndButtons` routine. The event loop is implemented in `processEvents`, described later.

The variables that follow are used to record the number of buttons and number of dials (valuators) associated with the dial-and-button box device (if one is found). `dialsResolution` is an array of size `numDials` that records the magnitude of a complete dial rotation.

```
int numButtons;
int numDials;
int *dialsResolution;

static void
initDialsAndButtons(void)
{
  XExtensionVersion *version;
  XDeviceInfoPtr deviceInfo, device;
  XAnyClassPtr any;
  XButtonInfoPtr b;
  XValuatorInfoPtr v;
  XAxisInfoPtr a;
  int numDevices, numButtons, numDials;
  int i, j, k;
  XEventClass eventList[4];
  version = XGetExtensionVersion(dpy, "XInputExtension");
  if (version != NULL && ((int) version) != NoSuchExtension) {
    XFree(version);
    deviceInfo = XListInputDevices(dpy, &numDevices);
    if (deviceInfo) {
      for (i = 0; i < numDevices; i++) {
        device = &deviceInfo[i];
        any = (XAnyClassPtr) device->inputclassinfo;
        if (!strcmp(device->name, "dial+buttons")) {
```

```
    v = NULL;
    b = NULL;
    for (j = 0; j < device->num_classes; j++) {
      switch (any->class) {
      case ButtonClass:
        b = (XButtonInfoPtr) any;
        numButtons = b->num_buttons;
        break;
      case ValuatorClass:
        v = (XValuatorInfoPtr) any;
        numDials = v->num_axes;
        dialsResolution = (int *) malloc(sizeof(int) * numDials);
        a = (XAxisInfoPtr) ((char *) v + sizeof(XValuatorInfo));
        for (k = 0; k < numDials; k++, a++) {
          dialsResolution[k] = a->resolution;
        }
      }
      any = (XAnyClassPtr) ((char *) any + any->length);
    }
```

This code should look very similar to the code in xdevices.c. The code determines whether the X Input extension is supported. If the extension is not supported or if a device called dial+buttons cannot be found, dials displays its window but will not accept any input.

If the device is found, the number of buttons and dials and the resolution of each full dial rotation is recorded. The dial resolution will be used to scale the dial values from valuator motion events between 0 and 360 by scaleDialValue.

```
    dialsDevice = XOpenDevice(dpy, device->id);
    if (dialsDevice) {
      DeviceMotionNotify(dialsDevice, deviceMotionNotify,
        eventList[0]);
      DeviceButtonPress(dialsDevice, deviceButtonPress,
        eventList[1]);
      DeviceButtonPressGrab(dialsDevice, deviceButtonPressGrab,
        eventList[2]);
      DeviceButtonRelease(dialsDevice, deviceButtonRelease,
        eventList[3]);
      XSelectExtensionEvent(dpy, win, eventList, 4);
```

XOpenDevice is used to open the dial-and-button box device. If the open succeeds, look up the event type values for each event to be requested and the event class that

is later passed in an array to `XSelectExtensionEvent` to select the events in
dials's window.

```
        break;
      }
    }
  }
  XFreeDeviceList(deviceInfo);
    }
  }
}


static int
scaleDialValue(int axis, int rawValue)
{
  return (rawValue * 360.0) / dialsResolution[axis];
}
```

`scaleDialValue` scales a raw valuator event value (`rawValue`) between 0 and 360
degrees for the specified dial (`axis`). `processEvents` uses this routine.

```
static void
processEvents(void)
{
  int needRedraw = 1;
  XEvent event;

  while (1) {
    do {
      XNextEvent(dpy, &event);
      switch (event.type) {
      case ConfigureNotify:
        resize(event.xconfigure.width, event.xconfigure.height);
        /* Fall through... */
      case Expose:
        needRedraw = 1;
        break;
      case ClientMessage:
        if (event.xclient.data.l[0] == wmDeleteWindow)
          exit(0);
        break;
```

These events are handled in the same way as `glxdino.c` when the window is resized, exposed, or told to quit.

```
default:
  if (deviceMotionNotify && event.type == deviceMotionNotify) {
    XDeviceMotionEvent *devmot = (XDeviceMotionEvent *)event;

    if (devmot->deviceid == dialsDevice->device_id &&
          devmot->window == win) {
      int i, first = devmot->first_axis,
        count = devmot->axes_count;

      for (i = first; i < first + count; i++) {
        if (i <= NUM_DIALS) {
          dials[i] = scaleDialValue(i, devmot->axis_data[i -
            first]) % 360;
        }
      }
      needRedraw = 1;
    }
```

Note that X Input extension events are not handled using the `case` construct, because the X Input event types are not constant, but rather dynamically assigned because they are extension event types. For dial motion, the event pointer must be cast as an `XDeviceMotionEvent*` to inspect the event fields.

The code demonstrates how to make sure that the event corresponds to a particular window and device. Note that events of the same type can be generated by different devices and selected for by multiple windows. This is overkill in the case of `dials`, since there is only a single window and a single open X Input extension device.

An `XDeviceMotionEvent` indicates that one or more axes have changed. For some devices, such as tablets and Spaceballs, it is natural for multiple axes to be reported simultaneously by a single event, since the event represents a position or coordinate. In the case of a dial-and-button box, it is very likely that each dial change is a distinct valuator event. Still, `dials` should be prepared to handle the updates from multiple dials in a single `XDeviceMotionEvent`. The `dials` array is updated to reflect each updated dial's angle of rotation. Notice that the window's display is not immediately redisplayed; instead, `needRedraw` is set so that multiple state updates can be batched into a single redraw.

```
  } else if (deviceButtonPress
    && event.type == deviceButtonPress) {
    XDeviceButtonEvent *devbtn = (XDeviceButtonEvent *) & event;
```

```
      if (devbtn->deviceid == dialsDevice->device_id
        && devbtn->window == win) {
        buttons[devbtn->button - 1] = PRESS;
        needRedraw = 1;
      }
  } else if (deviceButtonRelease
      && event.type == deviceButtonRelease) {
      XDeviceButtonEvent *devbtn = (XDeviceButtonEvent *)event;

      if (devbtn->deviceid == dialsDevice->device_id
        && devbtn->window == win) {
        buttons[devbtn->button - 1] = RELEASE;
        needRedraw = 1;
      }
  }
```

Unlike valuator events, each dial-and-button-box event comes in a single event. As in the valuator event case, the event's device ID and window are checked to make sure that it is destined for dials's window. The buttons array is updated with the button's current state and needRedraw is set.

```
      }
  } while (XPending(dpy)); /* Loop to compress events. */
  if (needRedraw) {
    display();
    needRedraw = 0;
  }
 }
}
```

Events are processed repeatedly until there is a lull in the event stream. Then, if a redraw is requested, display is called to redraw the window and the needRedraw flag is cleared.

```
static void
resize(int w, int h)
{
  glViewport(0, 0, w, h);
  glMatrixMode(GL_PROJECTION);
  glLoadIdentity();
  gluOrtho2D(0, w, 0, h);
  glScalef(1, -1, 1);
  glTranslatef(0, -h, 0);
}
```

The scene rendered by dials is strictly two-dimensional. The resize routine updates both OpenGL's viewport and its projection matrix. The projection matrix maps the rendering space in pixel coordinates, with the origin at the upper left corner of the window. This coordinate space is identical to the window coordinate system used by X rendering. Loading the projection matrix in this way makes it easy to mix OpenGL with X rendering. In the case of dials, loading the projection matrix this way simplifies the layout of the window contents.

The routines that follow display the graphical representation of the dial-and-button box state.

```
static void
drawCircle(int x, int y, int r, int dir)
{
  float angle;

  glPushMatrix();
  glTranslatef(x, y, 0);
  glBegin(GL_TRIANGLE_FAN);
  glVertex2f(0, 0);
  for (angle = 2 * PI; angle >= 0; angle -= PI / 12) {
    glVertex2f(r * cos(angle), r * sin(angle));
  }
  glEnd();
  glColor3f(0, 0, 1);
  glBegin(GL_LINES);
  glVertex2f(0, 0);
  glVertex2f(r * cos(dir * PI / 180), r * sin(dir * PI / 180));
  glEnd();
  glPopMatrix();
}

static void
displayDials(void)
{
  int i;

  for (i = 0; i < NUM_DIALS; i++) {
    glColor3f(0, 1, 0);
    drawCircle(60 + ((i + 1) % 2) * 100, 60 + (i / 2) * 100,
      40, dials[NUM_DIALS - 1 - i] - 90);
  }
}
```

displayDials displays the eight dials on the left side of the window. Each dial is rendered by calling drawCircle. The circle for each dial is drawn as a triangle fan. A line is drawn on top of the circle to indicate the current dial orientation.

```
static void
displayButtons(void)
{
  int i, n;

  for (i = 0, n = 0; i < NUM_BUTTONS; i++, n++) {
    switch (n) {
    case 0:     /* No button in device's upper left corner. */
    case 5:     /* No button in device's upper right corner. */
    case 30:    /* No button in device's lower left corner. */
      n++;      /* Skip drawing this location. */
    }
    if (buttons[i] == PRESS) {
      glColor3f(1, 0, 0);
    } else {
      glColor3f(1, 1, 1);
    }
    glRecti((n % 6) * 40 + 240, (n / 6) * 40 + 20,
      (n % 6) * 40 + 260, (n / 6) * 40 + 40);
  }
}
```

displayButtons renders a rectangle for each button. The rectangle is red if the button is currently pressed and white if it is released.

```
static void
display(void)
{
  glClear(GL_COLOR_BUFFER_BIT);
  displayDials();
  displayButtons();
  glXSwapBuffers(dpy, win);
}
```

display regenerates the window's display based on the current state of the dials and buttons arrays. The window is cleared, then the dials are rendered, then the buttons, and finally a buffer swap is performed.

6.2.8 X Toolkit Support for Extension Events

Using the X Input extension with the X Toolkit is more involved than using the X Input extension with pure Xlib programs. This is because the X Toolkit's main loop takes responsibility for dispatching all X events. Unfortunately, the original X Toolkit design did not provide any facility to dispatch X extension events.

Not until the X11R6 version of the X Toolkit was an interface provided for selecting, dispatching, and registering callbacks for X extension events.[3] The interface consists of three routines, prototyped as follows:

```
void XtRegisterExtensionSelector(Display *dpy,
  int min_event_type, int max_event_type,
  XtExtensionSelectProc proc, XtPointer client_data);

XtEventDispatchProc XtSetEventDispatcher(Display *dpy,
  int event_type, XtEventDispatchProc proc);
void XtInsertEventTypeHandler(Widget widget,
  int type, XtPointer select_data,
  XtEventHandler proc, XtPointer closure,
  XtListPosition position);
```

The `XtRegisterExtensionSelector` registers a routine that the X Toolkit can use to inform the X server when extension events are selected by a client. The `XtSetEventDispatcher` tells the X Toolkit that the specified X extension event should be dispatched by the X Toolkit (instead of simply discarded) and supplies a routine that determines the widget to which the event should be dispatched. `XtInsertEventTypeHandler` tells the X Toolkit that a specific widget is interested in receiving extension events and supplies a callback routine to handle such events when they are dispatched. The closure argument of `XtInsertEventTypeHandler` is a handle to extension-specific data passed along to the routine registered by `XtRegisterExtensionSelector` so that the event can be selected.

When this new interface is not available, X Toolkit programs must rewrite the application main loop to intercept X extension events.

If this sounds complicated, it is. The example in the next section demonstrates how these new X Toolkit routines are used to select for X Input extension events. If the new routines are not supported by your version of the X Toolkit, another version of the example shows how to rewrite the main loop to intercept the events.

6.2.9 *Motif-based OpenGL Examples*

The following example program, called `new_xt_tablet`, demonstrates the use of the X Input extensions in conjunction with the new X11R6 X Toolkit interfaces for selecting extension events. The program displays a virtual tablet puck in its OpenGL rendering area. The virtual puck moves in response to the actual tablet

---

3. The original X11R6 implementation suffered from a memory allocation bug. Before the X11R6 facility, X extension events were simply discarded by the X Toolkit. A source code patch for the bug was released by the X Consortium; the fix is integrated into the X11R6.1 release.

device. The buttons on the virtual puck are outlines when the actual buttons are released and filled when they are pressed. Figure 6.14 shows a screen snapshot of `new_xt_tablet`.

The `old_xt_tablet` example presented later, on page 343 is essentially the same program except that it works with any X Toolkit version. For it to do so, the standard `XtAppMainLoop` is replaced with a custom application main loop that intercepts X Input extension events.

6.2.9.1 `new_xt_tablet.c`

Include the required C library, Motif, X Toolkit, Xlib, OpenGL, and X Input extension header files.

```
#include <stdlib.h>
#include <stdio.h>
#include <Xm/Frame.h>
#include <Xm/RowColumn.h>
#include <X11/GLw/GLwMDrawA.h>
#include <X11/keysym.h>
#include <X11/Xutil.h>
#include <X11/extensions/XInput.h>
```

Figure 6.14 Screen snapshot showing the `new_xt_tablet` example. The yellow, white, and green buttons are filled, indicating that they are currently pressed.

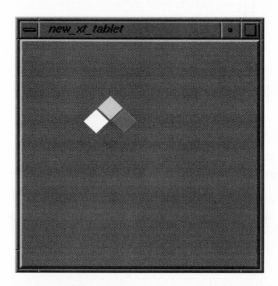

```
#include <X11/extensions/XIproto.h> /* For IEVENTS,
                                       unfortunately not in
                                       XInput.h */
```

Various global variables are used.

```
int attribs[] = {GLX_RGBA, GLX_DOUBLEBUFFER, None};
String fallbackResources[] = {
  "*glxwidget*width: 300", "*glxwidget*height: 300",
  NULL
};
Display *dpy;
XtAppContext appctx;
Widget toplevel, frame, glxwidget;
XDevice *tablet;
int tabletMotionNotify, tabletPressNotify, tabletReleaseNotify;
GLenum btnState[4] = {GL_LINE, GL_LINE, GL_LINE, GL_LINE};
int axisMin[2], axisRange[2];
int tabletPos[2] = {2000, 2000};
Bool direct, redisplayPosted = False;
```

The main routine relies on three other routines. Two are callbacks registered for the OpenGL rendering area widget to handle window exposes and resizes. `initialize-Tablet` is called by `main` and takes care of all the tablet-related initialization using the X Input extension and the X Toolkit's extension event selection mechanism.

```
void expose(Widget w, XtPointer client_data, XtPointer call);
void resize(Widget w, XtPointer client_data, XtPointer call);
void initializeTablet(void);

main(int argc, char *argv[])
{
  XVisualInfo *visinfo;
  GLXContext glxcontext;
```

Set up the program's widget instance hierarchy. A Motif OpenGL drawing area widget is nested in a frame widget that is nested in the application's top-level widget. Then the tablet is initialized.

```
  toplevel = XtOpenApplication(&appctx, "tablet", NULL, 0, &argc, argv,
    fallbackResources, applicationShellWidgetClass, NULL, 0);
  dpy = XtDisplay(toplevel);
```

```
frame = XmCreateFrame(toplevel, "frame", NULL, 0);
XtManageChild(frame);

/* Specify visual directly. */
if (!(visinfo = glXChooseVisual(dpy, DefaultScreen(dpy), attribs)))
  XtAppError(appctx, "no suitable RGB visual");

glxwidget = XtVaCreateManagedWidget("glxwidget",
  glwMDrawingAreaWidgetClass, frame
  GLwNvisualInfo, visinfo, XtNwidth, 300, XtNheight,
  300, NULL);
XtAddCallback(glxwidget, GLwNexposeCallback, expose, NULL);
XtAddCallback(glxwidget, GLwNresizeCallback, resize, NULL);

initializeTablet();
```

Realize the widget instance hierarchy. Once the hierarchy is realized, the OpenGL widget has an associated X window to which an OpenGL rendering context can be made current. The context's projection matrix is specified to be a 4,000-by-4,000-unit region.

```
XtRealizeWidget(toplevel);

glxcontext = glXCreateContext(dpy, visinfo, 0, GL_TRUE);
direct = glXIsDirect(dpy, glxcontext);
GLwDrawingAreaMakeCurrent(glxwidget, glxcontext);
glMatrixMode(GL_PROJECTION);
glOrtho(0, 4000, 0, 4000, 0, 1);
glMatrixMode(GL_MODELVIEW);
glClearColor(0.5, 0.5, 0.5, 0.);
```

Begin the X Toolkit's application main loop. Notice the standard `XtAppMainLoop`, since the X11R6 interfaces for selecting extension events are used. No custom application main loop is needed to intercept extension events.

```
XtAppMainLoop(appctx);
}
```

The three following callbacks are registered by `initializeTablet` for selecting and dispatching X Input extension events:

```
void selectXInputEvents(Widget w, int *event_types,
  XtPointer * select_data, int count, XtPointer client_data);
```

```
Boolean dispatchXInputEvent(XEvent * event);
void tabletHandler(Widget w, XtPointer client_data,
  XEvent * event, Boolean * continue_to_dispatch);

void
initializeTablet(void)
{
  Bool exists;
  XExtensionVersion *version;
  XDeviceInfoPtr deviceInfo, device;
  XAnyClassPtr any;
  XEventClass tabletMotionClass, tabletPressClass,
    tabletPressGrabClass,
    tabletReleaseClass;
  XButtonInfoPtr b;
  XValuatorInfoPtr v;
  XAxisInfoPtr a;
  int opcode, eventBase, errorBase;
  int numDev;
  int i, j, k;
```

Make sure the X Input extension is supported by the X server. If the extension is not supported, the program reports that no tablet could be found and runs in a crippled mode, not supporting tablet input.

```
  exists = XQueryExtension(dpy, "XInputExtension", &opcode,
    &eventBase, &errorBase);
  if (!exists) {
    goto noDevices;
  }
  version = XGetExtensionVersion(dpy, "XInputExtension");
  if (version == NULL || ((int) version) == NoSuchExtension) {
    goto noDevices;
  }
  XFree(version);
```

List all the devices supported.

```
  deviceInfo = XListInputDevices(dpy, &numDev);
  if (deviceInfo) {
    for (i = 0; i < numDev; i++) {
      device = &deviceInfo[i];
      any = (XAnyClassPtr) device->inputclassinfo;
```

For each device listed, look for a device called `tablet`.

```
if (!strcmp(device->name, "tablet")) {
  v = NULL;
  b = NULL;
  for (j = 0; j < device->num_classes; j++) {
    switch (any->class) {
    case ButtonClass:
    b = (XButtonInfoPtr) any;
    /* Sanity check: at least 1 button (normally 4). */
    if (b->num_buttons < 1) {
      goto skipDevice;
    }
    break;
  case ValuatorClass:
    v = (XValuatorInfoPtr) any;
    /* Sanity check: exactly 2 valuators? */
    if (v->num_axes != 2) {
      goto skipDevice;
    }
```

Once a device named `tablet` is located, a further check ensures that the device has at least one button and exactly two valuators (the *X* and *Y* axes). If so, the tablet's *X* and *Y* axis ranges are recorded so that the motion events from the tablet *X* and *Y* axes can be normalized:

```
a = (XAxisInfoPtr) ((char *) v + sizeof(XValuatorInfo));
for (k = 0; k < 2; k++, a++) {
  axisMin[k] = a->min_value;
  axisRange[k] = a->max_value - a->min_value;
}
break;
}
any = (XAnyClassPtr) ((char *) any + any->length);
}
```

If such a device is found, `XOpenDevice` opens it.

```
tablet = XOpenDevice(dpy, device->id);
if (tablet) {
```

Assuming the open succeeds, extract the type and class of the motion notify, button press, and button release events for the tablet device.

```
DeviceMotionNotify(tablet,
  tabletMotionNotify, tabletMotionClass);
DeviceButtonPress(tablet,
  tabletPressNotify, tabletPressClass);
DeviceButtonPressGrab(tablet,
  notUsedByMacro, tabletPressGrabClass);
DeviceButtonRelease(tablet,
  tabletReleaseNotify, tabletReleaseClass);
```

Register an event selection routine for the X Input extension events so the X Toolkit will know how to select for these events for a specific widget when `Xt-InsertEventTypeHandler` is used to supply an event handler for a given X Input extension event for a given widget.

```
XtRegisterExtensionSelector(dpy, eventBase,
  eventBase + IEVENTS - 1, selectXInputEvents, NULL);
```

Register a dispatch procedure for the various X Input extension events to which `new_xt_tablet` will respond. This tells the X Toolkit how to dispatch these events instead of discarding them.

```
XtSetEventDispatcher(dpy, tabletMotionNotify,
  dispatchXInputEvent);
XtSetEventDispatcher(dpy, tabletPressNotify,
  dispatchXInputEvent);
XtSetEventDispatcher(dpy, tabletReleaseNotify,
  dispatchXInputEvent);
```

Provide an event handler for the OpenGL drawing area widget for the desired X Input extension events. The single routine, `tabletHandler`, will dispatch all tablet-generated events. The event classes determined earlier will be passed to `selectX-InputEvents` which tells the X server to send the selected X Input extension events to this client. Notice that the pseudo-event class `tabletPressGrabClass` ensures that a passive grab is activated after a tablet button press, so that every press is guaranteed to be followed by the associated release.

```
XtInsertEventTypeHandler(glxwidget, tabletMotionNotify,
  /* select_data */ (XtPointer) tabletMotionClass,
  tabletHandler, NULL, XtListTail);
XtInsertEventTypeHandler(glxwidget, tabletPressNotify,
  /* select_data */ (XtPointer) tabletPressClass,
  tabletHandler, NULL, XtListTail);
XtInsertEventTypeHandler(glxwidget, tabletPressNotify,
```

```
        /* select_data */ (XtPointer) tabletPressGrabClass,
        tabletHandler, NULL, XtListTail);
      XtInsertEventTypeHandler(glxwidget, tabletReleaseNotify,
        /* select_data */ (XtPointer) tabletReleaseClass,
        tabletHandler, NULL, XtListTail);
```

At this point, the tablet device is successfully opened and initialized for use. There is no need to look any farther through the device list, so free it and return.

```
        XFreeDeviceList(deviceInfo);
        return;
      }
    }
  skipDevice:;
  }
```

At this point, all the devices have been inspected, but no suitable tablet has been found. Free the device list.

```
  XFreeDeviceList(deviceInfo);
}
```

Either the X Input extension is not supported or a tablet device was not found. Either way, report that new_xt_tablet is running without tablet support.

```
noDevices:
  fprintf(stderr, "new_xt_tablet: no tablet device found!\n");
  fprintf(stderr, " continuing without tablet support.\n");
  return;
}
```

The selectXInputEvents routine is called when the X Toolkit needs to tell the X server to select a set of extension events (within the X Input extension range of event types) for a particular widget to be sent to this client. client_data is an array of size count, composed of select_data from the calls to XtInsertEvent-TypeHandler. In this case, each client_data element is of type XEventClass and is passed to XSelectExtensionEvent.

```
void
selectXInputEvents(Widget w, int *event_types,
  XtPointer * select_data, int count, XtPointer client_data)
{
  XEventClass *xcp = (XEventClass *) select_data;
```

```
      XSelectExtensionEvent(XtDisplay(w), XtWindow(w), xcp, count);
}
```

The `dispatchXInputEvent` routine is called when the X Toolkit receives a tablet motion, press, or release event. The routine determines to which widget the event will be routed for dispatching. Such an event will be routed to the widget associated with the event's window. For an input device such as a numeric keypad device, it may be useful to route the event to the window with keyboard focus (determined by calling `XtGetKeyboardFocusWidget`).

```
Boolean
dispatchXInputEvent(XEvent * event)
{
  Widget w;
  XAnyEvent *xany = (XAnyEvent *) event;

  w = XtWindowToWidget(xany->display, xany->window);

  if (!XFilterEvent(event, (w == NULL) ? None : XtWindow(w))) {
    return XtDispatchEventToWidget(w, event);
  } else {
    return True;
  }
}
```

`tabletPosChange` updates the tablet puck's position based on tablet motion notify events. `postRedisplay` will make sure the OpenGL rendering area is redrawn to reflect the current input state.

```
void tabletPosChange(int first, int count, int *data);
void postRedisplay(void);
```

`tabletHandler` dispatches X Input extension motion, press, and release events. Motion events cause the axis motion data to be passed to `tabletPosChange`. Press events will cause the puck's onscreen image to be a filled diamond, instead of the outline of a diamond shown when the tablet button is released. `postRedisplay` is called to force a redisplay of the window based on the new state.

```
void
tabletHandler(Widget w, XtPointer client_data,
  XEvent * event, Boolean * continue_to_dispatch)
{
  if (event->type == tabletMotionNotify) {
```

```
    XDeviceMotionEvent *devmot = (XDeviceMotionEvent *) event;
    tabletPosChange(devmot->first_axis, devmot->axes_count,
      devmot->axis_data);
  } else if (event->type == tabletPressNotify) {
    XDeviceButtonPressedEvent *devbtn = (XDeviceButtonEvent *) event;

    btnState[devbtn->button - 1] = GL_FILL;
    postRedisplay();
  } else if (event->type == tabletReleaseNotify) {
    XDeviceButtonReleasedEvent *devbtn = (XDeviceButtonEvent *) event;

    btnState[devbtn->button - 1] = GL_LINE;
    postRedisplay();
  }
}
```

normalizeTabletPos maps the x and y positions returned by a tablet motion
notify event to a range between 0 and 4000, inclusive. Remember that the projection matrix has been established to map this same range to window coordinates.
queryTabletPos queries the absolute location of the tablet axes.

```
int normalizeTabletPos(int axis, int rawValue);
void queryTabletPos(void);
```

If only a subset of the valuators of an X Input device has changed, only the changed
values may be reported. For some valuators such as the dials on a dial-and-button
box, this behavior is reasonable, since the valuators change independently. For a
device such as a tablet, where the valuators represent closely coupled axes, reporting only x changes when the y axis stays constant is less reasonable, but a client
should be prepared for the axes to be reported independently.

```
void
tabletPosChange(int first, int count, int *data)
{
  int i, value, genEvent = 0;

  for (i = first; i < first + count; i++) {
    switch (i) {
    case 0: /* X axis */
    case 1: /* Y axis */
      value = normalizeTabletPos(i, data[i - first]);
      if (value != tabletPos[i]) {
        tabletPos[i] = value;
        genEvent = 1;
```

```
      }
      break;
    }
  }
```

It is possible that a client will receive a single-axis update without any previous knowledge of the other axis. In this case, `queryTabletPos` queries the combined location.[4]

```
  if (tabletPos[0] == -1 || tabletPos[1] == -1) {
    queryTabletPos();
    genEvent = 1;
  }
```

A redisplay is posted only if the tablet location has changed (in *normalized* coordinates) since the last tablet position change.

```
  if (genEvent) {
    postRedisplay();
  }
}
```

```
int
normalizeTabletPos(int axis, int rawValue)
{
  /* Normalize rawValue to between 0 and 4000. */
  return ((rawValue - axisMin[axis]) * 4000) /
    axisRange[axis];
}
```

`queryTabletPos` calls `XQueryDeviceState` to query the current state for each input class of the specified device.

```
void
queryTabletPos(void)
{
```

---

4. The X Input extension's `DeviceStateNotify` event (analogous to the core `KeymapNotify` event) permits an up-to-date accounting of a device's state for all its supported input classes immediately following a window's `DeviceFocusIn` or `EnterNotify` event. Using `DeviceStateNotify`, a client could track device state without ever resorting to queries. Unfortunately, the `DeviceStateNotify` event remains unimplemented in X servers based on X releases through X11R6.

```
XDeviceState *state;
XInputClass *any;
XValuatorState *v;
int i;

state = XQueryDeviceState(dpy, tablet);
any = state->data;
for (i = 0; i < state->num_classes; i++) {
  switch (any->class) {
  case ValuatorClass:
    v = (XValuatorState *) any;
    if (v->num_valuators < 2)
      goto end;
    if (tabletPos[0] == -1)
      tabletPos[0] = normalizeTabletPos(0, v->valuators[0]);
    if (tabletPos[1] == -1)
      tabletPos[1] = normalizeTabletPos(1, v->valuators[1]);
  }
  any = (XInputClass *) ((char *) any + any->length);
}
```

XFreeDeviceState should be used to free the device state returned by XQuery-
DeviceState when no longer needed.

```
end:
  XFreeDeviceState(state);
}
```

So far, in `new_xt_tablet`'s code, when the OpenGL rendering area's contents
should be updated, the rendering is not done directly; instead, `postRedisplay` is
called. The code that follows shows what happens when a redisplay is posted.

Posting a redisplay is generally more efficient than redisplaying the scene on
demand every time the window's underlying scene state changes. Consider
`new_xt_tablet`'s display. `new_xt_tablet`'s OpenGL rendering area should be
updated when the tablet's puck moves, but quickly sliding the puck across the tablet's surface may generate hundreds of `DeviceMotionNotify` events over a very
short period of time. If the scene cannot be redisplayed as quickly as the events are
generated, a considerable lag builds up between the events generated and the state
of displayed window. A way to avoid this lag is to delay redisplaying the window
until all pending events have been processed, by "posting a redisplay" in response to
each event instead of actually redrawing the scene in response to every event. In this
way, many pending event-caused state changes are batched and the result is
reflected in a single scene update.

The code that follows shows how `new_xt_tablet` implements a facility for posting redisplays.

When a redisplay is actually required, `drawScene` will render the scene based on the current program state. The `doRedisplay` routine is called when a redisplay is actually "posted"; when this happens, `drawScene` is called and the `redisplayPosted` flag is cleared.

```
void drawScene(void);

void
doRedisplay(void *client_data, XtIntervalId * id)
{
  drawScene();
  redisplayPosted = False;
}
```

When `postRedisplay` is called, the effect is to register an application timeout using `XtAppAddTimeOut` for 5 milliseconds in the future and the `redisplayPosted` flag is set. If the flag is already set (indicating that a redisplay is already pending), the routine returns immediately.

```
void
postRedisplay(void)
{
  if (!redisplayPosted) {
    redisplayPosted = True;
    XtAppAddTimeOut(appctx, 5, doRedisplay, NULL);
  }
}
```

`new_xt_tablet`'s facility for posting redisplays unifies redisplays caused by program state changes affecting the way the scene should appear *and* redisplays caused by `Expose` events generated by the window system. So the `expose` callback operates by calling `postRedisplay`.

```
void
expose(Widget w, XtPointer client_data, XtPointer call)
{
  postRedisplay();
}
```

`new_xt_tablet`'s OpenGL drawing area is redisplayed by rendering four diamonds (each rendered by `diamond`) as a virtual representation of the tablet's puck (rendered by `puck`). Each diamond is either filled or drawn as an outline depending on the `btnState` array, which is updated in response to `DeviceButtonPress` and `DeviceButtonRelease` events in `tabletHandler`. `drawScene` clears the window, draws the puck at the current normalized tablet position (as maintained by `tablet-Pos`), and performs a buffer swap.

```
void
diamond(GLenum mode)
{
  glPushMatrix();
  glPolygonMode(GL_FRONT_AND_BACK, mode);
  glRotatef(45., 0., 0., 1.);
  glRectf(-0.5, -0.5, 1, 1);
  glPopMatrix();
}

void
puck(void)
{
  /* Make a puck out of 4 diamonds. */

  glTranslatef(0, 1.2, 0);
  glColor3f(1.0, 1.0, 0.0);
  diamond(btnState[0]);

  glTranslatef(-1.2, -1.2, 0);
  glColor3f(1.0, 1.0, 1.0);
  diamond(btnState[1]);

  glTranslatef(1.2, -1.2, 0);
  glColor3f(0.0, 0.0, 1.0);
  diamond(btnState[2]);

  glTranslatef(1.2, 1.2, 0);
  glColor3f(0.0, 1.0, 0.0);
  diamond(btnState[3]);
}

void
drawScene(void)
{
  glClear(GL_COLOR_BUFFER_BIT);
  glPushMatrix();
  glTranslatef(tabletPos[0], tabletPos[1], 0);
  glScalef(200, 200, 1);
```

```
    puck();
    glPopMatrix();
    GLwDrawingAreaSwapBuffers(glxwidget);
```

To improve interactivity when the OpenGL context is indirect, call `glFinish` to ensure that the scene completes.

```
    if (!direct)
      glFinish();
}
```

When the OpenGL rendering area is resized, the OpenGL rendering context's viewport should be updated to reflect the new window size.

```
void
resize(Widget w, XtPointer client_data, XtPointer call)
{
  GLwDrawingAreaCallbackStruct *call_data;
  call_data = (GLwDrawingAreaCallbackStruct *) call;

  glXWaitX();
  glViewport(0, 0, call_data->width, call_data->height);
}
```

6.2.9.2 old_xt_tablet.c

Before the new Xt extension event-handling interfaces were introduced in X11R6, Xt's event-dispatching logic would simply discard extension events. To work around this fate, Xt's `XtAppMainLoop` *must* be rewritten to intercept X Input extension events. `xiEventBase` must be a global integer initialized to the X Input extension's event base.

```
void tabletHandler(Widget w, XtPointer client_data,
  XEvent * event, Boolean * continue_to_dispatch);
int xiEventBase;

void
MyAppMainLoop(XtAppContext app)
{
  XEvent event;
  Boolean continue_to_dispatch;

  while (1) {
    XtAppNextEvent(app, &event);
```

```
      if ((event.xany.type >= xiEventBase)
        && (event.xany.type < xiEventBase + IEVENTS)) {
      tabletHandler(
        XtWindowToWidget(event.xany.display, event.xany.window),
        NULL, &event, &continue_to_dispatch);
      continue;
    }
    XtDispatchEvent(&event);
  }
}
```

The code in `initialize_tablet` remains mostly unchanged except for the code that handles initializing the tablet once it is located and opened. First the X Input extension event base is saved in the `xiEventBase` global for `MyAppMainLoop`. Then the desired X Input events must be selected. Without the new R6 Xt interfaces, `XSelectExtensionEvent` must be called directly.

```
    tablet = XOpenDevice(dpy, device->id);
    if (tablet) {
      XEventClass eventList[4];

      xiEventBase = eventBase;

      DeviceMotionNotify(tablet,
        tabletMotionNotify, tabletMotionClass);
      DeviceButtonPress(tablet,
        tabletPressNotify, tabletPressClass);
      DeviceButtonPressGrab(tablet,
        notUsedByMacro, tabletPressGrabClass);
      DeviceButtonRelease(tablet,
        tabletReleaseNotify, tabletReleaseClass);
      XtRealizeWidget(toplevel);
```

Since `XSelectExtensionEvent` requires a window ID, the widget hierarchy must be realized before `XSelectExtensionEvent` can be called.

```
      eventList[0] = tabletMotionClass;
      eventList[1] = tabletPressClass;
      eventList[2] = tabletPressGrabClass;
      eventList[3] = tabletReleaseClass;
      XSelectExtensionEvent(dpy, XtWindow(glxwidget), eventList, 4);

      XFreeDeviceList(deviceInfo);
      return;
    }
```

More code using the X Input extension is found in the implementation of the support for the dial-and-button box, tablet, and Spaceball within the source code for the GLUT library, because GLUT accesses these input devices through the X Input extension.

6.3 USING OVERLAYS

Many OpenGL implementations are likely to support graphics hardware that provides overlay and possibly underlay planes. Overlays are a common feature of high-end graphics systems. Overlays act as an alternate set of frame buffer bitplanes that can be preferentially displayed instead of the standard set of bitplanes (usually called the *normal plane*). Rendering in the overlay avoids damage to an image retained in the normal plane. Pop-up menus, dialogs, rubber-banding, and text annotation are all common interactions that can make use of overlays to minimize screen damage.

Because scenes rendered with OpenGL are often expensive to redraw, using overlays minimizes screen damage and facilitates more responsive user interfaces. For example, normally when pop-up and pull-down menus are dismissed, they force the windows behind them to be redrawn. If menus are created in the overlays, use of the menus does not damage the application's normal plane windows, so potentially expensive redraws to windows with OpenGL rendering are eliminated.

It is worth noting that overlays can be generalized to an arbitrary number of frame buffer *layers*. Underlays are bitplanes that can defer their pixel values to the pixel values in the normal plane. In addition, multiple sets of overlay and underlay layers are possible.

Only overlays are discussed, because overlays tend to be both more common and more useful. Keep in mind that the same basic mechanisms described can also be used to support underlay planes.

This section describes the *server overlay visuals convention*, sometimes is referred to as SOV. While the convention is not an official X Consortium standard, nearly all X vendors that support overlays do so using this convention, including Digital Equipment Corp., Hewlett-Packard, IBM, and Silicon Graphics. Phil Karlton (Silicon Graphics) initially proposed the server overlay visuals convention to the X Consortium. David Wiggins (Intergraph) contributed to the proposal. Todd Newman (Silicon Graphics) did the first implementation of server overlay visuals; Peter Daifuku (Silicon Graphics) implemented and described a fully functional implementation of the convention.

6.3.1 Utility of Overlays

Overlays can be used in a number of different ways, but in all cases their benefits are of two sorts. Overlay planes can reduce screen repainting and permit efficient overlaid transparency effects.

6.3.1.1 Minimizing Screen Repaint Costs

Anyone familiar with X, or almost any other window system, understands that programs must be able to "repair" damaged or freshly exposed regions of their windows. For most simple 2D applications, regenerating a portion of a window is not very arduous. However, with 3D or imaging applications, redraws can be significantly more expensive, so it makes sense to find ways to avoid damaging the frame buffer contents.

The core X protocol supports a notion of *backing store*, which can minimize the client costs of regenerating windows, but it greatly increases the X server's burden by asking the server to maintain the contents of obscured or unmapped windows in offscreen memory. A related core X protocol capability, known as *save-unders*, saves the contents of windows obscured by a window using save-unders.

Unfortunately, backing store and save-unders are not well suited to OpenGL. An OpenGL frame buffer holds much more information than just the pixel's color. It also may contain alpha buffer, accumulation buffer, stencil buffer, and depth buffer information. "Deep" frame buffers magnify the costs of moving data offscreen and then back into the frame buffer again. With OpenGL direct rendering, backing store can become impossible for an X server to maintain, because the server is not involved in the rendering, making it impossible to retain backing store for such windows.

Overlays provide another means of minimizing window regeneration. It is notable that a significant amount of window damage is caused by "popping up" transient windows such as pop-up or pull-down menus and dialog boxes. Creating such transient windows in the overlays avoids damage to underlying, more permanent windows. Notice that overlays gain advantage in the same way as save-unders do: they both avoid damage to underlying windows.

Because hardware is used to implement overlays, there is little overhead in using them. Backing store and save-unders both have high software overhead. For save-unders, even though the client does not need to be aware that windows are being damaged, the server must still save the pixels in the frame buffer and be ready to rewrite them to the frame buffer. But in the overlay case, the pixels in the underlying window *never* need to be copied or redrawn, even by the server.

In addition, rendering to a window obscured by an overlay still makes use of the graphics hardware's faster rendering path instead of diverting rendering into often slower offscreen pixmaps as backing store does.

6.3.1.2 Overlaid Transparency

Along with minimizing screen repainting, overlays can be used to generate overlaid transparency effects efficiently. Usually overlay hardware supports a special *transparent* pixel value. If this value is drawn into the window, the pixel value in the layer below "shows through."

This type of *overlaid* transparency should be differentiated from the *rendering* transparency based on alpha values that is described in Section 5.3. The transparency supported by overlays involves no blending of pixels, but instead works by deferring display of transparent pixels in a higher frame buffer layer to an underlying pixel in a lower layer.

Consider an application that generates annotated weather maps of the United States. The map of the United States itself is unchanging, but the front lines and temperatures and the other symbols that are painted on top of the static map do change.

If overlays are used, the weather patterns can quickly be changed by redrawing only the meteorological annotations for the map. To do this, we draw the static map in a window located in the normal plane. Then we create an overlay window as a child of the static map's window. The background pixel for this window is the overlay's transparent pixel. Effectively, we see through the overlay to the map. Now we can draw the annotations in the overlay window. When a new set of annotations is to be drawn, we clear only the overlay window, leaving the static map untouched, and redraw a new set of annotations. (See Figure 6.18.)

Of course, the same application could be written without overlays, but overlays allow a much more efficient implementation by eliminating redrawing of the static map.

Video-game-style animation can also be implemented efficiently using overlays. Spaceships, asteroids, and sneaker-wearing hedgehogs can be drawn into an overlay window while an intricate background window scrolls by in a normal plane window.

6.3.1.3   A Single-Window Hierarchy

One thing worth noting about windows that exist in overlays is that such windows should exist in the *same* window hierarchy as the normal plane windows. Input event distribution should work the same for windows in different layers. A user should be able to push/pop a window at will, regardless of what layer it is in. There should be no restrictions about the ways windows in different layers should be parented. Layered windows should observe the same protocol semantics as normal single-layer X server implementations. The only ways layered windows should affect the server are that higher layers do not clip layers beneath them and that there is a transparent pixel.

This mode of operation ensures that X application need not be aware of what layer a window resides in and is not exposed to any layering artifacts, except when rendering a transparent pixel.

6.3.2   The Server Overlay Visuals Convention

One might expect that overlay support for X would require an extension. In fact, no additional requests or events are needed to support overlays, so a true X extension is unnecessary. The core X protocol's visual mechanism provides a way to create windows of different types, and this mechanism can be overloaded with overlay information. This overloading is similar to the overloading done by GLX to indicate the GLX attributes that are provided by different visuals. The only thing required is an X property on the root window of each screen, encoding which visuals are overlay visuals, since the core X notion of a visual does not include layer information. This can be done without a new extension request.

Using the property, it is up to the client to find an overlay visual appropriate to the client's needs. Once an overlay visual is found, the standard `XCreateWindow` routine, given the overlay visual, can be used to create an overlay window.

The property specified by the server overlay visuals convention is called `SERVER_OVERLAY_VISUALS`. You can determine whether your X server supports the convention by inspecting the root window for the property like this:

```
% xprop -root | grep SERVER_OVERLAY_VISUALS
SERVER_OVERLAY_VISUALS(SERVER_OVERLAY_VISUALS) = 0x20, 0x1, 0x0, 0x2,
0x26, 0x1, 0x0, 0x1
```

If a property called `SERVER_OVERLAY_VISUALS` is listed like this one, your X server supports the convention.

The X server itself creates the `SERVER_OVERLAY_VISUALS` property. The property has a standard format, described in Table 6.2. It consists of elements that specify a visual, the type of transparency supported by the visual, the layer the visual resides in, and a transparency value that is treated as a mask or a pixel value depending on the type of transparency supported. The `SERVER_OVERLAY_VISUALS` root window property is expected to be of type `SERVER_OVERLAY_VISUALS` and must be 32-bit in format.

The transparency type is an enumerated value indicating how transparency works for the visual. The following transparency types are possible:

Table 6.2 `SERVER_OVERLAY_VISUALS` Property Entry Format

Name	Type	Description
overlay_visual	VISUALID	Visual ID of visual.
transparent_type	CARD32	None (0). TransparentPixel (1). TransparentMask (2).
value	CARD32	Pixel value or transparency mask.
layer	INT32	The layer the visual resides in.

None There are no transparent pixels. The value field should be ignored.

TransparentPixel The value field explicitly names a transparent pixel value.

TransparentMask Any pixel value that has at least the same bits set as the value field is transparent.

The same visual may appear more than once in the list. In this case, the union of the pixel values described by the transparent type and value fields should all be transparent. The value of the layer field will be the same across all instances of the multiply listed visual. Generally, there is only one transparent pixel. Use of the transparent mask by SOV implementations is very rare; most implementations use the transparent pixel transparency type.

6.3.3 An SOV Programming Interface

The convention does not specify an Xlib interface to query the SERVER_OVERLAY_VISUALS property. X programmers wishing to use overlay windows have been forced to query and decode the property without help from utility routines. This section includes routines that mimic the Xlib XGetVisualInfo and XMatchVisualInfo routines, but are augmented so that they also provide support for querying the layering and transparency capabilities of visuals.

sovGetVisualInfo works like XGetVisualInfo, but instead of using an XVisualInfo structure as a template and returning information on each visual, it uses a sovVisualInfo structure, which has the XVisualInfo structure embedded in it but also contains fields for layer and transparency. The normal visual information mask bits are extended to support the new fields. The routine hides all the work done to query and interpret the SERVER_OVERLAY_VISUALS property.

sovMatchVisualInfo works like XMatchVisualInfo, but is extended in the same way as sovGetVisualInfo, using the sovVisualInfo structure. You can supply an additional layer parameter for matching a visual in a specified layer.

As mentioned earlier, a single overlay visual may support several transparency values. These routines return only a single transparency type and value.

6.3.3.1 sovLayerUtil.h
Here is the sovLayerUtil.h header file:

```
#include <X11/Xlib.h>
#include <X11/Xutil.h>
#include <X11/Xmd.h>
```

```
/* Transparent type values. */
/* None                    0 */
#define TransparentPixel    1
#define TransparentMask     2

/* Layered visual info template flags. */
#define VisualLayerMask 0x200
#define VisualTransparentType 0x400
#define VisualTransparentValue 0x800
#define VisualAllLayerMask 0xFFF

/* Layered visual info structure. */
typedef struct _sovVisualInfo {
  XVisualInfo vinfo;
  int layer;
  int type;
  unsigned long value;
} sovVisualInfo;

/* SERVER_OVERLAY_VISUALS property element. */
typedef struct _sovOverlayInfo {
  long overlay_visual;
  long transparent_type;
  long value;
  long layer;
} sovOverlayInfo;

extern sovVisualInfo *sovGetVisualInfo(
  Display *display,
  long lvinfo_mask,
  sovVisualInfo *lvinfo_template,
  int *nitems_return);
extern Status sovMatchVisualInfo(
  Display *display,
  int screen,
  int depth,
  int class,
  int layer,
  sovVisualInfo *lvinfo_return);
```

6.3.3.2 sovlayerutil.c

Here is the implementation of the sovGetVisualInfo and sovMatchVisualInfo routines:

```
#include <stdlib.h>
#include "sovLayerUtil.h"

static Bool layersRead;
static Atom overlayVisualsAtom;
static sovOverlayInfo **overlayInfoPerScreen;
static int *numOverlaysPerScreen;

sovVisualInfo *
sovGetVisualInfo(Display *display, long lvinfo_mask,
  sovVisualInfo *lvinfo_template, int *nitems_return)
{
  XVisualInfo *vinfo;
  sovVisualInfo *layerInfo;
  Window root;
  Status status;
  Atom actualType;
  unsigned long sizeData, bytesLeft;
  int actualFormat, numVisuals, numScreens, count, i, j;

  vinfo = XGetVisualInfo(display, lvinfo_mask & VisualAllMask,
    &lvinfo_template->vinfo, nitems_return);
  if (vinfo == NULL)
    return NULL;
  numVisuals = *nitems_return;
  if (layersRead == False) {
    overlayVisualsAtom = XInternAtom(display,
    "SERVER_OVERLAY_VISUALS", True);
    if (overlayVisualsAtom != None) {
    numScreens = ScreenCount(display);
    overlayInfoPerScreen = (sovOverlayInfo **)
      malloc(numScreens * sizeof(sovOverlayInfo *));
    numOverlaysPerScreen = (int *) malloc(numScreens * sizeof(int));
    if (overlayInfoPerScreen != NULL && numOverlaysPerScreen != NULL) {
      for (i = 0; i < numScreens; i++) {
        root = RootWindow(display, i);
        status = XGetWindowProperty(display, root, overlayVisualsAtom,
          0L, (long) 10000, False, overlayVisualsAtom,
          &actualType, &actualFormat,
          &sizeData, &bytesLeft,
          (char **) &overlayInfoPerScreen[i]);
        if (status != Success || actualType != overlayVisualsAtom ||
          actualFormat != 32 || sizeData < 4)
```

```
              numOverlaysPerScreen[i] = 0;
          else
            numOverlaysPerScreen[i] = sizeData /
              (sizeof(sovOverlayInfo) / 4);
        }
        layersRead = True;
      } else {
        if (overlayInfoPerScreen != NULL)
          free(overlayInfoPerScreen);
        if (numOverlaysPerScreen != NULL)
          free(numOverlaysPerScreen);
      }
    }
  }
  layerInfo = (sovVisualInfo *)
    malloc(numVisuals * sizeof(sovVisualInfo));
  if (layerInfo == NULL) {
    XFree(vinfo);
    return NULL;
  }
  count = 0;
  for (i = 0; i < numVisuals; i++) {
    XVisualInfo *pVinfo;
    int screen;
    sovOverlayInfo *overlayInfo;

    pVinfo = &vinfo[i];
    screen = pVinfo->screen;
    overlayInfo = NULL;
    if (layersRead) {
      for (j = 0; j < numOverlaysPerScreen[screen]; j++)
        if (pVinfo->visualid ==
          overlayInfoPerScreen[screen][j].overlay_visual) {
          overlayInfo = &overlayInfoPerScreen[screen][j];
          break;
        }
    }
    if (lvinfo_mask & VisualLayerMask)
      if (overlayInfo == NULL) {
      if (lvinfo_template->layer != 0)
        continue;
      } else if (lvinfo_template->layer != overlayInfo->layer)
      continue;
```

```
  if (lvinfo_mask & VisualTransparentType)
    if (overlayInfo == NULL) {
    if (lvinfo_template->type != None)
      continue;
    } else if (lvinfo_template->type !=
    overlayInfo->transparent_type)
    continue;
  if (lvinfo_mask & VisualTransparentValue)
    if (overlayInfo == NULL)
      /* non-overlay visuals have no sense of
      TransparentValue */
      continue;
    else if (lvinfo_template->value != overlayInfo->value)
      continue;
  layerInfo[count].vinfo = *pVinfo;
  if (overlayInfo == NULL) {
    layerInfo[count].layer = 0;
    layerInfo[count].type = None;
    layerInfo[count].value = 0;  /* meaningless */
  } else {
    layerInfo[count].layer = overlayInfo->layer;
    layerInfo[count].type = overlayInfo->transparent_type;
    layerInfo[count].value = overlayInfo->value;
  }
  count++;
}
XFree(vinfo);
*nitems_return = count;
if (count == 0) {
  XFree(layerInfo);
  return NULL;
} else
  return layerInfo;
}


Status
sovMatchVisualInfo(Display *display, int screen,
  int depth, int class, int layer, sovVisualInfo *lvinfo_return)
{
  sovVisualInfo *lvinfo;
  sovVisualInfo lvinfoTemplate;
  int nitems;
```

```
    lvinfoTemplate.vinfo.screen = screen;
    lvinfoTemplate.vinfo.depth = depth;
    lvinfoTemplate.vinfo.class = class;
    lvinfoTemplate.layer = layer;
    lvinfo = sovGetVisualInfo(display,
      VisualScreenMask|VisualDepthMask|VisualClassMask|VisualLayerMask,
      &lvinfoTemplate, &nitems);
    if (lvinfo != NULL && nitems > 0) {
      *lvinfo_return = *lvinfo;
      return 1;
    } else
      return 0;
}
```

6.3.4   Listing Overlay Visuals: `sovinfo.c`

To find out what overlay visuals are provided by a particular X server, the `sovinfo`
command uses the `sovGetVisualInfo` routine to decipher the SERVER_OVERLAY_
VISUALS and report the results. Here is the implementation of the `sovinfo` command:

```
#include <stdio.h>
#include <stdlib.h>
#include <string.h>
#include "sovLayerUtil.h"

int
main(int argc, char *argv[])
{
  Display *dpy;
  char *display_name, *arg, *class;
  sovVisualInfo template, *lvinfo;
  int nVisuals, i, overlaysOnly = 0;

  display_name = NULL;
  for (i = 1; i < argc; i++) {
    arg = argv[i];
    if (!strcmp(arg, "-display")) {
      if (++i >= argc) {
        fprintf(stderr, "sovinfo: missing argument to -display\n");
        exit(1);
      }
      display_name = argv[i];
```

```
   } else if (!strcmp(arg, "-overlays_only")) {
     overlaysOnly = 1;
   } else {
     fprintf(stderr,
       "usage: sovinfo [-display dpy] [-overlays_only]\n");
     exit(1);
   }
}
dpy = XOpenDisplay(display_name);
if (dpy == NULL) {
  fprintf(stderr, "sovinfo: cannot open display %s\n",
    XDisplayName(NULL));
  exit(1);
}
lvinfo = sovGetVisualInfo(dpy, 0L, &template, &nVisuals);
for (i = 0; i < nVisuals; i++) {
  if (!overlaysOnly || lvinfo[i].layer > 0) {
    printf(" Visual ID: 0x%x\n", lvinfo[i].vinfo.visualid);
    printf(" screen: %d\n", lvinfo[i].vinfo.screen);
    printf(" depth: %d\n", lvinfo[i].vinfo.depth);
    switch (lvinfo[i].vinfo.class) {
    case StaticGray:
      class = "StaticGray";
      break;
    case GrayScale:
      class = "GrayScale";
      break;
    case StaticColor:
      class = "StaticColor";
      break;
    case PseudoColor:
      class = "PseudoColor";
      break;
    case TrueColor:
      class = "TrueColor";
      break;
    case DirectColor:
      class = "DirectColor";
      break;
    default:
      class = "Unknown";
      break;
    }
```

```
      printf(" class: %s\n", class);
      switch (lvinfo[i].type) {
      case None:
        printf(" transparent type: None\n");
        break;
      case TransparentPixel:
        printf(" transparent type: TransparentPixel\n");
        printf(" pixel value: %d\n", lvinfo[i].value);
        break;
      case TransparentMask:
        printf(" transparent type: TransparentMask\n");
        printf(" transparency mask: %0x%x\n", lvinfo[i].value);
        break;
      default:
        printf(" transparent type: Unknown or invalid\n");
        break;
      }
      printf(" layer: %d\n", lvinfo[i].layer);
    }
  }
  return 0;
}
```

Figure 6.15 shows the output of sovinfo -overlays_only run on a 24-bit Silicon Graphics Indy. Notice that there are actually two overlays, an 8-bit overlay in

Figure 6.15 Output of sovinfo -overlays_only, showing overlays visuals supported on a 24-bit Silicon Graphics Indy.

```
Visual ID: 0x20
  screen: 0
  depth: 2
  class: PseudoColor
  transparent type: TransparentPixel
  pixel value: 0
  layer: 2
Visual ID: 0x26
  screen: 0
  depth: 8
  class: PseudoColor
  transparent type: TransparentPixel
  pixel value: 0
  layer: 1
```

layer 1 and a 2-bit overlay in layer 2. Also, notice that these visuals match the visuals in Figure 2.7, including the layer reported by GLX_LEVEL.

6.3.5 An Xlib-Only Overlay Example

To illustrate how to use an overlay window, the following layerdemo example uses the routines described previously to query the server for an overlay visual and then creates a normal plane window with a child in the overlays completely overlapping its parent. The background pixel value is set to a transparent pixel. Then, as in the weather map example mentioned earlier, a semi-intricate black-on-white image is drawn in the normal planes and red text annotation is drawn in the overlay planes. Each time a mouse button is clicked, the overlay planes are cleared and the text is redrawn in a different position. The example demonstrates how the overlays can be modified without disturbing the image in the normal plane. Figure 6.16 shows the output of layerdemo.

The example tries to find two appropriate visuals to use in making its "layer sandwich." The code first looks at the default visual and tries to find a visual "above" it with transparency supported. If such a visual is not found, the code looks for a visual "below" the default visual to use, but this requires that the default visual supports transparency. Note that this strategy could fail to find an appropriate pair of visuals in some cases, even when two potentially layerable visuals are present on

Figure 6.16 Screen snapshot of layerdemo. The text in the lower left-hand corner is rendered in the overlay.

a given server. The code is meant to be a relatively short, simple example to illustrate how to use layers in X; it is not intended to be a piece of production code.

The window created in the lower layer is the parent; the window created in the higher layer must be the child. It is important that this ordering not be reversed. The layered transparency effect implies that lower layers show through the transparent pixels of higher levels, rather than the other way around.

Because the overlay window is a child of the top-level normal plane window, if we move the client's top-level window, the overlay window moves too. Even though the windows are in different layers, the window hierarchy still dictates the way windows move and interact.

Also consistent with the window hierarchy is the way events are distributed for overlay windows. In our example, the child covers the entire normal plane window so it receives all button clicks. Note that an overlay window, receives mouse clicks even if the mouse is located on a transparent pixel. Transparency just affects how the pixel is displayed. Transparency does *not* affect the clipping region of a window. Similarly, if a transparent pixel is read from an overlay window using XGetImage, the value read is *not* the displayed value but the transparent value for the pixel. So transparency does not change the value of the pixel in the window; it only affects the color displayed on the screen.

6.3.5.1 `layerdemo.c`

Here is the implementation of `layerdemo`:

```
#include <stdio.h>
#include <stdlib.h>
#include <math.h>
#include "sovLayerUtil.h"

#define SIZE 400 /* Width and height of window. */

Display *dpy;
Window root, win, overlay;
Colormap cmap;
Visual *defaultVisual;
int screen, black, white, red, nVisuals, i, status;
GC normalGC, overlayGC;
XEvent event;
sovVisualInfo template;
sovVisualInfo *otherLayerInfo, *defaultLayerInfo;
XSetWindowAttributes winattrs;
XGCValues gcvals;
XColor color, exact;
int x = 0, y = SIZE / 2;
```

```
void
redrawNormalPlanes(void)
{
  /* Draw a black 43-legged octopus. */
  for (i = 0; i < 43; i++)
    XDrawLine(dpy, win, normalGC, SIZE / 2, SIZE / 2,
      (int) (cos(i * 0.15) * (SIZE / 2 - 5)) + SIZE / 2,
      (int) (sin(i * 0.15) * (SIZE / 2 - 12)) + SIZE / 2);
}


#define MESSAGE1 "This text is in the"
#define MESSAGE2 "OVERLAY PLANES"

void
redrawOverlayPlanes(void)
{
  XDrawString(dpy, overlay, overlayGC, x, y,
    MESSAGE1, sizeof(MESSAGE1) - 1);
  XDrawString(dpy, overlay, overlayGC, x, y + 15,
    MESSAGE2, sizeof(MESSAGE2) - 1);
}


void
fatalError(char *message)
{
  fprintf(stderr, "layerdemo: %\sn", message);
  exit(1);
}


void
main(int argc, char *argv[])
{
  dpy = XOpenDisplay(NULL);
  if (dpy == NULL)
    fatalError("cannot open display");
  screen = DefaultScreen(dpy);
  root = RootWindow(dpy, screen);
  defaultVisual = DefaultVisual(dpy, screen);
  /* Find layer of default visual. */
  template.vinfo.visualid = defaultVisual->visualid;
  defaultLayerInfo = sovGetVisualInfo(dpy, VisualIDMask,
    &template, &nVisuals);
```

```
/* Look for visual in layer "above" default visual with
   transparent pixel. */
template.layer = defaultLayerInfo->layer + 1;
template.vinfo.screen = screen;
template.type = TransparentPixel;
otherLayerInfo = sovGetVisualInfo(dpy,
  VisualScreenMask | VisualLayerMask | VisualTransparentType,
  &template, &nVisuals);
if (otherLayerInfo == NULL) {
  /* Make sure default visual has transparent pixel. */
  if (defaultLayerInfo->type == None)
    fatalError("unable to find expected layer visuals");
  /* Visual not found "above" default visual, try looking
     "below". */
  template.layer = defaultLayerInfo->layer - 1;
  template.vinfo.screen = screen;
  otherLayerInfo = sovGetVisualInfo(dpy,
    VisualScreenMask | VisualLayerMask, &template, &nVisuals);
  if (otherLayerInfo == NULL)
    fatalError("unable to find layer below default visual");
  /* XCreateColormap uses AllocNone for two reasons: (1)
     haven't determined class of visual, visual could have
     static colormap, and, more important, (2) transparent
     pixel might make AllocAll impossible. */
  cmap = XCreateColormap(dpy, root,
    otherLayerInfo->vinfo.visual, AllocNone);
  /* Not default colormap, must find our own black and white. */
  status = XAllocNamedColor(dpy, cmap, "black", &color, &exact);
  if (status == 0)
    fatalError("could not allocate black");
  black = color.pixel;
  status = XAllocNamedColor(dpy, cmap, "white", &color, &exact);
  if (status == 0)
    fatalError("could not allocate white");
  white = color.pixel;
  winattrs.background_pixel = white;
  winattrs.border_pixel = black;
  winattrs.colormap = cmap;
  win = XCreateWindow(dpy, root, 10, 10, SIZE, SIZE, 0,
    otherLayerInfo->vinfo.depth,
    InputOutput, otherLayerInfo->vinfo.visual,
    CWBackPixel | CWBorderPixel | CWColormap, &winattrs);
  status = XAllocNamedColor(dpy, DefaultColormap(dpy, screen),
    "red", &color, &exact);
```

```
    if (status == 0)
      fatalError("could not allocate red");
    winattrs.background_pixel = defaultLayerInfo->value;
    winattrs.border_pixel = 0;
    winattrs.colormap = DefaultColormap(dpy, screen);
    overlay = XCreateWindow(dpy, win, 0, 0, SIZE, SIZE, 0,
      DefaultDepth(dpy, screen),
      InputOutput, defaultVisual,
      CWBackPixel | CWBorderPixel | CWColormap, &winattrs);
  } else {
    /* Create lower window using default visual. */
    black = BlackPixel(dpy, screen);
    white = WhitePixel(dpy, screen);
    win = XCreateSimpleWindow(dpy, root, 10, 10, SIZE, SIZE, 1,
      black, white);
    /* See note above about AllocNone. */
    cmap = XCreateColormap(dpy, root,
      otherLayerInfo->vinfo.visual, AllocNone);
    status = XAllocNamedColor(dpy, cmap, "red", &color, &exact);
    if (status == 0)
      fatalError("could not allocate red");
    red = color.pixel;
    /* Use transparent pixel. */
    winattrs.background_pixel = otherLayerInfo->value;
    winattrs.border_pixel = 0; /* No border but still
                                  necessary to avoid BadMatch. */
    winattrs.colormap = cmap;
    overlay = XCreateWindow(dpy, win, 0, 0, SIZE, SIZE, 0,
      otherLayerInfo->vinfo.depth,
      InputOutput, otherLayerInfo->vinfo.visual,
      CWBackPixel | CWBorderPixel | CWColormap, &winattrs);
  }
XSelectInput(dpy, win, ExposureMask);
XSelectInput(dpy, overlay, ExposureMask | ButtonPressMask);
XSetWMColormapWindows(dpy, win, &overlay, 1);
gcvals.foreground = black;
gcvals.line_width = 8;
gcvals.cap_style = CapRound;
normalGC = XCreateGC(dpy, win,
  GCForeground | GCLineWidth | GCCapStyle, &gcvals);
gcvals.foreground = red;
overlayGC = XCreateGC(dpy, overlay, GCForeground, &gcvals);
XMapSubwindows(dpy, win);
XMapWindow(dpy, win);
```

```
while (1) {
  XNextEvent(dpy, &event);
  switch (event.type) {
  case Expose:
    if (event.xexpose.window == win)
      redrawNormalPlanes();
    else
      redrawOverlayPlanes();
    break;
  case ButtonPress:
    x = random() % SIZE / 2;
    y = random() % SIZE;
    XClearWindow(dpy, overlay);
    redrawOverlayPlanes();
    break;
  }
}
}
```

6.3.6 Vendor Support for Overlays

Silicon Graphics was the first vendor to implement X overlays using the server overlay visuals convention. In IRIX 4.0,[5] overlay support was introduced. Silicon Graphics's 4Dwm Motif-based window manager and other Silicon Graphics X clients, such as the xwsh terminal emulator, make use of the overlays to speed pop-up menus and support efficient rubber-banding. In addition, the IRIS Graphics Library allows rendering into the overlays. With the IRIX 5.0 release, the Silicon Graphics X product's overlay support was substantially reengineered to improve on the original implementation.

Hewlett-Packard [20, 34] also supports overlays on some of its workstations, in particular those with CRX24 and CRX48Z graphics hardware. Hewlett-Packard implements overlays by causing the default visual to be in an 8-bit overlay (supporting a transparent pixel). This approach means that most X clients automatically run in the overlay planes.

Other vendors, such as IBM and Digital Equipment Corp., have also implemented overlays for X. Supporting layered frame buffers in the X11R5 and the previous MIT release of X was difficult because the Device Independent X (DIX) code in the server implicitly assumes that all windows reside in the same layer. For overlays, this assumption is not true. The code to do window tree validation inside the X server is complicated by layers. With X11R6, hooks were added to the DIX layer

---

5. IRIX is Silicon Graphics's version of the Unix operating system.

to support frame buffer layers without vendor modification to the DIX layer. This should help make overlay implementations more commonplace.

The GLUT library, described in Chapter 4, will automatically use overlays for its pop-up menus if the server overlay visuals convention is supported.

6.3.7 Usage Considerations

A number of considerations should be kept in mind when you are using overlay windows.

6.3.7.1 Shallower Depths

It is common for an overlay frame buffer not to be as deep as the normal plane frame buffer. For example, the Indigo with Entry graphics and 8-bit Indy graphics (Silicon Graphics's lowest-end graphics options) support an 8-bit normal plane frame buffer, but provide only a 2-bit overlay. Mid-range Silicon Graphics graphics platforms support 4-bit and 8-bit overlays; the normal plane supports up to 24-bit deep normal plane windows. You can expect deeper overlays to be more common in the future, but do not be surprised by shallow overlay visuals. Hewlett-Packard avoids this issue of shallow depths by providing 8-bit overlays.

When you write a program to use overlays, you should remember that the overlays may be substantially shallower than the default visual. In the case of a 2-bit overlay visual, keep in mind that you probably have only three colors to use (since one is transparent). Efficient use of color resources is important.

Also, be aware that creating windows in the overlays generally means using visuals other than the default visual. You must always specify a colormap and a border pixel color or pixmap when creating a window not using the default visual. Otherwise, a `BadMatch` protocol error will occur. (See Section 2.8.2.)

6.3.7.2 Overlay Colormaps

Colormaps create another area of concern. Normally, if you create windows using the default visual, you use the default colormap and allocate colors from it. Since most windows use the default colormap, occasions when the colormap is not installed are rare. Because overlays cannot typically use the default colormap and each client ends up needing to create a unique colormap to be used with its overlay windows, it is easy to create colormap flashing problems in the overlay planes. And, generally, overlays do not support multiple simultaneous colormaps.

However, it is generally true that the overlays have a distinct hardware colormap from the normal plane. This means that usually a colormap for the overlays and a colormap for the normal plane can be installed simultaneously. This is the case on Silicon Graphics graphics hardware.

If you are new to the practice of using nondefault colormaps, you should note that `BlackPixel` and `WhitePixel` return pixel values for the *default* colormap.

Colormaps created with `XCreateColormap` are not created with preallocated black and white pixels. If you need black and white pixels, you should allocate them yourself.

Also remember to use `XSetWMColormapWindows` if you have a window using a colormap that is not the same as the colormap of your top-level window. This allows a window manager to install the appropriate colormaps for your client. (See Section 2.3.)

There is one more caveat for using overlay colormaps. Because Silicon Graphics hardware uses 0 for the overlay transparent pixel, the Silicon Graphics X server reserves pixel 0 in overlay colormaps. It is therefore impossible to allocate all the colormap cells in a Silicon Graphics overlay colormap. If a colormap for an overlay visual is created with the `AllocAll` parameter, Silicon Graphics has opted to generate a `BadAlloc` error. To avoid such errors, client programs should use `AllocNone` when creating overlay colormaps and allocate colormap cells individually.

Some vendors, such as Hewlett-Packard, put the default visual in the overlays, making it possible to use the default colormap. However, do not assume this will be the case for most overlay-capable X servers.

6.3.7.3 *Window Manager Interactions*

Window managers are another consideration when you are programming with overlays. Depending on the window manager, border decoration may or may not be created to be present in the overlays. If the borders are not in the overlays, `Expose` events for underlying normal plane windows will still be generated when an overlay window is moved or unmapped, because of the damage caused by the window manager borders. The chief advantage of creating overlay windows is removed. But if the window manager does create the borders in the overlays, the colormap used by the window manager will be different from the colormap for the client window, nearly guaranteeing colormap flashing.

The problem is not as bad as it seems. Since most uses of the overlay planes are for transient or non-top-level windows and in many cases only one client at a time is using the overlay planes, the problems of colormap clashes can be kept to a minimum.

The best advice is to create top-level overlay windows enabling override-redirect or without any window manager decoration. Since most uses of top-level overlays are for transient windows, this advice is generally easy to follow.

Another issue for override-redirect overlay windows is colormap installation. When you map override-redirect overlay windows such as pop-up menus, the window manager cannot control the way the window is mapped and therefore the time when the colormap is installed. This means that before you map an override-redirect overlay window, you should be sure to use `XInstallColormap` to install its colormap.

6.3.8 Using Overlays with Motif Menus

A common use of overlays in OpenGL programs is for pull-down and pop-up menus. Use of overlay menus does not damage expensive normal plane OpenGL rendering, so programs set up to use overlay menus typically have faster menu interactions. The following code fragments show how to create overlay Motif menus when available.

The detectOverlayMenuSupport routine below returns a non-zero value if the X server supports overlays suitable for use by Motif for menus. It uses the sovGetVisualInfo routine, from Section 6.3.3, to query what overlay visuals are available. If a suitable overlay visual is found, the pVisual, pDepth, and pColormap locations are updated with the visual, depth, and colormap information for the menu overlay visual. This information can then be used when creating menu widgets.

```
int
detectOverlayMenuSupport(Display *dpy, int screen,
  Visual **pVisual, int *pDepth, Colormap *pColormap)
{
  sovVisualInfo template, *overlayVisuals;
  int layer, nVisuals, i, entries;

  /* Need more than two colormap entries for reasonable menus. */
  entries = 2;
  for (layer = 1; layer <= 3; layer++) {
    template.layer = layer;
    template.vinfo.screen = screen;
    overlayVisuals = sovGetVisualInfo(dpy,
      VisualScreenMask | VisualLayerMask, &template, &nVisuals);
    if (overlayVisuals) {
      for (i = 0; i < nVisuals; i++) {
        if (overlayVisuals[i].vinfo.visual->map_entries > entries) {
          *pVisual = overlayVisuals[i].vinfo.visual;
          *pDepth = overlayVisuals[i].vinfo.depth;
          entries = (*pVisual)->map_entries;
        }
      }
      XFree(overlayVisuals);
    }
  }
  if (*pVisual) {
    if (DefaultVisual(dpy, screen)->visualid
        == (*pVisual)->visualid) {
      *pColormap = DefaultColormap(dpy, screen);
```

```
    } else {
      *pColormap = XCreateColormap(dpy,
        DefaultRootWindow(dpy), *pVisual, AllocNone);
    }
    return 1;
  } else {
    return 0;
  }
}
```

Here is an example using `detectOverlayMenuSupport` during the creation of a Motif pull-down menu. Observe that if `detectOverlayMenuSupport` succeeds, the returned visual, depth, and colormap are used when creating the pull-down menu. The same information can be used when any other overlay menus required by the program are created.

```
Widget menubar, menupane;
Visual *overlayVisual;
Colormap overlayColormap;
int menuInOverlay, overlayDepth;


menuInOverlay = detectOverlayMenuSupport(dpy, DefaultScreen(dpy),
  &overlayVisual, &overlayDepth, &overlayColormap);
if (menuInOverlay) {
  XtSetArg(args[0], XmNvisual, overlayVisual);
  XtSetArg(args[1], XmNdepth, overlayDepth);
  XtSetArg(args[2], XmNcolormap, overlayColormap);
  menupane = XmCreatePulldownMenu(menubar, "menupane", args, 3);
  XtAddCallback(XtParent(menupane), XmNpopupCallback,
    ensureMenuColormapInstalled, NULL);
} else {
  menupane = XmCreatePulldownMenu(menubar, "menupane", NULL, 0);
}
```

Notice that the `ensureMenuColormapInstalled` is registered to be called when the pull-down menu is popped up. Because the overlay menu may not be using the default colormap and the window manager cannot be responsible for installing menu colormaps, an `ensureMenuColormapInstalled` callback makes sure the menu's colormap is installed before the menu is mapped.

The `ensureMenuColormapInstalled` routine just calls `XInstallColormap` on the menu's colormap.

```
void
ensureMenuColormapInstalled(Widget w, XtPointer clientData,
  XtPointer callData)
{
  Colormap cmap;
  XtVaGetValues(w, XtNcolormap, &cmap, NULL);
  /* Ensure that overlay pulldown menu's colormap is installed. */
  XInstallColormap(dpy, cmap);
}
```

By using this technique when creating Motif menus, your applications can eliminate expensive OpenGL redraws resulting from pop-up and pull-down menu interactions when overlays are available. Users will appreciate the faster program responsiveness.

6.4 PORTABILITY AND INTEROPERABILITY

Because OpenGL is a standard programming interface, code you write using OpenGL can easily be ported to different OpenGL-capable graphics workstations.

Portability is related to the issue of *interoperability*. Interoperability means that your OpenGL program will work as expected when run against different OpenGL implementations. Because X applications are network-extensible, you should keep in mind that users will try to run your OpenGL application over the network to display it on an OpenGL implementation that you may not have specifically tested your application against. Interoperability issues can also arise because many vendors use OpenGL in conjunction with shared libraries to provide a single 3D interface across a range of different types of graphics hardware.

6.4.1 Portability Issues

OpenGL rendering code can be ported to window systems other than X that support OpenGL, such as Windows 95 and NT, OS/2, and the Power Macintosh. Of course, there is more to an application than OpenGL-based rendering code. Any window system dependent code (such as any code using Motif, Xlib, or GLX) in your application will need to be reimplemented when you port to another window system. If you expect to port your application to another window system, try to isolate your windowing code from your OpenGL rendering code. If you structure your code well, nearly all the OpenGL rendering code you write can simply be recompiled when you port to another window system.

When you plan to port your OpenGL code to different platforms or window systems, here are some things to keep in mind:

- Many C compilers, particularly for PCs, treat `near` and `far` as keywords. Avoid using `near` or `far` (or either of these words in uppercase or in combined uppercase and lowercase) as variable or macro names, even though they are obvious names when you are working with projection matrices or depth buffer ranges.

- Unix workstations typically support large stacks, but other operating systems, such as Windows, use (by default) a relatively small stack. Avoid allocating large arrays on the stack.

- The Windows 95 and NT binding API for OpenGL does not have an equivalent of `glXCopyContext`.

- If you use `glXUseXFont`, know that the fonts you access are window system dependent. Other windows systems, such as Windows NT and OS/2, have routines similar to `glXUseXFont`, but the way fonts can be accessed, and which ones, will be different.

- Code that manipulates images and texture data is often susceptible to byte-order assumptions. DEC and Intel-based systems place the least significant byte first in a word (often referred to as *little-endian*), while MIPS, PowerPC, and SPARC-based systems place the most significant byte first (often referred to as *big-endian*).

- If you use GLUT (see Chapter 4) and the platform you are porting to supports GLUT, you will not have to port the window system independent GLUT code you have written. In addition to the X implementation of GLUT, implementations exist for Windows NT and OS/2.

The OpenGL Utility (GLU) library is a standard library, common to all OpenGL implementations, so portable programs can rely on its existence. If you require any GLU 1.1 or 1.2 routines, make sure the system you are porting to supports the same version of the GLU interface.

OpenGL does have its own basic types (described previously in Table 1.2 data-types). While it will almost always be the case that the OpenGL version of a type will match to the corresponding C type (for example, `GLfloat` will be a `typedef` for `float`), it is possible for an OpenGL implementation to do otherwise. You should not need to cast explicitly OpenGL data types to C data types and vice versa for assignments and correctly prototyped functions. The time when you need to be careful is when pointers to OpenGL data types are expected. If the size of a basic C type is different from that of the corresponding OpenGL type, you could get into trouble. For example:

```
float vertex[3] = { 0.0, 1.0, 0.0 } ; /* WRONG type! */

glVertex3fv(vertex);
```

If `sizeof(GLfloat)` is not equal to `sizeof(float)`, you will be in trouble. If `vertex` is declared to be of type `GLfloat`, you are sure to avoid trouble. In practice, it is rather unlikely that you will ever encounter an OpenGL implementation in which the above code would cause a problem.

6.4.2   Interoperability Issues

OpenGL goes a long way to ensure that OpenGL code will operate as expected independent of the implementation it is running on. OpenGL dictates the set of rendering capabilities that compliant implementations must provide. When you write OpenGL code, you can count on *all* core OpenGL rendering capabilities being available. However, OpenGL's specification does give OpenGL implementations leeway in a number of areas. For the most part, these allowances will only rarely adversely affect the operation of OpenGL programs, but you should be aware of what allowances are permissible so you do not unintentionally rely on subtle implementation dependent behaviors.

The ways in which OpenGL implementations are permitted to vary are

- Exceeding minimum rendering implementation requirements.
- Allowed tolerances for rendering.
- Behavior when `GL_OUT_OF_MEMORY` error occurs.
- Varying frame buffer capabilities provided.
- Whether direct rendering is supported.
- Set of supported extensions.
- `glGetString` returns implementation dependent values.

Each of these differences deserves examination in more detail. The first three differences are in implementation capacity and quality; the remaining differences are in implementation capability.

6.4.2.1   Differences of Implementation Capacity and Quality

Implementations are permitted to exceed minimum limits on the capacity of certain rendering capabilities. For example, all implementations must implement a minimum attribute stack depth of 16 entries, but applications are permitted to support more. Table 6.3 shows OpenGL's minimum mandated implementation dependent values for rendering.

You can use `glGetIntegerv` (or `glGetFloatv` for the point size and line width ranges) to determine a particular implementation's limits. To make it portable, write your code so it will still operate correctly if an implementation implements only the minimum value for a limit. Limits to be particularly wary of exceeding

Table 6.3 Minimum implementation dependent rendering values for OpenGL implementations.* The viewport maximum size must be greater than or equal to the visible dimensions of the display being rendered to.

Description	Minimum value	Get value
Maximum number of lights	8	`GL_MAX_LIGHT`
Maximum user clipping planes	6	`GL_MAX_CLIP_PLANES`
Maximum modelview matrix stack depth	32	`GL_MAX_MODELVIEW_STACK_DEPTH`
Maximum projection matrix stack depth	2	`GL_MAX_PROJECTION_STACK_DEPTH`
Maximum texture matrix stack depth	2	`GL_MAX_TEXTURE_STACK_DEPTH`
Number of bits of subpixel precision in x and y	4	`GL_SUBPIXEL_BITS`
Maximum height or width of a texture image (without borders)	64	`GL_MAX_TEXTURE_SIZE`
Maximum size of a `glPixelMap` translation table	32	`GL_MAX_PIXEL_MAP_TABLE`
Maximum selection name stack depth	64	`GL_MAX_NAME_STACK_DEPTH`
Maximum display list call nesting	64	`GL_MAX_LIST_NESTING`
Maximum evaluator polynomial order	8	`GL_MAX_EVAL_ORDER`
Maximum viewport dimensions	*	`GL_MAX_VIEWPORT_DIMS`
Maximum attribute stack depth	16	`GL_MAX_ATTRIB_STACK_DEPTH`
Range of antialiased point sizes	1, 1	`GL_POINT_SIZE_RANGE`
Range of antialiased line widths	1, 1	`GL_LINE_WIDTH_RANGE`

are the projection and texture matrix maximum stack depths (since the limit is two), the maximum texture dimensions, and the maximum display list nesting. OpenGL 1.1's texture proxy mechanism, described on page 291 can assist in determining texture memory limits.

If you suspect you are running into an implementation limit, you can use `glGet-Error` to watch for `GL_STACK_OVERFLOW` or `GL_INVALID_VALUE` errors. It is always a good practice to occasionally poll for OpenGL errors while developing new code or running your code on a new OpenGL implementation. See Section 2.8.1.

What happens when a `GL_OUT_OF_MEMORY` occurs depends on the OpenGL implementation. While typically you should try to have enough memory to avoid ever getting a `GL_OUT_OF_MEMORY`, be aware that what implementations do once an out-of-memory condition occurs varies from one implementation to another.

OpenGL is not a *pixel-exact* rendering interface. OpenGL therefore does not guarantee an exact match between images produced by different OpenGL implementations. Do not depend on your program to generate exactly the same image on two different OpenGL implementations. OpenGL does specify an ideal for rendering, but because OpenGL transformations depend on floating-point calculations that can vary in precision depending on the precision of the underlying floating-point representation used, the quality of the generated picture can vary slightly.

While OpenGL does not have exact pixelization rules, do not get the false impression that there are no rules. Conformance to the OpenGL standard does require that implementations render the same results, with some bounded leeway for variation. Also, the OpenGL specification mandates some cases in which images rendered by the same implementation must match exactly.[6] Rendering conformance is enforced by the requirement that OpenGL implementations must pass OpenGL's conformance suite.

6.4.2.2 Differences of Implementation Capability

The biggest challenge for interoperability lies in the differences in frame buffer capabilities between OpenGL implementations. OpenGL mandates that its core rendering functionality be implemented fully; however, the type and resolution of frame buffer state are not strictly mandated. Implementations can provide any number of frame buffer configurations of varying capability, provided that there exist frame buffer configurations that meet or exceed the base required configurations (see Section 2.2.1).

Look for the most appropriate visual for your application, but if you cannot locate such a visual, scale back your requirements until you find a configuration that is supported. Determine the minimum reasonable frame buffer configuration your application requires. If possible, use the base RGBA visual required by GLX as your minimum visual. Avoid requiring a color index visual, since GLX does not require one.

Double buffering is not required by GLX. Try to fall back to single buffering if double buffering is not supported. If you need a single buffered visual and no single buffered visual matches your requirements, try looking for a double buffered visual and just render to the front buffer. Some X servers advertise only double buffered GLX visuals. `glXChooseVisual` will not automatically return double buffered visuals (boolean attributes must match exactly) if you request a single buffered visual, so you will have to use two calls. If `glXChooseVisual` does not meet your needs for visual selection, you can implement your own heuristic with GLX attribute information returned by `glXGetConfig`.

Frame buffer features like stereo and the Silicon Graphics multisampling extension will not be available on most workstations. Fall back to monoscopic mode if stereo is unavailable, or simply do not use multisampling.

---

6. These cases are described in an appendix to the OpenGL specification, titled "Invariance."

The bottom line is that you should make your best effort to ensure that your OpenGL application will run on hardware with varying frame buffer configurations. If you have access to low-end and high-end graphics workstations or workstations from different vendors, make sure you try your application on different OpenGL implementations. You cannot try your application on every OpenGL implementation, but you can verify that your visual selection code chooses reasonable frame buffer configurations for different implementations.

Direct rendering is not always supported. If you develop your application on an OpenGL implementation that supports direct rendering, you should occasionally run your application without benefit of direct rendering or try running your application from a remote machine (this ensures that you use direct rendering). The fact that you are developing your application on a local workstation that supports fast direct rendering does not necessarily mean that this will be the only way your application is used.

The difference between direct rendering and indirect rendering should be only a difference of performance; however, if you never consider the indirect rendering case, you may find the indirect rendering performance of your application is considerably worse than it needs to be. OpenGL commands that retrieve OpenGL state (such as `glGetIntegerv`) become considerably more expensive when using indirect- rendering. While a direct rendering program can quickly return state with little overhead, an indirect rendering program must send a request to the X server and wait for a reply for each piece of state requested. Sometimes state retrievals can be replaced by pushing and popping of matrices and attributes. Sometimes the program can track the state without having to query it from OpenGL at all.

Also, your program might greatly benefit from using display lists or texture objects to minimize the amount of information sent using GLX protocol to the X server.

The set of extensions provided by an implementation will clearly vary from implementation to implementation. If possible, your program should be prepared to operate without an extension. See Section 5.6 for more help with properly detecting and using extensions.

So far, the interoperability problems discussed have been due to allowed differences between implementations. It is also possible that problems result from bugs in certain OpenGL implementations that your application is aware of and can work around.

Using `glGetString`, you can (in addition to determining the list of supported extensions) retrieve implementation dependent data about the company responsible for the implementation (GL_VENDOR), the graphics hardware configuration (GL_RENDERER), and the release number or version of the implementation (GL_VERSION).

The conventions for the format of the strings returned by `glGetString` (except for GL_EXTENSIONS) vary from vendor to vendor. Along with working around known bugs, you can also use the information returned to recognize known platforms to modify your application's OpenGL usage based on the performance characteristics of the platform in use.

A final but important interoperability concern (particularly when you are connecting to a remote display) is that OpenGL's GLX extension is not supported by all X servers, particularly older workstations and low-end X terminals. When your application runs into this situation, the minimal thing to do is print a message saying that OpenGL is not supported and terminate. To be more user-friendly, you can display a window with your message instead of simply printing it. However, if 3D graphics is not fundamental to the program (say, a spreadsheet with a 3D graphing capability implemented in OpenGL), your users will probably prefer that the application run despite the lack of OpenGL and simply disable whatever features depend on OpenGL rendering.

6.5 HARDWARE FOR ACCELERATING OPENGL

OpenGL is intended for interactive graphics where specialized graphics hardware can greatly improve performance. OpenGL is also designed to be appropriate for a wide variety of graphics systems. The same OpenGL standard should achieve good performance on computers ranging from PCs to tomorrow's fastest graphics supercomputers. This is despite a difference of two or more orders of magnitude between both the expected performance and the cost at each extreme of such a range of computers. If you are going to program with OpenGL extensively, it is good to understand a bit about graphics hardware architecture in the same way as it helps to understand basic computer architecture for general-purpose programming.

One view of OpenGL is that OpenGL is a high-level description of the functionality that an OpenGL-capable graphics subsystem must implement. Within OpenGL's prescribed functionality, there are numerous approaches for implementing OpenGL at various price/performance levels.

The process of rendering interactive computer graphics is a highly specialized task that benefits greatly from graphics hardware designed to support the basic operations that occur repeatedly during graphics operations. As a rule, effectively utilized graphics hardware results in better graphics performance. At the same time, adding specialized hardware to a computer system increases the cost of the system. The decision as to how many dollars should be devoted to hardware for accelerating graphics operations is determined by the price/performance requirements of the complete system.

At a minimum, displaying OpenGL graphics requires video display hardware connected to a *frame buffer*. A frame buffer is a bank of memory designed to hold an array of image pixels that can be continuously scanned out to video display hardware. Beyond this minimum hardware support for displaying graphics, varying degrees of additional hardware can accelerate OpenGL rendering.

6.5.1 The Graphics Pipeline

In simple terms, OpenGL describes a *graphics pipeline* for performing graphics operations (OpenGL commands) to affect pixels in a frame buffer. A graphics pipeline is a logical model for decomposing graphics operations. In general, all graphics systems are organized using some type of pipeline partitioning scheme. In a broader sense (not limited to OpenGL), the general graphics pipeline can be partitioned into five stages:

- **Generation** (G), creation, acquisition, or modification of the information to be displayed and organization of this information into application data structures.

- **Traversal** (T) of application data structures, passing on the appropriate graphics data.

- **Transformation** (X) of the graphics data from object-space coordinates into eye-space coordinates, performing requested lighting operations, then clipping the transformed data in clip-space and projection of the resulting coordinates into window-space.

- **Rasterization** (R) renders window-space primitives (such as points, lines, and polygons) into a frame buffer. Iteration of per-vertex shading calculations, texture lookups and calculations, and per-pixel operations such as depth testing are performed during this stage.

- **Display** (D) scans the resulting pixels in the frame buffer, typically to a display monitor.

The stages make up a rendering pipeline because the outputs from one stage are the inputs for the next stage. The letters *G*, *T*, *X*, *R*, and *D* are used to abbreviate these stages.

An OpenGL graphics pipeline is actually a subset of the general graphics pipeline, specifying the last three stages. OpenGL leaves the generation and traversal stages to the application program, since these stages are highly dependent on the particular data to be displayed and the way it is organized. Tasks that are varied and highly application-dependent are best left to the system's general-purpose processor.[7] Figure 6.17 shows how the components of the OpenGL state machine map to the general graphics pipeline. Observe that this figure is a more involved version of Figure 1.1. Higher-level libraries such as Open Inventor [40] and IRIS Performer [35] can assist applications with the generation and traversal stages.

---

7. In principle, OpenGL's display list facility does support limited traversal, but OpenGL's display list functionality is not a general-purpose traversal facility.

6.5.2   A Taxonomy for Graphics Hardware

Using the pipeline framework, OpenGL implementations can be classified by the extent to which the OpenGL pipeline for each is implemented using specialized graphics hardware.

In graphics hardware architecture, a computer's general-purpose processor that drives the graphics hardware is called the *host*. The decision as to which stages in the graphics pipeline should be performed on the host and in which specialized graphics hardware is an important one when you are designing or evaluating a computer's graphics subsystem. Often, tasks performed on the host are said to be "implemented in software", meaning that no specialized hardware is used to perform the stages. Tasks performed by specialized graphics hardware are said to be "implemented in hardware", because dedicated hardware is used to accelerate the tasks.[8]

Kurt Akeley, a coauthor of the OpenGL specification [36], has described a useful taxonomy and associated nomenclature for classifying graphics subsystems based on the way the general graphics pipeline stages are partitioned between software implementation on the host and dedicated graphics hardware [1].[9] The string of letters *GTXRD* is an abbreviation indicating the general pipeline stages. A hyphen is used to indicate which stages are (largely) implemented in hardware. For example, a PC graphics board such as the standard VGA adapter would be an example of a *GTXR-D* architecture, since only the display stage is implemented in hardware. Table 6.4 describes various graphics subsystems using Akeley's taxonomy. In

Figure 6.17 How the OpenGL state machine maps to the general graphics pipeline.

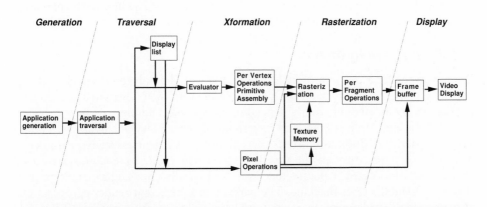

---

8. In practice, some graphics hardware does have specialized software known as microcode.
9. Akeley's original taxonomy, described in [1], referred to the rasterization stage as scan conversion.

Table 6.4 Various graphics subsystems described using Akeley's taxonomy for classifying graphics architectures.

Graphics Subsystem	Classification	Description
IBM VGA [12]	GTXR-D	Standard PC "dumb frame buffer"
Silicon Graphics Indigo Entry	GTX-RD	8-bit graphics option with line, span, and fill engine, 2-bit overlay, 4-bit double buffering
Silicon Graphics Indy 24 [37]	GTX-RD	24-bit graphics option with line, span, and fill engine, 8-bit overlay, 12-bit double-buffering
Sun Leo [8]	GT-XRD	210K 100-pixel triangles/sec, 4 parallel custom floating-point processors, and 5-way parallel raster subsystem using hyper-pipelining
SGI Indigo Extreme [18]	GT-XRD	500K triangle/sec and 80M pixels/sec, shaded and depth-buffered using 8 SIMD processors and two-way parallel raster subsystem
SGI Onyx Reality-Engine^2 [2]	GT-XRD	12 MIMD i860 processors for geometry processing, highly parallel rendering subsystem, trilinear texture mapping, and real-time full-scene antialiasing
SGI Onyx InfiniteReality	GT-XRD	8 custom geometry processors, 10+ million polygons/second, 200M to 800M pixels/sec, video resizing, multisampling
Evans and Sutherland ESIG4000	G-TXRD	High-end visual simulation system, including special terrain traversal and level-of-detail-rendering algorithms

practice, the taxonomy is a coarse one because there is variability in the extent to which specific functionality is implemented in hardware.

6.5.3 Rendering Paths

When you render a polygon using OpenGL, the way the polygon is actually drawn depends on the currently enabled OpenGL modes and their associated parameters. A polygon is rendered differently depending on the ways lighting, texturing, blending, antialiasing, depth testing, and a plethora of other OpenGL modes are configured. It is useful to think of sets of rendering modes and their associated parameters as *rendering paths* through the OpenGL implementation. By enabling rendering modes and selecting their parameters, you are logically choosing a rendering path through OpenGL's state machine. The performance of actual rendering operations along a specific rendering path depends on how well that path is optimized and supported in hardware by your specific OpenGL implementation.

The *GTXRD* taxonomy is useful for obtaining a high-level, coarse view of the types of operations that are potentially supported in hardware.

In practice, a system that is considered a *GT-XRD* architecture may incompletely support OpenGL's full transformation and rasterization functionality in hardware. For example, a *GT-XRD* system may not have support for texture mapping in its rasterization hardware. This means that any rendering path with texturing enabled will fall back to a software path. Falling back to software means that tasks in the transformation stage that could potentially have been done in hardware without texturing enabled must also fall back to software. It is important to realize that having a feature supported in hardware does not ensure that the hardware can be used on every rendering path.

Even when rendering paths for two different sets of modes are supported via specialized hardware, you are still very likely to find that one path is faster than another. For example, when OpenGL lighting is enabled, enabling a single light is quite likely to be faster than enabling all eight possible lights. And even though depth testing is supported in hardware, a rendering path with depth testing disabled is likely to run faster than one without depth testing.

At a high level, the *GTXRD* nomenclature is a good way to broadly classify the extent of hardware acceleration for a graphics hardware architecture. At the level of a specific application's graphics usage, however, it is better to consider the actual rendering paths exercised by the application and decide whether a given OpenGL implementation sufficiently optimizes those paths and whether the available hardware is effectively utilized.

When you are evaluating an OpenGL implementation for a specific application, find out what graphics functionality is implemented in hardware and what is implemented in software. Be careful not to expect every OpenGL feature to be supported in hardware. Instead, match your choice of system to your application performance demands and cost constraints. Be particularly careful about being misled by "standard" benchmarks, since they may measure graphics performance for a rendering path that is not particularly important to your application. There is no substitute for your own benchmarking of the particular rendering paths you care about most.

Considering the performance of specific paths without the context of a specific application is difficult when you are evaluating OpenGL performance in the overall selection of a graphics workstation. Instead, let general considerations guide you such as the *GTXRD* classification of the machine and general questions such as whether a depth buffer is supported in hardware or what type of texture mapping hardware is provided (assuming these capabilities are broadly desirable for the system you are selecting). Benchmarks can be useful, but be wary, because sometimes benchmarks are selected to show off particularly efficient rendering paths, and benchmarks more often demonstrate maximum performance than typical performance. More on benchmarks later.

The remainder of this section describes the stages of the OpenGL graphics pipeline in more detail and considers window system features for enhancing OpenGL's window system integration.

6.5.4 Hardware for OpenGL Stages

If you use a PC or a low-end 2D graphics workstation, you almost certainly have graphics hardware in your system, but it is likely to be of the *GTXR-D* variety. Primarily, PC and low-end workstation 2D graphics options are evaluated on the basis of screen and color resolution and read/write bandwidth to the frame buffer. When such systems do have hardware acceleration, it is likely for simple primitives like 2D lines and rectangles. The benchmarks cited for this class of hardware are typically 2D. The 2D transformation and rasterization stages are considerably simpler than the corresponding stages in 3D graphics. Typically, in 2D graphics, calculations are done in window coordinates so the transformation stage is sometimes nothing more than a logical placeholder.

Graphics hardware designed for 3D is more sophisticated. In addition to color values, the frame buffers for 3D hardware tend to have ancillary buffers for per-pixel data such as depth and stencil values. Rasterization and often transformation tasks are off loaded from the host processor and into the graphics hardware. To support multiple programs concurrently sending 3D graphics commands to the graphics subsystem, hardware features are often provided to better integrate 3D graphics with the window system.

The following sections consider the graphics pipeline, working in reverse order from the display stage to the transformation stage.

6.5.5 Display Options

OpenGL machines typically have more sophisticated display hardware than 2D graphics hardware. Display hardware for a 2D system typically displays the frame buffer in a uniform pixel format for every pixel on the screen.

6.5.5.1 Pixel Formats

As described in Section 1.2.3, OpenGL has two color models: RGBA and color index. Typically, OpenGL implementations support windows of both color models on the screen simultaneously. The "depth", or amount of color resolution, for each window may also vary. So for instance, 8-bit color index windows and 24-bit RGBA windows may coexist on the screen at the same time. Such display hardware needs to scan out not only the value of each pixel in the frame buffer, but also each pixel's format, to determine what color to display.

6.5.5.2 Double Buffering

OpenGL supports per-window double buffering. A double buffered window has two color buffers, designated the *front* and the *back* buffer. The front buffer is the displayed buffer; the back buffer is used to compose the next image to be displayed.

When a *buffer swap* is requested, the contents of the back buffer are logically transferred to the front buffer. Double buffering is very important for 3D, since it enables smooth animation of rendered frames.

Hardware support obviates the expense of a physical data transfer and allows the buffer swap to be timed with the monitor's vertical retrace interval (when the CRT's gun is moving back to the top of the screen to begin scanning out the next frame of video). Timing the buffer swap with vertical retrace avoids a visual artifact known as *tearing*, which occurs when the buffer swap occurs in the midst of the window's being scanned to the monitor, getting a portion of the image from the old front buffer and a portion from the new front buffer.

Without hardware support, the back buffer is normally allocated from host memory. In this case, a buffer swap requires a copy from host memory to the frame buffer. It is also more difficult to synchronize with vertical retrace. Because rendering to off screen memory normally makes it impossible to makes use of graphics hardware acceleration, double buffering hardware is typical for 3D *GTX-RD* and *GT-XRD* systems.

Normally, hardware double buffering is implemented by dividing the frame buffer into two color buffers: for example, a 24-bit frame buffer when single buffered would support 12-bit double buffered windows. This introduces additional pixel formats, not only for 12-bit depth, also to describe which 12-bit buffer is currently considered the front buffer for specific windows.

6.5.5.3 Overlays

Often OpenGL scenes are intricate and take time and resources to redraw. Overlays are another frame buffer layer that can be displayed preferentially relative to the normal plane frame buffer. Overlays are common for OpenGL-capable hardware. Overlays can be supported as part of the X Window System, independent of OpenGL, as described in Section 6.3.

Pop-up and pull-down menus using the overlays can avoid damaging OpenGL windows that are expensive to redraw. Overlays can also provide a way to perform rubber-banding and annotation of OpenGL windows. Figure 6.18 shows how overlay planes can be used for annotation.

6.5.5.4 *Multiple Colormaps*

Because OpenGL systems often support multiple pixel formats and different color models, display hardware suitable for OpenGL often includes support for multiple hardware colormaps. This means that multiple windows using differently loaded colormaps can operate simultaneously without *colormap flashing*. Otherwise, the colormaps for some windows will not be installed, forcing those windows to be displayed with invalid colors. This problem is discussed in Section 2.3. Be careful though, because even with multiple hardware colormaps, you can still exceed the number of physical colormaps and get colormap flashing.

Figure 6.18 Overlay planes used to annotate a complex underlying image.

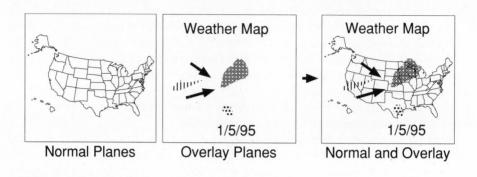

6.5.5.5   Per-Window Stereo

A 3D graphics system such as OpenGL is complemented by display hardware that supports stereo output. Usually, this is done using a monitor with twice the normal refresh rate and special goggles that rapidly switch LCD shutters between the two eyes in synchronization with the video frame rate. The display continuously scans out the left-eye view, then the right-eye view, synchronized with the LCD goggle shutters.

OpenGL supports a quad buffering scheme (stereo is almost always double buffered; stereo also adds left and right buffers in addition to front and back). Rendering to the various buffers is controlled with `glDrawBuffer`. Quad buffered stereo requires extra frame buffer memory and fast monitor refresh rates, so OpenGL stereo support is not currently common. To get the stereo effect, OpenGL applications rendering to a stereo window must render both the right and left views, each from a slightly different eye-point.

6.5.6   Rasterization

Rasterization is the process of converting primitives such as lines and triangles (already converted into window coordinates by the transformation stage) into updates to pixel values in the window's drawable frame buffer region. OpenGL's rasterization stage can be divided into four substages: primitive decomposition, texturing, fog, and per-fragment operations.

6.5.6.1   Primitive Decomposition

Primitive decomposition handles geometric primitives such as points, lines, and polygons, as well as image primitives such as pixel rectangles and bitmaps, by transforming the primitives into window coordinates and determining which pixel locations are occupied by each primitive. For each occupied pixel location, a fragment is generated. A fragment is a pixel location accompanied by assigned color, depth, and texture coordinates as required. The per-fragment operations that follow primitive decomposition use the fragment's associated data to update the pixel in the frame buffer that corresponds to the fragment.

OpenGL's rasterization state affects primitive decomposition. Factors affecting decomposition include antialiasing, line width, stippling, culling, and the pixel path modes.

A primitive such as a polygon is typically decomposed into a set of *spans*. A span is a one-pixel-high horizontal line defined by a pixel location and a width. Spans can easily be converted into fragments by iterating across the span. Color, depth, and texture coordinates may be interpolated between the two span endpoints.

A polygon span converter can be implemented in hardware. The results from the span converter can then be fed to a hardware span engine that iterates across the generated spans, doing depth and color interpolations as necessary. To lower the hardware cost of a *GTX-RD* system, the polygon span conversion may be done on the host so that the primitive decomposition hardware is limited to a span engine. Figure 6.19 demonstrates how a polygon span converter and a span iteration engine

Figure 6.19 Example of decomposing a smooth-shaded polygon to spans, then iterating across one of the generated spans, interpolating depth and color between the endpoints.

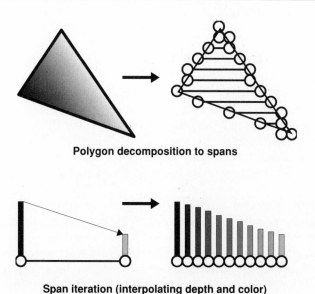

Polygon decomposition to spans

Span iteration (interpolating depth and color)

combine to render a triangle into fragments. Other primitives, such as points or lines, can also be converted to spans, or supported by special point and line drawing engines. Similarly, what are known as *bit-blit* engines can efficiently render image rectangles and bitmaps. To further minimize the host overhead, graphics hardware may support direct memory access (DMA) of primitives (particularly effective for image primitives). DMA lets the graphics hardware obtain data directly from host memory with minimal host overhead, thereby increasing the transfer speed to the graphics hardware. OpenGL 1.1's vertex array facility is designed to take advantage of DMA.

6.5.6.2 Texturing and Fog

Between scan conversion and processing of fragment operations, the fragment color can be modified by texturing and fog. Texturing maps a portion of a specified image (called a *texture*) onto each primitive for which texturing is enabled. Texturing is analogous to applying wallpaper over a surface. Based on the fragment's *texture coordinates*, the associated texture sample (or *texel* value) within the texture is combined with the fragment's color based on the texture function. Textures can be either 1D or 2D, and a host of texturing modes are available in OpenGL.

Then, fog (if enabled) blends the fragment's post-texturing color with the current fog color based on the eye-coordinate distance and fog mode. The post-fog fragment is then used to update the fragment's associated frame buffer pixel.

Texture mapping hardware tends to be expensive, because texturing is a per-pixel operation and requires fast memory to store and retrieve the texture image. Texture mapping hardware is only now becoming available on midrange to low-end workstations.

6.5.6.3 Per-Fragment Operations

The frame buffer in OpenGL contains more than color values. Logically, there are also *ancillary* (or helper) buffers that hold per-pixel information in the depth, stencil, accumulation, alpha, and auxiliary buffers. And, as discussed in the section on the display stage, there may be multiple color buffers for double buffering (front, back) and stereo (left, right). As long as the minimum GLX requirements for OpenGL's frame buffer functionality are met, an implementation may support a wide variety of frame buffer configurations with varying buffers and numbers of bit planes.

These ancillary buffers may be provided by the graphics hardware, usually in dedicated graphics memory. The alternative is for the host to allocate these buffers from host memory.

Some per-fragment operations (such as the depth test) affect ancillary buffers while some such as the scissor test, do not use ancillary buffers. The per-fragment operations form a pipeline, as shown in Figure 6.20. The operations that are most expensive are those that require an ancillary buffer read-modify-write, such as the depth buffer and stencil tests.

Figure 6.20 OpenGL per-fragment operations.

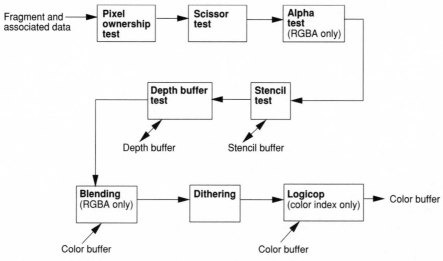

Performing per-fragment operations is particularly parallelizable, since each fragment's pixel update operations can be performed independently of other updates to different pixels. An effective technique for accelerating pixel updates is replication of numerous pixel processors, each processor updating a subset of the screen's pixels. Figure 6.21 shows an example of how 20 pixel processors might be used to parallelize fragment processing.

There are cost/performance limits to replicating pixel processors. Suppose every pixel on the screen had its *own* pixel processor. Because most pixels are not being updated at any given moment in time and many polygons tend to be small (less than 40 pixels or so), most of the screen's pixel processors would be underutilized, so the approach would likely not be cost-effective.

6.5.7 Transforming Geometry

Vertices for OpenGL polygons, lines, and other rendering primitives are specified in object coordinates. These coordinates and other parameters such as surface normals and texture coordinates are typically manipulated internally to OpenGL as floating-point values. OpenGL does permit a wide variety of input formats, so conversion to the OpenGL implementation's internal format may be necessary. After conversion, the purpose of the transformation stage is to take the vertices, normals, texture coordinates, and other parameters and convert these to primitives in window coordinates.

Table 6.5 Floating-point operations required to transform a single vertex using single-source lighting.

Operation	Floating-Point Operations
Vertex transformation	28
Normal transformation	15
Single-source lighting	28
Clip testing	6
Projection	11
Map to window space	9
Total	97

Like rasterization, transformation can be broken into several substages:

- **Modeling transformation.** Object coordinates are converted to world coordinates using OpenGL's current modelview matrix. Surface normals are also transformed and possibly normalized. This substage maintains the modelview matrix stack.

- **Lighting calculations.** If lighting is enabled, OpenGL performs per-vertex lighting calculations based on various lighting parameters.

Figure 6.21 Example of a triangle being rasterized into a frame buffer using a 20-way image processor configuration.

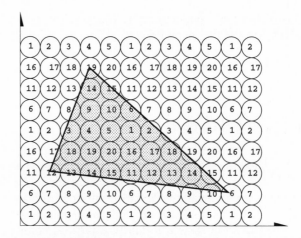

- **Clip testing**. Primitives are clipped to the current clip volume. In addition, OpenGL allows specifying user-defined clip planes.

- **Perspective division**. To maintain correct 3D perspective, OpenGL manipulates homogenous coordinates (meaning that a 3D coordinate is represented as four floating-point values: x, y, z, and w). This requires x, y, and z each to be divided by w to homogenize the result into a standard (x, y, z) form.

- **Viewport transformation**. Finally, the vertex coordinates must be converted to window space based on the viewport.

These substages are computationally intensive and are repeated for every vertex that is transformed. The number of floating-point operations required to transform a single 3D vertex lit by a single simple light source is roughly 100. See Table 6.5 for a breakdown. This means rendering a scene consisting of 10,000 triangles 30 times per second would require approximately 90 million floating-point operations per second ($30 \times 3 \times 10,000 \times 97$) just to transform the geometry. Offloading geometry transformation from the host processor and into specialized graphics hardware makes good sense for applications that demand very high polygon-rendering rates.

6.5.7.1 Pipelining and Parallelism

Geometry transformation can be done using specialized hardware. Obtaining the required rates of floating-point computation to achieve a given level of transformation performance at a reasonable cost is challenging. Two techniques are typically used to increase the throughput of transformation hardware:

- **Pipelining** is a technique used when the stages in a task (such as geometry transformation) are arranged as if in an assembly line. Specialized hardware performs the operations for each stage and passes the results on to the subsequent stage. Theoretically, pipelining allows a process to speed up in proportion to the number of pipeline stages added.

- **Parallelism** is a technique used when the hardware to do a task can be replicated several times (parallel processors) and the task is divisible into largely independent units. Each unit of work is then doled out to an available hardware unit. Instead of an assembly line, think of parallelism as in the case of bank tellers servicing the queue of customers waiting for service. Theoretically, four tellers can service bank customers four times faster.

Pipelining is appropriate when a task can be broken down into stages that can be processed in linear order. Parallelism works best when the unit of work (transforming a vertex, for example) is relatively self-contained and all the units of work take similar amounts of effort. Graphics operations tend to fit both of these descriptions. Figure 6.22 portrays both a pipelined and a parallel architecture.

Figure 6.22 (a) portrays a pipelined architecture with four stages; (b) portrays a parallel architecture with four tasks.

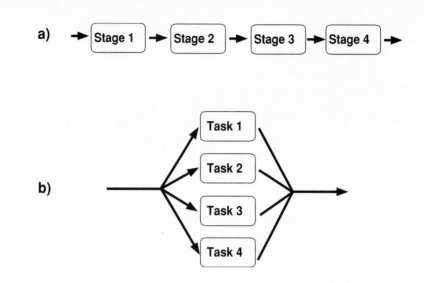

While pipelining and parallelism are discussed here in the context of geometry transformation (a particularly applicable stage in the general graphics pipeline), these two techniques can be used throughout the graphics pipeline. The example of per-fragment operations being performed by multiple image processors shown in Figure 6.20 is an example of parallelism. In addition, the general graphics pipeline itself is amenable to pipelining (hence the name).

While pipelining is straightforward, it is not always as flexible as parallelism. The stages in a hardware pipeline tend to be hardwired, meaning that it is difficult to add new stages and, if the work required for any single stage grows out of proportion to that for the other stages, that stage can undermine the efficiency of the pipeline. For example, OpenGL supports up to eight light sources. If a single pipeline stage performs all lighting calculations, that stage might back up the pipeline. The problem could be solved by dividing the lighting stage into eight separate hardware stages. While this is feasible, most of the time eight lights are not enabled, so the extra lighting stages would go largely unused.

Parallelism may be more flexible than pipelining, since each unit of work is executed largely independently of work executing on other parallel processors. So in the case of eight lights, each processor simply does more lighting calculations than the number required for a single light. Unlike a hardware pipeline, parallel processors can absorb the extra work without leaving other hardware underutilized.

Appreciate that pipelining and parallelism are not conflicting techniques, but can be complementary. For example, inside each parallel geometry processor, you are likely to find a floating-point pipeline executing.

Another trade-off when you are designing geometry transformation hardware is the decision as to whether you will *hardwire* the hardware to do its specific task, or design the hardware in a more general way so that it executes its tasks based on specialized software, normally called *microcode*. Generally, hardwired hardware can run faster, but is very inflexible and, when it is very complicated, can be harder to design. Hardwired hardware is more suitable for tasks that are well defined and very unlikely to change. Rasterization and display hardware is often hardwired. Usually hardware for geometry transformation is microcoded.

6.5.7.2 Types of Parallelism

There are two common ways to implement microcoded parallel processors: *lockstep* or *independent* processors. Independent processors let each parallel processor execute a different sequence of instructions. In the bank teller example, this might amount to one teller's processing a deposit and another teller's processing a withdrawal. In graphics (which is unlike a bank in this respect), it is often true that the preceding task is very similar to the current and immediately following tasks. For example, a triangle to be rendered is likely to be followed by several more triangles to be rendered the same way, but with different coordinates. Parallel processors can take advantage of the *homogeneous* nature of graphics calculations by running in lockstep. Each graphics processor working on one of a set of triangles of exactly same type can execute the identical transformation, lighting, and clip testing microcode, but execute the code on the coordinates of its triangle.

The advantage of lockstep execution is that a single microcode memory store is necessary and the complexity of programming lockstep processors can be lower than that of programming independent processors. Having a single microcode memory store is generally cheaper than having an independent microcode store per processor. Lock-step execution works well when the workload is homogeneous. If eight lockstep processors can all be working on different triangles of the same type, theoretically the triangles can be transformed eight times faster than with a single processor. But, if there is an OpenGL mode change so that each triangle is not of the same type, the advantage of lockstep parallelism breaks down.

Lockstep processors are called *SIMD* processors, meaning they have a *Single Instruction* stream for *Multiple Data* streams. Likewise, independent processors are referred to as *MIMD* processors, meaning they have *Multiple Instruction* streams for *Multiple Data* streams. The terms SIMD and MIMD are often used to describe the architectures of geometry transformation hardware. If other performance factors are equal (though they never are!), a SIMD architecture is likely to be less expensive than a MIMD architecture, though the MIMD architecture is potentially better with less homogeneous workloads.

In a pipelined or parallel system, an N-stage pipeline or N-way parallelism does not necessarily imply a speedup of N times. When the state within a hardware pipeline changes, it is likely to require the introduction of *stalls* into the pipeline. These stalls undermine performance, since all the stages are not kept busy with work. Likewise, for a parallel system, there may not be enough work to keep all N processors busy or there may be communication overhead that is necessary to coordinate the parallel processors.

6.5.8 Hardware for Window System Requirements

So far, this discussion of graphics hardware has focused on the problems of rendering and displaying graphics without concern for multiple programs trying to render graphics concurrently. Graphics workstations generally allow multiple programs to run at the same time and share access to the graphics acceleration hardware. This sharing is generally managed by the window system—in the case of the X Window System, the X server.

6.5.8.1 Graphics Context Switching

The approach that the X Window System takes to sharing the graphics hardware is to allow only a single program, namely the X server, to manipulate the graphics hardware directly. X clients send rendering requests to the X server to be dispatched. Effectively, the X server process acts as a rendering proxy for all X clients. For accelerated OpenGL graphics hardware, this approach has two problems.

First, OpenGL has a large amount of rendering state that is typically maintained in hardware by *GTX-RD* systems and even more state is maintained by *GT-XRD* systems. For typical 2D X operations, each rendering operation downloads its necessary hardware state, since this setup overhead is small. For OpenGL, the state is potentially quite large when all the lighting parameters, matrices, modes, and texture memory are considered. For *GTX-RD* systems, and particularly for *GT-XRD* systems, for OpenGL to be feasible within a window system, there must be a way to context-switch the graphics hardware efficiently.

Second, when accelerated graphics hardware is sufficiently fast, the overhead of generating, sending, and dispatching X protocol requests as compared to the hardware's rendering speed is high. A fast graphics subsystem cannot meet its performance potential if it cannot obtain OpenGL commands fast enough. To remedy this situation, OpenGL's GLX extension that integrates X with OpenGL provides OpenGL implementations with the option of supporting *direct rendering* so that local OpenGL programs can render directly to the graphics hardware.

When the X server does all rendering to the hardware, the X server context switches the hardware as necessary. But when direct rendering is supported, graphics context switching has to be managed among unrelated processes in separate address spaces. If the graphics hardware supports context switching asynchronous to rendering, the kernel and window system can "conspire" to virtualize graphics for OpenGL programs without those programs' knowing [25].

Another approach to speeding context switching is to support multiple contexts within the graphics hardware. This can be expensive, because OpenGL contexts can be large and supporting multiple contexts in hardware requires hardware resources. Devoting hardware resources can be hard to justify, since multiple contexts do not speed up the performance case of a single renderer. Even with multiple hardware contexts, the system may still run out of hardware contexts, so context-switching OpenGL state to and from host memory must still be supported.

6.5.8.2 Fast and Arbitrary Window Clipping

In Figure 6.20, showing the per-fragment pipeline, the pixel ownership test is where fragments are thrown away if they fall outside the window's drawable region. The drawable region of a window is often called the window's *clip*.

When the X server performs 2D X rendering, the X server can perform window clipping in software based on its special knowledge of every window's clip. But in *GTX-RD* and *GT-XRD* architectures, typically the hardware must enforce window clipping because the pixel ownership test occurs late in the graphics pipeline. Also, when using direct rendering, an OpenGL program does not generally have knowledge of its current window clip. In such cases, window clipping is typically supported in the hardware, with the hardware clipping information updated by the X server as the window layout changes.

There are two common approaches to supporting window clipping in hardware:

- **Clip rectangles** define the window's clip as a limited number of rectangles (one to four available clip rectangles is typical). Windows with simple clips, representable with the available number of available clip rectangles, can be clipped this way.

- **Clip ID planes** encode per-pixel state about the window to which a given frame buffer pixel belongs. The hardware rendering state maintains a current clip ID value that can be compared with the clip value in the clip ID planes for every generated OpenGL fragment. When clip ID clipping is enabled, the fragment is rendered only if the current clip ID matches the pixel's clip value. Typically, 2 to 4 bits of clip ID planes are supported, providing 3 to 15 clip ID values.[10]

---

10. Four clip ID planes would provide sixteen possible clip values, but one clip value is reserved for the screen region not assigned to any particular clip-ID-assigned window, leaving only fifteen clip values assignable.

Clip ID planes work for arbitrary clips,[11] while clip rectangles work only for simple clips. Clip ID planes are generally slower than clip rectangles, since every fragment clipped using clip ID planes must be tested against the pixel's clip ID, which must be retrieved from frame buffer memory. Because the case of an unobscured window is the most important performance case *and* arbitrary clips must be supported, a hybrid approach combining both clip rectangles and clip ID planes is common. Figure 6.23 shows clip rectangles and clip ID planes used simultaneously.

The clip ID and clip rectangle hardware state must be maintained and updated as necessary by the X server when window clips change. Note that there are a limited number of clip ID values, so the X server must be ready to virtualize clip ID use if too many windows have complex clips that require clip IDs.

Clip rectangles are also useful for implementing the OpenGL scissor test.

Figure 6.23 Clip rectangles define the clips for the two windows with simple drawable regions. One clip rectangle is needed for the rectangular window; two clip rectangles are needed for the L-shaped window. Three clip IDs are assigned to the three windows with irregular clips. Notice that clip ID 0 is used as a "slop" clip ID for the screen region not assigned to the clip ID windows (which includes the windows clipped using clip rectangles).

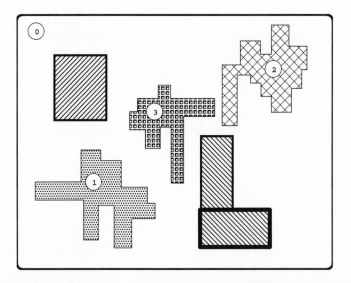

11. With the X Window System's Shape extension, arbitrarily shaped windows are easy to create, but even in a window system that only supports rectangular windows, complex overlappings can still define arbitrary clips so the case of arbitrary clips must be addressed.

6.5.8.3   Hardware Cursors

Window systems use cursors to track mouse motion. A *hardware cursor* means that the hardware provides special support for merging the current cursor image at the current cursor location into the displayed frame buffer image. If a hardware cursor is not supported, the X server must draw the cursor image into the frame buffer. When rendering is done or under a software-rendered cursor, the cursor must be undrawn and redrawn between rendering commands. Not only does this result in a flickering cursor, but it means that programs rendering to the hardware must know the cursor location to draw and undraw the cursor. This greatly complicates 3D rendering, so hardware cursors are extremely common for accelerated OpenGL graphics hardware.

6.5.9   Graphics Subsystem Bottlenecks

A *bottleneck* occurs when one task in a system limits the overall system performance to the extent that other tasks in the system cannot reach their performance potential. There is inevitably some task or tasks that limit system performance, but the goal is to balance the limitations to avoid over engineering some tasks while other tasks become bottlenecks.

The motivation for adding hardware to accelerate OpenGL is to achieve better overall graphics performance. However, if hardware is added in an unbalanced fashion, expensive hardware resources will go underutilized because of bottlenecks in the system and overall performance will suffer.

6.5.9.1   Host versus Transform versus Fill Limits

Looking at the general *GTXRD* graphics pipeline, there are three broad types of graphics performance bottlenecks:

> **Fill limits** occur in the rasterization stage. Fill-limited programs are limited by the rate at which pixels in the frame buffer can be updated. Visual simulation applications such as flight simulators, which draw large, textured polygons, are often fill-limited. The hardware fill-limit is often expressed in millions of pixels per second, and the limit depends on what rasterization modes (such as depth buffering) are enabled.
>
> **Transform limits** occur in the transformation stage. Transform-limited programs are limited by the rate at which vertices can be lighted, transformed, and clipped. A molecule visualization program that renders thousands of atoms as finely tessellated spheres is likely to be transform, limited. The hardware transform limit is often expressed in thousands of polygons per second, and the limit depends on what transformation modes (such as the number of lights) are enabled.
>
> **Host limits** occur in the generation and traversal stages. Host limits reflect the maximum rate at which the host computer can generate graphics commands so they can be processed by the graphics subsystem. Some tasks, such as the

finite element analysis of a car crash, cannot be done in real time and are therefore clearly host-limited, but even programs designed to be interactive may starve a fast graphics pipe if the program has too much overhead.

Notice that what limits a program's performance depends in large part on the application. Some applications may demand a machine with excellent fill performance; other applications may demand a machine with excellent transform performance. A system architect must make compromises based on the machine's intended purpose.

A good technique for determining whether a program is fill-limited is to resize the window down to a very small size. If the program speeds up, the program is very likely fill-limited. Likewise, if resizing the window to the full screen size has no effect on the program's graphics performance, the program is likely to be host- or transform-limited. More practical advice for dealing with graphics bottlenecks can be found in the following sections, particularly Section 6.6.1.

Other limits that do not cleanly fit into the above categories are also possible. If programs change OpenGL state frequently enough, these mode changes become a bottleneck. Downloading texture maps into the hardware is another potential bottleneck.

Understanding the bottlenecks for a given application on a given system is important for tuning the application. A program that is fill-limited may be able to make use of better lighting and finer tessellation without affecting application performance. Likewise, a transform-limited program may achieve better performance by limiting the number of polygons transformed by using coarser tessellations.

6.5.9.2 OpenGL Command Bandwidth

Another performance bottleneck is the rate at which commands are transferred from the host to the OpenGL implementation. The easiest way to improve OpenGL command bandwidth is to use direct rendering if the application is running on the local graphics workstations.

One way to minimize the OpenGL command bandwidth is to use OpenGL display lists. When you are rendering indirectly, display lists are downloaded into the X server so that when they are executed, only the command to execute the display list must be transferred to the X server. This can greatly reduce the network overhead of indirect rendering. Display lists may also be downloaded into the graphics hardware so they can be executed with no host overhead to drive the display list.

It is possible for a fast computer and a fast graphics subsystem to be starved by the interface between them. Make sure that the host's peripheral bus that is used to connect the graphics subsystem has sufficient bandwidth to drive the graphics at your required performance.

6.6 MAXIMIZING OPENGL PERFORMANCE

The essence of computer graphics is letting computer users visualize their data by creating computer-generated scenes that mimic the sense of reality we find in the world around us. Because the real world is infinitely more complex than what can be interactively computed on a graphics workstation, computer graphics is always an approximation. No matter how much effort is put into computing a computer-generated scene, there is always room for a bit more realism. Along with *realistic* rendering, users want *interactive* rendering. Extra time spent generating a more realistic rendering is lost interactivity, so there is always a trade-off.

Fortunately, the continuing advance of computer graphics hardware makes for faster and faster systems, improving both the realism and the interactivity of graphics applications.

But fast hardware helps only if it is properly utilized. To improve the realism and interactivity of your applications, you should learn how to tune your OpenGL rendering code to match the performance characteristics of the OpenGL implementations you use. This section provides practical advice on tuning your applications to maximize OpenGL rendering performance.

6.6.1   Pipeline-based Tuning

Software performance tuning is not unique to computer graphics applications. All computer programs can benefit from performance analysis and tuning. The traditional performance tuning methodology, known as *hot-spot* tuning, is based on the observation that computer programs tend to spend most of their time in a small fraction of the program's instructions. Often, this is stated as follows: "Ninety percent of the time is spent running 10% of the code." The exact percentage may vary, but the idea is still the same. These areas of programs where most of the time is spent are called *hot-spots*. If you concentrate your tuning efforts on these areas of a program that is being tuned, the improvements you make will have a substantial effect on the program's overall performance.

6.6.1.1   The Problem of Graphics Bottlenecks

While graphics applications will exhibit this same sort of *execution locality* resulting in hot spots, there is also another performance phenomenon at work in graphics applications that use specialized, pipelined 3D graphics hardware such as the sort described in the preceding section. As discussed in Section 6.5.9, pipelines are prone to *bottlenecks*, which limit overall rendering throughput because some stage of the pipeline is slower than the other pipeline stages.

A bottleneck is in many ways more severe than a hot spot. If you tune code outside the program's hot spots, you may get some marginal performance increase, but when a bottleneck exists, no amount of tuning in other pipeline stages will help if the tuning does not unjam the bottleneck. Still worse, since pipeline stages tend to be implemented with dedicated, often expensive hardware, a bottlenecked program leaves expensive resources under utilized, and because the bottleneck itself may exist in a piece of hardware, it is not so easy to "reimplement" the bottlenecked operation. Finally, even if you can reduce a bottleneck, there is typically some other limit that will create a new bottleneck. In a program with a hot spot, if you can halve the time spent in a 90% hot spot, you can increase your program's execution speed by 80%. Rarely will you find a bottleneck so severe that unjamming the bottleneck creates that kind of improvement, because there is probably another bottleneck that you will expose.

It is worth pointing out that *all* types of computer systems are prone to bottlenecks. A very common bottleneck is the bandwidth and latency getting to main memory, sometimes called the *von Neumann bottleneck* after the computer scientist who described today's standard processor- and memory-based computer architecture. Typically, fast memory caches are used to minimize this bottleneck. Caches reduce the memory access bottleneck because the hot spots discussed above tend to create memory locality that caches exploit. Pipelined RISC processors also encounter bottlenecks in their fine-grain execution of instructions. For most programmers, the scheduling of RISC instructions to avoid bottlenecks is a problem best left to compilers, since the scheduling of RISC instructions for optimal pipelined performance is better suited for computers, not for people.

With accelerated graphics hardware, the problem of bottlenecks is more prominent because the graphics pipeline (see Section 6.5.1) has more stages and different application use patterns are certain to place more stress on different stages. For example, when a program clears the frame buffer (meaning that every pixel in the entire frame buffer memory must be written all at once), this operation can easily create a rasterization bottleneck. It takes far less time to issue a `glClear` command than to perform the actual clear operation.

6.6.1.2   Dealing with Bottlenecks

An ideal pipeline would balance the work done in each stage to maximize the utilization of the pipeline stages. In general, designers of computer graphics hardware try to design a balanced architecture, but the dynamic nature of graphics and the need to construct general-purpose machines mean that bottlenecks will be encountered. Section 6.5.9 has already discussed the major types of graphics hardware bottlenecks: fill limits, transform limits, host limits, and OpenGL command bandwidth limits.

There are two approaches to dealing with bottlenecks. One is to try to reduce the bottleneck by reimplementing the work so that it stresses the bottlenecked pipeline stage less. The other is to make more use of the under utilized nonbottlenecked stages.

Here is a case in which work can be reimplemented to reduce stress on a bottleneck: Consider a system where the bus connecting the processor to the graphics subsystem is slow relative to the speed of the graphics subsystem and the processor. The bus is the bottleneck. If a graphics application is rendering detailed curved surfaces, trying to tessellate the surfaces into thousands of minute triangles will easily saturate the bus, leaving the graphics subsystem underutilized. But using OpenGL's evaluator mechanism, described in Section 5.5.2, *and assuming* evaluators are implemented within the graphics subsystem, the surfaces can be respecified as Bézier surface patches that greatly reduce the bus bandwidth necessary to specify the surfaces. Also, if the geometry is static, display lists implemented within the graphics subsystem can be another means to reduce host-to-graphics-subsystem bus bandwidth.

Here is an example of finding work for underutilized nonbottlenecked stages: Consider a CAD program rendering detailed mechanical parts on a high-end graphics subsystem supporting multisampling (see page 298). Because the program renders hundreds of finely detailed parts, the program is transform-limited. Using multisampling for high-quality antialiasing requires the rasterization subsystem to do significantly more work, but if the overall throughput is limited by geometry transformation, the CAD application may be able to enable multisampling with no loss of performance, yet render a much higher-quality image.

Keep in mind that if you use OpenGL implementations with little or no pipelined hardware acceleration (such as *GTXR-D* or *GTX-RD* architectures), graphics subsystem bottlenecks are less likely, since more of OpenGL is implemented on the host processor. This situation is better suited to traditional hot-spot tuning methods. In this case, you will likely find that much of the time rendering is spent *within* the OpenGL library. Since you do not control the implementation of the library, you will need to tune by controlling the choice of calls you make into the library. Traditional software profiling tools are useful in this case, to determine where your processor is spending its time.

One of the problems with pipelined graphics architectures is that tools such as traditional host-based software profilers are not useful for detecting bottlenecks within graphics subsystem hardware. That is why it is important to understand the hardware architecture of the graphics subsystems you are working with. Most vendors of high-end graphics subsystems will offer valuable tuning advice to help you maximize the hardware's performance.

While some advice may be very system-specific, there is plenty of good OpenGL tuning advice to be offered that is appropriate to a wide range of hardware architectures. The rest of this section discusses practical OpenGL performance tuning without delving into any particular hardware architecture.

6.6.2 Reducing OpenGL Command Overhead

The first potential bottleneck in OpenGL is the cost of transferring data to OpenGL. This is the bottleneck most apparent to the OpenGL programmer, since the data is passed explicitly by the OpenGL calls written by the programmer. Per-vertex data, image, and texture data all require moving large amounts of data quickly from the host processor to the graphics subsystem.

There are five common approaches for optimizing vertex transfers: display lists, OpenGL 1.1's vertex arrays, evaluators, smaller vertex data formats, and using connected primitives.

6.6.2.1 Display Lists

The most general-purpose way to reduce the overhead of OpenGL command transfer involves using display lists, but it works well only when static sets of commands need to be frequently reissued. It also requires that the OpenGL implementation make a copy of the data put into display lists. If you construct numerous or large display lists, a sizable amount of memory can be taken up storing the display lists. Be judicious about what it makes sense to compile as a display list.

When applications use indirect rendering, display lists have a *big* advantage over immediate mode rendering, because the display lists reside within the X server and the overhead to copy OpenGL commands from the application to the X server is substantial, particularly if the application and the X server are running on different machines.

Display lists are not a cure-all even when command sequences are largely static. In the worst case, display lists *can* be worse than immediate mode rendering. Take, for example, a display list containing a sphere tessellated as *two million* polygon vertices. If each vertex specifies a floating-point position and a normal vector (12 bytes for the position and 12 bytes for the normal), the entire display list will take up over 48 megabytes of memory. An OpenGL implementation executing this display list will have to traverse all this memory. Because modern computers rely on good memory locality for good performance, traversing 48 megabytes of memory may severely affect the overall system performance. It is very likely that a fast algorithm that computes each vertex on the fly will be more efficient than the monster display list. Consider the effects of *data expansion* when creating display lists.

Be aware that there is some extra calling overhead associated with each display list you create. Minimize the use of display lists containing fewer than 10 or so primitives, though the precise break-even point depends on your implementation and is probably lower when programs use indirect rendering.

6.6.2.2 Vertex Arrays

OpenGL 1.1's vertex array facility eliminates most of the procedure call overhead associated with OpenGL's basic approach of providing a procedure call per item of vertex data. The information about using vertex arrays starts on page 283. Like display lists, vertex arrays have setup costs, so vertex arrays may not be faster when you are using small vertex array transfers.

In the future, higher-level 3D programming interfaces will probably use vertex arrays as their primary mechanism for transferring vertex data to OpenGL.

6.6.2.3 Evaluators

When you render curves and surfaces that can be described by rational polynomials, evaluators, as described in Section 5.5.2, offer a way to offload the polynomial evaluation to the graphics subsystem. This can *greatly* reduce the overhead for describing curves and surfaces and give you control over how finely the curves and surfaces are tessellated.

While evaluators provide the opportunity for evaluator calculations to be off-loaded to the graphics subsystem, not all OpenGL implementations will implement evaluators this way. Many OpenGL implementations will perform the evaluator calculations on the host. Even when hardware will offload evaluator calculations, higher-order polynomial evaluators may not be offloaded.

6.6.2.4   Send Less Per-Vertex Data

Do not send per-vertex data that is unnecessary. If you are not using lighting, do not send normals. If you are not using texturing, do not send texture coordinates. Avoid frequent material changes. Try enabling `GL_COLOR_MATERIAL` if you need frequently changing materials. If you are using lighting but not `GL_COLOR_MATERIAL`, do not set current colors. Avoid sending extra components, such as alpha for colors or the z and w coordinates for 2D texture and vertex coordinates, when you are sending default values for these extra components or coordinates.

Most OpenGL applications use floating-point values to specify per-vertex data, but OpenGL permits vertex data to be passed in several formats. For normal vectors, consider using `glNormal3b` to represent each normal with 3 bytes, instead of 12 bytes, if floating-point values are used. In many cases, the lower precision of byte-specified normals has an imperceptible affect on resulting lighting calculations.

Even if you use smaller vertex formats, most OpenGL implementations will promote your data to floating-point for the calculations being performed. The advantage of smaller vertex formats is largely to save memory when storing vertex data, creating display lists, and transferring the data across the network.

6.6.2.5   Use Connected Primitives

You can reduce the number of vertices you send if you can structure your geometric data as connected primitives (see Figure 1.2). The connected primitives are line strips, triangle strips, triangle fans, and quad strips. Because vertices are reused in connected primitives, fewer vertices are transferred to draw more primitives.

While it depends on the implementation, try to put about eight or more vertices into each connected primitive. You may have to reformat your data to use connected primitives with common vertices, but the performance benefit is generally worth it. If you do need to generate unconnected primitives (triangles, quads, or lines), try to send multiple primitives per `glBegin` and `glEnd`.

Try to generate convex and planar polygons with only three or four vertices. More complex polygons should be respecified as connected primitives. Any concave or self-intersecting polygons will need to be tessellated with the GLU tessellator (see Section 2.1.2).

6.6.3   Minimize OpenGL Mode Changes

Changing rendering modes with routines such as `glEnable` and `glDisable` can reduce rendering performance, because the OpenGL implementation may need to resynchronize internal state based on the mode change. It is best to avoid unnecessary mode changes. It can even be advantageous to sort the data for your scene based on the OpenGL modes they require to minimize mode changes.

The cost of reconfiguring OpenGL internal state is typically significant relative to the speed at which vertex data can be issued. Often the effect of a mode change is to introduce a stall into the graphics pipeline while the mode change takes place. This stall hurts performance.

The expense of a particular mode change depends on the mode itself. Certain mode changes such as texture changes tend to be significantly more expensive than others. A rough ordering of geometry mode grouping, listed from most expensive to change to least expensive to change, is: texturing, evaluators, projection matrices, lighting, clipping, fog, modelview matrices, per-fragment modes.

Most OpenGL implementations operate by selecting different rendering paths (see Section 6.5.3) based on the currently configured OpenGL state. When a mode is implemented by software or microcode, changing the mode may not immediately cause the new rendering path to be selected. Instead, internal rendering state is invalidated. When the invalidated rendering path is next used, the OpenGL implementation first recalculates any internal state used by the rendering path based on OpenGL's currently configured state. Because of this validation process, it may be cheaper to change multiple related modes as a group.

Be careful when you are using the matrix and attribute stacks. If you are making a simple attribute change, it will likely be cheaper to make the change and restore the original state (assuming you know the current state and do not need to read it with a glGet*) instead of using glPushAttrib and glPopAttrib. Try to use glPushAttrib and glPopAttrib only when you are making multiple state changes or the code making the change does not know how to restore the state explicitly. The same applies to the matrix stacks. Typically, changes to the projection matrix are more expensive than modelview matrix changes because substantial internal lighting and clipping state may need updating when the projection matrix changes.

In general, avoid calling all OpenGL routines (typically the glGet* routines) that return OpenGL state. These routines often result in a complete stalling of the graphics hardware pipeline. When developing code, you should use glGetError to detect OpenGL errors, but retrieving errors is typically expensive and unnecessary for debugged programs.

6.6.4 Improving Transformation Performance

A significant amount of computation is done in the transformation stage of the graphics pipeline, making it a likely source of bottlenecks. Some of the preceding advice, such as using connected primitives and minimizing mode changes, will reduce transformation overhead.

6.6.4.1 Optimizing Lighting

The cost of OpenGL's lighting model varies significantly with the parameters specified. Assuming an RGBA color model, here is the most basic and highest-performance lighting configuration:

- A single enabled infinite light.
- glLightModeli(GL_LIGHT_MODEL_LOCAL_VIEWER, GL_FALSE), the default.
- glLightModeli(GL_LIGHT_MODEL_TWO_SIDE, GL_FALSE), the default.
- glDisable(GL_COLOR_MATERIAL), the default.
- glDisable(GL_NORMALIZE), the default.

Be careful about leaving GL_NORMALIZE disabled, because it places the burden of ensuring properly normalized vectors on your application. When it is disabled, if you scale objects using the modelview matrix, you risk disturbing your normal vectors and messing up the lighting calculations. With GL_NORMALIZE enabled, OpenGL will automatically normalize normal vectors sent (at some small performance cost).

When you enable more lighting parameters, keep these performance hints in mind:

- Many OpenGL implementations optimize the single-light case. Enabling a second light can noticeably hurt lighting performance; however, any additional lights after two incur a more gradual associated performance drop.
- Infinite lights have better performance than local lights, because their lighting effect is easier to compute. If the light source is far away from the objects being rendered, approximate it with an infinite light.
- Avoid changing material parameters. Try to use GL_COLOR_MATERIAL if you need changing materials. The GL_SHININESS material parameter is particularly expensive to change. Definitely avoid material changes with glMaterial* calls between a glBegin and a glEnd.
- Use the local viewer and two-sided lighting models with care, because they can significantly reduce lighting performance.

6.6.4.2 Reducing Polygon Counts

The best way to avoid a transformation bottleneck is to send less geometric data. There are three good approaches to doing this: use coarser tessellations of objects, replace complex geometry with simpler textured geometry, and cull polygons within the application.

If the models you are rendering permit you to control the level at which they are tessellated, you can quickly reduce the polygon count of scenes you are rendering by substituting a coarser tessellation. For example, glutSolidSphere(1.0, 15, 15) instead of glutSolidSphere(1.0, 20, 20) immediately reduces the polygon count of the sphere by almost 45%. Figure 6.24 shows the difference in quality. This is a trade-off of speed and rendering quality, and it is up to the programmer to balance the two. Consider adaptively adjusting the tessellation coarseness based on the desired rendering rate.

When tessellations are done automatically (for example, by the GLU NURBS and polygon tessellators), it is often worthwhile to inspect the resulting tessellations by calling glPolygonMode(GL_FRONT_AND_BACK, GL_LINE). You may find that the tessellation is far too fine or that minor adjustments to the input data can result in greatly simplified tessellations.

When fast texture mapping is available, textured polygons can be used to replace complex geometry. Rendering a brick wall will be made considerably faster by rendering the entire wall as a single polygon textured with a brick pattern instead of drawing the wall brick by brick. A complex, irregularly shaped object can be defined as a texture with the texture's alpha component used to mask the shape of the object. Texels not belonging to the object can be assigned alpha values of 0. Then, with GL_ALPHA_TEST enabled, the object can be rendered with a single polygon. This technique is sometimes called *billboarding*. It is up to the application to ensure that the billboard texture properly faces the viewer. Objects such as trees, which are very difficult to render realistically only with geometry, are efficiently rendered with this technique.

If an application sends data to OpenGL outside OpenGL's viewing volume, the polygons are eliminated during OpenGL's clipping stage. A great deal of computation can be saved if the application avoids sending geometry to OpenGL that the application can predetermine is outside the viewing volume. Using *application-level culling* is very important for visual simulation and virtual reality applications, because a large portion of the virtual surroundings is not viewed at any given point in time.

Figure 6.24 Two spheres rendered at different tessellations. The left sphere uses 400 polygons; the right sphere uses 225 polygons.

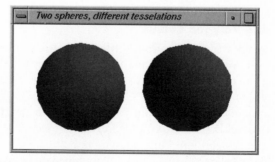

Various techniques exist for application-level culling, depending on the way the application organizes its data. This type of culling is an important optimization and one that is best left to the application. On multiprocessor workstations, the task of application-level culling is sometimes assigned to a dedicated processor, with the resulting nonculled geometry rendered by a processor dedicated to OpenGL rendering.

6.6.5   Improving Rasterization Performance

Once polygons have been transformed, they must be rasterized; the resulting fragments are used to update the frame buffer. Because a single large polygon can result in many thousands of fragments, the rasterization subsystem can easily become a performance bottleneck. While the rate at which polygons are transformed is often touted as the measure of a graphics subsystem's raw performance, the raster subsystem's ability to update pixels in the frame buffer is just as important.

There is an easy way to determine whether your program is fill-limited. Resize your rendering window as small as possible. If this improves your application's rendering performance, you know that your application is fill-limited.

6.6.5.1   The Relative Expensive of Per-Fragment Operations

Because per-fragment operations are done per-pixel, the expense of any enabled per-fragment operation is multiplied by the number of pixels it must be applied to. Below is a ranking of per-fragment operations, with the OpenGL commands used to enable each operation, beginning with the least expensive operation and proceeding through the most expensive:

1. Flat shading: glShadeModel(GL_FLAT).
2. Gouraud shading: glShadeModel(GL_SMOOTH).
3. Depth testing: glEnable(GL_DEPTH_TEST).
   Stencil testing: glEnable(GL_STENCIL_TEST).
   Logic operations: glEnable(GL_LOGIC_OP).
4. Alpha blending: glEnable(GL_BLEND).
5. Texture mapping: glEnable(GL_TEXTURE_2D) and glEnable(GL_TEXTURE_1D).
6. Multisampling: glEnable(GL_MULTISAMPLE_SGIS).

Except for flat and Gouraud shading, these different operations can be combined at increased expense. Per-fragment operations are typically more expensive if they require both a read and a write of frame buffer memory. Much of the reason depth buffering is expensive is that it requires the pixel's depth value to be read, and if the depth test passes, the fragment's depth value must be written into the frame buffer memory. Alpha blending, depth, and stencil operations that require a frame buffer read and write are more expensive than versions of these operations that do not require both the read and the write.

On different hardware architectures, the ordering of this list may change. For example, on machines with hardware texture mapping support, alpha blending may be more expensive than texture mapping. One reason texture mapping is more expensive without special hardware is that transformation work that might otherwise occur inside the graphics subsystem will need to be done on the host processor, where texture lookups must be performed out of host memory.

Here is some advice for efficiently using per-fragment operations:

- Use alpha blending with care. When you are rendering opaque non-antialiased primitives, you probably do not need blending enabled.
- Disable per-fragment operations you do not need, but avoid toggling operations excessively.
- While dithering is not typically very expensive, it is enabled by default. If you know you do not want dithering, try disabling it.
- It may be faster to enable per-fragment operations by changing the operation's mode instead of using `glEnable` and `glDisable`. For example, `glDepthFunc(GL_ALWAYS)` may be faster than `glDisable(GL_DEPTH_TEST)`.

6.6.5.2 Depth Buffer Tuning

Sometimes applications render large, and therefore expensive, polygons in the background of the scene. Flight simulators often do this to render the terrain and sky. It may be advantageous to disable depth buffering when you are rendering large background polygons if you can properly sort them, rendering backmost polygons first (it is best if there are only a few such large background polygons). This can significantly improve your rendering performance.

6.6.5.3 Use Backface Culling

Backface culling (see Section 2.1.2) is a very important optimization because it can typically eliminate half the polygons in your scenes assuming the numbers of back- and front-facing polygons are about equal. While the polygons must be transformed, culled polygons are not rasterized. This is most helpful for fill-limited applications.

6.6.5.4 Efficient Clears

Clearing is an important rendering operation, so OpenGL provides a special `glClear` command. Multiple ancillary buffers can be simultaneously cleared. For example:

```
glClear(GL_COLOR_BUFFER_BIT | GL_DEPTH_BUFFER_BIT);
```

Be sure to clear all the buffers you need cleared with a single `glClear`. Many graphics subsystems implement special "fast" clearing hardware that clears multiple buffers in parallel. Some systems also use special tag bits to indicate when a pixel is cleared instead of writing the entire pixel's color value. Rendering a window-sized polygon is not a good substitute for `glClear`.

6.6.6 Improving Imaging Performance

Tuning OpenGL's imaging operations (`glDrawPixels`, `glBitmap`, `glCopyPixels`, and `glReadPixels`) is very important for imaging applications. Because OpenGL has a fairly sophisticated pixel path (see Section 5.4.1), you should be sure not to have unintended operations enabled, because they can greatly degrade pixel throughput.

Here is some advice for using OpenGL imaging operations:

- In general, it is more efficient to work with larger images.
- Using `glPixelZoom` to magnify a large image is typically fill-limited.
- Some pixel path operations may use DMA to transfer quickly images from host memory to the graphics subsystem, but typically this is only for basic OpenGL pixel path configurations. If you enable a pixel path mode that does not support DMA transfers, performance may be greatly reduced. The pixel path configurations implemented via DMA vary, and some systems may not support DMA transfers at all.
- Byte-sized components, particularly unsigned bytes, tend to be well optimized.
- Use fewer components when possible: `GL_LUMINANCE_ALPHA` or `GL_LUMINANCE`.

6.6.6.1 Getting Fastest Image Performance

When you want to read, draw, or copy pixels as fast as possible, remember to disable pixel path and per-fragment operations that would slow down imaging performance. Here is a sequence of OpenGL calls that will turn off all pixel path and per-fragment operations that would slow down the pixel path performance:

```
  glDisable(GL_ALPHA_TEST);
  glDisable(GL_BLEND);
  glDisable(GL_DEPTH_TEST);
  glDisable(GL_DITHER);
  glDisable(GL_FOG);
  glDisable(GL_LIGHTING);
  glDisable(GL_LOGIC_OP); /* color index only */
#ifdef GL_COLOR_LOGIC_OP
  glDisable(GL_COLOR_LOGIC_OP); /* OpenGL 1.1, RGBA only */
#endif
  glDisable(GL_STENCIL_TEST);
  glDisable(GL_TEXTURE_1D);
```

```
glDisable(GL_TEXTURE_2D);
glPixelTransferi(GL_MAP_COLOR, GL_FALSE);
glPixelTransferi(GL_RED_SCALE, 1);
glPixelTransferi(GL_RED_BIAS, 0);
glPixelTransferi(GL_GREEN_SCALE, 1);
glPixelTransferi(GL_GREEN_BIAS, 0);
glPixelTransferi(GL_BLUE_SCALE, 1);
glPixelTransferi(GL_BLUE_BIAS, 0);
glPixelTransferi(GL_ALPHA_SCALE, 1);
glPixelTransferi(GL_ALPHA_BIAS, 0);
glPixelZoom(1.0, 1.0);

#ifdef GL_EXT_convolution
  glDisable(GL_CONVOLUTION_1D_EXT); glDisable(GL_CONVOLUTION_2D_EXT);
  glDisable(GL_SEPARABLE_2D_EXT);
#endif

#ifdef GL_EXT_histogram
  glDisable(GL_HISTOGRAM_EXT);
  glDisable(GL_MINMAX_EXT);
#endif

#ifdef GL_EXT_texture
  glDisable(GL_TEXTURE_3D_EXT);
#endif

#ifdef GL_SGIS_multisample
  /* Multisample-capable visuals only. */
  glDisable(GL_MULTISAMPLE_SGIS);
#endif
```

For good measure, the routines at the end of the sequence demonstrate disabling a few common OpenGL extensions. Remember that there are numerous OpenGL extensions to the pixel path, and if you use them, you should disable them when you desire the fastest possible pixel performance and do not need them.

In practice, you do not need to disable things that you do not use so you can probably eliminate most of the calls above in an actual program.

6.6.7 Improving Texturing Performance

When you are using texture mapping, the most important issue is whether the hardware you are running on supports texture mapping with specialized hardware. While such hardware will likely be commonplace in the near to medium future, at present many machines do not support texture mapping in hardware.

When texture mapping is not supported in hardware, it may make sense to provide an option to disable texture mapping if it is not critical to your application. While the existence of texture-mapping hardware gives a significant performance boost to texture-mapping speed, OpenGL does not attempt to characterize performance aspects of OpenGL implementations. An ad hoc solution is to base a program's behavior on the GL_RENDERER string returned by glGetString. A more adaptive approach is to measure the speed of texture-mapping operations and base the program's configuration on these measurements.

Here is some advice for using texture mapping:

- Because textures flow through the pixel path, all the advice for efficiently configuring the pixel path in the preceding section applies when you are downloading textures.

- For OpenGL 1.0, it is generally advantageous to make display lists containing repeatedly used texture definitions done by either glTexImage2D or glTexImage1D. Better yet is to use the texture object extension described in Section 5.6.2 if it is available. With OpenGL 1.1, programs should definitely use the texture object capabilities described on page 293.

- Accelerated texture memory is generally a limited resource. OpenGL implementations with specialized texture memory will try to keep commonly used textures resident in texture memory. It is faster to switch to a texture already resident in texture memory.

- Use OpenGL 1.1's glPrioritizeTextures to help inform OpenGL as to which textures are most important to keep resident.

- Use OpenGL 1.1's internal texture formats to improve performance, conserve texture memory, and probably improve your textured pixel fill rate. The GL_LUMINANCE and GL_LUMINANCE_ALPHA formats are also good ways to speed texture loading.

- OpenGL supports different texture filtering methods. The GL_NEAREST mode is the simplest and lowest-quality. The GL_LINEAR_MIPMAP_LINEAR is the highest-quality, but may be slower. Try using lower-quality texture filtering methods to improve performance.

In general, texture management is significantly improved in OpenGL 1.1, so heavily texture-oriented applications should use OpenGL 1.1, or the texturing extensions subsumed by OpenGL 1.1, when available.

6.6.8 Constructing Application-specific Benchmarks

Mere advice for performance tuning can go only so far. When you are tuning a specific OpenGL program's rendering performance, there is no substitute for benchmarking the rendering code you are tuning. If you can isolate the routines in your program that do rendering, you can benchmark the time they take, change things, rebenchmark, and see what works best. As a rule, empirical benchmarking is superior to guessing what will probably go fast.

Keep in mind that tuning by benchmarks often means tuning to the particular OpenGL implementation you are using. Tuning to get the best performance from one OpenGL implementation may not get the best performance from another implementation. You might consider running your benchmark on several different OpenGL implementations with varying degrees of hardware acceleration. If differences between OpenGL implementations are substantial, you can even let your application select its best rendering method based on the OpenGL implementation it is using by testing the GL_RENDERER and GL_VENDOR strings returned by glGetString.

Writing application-specific benchmarks also lets you estimate the performance benefit of new graphics hardware without porting your entire application to the new platform. Using such benchmarks, you can intelligently evaluate vendors' claims of rendering performance based on the rendering operations that are most important to your application.

6.6.8.1 Using the GLUT-based Benchmark Harness

GLUT is a good library to use when constructing such application-specific benchmarks. The glutTimerFunc routine lets you see how many iterations of your rendering routine can complete in at least a given period of time. Also, GLUT's portability and availability make it easy to compile your benchmark on different platforms.

The end of this section includes a GLUT-based "harness" for constructing application-specific benchmarks. It handles the common details such as parsing common benchmark command line options, iterating your rendering routine for at least some specified period of time, making sure the window was not damaged or obscured during the test, reporting OpenGL errors that occurred during the benchmark, and reporting the results.

You write two routines:

testInit initializes OpenGL state in preparation for running your rendering benchmark.

testRender performs the OpenGL rendering to be benchmarked.

The testInit routine is passed argc- and argv-style variables providing command line options for your benchmark. First, any GLUT and test harness command line arguments are stripped out, so you need only parse the remaining options for any test options for your benchmark. The testInit routine is also passed the test window's width and height in pixels.

Here is an example testInit and testRender routine that draws a torus. The -light and -depth command line options are used to enable lighting and depth testing.

```
#include <string.h>
#include <GL/glut.h>
```

```
/* Modify these variables if necessary to control the number of
   iterations for per time sample, the GLUT display mode for the
   window, and the minimum test running time in seconds. */
extern int testIterationsStep,
   testDisplayMode, testMinimumTestTime;

void
testInit(int argc, char **argv, int width, int height)
{
  static GLfloat light_diffuse[] = {1.0, 0.0, 0.0, 1.0};
  static GLfloat light_position[] = {1.0, 1.0, 1.0, 0.0};
  int i;

  glViewport(0, 0, width, height);
  glMatrixMode(GL_PROJECTION);
  gluPerspective(25.0, width/height, 1.0, 10.0);
  glMatrixMode(GL_MODELVIEW);
  gluLookAt(0.0, 0.0, 5.0,
    0.0, 0.0, 0.0,
    0.0, 1.0, 0.);
  glTranslatef(0.0, 0.0, -1.0);

  glColor3f(1.0, 0.0, 0.0);
  glLightfv(GL_LIGHT0, GL_DIFFUSE, light_diffuse);
  glLightfv(GL_LIGHT0, GL_POSITION, light_position);
  for (i = 1; i < argc; i++) {
    if (!strcmp("-light", argv[i])) {
      glEnable(GL_LIGHTING);
      glEnable(GL_LIGHT0);
    } else if (!strcmp("-depth", argv[i])) {
      glEnable(GL_DEPTH_TEST);
    }
  }
  glNewList(1, GL_COMPILE);
  glutSolidTorus(0.25, 0.75, 100, 100);
  glEndList();
}

void
testRender(void)
{
  glClear(GL_COLOR_BUFFER_BIT | GL_DEPTH_BUFFER_BIT);
  glCallList(1);
}
```

This code is then linked with the harness code at the end of the section to make your benchmark executable. You can compile the harness into an object file called `gl_harness.o`. To compile your benchmark, you would use a compile command line like this:

```
cc -o torus_test torus.c gl_harness.o -lglut -lGLU -lGL -lXmu \
   -lXext -lX11
```

Now you run the `torus_test` executable to measure the torus rendering speed. With different command line options, you can vary the test being performed. Here are some sample runs of the `torus_test` benchmark:

```
% torus_test
Renders/second = 2.90951
  after 30 iterations over 10.311 seconds

% torus_test -iters 40
Renders/second = 2.90846
  after 40 iterations over 13.753 seconds

% torus_test -time 5 -depth
Renders/second = 2.53678
  after 15 iterations over 5.913 seconds

% torus_test -depth -light
Renders/second = 1.82515
  after 20 iterations over 10.958 seconds

% torus_test -geometry 100x100 -depth -light
Renders/second = 2.00981
  after 25 iterations over 12.439 seconds
```

Notice that different options control the rate of rendering reported. The last two runs of `torus_test` indicate that the torus is very transform-limited. All the runs except the last render into GLUT's default 300-by-300-pixel window. The last run uses a 100-by-100-pixel window. Despite updating nine times fewer pixels, the 100-by-100-pixel window rendering rate is only about 10% faster than the 300-by-300 rate. It is not surprising that the torus test is transform-limited, considering that the torus is tessellated very finely to contain 10,000 polygons.

Two harness-specific options are supported. The `-time` option specifies the minimum amount of time, in seconds, that the test should run. The `-iters` option lets you specify how many iterations of your rendering routine should be called between checking whether the test time for the test has been exceeded and checking again. You might want a larger iteration count if the time required to execute your rendering routine is very short, to minimize the harness overhead included in the test result. The default iteration count is 10. From the results shown, you can see that increasing the count to 40 did little to change the benchmark results, since the harness overhead is fairly low. There is also a `-mode` option that lets you pass in the value of GLUT's display mode mask if you would like to test the program with a different frame buffer configuration.

6.6.8.2 *The GLUT Benchmark Harness*

The source code for the test harness will be shown next. The only tricky part of the harness is to make sure that the window was not disturbed while the test was run. At the end of the test, the window is raised. If the window has been obscured by another window, this generates a display callback to repair the damage. To guarantee that the window raise occurs and we receive any damage that might be reported, a second (dummy) window is created.

Also, notice that OpenGL errors are queried after the test. You would not want to query errors during the test because it might influence the test. If OpenGL errors happen or if the window is disturbed during the test, a message is output, when the test results are reported, that indicates that the rendering rate is questionable. This helps you to ensure that the test is properly run.

One thing the test does not ensure is that no other programs are running concurrently that might steal processor time or cause work for the graphics hardware. It is up to you to make sure nothing else is competing for the processor or graphics hardware when the benchmark is running.

```
#include <stdlib.h>
#include <stdio.h>
#include <string.h>
#include <GL/glut.h>

extern testInit(int argc, char **argv, int width, int height);
extern testRender(void);

int testIterationsStep, testDisplayMode, testMinimumTestTime;
float end, start;
int error;
int renders = 0, damaged = 0;
void

report(int value)
{
  float duration;

  duration = (end - start) / 1000.0;
  printf("Renders/second = %g\n",
      renders / duration);
```

```
    printf(" after %d iterations over %g seconds\n",
      renders, duration);
    if (error != GL_NO_ERROR)
      printf(
        "OpenGL errors occurred during test; RESULTS ARE DUBIOUS.\n");
    if (damaged != 1)
      printf("Window disturbed during test; RESULTS ARE DUBIOUS.\n");
    printf("\n");
    exit(damaged != 1);
}

void
ensureEventsGotten(int value)
{
  /* Hack. Creating a new window _ensures_ that any outstanding
     expose event from popping the window will be retrieved. */
  glutCreateWindow("dummy");
  glutHideWindow();
  glutTimerFunc(1, report, 0);
}

void
displayDone(void)
{
  if (glutLayerGet(GLUT_NORMAL_DAMAGED))
    damaged++;
}

void
done(int value)
{
  glFinish();
  end = glutGet(GLUT_ELAPSED_TIME);
  error = glGetError();

  /* Pop the window. If the window was obscured by another
     window during the test, raising the window should generate
     an expose event we want to catch. */
  glutPopWindow();

  /* The test is over, so only notice an expose and do not run
     the testRender routine. */
  glutDisplayFunc(displayDone);
  glutTimerFunc(1, ensureEventsGotten, 0);
}
```

```
void
display(void)
{
  int i;

  if (glutLayerGet(GLUT_NORMAL_DAMAGED)) {
    damaged++;
    if (damaged == 1) {
      glutTimerFunc(testMinimumTestTime * 1000, done, 0);
      start = glutGet(GLUT_ELAPSED_TIME);
    }
  }
  for (i = 0; i < testIterationsStep; i++) {
    testRender();
    renders++;
  }
  glutPostRedisplay();
}

void
visible(int state)
{
  if (state == GLUT_NOT_VISIBLE)
    damaged++;
}

int
main(int argc, char **argv)
{
  char *newArgv[100];
  int newArgc, i;

  /* Defaults; testInit may override these. */
  testIterationsStep = 5;
  testDisplayMode = GLUT_SINGLE | GLUT_RGB | GLUT_DEPTH;
  testMinimumTestTime = 10; /* seconds */

  glutInit(&argc, argv);
  newArgc = 1;
  newArgv[0] = argv[0];
  for (i = 1; i < argc; i++) {
    if (!strcmp("-time", argv[i])) {
      i++;
      if (argv[i] == NULL) {
        fprintf(stderr, "%s: -time option needs argument\n", argv[0]);
        exit(1);
```

```
      }
      testMinimumTestTime = strtol(argv[i], NULL, 0);
    } else if (!strcmp("-mode", argv[i])) {
      i++;
      if (argv[i] == NULL) {
        fprintf(stderr, "%s: -mode option needs argument\n", argv[0]);
        exit(1);
      }
      testDisplayMode = strtol(argv[i], NULL, 0);
    } else if (!strcmp("-iters", argv[i])) {
      i++;
      if (argv[i] == NULL) {
        fprintf(stderr, "%s: -mode option needs argument\n", argv[0]);
        exit(1);
      }
      testIterationsStep = strtol(argv[i], NULL, 0);
    } else {
      newArgv[newArgc] = argv[i];
      newArgc++;
    }
  }
  newArgv[newArgc] = NULL;

  glutInitDisplayMode(testDisplayMode);
  glutCreateWindow("OpenGL performance test");
  glutDisplayFunc(display);
  glutVisibilityFunc(visible);
  testInit(newArgc, newArgv,
    glutGet(GLUT_WINDOW_WIDTH), glutGet(GLUT_WINDOW_HEIGHT));
  glutMainLoop();
  return 0; /* ANSI C requires main to return int. */
}
```

6.6.9 Beware of Standard Benchmarks

Beware of "standard" graphics benchmarks. The performance that matters is the performance of your application. That is why the method described in the preceding section for constructing application-specific benchmarks is so important. Vendor-supplied benchmark numbers are often difficult to interpret, because not enough parameters are specified. For example, a vendor may claim "10 million 3D lines per second." While this number is high, it does not say whether the lines are depth-buffered, whether the lines are connected or unconnected,[12] whether the lines are shaded or textured, and so on. Also, if your application is rendering polygons, line rendering speed is probably irrelevant.

Standard graphics benchmarks often rely on synthetic workloads. Real graphics programs do not simply render millions of 3D lines. Instead, real programs switch between various primitives and use various modes. This switching overhead is rarely measured by benchmarks. Real programs also spend time generating the data to be rendered, a task not performed in benchmarks. Treat vendor-supplied benchmark numbers as "not to be exceeded" rendering performance for the particular rendering task measured; do not expect real applications to achieve benchmark results.

Finally, when you compare OpenGL implementations, either with benchmarks or in side-by-side comparisons running applications, there are a number of "tricks" to be wary of:

- Are the two OpenGL implementations updating pixels of the same depth? For example, comparing a machine updating 24-bit pixels with another updating 8-bit pixels means the 8-bit system is really only updating one third the number of bits. This warning applies to ancillary buffer depth, too.

- Is the benchmark running "full-screen"? If so, make sure the two screens actually have the same resolution. Do not assume this just because the monitors are the same size. For example, a 1024-by-768 screen has 40% fewer pixels than a 1280-by-1024 screen. That is fewer pixels to update, meaning less work to do. Lower screen resolutions are one reason games on PCs appear to have faster 3D graphics than workstation graphics.

- Does the vendor claim a high raw-polygon or raw-pixel fill rate, but not mention both rates? This may be an indication that the system's transformation and rasterization rates are not well balanced. The ability to render a million polygons per second may not be as interesting if the polygons have to be tiny in order not to exceed the machine's fill rate.

- Favor performance demonstrations that use dynamically changing scenes over the "static object spinning in 3D" demonstrations. Real applications change what they are rendering. Not only are you not seeing the effect of mode changes on performance, but you are likely looking at an OpenGL rendering path specially tuned for benchmarks.

---

12. Rendering N unconnected lines requires $2 \times N$ vertices; rendering connected lines means that each line starts where the last one ended, so only $N + 1$ vertices are required. Rendering connected lines requires half the per-vertex bandwidth of rendering unconnected lines.

- Be wary of "least common denominator" comparisons. What is not being compared may be just as important as what is being compared. For example, a vendor may compare a machine without hardware texture mapping to a machine with hardware texture mapping, but never include any performance comparisons of texture mapping speeds.

- This can also be more subtle, as when a machine supports high-quality texture sampling modes at the same rates as lower-quality texture sampling modes, but a second vendor's "apples-to-apples" comparison uses only the lower-quality texture mapping when the higher-quality texture mapping is "for free" on the first machine.

- When hardware texture mapping is demonstrated, favor performance demonstrations that show multiple textures in use, particularly changing textures. Showing a small set of static textures may be an indication that the system cannot download textures quickly. Ask what the raw texture download rate is.

- Be *extremely* careful when evaluating the results of double buffered benchmarks. Consider a high-end graphics workstation that is 100 times faster than a given low-end workstation. However, the low-end workstation vendor constructs a naive double buffered benchmark that runs on the low-end workstation at 6 frames per second and on the high-end workstation at 60 frames per second. According to the benchmark, the low-end workstation appears to be only 10 times slower than the high-end workstation, not 100 times slower as the high-end vendor claims.

  Good double buffering hardware synchronizes the buffer swap operation to the display's vertical refresh to avoid visual artifacts. If you think about it, it makes no sense to animate scenes faster than the images can be displayed to the monitor. This typically means that double buffered rendering will not go any faster than 60 frames per second (the typical monitor refresh rate).

  When the benchmark is run, the high-end workstation is idle most of the time because the benchmark is so simple (for the high-end workstation, at least) that a frame of animation renders in one tenth of the monitor refresh interval. If the `glXSwapBuffers` calls were removed from the benchmark, the raw rendering performance would validate the high-end vendor's claim that the high-end workstation is indeed 100 times faster than the low-end workstation.

Benchmarks are useful to the extent that they measure the speed of operations that are important to your application's performance. Few, if any, graphics applications will replicate the mix of operations measured by vendor benchmarks. It is difficult to overstate the importance of using application-specific rendering benchmarks when you compare the performance of different OpenGL implementations.

7

An Example Application

This chapter combines the techniques explained in the previous chapters to demonstrate a simple but interesting OpenGL application using Motif for viewing 3D representations of molecules. The program, called `molview`, demonstrates the following:

- It implements a Motif user interface that includes pop-up and pull-down menus that make use of overlay planes, if available, to minimize screen redraws caused by menu removal.

- When the user "picks" an atom by clicking on it with the mouse, OpenGL's selection mechanism is used to report the atom's name, location, and radius.

- To reduce successive window repaints, X Toolkit timers and work procs efficiently schedule window redisplay.

- Spinning the molecule is done with a "virtual" trackball routine to ensure intuitive rotations.

- To improve interactivity, the molecule is rendered at two different levels of detail. A coarse sphere model is used for interactive viewing, but with an "Auto HiRes" feature, 2 seconds after the scene stops moving, the scene is redrawn with detailed spheres.

- The program uses `glXUseXFont` for rendering text in an OpenGL window.

- It requests the GLX multisample extension, when available, for "painless" antialiasing.

415

7.1 RUNNING `molview`

The `molview` application has a standard Motif look and feel. Figure 7.1 shows `molview` displaying a molecule. When a molecule is displayed, it can be rotated by holding down the left mouse button. Clicking the middle mouse button on an atom reports the atom's name, location, and radius in Motif text fields below the viewing window.

The right button displays a pop-up menu providing the user with a way to switch between solid and wireframe renderings of the molecule. Two toggle buttons on the menu independently enable "Spin Momentum" and "Auto HiRes." The "Spin Momentum" feature keeps the molecule rotating once it is set in motion by spinning the molecule with the left mouse button. The "Auto HiRes" feature redisplays the molecule at a higher tessellation if the molecule spends 2 seconds without rotating. This adaptive behavior makes the molecule fast to rotate, but also improves its appearance when it is displayed statically. OpenGL lighting enhances the 3D appearance of the molecule, particularly when displayed at the higher tessellation. The menu is shown in Figure 7.7.

A pull-down menu bar at the top of `molview`'s main window has a single pull-down menu called File. It includes options to either "Quit" or "Open a molecule..." Selecting "Open a molecule..." brings up a file chooser dialog box with which the user can open a `.mol` molecule description file, as shown in Figure 7.2.

Figure 7.1 Screen snapshot of `molview` displaying the chemical structure of *taxol*, an extract from the bark of the Pacific yew tree.

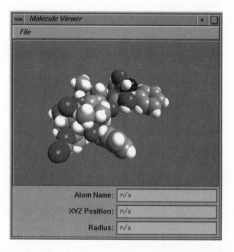

Figure 7.2 Screen snapshot of `molview` with its file chooser displayed. The text reading "No molecule loaded." that is displayed when `molview` starts up is rendered with OpenGL character bitmaps generated with `glXUseXFont`.

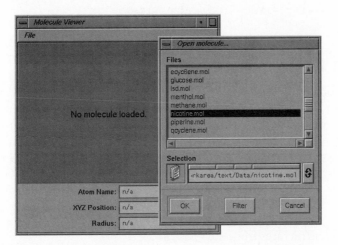

This chapter presents the source code that implements `molview`. The program is written with several source files. Here are the files, listed in the order in which they are presented, each with a brief description of the file's purpose:

> `molview.h` contains the common structures implementing the molecule data structure used by most of the source files.
>
> `mol_file.c` implements a reader for .mol files. A .mol file describes the 3D positions, sizes, and colors of the atoms within a molecule.
>
> `trackball.c` implements a "virtual" trackball to provide a means for rotating the molecule.
>
> `render.c` renders the loaded molecule with OpenGL.
>
> `pick.c` implements a picking mechanism that reports to the user what atom within the loaded molecule is "picked" using OpenGL's selection mechanism.
>
> `gui_init.c` initializes `molview`'s Motif widget hierarchy, including the OpenGL rendering area widget, and begins `molview`'s event processing loop.
>
> `gui_run.c` implements the callbacks for interacting with `molview`.

To place `molview`'s pop-up and pull-down menus in the overlay planes, `molview` also links with the `sovlayerutil.c` routines described in Section 6.3.3.

The command line to compile `molview` would look something like this:

```
cc -o molview mol_file.c gui_init.c gui_run.c \
  trackball.c render.c pick.c sovlayerutil.c \
  -lGLw -lXm -lXt -lXmu -lGL -lGLU -lXext -lX11 -lm
```

7.2 THE MOLECULE DATA STRUCTURE: `molview.h`

The data structure used to represent the molecule displayed by `molview` is a structure with two linked lists. The first, a list of atom types (hydrogen, oxygen, carbon, and so on), describes the color and radius of each particular type of atom. The second is the atom instance list that holds the (x, y, z) position of each atom instance. The extents of the molecule's atoms are also calculated to help center the atom within the viewing area. To support picking of atoms using OpenGL's selection mechanism, a selection buffer large enough to hold selection entries for every atom in the molecule is allocated. Figure 7.3 shows the data structure `molview` uses to represent a methane (CH_4) molecule.

Here are the structures from `molview.h`:

```
typedef struct _AtomType AtomType;
struct _AtomType {
  char *name;
  float radius;
  GLubyte color[3]; /* red, green, blue */
```

Figure 7.3 `molview` data structure representing a methane molecule.

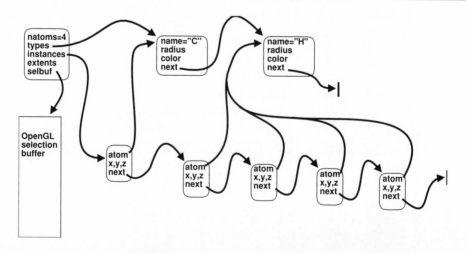

```
  AtomType *next;
};

typedef struct _AtomInstance AtomInstance;
struct _AtomInstance {
  AtomType *atom;
  float x, y, z;
  AtomInstance *next;
};

typedef struct {
  int natoms;
  AtomType *types;
  AtomInstance *instances;
  float xmin, ymin, zmin;
  float xsize, ysize, zsize;
  float maxdim;
  GLuint *selbuf;
} Molecule;
```

The spheres rendered by `molview` are at two different tessellation levels, depending on whether the molecule is moving or not. A coarser tessellation results in faster animation, but the finer tessellation looks better when the model is displayed statically. The `molview.h` header also contains symbolic constants for these two display lists:

```
#define HI_RES_SPHERE 1
#define LO_RES_SPHERE 2
```

The remainder of `molview.h` contains declarations for routines that are used in source files different from those where the routines are defined.

Figure 7.4 A .mol file description of a methane (CH_4) molecule.

```
;   description of methane, CH4
Carbon =      1.5 (.5,.5,.5)
Hydrogen =    0.9 (1.,1.,1.)
Carbon:       0.257   -0.363    0.000
Hydrogen:     0.257    0.727    0.000
Hydrogen:     0.771   -0.727    0.890
Hydrogen:     0.771   -0.727   -0.890
Hydrogen:    -0.771   -0.727    0.000
```

7.3 DATA FILE READER: `mol_file.c`

The molecule descriptions that `molview` reads, typically from files ending with .mol, have a very simple format. There are three types of lines in a .mol file: atom type lines, atom instance lines, and comment lines. Atom type lines are listed before atom instance lines and describe the name, radius, and color of a type of atom, such as carbon. For example:

```
Carbon = 1.5 (.5,.5,.5)
```

An atom instance line names an atom instance and specifies an (x, y, z) position for it. For example:

```
Carbon:     0.257 -0.363 0.000
```

Comment lines are prefixed with semicolons.

The .mol file describing a methane molecule is shown in Figure 7.4.

The `fileLoadMolecule` routine loads a .mol file into `molview`'s molecule data structure. The `addAtomType` and `addAtomInstance` routines parse the different line types. Once they are parsed, `calculateMoleculeExtents` determines a bounding box for the molecule used to fit the rendering of the molecule into `molview`'s viewing area. The `freeMolecule` routine frees a previously loaded molecule if a new molecule is loaded successfully. If `fileLoadMolecule` succeeds, `NULL` is returned; otherwise, a text message is returned that will be displayed in a dialog box to the user to explain why the file could not be loaded.

Here is the source code for `mol_file.c`:

```c
#include <stdio.h>
#include <stdlib.h>
#include <string.h>
#include <GL/gl.h>

#include "molview.h"

/* Helper routines for fileLoadMolecule. */
static char *addAtomType(Molecule * mol, char *name, float radius,
  float red, float green, float blue);
static char *addAtomInstance(Molecule * mol, char *name,
  float x, float y, float z);
static void freeMolecule(Molecule * mol);
static char *calculateMoleculeExtents(Molecule * mol);

#define MAX_LEN 256
```

```c
char *
fileLoadMolecule(char *filename, Molecule ** return_mol)
{
  FILE *file;
  char line[MAX_LEN], name[MAX_LEN];
  float radius, red, green, blue, x, y, z;
  char *error, fchar;
  Molecule *mol;
  int cnt;
  file = fopen(filename, "r");
  if (!file)
    return "Could not open file.";
  mol = (Molecule *) malloc(sizeof(Molecule));
  if (!mol) {
    fclose(file);
    return "Memory allocation failure";
  }
  mol->natoms = 0;
  mol->types = NULL;
  mol->instances = NULL;
  mol->selbuf = NULL;
  for (;;) {
    if (!fgets(line, MAX_LEN, file))
      break;
    fchar = line[0];
    if (fchar == '!' || fchar == ';' || fchar == '\n')
      continue;  /* Comment or blank line. */
    cnt = sscanf(line, "%[A-Za-z] = %f ( %f, %f, %f )",
      name, &radius, &red, &green, &blue);
    if (cnt == 5) {
      error = addAtomType(mol, name, radius, red, green, blue);
      if (error)
        goto ReadError;
      continue;
    }
    cnt = sscanf(line, "%[A-Za-z] : %f %f %f", name, &x, &y, &z);
    if (cnt == 4) {
      error = addAtomInstance(mol, name, x, y, z);
      if (error)
        goto ReadError;
      continue;
    }
    error = "File format incorrect.";
```

```
          goto ReadError;
    }
    error = calculateMoleculeExtents(mol);
    if (error)
      goto ReadError;

    /* Select buffer should have room for 4 entries
       (#,z1,z2,name) for each atom. */
    mol->selbuf = (GLuint *) malloc(4 * mol->natoms * sizeof(GLuint));
    if (mol->selbuf == NULL) {
      error = "Memory allocation failure";
      goto ReadError;
    }
    fclose(file);
    if (*return_mol)
      freeMolecule(*return_mol); /* Free old molecule if
                                    necessary. */
    *return_mol = mol;
    return NULL;

ReadError:
    freeMolecule(mol);
    fclose(file);
    return error;
}

static char *
addAtomType(Molecule * mol, char *name, float radius,
    float red, float green, float blue)
{
    AtomType *type;

    type = mol->types;
    while (type) {
      if (!strcmp(type->name, name))
        return "Duplicate atom type encountered.";
      type = type->next;
    }
    type = (AtomType *) malloc(sizeof(AtomType));
    if (!type)
      return "Memory allocation failure.";
    type->name = strdup(name);
    if (!type->name) {
```

```
    free(type);
    return "Memory allocation failure.";
  }
  type->radius = radius;
  type->color[0] = red * 255;
  type->color[1] = green * 255;
  type->color[2] = blue * 255;
  type->next = mol->types;
  mol->types = type;
  return NULL;
}

static char *
addAtomInstance(Molecule * mol, char *name, float x, float y, float z)
{
  AtomInstance *inst;
  AtomType *type;

  type = mol->types;
  while (type) {
    if (!strcmp(type->name, name)) {
      inst = (AtomInstance *) malloc(sizeof(AtomInstance));
      if (!inst)
        return "Memory allocation failure.";
      inst->atom = type;
      inst->x = x;
      inst->y = y;
      inst->z = z;
      inst->next = mol->instances;
      mol->instances = inst;
      mol->natoms++;
      return NULL;
    }
    type = type->next;
  }
  return "Name of atom instance not already encountered.";
}

static void
freeMolecule(Molecule * mol)
{
  AtomType *type, *next_type;
  AtomInstance *inst, *next_inst;
```

```
  type = mol->types;
  while (type) {
    free(type->name);
    next_type = type->next;
    free(type);
    type = next_type;
  }
  inst = mol->instances;
  while (inst) {
    next_inst = inst->next;
    free(inst);
    inst = next_inst;
  }
}

#define MAX(a,b) ((a)>(b)?(a):(b))
#define MIN(a,b) ((a)<(b)?(a):(b))

static char *
calculateMoleculeExtents(Molecule * mol)
{
  AtomInstance *inst;
  float xmin, xmax, ymin, ymax, zmin, zmax;
  float radius;
  inst = mol->instances;
  if (!inst)
    return "Must have at least one atom.";
  radius = inst->atom->radius;
  xmin = inst->x - radius;
  xmax = inst->x + radius;
  ymin = inst->y - radius;
  ymax = inst->y + radius;
  zmin = inst->z - radius;
  zmax = inst->z + radius;
  inst = inst->next;
  while (inst) {
    radius = inst->atom->radius;
    xmin = MIN(inst->x - radius, xmin);
    xmax = MAX(inst->x + radius, xmax);
    ymin = MIN(inst->y - radius, ymin);
    ymax = MAX(inst->y + radius, ymax);
    zmin = MIN(inst->z - radius, zmin);
    zmax = MAX(inst->z + radius, zmax);
    inst = inst->next;
```

```
    }
    mol->xmin = xmin;
    mol->ymin = ymin;
    mol->zmin = zmin;
    mol->xsize = xmax - xmin;
    mol->ysize = ymax - ymin;
    mol->zsize = zmax - zmin;
    mol->maxdim = MAX(MAX(mol->xsize, mol->ysize), mol->zsize);
    return NULL;
}
```

7.4 VIRTUAL TRACKBALL: `trackball.c`

The user can spin a loaded molecule model with left mouse button motion. Through the mouse, the user supplies incremental rotations that must be accumulated to maintain the accurate orientation for the model. The means to accumulate these incremental rotations are surprisingly complicated.

A naive approach is to perform `glRotatef` calls for each incremental rotation around the modelview X axis, and then the Y axis. There are a couple of problems with this approach. Accumulating multiple rotations directly on OpenGL's modelview matrix can accumulate floating-point errors. Over time, the model may shrink or grow in size as the errors accumulate. Also, accumulating rotations on the modelview stack may work for one rotating object, but makes it difficult to maintain multiple rotating objects. Both problems could be overcome by reading back the modelview matrix. The first problem could be solved by renormalizing the matrix occasionally to make sure errors do not accumulate. The second problem is solved by saving and restoring multiple modelview matrices for each rotating object. Reading back OpenGL state often hurts OpenGL rendering performance, so a method that accumulates rotations without relying on reading back OpenGL state is preferable.

Another naive approach is to represent each model orientation as three angles, each representing rotation around the X, then the Y, then the Z modelview axis. Each absolute angle would be updated as the user rotates the model. The problem is that rotations do not commute in the mathematical sense. (A set of translations and scalings of objects can be reordered and they will have the same effect, but this is not true of rotations.) Not only is the result of accumulating rotations this way incorrect, but you can stumble across a situation known as *gimbal lock*, in which an axis is "folded" into another axis such that a degree of rotational freedom is lost. The `glxsimple.c` example in Section 1.5 performs rotations this way and it is possible to encounter a gimbal lock when playing with `glxsimple`.

A third approach, based on a clever mathematical parameterization of rotations called a *quaternion* can represent the accumulation of incremental angles in a way that is both mathematically stable and free from gimbal locks and other anomalies.

While the theory underlying quaternions is beyond the scope of this book, `molview`'s `trackball.c` implements a set of routines for converting rotations to quaternions, accumulating quaternions, and converting a quaternion representation of a rotation to a rotation matrix suitable for multiplying with the current OpenGL modelview matrix. The source file to implement quaternion math is called `trackball.c`, because using quaternions lets `molview` spin the molecule models as if the model were controlled by a trackball.

A set of routines for basic vector operations such as zeroing vectors (`vzero`), adding vectors (`vadd`), multiplying vectors to calculate dot- or cross-products (`vdot` and `vcross`), and normalizing vectors (`vnormal`) are defined for use in converting among angle increments, quaternions, and matrix representations of rotations.

Each quaternion is represented by four floating-point values. The quaternion representing an incremental angle can be generated by calling `trackball`. The routine is passed beginning and ending window coordinates translated to the center of rotation and normalized to be between negative and positive 1. An array of four floating-point values returns the resulting quaternion. For example, to generate a quaternion representing a small rotation around the X axis, make the following call:

```
float deltaQuat[4];

trackball(deltaQuat,
   0.0,    -0.1,    /* starting X,Y */
   0.0,     0.3);   /* ending X,Y */
```

You can accumulate one quaternion with another by calling `add_quats`. The first two arguments supply the quaternions to be accumulated; the result is placed in the floating-point array named by the third argument. For example, to accumulate some current quaternion with the quaternion calculated above, call

```
float currentQuat[4];

add_quats(deltaQuat, currentQuat, currentQuat);
```

After a given number of calls to `add_quats`, the resulting quaternion is renormalized to keep the orientation vector from growing or shrinking in magnitude.

Finally, an accumulated quaternion can be converted with `build_rotmatrix` to a rotation matrix that can be multiplied by OpenGL's modelview matrix to affect the quaternion's rotation. For example:

```
GLfloat rotationMatrix[4][4];

build_rotmatrix(rotationMatrix, currentQuat);
glPushMatrix();
```

```
glMultMatrixf(&m[0][0]);
/* Render model. */
glPopMatrix();
```

If your 3D applications use rotations with a full three degrees of freedom, these
routines are very valuable. The code that follows was originally implemented by
Gavin Bell [33, 39, 41]. More information about quaternions and their applications to computer graphics can be found in more comprehensive graphics texts
[43].

Here is the source code for `trackball.c`:

```
#include <math.h>
#include <GL/gl.h>
#include "molview.h"

/* This size should really be based on the distance from the
   center of rotation to the point on the object underneath the
   mouse. That point would then track the mouse as closely as
   possible. This is a simple example, though, so that is left
   as an Exercise for the Programmer. */
#define TRACKBALLSIZE (0.8)

static float tb_project_to_sphere(float, float, float);
static void normalize_quat(float[4]);

void
vzero(float *v)
{
  v[0] = 0.0;
  v[1] = 0.0;
  v[2] = 0.0;
}

void
vset(float *v, float x, float y, float z)
{
  v[0] = x;
  v[1] = y;
  v[2] = z;
}

void
vsub(const float *src1, const float *src2, float *dst)
```

```
{
  dst[0] = src1[0] - src2[0];
  dst[1] = src1[1] - src2[1];
  dst[2] = src1[2] - src2[2];
}

void
vcopy(const float *v1, float *v2)
{
  register int i;
  for (i = 0; i<3; i++)
    v2[i] = v1[i];
}

void
vcross(const float *v1, const float *v2, float *cross)
{
  float temp[3];

  temp[0] = (v1[1] * v2[2]) - (v1[2] * v2[1]);
  temp[1] = (v1[2] * v2[0]) - (v1[0] * v2[2]);
  temp[2] = (v1[0] * v2[1]) - (v1[1] * v2[0]);
  vcopy(temp, cross);
}

float
vlength(const float *v)
{
  return sqrt(v[0] * v[0] + v[1] * v[1] + v[2] * v[2]);
}

void
vscale(float *v, float div)
{
  v[0] *= div;
  v[1] *= div;
  v[2] *= div;
}

void
vnormal(float *v)
{
  vscale(v, 1.0 / vlength(v));
}
```

```c
float
vdot(const float *v1, const float *v2)
{
  return v1[0] * v2[0] + v1[1] * v2[1] + v1[2] * v2[2];
}


void
vadd(const float *src1, const float *src2, float *dst)
{
  dst[0] = src1[0] + src2[0];
  dst[1] = src1[1] + src2[1];
  dst[2] = src1[2] + src2[2];
}


void
trackball(float q[4], float p1x, float p1y, float p2x, float p2y)
{
  float a[3];      /* Axis of rotation. */
  float phi;       /* How much to rotate about axis. */
  float p1[3], p2[3], d[3];
  float t;

  if (p1x == p2x && p1y == p2y) {
    /* Zero rotation */
    vzero(q);
    q[3] = 1.0;
    return;
  }
  /* First, figure out z-coordinates for projection of P1 and
     P2 to deformed sphere. */
  vset(p1, p1x, p1y, tb_project_to_sphere(TRACKBALLSIZE, p1x, p1y));
  vset(p2, p2x, p2y, tb_project_to_sphere(TRACKBALLSIZE, p2x, p2y));

  /* Now we want the cross product of P1 and P2. */
  vcross(p2, p1, a);

  /* Figure out how much to rotate around that axis. */
  vsub(p1, p2, d);
  t = vlength(d) / (2.0 * TRACKBALLSIZE);

  /* Avoid problems with out-of-control values. */
  if (t>1.0)
```

```
      t = 1.0;
   if (t<-1.0)
      t = -1.0;
   phi = 2.0 * asin(t);

   axis_to_quat(a, phi, q);
}


/* Given an axis and angle, compute quaternion. */
void
axis_to_quat(float a[3], float phi, float q[4])
{
   vnormal(a);
   vcopy(a, q);
   vscale(q, sin(phi / 2.0));
   q[3] = cos(phi / 2.0);
}


/* Project an x,y pair onto a sphere of radius r OR a
   hyperbolic sheet if we are away from the center of the
   sphere. */
static float
tb_project_to_sphere(float r, float x, float y)
{
   float d, t, z;

   d = sqrt(x * x + y * y);
   if (d<r * 0.70710678118654752440) { /* Inside sphere. */
      z = sqrt(r * r - d * d);
   } else {        /* On hyperbola. */
      t = r / 1.41421356237309504880;
      z = t * t / d;
   }
   return z;
}


/* Given two rotations, e1 and e2, expressed as quaternion
   rotations, figure out the equivalent single rotation and
   stuff it into dest. This routine also normalizes the result every
   RENORMCOUNT times it is called, to keep error from creeping in.
   NOTE: This routine is written so that q1 or q2
   may be the same   as dest (or each other). */
```

```
#define RENORMCOUNT 97

void
add_quats(float q1[4], float q2[4], float dest[4])
{
  static int count = 0;
  float t1[4], t2[4], t3[4];
  float tf[4];

  vcopy(q1, t1);
  vscale(t1, q2[3]);

  vcopy(q2, t2);
  vscale(t2, q1[3]);

  vcross(q2, q1, t3);
  vadd(t1, t2, tf);
  vadd(t3, tf, tf);
  tf[3] = q1[3] * q2[3] - vdot(q1, q2);

  dest[0] = tf[0];
  dest[1] = tf[1];
  dest[2] = tf[2];
  dest[3] = tf[3];

  if (++count > RENORMCOUNT) {
    count = 0;
    normalize_quat(dest);
  }
}

/* Quaternions always obey: a^2 + b^2 + c^2 + d^2 = 1.0 If they
   don't add up to 1.0, dividing by their magnitude will renormalize
   them. */
static void
normalize_quat(float q[4])
{
  int i;
  float mag;

  mag = (q[0] * q[0] + q[1] * q[1] + q[2] * q[2] + q[3] * q[3]);
  for (i = 0; i < 4; i++)
```

```
        q[i] /= mag;
}


/* Build a rotation matrix, given a quaternion rotation. */
void
build_rotmatrix(GLfloat m[4][4], float q[4])
{
  m[0][0] = 1.0 - 2.0 * (q[1] * q[1] + q[2] * q[2]);
  m[0][1] = 2.0 * (q[0] * q[1] - q[2] * q[3]);
  m[0][2] = 2.0 * (q[2] * q[0] + q[1] * q[3]);
  m[0][3] = 0.0;

  m[1][0] = 2.0 * (q[0] * q[1] + q[2] * q[3]);
  m[1][1] = 1.0 - 2.0 * (q[2] * q[2] + q[0] * q[0]);
  m[1][2] = 2.0 * (q[1] * q[2] - q[0] * q[3]);
  m[1][3] = 0.0;

  m[2][0] = 2.0 * (q[2] * q[0] - q[1] * q[3]);
  m[2][1] = 2.0 * (q[1] * q[2] + q[0] * q[3]);
  m[2][2] = 1.0 - 2.0 * (q[1] * q[1] + q[0] * q[0]);
  m[2][3] = 0.0;

  m[3][0] = 0.0;
  m[3][1] = 0.0;
  m[3][2] = 0.0;
  m[3][3] = 1.0;
}
```

7.5 MOLECULE RENDERER: `render.c`

A molecule is rendered by `molview` as an arrangement of spheres in 3D space. The code in `render.c` implements the code to initialize the OpenGL rendering context and render the scene displayed in an OpenGL drawing area widget.

The routine to initialize the OpenGL rendering context is `renderInit`. The routine initializes a quaternion to track the molecule's rotation, enables OpenGL rendering modes including setting up lighting parameters, sets up the modeling space, and establishes two display lists. One of the display lists renders a sphere at a fine degree of tessellation, for when the molecule is shown statically; the other display list renders a sphere at a coarse degree of tessellation, to be used when the model is spinning.

Two lights are used. A specular highlight is specified to capture a white spot on the spheres to help indicate the light direction. Back-face culling is used to speed rendering by eliminating any back-facing spheres. Normalization of surface normals is enabled because `glScalef` is used to scale the atoms to fit the viewing area.

A second initialization routine, `renderReshape`, is called when the drawing area changes size. The routine updates the viewport and adjusts the aspect ratio of the projection matrix.

The `renderScene` routine redraws the scene by clearing the screen, rendering the scene contents, and swapping the back buffer to make it visible if double-buffered. The way the scene is rendered depends on whether a molecule is loaded or not. The `renderNoMolecule` routine is called when no molecule is loaded, to display a message saying "No molecule loaded." The display lists created by `glXUseXFont` are rendered by `glCallLists` to display the message. Xlib's `XTextWidth` routine is used to calculate the width of the message in pixels based on the font information returned by `XLoadQueryFont`.

When a molecule is loaded, `renderMolecule` is called. The modelview matrix stack is pushed so that the current quaternion can be converted to a rotation matrix to orient the molecule based on the current accumulated rotations. The `render-Atoms` routine scales and translates the model based on the extents calculated when the model was loaded. Each atom on the instance list is rendered at its specified position with its material color and radius determined by the atom instance's type. The `sphereVersion` variable is either `HI_RES_SPHERE` or `LO_RES_SPHERE`, depending on whether the model is static or in motion.

`renderInit` is called once from `main` after the OpenGL rendering context is created. `renderReshape` is called during `main` and whenever the drawing area widget is resized. `renderScene` is called when the drawing area is damaged or the scene needs to be otherwise updated.

Here is the source code for `render.c`:

```
#include <GL/gl.h>
#include <GL/glx.h>
#include <GL/glu.h>

#include <stdio.h>

#include "molview.h"

int sphereVersion = LO_RES_SPHERE;
float curquat[4];
float lastquat[4];
static float mat_specular[] = {.72, .8, .93, 1.0};
static float mat_diffuse[] = {1.0, 1.0, 1.0, 1.0};
static float mat_shininess[] = {128.0};
```

```
static float light_ambient[] = {0.1, 0.1, 0.1, 1.0};
static float light_diffuse[] = {1.0, 1.0, 1.0, 1.0};
static float light_specular[] = {1.0, 1.0, 1.0, 1.0};
static float light_position[] = {1.0, 1.0, 1.5, 0.0};
static float light0_position[] = {-1.0, -1.0, 1.5, 0.0};

void
renderInit(void)
{
  GLUquadricObj *quadObj;

  quadObj = gluNewQuadric();
  gluQuadricDrawStyle(quadObj, GLU_FILL);
  gluQuadricOrientation(quadObj, GLU_OUTSIDE);
  gluQuadricNormals(quadObj, GLU_SMOOTH);

  /* hi-detail sphere */
  glNewList(HI_RES_SPHERE, GL_COMPILE);
  gluSphere(quadObj, 1.0, 32, 32);
  glEndList();

  /* lo-detail sphere */
  glNewList(LO_RES_SPHERE, GL_COMPILE);
  gluSphere(quadObj, 1.0, 6, 6);
  glEndList();

  gluDeleteQuadric(quadObj);

  glEnable(GL_DEPTH_TEST);
  glEnable(GL_CULL_FACE);
  glClearColor(0.4, 0.4, 0.4, 0.0);
  glClearDepth(1.0);
  glEnable(GL_NORMALIZE);
  glShadeModel(GL_SMOOTH);

  glLightfv(GL_LIGHT1, GL_AMBIENT, light_ambient);
  glLightfv(GL_LIGHT1, GL_DIFFUSE, light_diffuse);
  glLightfv(GL_LIGHT1, GL_POSITION, light_position);
  glLightfv(GL_LIGHT1, GL_SPECULAR, light_specular);
  glLightfv(GL_LIGHT0, GL_POSITION, light0_position);
  glMaterialfv(GL_FRONT, GL_SPECULAR, mat_specular);
  glMaterialfv(GL_FRONT_AND_BACK, GL_SHININESS, mat_shininess);
  glMaterialfv(GL_FRONT, GL_DIFFUSE, mat_diffuse);
```

```c
  glColorMaterial(GL_FRONT, GL_AMBIENT_AND_DIFFUSE);
  glEnable(GL_LIGHT1);
  glEnable(GL_LIGHTING);

  glMatrixMode(GL_MODELVIEW);
  glLoadIdentity();
  glTranslatef(0, 0, -4);

  trackball(curquat, 0.0, 0.0, 0.0, 0.0);
}

static GLfloat winWidth, winHeight;

void
renderReshape(int width, int height)
{
  float aspect;

  winWidth = width;
  winHeight = height;
  glViewport(0, 0, winWidth, winHeight);
  glMatrixMode(GL_PROJECTION);
  glLoadIdentity();
  aspect = ((float) winWidth) / winHeight;
  gluPerspective(60.0, aspect, 1.0, 7.0);
  glMatrixMode(GL_MODELVIEW);
}

void
renderAtoms(Molecule * mol)
{
  AtomInstance *atom;
  float radius;
  int name;

#define SCALE_FACTOR 4.0

  atom = mol->instances;

  glEnable(GL_COLOR_MATERIAL);
  glScalef(SCALE_FACTOR / mol->maxdim,
    SCALE_FACTOR / mol->maxdim,
    SCALE_FACTOR / mol->maxdim);
```

```
      glTranslatef(-(mol->xmin + mol->xsize / 2),
        -(mol->ymin + mol->ysize / 2),
        -(mol->zmin + mol->zsize / 2));

    name = 0;
    while (atom) {
      glLoadName(name);
      glPushMatrix();
      glTranslatef(atom->x, atom->y, atom->z);
      radius = atom->atom->radius;
      glScalef(radius, radius, radius);
      glColor3ubv(atom->atom->color);
      glCallList(sphereVersion);
      glPopMatrix();
      atom = atom->next;
      name++;
    }
    glDisable(GL_COLOR_MATERIAL);
}

#ifdef DEBUG
void
sniff_for_opengl_errors(void)
{
  int error;
  printf("sniff\n");
  while ((error = glGetError()) != GL_NO_ERROR)
    fprintf(stderr, "GL error: %s\n ", gluErrorString(error));
}
#endif

void
renderMolecule(Molecule * mol)
{
  GLfloat m[4][4];

  glPushMatrix();
  build_rotmatrix(m, curquat);
  glMultMatrixf(&m[0][0]);
  renderAtoms(mol);
  glPopMatrix();
#ifdef DEBUG
```

```c
    sniff_for_opengl_errors();
#endif
}

void
renderNoMolecule(void)
{
  extern XFontStruct *fontInfo;
  static char message[] = "No molecule loaded.";
  static int width = 0;
  if (width == 0)
    width = XTextWidth(fontInfo, message, sizeof(message));
  glPushMatrix();
  glLoadIdentity();
  glMatrixMode(GL_PROJECTION);
  glDisable(GL_LIGHTING);
  glPushMatrix();
  glLoadIdentity();
  gluOrtho2D(0, winWidth, 0, winHeight);
  glColor3f(0.0, 0.0, 0.0);
  glRasterPos2i(0, 0);
  glBitmap(0, 0, 0, 0,
    winWidth / 2 - width / 2,
    winHeight / 2 - (fontInfo->ascent + fontInfo->descent) / 2, 0);
  glCallLists(sizeof(message), GL_UNSIGNED_BYTE, message);
  glPopMatrix();
  glMatrixMode(GL_MODELVIEW);
  glPopMatrix();
  glEnable(GL_LIGHTING);
}

void
renderScene(Molecule * mol)
{
  glClear(GL_DEPTH_BUFFER_BIT | GL_COLOR_BUFFER_BIT);
  if (mol) {
    renderMolecule(mol);
  } else {
    renderNoMolecule();
  }
  swap();
}
```

7.6 PICKING: `pick.c`

When the user "picks" an atom by clicking on it with the mouse, OpenGL's selection mechanism is used to report the picked atom's name, location, and radius. The code to do this is found in `pick.c`.

The `pickScene` routine takes a molecule data structure and an (*x,y*) pixel position within the view window. The position is relative to the upper left-hand corner of the window. The routine returns an `AtomInstance*` for the atom at the specified position. `NULL` is returned if no atom is located at the specified position.

To assist in identifying objects rendered by OpenGL within a scene, OpenGL provides a mode of operation called *selection*. The default mode of operation is *render* mode. In this mode, OpenGL rendering commands are used to update the image in the frame buffer. In selection mode, the frame buffer is not modified. Instead, *hit records* are generated for generated OpenGL primitives that intersect with the viewing volume. Each primitive that intersects with the volume causes a selection *hit*. The hit records are saved in the selection buffer specified by `glSelectBuffer`.

By restricting the viewing volume to a small region of the viewport, you can determine what primitives fall within that region. You can identify objects at the current cursor location by specifying a restricted viewport region around that location. Each hit record has a list of associated integer-valued *names* that help identify the object to which a selected primitive belongs.

OpenGL's selection mode is the way `pickScene` determines what atom is at the specified window position. Picking is set up by setting up a selection buffer (`glSelectBuffer`), switching to the selection mode of operation (`glRenderMode`), initializing the name stack (`glInitNames` and `glPushName`), loading the projection matrix, and multiplying the projection matrix by a specially constructed pick matrix. The pick matrix is generated by `gluPickMatrix` based on the viewport and (*x,y*) position.

Once picking is initialized, the scene is regenerated using the same OpenGL commands that would be used to redraw the scene. The `renderMolecule` routine is called, just as for redrawing the scene. Looking back at `renderMolecule`, you will notice a call to `glLoadName` before each atom is rendered. Each call to `glLoadName` tags the primitives for each atom being rendered with the atom's integer index into the molecule's list. These per-atom names are stashed in selection hit records when the scene is rendered in selection mode. Exiting selection mode (resuming render mode) finalizes the selection buffer contents.

The finalized selection buffer is then processed by `processHits` to determine what atom was picked. Zero hits in the hit buffer indicate that no atoms were picked. If there are multiple hit records, the hit record with the lowest depth value (that is, the hit record for primitives closest to the viewer) is the picked atom. The `atomInfo` routine searches the molecule's atom list to find the picked atom by matching its index.

The code in `processHits` that is marked `#ifdef DEBUG` helps debug selection problems by decoding the hit records in the selection buffer.

Here is the source code for `pick.c`:

```
#include <stdio.h>
#include <GL/gl.h>
#include <GL/glu.h>

#include "molview.h"

static AtomInstance *processHits(Molecule *mol,
  GLint hits, GLuint buffer[]);

AtomInstance *
pickScene(Molecule * mol, int x, int y)
{
  GLint viewport[4];
  float aspect;
  int hits;

  glGetIntegerv(GL_VIEWPORT, viewport);
  glSelectBuffer(4*mol->natoms, mol->selbuf);
  (void) glRenderMode(GL_SELECT);
  glInitNames();
  glPushName(-1);

  glMatrixMode(GL_PROJECTION);
  glPushMatrix();
  glLoadIdentity();
  gluPickMatrix(x, viewport[3] - y, 1.0, 1.0, viewport);
  aspect = ((float) viewport[2])/viewport[3];
  gluPerspective(60.0, aspect, 1.0, 7.0);
  glMatrixMode(GL_MODELVIEW);
  renderMolecule(mol);
  glMatrixMode(GL_PROJECTION);
  glPopMatrix();
  glMatrixMode(GL_MODELVIEW);
  hits = glRenderMode(GL_RENDER);
  return processHits(mol, hits, mol->selbuf);
}

static AtomInstance *
atomInfo(Molecule *mol, int picked)
```

```
{
  AtomInstance *atom;
  int name;

  name = 0;
  atom = mol->instances;
  while (picked != name) {
    atom = atom->next;
    name++;
  }
  return atom;
}


AtomInstance *
processHits(Molecule *mol, GLint hits, GLuint buffer[])
{
  AtomInstance *atom;
  unsigned int i;
  GLint names;
  GLuint *ptr;
  GLuint minz, z, match;

  if(hits < 0 ) {
    fprintf(stderr, "WARNING: select buffer overflow!\n");
    return NULL;
  }
#ifdef DEBUG
  printf("hits = %d\n", hits);
  ptr = (GLuint *) buffer;
  for (i = 0; i < hits; i++) { /* for each hit */
    int j;

    names = *ptr;
    printf(" number of names for hit = %d\n", *ptr);
    ptr++;
    printf("  z1 is %g;", (float) *ptr/0xffffffff);
    ptr++;
    printf("  z2 is %g\n", (float) *ptr/0xffffffff);
    ptr++;
    printf("  the name is ");
    for (j = 0; j < names; j++) { /* for each name */
      printf("%d ", *ptr);
      ptr++;
```

```
    }
    printf("\n");
  }
#endif
  if(hits == 0)
    return NULL;
  minz = 0xffffffff;
  ptr = (GLuint *) buffer;
  for (i = 0; i < hits; i++) {  /* for each hit */
    names = *ptr;
    ptr++;
    z = *ptr;
    ptr++;
    ptr++;
    if(z <= minz) {
      minz = z;
      match = *ptr;
    }
    ptr += names;
  }
  atom = atomInfo(mol, match);

  return atom;
}
```

7.7 USER INTERFACE INITIALIZATION: `gui_init.c`

The `main` entry point for `molview` is found in `gui_init.c`. Within `main`, the basic widget hierarchy is established. This includes creating the application main window containing an OpenGL drawing area widget. The widget hierarchy created by `main` for `molview` is shown in Figure 7.5.

If the OpenGL implementation supports the GLX multisampling extension for hardware antialiasing, `molview` tries to find a visual that supports multisampling. Since GLX extensions are supported only in GLX 1.1, the helper routine `isSupportedByGLX` finds out whether the named extension passed to it is supported, first finding out whether GLX 1.1 or higher is supported. C preprocessor directives are used to control compilation of `isSupportedByGLX` and the multisampling detection code, based on whether the client supports GLX 1.1 and the GLX multisampling extension, respectively.

A second helper routine, `detectOverlaySupport`, uses the `sovGetVisualInfo` routine described in Section 6.3.3 to find an overlay visual appropriate for `molview`'s Motif pop-up and pull-down menus. If an appropriate overlay visual is found, the

Figure 7.5 Widget hierarchy for `molview` once it is initialized by `main`.

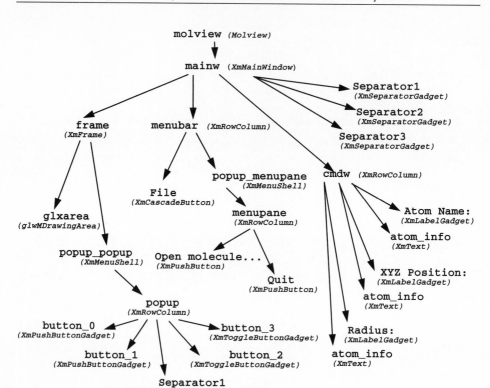

visual, depth, and appropriate colormap are created and passed to XmCreate-PulldownMenu and XmCreateSimplePopupMenu. See Section 6.3.8 for details about utilizing Motif overlay menus.

At the end of main, but before XtAppMainLoop is entered, XLoadQueryFont and glXUseXFont are used to establish a set of character display lists for rendering with OpenGL the "No molecule loaded." message when the program first starts. Only display lists for the displayable 7-bit ASCII characters are generated. glListBase is used to set the display list base so that glCallLists can be used to render character arrays as text.

Here is the source code for `gui_init.c`:

```
#include <stdlib.h>
#include <stdio.h>
#include <Xm/MainW.h>
#include <Xm/RowColumn.h>
```

```c
#include <Xm/PushB.h>
#include <Xm/ToggleB.h>
#include <Xm/CascadeB.h>
#include <Xm/Frame.h>
#include <Xm/FileSB.h>
#include <Xm/Text.h>
#include <Xm/MessageB.h>
#include <Xm/LabelG.h>
#include <X11/GLw/GLwMDrawA.h>  /* Motif OpenGL drawing area
                                      widget */
#include <GL/glx.h>

#include "molview.h"
#include "sovLayerUtil.h"

static int config[] = {
  None, None,          /* Space for multisampling GLX
                           attributes if supported. */
  GLX_DOUBLEBUFFER, GLX_RGBA, GLX_DEPTH_SIZE, 12,
  GLX_RED_SIZE, 1, GLX_GREEN_SIZE, 1, GLX_BLUE_SIZE, 1,
  None
};
static int *dblBuf = &config[2];
static int *snglBuf = &config[3];
static String fallbackResources[] = {
  "*sgiMode: true",   /* Try to enable Indigo Magic look & feel */
  "*useSchemes: all", /* and SGI schemes. */
  "*title: Molecule Viewer",
  "*filebox_popup*title: Open molecule...",
  "*glxarea*width: 400",
  "*glxarea*height: 300",
  NULL
};
static XtActionsRec actionsTable[] = {
  {"startRotation", startRotation},
  {"rotation", rotation},
  {"doPick", doPick},
};

XtAppContext app;
Display *dpy;
Bool doubleBuffer = True, madeCurrent = False;
Widget toplevel, mainw, menubar, menupane, btn, cascade,
  frame, glxarea, dialog, popup, cmdw;
```

```
WidgetList menuWidgets;
Window glxwin;
GLXContext cx;
XVisualInfo *vi = NULL;
Arg args[10];
XFontStruct *fontInfo;
Dimension viewWidth, viewHeight;
char *textLabels[] = {"Atom Name:", "XYZ Position:", "Radius:"};
Widget labels[XtNumber(textLabels)];
Visual *overlayVisual = NULL;
int overlayDepth;
Colormap overlayColormap;

static void
detectOverlaySupport(Display *dpy)
{
  sovVisualInfo template, *overlayVisuals;
  int layer, nVisuals, i, entries;

  /* Need more than two colormap entries for reasonable menus. */
  entries = 2;
  for (layer = 1; layer <= 3; layer++) {
    template.layer = layer;
    template.vinfo.screen = DefaultScreen(dpy);
    overlayVisuals = sovGetVisualInfo(dpy,
      VisualScreenMask | VisualLayerMask, &template, &nVisuals);
    if (overlayVisuals) {
      for (i = 0; i < nVisuals; i++) {
        if (overlayVisuals[i].vinfo.visual->map_entries>entries) {
          overlayVisual = overlayVisuals[i].vinfo.visual;
          overlayDepth = overlayVisuals[i].vinfo.depth;
          entries = overlayVisual->map_entries;
        }
      }
      XFree(overlayVisuals);
    }
  }
  if (overlayVisual)
    overlayColormap = XCreateColormap(dpy, DefaultRootWindow(dpy),
      overlayVisual, AllocNone);
}

static int
isSupportedByGLX(Display * dpy, char *extension)
```

```
{
#if defined(GLX_VERSION_1_1)
  static const char *extensions = NULL;
  const char *start;
  char *where, *terminator;
  int major, minor;

  glXQueryVersion(dpy, &major, &minor);
  /* Be careful not to call glXQueryExtensionsString if it
     looks like the server doesn't support GLX 1.1.
     Unfortunately, the original GLX 1.0 didn't have the notion
     of GLX extensions. */
  if ((major == 1 && minor >= 1) || (major>1)) {
    if (!extensions)
      extensions = glXQueryExtensionsString(dpy, DefaultScreen(dpy));
    /* It takes a bit of care to be foolproof about parsing
       the GLX extensions string. Don't be fooled by
       substrings, etc. */
    start = extensions;
    for (;;) {
      where = strstr(start, extension);
      if (!where)
        return 0;
      terminator = where + strlen(extension);
      if (where == start || *(where - 1) == ' ') {
        if (*terminator == ' ' || *terminator == '\0') {
          return 1;
        }
      }

      start = terminator;
    }
  }
#else
  /* No GLX extensions before GLX 1.1 */
#endif
  return 0;
}

int
main(int argc, char *argv[])
{
  static XmButtonType buttonTypes[] =
```

```
  {
    XmPUSHBUTTON, XmPUSHBUTTON, XmSEPARATOR, XmCHECKBUTTON,
                XmCHECKBUTTON,
  };
  XmString buttonLabels[XtNumber(buttonTypes)];
  int n, i;

  toplevel = XtAppInitialize(&app, "Molview", NULL, 0, &argc, argv,
    fallbackResources, NULL, 0);
  XtAppAddActions(app, actionsTable, XtNumber(actionsTable));
  dpy = XtDisplay(toplevel);

#if defined(GLX_VERSION_1_1) && defined(GLX_SGIS_multisample)
  if (isSupportedByGLX(dpy, "GLX_SGIS_multisample")) {
    config[0] = GLX_SAMPLES_SGIS;
    config[1] = 4;
    vi = glXChooseVisual(dpy, DefaultScreen(dpy), config);
  }
#endif

  if (vi == NULL) {
    /* Find an OpenGL-capable RGB visual with depth buffer. */
    vi = glXChooseVisual(dpy, DefaultScreen(dpy), dblBuf);
    if (vi == NULL) {
      vi = glXChooseVisual(dpy, DefaultScreen(dpy), snglBuf);
      if (vi == NULL)
        XtAppError(app, "no RGB visual with depth buffer");
      doubleBuffer = False;
    }
  }
  /* Create an OpenGL rendering context. */
  cx = glXCreateContext(dpy, vi, /* No display list sharing */ None,
  /* Favor direct rendering */ True);
  if (cx == NULL)
    XtAppError(app, "could not create rendering context");
  mainw = XtVaCreateWidget("mainw", xmMainWindowWidgetClass,
    toplevel,
    XmNcommandWindowLocation, XmCOMMAND_BELOW_WORKSPACE,
    NULL);
  XtManageChild(mainw);

  XtAddEventHandler(toplevel, StructureNotifyMask, False,
    mapStateChanged, NULL);
```

```
/* Try to find a good overlay visual for pull-down and pop-up
   menus. */
detectOverlaySupport(dpy);


/* Create menu bar. */
menubar = XmCreateMenuBar(mainw, "menubar", NULL, 0);
XtManageChild(menubar);
n = 0;
if (overlayVisual) {
  XtSetArg(args[n], XmNvisual, overlayVisual);
  n++;
  XtSetArg(args[n], XmNdepth, overlayDepth);
  n++;
  XtSetArg(args[n], XmNcolormap, overlayColormap);
  n++;
}
menupane = XmCreatePulldownMenu(menubar, "menupane", args, n);
if (overlayVisual) {
  XtAddCallback(XtParent(menupane), XmNpopupCallback,
    ensurePull-downColormapInstalled, NULL);
}
btn = XmCreatePushButton(menupane, "Open molecule...", NULL, 0);
XtAddCallback(btn, XmNactivateCallback, openMolecule, NULL);
XtManageChild(btn);
btn = XmCreatePushButton(menupane, "Quit", NULL, 0);
XtAddCallback(btn, XmNactivateCallback, quit, NULL);
XtManageChild(btn);
XtSetArg(args[0], XmNsubMenuId, menupane);
cascade = XmCreateCascadeButton(menubar, "File", args, 1);
XtManageChild(cascade);


/* Create framed drawing area for OpenGL rendering. */
frame = XmCreateFrame(mainw, "frame", NULL, 0);
XtManageChild(frame);
glxarea = XtVaCreateManagedWidget("glxarea",
  glwMDrawingAreaWidgetClass,
  frame, GLwNvisualInfo, vi, NULL);
XtVaGetValues(glxarea, XtNwidth, &viewWidth, XtNheight,
  &viewHeight, NULL);
XtAddCallback(glxarea, XmNexposeCallback, draw, NULL);
XtAddCallback(glxarea, XmNresizeCallback, resize, NULL);
XtAddCallback(glxarea, GLwNginitCallback, init, NULL);
```

```
/* Create atom pick result text field. */
cmdw = XtVaCreateWidget("cmdw", xmRowColumnWidgetClass, mainw,
  XmNpacking, XmPACK_COLUMN,
  XmNnumColumns, XtNumber(textLabels),
  XmNisAligned, True,
  XmNentryAlignment, XmALIGNMENT_END,
  XmNorientation, XmHORIZONTAL,
  NULL);
for (i = 0; i < XtNumber(textLabels); i++) {
  XtVaCreateManagedWidget(textLabels[i],
    xmLabelGadgetClass, cmdw, NULL);
  labels[i] = XtVaCreateManagedWidget("atom_info",
    xmTextWidgetClass, cmdw,
    XmNeditable, False,
    XmNcursorPositionVisible, False,
    XmNtraversalOn, False,
    XmNcolumns, 25,
    NULL);
}
clearPickInfo();
XtManageChild(cmdw);

/* Create pop-up menu. */
buttonLabels[0] = XmStringCreateLocalized("Solid");
buttonLabels[1] = XmStringCreateLocalized("Wireframe");
buttonLabels[2] = NULL;
buttonLabels[3] = XmStringCreateLocalized("Spin Momentum");
buttonLabels[4] = XmStringCreateLocalized("Auto HiRes");
n = 0;
XtSetArg(args[n], XmNbuttonCount, XtNumber(buttonTypes)); n++;
XtSetArg(args[n], XmNbuttons, buttonLabels); n++;
XtSetArg(args[n], XmNbuttonType, buttonTypes); n++;
XtSetArg(args[n], XmNbuttonSet, 4); n++;
XtSetArg(args[n], XmNsimpleCallback, processMenuUse); n++;
if (overlayVisual) {
  XtSetArg(args[n], XmNvisual, overlayVisual); n++;
  XtSetArg(args[n], XmNdepth, overlayDepth); n++;
  XtSetArg(args[n], XmNcolormap, overlayColormap); n++;
}
popup = XmCreateSimplePopupMenu(frame, "popup", args, n);
XtAddEventHandler(frame, ButtonPressMask, False, activateMenu,
  &popup);
XmStringFree(buttonLabels[0]);
XmStringFree(buttonLabels[1]);
XmStringFree(buttonLabels[3]);
XmStringFree(buttonLabels[4]);
```

```
XtVaGetValues(popup, XmNchildren, &menuWidgets, NULL);
XmToggleButtonSetState(menuWidgets[3], True, False);
XmToggleButtonSetState(menuWidgets[4], True, False);

/* Set up application's window layout. */
XmMainWindowSetAreas(mainw, menubar, cmdw, NULL, NULL, frame);
XtRealizeWidget(toplevel);

/* Once widget is realized (i.e., associated with a created X
   window), we can bind the OpenGL rendering context to the
   window.*/

glXMakeCurrent(dpy, XtWindow(glxarea), cx);
madeCurrent = True;

/* Get font for reporting no atom loaded. */
fontInfo = XLoadQueryFont(dpy,
   "-adobe-helvetica-medium-r-normal--18-*-*-*-p-*-iso8859-1");
if (fontInfo == NULL) {
  fontInfo = XLoadQueryFont(dpy, "fixed");
  if (fontInfo == NULL)
    XtAppError(app, "no X font available?");
}
glXUseXFont(fontInfo->fid, 32, 96, 1024 + 32);
glListBase(1024);

XtAppMainLoop(app);
return 0;
}
```

7.8 USER INTERFACE OPERATION: `gui_run.c`

All the user interface callbacks are contained in `gui_run.c`. This includes callbacks for the pop-up and pull-down menus, the file selection box, molecule rotation, molecule picking, and continuous animation. Figure 7.6 shows `molview` with interactive and finely detailed tessellations.

Here is the source code for `gui_run.c`:

```
#include <stdlib.h>
#include <stdio.h>
#include <unistd.h>
#include <math.h>
#include <X11/Intrinsic.h>
#include <Xm/RowColumn.h>
```

Figure 7.6 Two screen snapshots of `molview` tessellated differently. The left methane molecule is coarsely tessellated for good interactive animation. The right methane molecule is finely tessellated. Also notice that each set of pick fields is returning information about a specific atom picked by the user.

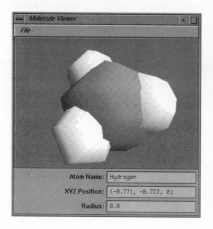
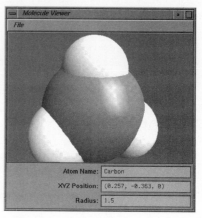

Figure 7.7 A screen snapshot of `molview` with its pop-up menu. The LSD molecule is shown in wireframe mode to show the high degree of tessellation.

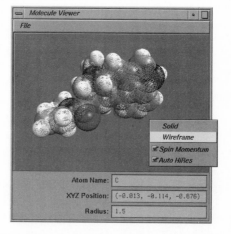

```
#include <Xm/FileSB.h>
#include <Xm/Text.h>
#include <Xm/MessageB.h>
#include <X11/GLw/GLwMDrawA.h> /* Motif OpenGL drawing area
                                      widget */
#include <X11/keysym.h>
#include <GL/gl.h>
#include <GL/glu.h>
#include <GL/glx.h>
#include "molview.h"

Molecule *mol = NULL;
XtWorkProcId animateID, hiResID, redisplayID;
int spinning;
int pendingAutoHiRes;
int beginx, beginy;
int autoHiRes = 1;
int momentum = 1;
XtTranslations trans = NULL;

static int redisplayPending = 0;

void postRedisplay(void);

void
stopSpinning(void)
{
  if (spinning) {
    spinning = 0;
    XtRemoveTimeOut(animateID);
  }
}

void
stopAutoHiRes(void)
{
  if(pendingAutoHiRes) {
    XtRemoveTimeOut(hiResID);
    pendingAutoHiRes = 0;
  }
}
```

```
void
makeHiRes(void)
{
  sphereVersion = HI_RES_SPHERE;
  postRedisplay();
}

void
hiresTimeout(XtPointer closure, XtIntervalId *id)
{
  makeHiRes();
}

void
makeLoRes(void)
{
  stopAutoHiRes();
  sphereVersion = LO_RES_SPHERE;
}

Boolean
handleRedisplay(XtPointer closure)
{
  renderScene(mol);
  if(autoHiRes && !spinning && !pendingAutoHiRes) {
    pendingAutoHiRes = 1;
    hiResID = XtAppAddTimeOut(app, 2000, hiresTimeout, 0);
  }
  redisplayPending = 0;
  return True;
}

void
postRedisplay(void)
{
  if(!redisplayPending) {
    redisplayID = XtAppAddWorkProc(app, handleRedisplay, 0);
    redisplayPending = 1;
  }
}

void
animate(XtPointer closure, XtIntervalId *id)
{
```

```
    add_quats(lastquat, curquat, curquat);
    postRedisplay();
    animateID = XtAppAddTimeOut(app, 1, animate, 0);
}

void
startRotation(Widget w, XEvent * event, String * params,
  Cardinal * num_params)
{
  int x, y;

  x = event->xbutton.x;
  y = event->xbutton.y;
  beginx = x;
  beginy = y;
  stopSpinning();
}

void
rotation(Widget w, XEvent * event, String * params,
  Cardinal * num_params)
{
  int x, y;

  x = event->xbutton.x;
  y = event->xbutton.y;
  trackball(lastquat,
    (2.0*beginx - viewWidth) / viewWidth,
    (viewHeight - 2.0*beginy) / viewHeight,
    (2.0*x - viewWidth) / viewWidth,
    (viewHeight - 2.0*y) / viewHeight
    );
  beginx = x;
  beginy = y;
  if (momentum) {
    if(!spinning) {
      spinning = 1;
      makeLoRes();
      animateID = XtAppAddTimeOut(app, 1, animate, 0);
    }
  } else {
    makeLoRes();
    add_quats(lastquat, curquat, curquat);
    postRedisplay();
```

```
    }
  }

  void
  updatePickInfo(AtomInstance *atom)
  {
    char buf[64];

    if(atom) {
      XmTextSetString(labels[0], atom->atom->name);
      sprintf(buf, "(%.3g, %.3g, %.3g)", atom->x, atom->y, atom->z);
      XmTextSetString(labels[1], buf);
      sprintf(buf, "%g", atom->atom->radius);
      XmTextSetString(labels[2], buf);
    } else {
      XmTextSetString(labels[0], "n/a");
      XmTextSetString(labels[1], "n/a");
      XmTextSetString(labels[2], "n/a");
    }
  }

  void
  clearPickInfo(void)
  {
    updatePickInfo(NULL);
  }

  void
  doPick(Widget w, XEvent * event, String * params,
    Cardinal * num_params)
  {
    AtomInstance *atom;
    int x, y;

    x = event->xbutton.x;
    y = event->xbutton.y;
    atom = pickScene(mol, x, y);

    updatePickInfo(atom);
  }

  void
  activateMenu(Widget w, XtPointer clientData, XEvent *event,
    Boolean *cont)
```

```
{
  if(overlayVisual) {
    /* Ensure that overlay popup menu's colormap is installed. */
    XInstallColormap(dpy, overlayColormap);
  }
  XmMenuPosition(popup, &event->xbutton);
  XtManageChild(popup);
}

static char *glxareaTranslations =
  "#override\n\
  <Btn1Down>:startRotation()\n\
  <Btn1Motion>:rotation()\n\
  <Btn2Down>:doPick()\n";

void
draw(Widget w, XtPointer data, XtPointer callData)
{
  postRedisplay();
}

void
resize(Widget w, XtPointer data, XtPointer callData)
{
  GLwDrawingAreaCallbackStruct *resize =
    (GLwDrawingAreaCallbackStruct*) callData;

  if (madeCurrent) {
    viewWidth = resize->width;
    viewHeight = resize->height;
    glXMakeCurrent(dpy, glxwin, cx);
    glXWaitX();
    renderReshape(viewWidth, viewHeight);
  }
}

void
fileBoxOk(Widget w, XtPointer data, XtPointer callData)
{
  XmFileSelectionBoxCallbackStruct *info =
    (XmFileSelectionBoxCallbackStruct *) callData;
  char *filename, *error;

  XmStringGetLtoR(info->value, XmSTRING_DEFAULT_CHARSET, &filename);
  error = fileLoadMolecule(filename, &mol);
```

```
      if (filename)
        XtFree(filename);
      if (error) {
        XmString text;

        if (!dialog) {
          dialog = XmCreateErrorDialog(w, "error", NULL, 0);
          XtUnmanageChild(XmMessageBoxGetChild(dialog,
            XmDIALOG_CANCEL_BUTTON));
          XtUnmanageChild(XmMessageBoxGetChild(dialog,
            XmDIALOG_HELP_BUTTON));
        }
        text = XmStringCreateSimple(error);
        XtVaSetValues(dialog, XmNmessageString, text, NULL);
        XmStringFree(text);
        XtManageChild(dialog);
        XtPopup(XtParent(dialog), XtGrabNone);
        return;
      }
      XtPopdown(XtParent(w));
      if (dialog)
        XtPopdown(XtParent(dialog));

      /* Delay setting up user interaction translation until there
         is data to interact with. */
      if (trans == NULL) {
        trans = XtParseTranslationTable(glxareaTranslations);
        XtOverrideTranslations(glxarea, trans);
      }

      updatePickInfo(NULL);
      postRedisplay();
    }

    void
    fileboxCancel(Widget w, XtPointer data, XtPointer callData)
    {
      XtPopdown(XtParent(w));
      if (dialog)
        XtPopdown(XtParent(dialog));
    }

    void
    openMolecule(Widget w, XtPointer data, XtPointer callData)
```

```
{
  static Widget filebox = NULL;
  Widget button;
  Arg args[1];

  if (filebox == NULL) {
    XtSetArg(args[0], XmNpattern, XmStringCreate("*.mol",
      XmSTRING_DEFAULT_CHARSET));
    filebox = XmCreateFileSelectionDialog(toplevel, "filebox",
      args, 1);
    XtAddCallback(filebox, XmNcancelCallback, fileboxCancel, 0);
    XtAddCallback(filebox, XmNokCallback, fileBoxOk, 0);
    /* Remove help button. */
    button = XmFileSelectionBoxGetChild(filebox,
      XmDIALOG_HELP_BUTTON);
    XtUnmanageChild(button);
  }
  XtManageChild(filebox);
  XtPopup(XtParent(filebox), XtGrabNone);
}

void
quit(Widget w, XtPointer data, XtPointer callData)
{
  exit(0);
}

void
swap(void)
{
  glXSwapBuffers(dpy, glxwin);
}

void
init(Widget w, XtPointer data, XtPointer callData)
{
  glxwin = XtWindow(w);
  glXMakeCurrent(XtDisplay(w), XtWindow(w), cx);
  renderInit();
  renderReshape(viewWidth, viewHeight);
}

void
processMenuUse(Widget w, XtPointer clientData, XtPointer callData)
```

```
{
  int button = (int) clientData;
    switch (button) {
    case 0:
      glPolygonMode(GL_FRONT_AND_BACK, GL_FILL);
      break;
    case 1:
      glPolygonMode(GL_FRONT_AND_BACK, GL_LINE);
      break;
    case 2:
      momentum = 1 - momentum;
      stopSpinning();
      break;
    case 3:
      autoHiRes = 1 - autoHiRes;
      if(autoHiRes && !spinning)
        makeHiRes();
      else
        makeLoRes();
      break;
    }
    postRedisplay();
}

void
ensurePulldownColormapInstalled(Widget w, XtPointer clientData,
  XtPointer callData)
{
  /* Ensure that overlay pulldown menu's colormap is installed. */
  XInstallColormap(dpy, overlayColormap);
}

void mapStateChanged(Widget w, XtPointer data, XEvent * event,
  Boolean * cont)
{
    switch (event->type) {
    case MapNotify:
      if (spinning) animateID = XtAppAddTimeOut(app, 1, animate, 0);
      break;
    case UnmapNotify:
      if (spinning) XtRemoveTimeOut(animateID);
      break;
    }
}
```

Obtaining GLUT, Mesa, and the Book's OpenGL Example Code

A.1 GLUT AND THE BOOK'S EXAMPLE CODE

The source code discussed in this book is available via ftp (file transfer protocol) using the Internet. If you have access to the Internet, you can use ftp to retrieve the source code.

First use your system's `ftp` command to go to the host `ftp.sgi.com`. Specify anonymous as your user name and your electronic mail address as the password. Then type the following:

```
cd pub/opengl/opengl_for_x
binary
get glut.tar.Z
get xlib-examples.tar.Z
get motif-examples.tar.Z
bye
```

Or, using the World Wide Web, you retrieve these same files by accessing the World Wide Web URL:

```
ftp://ftp.sgi.com/pub/opengl/opengl_for_x/
```

The files you will retrieve are compressed Unix `tar` files. Assuming you are using a Unix workstation, unpack the files like this:

```
uncompress glut.tar.Z
tar xvf glut.tar
```

The files and subdirectories in each compressed Unix `tar` file are extracted as subdirectories from wherever your current directory is.

The sample code is divided up among the three compressed Unix tar files named above. The contents of the files are

> `glut.tar.Z` The OpenGL Utility Toolkit source code distribution as described in Chapters 4 and 5 and Appendices B and C. The distribution contains source code for the GLUT library, example GLUT programs, test GLUT programs, and GLUT documentation.
>
> `xlib-examples.tar.Z` The Xlib-based OpenGL examples found in Chapters 1, 2, and 6.
>
> `motif-examples.tar.Z` The Motif-based OpenGL examples discussed in Chapters 3, 6, and 7.

Instructions explaining how to build the code are included with each distribution. Look for the file called README.

These same files can also be retrieved from the Addison-Wesley ftp server. Look on the aw.com ftp server in the `TCB/authors/kilgard` subdirectory for the same files described above. Or, using the World Wide Web, retrieve the files by accessing this URL:

```
ftp://aw.com/TCB/authors/kilgard
```

A.2 OBTAINING MESA

If your machine does not support OpenGL, you can use the freely available Mesa library that implements the OpenGL API. Mesa was written by Brian Paul at the University of Wisconsin. Mesa is distributed via the Internet with the GNU Public License. Because Mesa is not a licensed OpenGL implementation and has not passed the OpenGL conformance suite, it cannot be officially called "OpenGL."

Information about Mesa can be retrieved using the following World Wide Web URL:

```
http://www.ssec.wisc.edu/~brianp/Mesa.html
```

To join the Mesa mailing list, send electronic mail to `listproc@iqm.unicamp.br` with a message body reading:

```
subs mesa (your name)
```

For example:

```
subs mesa Jane Doe
```

You will receive a welcome message from the mailing list server that tells you how to post messages to the list.

Functional Description of the GLUT API

This appendix describes version 3 of the GLUT programming interface. Routines are grouped according to functionality.

B.1 INITIALIZATION

Routines beginning with the `glutInit-` prefix are used to initialize GLUT state. The primary initialization routine is `glutInit`, which should only be called exactly once in a GLUT program. No non- `glutInit-` prefixed GLUT or OpenGL routines should be called before `glutInit`.

The other `glutInit-` routines may be called before `glutInit`. The reason is that these routines can be used to set default window initialization state that might be modified by the command processing done in `glutInit`. For example, `glutInitWindowSize(400, 400)` can be called before `glutInit` to indicate that 400 by 400 is the program's default window size. Setting the *initial window size* or *position* before `glutInit` allows the GLUT program user to specify the initial size or position using command line arguments.

B.1.1 `glutInit`

`glutInit` is used to initialize the GLUT library.

B.1.1.1 Usage

```
void glutInit(int *argcp, char **argv);
```

> argcp A pointer to the program's *unmodified* argc variable from main. Upon return, the value pointed to by argcp will be updated, because glutInit extracts any command line options intended for the GLUT library.
>
> argv The program's *unmodified* argv variable from main. As with argcp, the data for argv will be updated because glutInit extracts any command line options understood by the GLUT library.

B.1.1.2 Description

glutInit will initialize the GLUT library and negotiate a session with the window system. During this process, glutInit may cause the termination of the GLUT program with an error message to the user if GLUT cannot be properly initialized. Examples of this situation include failure to connect to the window system, lack of window system support for OpenGL, and invalid command line options.

glutInit also processes command line options, but the options parsed are window system dependent.

B.1.1.3 X Implementation Notes

The X Window System–specific options parsed by glutInit are as follows:

> -display *DISPLAY* Specify the X server to connect to. If this is not specified, the value of the DISPLAY environment variable is used.
>
> -geometry *WxH+X+Y* Determines where windows should be created on the screen. The parameter following -geometry should be formatted as a standard X geometry specification. The effect of using this option is to change the GLUT *initial size* and *initial position* just as if glutInitWindowSize or glutInitWindowPosition were called directly.
>
> -iconic Requests that all top-level windows be created in an iconic state.
>
> -indirect Forces the use of *indirect* OpenGL rendering contexts.
>
> -direct Forces the use of *direct* OpenGL rendering contexts (not all GLX implementations support direct rendering contexts). A fatal error is generated if direct rendering is not supported by the OpenGL implementation.
>
> If neither -indirect or -direct is used to force a particular behavior, GLUT will attempt to use direct rendering if possible, and otherwise will fall back to indirect rendering.
>
> -gldebug After processing callbacks and/or events, find out whether there are any OpenGL errors by calling glGetError. If an error is reported, print out a warning by looking up the error code with gluErrorString. Using this option is helpful in detecting runtime errors.

`-sync` Enables synchronous X protocol transactions. This option makes it easier to track down potential X protocol errors.

B.1.2 `glutInitWindowPosition, glutInitWindowSize`

`glutInitWindowPosition` and `glutInitWindowSize` set the *initial window position* and *size*, respectively.

B.1.2.1 Usage

```
void glutInitWindowSize(int width, int height);
void glutInitWindowPosition(int x, int y);
```

   `width` Width in pixels.

   `height` Height in pixels.

   x Window X location in pixels.

   y Window Y location in pixels.

B.1.2.2 Description

It will be requested that windows created by `glutCreateWindow` be created with the current *initial window position* and size.

   The initial value of the initial window position GLUT state is –1 and –1. If either the *x* or *y* component to the *initial window position* is negative, the actual window position is left to the window system to determine. The initial value of the *initial window size* GLUT state is 300 x 300. The *initial window size* components must be greater than 0.

   The intent of the *initial window position* and *size* values is to provide a suggestion to the window system for a window's initial size and position. The window system is not obligated to use this information. Therefore, GLUT programs should not assume the window was created at the specified size or position. A GLUT program should use the window's reshape callback to determine the true size of the window.

B.1.3 `glutInitDisplayMode`

`glutInitDisplayMode` sets the *initial display mode*.

B.1.3.1 Usage

```
void glutInitDisplayMode(unsigned int mode);
```

   `mode` Display mode, normally the bitwise *or*-ing of GLUT display mode bitmasks. See values below:

GLUT_RGBA   Bitmask to select an RGBA mode window. This is the default if neither GLUT_RGBA nor GLUT_INDEX is specified.

GLUT_RGB   An alias for GLUT_RGBA.

GLUT_INDEX   Bitmask to select a color index mode window. This overrides GLUT_RGBA if it is also specified.

GLUT_SINGLE   Bitmask to select a single-buffered window. This is the default if neither GLUT_DOUBLE nor GLUT_SINGLE is specified.

GLUT_DOUBLE   Bitmask to select a double-buffered window. This overrides GLUT_SINGLE if it is also specified.

GLUT_ACCUM   Bitmask to select a window with an accumulation buffer.

GLUT_ALPHA   Bitmask to select a window with an alpha component to the color buffer(s).

GLUT_DEPTH   Bitmask to select a window with a depth buffer.

GLUT_STENCIL   Bitmask to select a window with a stencil buffer.

GLUT_MULTISAMPLE   Bitmask to select a window with multisampling support. If multisampling is not available, a non-multisampling window will automatically be chosen. **Note:** both the OpenGL client-side and server-side implementations must support the GLX_SAMPLE_SGIS extension for multisampling to be available.

GLUT_STEREO   Bitmask to select a stereo window.

B.1.3.2   Description

The *initial display mode* is used when creating top-level windows, subwindows, and overlays to determine the OpenGL display mode for the to-be-created window or overlay.

Note that GLUT_RGBA selects the RGBA color model, but it does not request that any bits of alpha (sometimes called an *alpha buffer* or *destination alpha*) be allocated. To request alpha, specify GLUT_ALPHA.

B.2   BEGINNING EVENT PROCESSING

After a GLUT program has done initial setup, such as creating windows and menus, GLUT programs enter the GLUT event processing loop by calling glutMainLoop.

B.2.1 `glutMainLoop`

`glutMainLoop` enters the GLUT event processing loop.

B.2.1.1 Usage

```
void glutMainLoop(void);
```

B.2.1.2 Description

`glutMainLoop` enters the GLUT event processing loop. This routine should be called at most once in a GLUT program. Once called, this routine will never return. It will call, as necessary, any callbacks that have been registered.

B.3   WINDOW MANAGEMENT

GLUT supports two types of windows: top-level windows and subwindows. Both types support OpenGL rendering and GLUT callbacks. There is a single identifier space for both types of windows.

B.3.1 `glutCreateWindow`

`glutCreateWindow` creates a top-level window.

B.3.1.1 Usage

```
int glutCreateWindow(char *name);
```

> name   ASCII character string for use as window name.

B.3.1.2 Description

`glutCreateWindow` creates a top-level window. name will be provided to the window system as the window's name. The intent is that the window system will label the window with name.

Implicitly, the *current window* is set to the newly created window.

Each created window has a unique associated OpenGL context. State changes to a window's associated OpenGL context can be made immediately after the window is created.

The *display state* of a window is initially for the window to be shown. But the window's display state is not actually acted upon until `glutMainLoop` is entered. This means that until `glutMainLoop` is called, rendering to a created window has no effect, because the window cannot yet be displayed.

The value returned is a unique small-integer identifier for the window. The range of allocated identifiers starts at 1. This window identifier can be used when calling `glutSetWindow`.

B.3.1.3 X Implementation Notes

The proper X Inter-Client Communication Conventions Manual (ICCCM) top-level properties are established. The `WM_COMMAND` property, which lists the command line used to invoke the GLUT program, is established only for the first window created.

B.3.2 `glutCreateSubWindow`

`glutCreateSubWindow` creates a subwindow.

B.3.2.1 Usage

```
int glutCreateSubWindow(int win,
   int x, int y, int width, int height);
```

> win   Identifier of the subwindow's parent window.
>
> x   Window *X* location in pixels relative to parent window's origin.
>
> y   Window *Y* location in pixels relative to parent window's origin.
>
> width   Width in pixels.
>
> height   Height in pixels.

B.3.2.2 Description

`glutCreateSubWindow` creates a subwindow of the window identified by `win`, of size `width` and `height` at location `x` and `y` within the *current window*. Implicitly, the current window is set to the newly created subwindow.

Each created window has a unique associated OpenGL context. State changes to a window's associated OpenGL context can be made immediately after the window is created.

The *display state* of a window is initially for the window to be shown. But the window's display state is not actually acted upon until `glutMainLoop` is entered. This means that until `glutMainLoop` is called, rendering to a created window has no effect. Subwindows can not be iconified.

Subwindows can be nested arbitrarily deep.

The value returned is a unique small-integer identifier for the window. The range of allocated identifiers starts at 1.

B.3.3 `glutSetWindow`, `glutGetWindow`

`glutSetWindow` sets the *current window*; `glutGetWindow` returns the identifier of the *current window*.

B.3.3.1 Usage

```
void glutSetWindow(int win);
int glutGetWindow(void);
```

> win   Identifier of GLUT window to make the current window.

B.3.3.2 Description

`glutSetWindow` sets the current window; `glutGetWindow` returns the identifier of the current window. If no windows exist or the previously current window was destroyed, `glutGetWindow` returns 0. `glutSetWindow` does *not* change the *layer in use* for the window; this is done using `glutUseLayer`.

B.3.4 `glutDestroyWindow`

`glutDestroyWindow` destroys the specified window.

B.3.4.1 Usage

```
void glutDestroyWindow(int win);
```

> win   Identifier of GLUT window to destroy.

B.3.4.2 Description

`glutDestroyWindow` destroys the window specified by win and the window's associated OpenGL context, logical colormap (if the window is color index), and overlay and related state (if an overlay has been established). Any subwindows of destroyed windows are also destroyed by `glutDestroyWindow`. If win was the *current window*, the *current window* becomes invalid (`glutGetWindow` will return 0).

B.3.5 `glutPostRedisplay`

`glutPostRedisplay` marks the *current window* as needing to be redisplayed.

B.3.5.1 Usage

```
void glutPostRedisplay(void);
```

B.3.5.2 Description

Mark the normal plane of the *current window* as needing to be redisplayed. During the next iteration through `glutMainLoop`, the window's display callback will be called to redisplay the window's normal plane. Multiple calls to `glutPostRedisplay` before the next display callback opportunity generate only a single redisplay callback. `glutPostRedisplay` may be called within a window's display or overlay display callback to re-mark that window for redisplay.

Logically, normal plane damage notification for a window is treated as a `glut-PostRedisplay` on the damaged window. Unlike damage reported by the window system, `glutPostRedisplay` will *not* set to true the normal plane's damaged status, returned by `glutLayerGet(GLUT_NORMAL_DAMAGED)`.

Also, see `glutPostOverlayRedisplay`.

B.3.6 `glutSwapBuffers`

`glutSwapBuffers` swaps the buffers of the current window if it is double-buffered.

B.3.6.1 Usage

```
void glutSwapBuffers(void);
```

B.3.6.2 Description

Performs a buffer swap on the *layer in use* for the *current window*. Specifically, `glutSwapBuffers` promotes the contents of the back buffer of the layer in use of the *current window* to become the contents of the front buffer. The contents of the back buffer then become undefined. The update typically takes place during the vertical retrace of the monitor, rather than immediately after `glutSwapBuffers` is called.

An implicit `glFlush` is done by `glutSwapBuffers` before it returns. Subsequent OpenGL commands can be issued immediately after calling `glutSwapBuffers`, but are not executed until the buffer exchange is completed.

If the layer in use is not double-buffered, `glutSwapBuffers` has no effect.

B.3.7 `glutPositionWindow`

`glutPositionWindow` requests a change to the position of the *current window*.

B.3.7.1 Usage

```
void glutPositionWindow(int x, int y);
```

x New *x* location of window in pixels.

y New *y* location of window in pixels.

B.3.7.2 Description

`glutPositionWindow` requests a change in the position of the *current window*. For top-level windows, the x and y parameters are pixel offsets from the screen origin. For subwindows, the x and y parameters are pixel offsets from the window's parent window origin.

A request by `glutPositionWindow` is not processed immediately. The request is executed after returning to the main event loop. This allows multiple `glutPositionWindow`, `glutReshapeWindow`, and `glutFullScreen` requests to the same window to be coalesced.

In the case of top-level windows, a `glutPositionWindow` call is considered only a request for positioning the window. The window system is free to apply its own policies to top-level window placement. The intent is that top-level windows should be repositioned according to `glutPositionWindow`'s parameters.

`glutPositionWindow` disables the full-screen status of a window if it has previously been enabled.

B.3.8 `glutReshapeWindow`

`glutReshapeWindow` requests a change to the size of the *current window*.

B.3.8.1 Usage

```
void glutReshapeWindow(int width, int height);
```

width   New width of window in pixels.

height   New height of window in pixels.

B.3.8.2 Description

`glutReshapeWindow` requests a change in the size of the *current window*. The `width` and `height` parameters are size extents in pixels. `width` and `height` must be positive values.

A request by `glutReshapeWindow` is not processed immediately. The request is executed after returning to the main event loop. This allows multiple `glutReshapeWindow`, `glutPositionWindow`, and `glutFullScreen` requests to the same window to be coalesced.

In the case of top-level windows, a `glutReshapeWindow` call is considered only a request for sizing the window. The window system is free to apply its own policies to top-level window sizing. The intent is that top-level windows should be reshaped according to `glutReshapeWindow`'s parameters. Whether a reshape actually takes effect and, if so, the reshaped dimensions are reported to the program by a reshape callback.

`glutReshapeWindow` disables the full-screen status of a window if it has previously been enabled.

B.3.9 `glutFullScreen`

`glutFullScreen` requests that the *current window* be made full-screen.

B.3.9.1 Usage

```
void glutFullScreen(void);
```

D.3.9.2   Description

`glutFullScreen` requests that the *current window* be made full-screen. The exact semantics of what full-screen means may vary according to the window system. The intent is to make the window as large as possible and disable any window decorations or borders added by the window system. The window width and height are not guaranteed to be the same as the screen width and height, but that is the intent of making a window full-screen.

`glutFullScreen` is defined to work only on top-level windows.

A `glutFullScreen` request is not processed immediately. The request is executed after returning to the main event loop. This allows multiple `glut-ReshapeWindow`, `glutPositionWindow`, and `glutFullScreen` requests to the same window to be coalesced.

Subsequent `glutReshapeWindow` and `glutPositionWindow` requests on the window will disable the full-screen status of the window.

D.3.9.3   X Implementation Notes

In the X implementation of GLUT, full-screen is implemented by sizing and positioning the window to cover the entire screen and posting the `_MOTIF_WM_HINTS` property on the window, requesting absolutely no decorations. Non-Motif window managers may not respond to `_MOTIF_WM_HINTS`.

D.3.10   `glutPopWindow`, `glutPushWindow`

`glutPopWindow` and `glutPushWindow` change the stacking order of the *current window* relative to its siblings.

D.3.10.1   Usage

```
void glutPopWindow(void);
void glutPushWindow(void);
```

D.3.10.2   Description

`glutPopWindow` and `glutPushWindow` work on both top-level windows and subwindows. The effect of pushing and popping windows does not take place immediately. Instead, the push or pop is saved for execution on return to the GLUT event loop. A subsequent push or pop requests on a window replaces the previously saved request for that window. The effect of pushing and popping top-level windows is subject to the window system's policy for restacking windows.

D.3.11   `glutShowWindow`, `glutHideWindow`, `glutIconifyWindow`

`glutShowWindow`, `glutHideWindow`, and `glutIconifyWindow` change the display status of the *current window*.

B.3.11.1 Usage

```
void glutShowWindow(void);
void glutHideWindow(void);
void glutIconifyWindow(void);
```

B.3.11.2 Description

`glutShowWindow` will show the *current window* (though it still may not be visible if it is obscured by other shown windows). `glutHideWindow` will hide the *current window*. `glutIconifyWindow` will iconify a top-level window, but GLUT prohibits iconification of a subwindow. The effect of showing, hiding, and iconifying windows does not take place immediately. Instead, the requests are saved for execution on return to the GLUT event loop. Subsequent show, hide, or iconification requests on a window replace the previously saved request for that window. The effect of hiding, showing, or iconifying top-level windows is subject to the window system's policy for displaying windows.

B.3.12 `glutSetWindowTitle, glutSetIconTitle`

`glutSetWindowTitle` and `glutSetIconTitle` change the window or icon title, respectively, of the current top-level window.

B.3.12.1 Usage

```
void glutSetWindowTitle(char *name);
void glutSetIconTitle (char *name);
```

> name   ASCII character string for the window or icon name to be set for the window.

B.3.12.2 Description

These routines should be called only when the *current window* is a top-level window. On creation of a top-level window, the window and icon names are determined by the `name` parameter of `glutCreateWindow`. Once the window is created, `glutSetWindowTitle` and `glutSetIconTitle` can change the window and icon names, respectively, of top-level windows. Each call requests that the window system change the title appropriately. Requests are not buffered or coalesced. The policy by which the window and icon name are displayed is window system dependent.

B.3.13 `glutSetCursor`

`glutSetCursor` changes the cursor image of the *current window*.

B.3.13.1 Usage

```
void glutSetCursor(int cursor);
```

cursor   Name of cursor image to change to.

GLUT_CURSOR_RIGHT_ARROW   Arrow pointing up and to the right.

GLUT_CURSOR_LEFT_ARROW   Arrow pointing up and to the left.

GLUT_CURSOR_INFO   Pointing hand.

GLUT_CURSOR_DESTROY   Skull and crossbones.

GLUT_CURSOR_HELP   Question mark.

GLUT_CURSOR_CYCLE   Arrows rotating in a circle.

GLUT_CURSOR_SPRAY   Spray can.

GLUT_CURSOR_WAIT   Wristwatch.

GLUT_CURSOR_TEXT   Insertion point cursor for text.

GLUT_CURSOR_CROSSHAIR   Simple crosshair.

GLUT_CURSOR_UP_DOWN   Bidirectional pointing up and down.

GLUT_CURSOR_LEFT_RIGHT   Bidirectional pointing left and right.

GLUT_CURSOR_TOP_SIDE   Arrow pointing to top side.

GLUT_CURSOR_BOTTOM_SIDE   Arrow pointing to bottom side.

GLUT_CURSOR_LEFT_SIDE   Arrow pointing to left side.

GLUT_CURSOR_RIGHT_SIDE   Arrow pointing to right side.

GLUT_CURSOR_TOP_LEFT_CORNER   Arrow pointing to top left corner.

GLUT_CURSOR_TOP_RIGHT_CORNER   Arrow pointing to top right corner.

GLUT_CURSOR_BOTTOM_RIGHT_CORNER   Arrow pointing to bottom right corner.

GLUT_CURSOR_BOTTOM_LEFT_CORNER   Arrow pointing to bottom left corner.

GLUT_CURSOR_FULL_CROSSHAIR   Full-screen crosshair cursor (if possible, otherwise GLUT_CURSOR_CROSSHAIR).

GLUT_CURSOR_NONE   Invisible cursor.

GLUT_CURSOR_INHERIT   Use parent's cursor.

B.3.13.2   Description

glutSetCursor changes the cursor image of the *current window*. Each call requests that the window system change the cursor appropriately. The cursor image when a window is created is GLUT_CURSOR_INHERIT. The exact cursor images used are implementation-dependent. The intent is for the image to convey the meaning of the cursor name. For a top-level window, GLUT_CURSOR_INHERIT uses the default window system cursor.

B.3.13.3   X Implementation Notes

GLUT for X uses Silicon Graphics's _SGI_CROSSHAIR_CURSOR convention [23] to access a full-screen crosshair cursor if possible.

B.4 OVERLAY MANAGEMENT

When overlay hardware is available, GLUT provides a set of routines for establishing, using, and removing an overlay for GLUT windows. When an overlay is established, a separate OpenGL context is also established. A window's overlay OpenGL state is kept distinct from the normal plane's OpenGL state.

B.4.1 `glutEstablishOverlay`

`glutEstablishOverlay` establishes an overlay (if possible) for the *current window*.

B.4.1.1 Usage

```
void glutEstablishOverlay(void);
```

B.4.1.2 Description

`glutEstablishOverlay` establishes an overlay (if possible) for the *current window*. The requested display mode for the overlay is determined by the *initial display mode*. `glutLayerGet(GLUT_OVERLAY_POSSIBLE)` can be called to determine whether an overlay is possible for the *current window* with the current *initial display mode*. Do not attempt to establish an overlay when one is not possible; GLUT will terminate the program.

If `glutEstablishOverlay` is called when an overlay already exists, the existing overlay is first removed and then a new overlay is established. The state of the old overlay's OpenGL context is discarded.

The initial display state of an overlay is shown; however, the overlay is actually shown only if the overlay's window is shown.

Implicitly, the window's *layer in use* changes to the overlay immediately after the overlay is established.

B.4.1.3 X Implementation Notes

GLUT for X uses the `SERVER_OVERLAY_VISUALS` convention to determine whether overlay visuals are available. While the convention allows for opaque overlays (no transparency) and overlays with the transparency specified as a bitmask, GLUT overlay management provides access only to transparent pixel overlays.

Until RGBA overlays are better understood, GLUT supports only color index overlays.

B.4.2 `glutUseLayer`

`glutUseLayer` changes the *layer in use* for the *current window*.

B.4.2.1 Usage

```
void glutUseLayer(GLenum layer);
```

layer   Either GLUT_NORMAL or GLUT_OVERLAY, selecting the normal plane or overlay, respectively.

B.4.2.2 Description

glutUseLayer changes the per-window layer in use for the *current window*, selecting either the normal plane or the overlay. The overlay should be specified only if an overlay exists; however, windows without an overlay may still call glutUse-Layer(GLUT_NORMAL). OpenGL commands for the window are directed to the current layer in use.

To query the layer in use for a window, call glutLayerGet(GLUT_LAYER_IN_USE).

B.4.3   glutRemoveOverlay

glutRemoveOverlay removes the overlay (if one exists) from the *current window*.

B.4.3.1 Usage

void glutRemoveOverlay(void);

B.4.3.2 Description

glutRemoveOverlay removes the overlay (if one exists). It is safe to call glutRemove-Overlay even if no overlay is currently established—it does nothing in this case. Implicitly, the window's *layer in use* changes to the normal plane immediately once the overlay is removed.

If the program intends to reestablish the overlay later, it is typically faster and less resource-intensive to use glutHideOverlay and glutShowOverlay to change the display status of the overlay.

B.4.4   glutPostOverlayRedisplay

glutPostOverlayRedisplay marks the overlay of the *current window* as needing to be redisplayed.

B.4.4.1 Usage

void glutPostOverlayRedisplay(void);

B.4.4.2 Description

Mark the overlay of the *current window* as needing to be redisplayed. The next iteration through glutMainLoop, the window's overlay display callback (or simply the display callback, if no overlay display callback is registered) will be called to redisplay the window's overlay plane. Multiple calls to glutPostOverlayRedisplay before the next display callback opportunity, (or overlay display callback opportunity, if one is registered) generate only a single redisplay. glutPostOverlay-

`Redisplay` may be called within a window's display or overlay display callback to re-mark that window for redisplay.

Logically, overlay damage notification for a window is treated as a `glutPost-OverlayRedisplay` on the damaged window. Unlike cases in which damage is reported by the window system, `glutPostOverlayRedisplay` will not set to true the overlay's damaged status, returned by `glutLayerGet(GLUT_OVERLAY_DAMAGED)`.

Also, see `glutPostRedisplay`.

B.4.5 `glutShowOverlay`, `glutHideOverlay`

`glutShowOverlay` shows the overlay of the *current window*; `glutHideOverlay` hides the overlay.

B.4.5.1 Usage
```
void glutShowOverlay(void);
void glutHideOverlay(void);
```

B.4.5.2 Description
`glutShowOverlay` shows the overlay of the *current window*; `glutHideOverlay` hides the overlay. The effect of showing or hiding an overlay takes place immediately. Note that `glutShowOverlay` will not actually display the overlay unless the window is also shown (and even a shown window may be obscured by other windows, thereby obscuring the overlay). It is typically faster and less resource-intensive to use these routines to control the display status of an overlay than to remove and re-establish the overlay.

B.5 MENU MANAGEMENT

GLUT supports simple cascading pop-up menus. They are designed to let a user select various modes within a program. The functionality is simple and minimalistic and is meant to be that way. Do not mistake GLUT's pop-up menu facility for an attempt to create a full-featured user interface.

It is illegal to create or destroy menus, or to change, add, or remove menu items while a menu (and any cascaded submenus) are in use (that is, popped up).

B.5.1 `glutCreateMenu`

`glutCreateMenu` creates a new pop-up menu.

B.5.1.1 Usage
```
int glutCreateMenu(void (*func)(int value));
```

func The callback function for the menu that is called when a menu entry from the menu is selected. The value passed to the callback is determined by the value for the selected menu entry.

D.5.1.2 Description

glutCreateMenu creates a new pop-up menu and returns a unique small-integer identifier. The range of allocated identifiers starts at 1. The menu identifier range is separate from the window identifier range. Implicitly, the *current menu* is set to the newly created menu. This menu identifier can be used when you are calling glut-SetMenu.

When the menu callback is called because a menu entry is selected for the menu, the *current menu* will be implicitly set to the menu with the selected entry before the callback is made.

D.5.1.3 X Implementation Notes

If available, GLUT for X will take advantage of overlay planes for implementing pop-up menus. The use of overlay planes can eliminate display callbacks when pop-up menus are deactivated. The SERVER_OVERLAY_VISUALS convention is used to determine whether overlay visuals are available.

D.5.2 glutSetMenu, glutGetMenu

glutSetMenu sets the *current menu*; glutGetMenu returns the identifier of the *current menu*.

D.5.2.1 Usage

```
void glutSetMenu(int menu);
int glutGetMenu(void);
```

menu   The identifier of the menu to make the current menu.

D.5.2.2 Description

glutSetMenu sets the *current menu*; glutGetMenu returns the identifier of the *current menu*. If no menus exist or the previous *current menu* was destroyed, glut-GetMenu returns 0.

D.5.3 glutDestroyMenu

glutDestroyMenu destroys the specified menu.

D.5.3.1 Usage

```
void glutDestroyMenu(int menu);
```

menu   The identifier of the menu to destroy.

B.5.3.2 Description

`glutDestroyMenu` destroys the specified menu by menu. If menu was the *current menu,* the *current menu* becomes invalid and will return 0.

B.5.4 `glutAddMenuEntry`

`glutAddMenuEntry` adds a menu entry to the bottom of the *current menu.*

B.5.4.1 Usage

`void glutAddMenuEntry(char *name, int value);`

> name   ASCII character string to display in the menu entry.
>
> value   Value to return to the menu's callback function if the menu entry is selected.

B.5.4.2 Description

`glutAddMenuEntry` adds a menu entry to the bottom of the *current menu.* The string `name` will be displayed for the newly added menu entry. If the menu entry is selected by the user, the menu's callback will be called, passing `value` as the callback's parameter.

B.5.5 `glutAddSubMenu`

`glutAddSubMenu` adds a submenu trigger to the bottom of the *current menu.*

B.5.5.1 Usage

`void glutAddSubMenu(char *name, int menu);`

> name   ASCII character string to display in the menu item from which to cascade the submenu.
>
> menu   Identifier of the menu to cascade from this submenu menu item.

B.5.5.2 Description

`glutAddSubMenu` adds a submenu trigger to the bottom of the *current menu.* The string `name` will be displayed for the newly added submenu trigger. If the submenu trigger is entered, the submenu numbered `menu` will be cascaded, allowing submenu menu items to be selected.

B.5.6 `glutChangeToMenuEntry`

`glutChangeToMenuEntry` changes the specified menu item in the *current menu* into a menu entry.

B.5.6.1 Usage

```
void glutChangeToMenuEntry(int entry, char *name, int value);
```

> entry Index into the menu items of the *current menu* (1 is the topmost menu item).
>
> name ASCII character string to display in the menu entry.
>
> value Value to return to the menu's callback function if the menu entry is selected.

B.5.6.2 Description

glutChangeToMenuEntry changes the specified menu entry in the *current menu* into a menu entry. The entry parameter determines which menu item should be changed, with 1 being the topmost item. entry must be between 1 and glut-Get(GLUT_MENU_NUM_ITEMS) inclusive. The menu item to change need not already be a menu entry. The string name will be displayed for the newly changed menu entry. value will be returned to the menu's callback if this menu entry is selected.

B.5.7 glutChangeToSubMenu

glutChangeToSubMenu changes the specified menu item in the *current menu* into a submenu trigger.

B.5.7.1 Usage

```
void glutChangeToSubMenu(int entry, char *name, int menu);
```

> entry Index into the menu items of the *current menu* (1 is the topmost menu item).
>
> name ASCII character string to display in the menu item to cascade the submenu from.
>
> menu Identifier of the menu to cascade from this submenu menu item.

B.5.7.2 Description

glutChangeToSubMenu changes the specified menu item in the *current menu* into a submenu trigger. The entry parameter determines which menu item should be changed, with 1 being the topmost item. entry must be between 1 and glut-Get(GLUT_MENU_NUM_ITEMS) inclusive. The menu item to change need not be a submenu trigger. The string name will be displayed for the newly changed submenu trigger. The menu identifier names the submenu to cascade from the newly added submenu trigger.

B.5.8 glutRemoveMenuItem

glutRemoveMenuItem removes the specified menu item.

B.5.8.1 Usage
void glutRemoveMenuItem(int entry);

> entry   Index into the menu items of the *current menu* (1 is the topmost menu item).

B.5.8.2 Description
glutRemoveMenuItem removes the entry menu item, whether it is a menu entry or a submenu trigger. entry must be between 1 and glutGet(GLUT_MENU_NUM_ITEMS) inclusive. Menu items below the removed menu item are renumbered.

B.5.9 glutAttachMenu, glutDetachMenu

glutAttachMenu attaches a mouse button for the *current window* to the identifier of the *current menu*; glutDetachMenu detaches an attached mouse button from the *current window*.

B.5.9.1 Usage
void glutAttachMenu(int button);
void glutDetachMenu(int button);

> button   The button to attach or detach a menu,

B.5.9.2 Description
glutAttachMenu attaches a mouse button for the *current window* to the identifier of the *current menu*; glutDetachMenu detaches an attached mouse button from the *current window*. If a menu identifier is attached to a button, the named menu will be popped up when the user presses the specified button. button should be one of GLUT_LEFT_BUTTON, GLUT_MIDDLE_BUTTON, and GLUT_RIGHT_BUTTON. Note that the menu is attached to the button by identifier, not by reference.

B.6 CALLBACK REGISTRATION

GLUT supports a number of callbacks to respond to events. There are three types of callbacks: window, menu, and global. Window callbacks indicate when to redisplay or reshape a window, when the visibility of the window changes, and when input is available for the window. The menu callback is set by the glutCreateMenu call described earlier. The global callbacks manage the passing of time and menu use. The calling order of callbacks between different windows is undefined.

Callbacks for input events should be delivered to the window the event occurs in. Events should not propagate to parent windows.

B.6.0.1 X Implementation Notes
The X GLUT implementation uses the X Input extension [31, 32] to support sophisticated input devices: spaceball, dial-and-button box, and digitizing tablet.

Because the X Input extension does not mandate the ways particular types of devices are advertised through the extension, it is possible that GLUT for X will not correctly support input devices that would otherwise be of the correct type. The X GLUT implementation will support the Silicon Graphics spaceball, dial-and-button box, and digitizing tablet as advertised through the X Input extension.

B.6.1 `glutDisplayFunc`

`glutDisplayFunc` sets the display callback for the *current window*.

B.6.1.1 Usage

```
void glutDisplayFunc(void (*func)(void));
```

func   The new display callback function.

B.6.1.2 Description

`glutDisplayFunc` sets the display callback for the *current window*. When GLUT determines that the normal plane for the window that needs to be redisplayed, the display callback for the window is called. Before the callback, the *current window* is set to the window that needs to be redisplayed and (if no overlay display callback is registered) the *layer in use* is set to the normal plane. The display callback is called with no parameters. The entire normal plane region should be redisplayed in response to the callback (this includes ancillary buffers if your program depends on their state).

GLUT determines when the display callback should be triggered based on the window's redisplay state. The redisplay state for a window can be set either explicitly, by calling `glutPostRedisplay`, or implicitly, as the result of window damage reported by the window system. Multiple posted redisplays for a window are coalesced by GLUT to minimize the number of display callbacks called.

When an overlay is established for a window, but no overlay display callback is registered, the display callback is used for redisplaying *both* the overlay and the normal plane (that is, it will be called if either the redisplay state or the overlay redisplay state is set). In this case, the layer in use is *not* implicitly changed on entry to the display callback.

See `glutOverlayDisplayFunc` to understand how distinct callbacks for the overlay and normal plane of a window may be established.

When a window is created, no display callback exists for the window. It is the responsibility of the programmer to install a display callback for the window before the window is shown. A display callback *must* be registered for any window that is shown. If a window becomes displayed without a display callback's being registered, a fatal error occurs. Passing NULL to `glutDisplayFunc` is illegal as of GLUT 3.0; there is no way to "deregister" a display callback (though another callback routine can always be registered).

Upon return from the display callback, the *normal damaged* state of the window, returned by calling `glutLayerGet(GLUT_NORMAL_DAMAGED)`, is cleared. If no overlay display callback is registered, the *overlay damaged* state of the window, returned by calling `glutLayerGet(GLUT_OVERLAY_DAMAGED)`, is also cleared.

B.6.2   `glutOverlayDisplayFunc`

`glutOverlayDisplayFunc` sets the overlay display callback for the *current window.*

B.6.2.1   Usage

```
void glutOverlayDisplayFunc(void (*func)(void));
```

   func   The new overlay display callback function.

B.6.2.2   Description

`glutDisplayFunc` sets the overlay display callback for the *current window.* The overlay display callback is functionally the same as the window's display callback, except that the overlay display callback is used to redisplay the window's overlay.

When GLUT determines that the overlay plane for the window needs to be redisplayed, the overlay display callback for the window is called. Before the callback, the current window is set to the window that needs to be redisplayed and the *layer in use* is set to the overlay. The overlay display callback is called with no parameters. The entire overlay region should be redisplayed in response to the callback (this includes ancillary buffers if your program depends on their state).

GLUT determines when the overlay display callback should be triggered based on the window's overlay redisplay state. The overlay redisplay state for a window can be set either explicitly, by calling `glutPostOverlayRedisplay`, or implicitly, as the result of window damage reported by the window system. Multiple posted overlay redisplays for a window are coalesced by GLUT to minimize the number of overlay display callbacks called.

On return from the overlay display callback, the *overlay damaged* state of the window, returned by calling `glutLayerGet(GLUT_OVERLAY_DAMAGED)` is cleared.

The overlay display callback can be deregistered by passing NULL to `glut-OverlayDisplayFunc`. The overlay display callback is initially NULL when an overlay is established. See `glutDisplayFunc` to understand how the display callback alone is used if an overlay display callback is not registered.

B.6.3   `glutReshapeFunc`

`glutReshapeFunc`   sets the reshape callback for the current window.

B.6.3.1   Usage

```
void glutReshapeFunc(void (*func)(int width, int height));
```

   func   The new reshape callback function.

B.6.3.2 Description

glutReshapeFunc sets the reshape callback for the *current window*. The reshape callback is triggered when a window is reshaped. A reshape callback is also triggered immediately before a window's first display callback after the window is created or whenever an overlay for the window is established. The width and height parameters of the callback specify the new window size in pixels. Before the callback, the current window is set to the window that has been reshaped.

If a reshape callback is not registered for a window or NULL is passed to glutReshapeFunc (to deregister a previously registered callback), the default reshape callback is used. This default callback will simply call glViewport(0,0,width,height) on the normal plane (and on the overlay, if one exists).

If an overlay is established for the window, a single reshape callback is generated. It is the callback's responsibility to update both the normal plane and the overlay for the window (changing the layer in use as necessary).

When a top-level window is reshaped, subwindows are not reshaped. It is up to the GLUT program to manage the sizes and positions of subwindows within a top-level window. Still, reshape callbacks will be triggered for subwindows when their sizes are changed using glutReshapeWindow.

B.6.4 glutKeyboardFunc

glutKeyboardFunc sets the keyboard callback for the *current window*.

B.6.4.1 Usage

```
void glutKeyboardFunc(void (*func)(unsigned char key,
int x, int y));
```

func   The new keyboard callback function.

B.6.4.2 Description

glutKeyboardFunc sets the keyboard callback for the *current window*. When a user types into the window, each key press generating an ASCII character will generate a keyboard callback. The key callback parameter is the generated ASCII character. The state of modifier keys such as **Shift** cannot be determined directly; their only effect will be on the returned ASCII data. The x and y callback parameters indicate the mouse location, in window-relative coordinates, when the key was pressed. When a new window is created, no keyboard callback is initially registered, and ASCII keystrokes in the window are ignored. Passing NULL to glutKeyboardFunc disables the generation of keyboard callbacks.

During a keyboard callback, glutGetModifiers may be called to determine the state of modifier keys when the keystroke generating the callback occurred.

Also, see glutSpecialFunc for a means of detecting non-ASCII key strokes.

B.6.5 glutMouseFunc

glutMouseFunc   sets the mouse callback for the *current window*.

B.6.5.1 Usage

```
void glutMouseFunc(void (*func)(int button,
  int state, int x, int y));
```

func The new mouse callback function.

B.6.5.2 Description

glutMouseFunc sets the mouse callback for the *current window*. When a user presses and releases mouse buttons in the window, each press and each release generates a mouse callback. The button parameter is one of GLUT_LEFT_BUTTON, GLUT_MIDDLE_BUTTON, or GLUT_RIGHT_BUTTON. For systems with only two mouse buttons, it may not be possible to generate a GLUT_MIDDLE_BUTTON callback. For systems with a single mouse button, it may be possible to generate only a GLUT_LEFT_BUTTON callback. The state parameter is either GLUT_UP or GLUT_DOWN, indicating whether the callback resulted from a release or a press, respectively. The x and y callback parameters indicate the window-relative coordinates when the mouse button state changed. If a GLUT_DOWN callback for a specific button is triggered, the program can assume that a GLUT_UP callback for the same button will be generated (assuming the window still has a mouse callback registered) when the mouse button is released, even if the mouse has moved outside the window.

If a menu is attached to a button for a window, mouse callbacks will not be generated for that button.

During a mouse callback, glutGetModifiers may be called to determine the state of modifier keys when the mouse event generating the callback occurred.

Passing NULL to glutMouseFunc disables the generation of mouse callbacks.

B.6.6 glutMotionFunc, glutPassiveMotionFunc

glutMotionFunc and glutPassiveMotionFunc set the motion and passive motion callbacks respectively for the *current window*.

B.6.6.1 Usage

```
void glutMotionFunc(void (*func)(int x, int y));
void glutPassiveMotionFunc(void (*func)(int x, int y));
```

func The new motion or passive motion callback function.

B.6.6.2 Description

glutMotionFunc and glutPassiveMotionFunc set the motion and passive motion callbacks, respectively, for the *current window*. The motion callback for a window is called when the mouse moves within the window while one or more mouse buttons are pressed. The passive motion callback for a window is called when the mouse moves within the window while *no* mouse buttons are pressed.

The x and y callback parameters indicate the mouse location in window-relative coordinates.

Passing NULL to glutMotionFunc or glutPassiveMotionFunc disables the generation of the mouse or passive motion callback, respectively.

B.6.7 glutVisibilityFunc

glutVisibilityFunc sets the visibility callback for the *current window*.

B.6.7.1 Usage

```
void glutVisibilityFunc(void (*func)(int state));
```

func   The new visibility callback function.

B.6.7.2 Description

glutVisibilityFunc sets the visibility callback for the *current window*. The visibility callback for a window is called when the visibility of a window changes. The state callback parameter is either GLUT_NOT_VISIBLE or GLUT_VISIBLE, depending on the current visibility of the window. GLUT_VISIBLE does not distinguish between a window's being totally and partially visible. GLUT_NOT_VISIBLE means no part of the window is visible; that is, until the window's visibility changes, all further rendering to the window is discarded.

GLUT considers a window visible if any pixel of the window is visible *or* if any pixel of any descendant window is visible on the screen.

Passing NULL to glutVisibilityFunc disables the generation of the visibility callback.

If the visibility callback for a window is disabled and later reenabled, the visibility status of the window is undefined. Any change in window visibility will be reported; that is, if you disable a visibility callback and reenable the callback, you are guaranteed that the next visibility change will be reported.

B.6.8 glutEntryFunc

glutEntryFunc   sets the mouse enter/leave callback for the *current window*.

B.6.8.1 Usage

```
void glutEntryFunc(void (*func)(int state));
```

func   The new entry callback function.

B.6.8.2 Description

glutEntryFunc sets the mouse enter/leave callback for the *current window*. The state callback parameter is either GLUT_LEFT or GLUT_ENTERED, depending on whether the mouse pointer has last left or entered the window.

Passing NULL to glutEntryFunc disables the generation of the mouse enter/leave callback.

Some window systems may not generate accurate enter/leave callbacks.

B.6.8.3 X Implementation Notes

An X implementation of GLUT should generate accurate enter/leave callbacks.

B.6.9 `glutSpecialFunc`

`glutSpecialFunc` sets the special keyboard callback for the *current window*.

B.6.9.1 Usage

```
void glutSpecialFunc(void (*func)(int key, int x, int y));
```

  func   The new entry callback function.

B.6.9.2 Description

`glutSpecialFunc` sets the special keyboard callback for the *current window*. The special keyboard callback is triggered when keyboard function or directional keys are pressed. The key callback parameter is a GLUT_KEY_* constant for the special key pressed. The x and y callback parameters indicate the mouse in window-relative coordinates when the key was pressed. When a new window is created, no special callback is initially registered and special keystrokes in the window are ignored. Passing NULL to `glutSpecialFunc` disables the generation of special callbacks.

During a special callback, `glutGetModifiers` may be called to determine the state of modifier keys when the keystroke generating the callback occurred.

An implementation should do its best to provide ways to generate all the GLUT_KEY_* special keys. The available GLUT_KEY_* values are:

GLUT_KEY_F1	F1 key.
GLUT_KEY_F2	F2 key.
GLUT_KEY_F3	F3 key.
GLUT_KEY_F4	F4 key.
GLUT_KEY_F5	F5 key.
GLUT_KEY_F6	F6 key.
GLUT_KEY_F7	F7 key.
GLUT_KEY_F8	F8 key.
GLUT_Key_F9	F9 key.
GLUT_KEY_F10	F10 key.
GLUT_KEY_F11	F11 key.
GLUT_KEY_F12	F12 key.
GLUT_KEY_LEFT	Left directional key.

GLUT_KEY_UP   Up directional key.

GLUT_KEY_RIGHT   Right directional key.

GLUT_KEY_DOWN   Down directional key.

GLUT_KEY_PAGE_UP   **Page up** directional key.

GLUT_KEY_PAGE_DOWN   **Page down** directional key.

GLUT_KEY_HOME   **Home** directional key.

GLUT_KEY_END   **End** directional key.

GLUT_KEY_INSERT   **Ins** key.

Note that the escape, backspace, and delete keys are generated as ASCII characters.

B.6.10   glutSpaceballMotionFunc

glutSpaceballMotionFunc sets the spaceball motion callback for the *current window*.

B.6.10.1   Usage

void glutSpaceballMotionFunc(void (*func)(int x, int y, int z));

func   The new spaceball motion callback function.

B.6.10.2   Description

glutSpaceballMotionFunc sets the spaceball motion callback for the *current window*. The spaceball motion callback for a window is called when the window has spaceball input focus (normally, when the mouse is in the window) and the user generates spaceball translations. The x, y, and z callback parameters indicate the translations along the X, Y, and Z axes. The callback parameters are normalized to be within the range of –1000 to 1000 inclusive.

Registering a spaceball motion callback when a spaceball device is not available has no effect and is not an error. In this case, no spaceball motion callbacks will be generated.

Passing NULL to glutSpaceballMotionFunc disables the generation of spaceball motion callbacks. When a new window is created, no spaceball motion callback is initially registered.

B.6.11   glutSpaceballRotateFunc

glutSpaceballRotateFunc sets the spaceball rotation callback for the *current window*.

B.6.11.1 Usage

```
void glutSpaceballRotateFunc(void (*func)(int x, int y, int z));
```

> func   The new spaceball rotation callback function.

B.6.11.2 Description

glutSpaceballRotateFunc sets the spaceball rotate callback for the *current window*. The spaceball rotate callback for a window is called when the window has spaceball input focus (normally, when the mouse is in the window) and the user generates spaceball rotations. The x, y, and z callback parameters indicate the rotation along the X, Y, and Z axes. The callback parameters are normalized to be within the range of −1800 to 1800, inclusive.

Registering a spaceball rotate callback when a spaceball device is not available has no effect and is not an error. In this case, no spaceball rotate callbacks will be generated.

Passing NULL to glutSpaceballRotateFunc disables the generation of spaceball rotate callbacks. When a new window is created, no spaceball rotate callback is initially registered.

B.6.12 glutSpaceballButtonFunc

glutspaceballButtonFunc sets the spaceball button callback for the *current window*.

B.6.12.1 Usage

```
void glutSpaceballButtonFunc(void (*func)(int button, int state));
```

> func   The new spaceball button callback function.

B.6.12.2 Description

glutspaceballButtonFunc sets the spaceball button callback for the *current window*. The spaceball button callback for a window is called when the window has spaceball input focus (normally, when the mouse is in the window) and the user generates spaceball button presses. The button parameter will be the button number (starting at 1). The number of available spaceball buttons can be determined with glutDeviceGet(GLUT_NUM_SPACEBALL_BUTTONS). The state is either GLUT_UP or GLUT_DOWN, indicating whether the callback was due to a release or a press, respectively.

Registering a spaceball button callback when a spaceball device is not available has no effect and is not an error. In this case, no spaceball button callbacks will be generated.

Passing NULL to glutSpaceballButtonFunc disables the generation of spaceball button callbacks. When a new window is created, no spaceball button callback is initially registered.

B.6.13 glutButtonBoxFunc

glutButtonBoxFunc sets the dial-and-button box button callback for the *current window.*

B.6.13.1 Usage

```
void glutButtonBoxFunc(void (*func)(int button, int state));
```

   func   The new button box callback function.

B.6.13.2 Description

glutButtonBoxFunc sets the dial-and-button box button callback for the *current window.* The dial-and-button box button callback for a window is called when the window has dial-and-button box input focus (normally, when the mouse is in the window) and the user generates dial-and-button box button presses. The button parameter will be the button number (starting at 1). The number of available dial-and-button box buttons can be determined with glutDeviceGet(GLUT_NUM_BUTTON_BOX_BUTTONS). The state is either GLUT_UP or GLUT_DOWN, indicating whether the callback resulted from a release or a press, respectively.

Registering a dial-and-button box button callback when a dial-and-button box device is not available has no effect and is not an error. In this case, no dial-and-button box button callbacks will be generated.

Passing NULL to glutButtonBoxFunc disables the generation of dial-and-button box button callbacks. When a new window is created, no dial-and-button box button callback is initially registered.

B.6.14 glutDialsFunc

glutDialsFunc sets the dial-and-button box dials callback for the *current window.*

B.6.14.1 Usage

```
void glutDialsFunc(void (*func)(int dial, int value));
```

   func   The new dials callback function.

B.6.14.2 Description

glutDialsFunc sets the dial-and-button box dials callback for the *current window.* The dial-and-button box dials callback for a window is called when the window has dial-and-button box input focus (normally, when the mouse is in the window) and the user generates dial-and-button box dial changes. The dial parameter will be the dial number (starting at 1). The number of available dial-and-button box dials can be determined with `glutDeviceGet(GLUT_NUM_DIALS)`. `value` measures the absolute rotation in degrees. Dial values do not "roll over" with each complete rotation, but continue to accumulate degrees (until the `int` dial value overflows).

Registering a dial-and-button box dials callback when a dial-and-button box device is not available has no effect and is not an error. In this case, no dial-and-button box dials callbacks will be generated.

Passing `NULL` to `glutDialsFunc` disables the generation of dial-and-button box dials callbacks. When a new window is created, no dial-and-button box dials callback is initially registered.

B.6.15 `glutTabletMotionFunc`

`glutTabletMotionFunc` sets the special keyboard callback for the *current window*.

B.6.15.1 Usage

```
void glutTabletMotionFunc(void (*func)(int x, int y));
```

func   The new tablet motion callback function.

B.6.15.2 Description

`glutTabletMotionFunc` sets the tablet motion callback for the *current window*. The tablet motion callback for a window is called when the window has tablet input focus (normally, when the mouse is in the window) and the user generates tablet motion. The `x` and `y` callback parameters indicate the absolute position of the tablet "puck" on the tablet. The callback parameters are normalized to be within the range of 0 to 2000, inclusive.

Registering a tablet motion callback when a tablet device is not available has no effect and is not an error. In this case, no tablet motion callbacks will be generated.

Passing `NULL` to `glutTabletMotionFunc` disables the generation of tablet motion callbacks. When a new window is created, no tablet motion callback is initially registered.

B.6.16 `glutTabletButtonFunc`

`glutTabletButtonFunc` sets the special keyboard callback for the *current window*.

B.6.16.1 Usage

```
void glutTabletButtonFunc(void (*func)(int button, int state,
  int x, int y));
```

func   The new tablet button callback function.

B.6.16.2 Description

glutTabletButtonFunc sets the tablet button callback for the *current window*. The tablet button callback for a window is called when the window has tablet input focus (normally, when the mouse is in the window) and the user generates tablet button presses. The button parameter will be the button number (starting at 1). The number of available tablet buttons can be determined with glutDevice-Get(GLUT_NUM_TABLET_BUTTONS). The state is either GLUT_UP or GLUT_DOWN, indicating whether the callback resulted from a release or a press, respectively. The x and y callback parameters indicate the window-relative coordinates when the tablet button state changed.

Registering a tablet button callback when a tablet device is not available has no effect and is not an error. In this case, no tablet button callbacks will be generated.

Passing NULL to glutTabletButtonFunc disables the generation of tablet button callbacks. When a new window is created, no tablet button callback is initially registered.

B.6.17 glutMenuStatusFunc

glutMenuStatusFunc sets the global menu status callback.

B.6.17.1 Usage

```
void glutMenuStatusFunc(void (*func)(int status, int x, int y));
void glutMenuStateFunc(void (*func)(int status));
```

func   The new menu status callback function.

B.6.17.2 Description

glutMenuStatusFunc sets the global menu status callback so a GLUT program can determine when a menu is or is not in use. When a menu status callback is registered, it will be called with the value GLUT_MENU_IN_USE for its value parameter when the user is employing pop-up menus; the callback will be called with the value GLUT_MENU_NOT_IN_USE for its status parameter when pop-up menus are no longer in use. The x and y parameters indicate the location, in window coordinates, of the button press that caused the menu to go into use, or the location where the menu was released (may be outside the window). The func parameter names the callback function. Other callbacks (except mouse motion callbacks) continue to operate when pop-up menus are in use, so the menu status callback allows a program to suspend animation or other tasks when menus are in use. The cascading and unmapping of submenus from an initial pop-up menu does not generate menu status callbacks. There is a single menu status callback for GLUT.

When the menu status callback is called, the *current menu* will be set to the initial pop-up menu in both the GLUT_MENU_IN_USE and GLUT_MENU_NOT_IN_USE cases. The *current window* will be set to the window from which the initial menu was popped up, also in both cases.

Passing NULL to glutMenuStatusFunc disables the generation of the menu status callback.

glutMenuStateFunc is an obsoleted version of the glutMenuStatusFunc routine. The only difference is that the glutMenuStateFunc callback prototype does not deliver the two additional x and y coordinates.

B.6.18 glutIdleFunc

glutIdleFunc sets the global idle callback.

B.6.18.1 Usage

```
void glutIdleFunc(void (*func)(void));
```

func   The new idle callback function.

B.6.18.2 Description

glutIdleFunc sets the global idle callback to be func so a GLUT program can perform background processing tasks or continuous animation when window system events are not being received. If enabled, the idle callback is continuously called when events are not being received. The callback routine has no parameters. The *current window* and *current menu* will not be changed before the idle callback. Programs with multiple windows and/or menus should explicitly set the current window and/or current menu and not rely on their current settings.

The amount of computation and rendering done in an idle callback should be minimized to avoid affecting the program's interactive response. In general, not more than a single frame of rendering should be done in an idle callback.

Passing NULL to glutIdleFunc disables the generation of the idle callback.

B.6.19 glutTimerFunc

glutTimerFunc registers a timer callback to be triggered in a specified number of milliseconds.

B.6.19.1 Usage

```
void glutTimerFunc(unsigned int msecs,
  void (*func)(int value), value);
```

msecs   Milliseconds before triggering callback.

func   The timer callback function.

value   The timer's associated value.

B.6.19.2 Description

glutTimerFunc registers the timer callback func to be triggered in at least msecs milliseconds. The value parameter of the timer callback will be the value of the value parameter to glutTimerFunc. Multiple timer callbacks at the same time or at different times may be registered simultaneously.

The number of milliseconds is a lower bound on the time before the callback is generated. GLUT attempts to deliver the timer callback as soon as possible after the expiration of the callback's time interval.

There is no support for canceling a registered callback. Instead, ignore a callback based on its value parameter when it is triggered.

B.7 COLOR INDEX COLORMAP MANAGEMENT

OpenGL supports both RGBA and color index rendering. The RGBA mode is generally preferable to color index, because more OpenGL rendering capabilities are available and color index mode requires the loading of colormap entries.

The GLUT color index routines are used to write and read entries in a window's color index colormap. Every GLUT color index window has its own logical color index colormap. The size of a window's colormap can be determined by calling glutGet(GLUT_WINDOW_COLORMAP_SIZE).

GLUT color index windows within a program can attempt to share colormap resources by copying a single color index colormap to multiple windows using glutCopyColormap. If possible, GLUT will attempt to share the actual colormap. Though copying colormaps using glutCopyColormap can potentially allow sharing of physical colormap resources, logically each window has its own colormap. So changing a copied colormap of a window will force the duplication of the colormap. For this reason, color index programs should generally load a single color index colormap, copy it to all color index windows within the program, and then not modify any colormap cells.

Use of multiple colormaps is likely to result in colormap installation problems in which some windows are displayed with an incorrect colormap because of limitations on colormap resources.

B.7.1 glutSetColor

glutSetColor sets the color of a colormap entry in the *layer of use* for the *current window*.

B.7.1.1 Usage

void glutSetColor(int cell, GLfloat red, GLfloat green, GLfloat blue);

    cell   Color cell index (starting at 0).

    red   Red intensity (clamped between 0.0 and 1.0, inclusive).

green   Green intensity (clamped between 0.0 and 1.0, inclusive).

blue   Blue intensity (clamped between 0.0 and 1.0, inclusive).

B.7.1.2 Description

Sets the cell color index colormap entry of the *current window*'s logical colormap for the layer in use with the color specified by red, green, and blue. The layer in use of the *current window* should be a color index window. cell should be 0 or greater and less than the total number of colormap entries for the window. If the colormap of the *layer in use* was copied by reference, a glutSetColor call will force the duplication of the colormap. Do not attempt to set the color of an overlay's transparent index.

B.7.2 glutGetColor

glutGetColor retrieves a red, green, or blue component for a given color index colormap entry for the *layer in use*'s logical colormap for the *current window*.

B.7.2.1 Usage

GLfloat glutGetColor(int cell, int component);

cell   Color cell index (starting at 0).

component   One of GLUT_RED, GLUT_GREEN, or GLUT_BLUE.

B.7.2.2 Description

glutGetColor retrieves a red, green, or blue component for a given color index colormap entry for the *current window*'s logical colormap. The current window should be a color index window. cell should be 0 or greater, and less than the total number of colormap entries for the window. For valid color indexes, the value returned is a floating-point value between 0.0 and 1.0, inclusive. glutGet-Color will return −1.0 if the color index specified is an overlay's transparent index, less than 0, or greater or equal to the value returned by glut-Get(GLUT_WINDOW_COLORMAP_SIZE); that is, if the color index is transparent or outside the valid range of color indices.

B.7.3 glutCopyColormap

glutCopyColormap copies the logical colormap for the *layer in use* from a specified window to the *current window*.

B.7.3.1 Usage

void glutCopyColormap(int win);

win The identifier of the window from which the logical colormap should be copied.

B.7.3.2 Description

`glutCopyColormap` copies (lazily if possible, to promote sharing) the logical colormap from a specified window to the *current window*'s *layer in use*. The copy will be from the normal plane to the normal plane or from the overlay to the overlay (never across different layers). Once a colormap has been copied, avoid setting cells in the colormap with `glutSetColor`, since that will force an actual copy of the colormap if it was previously copied by reference. `glutCopyColormap` should be called only when both the current window and the win window are color index windows.

B.8 STATE RETRIEVAL

GLUT maintains a considerable amount of programmer visible state. Some (but not all) of this state may be directly retrieved.

B.8.1 glutGet

`glutGet` retrieves simple GLUT state represented by integers.

B.8.1.1 Usage

```
int glutGet(GLenum state);
```

state Name of state to retrieve.

GLUT_WINDOW_X *X* location in pixels (relative to the screen origin) of the *current window*.

GLUT_WINDOW_Y *Y* location in pixels (relative to the screen origin) of the current window.

GLUT_WINDOW_WIDTH Width in pixels of the *current window*.

GLUT_WINDOW_HEIGHT Height in pixels of the *current window*.

GLUT_WINDOW_BUFFER_SIZE Total number of bits for the *current window*'s color buffer. For an RGBA window, this is the sum of GLUT_WINDOW_RED_SIZE, GLUT_WINDOW_GREEN_SIZE, GLUT_WINDOW_BLUE _SIZE, and GLUT_WINDOW_ALPHA_SIZE. For color index windows, this is the number of bits for the color indexes.

GLUT_WINDOW_STENCIL_SIZE Number of bits in the *current window*'s stencil buffer.

GLUT_WINDOW_DEPTH_SIZE Number of bits in the *current window*'s depth buffer.

GLUT_WINDOW_RED_SIZE Number of bits of red stored in the *current window*'s color buffer. Zero if the window is color index.

`GLUT_WINDOW_GREEN_SIZE`   Number of bits of green stored in the *current window*'s color buffer. 0 if the window is color index.

`GLUT_WINDOW_BLUE_SIZE`   Number of bits of blue stored in the *current window*'s color buffer. 0 if the window is color index.

`GLUT_WINDOW_ALPHA_SIZE`   Number of bits of alpha stored in the *current window*'s color buffer. 0 if the window is color index.

`GLUT_WINDOW_ACCUM_RED_SIZE`   Number of bits of red stored in the *current window*'s accumulation buffer. 0 if the window is color index.

`GLUT_WINDOW_ACCUM_GREEN_SIZE`   Number of bits of green stored in the *current window*'s accumulation buffer. 0 if the window is color index.

`GLUT_WINDOW_ACCUM_BLUE_SIZE`   Number of bits of blue stored in the *current window*'s accumulation buffer. 0 if the window is color index.

`GLUT_WINDOW_ACCUM_ALPHA_SIZE`   Number of bits of alpha stored in the *current window*'s accumulation buffer. 0 if the window is color index.

`GLUT_WINDOW_DOUBLEBUFFER`   1 if the *current window* is double-buffered; 0 otherwise.

`GLUT_WINDOW_RGBA`   1 if the *current window* is RGBA mode; 0 otherwise (i.e., color index).

`GLUT_WINDOW_PARENT`   The window number of the *current window*'s parent; 0 if the window is a top-level window.

`GLUT_WINDOW_NUM_CHILDREN`   The number of subwindows the *current window* has (not counting children of children).

`GLUT_WINDOW_COLORMAP_SIZE`   Size of the *current window*'s color index colormap; 0 for RGBA color model windows.

`GLUT_WINDOW_NUM_SAMPLES`   Number of samples for multisampling for the *current window.*

`GLUT_WINDOW_STEREO`   1 if the *current window* is stereo, 0 otherwise.

`GLUT_WINDOW_CURSOR`   Current cursor for the *current window.*

`GLUT_SCREEN_WIDTH`   Width of the screen in pixels. 0 indicates that the width is unknown or not available.

`GLUT_SCREEN_HEIGHT`   Height of the screen in pixels. 0 indicates that the height is unknown or not available.

`GLUT_SCREEN_WIDTH_MM`   Width of the screen in millimeters. 0 indicates that the width is unknown or not available.

`GLUT_SCREEN_HEIGHT_MM`   Height of the screen in millimeters. 0 indicates that the height is unknown or not available.

`GLUT_MENU_NUM_ITEMS`   Number of menu items in the *current menu.*

`GLUT_DISPLAY_MODE_POSSIBLE`   Whether the *current display mode* is supported or not.

GLUT_INIT_DISPLAY_MODE   The *initial display mode* Bitmask.

GLUT_INIT_WINDOW_X   The X value of the *initial window position*.

GLUT_INIT_WINDOW_Y   The Y value of the *initial window position*.

GLUT_INIT_WINDOW_WIDTH   The width value of the *initial window size*.

GLUT_INIT_WINDOW_HEIGHT   The height value of the *initial window size*.

GLUT_ELAPSED_TIME   Number of milliseconds since glutInit called (or first call to glutGet(GLUT_ELAPSED_TIME)).

B.8.1.2 Description

glutGet retrieves simple GLUT state represented by integers. The state parameter determines what type of state to return. Window capability state is returned for the *layer in use*. GLUT state names beginning with GLUT_WINDOW_ return state for the *current window*. GLUT state names beginning with GLUT_MENU_ return state for the *current menu*. Other GLUT state names return global state. Requesting state for an invalid GLUT state name returns −1.

B.8.2   glutLayerGet

glutLayerGet retrieves GLUT state pertaining to the layers of the *current window*.

B.8.2.1 Usage

```
int glutLayerGet(GLenum info);
```

info   Name of device information to retrieve.

GLUT_OVERLAY_POSSIBLE   Whether an overlay could be established for the *current window* given the current *initial display mode*. If false, glut-EstablishOverlay will fail with a fatal error if called.

GLUT_LAYER_IN_USE   Either GLUT_NORMAL or GLUT_OVERLAY, depending on whether the normal plane or overlay is the *layer in use*.

GLUT_HAS_OVERLAY   If the *current window* has an overlay established.

GLUT_TRANSPARENT_INDEX   The transparent color index of the overlay of the current window; −1 is returned if no overlay is in use.

GLUT_NORMAL_DAMAGED   True if the normal plane of the *current window* has been damaged (by window system activity) since the last display callback was triggered. Calling glutPostRedisplay will not set this true.

GLUT_OVERLAY_DAMAGED   True if the overlay plane of the *current window* has been damaged (by window system activity) since the last display callback was triggered. Calling glutPostRedisplay or glutPostOverlayRedisplay will not set this true. Negative 1 is returned if no overlay is in use.

B.8.2.2 Description

`glutLayerGet` retrieves GLUT layer information for the *current window* represented by integers. The `info` parameter determines what type of layer information to return.

B.8.3 `glutDeviceGet`

`glutDeviceGet` retrieves GLUT device information represented by integers.

B.8.3.1 Usage

`int glutDeviceGet(GLenum info);`

info   Name of device information to retrieve.

`GLUT_HAS_KEYBOARD`   Nonzero if a keyboard is available; 0 if not available. For most GLUT implementations, a keyboard can be assumed.

`GLUT_HAS_MOUSE`   Nonzero if a mouse is available; 0 if not available. For most GLUT implementations, a keyboard can be assumed.

`GLUT_HAS_SPACEBALL`   Nonzero if a spaceball is available; 0 if not available.

`GLUT_HAS_DIAL_AND_BUTTON_BOX`   Nonzero if a dial-and-button-box is available; 0 if not available.

`GLUT_HAS_TABLET`   Nonzero if a tablet is available; 0 if not available.

`GLUT_NUM_MOUSE_BUTTONS`   Number of buttons supported by the mouse. If no mouse is supported, 0 is returned.

`GLUT_NUM_SPACEBALL_BUTTONS`   Number of buttons supported by the spaceball. If no spaceball is supported, 0 is returned.

`GLUT_NUM_BUTTON_BOX_BUTTONS`   Number of buttons supported by the dial-and-button box device. If no dial-and-button box device is supported, 0 is returned.

`GLUT_NUM_DIALS`   Number of dials supported by the dial-and-button box device. If no dial-and-button box device is supported, 0 is returned.

`GLUT_NUM_TABLET_BUTTONS`   Number of buttons supported by the tablet. If no tablet is supported, 0 is returned.

B.8.3.2 Description

`glutDeviceGet` retrieves GLUT device information represented by integers. The `info` parameter determines what type of device information to return. Requesting device information for an invalid GLUT device information name returns –1.

B.8.4 `glutGetModifiers`

`glutGetModifiers` returns the modifier key state when certain callbacks were generated.

B.8.4.1 Usage

```
int glutGetModifiers(void);
```

> GLUT_ACTIVE_SHIFT   Set if the **Shift** modifier or **CapsLock** is active.
>
> GLUT_ACTIVE_CTRL   Set if the **Ctrl** modifier is active.
>
> GLUT_ACTIVE_ALT   Set if the **Alt** modifier is active.

B.8.4.2 Description

`glutGetModifiers` returns the modifier key state at the time the input event for a keyboard, special, or mouse callback is generated. This routine may be called only while a keyboard, special, or mouse callback is being handled. The window system is permitted to intercept window-system defined modifier keystrokes or mouse buttons, in which case no GLUT callback will be generated. This interception will be independent of use of `glutGetModifiers`.

B.8.5 glutExtensionSupported

`glutExtensionSupported` helps to determine whether a given OpenGL extension is supported.

B.8.5.1 Usage

```
int glutExtensionSupported(char *extension);
```

> extension   Name of OpenGL extension.

B.8.5.2 Description

`glutExtensionSupported` helps to determine whether a given OpenGL extension is supported. The `extension` parameter names the extension to query. The supported extensions can also be determined with `glGetString(GL_EXTENSIONS)`, but `glutExtensionSupported;` does the correct parsing of the returned string.

`glutExtensionSupported` returns nonzero if the extension is supported, 0 if not supported.

There must be a valid *current window* to call `glutExtensionSupported`.

`glutExtensionSupported` returns information about OpenGL extensions only. This means that window system dependent extensions (for example, GLX extensions) are not reported by `glutExtensionSupported`.

B.9   FONT RENDERING

GLUT supports two types of font rendering: stroke fonts, in which each character is rendered as a set of line segments, and bitmap fonts, in which each character is a bitmap generated with `glBitmap`. Stroke fonts have the advantage that because they are geometry, they can be arbitrarily scaled and rendered. Bitmap fonts are less flexible, since they are rendered as bitmaps, but are usually faster than stroke fonts.

B.9.1 `glutBitmapCharacter`

`glutBitmapCharacter` renders a bitmap character using OpenGL.

B.9.1.1 Usage

```
void glutBitmapCharacter(void *font, int character);
```

font   Bitmap font to use.

character   Character to render (not confined to 8 bits).

B.9.1.2 Description

Without using any display lists, `glutBitmapCharacter` renders `character` in the named bitmap `font`. The available fonts are as follows:

GLUT_BITMAP_8_BY_13   A fixed-width font, each of whose characters fit into an 8-by-13 pixel rectangle. The exact bitmaps to be used are defined by the standard X glyph bitmaps for the X font called

`-misc-fixed-medium-r-normal--13-120-75-75-C-80-iso8859-1`

GLUT_BITMAP_9_BY_15   A fixed-width font, each of whose characters fits into a 9-by-15 pixel rectangle. The exact bitmaps to be used are defined by the standard X glyph bitmaps for the X font called

`-misc-fixed-medium-r-normal--15-140-75-75-C-90-iso8859-1`

GLUT_BITMAP_TIMES_ROMAN_10   A 10-point proportionally spaced Times Roman font. The exact bitmaps to be used are defined by the standard X glyph bitmaps for the X font called

`-adobe-times-medium-r-normal--10-100-75-75-p-54-iso8859-1`

GLUT_BITMAP_TIMES_ROMAN_24   A 24-point proportionally spaced Times Roman font. The exact bitmaps to be used are defined by the standard X glyph bitmaps for the X font called

`-adobe-times-medium-r-normal--24-240-75-75-p-124-iso8859-1`

GLUT_BITMAP_HELVETICA_10   A 10-point proportionally spaced Helvetica font. The exact bitmaps to be used are defined by the standard X glyph bitmaps for the X font called

`-adobe-helvetica-medium-r-normal--10-100-75-75-p-56-iso8859-1`

GLUT_BITMAP_HELVETICA_12   A 12-point proportionally spaced Helvetica font. The exact bitmaps to be used are defined by the standard X glyph bitmaps for the X font called

`-adobe-helvetica-medium-r-normal--12-120-75-75-p-67-iso8859-1`

GLUT_BITMAP_HELVETICA_18   A 18-point proportional spaced Helvetica font. The exact bitmaps to be used are defined by the standard X glyph bitmaps for the X font called:

`-adobe-helvetica-medium-r-normal--18-180-75-75-p-98-iso8859-1`

Rendering a nonexistent character has no effect. `glutBitmapCharacter` automatically sets the OpenGL unpack pixel storage modes it needs appropriately and saves and restores the previous modes before returning. The generated call to `glBitmap` will adjust the current raster position based on the width of the character.

B.9.2 `glutBitmapWidth`

`glutBitmapWidth` returns the width of a bitmap character.

B.9.2.1 Usage

`int glutBitmapWidth(GLUTbitmapFont font, int character)`

> `font`   Bitmap font to use.
>
> `character`   Character whose width should be returned (not confined to 8 bits).

B.9.2.2 Description

`glutBitmapWidth` returns the width in pixels of a bitmap character in a supported bitmap font. While the width of characters in a font may vary (though fixed-width fonts do not vary), the maximum height characteristics of a particular font are fixed.

B.9.3 `glutStrokeCharacter`

`glutStrokeCharacter` renders a stroke character using OpenGL.

B.9.3.1 Usage

`void glutStrokeCharacter(void *font, int character);`

> `font`   Stroke font to use.
>
> `character`   Character to render (not confined to 8 bits).

B.9.3.2 Description

Without using any display lists, `glutStrokeCharacter` renders `character` in the named stroke `font`. The available fonts are as follows:

GLUT_STROKE_ROMAN   A proportionally spaced Roman Simplex font for ASCII characters 32 through 127. The maximum character top in the font is 119.05 units; the maximum bottom descends 33.33 units.

GLUT_STROKE_MONO_ROMAN   A monospace Roman Simplex font (same characters as GLUT_STROKE_ROMAN) for ASCII characters 32 through 127. The maximum character top in the font is 119.05 units; the bottom descends 33.33 units. Each character is 104.76 units wide.

Rendering a nonexistent character has no effect. A glTranslatef is used to translate the current modelview matrix to advance the width of the character.

B.9.4 glutStrokeWidth

glutStrokeWidth   returns the width of a stroke character.

B.9.4.1 Usage

```
int glutStrokeWidth(GLUTstrokeFont font, int character)
```

font   Stroke font to use.

character   Character whose width should be returned (not confined to 8 bits).

B.9.4.2 Description

glutStrokeWidth returns the width in pixels of a stroke character in a supported stroke font. While the width of characters in a font may vary (though fixed-width fonts do not vary), the maximum height characteristics of a particular font are fixed.

B.10 GEOMETRIC OBJECT RENDERING

GLUT includes a number of routines for generating easily recognizable 3D geometric objects. These routines reflect functionality available in the aux toolkit described in the *OpenGL Programmer's Guide* and are included in GLUT to allow the construction of simple GLUT programs that render recognizable objects. These routines can be implemented as pure OpenGL rendering routines. The routines do *not* generate display lists for the objects they create.

The routines generate normals appropriate for lighting, but do not generate texture coordinates (except for the teapot).

B.10.1 glutSolidSphere, glutWireSphere

glutSolidSphere and glutWireSphere render a solid and a wireframe sphere, respectively.

B.10.1.1 Usage

```
void glutSolidSphere(GLdouble radius, GLint slices, GLint stacks);
void glutWireSphere(GLdouble radius, GLint slices, GLint stacks);
```

radius   The radius of the sphere.

slices   The number of subdivisions around the Z axis (similar to lines of longitude).

stacks   The number of subdivisions along the Z axis (similar to lines of latitude).

D.10.1.2 Description

glutSolidSphere and glutWireSphere render a solid or a wireframe sphere, respectively, centered at the modeling coordinates origin of the specified radius. The sphere is subdivided around the Z axis into slices and along the Z axis into stacks.

D.10.2 glutSolidCube, glutWireCube

glutSolidCube and glutWireCuberender a solid or a wireframe cube, respectively.

D.10.2.1 Usage

```
void glutSolidCube(GLdouble size);
void glutWireCube(GLdouble size);
```

size   Length of cube sides.

D.10.2.2 Description

glutSolidCube and glutWireCube render a solid or a wireframe cube, respectively. The cube is centered at the modeling coordinates origin with sides of length size.

D.10.3 glutSolidCone, glutWireCone

glutSolidCone and glutWireCone render a solid or a wireframe cone, respectively.

D.10.3.1 Usage

```
void glutSolidCone(GLdouble base, GLdouble height,
  GLint slices, GLint stacks);
void glutWireCone(GLdouble base, GLdouble height, GLint slices,
  GLint stacks);
```

base   The radius of the base of the cone.

height   The height of the cone.

slices   The number of subdivisions around the Z axis.

stacks   The number of subdivisions along the Z axis.

D.10.3.2 Description

glutSolidCone and glutWireCone render a solid or a wireframe cone, respectively, oriented along the Z axis. The base of the cone is placed at Z = 0, and the top at Z = height. The cone is subdivided around the Z axis into slices, and along the Z axis into stacks.

D.10.4 glutSolidTorus, glutWireTorus

glutSolidTorus and glutWireTorus render a solid or a wireframe torus (doughnut), respectively.

D.10.4.1 Usage
```
void glutSolidTorus(GLdouble
  innerRadius, GLdouble outerRadius, GLint nsides, GLint rings);
void glutWireTorus(GLdouble innerRadius,
  GLdouble outerRadius, GLint nsides, GLint rings);
```

> innerRadius Inner radius of the torus.
>
> outerRadius Outer radius of the torus.
>
> nsides Number of sides for each radial section.
>
> rings Number of radial divisions for the torus.

D.10.4.2 Description

glutSolidTorus and glutWireTorus render a solid or a wireframe torus (doughnut), respectively, centered at the modeling coordinates origin whose axis is aligned with the Z axis.

D.10.5 glutSolidDodecahedron, glutWireDodecahedron

glutSolidDodecahedron and glutWireDodecahedron render a solid or a wireframe dodecahedron (12-sided regular solid), respectively.

D.10.5.1 Usage
```
void glutSolidDodecahedron(void);
void glutWireDodecahedron(void);
```

D.10.5.2 Description

glutSolidDodecahedron and glutWireDodecahedron render a solid or a wireframe dodecahedron, respectively, centered at the modeling coordinates origin with a radius of $\sqrt{3}$.

D.10.6 glutSolidOctahedron, glutWireOctahedron

glutSolidOctahedron and glutWireOctahedron render a solid or wireframe octahedron (8-sided regular solid), respectively.

B.10.6.1 Usage

```
void glutSolidOctahedron(void);
void glutWireOctahedron(void);
```

B.10.6.2 Description

glutSolidOctahedron and glutWireOctahedron render a solid or a wireframe octahedron, respectively, centered at the modeling coordinates origin with a radius of 1.0.

B.10.7 glutSolidTetrahedron, glutWireTetrahedron

glutSolidTetrahedron and glutWireTetrahedron render a solid or a wireframe tetrahedron (4-sided regular solid), respectively.

B.10.7.1 Usage

```
void glutSolidTetrahedron(void);
void glutWireTetrahedron(void);
```

B.10.7.2 Description

glutSolidTetrahedron and glutWireTetrahedron render a solid or a wireframe tetrahedron, respectively, centered at the modeling coordinates origin with a radius of $\sqrt{3}$.

B.10.8 glutSolidIcosahedron, glutWireIcosahedron

glutSolidIcosahedron and glutWireIcosahedron render a solid or a wireframe icosahedron (20-sided regular solid), respectively.

B.10.8.1 Usage

```
void glutSolidIcosahedron(void);
void glutWireIcosahedron(void);
```

B.10.8.2 Description

glutSolidIcosahedron and glutWireIcosahedron render a solid or a wireframe icosahedron, respectively, centered at the modeling coordinates origin with a radius of 1.0.

B.10.9 glutSolidTeapot, glutWireTeapot

glutSolidTeapot and glutWireTeapot render a solid or a wireframe teapot,[1] respectively.

---

1. Yes, the *classic* computer graphics teapot modeled by Martin Newell in 1975 [6].

B.10.9.1 Usage

```
void glutSolidTeapot(GLdouble size);
void glutWireTeapot(GLdouble size);
```

size   Relative size of the teapot.

B.10.9.2 Description

`glutSolidTeapot` and `glutWireTeapot` render a solid or a wireframe teapot, respectively. Both surface normals and texture coordinates for the teapot are generated. The teapot is generated with OpenGL evaluators.

GLUT State

This appendix specifies precisely what programmer-visible state GLUT maintains. GLUT maintains three categories of programmer-visible state: global, window, and menu. The window and menu state categories are maintained for each created window or menu. Additional overlay-related window state is maintained when an overlay is established for a window for the lifetime of the overlay.

The tables below name each element of state, define its type, specify what GLUT API entry points set or change the state (if possible), specify what GLUT API entry point or glutGet, glutDeviceGet, or glutLayerGet state constant is used to get the state (if possible), and how the state is initially set. For details as to how any API entry point operates on the specified state, see the routine's official description. Footnotes for each category of state indicate additional caveats for the element of state.

C.1 TYPES OF STATE

These types are used to specify GLUT's programmer-visible state:

Bitmask A group of boolean bits.

Boolean True or false.

Callback A handle to a user-supplied routine invoked when the given callback is triggered (or NULL, which is the default callback).

ColorCell Red, green, and blue color component triple; an array of Color-Cells makes a colormap.

Cursor A GLUT cursor name.

Integer An integer value.

Layer Either normal plane or overlay.

MenuItem   Either a menu entry or a submenu trigger. Both subtypes contain a *String* name. A menu entry has an *Integer* value. A submenu cascade has an *Integer* menu name naming its associated submenu.

MenuState   Either in use or not in use.

Stacking   An ordering for top-level windows and subwindows that have the same parent. Higher windows obscure lower windows.

State   One of shown, hidden, and iconified.

String   A string of ASCII characters.

Timer   A triple of a timer *Callback*, an *Integer* callback parameter, and a time in milliseconds (which expires in real time).

C.2   GLOBAL STATE

There are two types of global state: program-controlled state, which can be modified directly or indirectly by the program, and fixed system-dependent state.

C.2.1   Program-Controlled State

Name	Type	Set/Change	Get	Initial
currentWindow	Integer	glutSetWindow[1]	glutGetWindow	0
currentMenu	Integer	glutSetMenu[2]	glutSetMenu	0
initWindow X	Integer	glutInit-WindowPosition	GLUT_INIT_WINDOW_X	−1
initWindow Y	Integer	glutInit-WindowPosition	GLUT_INIT_WINDOW_Y	−1
initWindow Width	Integer	glutInit-WindowSize	GLUT_INIT_WINDOW_WIDTH	300
init-Window-Height	Integer	glutInit-WindowSize	GLUT_INIT_WINDOW_HEIGHT	300
initDisplay-Mode	Bitmask	glutInit-DisplayMode	GLUT_INIT_DISPLAY_MODE	GLUT_RGB, GLUT_SINGLE, GLUT_DEPTH
idleCallback	Callback	glutIdleFunc	–	NULL
menuState	MenuState	–	[3]	NotInUse
menuState-Callback	Callback	glutMenu-EntryFunc	–	NULL
timerList	list of Timer	glutTimerFunc	–	none

1. The *currentWindow* is also changed implicitly by every window or menu callback (to the window triggering the callback) and by the creation of a window (to the window being created).
2. The *currentMenu* is also changed implicitly by every menu callback (to the menu triggering the callback) and by the creation of a menu (to the menu being created).
3. The menu state callback is triggered when the *menuState* changes.

C.2.2 Fixed System Dependent State

Name	Type	Get
screenWidth	Integer	GLUT_SCREEN_WIDTH
screenHeight	Integer	GLUT_SCREEN_HEIGHT
screenWidthMM	Integer	GLUT_SCREEN_WIDTH_MM
screenHeightMM	Integer	GLUT_SCREEN_HEIGHT_MM
hasKeyboard	Boolean	GLUT_HAS_KEYBOARD
hasMouse	Boolean	GLUT_HAS_MOUSE
hasSpaceball	Boolean	GLUT_HAS_SPACEBALL
hasDialAndButtonBox	Boolean	GLUT_HAS_DIAL_AND_BUTTON_BOX
hasTablet	Boolean	GLUT_HAS_TABLET
numMouseButtons	Integer	GLUT_NUM_MOUSE_BUTTONS
numSpaceballButtons	Integer	GLUT_NUM_SPACEBALL_BUTTONS
numButtonBoxButtons	Integer	GLUT_NUM_BUTTON_BOX_BUTTONS
numDials	Integer	GLUT_NUM_DIALS
numTabletButtons	Integer	GLUT_NUM_TABLET_BUTTONS

C.3 WINDOW STATE

For the purposes of listing the window state elements, window state is classified into three types: base state, frame buffer capability state, and layer state. The tags *top-level*, *subwin*, and *cindex* indicate that the table entry applies only to top-level windows, subwindows, or color index windows, respectively.

C.3.1 Base State

Name	Type	Set/Change	Get	Initial
number	Integer	–	glutGetWindow	*top-level:* glutCreate-Window [1] *subwin:* glut-CreateSubWindow [1]
x	Integer	glutPosition-Window	GLUT_WINDOW_X	*top-level:* initWindowX [2] *subwin:* glut-CreateSubWindow
y	Integer	glutPosition-Window	GLUT_WINDOW_Y	*top-level:* initWindowY [3] *subwin:* glut-CreateSubWindow
width	Integer	glut-ReshapeWindow	GLUT_WINDOW_WIDTH	*top-level:* initWindowWidth [4] *subwin:* glut-CreateSubWindow

Name	Type	Set/Change	Get	Initial
height	Integer	`glut-ReshapeWindow`	`GLUT_WINDOW_HEIGHT`	*top-level:* `initWindow-Height`[5] *subwin:* glutCreate-SubWindow
top-level: fullscreen	Boolean	`glutFullScreen` `glutPosition-Window` `glutReshape-Window`[6]		`False`
cursor	Cursor	`glutSetCursor`	`GLUT_WINDOW_CURSOR`	`GLUT_CURSOR_INHERIT`
stacking	Stacking	`glutPopWindow` `glutPushWindow`	—	top
displayState	State[7]	`glutShowWindow` `glutHideWindow` `glutIconify-Window`[8]	—	shown
visibility	Visibility	[9]	[10]	undefined
redisplay	Boolean	`glutPost-Redisplay`[11]	—	False
top-level: windowTitle	String	`glutWindow-Title`	—	`glutCreateWindow`
top-level: iconTitle	String	`glutIconTitle`	—	`glutCreateWindow`
displayCallback	Callback	`glutDisplay-Func`	—	`NULL`[12]
reshapeCallback	Callback	`glutReshape-Func`	—	`NULL`[13]
keyboardCallback	Callback	`glutKeyboard-Func`	—	`NULL`
mouseCallback	Callback	`glutMouseFunc`	—	`NULL`
motionCallback	Callback	`glutMotionFunc`	—	`NULL`
passiveMotion-Callback	Callback	`glutPassive-MotionFunc`	—	`NULL`
specialCallback	Callback	`glutSpecial-Func`	—	`NULL`
spaceballMotion-Callback	Callback	`glutSpaceball-MotionFunc`	—	`NULL`
spaceballRotate-Callback	Callback	`glutSpaceball-Rotatefunc`	—	`NULL`
spaceballButton-Callback	Callback	`glutSpaceball-ButtonFunc`	—	`NULL`
buttonBox-Callback	Callback	`glutButtonBox-Func`	—	`NULL`
dialsCallback	Callback	`glutDialsFunc`	—	`NULL`
tabletMotion-Callback	Callback	`glutTablet-MotionFunc`		`NULL`

Name	Type	Set/Change	Get	Initial
tabletButtonCallback	Callback	`glutTablet-ButtonFunc`	-	NULL
visibilityCallback	Callback	`glut-VisibilityFunc`	-	NULL
entryCallback	Callback	`glutEntryFunc`	-	NULL
cindex: colormap	array of Color-Cell	`glutSetColor` `glutCopyColor`	`glutGetColor`	undefined
windowParent	Integer		`GLUT_WINDOW_PARENT`	*top-level:* 0 *subwin*[14]
numChildren	Integer	`glutCreate-SubWindow` `glutDestroy-Window`	`GLUT_NUM_CHILDREN`	
leftMenu	Integer	`glutAttachMenu` `glutDetachMenu`	-	0
middleMenu	Integer	`glutAttachMenu` `glutDetachMenu`	-	0
rightMenu	Integer	`glutAttachMenu` `glutDetachMenu`	-	0

1. Assigned dynamically from unassigned window numbers greater than 0.
2. If *initWindowX* is greater than or equal to 0 *and initWindowY* is greater or equal to 0, then *initWindowX*, else window location left to window system to decide.
3. If *initWindowY* is greater than or equal to 0 *and initWindowX* is greater or equal to 0, then *initWindowY*, else window location left to window system to decide.
4. If *initWindowWidth* is greater than 0 *and initWindowHeight* is greater than 0, then *initWindowWidth*, else window size left to window system to decide.
5. If *initWindowHeight* is greater than 0 *and initWindowWidth* is greater than 0, then *initWindowHeight*, else window size left to window system to decide.
6. `glutFullScreen` sets to true; `glutPositionWindow` and `glutReshapeWindow` set to false.
7. Subwindows cannot be iconified.
8. Window system events can also change the *displayState*.
9. Visibility of a window can change for a window-system-dependent reason; for example, a new window may occlude the window. `glutPopWindow` and `glutPushWindow` can affect window visibility as a side effect.
10. The visibility callback set by `glutVisibilityFunc` allows the visibility state to be tracked.
11. The redisplay state can be enabled explicitly by `glutRedisplayFunc` or implicitly in response to normal plane redisplay events from the window system.
12. A window's *displayCallback* must be registered before the first display callback would be triggered (or the program is terminated).
13. Instead of being a no-op, as most NULL callbacks are, a NULL *reshapeCallback* sets the OpenGL viewport to render into the complete window, that is, `glViewport(0,0,width, height)`.
14. Determined by *currentWindow* at `glutCreateSubWindow` time.

C.3.2 Frame Buffer Capability State

Name	Type	get
Total number of bits in color buffer	Integer	`GLUT_WINDOW_BUFFER_SIZE`
Number of bits in stencil buffer	Integer	`GLUT_WINDOW_STENCIL_SIZE`
Number of bits in depth buffer	Integer	`GLUT_WINDOW_DEPTH_SIZE`
Number of bits of red stored in color buffer	Integer	`GLUT_WINDOW_RED_SIZE`
Number of bits of green stored in color buffer	Integer	`GLUT_WINDOW_GREEN_SIZE`
Number of bits of blue stored in color buffer	Integer	`GLUT_WINDOW_BLUE_SIZE`
Number of bits of alpha stored in color buffer	Integer	`GLUT_WINDOW_ALPHA_SIZE`
Number of bits of red stored in accumulation buffer	Integer	`GLUT_WINDOW_ACCUM_RED_SIZE`
Number of bits of green stored in accumulation buffer	Integer	`GLUT_WINDOW_ACCUM_GREEN_SIZE`
Number of bits of blue stored in accumulation buffer	Integer	`GLUT_WINDOW_ACCUM_BLUE_SIZE`
Number of bits of alpha stored in accumulation buffer	Integer	`GLUT_WINDOW_ACCUM_ALPHA_SIZE`
Color index colormap size	Integer	`GLUT_WINDOW_COLORMAP_SIZE`
If double-buffered	Boolean	`GLUT_WINDOW_DOUBLEBUFFER`
If RGBA color model	Boolean	`GLUT_WINDOW_RGBA`
If stereo	Boolean	`GLUT_WINDOW_STEREO`
Number of samples for multisampling	Integer	`GLUT_WINDOW_MULTISAMPLE`

A window's (normal plane) frame buffer capability state is derived from the global *initDisplayMode* state at the window's creation. A window's frame buffer capabilities cannot be changed.

C.3.3 Layer State

Name	Type	Set/Change	Get	Initial
hasOverlay	Boolean	`glutEstablishOverlay` `glutRemoveOverlay`[1]	`GLUT_HAS_OVERLAY`	False
overlayPossible	Boolean		`GLUT_OVERLAY_POSSIBLE`	False
layerInUse	Layer	`glutUseLayer`[2]	`GLUT_LAYER_IN_USE`	normal plane[3]
cindex: *transparentIndex*	Integer	–	`GLUT_TRANSPARENT_INDEX`	
overlayRedisplay	Boolean	`glutPostOverlayRedisplay`[4]	–	False

Name	Type	Set/Change	Get	Initial
overlayDisplay Callback	Callback	`glutOverlayDisplay-Func`	–	NULL
overlayDisplay-State	State	`glutShowOverlay` `glutHideOverlay`	–	shown
normalDamaged	Boolean	[5]	`GLUT_NORMAL_DAMAGED`	False
overlayDamaged	Boolean	[6]	`GLUT_OVERLAY_DAMAGED`	False

---

1. Whether an overlay is possible is based on the *initDisplayMode* state *and* the frame buffer capability state of the window.
2. The *layerInUse* is implicitly set to overlay after `glutEstablishOverlay`; likewise, `glutRemove-Overlay` resets the state to normal plane.
3. The *transparentIndex* is set when a color index overlay is established. It cannot be set; it may change if the overlay is reestablished. When no overlay is in use or if the overlay is not color index, the *transparentIndex* is –1.
4. The *overlayRedisplay* state can be explicitly enabled by `glutPostOverlayRedisplay` or implicitly in response to overlay redisplay events from the window system.
5. Set when the window system reports that a region of the window's normal plane is undefined (for example, damaged by another window moving or initially being shown). The specifics of when damage occurs are left to the window system to determine. The window's *redisplay* state is always set true when damage occurs. *normalDamaged* is cleared whenever the window's display callback returns.
6. Set when the window system reports that a region of the window's overlay plane is undefined (for example, damaged by another window moving or initially being shown). The specifics of when damage occurs are left to the window system to determine. The damage may occur independent of damage to the window's normal plane. The window's *redisplay* state is always set true when damage occurs. *normalDamaged* is cleared whenever the window's display callback returns.

When an overlay is established, *overlay* frame buffer capability state is maintained as described in Section C.3.2. The *layerInUse* determines whether `gluGet` returns normal plane or overlay state when an overlay is established.

C.4 MENU STATE

Name	Type	Set/Change	Get	Initial
number	Integer	–	`glutSetMenu`	`glutCreateMenu`[1]
select	Callback	–	–	`glutCreateMenu`
items	list of MenuItems	–	–	–
numItems	Integer	–	`GLUT_MENU_NUM_ITEMS`	0

---

1. Assigned dynamically from unassigned menu numbers greater than 0.

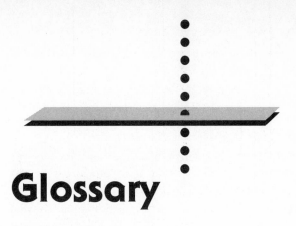

Glossary

Accumulation buffer A color buffer with extended color resolution, used to accumulate rendered images. Uses include motion blur, depth-of-field effects, and full-scene antialiasing.

Alpha A fourth color component in addition to red, green, and blue. Alpha is never displayed, but represents the degree of opacity of the color. An alpha of 0 represents a fully transparent color; an alpha of 1 represents a fully opaque color. Alpha is commonly used for blending colors together.

Ancillary buffer OpenGL has displayable color buffers for rendering color images, but OpenGL frame buffers also support additional ancillary, or helper, buffers to maintain depth, stencil, and other per-pixel information. See *accumulation buffer*, *depth buffer*, and *stencil buffer*.

Antialiasing Any technique for dealing with the artifacts that occur when data such as images or geometric primitives is sampled during rasterization. The most common example of this problem is the jagged, or "stair-step," appearance along the edges of lines and polygons. Polygon and line smoothing, accumulation buffers, and multisampling are all approaches to reducing the effects of aliasing. See *multisampling*.

Architectural Review Board This is the organization responsible for defining OpenGL. The board is composed of industry leaders, namely Digital Equipment Corporation, Evans and Sutherland, IBM, Intel, Intergraph, Microsoft, and Silicon Graphics.

Back-face culling A technique to reduce the rasterization overhead by not rendering polygons that are determined to be facing backwards. For example, a sphere represented by polygons has its back-facing polygons obscured by the front half of the sphere. Eliminating the back-facing polygons will improve rendering speed. Whether a polygon is back- or front-facing is determined by the clockwise or counterclockwise ordering of its vertices.

Bitmap font A representation of a character set in which each character is rendered as a bitmap. Bitmap characters are typically fast to render. Because bitmaps are images instead of geometry, they cannot be rotated, scaled, or projected. See *stroke font*.

Bottleneck A performance problem that results when one stage of a pipeline is slower than other pipeline stages. The result is that the slowest stage holds back the overall pipeline throughput.

Callback An application-supplied routine that is invoked by a toolkit or other library routine as needed. For example, a callback could be registered to handle key presses. Callbacks supply application-specific handling of events.

Clipping A process of eliminating primitives or portions of primitives that fall outside a given viewing space.

Color index One of the two color models for OpenGL. This model represents colors as color indices during rendering and within the frame buffer. See *RGBA*.

Colormap Every X window must have a colormap describing the way the window's pixel values are mapped to displayable colors. There are different types of colormaps for different types of visuals.

Component A single, continuous range that represents an intensity or quantity. For example, a color in the RGBA color model is a set of four components for red, green, blue, and alpha.

Convolution An image-processing operation allowing you to filter images. Among other uses, convolution can be used to blur and sharpen images. OpenGL has an extension to support convolution as part of its pixel path. See *pixel path*.

Current raster position The OpenGL state that determines where an image or bitmap primitive will be rendered. The raster position is specified in modeling coordinates.

Depth buffer This ancillary buffer maintains per-pixel depth information used for hidden-line and -surface removal. Enabling depth buffering is a simple way to make sure close objects in a scene properly obscure objects farther away.

DirectColor This X visual class is like TrueColor except that the red, green, and blue fields within the pixel value are each passed through modifiable colormaps. OpenGL's RGBA rendering model can render into DirectColor windows.

Display list A sequence of OpenGL commands identified by an integer name. Display lists are stored either within the X server or, sometimes, in the graphics hardware. Calling a display list issues the commands within the display list. Use of display lists can help improve performance.

Dithering A technique for increasing the perceived color resolution at the cost of spatial resolution. Dithering is similar to the way black and white pixels can be alternated to form regions that appear as shades of gray from a distance.

Double buffering A technique for animation that uses a front and a back color buffer. The front buffer is displayed while the back buffer is used to render the next frame of animation. A buffer swap operation performs an instantaneous or near-instantaneous copy of the back-buffer's contents to the front buffer.

Drawable A drawing surface maintained by the X server for X rendering; normally a window or a pixmap.

Encapsulated PostScript A set of conventions for using a subset of Adobe's page description language. Encapsulated figures and images can be embedded within PostScript documents.

Evaluator OpenGL can evaluate polynomials to generate vertex information. Evaluators are used for efficient curve and surface generation.

Extension An optional capability added to a software standard. OpenGL, X, and GLX all have mechanisms for supporting extensions. GLX is actually an extension to the X Window System, but GLX also supports extensions to itself.

Focus The ability to direct input events to a given window. Generally, the focus is set to the window where the cursor currently resides, but the focus can also be forced to a specific window.

Fragment Fragments are generated during the rasterization of primitives. Each fragment corresponds to a single pixel and includes color, depth, and sometimes texture coordinate information.

Frame buffer This is where rendered pixels are retained. In addition to one or more color buffers, a frame buffer may consist of a number of ancillary buffers. While graphics hardware contains a physical frame buffer, this memory is divided among displayed windows. Conceptually, OpenGL considers each window or GLXPixmap to have its own frame buffer. See *Drawable* and *GLXDrawable*.

Frame buffer capability Depth buffering, stereo, and double buffering are all examples of frame buffer capabilities.

Frame buffer configuration A set of frame buffer capabilities. GLX advertises supported frame buffer capabilities via X visuals. See *visual*.

GLU The OpenGL Utility library. The GLU contains a standard set of useful routines common in programming with OpenGL, including routines for polygon and NURBS tessellation, mipmap generation, and transforming coordinates.

GLUT The OpenGL Utility Toolkit. GLUT is a simple, window system independent toolkit for constructing portable OpenGL demos and examples. It is a good vehicle for learning and exploring OpenGL and is used in many of this book's examples. You can obtain GLUT free of charge over the Internet.

GLX The GLX extension to the X Window System is the means by which OpenGL is supported in the X environment.

GLX attribute One of the token/value pairs used by GLX to describe frame buffer capabilities. See *frame buffer capability*.

GLXDrawable A drawable supporting OpenGL rendering. See *drawable*, *GLXPixmap*, and *visual*.

GLXPixmap An enhanced X pixmap for OpenGL rendering. See *pixmap*.

GTXRD A taxonomy for describing graphics hardware architectures, proposed by Kurt Akeley. The letters GTXRD stand for generation, traversal, transformation, rasterization, and display.

Histogram A histogram over an image counts the occurrences of color component values and tracks the minimum and maximum values. This information is important for image processing operations such as color quantization. The histogram is supported by OpenGL as an extension to the pixel path. See *pixel path*.

Homogeneous Coordinates A set of n+1 coordinates used to represent points in n-dimensional projective space. Points in projective space can be thought of as points in Euclidean space together with some points at infinity. Homogeneous coordinates are very useful in computer graphics.

ICCCM The Inter-Client Communication Conventions Manual, an X standard describing the ways clients interact with each other and, in particular, with the window manager.

IRIS GL OpenGL is the successor to IRIS GL, the original graphics library developed by Silicon Graphics.

Menu entry In GLUT, a selectable menu item with a displayed name and a returned value.

Menu item In GLUT, an item listed within a pop-up menu. It can be either a menu entry or a submenu trigger.

Mesa A publicly available implementation of the OpenGL programming interface, written by Brian Paul at the University of Wisconsin. Mesa supports a large number of platforms. It is a great way to learn OpenGL if you do not have access to a true OpenGL implementation. You can obtain Mesa free of charge over the Internet.

Modelview matrix This 4-x-4 matrix transforms geometric primitives from object coordinates to eye coordinates. See *projection matrix* and *transformation*.

Motif The most widely used widget set for the X Toolkit. Developed by the Open Software Foundation. Motif is big and bloated, but it is also the most full-featured widget set available.

Multisampling An expensive technique for antialiasing that is fast and requires no enabling of involved program changes. Multisampling maintains multiple depth and color subsamples for each pixel in the frame buffer. These samples are blended to obtain the final displayed pixel. Typically, only high-end graphics hardware will support this feature. OpenGL supports it via an extension. See *antialiasing*.

Normal Per-vertex information indicating in what direction a polygon faces. Normals are used for calculating lighting effects.

Normal plane The default frame buffer layer. See *overlay*.

NURBS Non-Uniform Rational B-Splines, or NURBS, are common curve and surface representations used in computer graphics. Rendering NURBS can be accelerated with OpenGL evaluators. See *evaluator*.

Open Inventor A descriptive, object-oriented graphics library that renders using OpenGL.

Overlay A frame buffer layer displayed preferentially to the normal plane, usually providing a transparent pixel value that shows through to the normal plane. The overlay is often used for visual effects such as text annotation, rubber-banding, and pop-up menus. See *normal plane*.

PEX The other standard 3D graphics system for the X Window System.

Pixel path The pipeline of OpenGL image operations, applied during the drawing, copying, and reading of images and textures.

Pixmap An array of pixel values maintained in offscreen memory for X rendering. See *GLXPixmap*.

Pop-up menu In GLUT, a menu that can be activated by a button press. The menu appears at the current mouse position. If overlays are supported, pop-up menus use them to avoid damaging the underlying image when the menu is removed. See *menu item* and *submenu*.

Primitive A bitmap, an image, a line, a point, or a polygon.

Projection matrix This 4-x-4 matrix transforms geometric primitives from eye coordinates to clip coordinates. See *modelview matrix* and *transformation*.

PseudoColor An X visual class in which pixel values are converted to displayable red, green, and blue color components using a colormap. The colormap can be modified as necessary. PseudoColor is typically used for OpenGL color index rendering.

Quaternion A means of parameterizing orientation that avoids several nasty mathematical problems that arise from naive approaches to accumulating 3D rotations. Quaternions are often used in computer graphics for computing arbitrary rotations of objects.

Rasterization The process of converting primitives to fragments and updating pixels in the frame buffer appropriately. See *fragment* and *transformation*.

Rendering Jargon for making pretty pictures with computers.

Rendering context An instance of the OpenGL state machine. OpenGL programs must make current to a rendering context and GLXDrawable before OpenGL commands can be issued. Then OpenGL commands affect the current rendering context and drawable.

RGBA One of the two color models for OpenGL is RGBA, which stands for red, green, blue, and alpha. These are the components used to represent colors during rendering and within the frame buffer. This model is typically preferable to OpenGL's color index model because RGBA has more rendering capabilities and is easier to use. See *color index*.

Rubber-banding A technique used to select regions of an image by dragging the outline of a rectangle over the image. When performed in the overlays, rubber-banding can be done without disturbing the original image.

Server Overlay Visuals convention Nearly all X vendors that support overlays do so with the Server Overlay Visuals convention. Overlay windows are created using special overlay visuals advertised by the convention.

State machine A conceptual model for specifying OpenGL. Modes within OpenGL are considered to be state that is manipulated by OpenGL commands. Primitives are rendered based on OpenGL's current state. See *rendering context*.

Stencil buffer This ancillary buffer keeps per-pixel state that can be used to control the update of the pixel. The most common use for the stencil buffer is to constrain rendering to arbitrary regions within the frame buffer.

Stereo In the same way as double buffering supports a front and back buffer, stereo provides left and right buffers. Special goggles and display hardware synchronize the display of the alternating left and right buffers with the viewer's left and right eyes. If the scene is drawn twice, from a slightly adjusted perspective for each eye, the viewer sees the scene in stereo.

Stroke font A representation of a character set in which each character is rendered as a set of vectors. Because stroke fonts are represented as 3D geometry, they can be translated, rotated, and scaled within 3D scenes. See *bitmap font*.

Submenu GLUT allows a pop-up menu to cascade other menus, which are referred to as submenus.

Submenu trigger In GLUT, a menu item that cascades a submenu when entered with the mouse cursor. See *menu item*.

Tessellation The process of breaking geometric representations, such as complex polygons or surfaces, into primitive polygons.

Texture mapping A technique for combining images and geometry. The texture image is applied to a geometric primitive. For example, you could texture a brick pattern on a rectangle representing the surface of a wall.

Transformation The process of converting primitives from modeling coordinates to window coordinates and performing lighting calculations. See *primitive* and *rasterization*.

Transparent pixel value A special pixel value that "shows through" to frame buffer layers logically beneath the layer supporting transparency. See *overlay*.

TrueColor An X visual class that directly encodes pixels as RGB colors. OpenGL's RGBA color model typically uses TrueColor visuals. See *DirectColor*.

Underlay Like an overlay, except displayed deferentially or logically beneath the the normal plane. See *overlay* and *normal plane*.

Vertex A coordinate used to describe a geometric primitive's position in 3D space. The plural is *vertices*.

Viewport The viewport determines how normalized device coordinates are converted to window coordinates. You can think of it as the rectangle within your window that OpenGL rendering uses. Normally, the viewport is adjusted when the window is resized.

Visual The configuration for a window that describes the way pixel values within the window are converted to displayable colors. Each X server advertises a static set of visuals. GLX overloads X visuals with information about frame buffer capabilities.

Widget The basic user interface object for the X Toolkit.

Window A displayable drawable. In X, windows are lightweight objects maintained by the X server. See *drawable*.

Wireframe A solid object rendered as a set of lines. Typically, wireframe rendering is faster than rendering the object as a set of polygons.

X Consortium The organization that develops X Window System technology. OpenGL is not an X Consortium Standard. See *Architectural Review Board*.

X Input extension An X extension for controlling and querying X input devices other than the mouse and the keyboard.

X Toolkit This standard X library provides a framework for using user interface objects called widgets. The X Toolkit is also referred to as the Xt Intrinsics. See *Motif* and *widget*.

Xlib The lowest-level application programming interface for the X Window System. The chief responsibility of this interface is to hide the details of communicating with the X server via the X11 protocol.

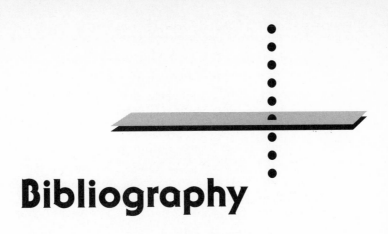

Bibliography

1. Akeley, Kurt. "The Silicon Graphics 4D/240GTX Superworkstation," *IEEE Computer Graphics and Applications*, July 1989.

2. Akeley, Kurt. "RealityEngine Graphics," *Proceedings of SIGGRAPH '93*, July 1993.

3. Akin, Allen. "Analysis of PEX 5.1 and OpenGL 1.0," Silicon Graphics, August 3, 1992.

4. Bartels, Richard et al. *An Introduction to Splines for Use in Computer Graphics and Geometric Modeling.* Morgan Kaufmann, 1987.

5. Burns, Derrick. *Dynamic Trimmed Surface Rendering*, Ph.D. dissertation, Stanford University, 1993.

6. Crow, F. C. "The Origins of the Teapot," *IEEE Computer Graphics and Applications*, January 1987.

7. Daifuku, Peter. "A Fully Functional Implementation of Layered Windows," *The X Resource: Proceedings of the 7th Annual X Technical Conference*, O'Reilly & Associates, Issue 5, January 1993.

8. Deering, Michael. "Leo: A System for Cost Effective 3D Shaded Graphics," *Proceedings of SIGGRAPH '93*, July 1993.

9. Farin, Gerald. *Curves and Surfaces for Computer-Aided Geometric Design*, Academic Press, 1990.

10. Ferguson, Paula. "The X Input Extension: A Tutorial," *The X Resource*, Issue 4, 1992.

11. Ferguson, Paula. ed., "The X Input Extension: Reference Pages," *The X Resource*, Issue 4, 1992.

12. Ferraro, Richard. *Programmer's Guide to the EGA and VGA Cards, 2d Ed.*, Addison-Wesley, 1990.

13. Foley, James, Andries van Dam, Steven Feiner, and John Hughes. *Computer Graphics: Principles and Practice*, 2d ed. Addison-Wesley, 1990.

14. Gabbard, Rob. "Addressing the Problems Facing the Integration of 3D Applications with Modern User Interfaces," SDRC Graphics and User Interface Group, unpublished, July 1992.

15. Gaskins, Tom. "Using PEXlib with X Toolkits," *PEXlib Programming Manual*, O'Reilly & Associates, 1992.

16. Haeberli, Paul, Kurt Akeley. "The Accumulation Buffer: Hardware Support for High-Quality Rendering," *Proceedings of SIGGRAPH '90*, August 1990, 309-318.

17. Haeberli, Paul, and Mark Segal. "Texture Mapping as a Fundamental Drawing Primitive," *Proceedings of the Fourth Eurographics Workshop on Rendering*, June 1993.

18. Harrel, Chandlee, and Farhad Fouladi. "Graphics Rendering Architecture for a High-Performance Desktop Workstation," *Proceedings of SIGGRAPH '93*, July 1993.

19. Heckbert, Paul. "Survey of Texture Mapping," *IEEE Computer Graphics and Applications*, November 1986.

20. Hiebert, Steven, John Lang, and Keith Marchington. "Sharding Overlay and Image Planes in the Starbase/X11 Merge System," *Hewlett-Packard Journal*, December 1989.

21. Karlton, Phil, and David Wiggins. "Describing Overlay Visuals," X Consortium communication, 1991.

22. Karlton, Phil. "Integrating the GL into the X Environment: A High-Performance Rendering Extension Working with and Not Against X," *The X Resource: Proceeding of the 6th Annual X Technical Conference*, O'Reilly & Associates, Issue 1, Winter 1992.

23. Kilgard, Mark J. "Going Beyond the MIT Sample Server: The Silicon Graphics X11 Server," *The X Journal*, SIGS Publications, January 1993.

24. Kilgard, Mark J., Simon Hui, Allen A. Leinwand, and Dave Spalding. "X Server Multi-rendering for OpenGL and PEX," *The X Resource: Proceedings of the 8th X Technical Conference*, O'Reilly & Associates, Issue 9, January 1994.

25. Kilgard, Mark, David Blythe, and Deanna Hohn. "System Support for OpenGL Direct Rendering," *Proceedings of Graphics Interface '95*, 1995.

26. Korobkin, Carl. "Interactive Geometric Image Transformation Using Texture Mapping," in press, Silicon Graphics, 1994.

27. McLendon, Patricia. *Graphics Library Programming Guide*, Silicon Graphics, 1991.

28. Neider, Jackie, Tom Davis, and Mason Woo. *OpenGL Programming Guide: The Official Guide to Learning OpenGL, Release 1*, Addison-Wesley, 1993.

29. Newman, Todd. "How Not to Implement Overlays in X," *The X Resource: Proceeding of the 6th Annual X Technical Conference*, O'Reilly & Associates, Issue 1, Winter 1992.

30. OpenGL Architecture Review Board. *OpenGL Reference Manual: The official reference document for OpenGL, Release 1*, Addison-Wesley, 1992.

31. Patrick, Mark and George Sachs. *X11 Input Extension Library Specification*, X Consortium Standard, X11R6, April 18, 1994.

32. Patrick, Mark and George Sachs. *X11 Input Extension Protocol Specification*, X Consortium Standard, X11R6, April 17, 1994.

33. Pletinckx, D. "Quaternion Calculus as a Basic Tool in computer Graphics," *The Visual Computer*, February 13, 1989.

34. Rhoden, Desi, and Chris Wilcox. "Hardware Acceleration for Window Systems," *Computer Graphics*, Association for Computing Machinery, vol. 23, no. 3, July 1989.

35. Rohlf, John, James Helman. "IRIS Performer: A High-Performance Multiprocessing Toolkit for Real-Time 3D Graphics," *Proceedings of SIGGRAPH '92*, July 1994.

36. Segal, Mark, and Kurt Akeley. *The OpenGL™ Graphics System: A Specification*, Version 1.0, Silicon Graphics, June 30, 1992.

37. Silicon Graphics. "Indy Graphics," *Indy™ Technical Report*, Version 1.0, 1993.

38. Silicon Graphics. *The OpenGL Porting Guide*, supplied with the IRIX 5.2 development option, 1994.

39. Shoemake, K. "Animating Rotation with Quaternion Curves," *Proceedings of SIGGRAPH '85*, August 1985, 245-254.

40. Strauss, Paul, and Rikk Carey. "An Object-Oriented 3D Graphics Toolkit," *Proceedings of SIGGRAPH '92*, July 1992, 341-347.

41. Chen, Michael, Joy Mountford, and Abigail Sellen, "A Study in Interactive 3D Rotation Using 2D Control Devices," *Proceedings of SIGGRAPH '88*, August 1988, 121-129.

42. Teschner, Michael. "Texture Mapping: a new dimension in scientific and technical visualization," *IRIS Universe*, Number 29, 1994.

43. Watt, Alan, and Mark Watt. *Advanced Animation and Rendering Techniques: Theory and Practice*, Addison-Wesley, 1992.

44. Wernecke, Josie. *The Inventor Mentor*, Addison-Wesley, 1993.

45. Womack, Paula, et al. "PEX Protocol Specification, Version 5.1," The X Consortium, August 31, 1992.

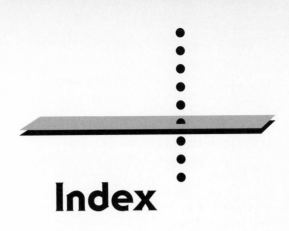

Index